FAMILY
Ministry

A COMPREHENSIVE
GUIDE

DIANA R.
GARLAND

InterVarsity Press
Downers Grove, Illinois

InterVarsity Press
P.O. Box 1400, Downers Grove, IL 60515
World Wide Web: www.ivpress.com
E-mail: mail@ivpress.com

InterVarsity Press® is the book-publishing division of InterVarsity Christian Fellowship/USA®, a student movement active on campus at hundreds of universities, colleges and schools of nursing in the United States of America, and a member movement of the International Fellowship of Evangelical Students. For information about local and regional activities, write Public Relations Dept., InterVarsity Christian Fellowship/USA, 6400 Schroeder Rd., P.O. Box 7895, Madison, WI 53707-7895.

Cover illustration: Mark Cooper/Stock Market
ISBN 0-8308-1585-6
Printed in the United States of America ∞

Library of Congress Cataloging-in-Publication Data
Garland, Diana S. Richmond, 1950–
   Family ministry : a comprehensive guide / Diana R. Garland.
      p.   cm.
   Includes bibliographical references.
   ISBN 0-8308-1585-6 (alk. paper)
   1. Church work with families—United States. 2. Family—Religious
aspects. I. Title.
BV4438.G38   1999
259'.1—dc21
                                                                      99-43127
                                                                      CIP

10	19	18	17	16	15	14	13	12	11	10	9	8	7	6	5	4	3	2	1
16	15	14	13	12	11	10	09	08	07	06	05	04	03	02	01	00	99		

For my faith sisters—Margaret,
Alice and Martha

PART TWO: LEADING FAMILY MINISTRY

Introduction

Christian congregations today are providing significant resources and support for families. Between 1994 and 1999 I assessed and consulted with more than 50 congregations and extensively interviewed more than 120 families.[1]

I learned a great deal from these congregations and their families; one of the most compelling findings is how strong many Christian families are. Their faith has not protected them from troubles or disappointments, but it has given them a framework for coping and even thriving in adverse circumstances. The strength of these families is rooted in their faith, and that faith is nurtured in their congregations. Congregations nurture families by instilling values that promote strong family life, values such as unconditional love and commitment, giving oneself for others, joy and celebration, forgiveness and grace.

In a culture that has largely lost the sense of community we used to find in our neighborhoods and extended families, the church often becomes a major community of support for the daily lives of families. Church teachings and programs offer parents, spouses and children practical guidance for family living. In the church, people find the support of friends who are journeying through the same stages and transitions of life. The church community also makes possible a wealth of crossgenerational relationships. In the context of the congregation, generations can learn from and care for one another. And in times of crisis, particularly illness, birth and death, churches provide entire families with meaningful and practical care.

So Christian families are strong not only because of their faith but also because of the church. And many of the wonderful things we do for families come simply as a part of being the church, and not from any special emphasis or program called family ministry. When we pray for one another in sickness and trouble, when we provide a place for families to worship or share a Wednesday-night supper together, when we give parents respite by offering vacation Bible school or church camp, churches minister to families.

---

[1]The initial findings of this research are reported in Yankeelov and Garland 1998.

This book defines family ministry as not only the programs and services congregations target to family needs but, more broadly, the ways our entire congregational life shapes and strengthens family relationships.

Of course we can do much more to help families live faithfully and joyfully. Some families find only loneliness in a congregation that seems to have no place for them. Our guidance and support may address some of the issues and relationships of family life but neglect others. Much of the rich potential for crossgenerational support never materializes because much of today's church programming is designed for homogeneous age groups. Some of the most painful burdens of family life—chronic conflict or violence, mental illness, unfaithfulness—seem shameful and thus often remain hidden. Congregations do sometimes shoot their wounded rather than caring for them. Couples going through divorce, or an unmarried woman who learns she is pregnant, may find it more comfortable to leave the church than to seek support and care there.

Surely these congregational failings create rather than ameliorate problems for families. Still, it is all too easy to catalog the list of problems and shortcomings of congregations. Lists of problems breed discouragement. Yes, there is much congregations ought to and can be doing. Congregations are more likely to embrace change, however, if they first identify their strengths. We can build better church communities on a foundation of congregational strength than we can on a litany of failings.

Family ministry in the United States too often begins with a cataloging of all that is wrong with families today and all that is wrong with a culture that seems hostile to Christian family living. Family ministry programs in congregations rarely begin with a quest for the strengths and resilience of families and the community. Instead we often begin by assessing the "needs" of families.

In large part, this focus on needs follows a model set by the helping professions—psychology, social work and pastoral care. Many of those shaping congregations' family ministry programs today came of age professionally during the 1960s and 1970s. During that time, professional services for families focused on providing family life education programs and treating problems with crisis intervention and family therapy. With a strong network of educational programs and counseling services, much family dysfunction could be averted—or at least that was the theory. Church leaders subsequently translated professional family services into church programs. "Family ministry" is the church version of need-based family life education and family counseling.

Many families have benefited enormously from marriage enrichment retreats, marital preparation courses, parent education seminars, support groups for adults caring for frail elderly parents, and the other services that congregations offer based on the perceived needs of families. The needs for ministry with families are myriad, however, and seem to be increasing exponentially year by year. No church can meet all the needs for educational services and counseling within its own membership, much less in the larger community. It also seems that these programs, as beneficial as they may be, are often too little, too late. They do not cut to the heart of the social forces that besiege and weaken families. By the same token, they do not take seriously enough the possibilities for shaping communities that would be more nurturing of family life. Most fundamentally, they define families as needy and vulnerable rather than as resilient and strong.

THIS BOOK'S STRUCTURE AND PURPOSE

This book is designed to provide church leaders with a foundation for designing and carrying out congregational ministries with and through families. Its basic premise is that *ministry leadership is most effective when it calls out and builds on the strengths of families and congregations.*

Part One: The Context for Family Ministry

Family ministry needs to be grounded in an understanding of family life in today's social and cultural context. Therefore part one begins by examining this context: who families are today and how they are shaped by and give shape to their physical and social environment. The second section turns to the developmental and relational processes that influence family life over time, day by day—how families form, change and transform; how they deal with communication, intimacy and conflict; how they distribute, maintain and challenge power among their members; how they define themselves with rituals, celebrations and memories; and what makes them strong.

This book assumes a basic knowledge of the sociology of marriage and family relationships. It does not provide a comprehensive treatment of family systems and the relationship of families to their communities and other institutions. Nor does it address the theory and methods of family therapy that church leaders who provide crisis intervention and counseling for families need to know. I leave that to the professional preparation and ongoing development of pastoral counselors, social workers and educators who minister with families. Instead this book addresses the interface between the church and these areas of knowledge, theory and method, the values that inform our practice and goals as family ministers. What are we aiming at? The values and motivation for family ministry must be clarified and understood before professionals can apply particular theories and methods in helping the church achieve its mission.

How the church has defined, related to and consequently shaped family life for the past two thousand years has significance for what we do and how we do it today. Section three examines this historical relationship between church and family, and suggests implications for current congregational leadership.

Section four of the first division functions as the heart of the book; here I explore the biblical themes and narratives that have shaped my approach to family ministry. The social, cultural, psychological and historical explorations of the previous chapters define the context from which I go to biblical narratives and teachings to seek understanding of what the term *family* means for Christians in today's world. I present my definition of family based on my understanding of the New Testament; this understanding has undeniably been shaped by my own professional and personal life experiences, which I describe below. Here is that definition: *Family is composed of those who choose to be followers of Jesus Christ and who are caregivers for one another—the "family of faith"* (Mk 3:31-35). I seek to define the purpose and meaning of family life in the teachings and stories of the Bible. I also explore how the Bible describes the roles family plays in the lives of the faithful, and what guidelines the Bible provides for discipleship through family living. These teachings need to be the central focus shaping the response of congregations to the families in their fellowship and community.

Part Two: Leading Family Ministry

The second major division of the book provides practical guidelines for planning, leading and evaluating family ministries, building on the foundation of the first division. Section five defines family ministry. It describes the processes of organizing for congregational family ministry, assessing the mission of the congregation, deciding on ministry priorities and planning what to do and how to evaluate it. Various categories of family ministry programs are delineated: support programs, resource programs, family life education and family advocacy. The sixth section of the book explores ministry issues with specific kinds of family relationships: the faith family, marriage, parents and children, and families facing extraordinary challenges.

RESOURCES FOR THIS BOOK

In writing this book, I have drawn on my own experiences as a social work educator, an editor of the journal *Family Ministry: Empowering Through Faith,* a congregational member, and a member in both my childhood family and my adulthood family. These have shaped my understanding of families and congregations, and you need to know more about these influences in order to understand my perspective and biases about family ministry and congregational life. It should be said at the outset that this book is unavoidably limited by my geographic and cultural rootedness in the United States. I encourage the reader to consider the relevance of my work to other cultural contexts.

I began my career as a social worker by providing counseling services to families on welfare, and through the years I have worked with client families in several church-related agencies. I served as a social worker in a Baptist residential child-care program, providing clinical services to children and their families. I then worked for almost a decade in a pastoral counseling agency, with families referred to me by pastors of several denominations. More recently, I provided clinical services for girls considered "severely emotionally disturbed" who were graduating from residential treatment as they completed high school. Many had been kicked about in the child welfare system for years as wards of the state before they found a home in this wonderful Catholic residential care program. Most of these girls longed to go home to their families, even though their families had long histories of physical and emotional abuse. It was my job to help them make good decisions about their futures, and I realized they could do so if they felt rooted in a family. If their biological families had failed them, then we were failing them, too, if we did not help them find new families where they could experience mutual love and commitment.

For two decades I have also been a social work educator in a seminary and now in a Baptist university, teaching students who want to provide professional services to children, families and congregations. This has been particularly challenging since there is very little professional literature defining social work practice in the context of the church and religious organizations. Nothing challenges one to think about what one knows and to attempt to organize it coherently more than trying to teach it to someone else.

I have also served as a congregational consultant in family ministry, most often with Southern Baptist churches and more recently with Presbyterians, United Methodists and National Baptists as well. This role has given me the privilege of participating in a number of congregations in addition to my own. My consultation with churches raised so many questions for me about families and congregations that I began a major research project to understand who the families of our congregations are and how congregations can minister with them more effectively. The Lilly Endowment has generously funded this research project, which is sponsored by Louisville Presbyterian Theological Seminary. Through the project, my research colleagues and I have conducted congregational surveys so that we might understand the kinds of families in our congregations; what their strengths, challenges and stressors are; and how they understand faith as a dimension of their life together. I have also engaged in two-hour interviews with more than 120 congregational families in their homes, trying to understand better how they live their faith together and the challenges they face.

These families' stories have woven their way into my understanding of family life, and I will share some of the accounts with you. Names and other identifying details have been changed, however, as well as information that would identify particular congregations, in order to protect their privacy. At times conversations have been edited to make them easier to read and understand, but not so as to change their meaning. If I identify a congregation or a person by their real name, it is because I have their permission to do so. This research is not completed and will be reported at length elsewhere, but already the life stories of these families have had a profound influence on my understanding of families, particularly families in congregations.

Crescent Hill Baptist Church in Louisville, Kentucky, was my community of faith and safe haven through most of the twenty-eight years my family lived in Kentucky. In the early workings of this book, they let me try out my half-baked ideas on them. Lovingly and patiently they encouraged me. I learned a great deal about what it means to be a church from the giants in the faith who have been part of that congregation decade after decade. During the denominational war that swirled around us over the last two decades, I came to appreciate deeply a congregation's potential roles as advocate and prophet. Crescent Hill has demonstrated both.

Since 1995 I have been serving as editor of the *Journal of Family Ministry;* its name has recently been changed to *Family Ministry: Empowering Through Faith.*

This involvement has exposed me to the work of many other congregations, as I have helped others think through and write about what they have learned about family ministry.

Probably most significant among all these influences, my own family experiences have been the ground of my experience, enriching my life with the daily challenges of living faithfully and lovingly with my beloveds, and overwhelming me with their love and care when I have least deserved it. Family living teaches experientially the meaning of grace and love, anger and sin, forgiveness and reconciliation and covenant. I have been especially privileged to have spent almost thirty years married to a New Testament scholar and teacher. David and I have written and spoken together on the topics of marriage and family life, and I borrow shamelessly from his knowledge of Scriptures and from his teachings. But I take full responsibility for my own forays into the meanings of biblical texts. David would tell you I can hold stubbornly to favorite ideas even when he attempts to persuade me otherwise.

In the pages of this book I frequently share stories from my family's private life. In every case I have obtained their permission, at least of those who are still living. As for the stories of those who have gone on before us, I think I know that my loved ones would smile at these stories of our life together.

ACKNOWLEDGMENTS

There is no way I can adequately thank all the persons and congregations who helped give shape to this book. I have already mentioned people and churches that have shaped my life and my understanding of congregations and families. The many families who shared their stories with me as a part of the research project enriched my understanding of families immeasurably. I am grateful to the Lilly Endowment and to President John M. Mulder and Louisville Presbyterian Theological Seminary for the generous support provided me for conducting research in family ministry. Dr. Mulder has been a source of vision, support and encouragement throughout the project and in the writing of this manuscript. And even though I had joined the faculty less than a year before, Baylor University granted me a summer research leave to complete the writing.

More than five years ago, Bob Dempsey asked me to become the family ministry consultant for the churches of the Montgomery Baptist Association. Bob believed I had something to offer churches there as they strove to develop ministries that would address the particular cultural and community contexts of local families. I learned a great deal about congregational assessment and family ministry planning through the support and collaboration offered by Bob and the congregational leaders of the Montgomery Baptist Association. It was in my work with them that most of the ideas in this book took shape.

I shared early renditions of this manuscript with students and with colleagues too many to name individually. They critiqued, questioned and encouraged. In particular, my dear friends John Mulder and Arthur Kelly put their considerable editorial skills to work in helping me reorganize the content. They were constant sources of insight and inspiration. Charles Scalise also provided useful guidance with the historical material.

Nothing springs from nothing, and this book is obviously no exception. Although most of the content of this book is new for me, it includes materials developed from ideas that I introduced in earlier publications. I am grateful to my husband, David, for his permission to use some of the material we earlier wrote together in *Beyond Companionship: Christians in Marriage,* published in 1986 by Westminster Press. Chapter four contains material previously published as "Creating and Nurturing Families" (Garland 1990) and *The Church's Ministry with Families* (Garland and Pancoast 1990).

David is not only my dearest friend but also my most reliable colleague. His gifts and skills in New Testament interpretation are a wonderful resource for me. He also is gifted at lovingly telling me when my ideas miss the mark. He faithfully read and edited portions of the manuscript in its multiple versions, even though he had pressing writing projects of his own.

You will read stories about my life as the wife of David, the mother of John and Sarah, the daughter of George and Dorsie, the daughter-in-law of Ruth and Ned, the sister of Elaine, the sister-in-law of Lou, the aunt of Amanda and Sydney, and the faith-sister of Martha and Margaret and Alice. Too many times to count, I have experienced God's grace through these beloveds.

Despite this wonderful community of beloveds, friends and colleagues, responsibility for the limitations of this book remains with me. I offer this as a beginning effort. So much more could be done. But there comes a time to write it down so that others can react and build upon and replace it with something better.

Part One

The Context
for Family Ministry

Section One

Families Today

W HEN I FIRST CONCEPTUALIZED THIS BOOK, I PLANNED TO begin by exploring biblical texts that serve as framework and rationale for my approach to family ministry. Surely what the Bible says about families and about the mission of the church should be most fundamental in shaping family ministry. To begin this way, however, suggests that my interpretation and even my selection of passages that seem most significant for family ministry are more enduring and bias-free than is most certainly is the case. I approach the Bible with specific questions and concerns that are shaped by my life experiences. We all do. Interpretation of Scripture always comes through filters of social and cultural experience. There is no way to stand above or beyond one's culture and community to interpret Scripture free of these filters, nor would it be somehow better if we could. Biblical interpretation must reflect an understanding of social and cultural realities if the church is to be faithful to God. God has historically worked in ways that are concrete and relevant and is still doing so in today's world. Thus the church responds to its social context, proactively seeking to shape society and culture. To be effective, it must understand this context.

In the twentieth century the social sciences, with their formal study of families, societies, cultures and, most recently, congregations, have contributed significantly to our understanding of families and churches. Not only have social scientists studied the institutions of family and church, but they have also significantly shaped the modern expressions of these institutions. The social sciences have become not only the primary means for understanding but also the foundation for intervening in and changing family and church life. Methods for studying communities, such as the community needs assessment process developed for use by the mental health professions, have been adapted by churches for studying the community in which they are ministering. Findings from studies of family strengths and dysfunctions have been used in Christian education programs and in pastoral counseling and the social ministries of congregations. And in an interesting conflation of the study of families and congregations, the social scientific study of the family is even being used as a theoretical framework for understanding and intervening in congregational life. This is most clearly illustrated in the application of Murray Bowen's family therapy approaches to the pastoral care of congregations (Friedman 1985).

The section that follows will explore the realities of family life in contemporary Western society. We will look at current social definitions of the family, the "ecology" of family life, and the significance of culture for families—the external culture of the community and society in which they live as well as the internal culture that each family creates.

Chapter 1

Families Today

THE FAMILY HAS BECOME A POWERFUL POLITICAL AND MORAL symbol in today's culture. Everyone is "profamily," even though there is sharp disagreement over what "the family" is and what being "for" it means. What one group believes will strengthen and help families is seen by another group as a frontal attack on "family values." Stephen Barton has suggested that "the family" has such enormous symbolic potential because

1. it represents what is traditional and stable, including society as a whole, because it has historically been seen as the building-block of civic community;

2. it is the most intimate form of social organization and thus carries high emotional voltage;

3. it is ubiquitous—almost everyone is touched by "family";

4. it is inextricably linked with a dynamic and complex set of moral-political concerns, such as male-female roles, children, work and economics; and

5. it is intimately linked with religion and thus is a potent symbol of a higher order of life (Barton 1996b:452).

Much of the current debate about families swirls around a lack of consensus on a definition of "the family." It seems obvious that no agreement will be reached on what families *need* if there is conflict over what a family *is*.

In churches, part of the conflict grows out of an unspoken disagreement over whether a definition of family should function as a description of what family "is" or of what a family "ought to be." The concern appears to be that if the term *family* is used to describe a never-married mother and her child, or unmarried partners living together (whether as celibate friends or as sexual partners), we are condoning these relationships. For some, however, these *are* families and thus, they believe, deserving of recognition as family. Whether we agree on the morality of their family's structure is beside the point. They are simply describing family. For others, it important to define these structures as something other than family. Of course, both kinds of definitions are important for family ministry: the *sociological reality* (i.e., what current reality is) and the *normative model* (i.e., the ideal, what "ought to be").

Those who want to reserve the term *family* for family structures believed to be moral have good reason to want to protect who has the right to be called "family." Definitions have the power to shape that which they appear to be simply defining. When something is given a definition, it becomes an acknowledged social reality—a norm. The definition of *family* shapes social and institutional responses to those called "families" and those deemed "not-families." Certain privileges come with the status of "family." Hospital intensive-care units often limit visitors to "immediate family," and zoning laws in a community may limit who can reside together in a single-family dwelling to "family members." Tax codes give breaks to persons recognized as family. Society holds people who are "family" responsible for one another legally and economically. So the argument over who is allowed to call themselves "family" is not an idle one.

In chapter twelve I will attempt to define a normative model— what ought to be—based on my reading and interpretation of biblical texts. This chapter presents the sociological reality of family as it is experienced in American culture today.

DESCRIBING TODAY'S FAMILIES

Much of the debate over how to define family has arisen because the diversity of human groups that call themselves families appears to be growing rapidly. These seem to be significantly different from, and some consider them even threatening to, what has been called the "traditional family." The traditional family is usually thought of as the "nuclear family," the sociological term for a household consisting of a married heterosexual couple and their children. Some definitions of the traditional family include the additional stipulations that (1) this is the first marriage for both spouses, (2) there are no children of either spouse from other unions, (3) the children are the biological descendants of both spouses (not adopted or in foster care), and/or (4) the wife is not employed outside the home. Of course, the more stipulations that are added to this definition, the smaller the number of families that can be considered "traditional." As we will see in chapter ten, variations on the nuclear family have always existed, and the "traditional" family, particularly as defined by the work patterns of the married couple, is a family form that was actually experienced on a large scale by middle-class American families only in the mid-twentieth century, not the standard throughout history. Nevertheless, it carries enormous emotional weight in our culture.

Regardless of how one feels about the myth or reality or value of traditional families, no one at the beginning of the third millennium A.D. can fool themselves into believing that the traditional family is the dominant family structure and all others are exceptions. Even if blended families (couples in second and later marriages with children from previous unions) are included, in the United States married couples with dependent children account for only 27 percent of families. Married couples without children are more prevalent than any other kind of household (30 percent). Many of these are couples whose children have grown up and left home. The remaining family households consist primarily of cohabiting couples and unmarried women and their children.

The proportion of households that are families is not nearly as high as once was the case in America. Today one out of four households (25 percent) consists of a single adult, compared with only 17 percent in 1970 (Rawlings 1994). The number of single adult households is almost equal to the number of households of married couples and their children. In 1977 there were 16 million Americans living alone; twenty years later there were 25 million (Harder 1997). During this same twenty-year period, the number of unmarried couples cohabiting more than tripled, from under 100,000 to more than 3.7 million (Harder 1997).

The increase in the number of U.S. families maintained by women alone has been one of the major changes in family composition. That proportion has been much higher among blacks than whites for many years, but the number of white women who are sole heads of households is now increasing more rapidly. In 1970 about 28 percent of black families were maintained by women alone, versus 9 percent of white families. In 1997 only 33 percent of black children and 76 percent of white children lived in a two-parent family (Harder 1997; Rawlings 1994:10-11).

Based on 1993 census data, families who have children under the age of eighteen have the structures shown in table 1.1 (Rawlings 1994; Saluter 1994:8-11; Strong and DeVault 1995).

There were an average of 2.63 persons per household in 1993 (Rawlings 1994:82). In 1790 American families lived in households with an average size of 5.8 persons, and about 36 percent of households at that time contained seven persons or more. By 1900 the average household size was 4.8, and 20 percent of households had seven persons or more. Today only 1 percent of households are this large.

What do all these statistics mean? Some fear that these changes portend the demise of the family: the decrease in the proportion of families that are nuclear indicates that this family form is being replaced. Others argue that such fears are based on myths about what families have been historically and what is happening today, as indicated in the book title *The Myth of Family Decline* (Kain 1990). The dramatic changes being reported in the diversity of families today actually reflect a mix of factors that involve both changes in our ways of seeing and interpreting social phenomena and changes in the phenomena themselves. A closer examination reveals that (1) we are seeing diversity that has existed all along, though perhaps not openly and as widespread, (2) changes in mortality and birth rates are contributing to a changing distribution among family types, and, indeed, (3) forces are at work within families and society that are creating new family forms and altering the development and endurance of families. All of these changes have evolved over time as a consequence of social forces that are continuing to give shape to our social and physical world.

biological nuclear families	45%
step-families	21%
single-parent families (87% with mothers, 13% with fathers)	27%
grandparent-headed families	5%
cohabiting couple families	2%

Table.1.1. **Structures of families with children**

1. We are seeing diversity that has existed all along. The powerful images of the nuclear family unit, with its husband and father, wife and mother, and child and sibling positions have defined family relationships throughout American history, and they continue to do so today. Even with increasingly diverse types of families, nuclear family terms still provide the root language for defining variations in family relationships—"like-a-*sister*," "adoptive *grandparent*," "foster *mother*," "step*child*." Nevertheless, the nuclear family, much less the traditional family with its additional requisites, has never been the only way families have constituted themselves. There have always been births outside of marriage, nonmarital cohabitation of heterosexual and same-sex couples, childless marriages, working wives, and separation and divorce.

The fact that something exists, however, does not mean that it is part of a culture's self-consciousness. Television entertainment provides a fascinating window into how U.S. society has viewed itself over the past fifty years. Television indicates what is valued and recognized in the culture, and because it is such a pervasive presence in American lives, it also influences our societal values. One can refer to television characters and be more sure that one's readers know them than one can to characters in a bestselling novel or, for that matter, a Bible story. More people share in the institution of television than any other institution of American society.

It has been often pointed out that the nuclear families of 1950s television show how our society saw itself—*Father Knows Best*, *Lassie* and *Leave It to Beaver* portrayed homemaker mothers, fathers as heads of household, and their dependent children. What television does *not* portray also provides an interesting perspective on how our culture sees itself. For example, *The Andy Griffith Show* was an all-time favorite from the 1950s that continues to be popular in reruns, presumably because of its humor, character development and homespun wisdom. Though it is set in a small town in the American South, there is not a single African-American to be seen in the series. During the 1950s, racial diversity was not a part of how Americans thought of their culture. Dominant white culture was *the* culture; others were invisible.

Of course, this same show exemplifies a nontraditional family. The lead character is a widower raising a son alone with the help of live-in Aunt Bee and his cousin Barney. On the other hand, Andy's status as a widower does tie the family to a traditional structure; the situation of single parenting was not created by divorce or birth outside of marriage, and the presence of a maiden aunt makes the family the functional equivalent of a nuclear family.

Another television series of the era, *My Three Sons,* presented the family of a widower raising three sons with the help of a live-in Uncle Charlie. This family stretched the definition a bit further because the household was all male. Nevertheless, Uncle Charlie was a full-time homemaker, gruff but lovable, wearing an apron and very much a "Mr. Mom." Then as well as now, few families probably could identify with having an uncle willing and capable of moving into the household to devote his full energies to raising three children. Part of the humor of this show came from its contrast with reality.

Juxtapose those families to the kinds of families depicted in the most highly rated shows on American television in the 1990s: Murphy Brown is an unmarried career mom, Grace in *Grace Under Fire* is a divorced working-class mother, *Friends* and *Seinfeld* depict groups of young single adults living together in a mix of sexual and nonsexual familylike relationships with no children, and Ellen of the eponymous show is a lesbian bookstore owner whose "family" seems to be her cousin, her employees and her patrons. *Frazier* depicts quite an assortment. A divorced father, whose son lives on the other side of the nation, lives with his own father and a live-in physical therapist. A divorced brother lives alone nearby, and a coworker/close friend is an unmarried single mother; these two are often a part of the family's activities. With the exception of *Grace Under Fire,* children put in only rare appearances in these shows.

At the same time, there are nuclear families, albeit with working women, such as in *Home Improvement, Roseanne* and *Cosby.* In each of these shows, the action is much more likely to be set in the home setting than in the workplace. Allusions to sexual activity are very much present but not as graphic as in the shows listed above; here such references are predominantly limited to the marital relationship. And children have central roles.

It is not so much that new family forms are being developed as that forms that in the past were either relatively rare or closeted are becoming much more common and visible. There were African-American families somewhere in Mayberry (setting of *Andy Griffith*), and the women in these families were probably employed outside the home because their income was needed for the family to survive. Poor women of all races have always worked outside the home to support their families. Although the majority of 1950s women lived in nuclear families with their husbands and children, significant numbers of both African-American and white women were single parents with children even during that heyday of the nuclear family. At the end of that decade, one out of three black children and one out of ten white children were *not* living in two-parent families.

Some alternative family systems still are not widely recognized in our culture, even though they have been present as long or longer than nuclear families. For example, many Native American cultures have historically viewed families as three generations, with parental functions shared among aunts and uncles as well as grandparents (Attneave 1982). Native American families have often gone to great lengths to sustain their own traditional family structures in a culture that defines the "traditional family" quite differently. African-American families have also been characterized by three-generation extended kinship networks. These networks carry the responsibilities that white middle-class America assigns to the nuclear family, including sharing economic resources and the responsibilities of child care and childrearing (Hines and Boyd-Franklin 1982). Mexican-American families have traditionally included *compadres*, godparents who share in the responsibilities of childrearing, contributing financially as well as providing security and support in times of crisis (Falicov 1982).

2. Changes in mortality and birth rates are contributing to a changing distribution among family types. Some of the changes in American family life are results of changes in mortality and birth rates that indirectly shift the proportions of family types. The biological family is "elongating," as measured by the number of living generations of which it is composed. In 1900, life expectancy was little more than forty-five years. By the end of the twentieth century, life expectancy had stretched to seventy-two years (Ahrons 1992). Currently, 13 percent of the U.S. population is sixty-five or older (Congregations 1997). In nineteenth–century America, the combination of high mortality rates and immigration made the three-generation family a rarity. Many people died before they could be grandparents, let alone great-grandparents. Today, four-generation families have become commonplace.

Historically, stepfamilies have been common. Until relatively recently, however, they were more likely to have been created through the death of a spouse than by divorce, which is the most common origin of stepfamilies today. It was not until 1973-1974 that the number of U.S. marriages that ended in divorce exceeded the number of marriages that ended in widowhood (Spanier 1989).

Furthermore, the birth rate has dropped dramatically in the last two hundred years. In the late eighteenth century, the average American family had eight children; by 1900 this number had dropped to three (Grabill, Kiser and Whelpton

1973). American families now average 1.8 children (Ahrons 1992), which is less than the rate needed to replace the current adult population. Because families are choosing to have fewer children, the number of years that are dedicated to raising dependent children has decreased. To raise all a family's children to age eighteen today takes only an average of nineteen years. When families averaged three or more children, childrearing involved twenty-four or more years. Raising the average of eight children in a family two hundred years ago filled the entire adult life span. Today, adults who bear children are childless for many more years than the years they are actively parenting.

Increasing numbers of children remain "only children"; relatively few have more than one sibling. An only child marrying an only child serves as the extreme example of this shrinking family; their children have no aunts, uncles or cousins—only the generations before and after them. Their family tree looks more like a tall, thin poplar than a spreading chestnut. These families appear nuclear in structure, but their limited membership creates a small pool of resources on which to draw, particularly for peer adult support. Family support comes from one generation to the next rather than from siblings and cousins. Consequently, many of these small families develop familylike relationships with friends and work colleagues that supplement the resources of the family. Thus the limitations of the nuclear family in this time of dropping birth rates leads indirectly to exploration of new forms of primary relationship that can supplement or even replace the shrinking family membership of age peers.

3. Forces at work within families and society are creating new family forms and altering the development and endurance of families. The shrinking size of the nuclear family is not the only force that encourages the development of new family forms. Divorce has had a dramatic impact on many families that otherwise might be characterized as "lean and long." Of those who divorce today, almost half do so relatively early in their marriage, many before they have children. The ex-spouses can anticipate a traditional-looking family in a second marriage, with few if any ties to the first spouse.

For the other half of divorcing persons, representing about 25 percent of marriages (Glick 1989), divorce has increased dramatically the "width" of the family, plumping it up with an array of stepsiblings, stepgrandparents, and assorted stepaunts and stepuncles. Nevertheless, these relationships are a matter more of choice than of ascription. Some persons choose to relate to these steprelations as "family"; many others do not, as indicated by the fact that even stepparents and stepchildren do not necessarily consider one another "family."

Indeed, the subtle but growing role of choice concerning who is and is not one's family may be the most significant theme underlying seemingly diverse family types. When a pregnancy occurs outside of marriage today, the couple experiences far less pressure to marry than they would have two generations ago. The individuals may choose to marry, but they may also choose single parenting, or abortion.

So parenting is much more a voluntary choice than it was two generations ago. Increasingly effective birth-control technologies enable women to time pregnancy according to their own choices. Remaining married is also much more a voluntary choice. "No-fault" divorce laws have removed the element of having to make a case against a marriage; spouses can simply choose to end their marriage based on their own reasons. Spouses who have career opportunities in different communities have the option to establish voluntarily a two-household marriage—a choice that would have created major community consternation thirty or forty years ago in middle-class America. Most significantly, procreation no longer defines family relationships as it did in the past, although purpose and common goals are still highly relevant. It would be virtually as unthinkable today for a spouse to seek divorce because their partner was infertile as it was in the nineteenth century for spouses to divorce because they "could not communicate."

All of this means that (1) families are increasingly defined by those persons *chosen* to be family, and (2) many families no longer define their primary purpose as bearing and raising children. The process of choosing family takes place over time and is revisited throughout our lives. We choose to marry, and when times are difficult we choose to continue, or not continue, the marriage. We choose to "be close" to family members who may be geographically distant by making efforts to visit, to phone, to "stay in touch"—or we choose not to make the effort. Certainly we can choose to grow friendships into familylike relationships—or not.

A 1989 poll found that Americans tend not to see the family in structural terms—that is, as defined by blood relationships, marriage or adoption. Instead they define their families in emotional terms, as a group of people who love and care for one another. The poll found that 10 percent of respondents included friends when listing close family members. On the other hand, half of those who had stepchildren did not consider them family members (O'Brien 1989). Increasingly, family relationships are not defined by the roles they represent (mother, father, sibling, etc.) but by the functions they serve (nurturance, discipline, intimacy, cooperation).

In Barbara Kingsolver's novel *Pigs in Heaven* (Kingsolver 1993), a young single woman, Taylor, is living with a man named Jax. She is mothering Turtle, a Native American child who was left as an infant in Taylor's care after being severely sexually abused by her own family. Taylor finally has been able to adopt Turtle. Taylor is talking to her mother, Alice:

> "When the social worker asked Turtle about her family today, you know what she said? She said she didn't have one."
>
> "That's not right! She was confused."
>
> "Yeah. She's confused, because I'm confused. I *think* of Jax and Lou Ann and Dwayne Ray, and of course you, and Mattie, my boss at the tire store, all those people as my family. But when you never put a name on things, you're just accepting that it's okay for people to leave when they feel like it."
>
> "They leave anyway," Alice says. "My husbands went like houses on fire."
>
> "But you don't have to *accept* it," Taylor insists. "That's what your family is, the people you won't let go of for anything." (p. 328)

Taylor names the people she works with at the tire store and friends, as well as her "of course" family—her mother—as those she thinks of as family. These are people who have *become* family to her through intended and unintended choices. Nevertheless, once people have become family, they are supposed to *act* like family, which for Taylor—and for our society—means an ongoing committed relationship that "you won't let go of for anything." Yet even people in traditional family relationships *do* let go, as Alice illustrates by alluding to her several husbands.

Kingsolver's character is not the only one confused by the changing way we define families. Choosing to be family means not letting go of one another, no matter what other choices later present themselves. At least that is the ideal. The reality is that many people do make the choice at some point to "let go."

Perhaps the only family relationship that does not allow at least a moderate level of continuing choice is that of parents to children. The hoopla raised over a case in which a child sued parents for a divorce indicates just how strong feelings are in our culture about the parent-child bond. Once children are born into a family, whether by choice or by accident, that child and parent have few choices about whether or not to be family for one another. Immediately after birth, a parent may choose to place the child for adoption by another family.

This is a very difficult choice that becomes even more difficult and socially unacceptable with time. This attitude is based on our understanding of children's dependence on family for health and well-being. Adults are able to maintain a "single" status and survive, but this is not possible for children. They must have a family or, in situations of abuse or neglect, a substitute family of some kind in order to survive. We reserve our most derogatory public language about family relationships—"deadbeat," "neglectful"—for parents who choose to walk away from parent-child relationships. Even in the case of infant adoption, our society expects the biological parents to maintain a secret love for and attachment to their child, and to want eventually to be reunited in some way. We find it almost unfathomable that a birth parent would reject contact with a child who is seeking to be reunited.

The hottest debate about families in American culture today swirls around the place and needs of children. Children are increasingly becoming a scarce resource in American and other Western cultures. Because of dropping birth rates, the work force is shrinking. The next generation of workers—today's children—will be paying taxes to support the current adult generation in their old age. The smallest cohort of adults (our current children) will supporting the largest group of aging adults two generations ahead of them (the baby boomers). Consequently, the significance of providing the support children need to grow into productive adults is dawning on current societal leaders, if only out of self-interest. We can expect to see an intensification of discussion about the roles of children and parenting in defining American family life, and ways society can support families bearing and raising children.

Finally, the role of choice is directly related to the American ideal of mobility. The pull of economic opportunities in other places has historically been more compelling to Americans than the tie to an extended family rooted in a particular place. America was—and still is—a society of immigrants. Often older generations were left behind in countries of emigration, in both Europe and Asia, and in Africa by involuntary emigrants from that continent. The westward movement in the United States also lured young families toward life on the frontier and away from families in the East. African-Americans from the South migrated toward the North seeking work, sometimes leaving children behind with relatives until economic viability could be established. Farm children migrated to the city.

This mobility as a feature of American family life has continued. As one indicator, census data show that the percentage of today's population that is foreign-born has almost doubled since 1970 to 8.8 percent; it is now at its highest level since prior to World War II (Congregations 1997).

WHY DEFINING THE FAMILY IS SO IMPORTANT

Defining family is more than an academic exercise. It has significance both for families and for the society and culture in which those families are embedded. Indeed, defining family does *create* family. It not only names reality, it *shapes* reality. If we believe a family relationship exists, then it does. Believing you are my brother leads to actions quite different on my part than believing you are a potential sexual partner, or employer, or friend.

The definition of family communicates what is considered "normal" and "right." It reflects subtle but very significant indicators of social acceptance. For example, in many professions, including that of church pastor in many Protestant denominations, preference is still given to men who have wives and children; this living situation is perceived to be most stable and supportive of a demanding career.

At the same time, a prospective employee who has dependent children may be considered less desirable, for children may intrude upon job concerns and schedule. Many young families identified with *Parenthood*, a movie released in 1989; it was a social commentary on the changing relationship between the world of work and the world of the family. In the film, a father who is active in his children's lives, and thus not freely available for extended work hours and undivided devotion to the company, is passed over for a promotion. The boss gives the promotion to another man, saying admiringly, "I don't know if he even *has* children."

Yet the boss comes across as the villain in this scene. Thirty years ago, it would have seemed appropriate for an employer to expect his subordinates to keep family concerns from interfering with work performance. But our values have changed. Today it is *right* for parents to be involved in their children's lives, even if it occasionally compromises their work performance. This is especially true for fathers, who had for several decades been seen as peripheral to their children's well-being but are being rediscovered as necessary ingredients in the lives of healthy, well-adjusted children. Laws have been passed forbidding job interviewers to ask questions about plans for pregnancy and childbearing, because such questions have been used to discriminate against potential employees. These laws reflect our society's belief about what is "good" and "moral," including the right and responsibility to give people time to bear and raise children.

Every society privileges certain activities and practices because they are valued. The definition of family matters because it is the basis for social privileges. These privileges are concretely represented in social policies.

The definition of family is important because it is the basis for government, legal and institutional policies. Grieving adults have been excluded from the bedside of a terminally ill lifelong partner because they were not "family." Stepparents are sometimes unable to obtain needed medical care for a stepchild because they are not "family." A stepmother may have functioned as the mother for the entire life of her stepchild; should her husband die, however, she may lose custody of the child to the paternal or maternal blood relatives because she is not "family" to the child. Zoning laws may keep two young single mothers from establishing a household together to pool their incomes and help one another raise their children. They are not related to one another and thus not legally allowed to share the same single-family dwelling, even though their combined household is no larger than a nuclear family with two children. Social assistance programs and publicly financed medical care are determined by family status. Tax codes may or may not give special allowances to families because they share a household or deductions to families that have "dependent members" to support.

In the church, too, the definition of family out of which we operate shapes our programs and ministries. It privileges those recognized as families by providing attention to their issues and needs. By ignoring other kinds of primary relationships not considered "family" by our definition, we de facto exclude them from the faith community. They do not receive the support and resources provided to other families. For example, churches have been using the traditional family as their definition for several decades, as reflected in the organization of family ministry programs in the categories of "married couples," "parents" and "single adults." Two sisters who share a household and are providing care for an old friend of the family with Alzheimer's disease who is living independently nearby will probably not receive the same level of support and care as a married couple providing care for a parent in a similar health and living situation. The sisters may receive encouragement and tangible support from members of their Sunday-school class and others in the church, but it will probably not fall under the category of "family ministry."

Congregations do indeed provide support and care for a diversity of families, but they do so in informal ways. Insofar as congregations are communities, much support and care for families come about informally. I interviewed a single mother of older teenage and young adult children who serves as an important lay leader in her congregation. At the time of our interview she had been divorced for thirteen years. (Even the fact that she was a divorced woman in a position of church leadership indicates the changes in congregational acceptance of diverse family structures.) Seven years after their divorce, her ex-husband, who was living in another city, committed suicide after his second marriage ended. This mother experienced enormous stress as she tried to help her children cope with the death of their father and her own anger that he would create this grief and loss for his own children.

But the death of an ex-spouse who is not a church member and not known by the congregation is not a typical situation calling for family ministry. Because the couple had been divorced for many years, many persons might not recognize the intensity of stress this situation presented for this mother and her children; she was, after all, not technically "widowed." Yet she described an outpouring of care from her congregation in ways that would be typical if she had been widowed:

> Everybody has been there for me. Our church was incredible. They helped in every way imaginable, from just being there to notes of encouragement, food. . . . Even now somebody will ask, "How are you? Are you really doing okay?" And it's wonderful to know that there's a history there, that those people are really concerned and caring.

The challenge for church leaders may be to recognize and support with our programs and church policies what congregations are already doing informally to care for the diversity of families in their circles of care.

SOCIOLOGICAL DEFINITIONS OF FAMILY

As we saw in the previous section, definitions of the nuclear family and the traditional family have been extremely significant not only in the study of families but also in shaping social responses to those primary groups defined as families and those that are not. *How* to define the family, however, has been a perennial debate. Ernest Burgess, a pioneer in family studies, described his work:

> This study of the patterns of personal relationships in family life led directly to the conception of the family as a unity of interacting persons. By a unity of interacting personalities is meant a living, changing, growing thing. I was about to call it a

superpersonality. At any rate, the actual unity of family life has its existence not in any legal conception, nor in any formal contract, but in the interacting of its members. (Burgess 1926:5)

Despite Burgess's concept, sociology and our society has more often defined family as a structure, a set of statuses and roles (such as parent-child, spouse-spouse) than as "patterned personal relationships."

A Structural Definition of the Family

The assumption implicit in a nuclear definition of the family is that family relationships are best defined by *structure*—how persons are related to one another by blood lineage or legal bonds of adoption and marriage. A *structural* definition of family defines primary groups as families when they consist of a married couple and their biological or adopted children, or any remnant of these relationships (such as a single parent and his or her children, or an elderly parent living with an adult child). The defining features for family in this schema are marriage and parenthood. It is the patterns (structures of relationship) created by marriage, adoption and parenthood that define what a family is. Persons are family because of legal relationship (marriage or adoption) or biological relationship with one another, regardless of the strength or quality of the relationship. It may have been twenty years since a person has seen a sister or parent, but that person is still defined as family, and that definition carries with it certain rights and responsibilities. For example, it would be acceptable for the sister to show up in town and call to see if she can stay overnight—or a week or more. By contrast, an acquaintance who has not been seen for twenty years would have much less social license to ask for such hospitality (although she still might ask!).

A structural definition is applicable to other types of families in addition to nuclear families, such as "extended families," "blended families" or "stepfamilies," and "fictive kin." "Extended family" is the kinship network that extends beyond primary relationships of marriage and parenthood, defined by relationship to either the marriage or parental status: grandparents, in-laws, aunts, uncles, cousins. Extended family is the "family tree." The "blending family" or "stepfamily" results when sections of family that did not originate there are "grafted" onto a family tree. This grafting usually takes place through the process of divorce and remarriage and usually is dependent on the presence of children from the first marriage of one or both spouses. If there are no children, frequently the new marriage dissolves any family ties to the first spouses' families. When there are children present, however, a remarriage results in the new roles of stepparent, stepsibling, stepgrandparent and other steprelatives. Like the nuclear family, all of these relationships are defined by marital and parenting relationships.

Finally, "fictive kin" are persons who relate to a family *as if* they were nuclear or extended family members, when in fact they are not related by either blood or marriage. This is the "Aunt Suzy" who participates in family events, who may even live in the family household, but the relationship is structurally friendship, not marriage or parenting. Perhaps she was Grandmother's best friend and gradually became more family than friend. The operative word here is *fictive:* this person may act like kin and may even be mistaken by others for kin, but the kinship is a "fiction."

A structural definition of the family posits a set of statuses that persons fill— parent, spouse, child. Note that these categories are *sociological;* that is, they are ways students of the family categorize family relationships and nonfamily relationships. They are not necessarily the ways persons would define themselves and their families. Undoubtedly Aunt Suzy would not consider her family membership a "fiction," nor would others in the family. Nevertheless, if pushed a little they might acknowledge that Aunt Suzy is not *really* a family member, because the structural definition permeates our culture's thinking about how to define family relationships. On the other side, the sociological category "blending families" may define persons as kinfolk who do not see themselves in that way. Older children in a newly created family system often do not see their stepparent and stepparent's relatives as "family."

Family Structure and Personal Well-Being

Alan Acock and David Demo have studied the hypothesis that family structure influences family relationships and personal well-being. Using a national random survey of more than thirteen thousand households in the late 1980s (Acock and Demo 1994), they examined a number of variables across four prevalent family structures: two-parent families in which both parents are in their first marriage, single-parent families headed by a divorced mother, two-parent stepfamilies with at least one child from the mother's previous marriage, and single-parent families of never-married mothers. The researchers identified several important patterns and themes in American families. First, they found more variation in key variables of family well-being *within* each type of family structure than there is *between* them. In other words, family structure is not significantly related to family well-being.

Second, women continue to perform a tremendous amount of the household labor, whether or not they are employed outside the home. They do two to three times as much housework as their husbands or cohabiting partners. Increasing family diversity has not changed the division of domestic labor. Although husbands and fathers are often physically present in the household, they tend not to be significantly involved in family life; parenting, like housework, is "gendered family labor" (p. 218). Although men are doing more than they did in the 1960s, they are doing only slightly more.

Third, mothers of all family types emphasize their rules and expectations for their children. "The evidence suggests that any problems associated with single-parent families cannot be attributed to 'poor' childrearing values, lack of rules, or low expectations for children. Instead, disadvantages for parents and children in single-parent families typically stem from sustained economic hardship" (p. 219).

Finally, intergenerational relationships in stepfamilies seem less satisfactory and more stressful for children, but may have many advantages for the adult partners in comparison to first marriages. Second marriages are marked by more frequent marital interaction and sexual intercourse and less arguing than first marriages are.

The researchers concluded that studying family *structure* is not as useful for understanding individual satisfaction with family life as is studying the *processes* of family life. For example, it is not the structure of the single-parent family that is as predictive of mother's happiness and children's well-being; more significant is the role the father plays—or does not play—in the lives of his children.

Although these findings are not particularly surprising to family therapists and family life educators, they do point to the possibility that we can address family needs effectively across different structures rather than having to address each kind of family uniquely. *All* families need to address household role expectations for men, women and children. *All* fathers, whether they are resident husbands of their children's mother, never-married fathers living separately from their children, or members of divorced two-household families, need to be encouraged and equipped to assume nurturing roles in the lives of their children.

A Functional Definition of Family

The structural definition of the family has dominated scientific and popular thought concerning families and has consequently had a significant influence in shaping families in our culture as well as describing them. But it is not the only way to define families. Families can also be defined by the ways persons behave toward one another, or how relationships *function* in the lives of people.

Instead of statuses to which one is assigned, a *functional* definition of family looks to the roles persons take with one another. In this definition, how people relate to one another in familylike ways determines family membership, not the formal and biological statuses they hold. Structure does not necessarily equal function: using a functional definition of family, Aunt Suzy is indeed *really* family. In the same way, two single adults who have lived as roommates for many years may share their tangible resources and support and care for one another in familylike ways. From a functional perspective, they are "family," not just "fictive kin." A grandmother who has custody of and is raising her grandchildren because the children's parents cannot do so for whatever reasons is really "mother" more than she is "grandmother." This functional role is at least as significant to understanding this family as is knowing the biological relationship of grandparent-grandchildren. In fact, it takes both definitions to understand the complexities of families.

The lack of terms for defining relationships presents a major challenge for a functional definition of family. The only family terms we have come from the structural definition of family relationships—*parent, grandparent, spouse, brother, sister, aunt, uncle.* Functional family relationships that are not overlays of existing structures thus have to modify these terms. For example, the structure of biological relationship between two sisters becomes the term they use to describe their bond as adults living together as a family—*sisters.* Two adult women who do not have this underlying biological relationship but who are also bonded together as adults in a nonsexual relationship, sharing their household and lives with one another, have no corresponding term to use to describe their bond, so they use the term *sister* with a qualifier such as *like*—"like sisters." This is a significantly different way of thinking about this relationship, however, than the structural term that would be relevant, "fictive kin." It points to the similarity of the relationship ("like") to what one would expect in the named biological relationship ("sisters") rather than highlighting the dissimilarity ("fictive").

The subtle but important distinction that the functional definition can make in defining family relationships can be seen in the case of families formed by second marriages with children from first marriages present. Some students of the family choose the term *blending,* with its implication of ongoing action, over the term *blended,* which assumes the process is complete, and *step,* which defines the family by its legal structure. This subtle difference in terms actually indicates a dramatic difference between the structural definition of family and the functional definition. The terms *blended* and *step* both imply that this relationship is created by the legal act of marriage. *Blending,* on the other hand, is a *functional* term. The action of "blending" is an ongoing process, not completed by the legal action of marriage. Indeed, in many blending families, persons never completely accept one another as full-fledged "family." One of the families I interviewed described the blending process they experienced, which extended over more than fifteen years:

> Ann's father died when she was twelve. Through Ann's teenage years, Ann's mother, Ruth, dated Sam, a family friend. They finally married when Ann was twenty and out of the home. The first years of Ann's relationship with Sam were rocky; both of them resented the attention Ruth gave the other. They tended to avoid one another and did not consider one another "family," but rather "my mother's new husband" and "my wife's daughter." It was only after Ann married and had children, and Ruth and Sam began caring for the children while Ann and her husband worked, that they began to feel like family to one another. Even though Sam is not biologically related to the grandchildren, the children call him Grandpa and clearly he functions in that role. And Ann now accepts Sam as her "father."

The functional definition of families requires defining the functions that family plays in persons' lives that are distinct from other interpersonal relations. Family is *the organization of relationships that endure over time and contexts through which persons attempt to meet their needs for belonging and attachment and to share life purposes, help and resources.* A family is thus defined by *observation of behavior,* not by role designations. Who does one share troubles with? share money with? Who lives together? eats together? Who takes care of each other during sickness? Who sticks together year after year, moving from one town to another to live with or be close to one another? The words *attempt to* in the definition communicate that families are not always successful in fulfilling these functions. Nevertheless, these are the relationships through which persons continue to *attempt* to live out what it means to be family. But each of the functions embedded in this definition needs further explication.

1. Organization of relationships. Families are organizations, whether they think of themselves in this way or not. As organizations, they are characterized by roles, rules and the distribution of power.

Members take on roles, both chosen and assigned, which they enact with another. These roles change over time, but as they are enacted and changed, they define relationships. For example, one member takes responsibility for the family finances, or this is a shared responsibility taken on together. However it is defined, if the family member who is *not* ascribed the role "financial manager" takes on the task of balancing the checkbook or completing the income tax forms, there will probably be surprise and even disorientation.

The family organization has spoken and unspoken rules. When family members break the rules, there are expected repercussions. Children are disciplined by spanking or the taking away of privileges. Families are the only place where persons are still given social permission to hit one another as a means of discipline, although this is increasingly being circumscribed by spouse-abuse and child-abuse laws. Adults are disciplined by withdrawal of affection or the use of other interpersonal sanctions. For example, the family cook may "discipline" another adult by serving something that person does not like, or by refusing to cook at all until the situation is rectified.

Family rules and roles are related to the distribution of power within the family. Power in families is often distributed in relationship to the gender and generational relationships in the family. Men tend to have more power than women, and adults have more power than children. Our cultural values dictate that family members use power in benevolent, nurturing ways that contribute to the well-being of all other family members. Nevertheless, power can be and often is abused, meaning that those with power take advantage of those with less power.

2. Enduring over time and contexts. Family relationships are not transitory. They last across time and space, whether there is frequent contact or involvement or not. Children are never adopted for a limited period, nor are marriages defined as temporary, although both kinds of relationships can indeed be disrupted and terminated. The exceptions only underscore the expectations for permanence. The very sense of the terms *disrupted* and *terminated* indicates that these relationships were expected to continue for a lifetime.

This feature of family life is common throughout the world. Although the ways families achieve permanence vary from culture to culture, the continuity of family units has been an important feature of virtually all cultures. For example, in Chinese society the ancestral chain permanently linking the living with their ancestors and their future unborn children provides an identification with a stable family unit that permeates Chinese life (Thornton 1996:81).

Perhaps permanence, more than any other characteristic of family, distinguishes the often subtle boundary between friendship and family. Friendships sometimes becomes family relationships. Thus the boundary is a fuzzy one, but it is still a real boundary. Friendships are usually more a matter of convenience than of lifetime commitment. Friendships are location-specific; retirees often attest to their surprise that long-term friendships in the workplace often fade upon retirement. Obviously, sometimes extraordinary lengths are taken to maintain friendships, and sometimes friends appear to be more like family members than are some relatives. For example, we allow relationships with unfavorite cousins or aunts and uncles to drift for years unnurtured. Perhaps we even lose their addresses and phone numbers so we could not relate to them if we wanted to, without seeking contact through others. Alternatively, some relationships between family members may take on characteristics of friendship. One young single mother exclaimed to me, "My parents aren't just parents; they are my best friends." These overlapping descriptions simply indicate that the boundaries between friendships and family are not crisply defined—not that there is no difference between the two kinds of relationship.

The crosscountry move, the major interpersonal conflict or the drifting of interests often defines the difference between friends and families. A defining moment in determining family membership comes when one family member considers moving to another community because of employment. In contrast with persons designated "friends," family members expect to be consulted about, or at very least included in, decisions and plans for such a move. If the family does not live in the same household, there are intentional and sometimes elaborate processes for maintaining the family relationships. Spouses employed in different cities spend great amounts of time and resources to be together on a regular basis. Estimates of college costs always factor in transportation to allow the student to travel home for holidays and school recesses.

Friends, on the other hand, may be informed and even consulted about a crosscountry move, but they do not expect to be included in the actual move, nor is it typical for elaborate plans and significant expenditures of family resources to be invested in maintaining a long-distance relationship. Phone calls, occasional letters and visits while back in town on business or on the way somewhere else are typical ways friends work at maintaining their relationships. Families, on the other hand, are more intentional—phone calls and letters (or e-mail) are regular, and regular visits are not as likely to happen because family members are "on the way," but rather for the specific purpose of being together.

Moving to a new community is often most wrenching because it implies leaving friends behind and establishing new friendships. It is socially acceptable for friends to allow relationships to become more tenuous in these circumstances, whereas families are expected to expend significant effort and resources to retain and nourish their relationships with one another.

3. Meeting needs for attachment and belonging. One of the most important functions of family is providing what John Bowlby has called a "secure base" (Bowlby 1988). Its members can venture out into the world more securely because they know that when they return home they will be welcomed, nourished physically and emotionally, and comforted if distressed. We can see this most readily in toddlers, who play happily and independently so long as parents are nearby, perhaps checking in periodically with verbal exchanges or even a quick run for physical contact and then returning to play. Whenever they are frightened, or tired, or hungry, however, they seek prolonged contact with the parent.

In this respect the family functions much like a military base from which an expeditionary force sets out and to which it can retreat if trouble is encountered. Only the military officer who is confident that the base is secure can press forward and take risks (Bowlby 1988:11).

Of course, it is not only children who need such a base. Adolescents and adults, too, need a place that feels secure, a place where they feel welcomed and where they belong. Indeed, such a secure base allows them to engage in work and play with much greater single-mindedness, creativity and even courage.

We can define a person's family by determining who populates that person's "secure base." One of the most telling ways to determine who family is for someone is to ask whom they would be concerned to locate first in the event of a disaster. In a nuclear war, a tornado or a hurricane that obliterates a community, whom would they search for first? Obviously, there is also concern for neighbors and friends, but there is a qualitative difference in the level of panic created by separation from family from that created when separated from friends. Family members are *attached* to one another; the family members feel like appendages of, a part of, the self. To lose that appendage is to lose a part of the self, and thus separation is a significant personal threat.

Bowlby defines *attachment* as "any form of behaviour that results in a person attaining or maintaining proximity to some other clearly identified individual who is conceived as better able to cope with the world" (1988:26-27). As we become adults, it may be that the other is not necessarily able to cope better, but that *together* we can cope with the world better than one can cope alone, often expressed in song lyrics and on T-shirts as "you and me against the world." Obviously, adults become attached to children as well as children becoming attached to adults. Although children may seem to contribute little in terms of coping, the meaning and purpose they give to an adult's life may indeed be central to that adult's ability and style of coping with life circumstances.

Bowlby has been the most significant theorist of attachment theory, developing it out of and distinct from psychoanalytic theory. He sees attachment as a fundamental form of behavior with its own internal motivation apart from feeding and sex, and just as important for survival. Thus he has challenged the pejorative connotation of "dependency" needs. He has also distinguished attachment from dependency. Dependency is considered a characteristic of children that will be grown out of, and of adults who have not matured. It manifests itself in many relationships. For example, the dependent adult may be considered clingy and even smothering by friends, family and acquaintances. By contrast, attachment manifests itself in a few emotionally charged relationships with very specific others and is not readily transferred to other relationships. Attachment takes time to develop, and the loss of an attachment figure is a major source of grief and despair. Attachment relationships are vital to healthy, functional, productive adulthood.

Attachment is demonstrated (1) when family members experience a need to be with one another when experiencing distress and find a sense of comfort and diminished anxiety in one another's presence and (2) when separation from the other and an inability to be reunited create anxiety, protest and despair (Bowlby 1969 and 1975; Weiss 1993). When we are upset by something, often the first thing we want to do is seek out the persons to whom we are attached. The very presence of the other is comforting, regardless of whether they can actually make any difference in the problem that confronts us. An anxious surgery patient may want the person to whom he is attached to hold his hand while he is prepped for surgery, or at least to be nearby.

The opposite is also true: separation from and inability to be reunited with the persons to whom we are attached creates enormous anxiety. We recognize attachment in the agitation a small child expresses when parents leave her for the first time in a new church nursery or daycare center. Not just any comforting figure will do; it is Mommy or Daddy who is desperately longed for and can provide the needed comfort. The grief over the loss of a lifetime partner is another painful expression of attachment; no one else can replace the attachment figure or comfort the loss. One widow found some small comfort in wrapping herself in her husband's old robe because it smelled like him and felt like him. No one could take his place. Even loving children's arms were not as comforting as the sleeves of that old robe—the best available representation of his presence.

Attachment takes place over time; it is perhaps the most significant indicator that a marriage relationship or a friendship or a caregiving relationship has become a family relationship. A marriage, for example, may be primarily a sexual relationship and/or a friendship, but the partners do not necessarily experience attachment with one another until long after the wedding. Young spouses may still turn to earlier attachment figures (usually their own parents) for comfort in times of stress, or at least may experience a greater sense of being "at home" in the parental home than in the new household they have founded. Couples often speak of the gradual process of transferring their sense of "at-homeness" to the new household. This is the attachment process.

New attachment figures do not replace other attachment figures; attachment figures cannot really be replaced. Spouses may find comfort in one another's presence but also seek out parents for comfort in times of great distress, even after the marital attachment is firm. A fifty-year-old adult happily married for a quarter of a century may still long for her mother's comfort during a time of great distress. Elderly persons with significant dementia may call out anxiously for parents or spouses or even children long dead.

It is interesting to conjecture that attachment may help explain why divorce rates are much higher during the early years of marriage, when we can hypothesize that attachment has not fully developed. After the couple has become family for one another, divorce means the loss not only of the partner but also of the secure base that partner represents.

Obviously, attachments also continue to be formed throughout life. They are not just a characteristic of the parent-child and marital bonds. In my own life, I experienced this development of attachment with my father-in-law, Ned. My mother-in-law, Ruth, developed cancer when I was pregnant with our second child; she died two years later. My husband is an only child, so we were Ned's only family. He lived in an apartment near us, and as his health began to fail, my husband and I took increasingly active roles in caring for him, with daily phone contact and bringing him to our home almost daily so he could eat dinner and spend the evening with us. As the years passed, he had to give up driving, so we provided transportation to doctors, to the store and to church.

Although Parkinson's disease gradually made it difficult for Ned to carry on conversations with strangers because of his difficulty when anxious with putting thoughts into words, his mind remained sharp, and we had long talks as we did chores together. He sat in the kitchen and talked with me or just watched while I prepared dinner or folded laundry. He listened to the joys and frustrations of my work. As a retired missionary and church pastor, he was a compassionate supporter of my work with congregations. I also listened to him as he talked about his experiences and sometimes gave me advice. He was proud of me, and it pleased me to please him. I washed his clothes, fussed over his not eating enough, and balanced his checkbook. He treated me like a daughter, and he felt like a father to me. In absent-minded moments in the last months of his life, he sometimes called me "Ruth," his wife's name. I felt honored, taking this as a sign that I was important to him and that I was doing the "family thing" as I needed and wanted to do. In short, we became attached to one another.

He died twelve years after Ruth. For more than two years after Ned's death, I found myself wanting to pick up the phone and call him to talk over the little events of my days, as I had for years. I experienced his absence at the dinner table and in our family's daily life as something almost palpable. I still miss him.

Intimacy refers to the sense of attachment and closeness one experiences with family members for whom one provides and from whom one receives physical and emotional care. It is expressed in the little acts of bodily care for another in infancy, illness and disability. Intimacy also develops when persons share meals or other resources, and when persons see one another's private selves not generally shared with others. I laugh to remember a camping trip in the Rocky Mountains my husband and I took with several children—our own and the children of friends. During a burping contest to celebrate wonderfully cold soft drinks after a long hike one hot afternoon, one little girl said, "My dad can outburp any of you!" Her father is a distinguished theologian and church leader whom I will not name here. I had not considered that he might have that particular talent. Families see the other side of us!

The result of attachment is the sense of belonging and "at-homeness" family members experience in one another's presence. We can be "ourselves" and still be accepted with these people. Although there are expectations that we fulfill certain roles with one another, we are more than simply roles in each other's lives. This is quite different from settings in which relationships are much more defined by role assignments: student-teacher, employer-employee and so on. Even friendships may be role specific: the persons who attend the same Sunday-school class, who play softball together, who work in the mail room.

When family members are treated as roles, on the other hand, there is a sense of being "used" or even mistreated. There are few spouses who want to be considered *just* as sexual partners, or parents who want to be considered *just* as the family cook or launderer, or grown children who want to be seen as *just* as the one who takes an elderly parent to the doctor or balances the checkbook. Family members fulfill roles, but in our culture they expect these roles to be incidental to the regard and concern they feel from others in the family.

4. Sharing life purposes. One of the most significant functions of a family is the integration and mutual care of the generations. No other aspect of our culture emphasizes the relationships between generations as families do. Even though not all families include persons of different generations all of the time, the care of one generation for another remains the responsibility of families. Every child must be attached to a family to survive and thrive, and this responsibility is unique to families. Even childless families often carry responsibility for generational care, because every person has parents.

This responsibility for caregiving is most visible at the interface of family with community. Families are expected to contribute to the community through the socialization and support of members, both adults and children. We expect workers to go home to families and be refreshed and strengthened there for the next day's work. We expect children to come to school with the experiences and nurture they need to prepare them adequately for formal learning.

Laws hold parents responsible for their children's conduct, whether or not they are at home. For example, parents whose children are chronically truant from school are liable to prosecution for child neglect, and some states have attempted to prosecute parents for the delinquency of their children. Similarly, adult children are expected to make decisions about when to resuscitate a critically ill aging parent who is not expected to recover, or to take legal responsibility for the affairs of an "incompetent" parent.

Caring for one another economically and physically often gives meaning and purpose to a family's life together. Families share in maintaining the family's living space and economic stability. There may be a "family chore" time when family members work together to do housework or maintenance.

Caregiving includes those not living in the same household. Nonresident children take down and put up screens and storm windows, paint, and in other ways maintain an older parent's home, or take the parent to the doctor or shopping, or bring in prepared food. In turn, older adults provide respite or after-school care for young children, or help young adults with the purchase of homes, autos or large appliances. They come to help out in times of childbirth, illness and other crises when more adult assistance is needed.

> Beth and Brian's first child Evan was born critically ill and remained in neonatal intensive care for almost three months. During that time, Beth's mother kept her refrigerator stocked and the house clean. She came to pick up their laundry and returned it clean to their drawers and closets. As Beth said, "Mom did everything so that I could stay at the hospital with Evan."

Yet caring for and bearing responsibility for one another is not the only social purpose of the family. Families also have responsibilities beyond their own boundaries for the social and physical world around them. We expect families to beautify the land or corner of the building or front door leading to the space they occupy. We expect them to participate in the community in ways that strengthen it, whether through community organizations, informal looking out for the needs of neighbors, or simply paying taxes. Families—and their members—carry responsibility not simply for themselves but also for their piece of the community and world.

This emphasis on both mutual caregiving and care for the social and physical environment points to the different ways families and other social institutions relate to time. In the workplace or on the sports field, people focus on doing one or a few related things at one time. They work toward specified or implicit goals. The time orientation tends to be *monochronic*, with an emphasis on activities organized linearly. In contrast, families have a *polychronic* time orientation, in which people are doing several things simultaneously—caring for children, doing housework, talking to a friend on the phone. Physical tasks of cooking and cleaning are interwoven with interpersonal, emotional and affective tasks of caregiving. Family activity normally consists of interruptions, messes, disarray, starting and stopping, and partially completed tasks (Beutler, Burr, Bahr and Herrin 1989). In family life, the *processes* of life are just as important as reaching established goals.

Obviously, the linear attitudes of the workplace often seep in, but these intrusions of a linear orientation are often met with dissatisfaction and frustration, as when burdened parents worry that they are so busy marching their families through daily routines that they don't have "quality time" together. They perceive that the processes of daily activities (talking with a small child riding in the child seat of a grocery cart, teaching the names of vegetables and counting or reading labels, and enjoying one another's company) may take more time and energy when done "well," but that these processes are just as important as the outcome (stocking the kitchen with needed groceries). The goal is not to purchase groceries as efficiently as possible but to instruct, nurture and enjoy the child *while* buying food. If asked which was more important, in fact, many family members would see the relationship being nurtured as more important than the outcome of the shared activity—grocery shopping completed. Families often worry about the extent they are "being family," or simply doing what has to be done; this concern indicates the significance of the expectation of a process orientation in family life.

5. Sharing help. When people need help, our culture expects them to turn first to their family and expects the family to help to the extent that it can. In sickness, financial need or emotional distress, families help one another. Families in our society are expected to operate as covenantal relationships, not as contractual setups. Obviously, they do not always achieve this ideal, but when they do not, this is seen as a failure of the family, not of the ideal. There is a sense of duty to one another that is more fundamental and compelling than paying one's debts.

Although family help is not considered contractual, our culture does expect mutuality over time in families. Children are not expected to repay parents for the cost of their rearing. Family members do not expect repayment for help they give one another. Instead there is the expectation that family members who give help can also call on the family when they are in distress. Or family members are expected to "pass it on" to the next generation. The message of parent to their children is often, at least implicitly, "As we have helped you as much as we can, so help your own children when that time comes."

Again, the distinction between friendship and family is important. Friendships tend to be sources of social support and limited tangible support. It is expected that a friend will loan a relatively small sum of money, but it is also expected that it will be paid back. A friend can be expected to buy your lunch once in a while, but probably cannot be counted on for support for four years of college.

6. Sharing resources. Finally, families share their resources with one another. Although adults may retain separate checking accounts, and teenage children are often allowed to keep at least a portion of their earnings from part-time jobs to spend as they see fit, families tend to share their financial and other resources. Families purchase groceries, toilet paper, laundry soap and other household supplies from the family budget. Cars, refrigerators and media equipment often belong to the family, not to single individuals. Even when family members do not share a household, there is still often a sense of "what is mine is yours." Members give or swap cars back and forth in ways that would be considered highly unusual for friends. If they sell things to one another or loan one another money, families rarely charge the going interest rate.

These six elements characterize what persons in our society *expect* from family relationships. They do not necessarily portray reality for all families; perhaps no family fulfills all these functions, particularly at any given time. Almost every family is at one time or another "dysfunctional" with regard to one or more of these characteristics.

Some have even considered that if a collection of people who view themselves as "family" are not fulfilling these functions, they are in a functional sense not really a family. Take this definition of a "family" published in 1937:

> The family is in essence, then, a fellowship that, acting through a great variety of combinations and modes of sharing significant interests, fosters growth and fulfillment in every member and yields meanings increasingly diversified and rich, for all its members and for their larger community. How much of a genuine family any one small group actually is will depend then, if these considerations are sound, upon how much of this type of fellowship is operative within that group. (Wieman 1937:58)

Does that mean that when a family group tends to squash personal fulfillment in some members rather than nourishing, it is not really a family? The structural definition runs the danger of excluding from the definition of "family" those who do not relate to one another in the requisite statuses, even though they *function* as family for one another. The functional definition runs the danger, on the other hand, of excluding those who may have the status of spouses, parents or children but nevertheless do not fulfill all the functions of a family.

It seems that neither of these definitions is adequate by itself. Together, however, structural and functional definitions complement one another and provide keys for understanding families in our culture.

CONCLUSION

Most family ministries have been based on a structural definition of family. Thus we have ministry with married couples, with parents, with single parents, with single adults, with empty-nest families and so on. No doubt these ministries have been helpful to families dealing with the various life-stage issues. On the other hand, this approach tends to cut up a congregation into homogenous groups, so that all the married couples are grouped for ministry, and all the singles, and so on. It also has the tendency toward congregational specialization, so that one congregation may become known as the congregation for young families, another the church for single adults, or for senior adults. Inevitably some types of families do not find a specialized ministry for them, because most congregations do not have enough specialized staff and other resources to maintain a host of specialized ministries for the diversity of family types included in the community.

Recognizing that the functional definition also has its limitations and needs to be complemented by the structural approach, I propose that family ministry will be better defined if we begin with a functional family definition as the ideal to which we strive. The functional definition seems to better fit Jesus' teachings about family. For followers of Christ are not to be bound by the structures of legally recognized or biologically based relationships. Rather, family relationships are defined by relationship processes—loving one another, being faithful to the same Lord, and adopting one another as brothers and sisters in the household of faith.

Taking a functional definition of family has a number of implications for family ministry.

☐ A functional definition means we expand our vision to see all the ways persons in our congregation and community live in family groups. "Family ministry" becomes sensitive to the life experiences of everyone, not just those living in nuclear families.

☐ We cannot always know who families are by looking at the church roll and seeing who is married to or parenting whom. Instead we must ask people to tell us who their families are. Here are some questions that help persons tell us who their families are: (1) If a tornado blew away our town, whom would you be most desperate to locate and make sure they were okay? (2) If you were moving a thousand miles away, who would move with you, or with whom would you go to all kinds of lengths to stay attached? (3) If you developed a long-term illness, whom could you count on to take care of you? (4) Who will be your family from now until you or they die? (5) Whom could you borrow money from and not feel like you had to pay it back immediately?

☐ Our Christian faith undoubtedly has much to say about the choices we make about who our families are and the choices we make to continue to be family for one another. These are issues of Christian discipleship.

☐ Because being defined as a family carries with it rights and responsibilities, groups that consider themselves family but are denied family status in social policies suffer a variety of losses. Congregations can speak out in behalf of more just social policies when they believe that the denial of family status is unjust.

☐ Congregations can give recognition to functional family relationships that do not have "names" in our cultural language, publicly recognizing and supporting families by giving them social significance.

☐ Families benefit from learning how families function. For example, it helps blending families to know that it is normal for the process of becoming family to take years. It helps busy families to understand that family time is "polychronic" and thus feels quite different from the "monochronic" time of the workplace. There is helpful content here for family life education.

Chapter 2

Families in Physical & Social Space

Early in my social work career, Jim and Sally, a married couple in their thirties, came to me for counseling. They complained of "not being able to communicate" with each other. Everything seemed to start an argument. Ten years after their marriage, their daughter had been born, and soon thereafter their struggles began. Both had experienced the divorce of their own parents, and they were afraid that they were headed in the same direction.

I hypothesized that the birth of this child had created a developmental crisis for this couple who had waited to have a child. Perhaps they had been ambivalent about sealing their commitment to be family with one another in this very significant way. Now that they had done so, the bonds their daughter's birth signified created anxiety for them, and each perceived the other to be responsible in some way for this increase in anxiety. In addition, the child's presence brought no small amount of disruption to their well-established routines. Babies mean sleep deprivation for parents, which means less creativity and energy for dealing with other stresses and anxieties. With these guesses about the causes of their distress in my mind, I began my work with them.

Since I guessed that their commitment to one another and to their child might be causing some anxiety for them, I decided to help them revisit the positive experiences that had led to their commitment in the first place. I led them to share what they remembered about their attraction to each other early in their courtship. I also asked them to think about and name what they really liked about their current relationship and wanted to hold on to, as well as what they would like to see changed. It was difficult for them to say positive things to each other without sliding in barbs. Their speech was dominated with blaming and "you" messages ("*you* never used to be that way"; "if *you* would just be more considerate of my feelings"; "if *you* would recognize that I get tired too").

We talked about the crisis of adding a child to their relationship, even though their daughter was very much planned and a joy in their lives. With both of them working, caring for her certainly added stress to their lives. Much of the responsibility seemed to be falling on the wife, and she had little energy left for intimacy with her husband.

It all fit everything I learned in graduate school about communication problems in marriage and about family development issues. The direction seemed clear to me—work on their communication skills, educate them about the psychological and interpersonal dynamics of becoming parents for the first time, and help with problem solving as they faced the new issues that were being presented to them. They agreed to the plan to work on their communication—after all, that was what they had asked for.

After the first two counseling sessions, Jim and Sally seemed to feel much better about themselves and their relationship. In the third session, however, it all fell apart. Jim had gone to a ball game with friends on Saturday, leaving Sally at home with the baby. For her, this was the last straw. She had planned for them to get a babysitter and go out together. They had argued. He wanted to spend time with her, but being with his friends was also important.

At that point an interesting piece of information came to light. Not only were they both employed, but they were working different shifts. She worked a 9:00 a.m. to 5:00 p.m. job; he worked the 3:00 p.m. to 11:00 p.m. shift. She was always asleep when he came home from work at midnight or after, because she had to get up at 6:30 in order to get herself ready for work and take the baby to a babysitter's. When she got up, he was asleep. They never saw one another awake except on the weekend! The only contact Jim had with his daughter was when he gave her a middle-of-the-night feeding. The weekends had become highly charged times during which Sally and Jim conducted all their business of being a family together, of being friends, of being lovers.

My graduate education had not taught me to ask about time together, about work schedules, about how a couple's life in the community supported what they were trying to do together. In fact, at the time I was in graduate school, families had just been discovered as the context in which individuals need to be understood. A counseling generation before me, no one would have considered seeing this young couple together; the problem would have been perceived to be located in each of their individual psyches. Perhaps there had been a lack of consistent nurture of one or both of them as infants, and this new child threatened the nurturing relationship they had developed with one another.

So, in fact, my focus on communication and other relationship issues was progressive. The boundary of attention was expanded from Sally and Jim as individuals to the relationship between them. Still, I was not prepared to see further than that. I had not been trained to see that the relationship with other systems *outside the family*—in this case, the work environment—might be not only critical for understanding the problems they were experiencing but also the target of our work together.

I began to scramble for ways to integrate this new piece of information into my conceptual framework. I began by emphasizing that perhaps the problem was not communication at all but the lack of *opportunity* for communication and simple presence with one another. Their work schedules had worked well for them as young adults who had "dates" with one another on weekends and then lived relatively independently during the week. But how did those schedules work for a family with an infant? We began to seek ways they could have time together while they considered whether and how they might bring about some structural change in their schedules.

Sally arranged with her employer to have an extended lunch (ninety minutes instead of the standard sixty) and then worked thirty minutes later in the afternoon. She went home for lunch, which was only fifteen minutes from her workplace, so that she and Jim could have this meal together. Many days he picked up the baby before lunch so that the three of them could be together. He then returned the baby to the babysitter in time for her nap, before he went to work. He delighted his wife by learning to cook simple lunches—something he had never done before. Sometimes she took the baby and a picnic and joined him at his place of employment for his supper break.

Sally and Jim then considered whether this approach to their time together was adequate to meet the changing needs of their family, or whether a more radical change—a different job arrangement for one of them—was needed. Jim liked working the evening shift, and the pay was better. He decided, however, to request a change to the "graveyard" shift—11:00 p.m. to 7:00 a.m. Now the family had both mornings and evenings together—Jim slept while Sally worked, and vice versa.

Taking a contextual perspective did not negate the psychological and interpersonal dynamics that may have been operative in this family; it simply placed these in the larger context of the family's social and physical world. The fact is, shift work has a negative effect on marriage. Research indicates that every indicator of marital quality is significantly and negatively affected. Over a three-year period, shift work also increases the probability of divorce from 7 percent to 11 percent (White and Keith 1990).

Jim and Sally may have found their new parenting role to create a psychological crisis because of early nurturing experiences of their own. They did struggle with some communication patterns that tended to thwart rather than facilitate their problem solving. One could even conjecture that they had sought a high degree of independence and for that reason had not sought ways to increase their time together before. It is interesting, though, that they so readily assumed that the problem was within themselves and their relationship that they did not even think it important to tell me about their family schedules—and I didn't think it important enough to ask. Yet their work outside the home was influencing their relationship with one another in ways that would be a challenge for *any* family, regardless of their communication and psychological makeup. This realization gave us a new viewpoint from which to examine their life together.

Family theorists call this viewpoint an "ecological perspective," or the "ecosystemic approach." It defines the family as a social system embedded in an ecological context and draws on both systems theory and the ecological sciences for understanding the family. Just as we cannot understand individuals without attending also to the family relationships that have nurtured and shaped them, neither can we understand families without looking beyond them to the social environment that nurtures, shapes and is influenced by the family.

The ecosystemic perspective uses ecology as a metaphor for the relationships human systems (families) have with their physical and social environments. An ecosystemic perspective looks at the way a family relates to, changes and is changed by its environment of social relationships and the physical world. It focuses not only on relationships within the family but also on how the family interacts with other persons, social systems and the physical environment. In addition, it looks *inside* the family, not only at the interactions between family members but also at the physical environment of the home, and then to the internal factors of each family member—their biological and psychological and spiritual selves. Thus the ecosystemic approach looks at systems within systems within systems, each system nested in the next larger system, and how this complexity of interacting layers of factors creates the internal and external environment in which families function (Garland 1989; Garland and Pancoast 1990; Hartman and Laird 1983). The following list shows just a few of the salient factors influencing the Woodley family.

□ *Extrafamilial physical environment:* the distance from work to home that allows the Woodleys to rendezvous during the workday; parks nearby where they can picnic or other places they can meet during the day; the quiet or noise level of their neighborhood and its effect on sleep and time together.

□ *Extrafamilial relationships with social systems:* the support or lack of it Sally and Jim each experience from the policies and practices of their employers (is there time for parental leave? how flexible are they willing to be in response to family needs?); availability of quality child care and medical care; friends and family who can be supportive of this young family as they learn their new roles; the blessing of a community that admires and loves their child and helps them to feel supported in their new responsibility.

□ *Extrafamilial interpersonal relationships:* the effect of this first grandchild on the relationship of Jim and Sally with their parents and siblings. How it has affected friendships (do their friends have babies? if not, are they experiencing a growing distance due to changed interests and responsibilities?); the availability of babysitters and quality care at church so that Sally and Jim can continue in activities that are important to them; the availability of activities and groups in their community and church where this time-stressed couple can go with their infant and be together as a family.

□ *Intrafamilial physical changes:* where the baby is sleeping and the physical intrusion the parents are experiencing; the adequacy of their home for providing both privacy for sleep (e.g., does the sound of the baby crying and then Jim's playing with her in the middle of the night disrupt Sally's sleep? what about in the morning, when Sally is preparing for work but Jim is still trying to sleep?).

□ *Intrafamilial relationships:* the need for increased cooperation and planning to meet the new demands on them as a couple; the relationship of each with the infant and the extent to which these relationships are meeting the needs of all three of them; the additional work and who has taken on what responsibilities and feelings about that (laundry, child care, feedings, etc.); whether or not Sally is nursing and how that affects Jim and Sally's relationship with one another and with the baby; the effects of pregnancy and parenthood on their sexual relationship.

□ *Psychological/spiritual:* the meaning and purpose of parenthood and marriage for each of them and for them as a couple; the memories and experiences that shape their view of themselves in this new parenting role; the match between their expectations for this child and what their child is actually like.

□ *Biological:* the biorhythms of each of these spouses, as well as their new infant, and how these fit their employment schedules and each other's needs; the postpartum changes Sally experiences; the baby's patterns of eating and sleeping; whether or not Sally is nursing and how that is being experienced by her and by the baby.

The ecosystemic approach is *transactional;* it assumes that the relationship between family and environment changes each. Not only does the workplace influence the Woodleys' family life, but they in turn have an influence on the workplace. As Jim began to be more aware of the impact his work schedule was having on his family life, he talked about it with workmates and found out he was not alone. They began to talk about changes that could be made. They negotiated with the boss successfully for a flexible dinner hour, and they also turned the employee lounge into a space that families could use for a meal together. They convinced management that helping evening-shift employees with the family issues created by their work schedules would provide for a more stable and satisfied work force.

The use of ecology as a metaphor suggests several concepts that can help us in understanding families: habitat, adaptation, stress and social networks.

HABITAT

In biology, a habitat is the physical place in which an organism lives. We have heard about the importance of habitat for the survival of endangered species, such as an owl that lives in old-growth forests in the Pacific Northwest. Families, too, live in habitats. The physical settings of the dwelling, the neighborhood and the community must support the social settings of the family itself and the family's community if families are to thrive. A family's habitat needs to provide for protection, security, courtship, intimacy, childrearing, eating together, restful sleep, solitude and interaction, working, learning and playing. When the habitat thwarts one or more of these dimensions of family life, family members experience feelings of stress. These feelings interfere with the family's ability to function well and, in turn, contribute what is needed to maintain the surrounding habitat.

For example, the poverty of low-income neighborhoods is often physically expressed in the ugly design and poor construction of low-income housing, garbage and graffiti, infestation with vermin, faulty plumbing and heating, lack of safe green spaces for play, and noise and air pollution from nearby industries. Such a physical environment undermines self-esteem by communicating via all the senses the lack of value society has for those who live there. Mothers fear the crime of the streets, and so children may be cooped up indoors with little to do but watch television. Thin walls and inadequate space make privacy difficult and contribute to stress levels. Thus families in poverty may be more at risk for violence and other forms of personal and interpersonal distress, which in turn make the habitat even less supportive of their own family life and the life of other families in the community.

The concept of habitat suggests the importance of the physical arrangement of the family home to ensure both privacy and time together. For example, some poor families do not have enough furniture to allow everyone to sit down to a meal together, or enough beds for the family to sleep in. Family members need "nests" within the home where they can have privacy just as much as they need space where they can be with others. An individual's nest may be no more than a few drawers in a dresser or a particular area of a bedroom, but it is nevertheless "private."

On the other hand, affluent families may have created individual nests so successfully that the family's time for interaction and sharing is minimal. Historical changes in the physical home environment have made this increasingly the case. When central heating arrived, families no longer had to spend all their time together in front of the central home-fire. The physical design of the home continues to evolve, with significant implications not only for how families want to live but, by implication, how they should live. In single-family dwellings in the United States, architectural support for privacy is evident. New houses designed for upper-middle-class families often have the equivalent of self-contained mini-apartments for family members.

Along with the benefits of greater privacy come costs. For the family that can afford the luxuries of the modern home, privacy encourages greater individual isolation. Family members no longer have to compromise on when to shower, how to share the phone, which music to listen to, which television show to watch or what to eat for dinner. Multiple bathrooms in the home, more than one phone line, headsets for music listening, televisions in bedrooms and individually packaged microwavable food make daily family negotiation and compromise largely a thing of the past for families able to afford these amenities. New technology contributes to the devolving of family life into individual autonomy. For example, the microwave oven, heralded at its introduction as a faster way to cook for a family (often shown with a turkey or some other such symbol of the family dinner), is in fact used most often for heating individual self-contained meal packages.

Outside the family home, the location of needed resources also affects family life in significant ways. If the family relies on public transportation, is it nearby, and does it provide easy access to medical care, employment, shopping and other resources? Can children walk to school and parents easily gain access to their children's teachers, or are children bused across town to schools their parents are rarely or never able to visit because of distance and work schedules? Are there parks where families who live in apartments can be outside, or is outside time expected to take place in enclosed back yards? If families are in suburbs with their own yards, is fencing the kind that encourages contact with neighbors, or is it high board fences that preclude any contact? Are there sidewalks that encourage walking in the neighborhood and visiting with neighbors?

Much of this seems commonsensical and even simplistic; consequently, family habitat has not been given much attention. Nevertheless, not only does the concept of family habitat help in understanding family life in our culture, but it can be a useful handle for families as they consider the stresses and challenges they face daily. Families often find an examination of their own habitat to be a creative and helpful exercise. They may not have thought about how important their environment is for understanding their life together. As it was for Jim and Sally, looking at the physical and social environment helps family members become a team working together rather than placing blame within the family for stress and trouble they experience.

ADAPTATION

Biological "adaptation" is the way organisms change their structure and function, insofar as possible, in order to survive and thrive in their environment. One cannot understand the color of a snowshoe rabbit, brown in summer and white in winter, without knowing the context of rock and snow to which it has adapted.

In the same way, we have to know a family's ecological context if we are to understand the way it is structured and the way its members live with one another. Consider a snowflake. All snowflakes are similar in some respects: they are crystals that are round, symmetrical and white. Yet they also differ dramatically, from large, loosely structured flakes to hard little balls of ice. In order to understand the difference, we have to examine the context in which the snowflakes were formed. Those little balls of ice—even in a freak hailstorm on a hot July day—came, we know, from a stormy, frigid context in which they were tossed over and over high up into the atmosphere. As they accumulated more moisture, they fell, only to be tossed high again and frozen. Their tight structure is a result of this harsh context. Those big flakes children try to copy with scissors and folded paper are beautiful, but they also break easily. They are formed in temperatures just below freezing—just cold enough to allow to them coalesce into such a structure at all. Which is the "normal" or "best" structure for snowflakes is simply a value judgment. Each is "normal" or "best" in the sense of having been formed as an adaptation to its environmental context.

The concept of ecological adaptation suggests that rather than deciding what shape of family life we like the best and want to build from the inside (changing patterns within the family), it is more effective to change the context to one that best grows the kinds of families we are attempting to create. Rather than changing the family, then, this approach attempts to change the *environment* of families.

For example, if we want to create families in which parents have primary roles in their preschool children's care, then we create structures that make possible and even encourage parent-child involvement. The ecological approach assumes that parents are working outside the home and entrusting child care to others because it is *functional* for them to do so. We can surmise that most parents are working primarily because their families need the financial support and that at least some find work to provide a sense of social significance and important adult interpersonal relationships.

Therefore, to make changes that will enable parents to provide greater amounts of child care, parents must have economic support, a sense of social contribution, and adult interpersonal relationships available to them in ways that fit their child care responsibilities. The changes that could be made to encourage parent-provided child care are myriad, such as a government-subsidized family allowance that enables one or both parents to take career leave or work part time during their children's preschool years; eligibility for fringe benefits and career benefits in part-time employment positions; flexible work scheduling so that two parents can together provide child care for at least a major portion of the day; flexible work that allows parents to take work home—and so on. This approach assumes that if the environment makes it *functional* for the family to provide its own child care, it will do so.

STRESS

Stress is defined as an upset in the usual or desired fit between an organism and its environment. Plants that need lots of water are stressed by drought; the environment and plant are out of "fit" with one another. For a family, destructive or painful stress arises when what the family perceives as a demand from the environment exceeds the family's capacity to meet that demand (McCubbin, Thompson, Pirner and McCubbin 1988). A large credit-card bill can be stressful if the family does not have money to pay it off and yet fears that if the bill is not paid the family's credit will be damaged. Stress is *transactional* (Leventhal and Tomarken 1987; McCubbin and Figley 1983). That is, stress is created by the *transaction* between demand and capability, not just by the demand itself. The large credit-card bill may not be stressful at all for a family with ample financial resources. Thus stress resides in the relationship between event/experience (receiving the credit-card bill) and the person or family's resources (bank account balance and expected income), not in the event/experience itself.

Stress is also *experiential;* a stressor is not a stressor until it is experienced as such (Boss 1988; Pearlin and Turner 1987). The experience of stress, however, does not have to be acknowledged or even conscious; physical or relationship tension can be experienced by a person or family without being realized consciously. An adult can come home and ignore family members or lash out at them without acknowledging to either self or others the stress from a bad day in the workplace. The stress was created by feeling that demands at work exceeded what was reasonable or even possible to do. That stress becomes an element in the family's life together, however, perhaps made worse now that the "incapability" at work now seems matched by a lack of ability to cope at home.

Stress can originate within the family as well as from the environment. New parents or adults caring for frail elders know well the stress that caregiving can create—new financial expenses, lost sleep, worry about whether the care being given is the right or best thing to do, trying to care for a family member who cannot communicate clearly. Often, however, stress from within the family is compounded with stress from the environment. The stress of caregiving, for example, may be compounded by attempts to balance these family responsibilities with employment demands, with a commute to work that has just been lengthened by thirty minutes because of road construction, and by the neighbor's barking dog that wakes up the whole family, including the infant/elder, in the wee hours of the morning. Individual factors can also compound family stress. Individual family members may be dealing with their own conflicted feelings about caregiving, or ill health, or resentment about the career sacrifices that are being made.

Work stress seems to be contagious; it spreads from the workplace to the home. The contagion of work stress into the home sets in motion a process of adjustment whereby family members try to modify their role assignments to compensate for the work stresses of their partners. Research indicates that wives tend to make these attempts in response to their husband's stress from the workplace more often than husbands attempt to respond to their wife's workplace stress (Bolger, DeLongis, Kessler and Wethington 1989; see also Rook, Dooley and Catalano, 1991).

Distress and Eustress

Not all stress is debilitating distress. Stress can also be strengthening, helping the family develop hardiness and ability to adapt and change. Such stress has been called "eustress." As families cope with stress successfully by changing themselves or their environment—or both—they develop a sense of "family efficacy." The stories of endurance and overcoming become a part of the family's story, a part of their identity. They serve not only as a source of identity and cohesion for the family-at-present but also as encouragement to the family that indeed they can survive and thrive, no matter what comes. Sometimes stress sends a family back to a reexamination of what is really important to them, what they value and what they are willing to sacrifice for what they value.

What makes the difference between distress and eustress? If stress is defined by the *interaction* of the stressor and the resources for coping with the stressor, then the family can turn distress into eustress—can cope successfully and grow stronger—in one of two ways. First, it can find ways to respond effectively to the demands being placed on it. Second, it can increase the family's resources from the environment to deal with the stressor. Often, successful family coping involves a combination of both strategies. Neither approach necessarily removes the stress-producing factor; both may simply help the family live with it more constructively. Jim and Sally, the couple with a new baby and dissonant work schedules, took on both the environmental demands being placed on them and their own strategies for coping, including their communication and empathy with one another and their problem-solving skills. Stress handled effectively not only contributes to the family's sense of itself; it also develops and strengthens the coping skills of the family.

Obviously, some stressors cannot be changed by the actions of a family, and to imply that families *can* create changes in their environment in these cases is to be unjust and even oppressive. The death of a family member brings on grief to be lived through and with for a long time, often for a lifetime. The traumatic after-effects of wartime experiences or childhood abuse or a chronic illness often cannot be erased; families must learn to live with and be supportive of members who bear these scars. Even in these immutable circumstances, however, coming to terms with what can and cannot be changed can help families manage their lives more effectively.

Many stressors *can* be tackled, although families need partners in their efforts. One family cannot make much of a dent in community violence, or the air pollution that exacerbates a child's asthma, or the poverty and despair of an inner-city ghetto that saps both children and adults of hope. They need a community of other families to join with them.

The concepts of distress and eustress are heavy with possibility for family ministry. Teaching families the skills they need to cope effectively with life stressors, helping them to discern what is reasonable and not reasonable to expect of themselves, providing a community where they can talk with and receive mutual support from other families dealing with similar stressors, being the community that together takes on the social and cultural systems that are creating distress for families—these are the essence of family ministry. In the language of the church, it is helping families live their covenants with one another; it is helping them to love in all the hard ways described in 1 Corinthians 13; it is helping them to "bear one another's burdens"; it is helping them "abide in the vine" (Jn 15) that gives them sustenance for hard times. It is helping them deal with the principalities and powers that oppress them and others like them.

Stress Factors

Several factors are involved in the interactional definition of stress (Boss 1988; McCubbin and Figley 1983a).

1. The degree to which the family is committed to whatever is creating the stress. The family that highly values education as the key to success will be more stressed by a child's failing grade than a family that defines success by other criteria. The family that is deeply committed to and involved in children's sports and music lessons will be more stressed by a conflict in soccer practice and violin lessons than a family that views such activities as "extracurricular" rather than essential.

2. The family that has chosen the stressor will be less stressed than the family who feels they had no choice. All other things being equal, overtime working hours that have been chosen by a parent after discussion with the family will create less stress than those that come as a nonnegotiable expectation of the employer. Even that which is chosen may produce stress, but that stress will be less than that which is not chosen.

3. The degree to which the family believes that what they are experiencing is normal, manageable and meaningful defines in part the extent to which they feel stressed. If other families are managing to handle the stress, and particularly if the family can learn coping strategies from others, they will perceive their stress to be less. If the stressful events have importance and meaning for the family, they will also not experience as much stress as when the stress seems meaningless and unimportant (Antonovsky and Sourani 1988). A parent who has hurried home to fix dinner early in order to be sure to get to the PTSA meeting at school will feel less stress if the meeting is truly helpful to the children's school experience. If the meeting seems simply to be "busywork" and does not give opportunity for parents to learn more about their children's schoolwork or to address issues they consider important, the meeting will feel much more stressful.

Stress can be created by demands from the environment or from within the family itself. Often stress results from demands from both directions. For example, the large credit-card bill becomes stressful when it is met by a checkbook balance below the amount needed and by family members who have different expectations about how credit cards should and should not be used. If one powerful member has demanded that credit cards be used only for emergencies and another family member has decided to use the credit card to take advantage of a seasonal sale on clothing, then the family is about to experience stress between members.

Chronic Stress

These factors suggest why some families experience *chronic stress* as a fact of life, something to be lived with rather than challenged. Some families simply have extraordinary ongoing demands placed on them by internal and external factors—a child with a physical or developmental disability; unemployment; a parent with Alzheimer's disease. Other families willingly choose to live with chronic stress because they have chosen the very factors that are stressing them. All the activities, demands and commitments are "good stuff": individual career goals, participating in church and community programs, serving on committees, playing in sports leagues, entertaining friends and work colleagues in the home, caring for home and garden, straining the family budget to be able to purchase what is wanted. These stressors are defined as a normal part of family life today, that which contributes to growth and development. As a consequence, the chronic stress families experience is relatively low volume, or to use another analogy, a few degrees more heat in the family climate. In fact, the stress grows almost imperceptibly because it is defined as voluntary, normal and enriching.

Stress operates over time (Leventhal and Tomarken 1987). I have heard that if a frog is put in a pan of hot water, it will immediately jump out. If the same frog is put into a pan of cold water and the heat beneath the pan is turned up only gradually, the frog will not respond to the temperature change and will sit there until it boils to death. Chronic family stress is insidious, somewhat like the slow rise in temperature of water on a burner set on low. It may be a noticeable change, perceptibly "warmer" and uncomfortable, but nothing to cause a family to jump out of their pot.

Chronic family stress does not in itself necessarily lead to crisis or dysfunction, but it limits the family's ability to cope with an additional stressful event (such as an illness or unexpected work demands). Chronic family stress lowers the family's emotional and physical resources and saps flexibility. Resources and flexibility are key components in effective crisis coping (McCubbin and McCubbin 1989). Chronic family stress may be thought of as family "high blood pressure." The family system stays in a state of ongoing stress, making it more vulnerable and less able to respond effectively to other kinds of stressors. Physical illness, emotional hurt, fear and depression are more easily aroused in families with chronic family stress (Bigbee 1992; McCubbin and Patterson 1981). Families are more vulnerable to a "family stroke" in response to additional internal or external stressful events, just as a person with high blood pressure may be more vulnerable to a stroke when exercising in an out-of-the-ordinary way. When someone becomes emotionally or physically ill, experiences a failure in work or school or socially, or experiences a spiritual crisis, the family cannot absorb the additional stress. The result may be the family system equivalent of a stroke—interpersonal violence, abuse of alcohol or drugs, marital crisis or divorce, the emotional or physical illness of one or more members, or the inability of family members to provide adequate protection and nurture for one another. These consequences of stress or crisis in families exacerbate the original state of chronic stress, leading to an ascending spiral of stress and a collapse in coping.

Not Enough Money

Chronic stress factors often have to do with two of the most basic resources for family life today—money and time. Because economics play such a significant role in family life, inadequate income is a stressor that permeates virtually all of a family's life together. Parents who are not able to provide what their children need—both basic physical needs and their felt needs, such as money for school field trips, for the "right" kinds of clothing or for college—may feel their role undermined. Partners struggling with chronic economic problems often are faced by more frequent conflict over using what resources they do have. Affluent families may resolve conflicting values by accommodating a variety of family desires; families in poverty do not have that luxury.

Family members often experience economic distress differently. Adults may be almost consumed by worry over economic stressors, whereas children may only be dimly aware of any problem. One adult may look at the checkbook balance and worry over whether there is enough cushion for some unforeseen economic circumstance. Another adult in the family may view the same checkbook balance with pleasure and fancy how the bit of surplus might be spent on something fun. In this situation the economic situation may be a stress for only one person, but partners' differing interpretations of their situation may create family conflict that contributes to the stress.

Not Enough Time

Many families are stressed by inadequate time to address all the responsibilities and commitments of life. Time is a family's currency as they try to organize complex and often competing timetables and responsibilities. The result is that there is sometimes competition for time in families in the same way that there is competition for money in the business world (Daly 1996).

The work of adults outside the household has created a dizzying pace and a sense of fragmentation. It is not simply adults, however, who feel as if they are running faster and faster. The formalization of children's play and extracurricular learning also contributes to time stresses on families. Two generations ago, children's play and learning took place mostly informally through board games, ball games on the vacant lot where children organized their own teams, and unstructured play with siblings and neighbor children, with perhaps a smattering of formal activities such as scouts and music lessons. Today middle-class children's play is formalized into leagues and lessons in art, music and dance, as well as scouting and other children's clubs.

This pace continues into adolescence. Furthermore, adolescents are now working outside the home in increasing numbers. Studies of American adolescents and work indicate that between 1947 and 1990, there was a 65 percent increase in the labor force participation of school-enrolled sixteen- and seventeen-year-old boys and a 240 percent increase among girls of the same age (Daly 1996:93). In generations past, poor and working-class adolescents worked to supplement the family income. Now middle-class adolescents are also working, but they are working to support their own consumer spending.

Coping with Stress

Families use a variety of physiological, psychological and behavioral strategies to cope with stress. Some of these strategies actually do something to change the stress producer; others simply help the family cope better, without addressing the continuing source of stress. For example, *physiological strategies* for dealing with a too-large credit-card bill include deciding to sit down together and relax before discussing what to do about the bill or grabbing something to eat or drink that is particularly comforting (eating lowers physiological stress). *Psychological strategies* may include talking about how unimportant this stress is in the grand scheme of things. ("After all, we have one another, and everything is really going well in other ways. This is just a bad time financially.") Such strategies may help for the moment to alleviate the sense of stress. They may even lower anxiety enough that the stressor can be handled more creatively, but they do not actually change the fit between environmental demand and capacity to respond. When the family's capacity to respond cannot be changed, these may be the only coping responses available. For example, if one spouse is temporarily unemployed or the family is paying large medical bills, changing the stressful event may be impossible and management of the stress may be the only coping strategy available.

Finally, however, *behavioral strategies* are often aimed at either (1) altering the demands of the environment (contacting the credit-card company and working out a payment plan) or (2) increasing the capacity of the family to respond to the demands (asking relatives for money to pay off the debt, selling something of value, going without necessities in order to collect the money needed, a family member taking an extra job or working overtime to increase income). If these strategies fail, stress may persist and intensify. In fact, coping strategies themselves sometimes lead to further stress. Doing without needed groceries, exhausted family members trying to work extra hours, and children's disappointment that a vacation or school field trip has to be scuttled all contribute to the overall family stress.

Therefore, *coping is also transactional.* Coping is not simply a personal or family attribute. Every family has strength in some environmental circumstances and vulnerability in others. Problems are the outcomes of the transaction of many complex variables. This is both bad news and good news. Because of the complexity of causes of many problems, one does not have to search for a single cause or cure. One can intervene at multiple levels to help families and environments adapt better to one another. In fact, change often needs to occur at several levels. When families have credit-card stress, therefore, a change strategy might include one or several of the following:

☐ teaching families how to use credit to help rather than create stress
☐ providing debt counseling services and repayment plans
☐ developing support programs in the church to help families live more simply
☐ developing resource programs that enable families to swap services (such as car repair and clothing mending) rather than paying for these
☐ establishing cooperatives for purchasing expensive items that are used only occasionally and thus can be shared among families (ice cream freezers, leaf shredders, folding tables for family reunions, etc.)

COMMUNITY

A family's most immediate social ecology is the community. Community is *the habitat external to the family's boundaries.* If "home" is the first layer of habitat for a family, then "community" is the next layer. When we talk about community, we mean *the set of personal contacts through which persons and families receive and give emotional and interpersonal support and nurture, material aid and services, information, and new social contacts.* W. G. Brueggemann has defined community as the "natural human associations based on ties of kinship, relationship, and/or shared experiences in which individuals voluntarily attempt to provide meaning in their lives, meet needs, and accomplish personal goals" (Brueggemann 1996:110).

The people in our community know us. They are people from whom we can borrow or who will take care of a child in an emergency, the persons from whom we can obtain news and gossip so that we gain the significant and not-so-significant information that gives shape to our lives, the persons who can help us find a new medical specialist or someone to work on our car. The community also consists of organizations that care for us and know us, as well as those to which we contribute. These are represented by the bank teller who remembers our name, the church where we have served and been served through the years, the children who were members of the scout troop one's spouse led.

Community includes the physical environment that also, by being familiar, communicates a sense of belonging. The smells of the river or the factory or the pine trees down the street are much like the smell of Grandma's house, part of the canvas of daily experience so familiar that it is hardly noticed until we are absent. We know the streets and do not need a map to find our way around. We sit in the same pew on Sunday and look at the same stained-glass windows from the same angle, and can predict who else will sit where. We know where to find tomato sauce and oregano in the grocery store without having to consult the store directory.

We hardly think about or recognize community until it is changed or we absent ourselves. Upon return from a long absence, the sights, smells and greetings from familiar people may flood us with emotion. All these point to the familiar niche that community is. It consists of people, organizations and the physical environment that keep us from depending solely on the persons within our family to meet all our personal, social, physical and spiritual needs, and who communicate, "This is your place; you belong here."

The African proverb "It takes a village to raise a child" became a political slogan pointing to the importance of community for children, but it does not quite go far enough. *All* persons, both children and adults, need community. Because children are so dependent on others for their survival, their vulnerability in the absence of community is more apparent. As James Garbarino has pointed out, children are like the canaries miners used to take with them into mineshafts. Canaries are particularly sensitive to poisonous gases, and if they succumbed, the miners knew the environment was dangerous (Garbarino 1995). Like canaries in mineshafts without adequate fresh air, children "succumb" without adequate communities of nurture and support. Adults, however, need to live in community as well. Some seem to need community more than others, but even self-sufficient adults seek the company of others and need a community when they become ill, injured or threatened.

Anyone who has moved from one community to another can testify to the vulnerability that families experience when stripped of their community. The simplest activities require greater effort; a trip to a grocery store or a laundry may require thirty minutes of preparation time spent with the telephone yellow pages in one hand and a city map in the other. It takes twice as long to find needed items in a strange grocery store. The very simple forms of mutual aid that typify functional communities are missing. There is no known neighbor who can watch one child while the other is taken to the emergency room for stitches. And which doctor is "good"? Informal sources of communication do not exist, and often what a family needs to know about its immediate social environment—like who the best doctors are—is available only through informal channels.

After twenty-seven years of living in the same community, we recently moved to a different region of the country. Normally I pride myself on being resourceful and competent as comanager of our household. Suddenly, however, what had been rather mindless and insignificant tasks required great thought and threatened to overwhelm me with a sense of being alone and vulnerable in a place I did not know or understand. When we were preparing to leave on a trip, there were no neighbors I knew to ask to pick up our mail and keep an eye on things while we were gone. I cleaned out the refrigerator before we left, but there was no one to whom I could give the half-carton of eggs, the piece of cheese and the fruit, so I had to throw them away. I didn't know any teenagers in the neighborhood whom I could ask to cut the grass and water the potted plants. *These are very small issues,* I thought to myself. *What if I were ill and needed help in caring for a toddler, or my husband were in an automobile accident and I needed transportation to the hospital? Whom could I call on to help me?*

Connections with others shape and reinforce a person's sense of competence and mastery. Not only does the above account of moving to a new community describe loneliness; it also describes a sense of vulnerability, of being unable to handle everyday life stressors with competence. In situations of difficulty, a community can provide a family with social support and tangible aid.

A community also provides opportunities for a family to serve others. Serving others contributes to a sense of competence. Families are strengthened through their efforts to make the world a better place, and the community is their most immediate world. Those efforts include such things as participating in the community's recycling program, tending the home and yard to make the community more attractive, providing leadership in local organizations, and helping others with social support and tangible assistance—even if only by sharing leftover groceries before a trip.

The personal sense of security derived from social connections helps us not only to manage life stresses but also, when needed, to muster the courage to make changes. A community provides models of others who have dealt with similar circumstances. A family is strengthened when it finds community connections with others who have cared for an older family member with Alzheimer's disease or an adult child with AIDS. A family with newborn twins may discover other parents of twins in the community happy to pass down strollers, other baby equipment and helpful advice.

When my toddler son was discovered to have serious allergies to wheat gluten and dairy products, I was at a loss. There are few typical toddler-type foods that do not contain one or the other. A close friend at church, however, knew someone who had a child with the same allergies. She put us in touch with one another, and soon I had tapped into a whole network of parents who had helpful advice and recipes for home-baked toddler biscuits and other foods that did not contain wheat or dairy products.

Communities Are Not Always Geographically Defined
Historically, communities have been defined geographically as the social and physical surrounds of the family household. The concept of "neighborhood" conveys that sense of geographic community. The neighborhood included the other households and social institutions with which the family shared a particular geographic

location. Indeed, neighborhoods still do function as communities, in some places more than others. Neighbors still help one another with care of their physical property and can often be called upon in an emergency.

But with the move of work and schooling out of the household, and the consequent daily travel of family members out of the immediate neighborhood, however, community has taken more of a social/functional than geographic definition. Magnet schools pull children from all over a region, replacing neighborhood schools. Children no longer walk to school through a familiar neighborhood of people who at least know them by sight. Now they ride school buses to regional schools located sometimes miles from home territory and far from easy involvement of parents and other community members. Regional shopping malls have supplanted small local businesses. Lower prices and much larger selection in megastores inadvertently have led to the end of the community relationships that existed in neighborhood shops. Bank machines operated from a central location have replaced neighborhood banks. Regional sports leagues have supplanted informal sandlot neighborhood play. Adults, like children going to regional schools, travel far from their neighborhood for the day's work and play.

One can imagine a time-exposed aerial photograph of a family's daily movements that would provide a map of the family's community—to various workplaces and schools, to shopping centers and grocery stores, to visit friends and family in other neighborhoods, to a fast-food restaurant for a family meal, to soccer practice or ballet lessons or the pediatrician. A family's automobile is the family encapsulated, moving from one node of community to another, often through "foreign" (not-part-of-the-family's-community) territory. The streets of the neighborhood used to be the place where neighbors met neighbors and community developed and functioned. Now streets are passageways that *connect* geographically separated nodes of community life, but they themselves are not locations of community.

As a consequence of all these changes, the neighborhood and the community have become separate entities. Particularly for middle-class families, community is often flung over a much larger region. Before the advent of the automobile, the symbols of community might have been the front porch swing, the unlatched kitchen screen door open to a neighbor stopping in for a cup of coffee or to borrow an egg, the pub or drugstore soda counter on the corner where people gathered "just to talk," the park bench. By contrast, today's symbol of community might be the minivan, transporting the family to the various places where members receive community services and make their own investment in the community.

This is particularly true of families with school-age children who require parental transportation in order to play with friends, play sports, take music lessons and so on. During this period in my own children's lives, many mornings I felt as if we were going on a trip rather than just living the day. Indeed, each day was a trip. Bags had to be packed for school for children and for work for parents, for the gym for a parent getting some exercise on lunch hour, for a child's soccer practice after school, for the other child's violin lesson. Many families leave the household not to return for ten or more hours. The automobile becomes the place where clothes are changed, meals are eaten, and important family conversations are held. For many families of school-age children, it seems a far distant past when the family was rooted in the household, when children and parents came home to eat lunch together, when children played across the back yards of the neighborhood rather than at appointed times at a regional soccer center, when birthday parties were held on the family picnic table rather than at the mall's pizza and game center.

Families in which all members drive themselves, however, often do not have this connection in the family vehicle. Instead family life is a set of community nodes with *no* connection to one another. Adult family members may meet for lunch or dinner, and the restaurant table (or the church supper) replaces the kitchen table as a node of family life. Many middle-class families take multiple cars to church and other activities, meeting and leaving each other there rather than coming and going together.

At the same time, perhaps this sense of mobility and scattered community points to the much greater significance of place given the family home today. "Cocooning," or staying in the home with videos to watch and a delivered pizza, has become the recreation of choice for many families tired from all the running to connect the dots of their scattered lives.

This "cocooning" has also moved community into a new dimension without geography—that of cyberspace. Instead of gathering on the street corner or on park benches or at the barbershop, Internet "buddies" gather in chat rooms via the World Wide Web without ever leaving home. There they write messages back and forth. This kind of community seems one-dimensional and impoverished when compared to a community where people see and touch one another, where babies are bounced on knees and arms are thrown around each other's shoulders. On the other hand, many persons who otherwise feel isolated and alone in their geographic community seems to find significant support and connection via the electronic community. Persons struggling with rare and debilitating illnesses can converse with others in the same struggle who live halfway around the world.

It should also be noted that families living in poverty, who do not own an automobile, much less one for every family member's use, often live in more geographically constrained communities. The vitality and support of the walking community is much more important for the health and well-being of these families (Vosler 1996).

Family Members Do Not Share the Same Communities

The last vestige of neighborhood as community has been rapidly fading since women began joining the work force. The demise of neighborhood as community began, however, when work first started being separated from home, when men packed lunchboxes and left home for the greater part of each day. They began developing collegial relationships in the workplace—away from the neighborhood—and neighboring decreased. Women who were still working in the home became the primary contact point for the family with its neighborhood/community. They still prepared lunch for children coming home from school; they served as volunteers in school and church and civic organizations; they visited with and cared for neighbors. Men increasingly relied on women to be the community connection for the family.

As women entered the workplace, however, the final reliable community contact began to fray. In the thirty years from 1960 to 1990, the proportion of U.S. families in which men are the sole breadwinner declined from 42 percent to 15 percent (Wilkie 1991). Schools began serving lunches. Those women still working at home found themselves in empty neighborhoods, except for senior adults and latchkey children who returned at the end of the schoolday. Meanwhile, like working men, women in the work force developed friendships through their places of employment, where they spent so much more of their time than the neighborhood.

The friendships adults form in the workplace are *individual* friendships, however, not family friendships. Work colleagues may have never seen a person's home or know who else lives there. One research study found that only about 25 percent of community relationships of one spouse are included in the community of the partner (Milardo 1989).

Therefore it is not simply that the changing ecology of family life has flung community more widely; it has endangered the very existence of community for many families. The most vulnerable families are those for whom mobility has meant moving from one location to another. Rodney Clapp (1993) has suggested that the image of family life, particularly in the American suburbs, is no longer the sturdy, intricately rooted tree. Instead it is a hydroponic plant that floats on the surface of water and easily adapts when moved from one tank to another. Trees contribute to and are nourished by their environment; a tree cannot be uprooted without serious damage both to itself and to the ecological niche from which it is removed. Hydroponic plants, on the other hand, can be moved with little effect either way. Rootless suburban families attempt to meet their community needs with several single-purpose pseudocommunities. Pseudocommunities are voluntary associations formed around shared interests—children's sporting leagues, self-help groups, Bible study.

These pseudocommunity connections are often formed by *individual* family members, not by the family as a whole. Each family member has his or her own set of outside relationships. These relationships are more tenuous and less supportive of the family as a group. As Clapp says, "If I play racquetball with you once a week or sit in your reading group once a month, what business is it of yours if I cheat on my wife?" (Clapp 1993:50).

Pseudocommunities bring together those who are socially, economically or culturally similar. Their chief purpose is to allow us to enjoy being with those who share our lifestyle (Brueggemann 1996). Self-help groups such as twelve step programs or weight-monitoring groups are "pseudocommunities" because they are based on one-dimensional commonality rather than the multisalient relationships that characterize a community.

Families are not hydroponic. They function best when they are deeply rooted and nurtured *as families* and not just as collections of individuals. We need the community to know us *as a family*. That is why marriages are public events; there is wisdom in publicly acknowledging the creation of a family as an entity. Betty Carter, a prominent family therapist, has argued that Americans are experiencing a massive collapse of community. "The current red herring—that divorce and any family structure that diverges from the traditional breadwinner male/homemaker female is causing social breakdown—is exactly backward. It is social breakdown—disappearance of community—that is undermining even strong and devoted families" (Carter 1995:33, 35). We have lost the informal sharing of work, recreation, resources and help in times of need. We have also lost the spiritual sense of belonging to something larger than our own small, separate family unit.

Carter has admonished family therapists to broaden their assessment of families to include their connections to the community. A good assessment should include questions like these: Is this family contributing anything beyond their own circle? Do they belong somewhere, besides sitting around their own dinner table (Carter 1995)? It is not just that families need communities; communities also need families to nurture and socialize their members for effective community participation.

Communities Are Not Always Supportive

Of course, just as families do not always function in optimal ways but may become stuck in less creative and even harmful patterns of relationships, so do communities. Communities may isolate and shun rather than support families, communicating to a family a sense of *not* belonging rather than a sense of place. A community may add to rather than share in the burden a family is trying to bear. One of the most significant ways churches can minister with families is to develop strong, functional communities. Even the best of communities, however, are not perfect. And all communities have significant costs as well as benefits for their members.

Just as families are nurtured and stressed by their community environments, so communities are nurtured and stressed by the larger society that is their environment. An inner-city slum is often a weak, unsupportive community because of social forces far beyond the members and physical resources of the community. Suburbs, city communities, rural towns and villages all are influenced by larger factors such as government policies, the practices of national and international corporations, the pollution of water and air by communities far distant from them.

The Costs of Community: Are They Worth It?

Stephanie Coontz describes her experience of parenting during a visit with Hawaiian-Filipino friends on the island of Lanai:

> My child was still in diapers, and I greatly appreciated the fact that nearly every community function, from weddings to baptisms to New Year's Eve parties, was open to children. I could sit and socialize and keep an eye on my toddler, and I

assumed that was what all the other parents were doing. Soon, however, I noticed that I was the only person jumping up to change a diaper, pick my son up when he fell, wipe his nose, dry his eyes, or ply him with goodies. Belatedly, I realized why: The other parents were *not* keeping an eye on their kids. Instead, each adult kept an eye on the *floor* around his or her chair. Any child who moved into that section of the floor and needed disciplining, feeding, comforting, or changing was promptly accommodated; no parent felt compelled to check that his or her *own* child was being similarly cared for. (Coontz 1992:210)

To mainland white Americans used to bearing almost total responsibility for their own children, this picture seems almost idyllic. But this reliance on the community does not come without a price. It means trusting others with our precious children, and that may mean knowing that others will not respond in just the way we would. How would the author have felt if someone else had disciplined her child more harshly than she considered acceptable? Reliance on community also means caring for other people's children. It means more responsibility for others and less for ourselves, more freedom from having to do it all ourselves but also less control. There are good reasons that Americans have embraced family autonomy and responsibility. There is much greater choice and freedom, although the cost is lessened support and nurture from the community.

The swapping of services and tangible resources carries obligations. Accepting help carries with it the expectation that the help will sooner or later be reciprocated, one way or another. Perhaps this obligation is that from which the middle class has sought freedom through its financial resources. For this reason, many families would much prefer purchasing the help they need—a carry-out meal during the family cook's illness, for example, rather than a covered-dish dinner from a Sunday school class.

Obligations may even become codified into unwritten principles of etiquette. The covered-dish dinner obligates the recipient to, at the very least, write a thank-you note and participate in similar care for others in time of need. In some communities, if the recipient is able to do so, the baking dish in which food has been offered in a time of crisis is returned full to its owner. That is, the recipient of the initial care prepares food to return in the dish as a way of saying thank you.

Living in community creates costs that are easily overlooked by persons weary of having to bear life burdens virtually alone. Most families with children today are adult-deprived; there do not ever seem to be enough hands and hours to do the chores of household management, caring for dependent members, and nurture of shared life. Daniel Yankelovich has suggested that our society seems to work on a "lurch and learn" principle. We have lurched from work embedded in community relationships to individual hedonism, only to learn that it resulted in isolation and the loss of community (Yankelovich 1996). Before we lurch back toward embracing more community, its costs must also be recognized.

Community does not mean simply being supported in times of stress and crisis; it also means supporting others. It means not only receiving welcome support and advice but also being the recipient of unwelcome advice and meddling from well-meaning, or not so well-meaning, community members. (One young mother expressed her despair at the constant stream of family members and friends at the hospital where her child was critically ill. "I just needed some time to be alone with my husband," she said.) And when neighbors share, items shared are sometimes damaged or not returned at all. That is the cost of community. In some ways communities are like children; they disrupt, stress and bring high price tags that are often not considered beforehand. On the other hand, they can bring a sense of fulfillment, rootedness and even joy.

Defining a Family's Community

Understanding the community of congregational families is a necessary foundation for family ministry, but not a particularly easy task. Although some communities still are defined by neighborhoods, most American families, particularly in urban areas, have communities with idiosyncratic definitions. Families themselves may not be aware of their community's definition, unless some crisis event activates it, or they move far away and then experience the community by its absence.

Observing a family in crisis. One of the ways families describe their community is through recalling times of crisis and the response of significant persons and social systems. This too is a time an outsider can glimpse what the community of a family is like. Church leaders often glean a great deal of insight about a family's community by observing who comes to visit and who provides chore services and other forms of support during the hospitalization of a family member. This also may be time the family subconsciously takes stock of its community. As a young mother of a child who had been critically ill for months told me, "You find out who your real friends are."

I experienced this very directly some years ago on a cold fall evening. I dropped my ten-year-old son, John, off for soccer practice, which was being held near a shopping center in another neighborhood in our city. I had to take his sister to a violin lesson, but I would be back, I said. I told him to walk to the nearby store, which had a snack bar, and wait for me there when practice ended. I handed him money to buy himself a snack.

When I returned an hour later, after racing to the violin lesson and back, John was not where I had told him to meet me. For almost an hour I frantically searched the nearby businesses and the surrounding neighborhood. It was now long past dark. Not knowing what else to do, I reported him missing to the police and waited while a police search, complete with a helicopter with floodlights and, later, a bloodhound, commenced. The police and I were convinced that John had been abducted. It was the most frightening experience of my life.

Almost three hours after my son was reported missing, the bloodhound tracked where he had run back and forth all over the soccer field during his practice and finally the route he had taken to a nearby store—the wrong one—where he was still waiting for me, frightened and alone. I had miscommunicated; I knew which store I meant, but he misunderstood because he had never been to that particular store. He did know of a snack bar in a store a block away, which was where he in good faith had gone to wait for me. I had guessed that he might go there, but evidently when I had earlier stopped in to look for him, he had been in the rest room.

The police officer brought him to me in the police cruiser. He was frightened and very embarrassed. His first words to me as I hugged him were "Mom, please don't tell anyone."

In the first hour of my search, one of my first stops had been the home of one of his friends, some six blocks from the soccer field. The friend had been with my son at the practice. The friend's parents quickly pulled on coats to help me look, while I returned to the place where I thought my son knew to meet me. It was then that I called the police. As I sat alone in the parking lot weeping, giving a report to the police officer and berating myself for being a neglectful mother, I felt terribly alone. Soon, however, the parents who had searched in vain joined me to wait while the police searched. A work colleague happened into the shopping center and saw me. He too stayed with me after learning what had happened, taking only a moment to go into the store and phone his wife, who in turn began making phone calls. Within thirty minutes, the community had been activated. Several friends came to wait with me in the cold parking lot. I learned later that prayer groups in our church were quickly organized. Work colleagues prayed together over the phone lines. The soccer players' parents gathered in one family's home by a citizen's band radio to listen to the police search activity. A store owner brought me hot chocolate. When my son was finally brought to me by the police officers and the dog, and we returned home at 11:30 p.m., one of the ministers from our church was sitting on the cold front steps waiting for us, to make sure we were all right. He had heard that John had been found but just wanted to check on us.

The community that became activated that evening is probably typical of the communities of many families with school-age children. It included friends from the workplace, parents of children's friends who play together on sports teams, a local business manager and the community's service personnel (and dog), and friends and church leaders from our family's congregation. The difference between community and neighborhood is apparent in at least two ways. First, many of these persons—including our family—did not live in the neighborhood where the soccer field and shopping center were located. Second, virtually the only connecting element for this network was the relationship with our family. The parents of children's friends were not members of our church, nor were the work colleagues part of either of the other two groups. Community today is a *social network* organized by relationships with a particular family much more than it is a set of relationships within a defined geographic or social boundary. In a well-integrated community, many families may share overlapping social networks. In a less integrated network, the community has definition primarily because of relationships with the nodal family.

Perhaps most notable, however, is how quickly this community was mobilized. One moment I was alone in the most frightening moments of my life. Thirty minutes later I was surrounded by friends, colleagues and community servants mobilized by my need. All of these were busy people; no one was sitting at home looking for something to do.

On the other hand, there was some price to being a part of this community. I felt shame to have lost my child because I had mismanaged our time and communication, and everyone in our community knew it. When John said, "Mom, please don't tell anyone," I had to respond, "John, everybody already knows. You'll just have to get your story ready, because people will ask you." I learned later that many children received instructions from anxious parents that night about what to do if they became lost. Thus our misadventure made some small contribution to the community, if only by providing a negative example. The price of community is that everyone knows more about us than sometimes we wish. It is harder to hide our less-than-noble moments when we live in a community.

The whole community paid a price for its involvement, too. Lots of people spent a cold November evening combing city streets for a lost child, or standing vigil with a distraught mother in a grocery-store parking lot, or phoning others and praying, when they could have been preparing their work for the next day, doing laundry, spending time with their own children, or cocooning with pizza and a television movie.

POSSIBILITIES AND COMPLEXITIES OF AN ECOSYSTEMIC APPROACH

This discussion of the physical and social space of family life has several implications for family ministry.

☐ Congregations can be a significant physical and social environment for families. The church as a physical environment can be an extension of the home, a place where families eat and play and talk and worship and serve others together in a context that supports and values their commitments to each other. It can also be a place where family members can gain privacy from one another and can find peer groups and friends who give balance to family life.

☐ Families find it helpful to think about the habitat in which they live—their home, neighborhood and community—and the ways that habitat supports or strains their life together. Sometimes they and their congregation can make significant changes to make family habitat more supportive for themselves and for other families in their community.

☐ Congregations can help families cope effectively with life stressors, helping them to discern what is reasonable and not reasonable to expect of themselves, providing a community where they can talk with and receive support from other families dealing with similar stressors, taking on the social and cultural systems that are creating distress for families.

☐ Families need to be rooted in a community, whether it be a geographic neighborhood or a network of physical nodes scattered geographically. Congregations can serve as significant community "nodes" where families can be nurtured and can contribute as families, not simply as individuals.

One of the frustrations of an ecosystemic framework for understanding family life is also its advantage—it is all-inclusive. It includes looking at physical characteristics of the environment such as the spatial arrangement of a home, the adequacy of neighborhood playgrounds, and air quality. It considers genetic and biological factors influencing family members, from food allergies that create agitation in a child to dementia in an aging family member. It addresses interpersonal skills, employment/family interfaces, and on and on. No matter how a family problem or challenge is defined, there is always another way to consider it. Ecosystemic thinking challenges churches to be sensitive to, and sometimes active in, the biological, physical, environmental, social-institutional and political-governmental levels of family ecology that have an impact on family life.

The complexity of an ecosystemic framework also points to all the possibilities for ministry with families. A church's ministry does not have to tackle every level of cultural, systemic, ecological, familial and biological system that has an impact on families. We can do something without having to do everything. On the other hand, an ecosystemic framework points to the danger of dealing with system levels with which we are most comfortable—family communication and personal psychology—as an escape from attending to the community and social systems that have an impact on the entire community of families. It seems easier to offer counseling family by family than to organize families or speak on their behalf to change larger community and social systems. It is easier to be priest than to be prophet.

If there were other prophetic voices in our society, perhaps the church's choice to be priest and prophet would not be of concern. But there are not. Families alone often do not have voices loud enough to challenge the oppression they experience as family stress, such as an economic system that virtually requires two spouses to work—and to work different shifts. They need to partner with other families, and sometimes they need the voice of an even larger system, such as their congregation, to help them work toward community and social changes. Family ministry, then, involves not only education and support but also collaboration and advocacy for social and cultural supports for family life.

Chapter 3

Families & Culture

CULTURE IS THE FAMILY'S STORY BASED ON WHO "THEIR PEOple" are—their ancestors and community historic and present. Several spheres and subspheres of ethnicity, class, religion and region/nation form a family's cultural identity. For example, my family is white, working/middle-class American Southerners. Each of those designations represents large spheres, however, that contain subspheres. To understand my family, one has to probe further within each sphere of cultural identity. Somewhere in the murk of history, our ancestors (on both sides of the family) immigrated to the United States from England and Ireland. Like many working- and middle-class white Americans, however, my family has only mild curiosity concerning who those ancestors were or when and why they came.

My family would probably agree that we are "Euro-Americans," but that designation seems a little fussy and unnecessary. Middle-class white Americans "like us" tend to live for the present and future, because we believe anything is possible, regardless of where you came from. The past is not determinative. The cultural identity "white" thus communicates something significant about our culture, in that it carries very little information about the ancestors from which we come. It carries the information that in this cultural group, the individual and the present are far more important than ancestors and the past. It also carries a not-so-subtle message about our place in a race-conscious society.

Some probing into "American Southerners" would also result in discovering much more complex information about this family that describes who we are. My husband's parents and grandparents were missionaries, although my in-laws returned to lived in Maryland shortly before David was born. My family lived in Oklahoma, although only a couple of generations. My grandparents moved to Oklahoma from the Deep South as children with their parents. My husband and I lived twenty-seven years in Kentucky and have just moved to central Texas, which is considered the western border of the American South. We also lived a year in Germany and another year in Australia. So although most of our lives have been lived in the American South, all of this mobility makes this family's identity, our sense of who "our people" are, significantly different from that of families who have lived for generations in the same Southern location where we now live.

Every family has such a story that weaves together themes of long-term residence or migration, connection and reorganization, and changing historical and geographic conditions. I have only related a few facts about my family, the ones that seem most important as illustration. Thus the story of a family's past is shaped and revised to fit the current family's values and needs. Family stories provide a framework for a family's values, for what they think and believe, for how they work and play, and for how family members relate to one another and the world around them.

FAMILIES IN CULTURE

Culture is the *core values of those who share an identity with a place, a religion or membership in an ethnic or class group.* Let's look at each of the terms in this definition.

Core values answer basic human questions—the relationship of individual and group, the meaning of time, the natural world, human nature, and the spiritual dimension of life. These values find expression in preferred strategies for handling daily expectations and challenges. Core values explain why families behave the way they do. A family may never express its core values in words; instead, those values can be inferred as we observe how the family invests its energies and other resources.

For example, some families work very hard and make considerable sacrifices to save money for children's college education, perhaps with one partner taking an additional part-time or full-time job. Others do not or cannot; children are expected to make their own way financially after completing high school, with only occasional or partial help from parents. Whether parents pay for a college education is certainly sometimes simply an issue of the availability of financial resources, but it also involves core values. Whether parents or children are responsible for the costs of college education is related to the core value of independence and when it is "supposed" be achieved. Whether the father takes a second job or a mother who has been a homemaker decides to go to work to provide funds for children's education involves issues of gender roles and family coping strategies. These too are core value issues.

Place may refer to a nation, a region (American South, Appalachia, Pacific Northwest), a community or even a neighborhood (the Bronx, the South End, the Flats). Living in that place carries with it certain life strategies that need to be learned for belonging, for survival or simply for living well. For example, in some communities wearing certain colors or hats turned certain directions indicates gang membership and may be dangerous. In some communities looking strangers in the face and smiling or speaking might be considered rude; in other communities *not* to do so is considered rude.

Religion is the social expression of an organized and shared belief system. It almost always is far more complex than the faith itself—Christian, Hindu—and even than religion subcategories of denomination—Presbyterian, Baptist. Within denominations there are often parties or other subgroups—moderates and conservatives, for example. These are not only religious groups; they are also cultural enclaves of values and beliefs about living rightly in community and in family.

Ethnicity refers to minority groups that are often thought of as subgroups of race, although the boundaries between racial groups are often fuzzier than the boundaries between ethnic groups. For example, *African-American* designates an ethnic group that includes persons descended from African slaves but also persons with mixed racial heritage who *identify* with and are seen by others as members of the African-American community. Every family belongs to at least one ethnic group, but ethnic group status is far more significant for minority populations than for the dominant population group. Many white Americans, for example, have to stop and think about their ethnic identity; it is not a part of how they are labeled or of their own sense of identity day in and day out.

Finally, *class* also often represents a distinct cultural identity, often in combination with *place*. For example, Will Campbell has pointed out that *redneck*, a class distinction for poor white rural people in the South, is the last cultural slur that has not been identified as politically incorrect to use (Campbell 1995). Other combinations of class groups with locators include suburban middle-class ("soccer moms") and the inner-city poor ("underclass").

Culture Is Constantly Changing

Culture is dynamic and constantly changing, often as a consequence of changing historic and physical conditions, but also as a consequence of interaction with other cultures. In a world increasingly connected via mass media and computer technology, the boundaries between cultures are becoming more and more permeable.

A simple examination of the food prepared and consumed by American families represents this dynamic quality of culture. In the almost thirty years since my marriage, the food I have prepared for my family unit has changed significantly. In the early years it reflected my own background in Oklahoma. Meat, usually beef, was the center of the meal, accompanied by potatoes. The kind of beef I served was influenced by our economic/class circumstances; it was usually ground beef, the cheapest meat available. I cannot remember eating Thai or Korean food as a child. But Mexican food was very much a part of our culture. When I married, I introduced my husband to Mexican food long before there was a single Mexican restaurant in the city where we had taken up residence. The Indian background of my husband's family introduced me to curry and rice, and these also found a way into our regular meals.

Historical factors have had an impact on the food on our table during the past three decades. Research about the benefits of a vegetable-centered diet and the dangers of too much red meat gradually changed our meals: more chicken and salad, less beef. Ours is a culture that puts great credence in scientific research. The development of agricultural and transportation technologies has made a greater diversity of vegetables available all year round. Even spirituality has had an impact on our family meals. Several years ago our teenage daughter became a vegetarian. This came about with the support of several friends in her church peer group, who believed that this is an important way to be good stewards of God's creation. After her decision, meat was served only every other day in our family, and then as a side dish for some family members. One-dish casseroles with meat no longer worked. Thus a complex interaction of forces have had a significant impact on what my family eats for dinner.

Culture Is Overlays of Adaptive Life Strategies

As a child, I loved the encyclopedia entry for "human anatomy." It consisted of several pages of color transparencies of the different systems of the body, beginning with the skeleton. As one turned each page on top of the skeleton, additional systems—circulatory, nervous, organs—were overlaid. This is a good way to think about culture. It begins with the skeleton (place). Then come the circulatory system (ethnicity), the organs (class) and the nervous system (religion). Each can be studied by itself, but one does not understand the functioning of the whole without seeing them overlaying one another. Each of these cultural overlays is an influence on the lives of families within a culture, but the strength of that influence varies from family to family, based on the alignment or conflict with other cultural overlays and with the ecological and historical context.

One could continue to add overlays. For example, Celia Falicov provides a wonderfully complex definition of culture as derived from "simultaneous membership and participation in a multiplicity of contexts, such as rural, urban or suburban setting; language, age, gender, cohort, family configuration, race, ethnicity, religion, nationality, socioeconomic status, employment, education, occupation, sexual orientation, political ideology; migration and stage of acculturation" (Falicov 1995:375). Because these cultural memberships are experienced in different combinations from family to family, cultural behavior is much less predictable.

Culture Defines What Is Important and What Is Valuable

Culture touches all aspects of family life—what people eat for dinner, how they handle differences, who has power by virtue of gender and role, whether persons believe that they control their own lives or that they are controlled by fate, and on and on. Each of these aspects of life relates to some understanding of what is important. It is "right" and "better" to eat a vegetable-centered diet; it is "right" that spouses should speak honestly and confront their differences; it is "right" for spouses to reach consensus rather than one making all final decisions in matters of finances. Values such as these are core values that are lived out in family behavior. Because they are our way, they are the "right" way. In other words, they are our understanding of truth.

The issues of culture bring us face to face with the reality that we can never take off our own culturally tinted lenses to see another culture "objectively"; we must recognize our biases and be responsible for wondering about what those biases keep us from seeing. Or as Paul says, we see "through a glass darkly" (1 Cor 13:12). Even the seemingly unimportant everyday decisions we make, such as what to eat for dinner, reflect our understanding of what is important and what is real. Is the earth ours to "subdue" and even "exploit," or is it ours to care for as stewards? This is a theological decision made in a cultural context. Do we believe the scientific reports that say rainforests are being destroyed by the raising of beef and that the American diet is not sustainable for the entire world? Americans tend to put great stock (excuse the pun) in science and research; it is part of our culture to accept scientific reports about rainforests and global warming as "truth," even when the conclusions clash with other cultural truths, such as the one I grew up with that a meal is not a meal without meat, preferably beef. The times are constantly changing, and so is culture, including the understanding of what is real and what is important. In fact, change almost always challenges some aspect of culture, of how a family and a culture experience reality.

Culture Defines How Families Socialize Their Members

Socialization is the process by which persons acquire the behaviors and values of their social world. It is the cultural training that goes on constantly in a family. We often think of children as being "socialized" by the family, but adults continue to be socialized throughout their lives. Marriage socializes the partners as they learn how to live and love together, and as they define the limits of what the relationship allows and expects them to do inside and outside the family. They, in turn, have been socialized into these marital roles by the families in which they grew up. Children contribute to that family socialization as well as being influenced by it. My daughter has now left home for college, but most of the meals I prepare are still vegetarian.

The three objectives of socialization are (1) impulse control, including the development of a conscience; (2) role preparation and performance, including occupational roles, gender roles and roles in institutions such as marriage and parenthood; and (3) the cultivation of sources of meaning—that is, what is important, what is to be valued, what is to be lived for (Arnett 1995:618). Socialization takes place in other social institutions besides the family—the workplace, school and church, for example. Nevertheless, the family is considered the major locus of socialization for children and adults.

Jeffrey Arnett has distinguished between two general types of cultural social-ization, broad and narrow (Arnett 1995). Cultures characterized by broad social-ization encourage individualism, independence and self-expression. In contrast, cultures characterized by narrow socialization hold obedience and conformity as the highest values and discourage deviation from cultural expectations. Broad socialization allows a relatively broad range of possibilities for individual differ-ences in paths of development. Narrow socialization, on the other hand, restricts the possibilities open to a person; the socialization presses persons toward confor-mity to a certain cultural standard.

Family practices reflect and transmit the values of the culture as a whole. For example, parents do not simply create their parenting practices on their own. Rather, they follow and are constrained by role requirements for parents in their culture, which they have learned through their own experiences of socialization. The extent to which parents are allowed to vary the cultural socialization differs from culture to culture (Arnett 1995:619). In American culture, parents have considerable freedom to define their own parenting practices. Short of physical abuse and neglect that might result in permanent physical damage, they are allowed to care for and discipline their children as they think best. An American parent usually can spank a child with a hand in public without anticipating any interference from onlookers. In some other countries they might be arrested for child abuse.

I experienced such a cultural difference when our daughter was a preschooler and we were living in a small town in southwestern Germany. We were walking down the street one day in late fall. Sarah, with her wonderful and very frustrat-ing sense of self-determination, refused to wear her sweater, though it was a brisk day, so I was carrying it under my arm. Suddenly in front of me appeared three older women—strangers—who with considerable agitation and firmness insisted that it was very cold and I must put the sweater on my daughter lest she become ill. I was embarrassed and tried to explain in my best German that she refused. Quite taken aback by this adult conversation, Sarah saw I was "in trouble" and quietly slipped the sweater from under my arm and put it on. The ladies, satis-fied, then walked on. I was left red-faced, thinking, *How dare they? This would never happen "at home."*

Only much later, after the embarrassment had worn off, did I begin to see the encounter from a different perspective. I am used to living in a culture where par-ents bear all the responsibility for deciding what is best for their children. I thus experienced the women's confrontation as a challenge of my parenting. Indeed it was: in some sense they perceived me to be neglecting the physical needs of my child. Their culture is somewhat narrower, in that there are general standards and the community is responsible for reinforcing them. Parents are not so alone. From their perspective, the women's confrontation could actually be viewed as *supportive* of me. After all, they were agreeing with my earlier statement to Sarah that it was cold and she should really wear her sweater. The result of their "interference" was that Sarah complied with my wishes. But the life strategy/parenting practice for reaching that end was not congruent with my own.

FAMILY CULTURE

There is yet another cultural overlay to the family, and that is the family's own *internal* culture. A family's culture develops in the context of and in response to the layers of place, ethnicity, class and religion, but as the family weaves these together in its own history and ecology, the family takes on a culture of its own—unique strategies and values for living. We can thus speak not only of the cultures in which families are embedded—the places, ethnicity, class and religious groups to which they belong—but also of the culture of the family itself. A family's culture is made up of shared stories and traditions, rituals, unique ways of communicating with one another, and patterns of living that extend back into the family's history and forward into its future. Every family has a distinct culture, just as every country has its own culture—Australian culture is different from English and American and Canadian and Liberian culture. Although we also share some characteristics and speak the same language, there are words and phrases and values that are different because we are American or Canadian and not Australian or Liberian. There are also words and phrases and values that are different because you are a Crowther or a García or a McMurphy or a Lee and not a Garland.

We sometimes think everyone communicates the way we do or lives their daily lives in the same way as our family. But every family has ways of communicating that may be like a foreign language to the outsider. One small example in our family is the "hand squeeze." When holding hands, one person squeezes the other's hand three times, which means, "I . . . love . . . you." The other squeezes back twice, meaning, "How . . . much?" And the first squeezer responds by squeezing as hard and as long as she wants—that stands for how much and for how long she will love the other. Usually hand squeezes are exchanged where words are not possible or would somehow mar the occasion: in a long meeting where children are trying to sit quietly, in the midst of a crowded shopping mall, or during an evening walk in the woods. Not all squeezes are hearty and long, either. Sometimes a wimpy, brief squeeze communicates "I'm miffed," usually accompanied by a smile—the beginning of resolution of some difference between two family members.

I do not know the origin of this little communication pattern. My mother-in-law used to "squeeze love" my husband's hand when he was a little boy sitting next to her in church. Perhaps it was used in the generations before that; I like to imagine that it was. My husband taught it to me when we were dating. It thus carries more than the simple message of love. It is a way of saying we belong to one another, and to Grandma who has gone on, and to other parents and children in our family before that, and, I hope, to generations yet to come.

Every family has such communication patterns. Perhaps they are words or stories that carry special meaning for the family but would have to be translated for the outsider. A gesture or glance can carry a paragraph's worth of meaning and can be clearly understood by all family members. A certain hesitation in speech, or silence, speaks a loud and clearly understood message. These are the family's language.

The Family's Values
Another aspect of family culture is a family's shared assumptions about the world. Despite conflict and disagreements, family members share these fundamental assumptions. "Indeed, the core of an individual's membership in his own family is his acceptance of, belief in, and creative elaboration of these abiding assumptions" (Reiss 1981:1). These assumptions may be about any aspect of family life—how family members relate to one another, family economics or religion, family commitments. A person may reject such an assumption cognitively yet struggle with the dissonance created by the emotions attached to the assumption.

These assumptions define what is valuable, and who is valuable, and in what ways that value is expressed. Margaret Blackburn, a mother in her late thirties who returned to school to work toward a college degree, wrote a paper for a class I was teaching. She tells of her experiences of growing up female in a working-class Euro-American family in Chicago in the 1960s and 1970s. She describes a culture that in some ways seems familiar yet in other ways may be quite different from mine and yours. Implicit in her account are gender roles and expectations, the way power is distributed and exercised in the family, and socialization with regard to husband-wife relationships and parent-child relationships. Families rarely make conscious decisions to shape their culture according to particular roles and norms. It simply "happens," as a part of the family's heritage as well as through interaction with the physical and social ecology in which the family finds itself. One of the characteristics of culture is that it does not necessarily have to be consciously known by its members.

I am the youngest of five children. I have a brother who is ten years older than I am. The rest of us are girls. I have sisters that are nine, six (deceased eight years ago), and two years older. My dad always wanted another boy and made no bones about it. He never treated us poorly, but he would really have liked another boy. An ongoing joke in our family when I was growing up was that as each girl was born he would say "Another split tail." I know that is pretty gross and I never understood it until I got older. I grew up in a suburb that butted up to Chicago. My mother, though, was born in South Carolina. She met my dad during World War II when she worked at a navy base. He was born in Alabama, but moved to northern Illinois/northwest Indiana as a boy. When they married they moved to Illinois because that is what a wife did—she followed her husband.

My family was pretty typical of the 50's and 60's. My dad worked a factory job and my mom stayed home. She could not drive and was in effect a prisoner in our subdivision. After she got us off to school she would sometimes go to a neighbor's house and have a cup of coffee. My dad worked the swing shift and my mom and all of us would have to adapt to his schedule. In the summertime if he worked nights we could not play in our yard because we might wake him up. I will always remember my mom combing her hair and putting on lipstick when it was time for him to come home from work. She always greeted him with a kiss, though she was not demonstrative to us kids. To make extra money for herself she would iron some neighbors' clothes, but she would have to hide it from my dad because he got mad and took it personally. She would set the ironing board up in the living room (our house only had a living room, kitchen, bathroom and two bedrooms) after he left or before he came home and iron the clothes she had hidden in the utility room. I always thought it pretty silly that she had to hide that way, but when we were young we did not express our feelings as much as kids do now.

When I was nine, though, my world changed. My father died. He was an alcoholic and his liver finally failed him at age thirty-nine, the age I am now. This may sound strange, but it was the best thing that happened to us kids at home, the three youngest. I loved him very much—he was never mean or cruel—but after he died there was money in the house. When he was alive we always had enough but never any extras. He drank the extra money. Now, though, we could buy Cokes and a candy bar. We even got to eat at McDonald's. I never had one until I was ten. But the biggest change was in my mom. I never remember her smiling until after my dad died. I don't mean that she didn't grieve—she did terribly—but now she wasn't a nervous wreck worrying about my dad. She became a room mother for me in sixth grade because she wasn't tied down at home.

But we had new problems facing us. My mom, who had never written a check or paid a bill, had to learn how. It fell to my sister who was six years older than me to help her. It also fell to my sister to pass her driver's license exam the day she turned sixteen so she could take my mom to the grocery store. My brother, in case you are wondering, had been drafted one month before my father died. We girls learned to mow the grass, cut the bushes, take the garbage out and fix things. One time our toilet tank broke. We had more money, but not enough to ever call a repair man unless it was an emergency. My mom and sister took the lid off and stood there looking down in the tank for a long time. I was out in the hallway sitting on the floor and finally asked them what they were looking at. They said they had no idea. It took two hours, but they finally fixed the chain with a bobby pin. It worked for a long time before they had to fix it again. That is how I finished growing up, finding out how to make do with things around the house. My mother never remarried. She always said that she loved my dad but she never wanted to do another man's laundry or have him tell her what to do. As my sister Kathy went off to college (she was the first to go to college, another change), my sister Grace took over the sharing of responsibility, and as Grace went to school, I shared the duties.

I don't ever remember my mom verbally telling us girls not to give up our independence after we married, but we three younger ones got the message. Sometimes I think she taught us two younger ones too well. My husband has learned never to "tell" me something to do. He makes suggestions. But I tell him what to do all the time! If something needs fixing I fix it, if I can, and it hurts him that I don't rely on him.

I think my family was a little different from our neighbors in that my mom tried to create a Southern home in the heart of all those damn Yankees. We girls were not to raise our voices when we were young. We grew up drinking ice tea, and heaven forbid if we even looked at a beer can at our uncle and aunt's house. My brother was and is the prince of our family. Even now whenever he comes over to my mom's she will hop up—well, as fast as a seventy-one-year-old can—and make him a cup of coffee. At Christmas she will fix him his plate of food and take it to him. She will not eat until he is all settled. We tease her and ask her what she is doing. She didn't raise us girls to wait on a man! And she will stand there and agree with us completely. Then she reminds us that one of her favorite sayings is "Don't do as I do, do as I say." (Margaret Blackburn, spring 1996)

Families are very much carriers of the broader culture in which they are embedded. Although Margaret Blackburn's family story is unique, the gender roles and values and ways power is distributed clearly have also been influenced by and express broader cultural values of the Euro-American working class in the Midwest and, even more broadly, the American values they hold in common with other ethnic, socioeconomic and regional groups. Culture defines gender roles and family relationships, and in turn, family relationships carry, define and shape the culture.

This family's culture clearly weaves together place (a Southern family in a Chicago suburb), class (a working-class traditional family adapting to financially difficult circumstances) and ethnicity (a Euro-American family with its values of hard work, self-sufficiency and male dominance). Religion is not mentioned, although the author is a Christian, and conservative Southern religion may be a factor throughout the story she weaves—the work ethic, the negative values about alcohol (father is an alcoholic but children are forbidden even to look at a beer can), the commitment to family even in hard times. There are other factors—historical and intrapersonal—that also become a part of the weaving of this family's culture—a father's alcoholism and early death; a mother's determination to make things better for her daughters; the historic events of two wars that created the circumstances that first brought this couple together and then, two decades later, resulted in the drafting of the only son, pushing the women in the family toward self-sufficiency after the father's death. Like all families' cultures, this family's culture is a process of ongoing change, building on and growing from previous lifeways in the context of current realities. The author is herself carrying on this process as she describes her independence, writing this paper as part of her college education during midlife.

Yet the same commitment to family and avoidance of conflict that was present in the previous generation leak from between the lines. This family values and respects family relationships even more than they do their "principles," such as the male-female equality that the author has adamantly tried to establish in her marriage. Change is coming and has been happening ever since Mother determined to take in ironing even though her husband did not want her to. Change, however, is balanced by commitment and care for one another. Mother took the ironing in, but she hid it out of respect for her husband's feelings, or out of fear of his anger, or out of her belief that subterfuge is better than conflict. Whatever her motivation, the change had to come second to interpersonal relationships. In this family, change is not worth risking conflict. The author believes in equal male-female relationships, but she tolerates in good humor her mother's solicitous care of her brother rather than pushing her mother to live by new gender role expectations.

The Family's Patterns of Living

A family's culture includes its patterns of living. Like a well-oiled machine, family members move in and out of rooms and one another's lives. They may not even realize that they are living in patterns, because the patterns have become habit. Who gets the bathroom first in the morning, what is a "reasonable" time to monopolize it, whether bedroom doors are open or shut, what is "appropriate" attire for walking through the house after a bath, what are the unspoken terms for borrowing an article of clothing from someone else, what is "private property" and what belongs to the family, how loud is "too loud" and what are the tolerated hours for listening to music—and on and on.

Because we live these patterns, we are hardly even aware of them. It is only when we visit overnight in another home that we realize what our patterns are— because they conflict with the patterns of our host family. The host family feels some disruption too. No matter how little "trouble" the guest is, the presence of a "foreigner" throws a kink into the family patterns.

The Family's Clock

American society is notoriously time-conscious. Clocks are everywhere: on our arms, our car dashboard, the corner of our computer screen, by our bed. Not long ago my watch broke. At first I was desperate; how would I ever control my day without it? Slowly I realized that at no time during my day was I out of view of a clock. They are everywhere.

As I write this, I am staying in a mountain cabin. Besides writing, my only responsibility during these days is to cook for my family. When we eat or sleep or work or play is really up to us. Yet when I realized that the clock high on the kitchen wall was off by ten minutes, I quickly moved a chair over, climbed up and adjusted it. Knowing the time—the correct time—is evidently a significant value for me.

There are other kinds of time than the minutes and seconds of a clock that are just as important. Linda Burton and Carol Stack have called the temporal scripts of family "kin-time" (Burton and Stack 1993). *Kin-time* refers to family members' shared understanding of when and in what sequence they should move from one role to another, taking on or giving up certain responsibilities. When "should" family members marry, bear children, care for aging adults? When should children be economically self-sufficient or "settle down"? When should a mother come in to help out after a grandchild is born, and how long should she stay? Often these norms of the family clock are not articulated, except when something occurs off schedule. Births before or outside of marriage are seriously out of sync with many families' norms about timing, but there may be just as much a sense of "bad timing" when a pregnancy occurs in late adulthood. Some families expect and even welcome young adults' periodic return to the parental home between completing school and finding a job, between jobs, between marriages. In other families, such a dependency on the parental home would be a serious breach of kin-time. Subtle expectations about how long is long enough, and how long is too long, are simply "known" without being put into words. A breach of these family rules, however, may result in grumbling behind closed bedroom doors, family phone gossip or outright conflict.

AFRICAN-AMERICAN FAMILY LIFE

The family life of African-Americans can illustrate the significance of the interaction between cultural heritage and current social and economic conditions in giving shape to family life. Of course, there are as many different ways to be family for African-Americans as there are for Euro-Americans. Nevertheless, the combination of African heritage, a history of slavery and oppression, and current conditions of systemic racism and limited economic capital and opportunities combine to create a distinctive set of influences that needs to be understood by those who minister with African-American families. A brief overview of some of these factors will highlight the significance of culture in understanding family life. This is not a full overview of African-American family life; it serves only to illustrate the importance of exploring and learning about the ways culture shapes family life for minority and ethnic groups.

African Culture
The family structures of western Africa, from which most people who became slaves in America were abducted, were primarily consanguineal (blood-related) rather than conjugal (marriage-related). That is, kinship was biologically based and rooted in blood ties, parent to child. African family structure tends to form

around cores of adult siblings that include their spouses and children (Smith 1985). In African tradition, marriage is not simply a union between two people but the uniting of two groups of people. That tradition is still very much alive in African-American families. Without the support and sanction of the two families, the new union is potentially less stable (Billingsley 1992). The relationship with extended family is so close that even after a divorce it is common for an ex-spouse to retain close relationships with the partner's family.

Similarly, childrearing is a task for the extended family, not just for parents. Ethnographic work in Africa shows that many children live at least part of the time with kin or close acquaintances rather than their parents. Sending children to live elsewhere is positively sanctioned in particular cases. Parents are considered likely to spoil children, and sharing the raising of children is a way of extending, maintaining and acknowledging extended family ties (McDaniel and Morgan 1996).

African peoples also practiced polygamy, a system that grew out of the frequent wars that decimated the male population. Polygamy ensured a high birth rate and thus survival of the people. It also provided protection for women who otherwise might not find a male partner and prevented prostitution among women with no other means of support (Smith 1985).

A History of Slavery and Oppression

In America, slavery began to supplant indentured servitude after 1670. At first, most imported slaves were men, a situation that led to uneven sex ratios. By the mid-eighteenth century, however, the African-American population began to reproduce itself (Freedman 1997). Even so, American slavery systematically attempted to destroy the African family. Marital partners were often separated, and children were sold away from their parents and other kin. In the face of such horrific practices, African-American families demonstrated amazing resilience and creativity, developing their own rituals for marriage and patterns of adoption that provided children separated from parents with love and nurture. Wallace Smith has described the black family as an "adoptionist community" (Smith 1985), and this quality has made an extraordinary contribution to black ecclesiology.

During the first half-century after emancipation, African-American families remained in the rural South, often sharecropping or working as laborers. Many went to extraordinary lengths to locate family members from whom they had been separated. Then came the Great Northern Drive, a mass migration from the South between 1900 and 1929. During this time the African-American population of New York increased by ninety-one thousand and that of Chicago by seventy-nine thousand. Other cities underwent a similar influx of African-Americans from the South. Two factors contributed to this migration: the boll weevil blight that caused an agricultural crisis in the rural South, and continued racial violence in the South.

For many families, migration consisted of a parent's leaving children with relatives or close friends while seeking work in the North. As soon as they could establish themselves, parents would send for their children, but this process was often much more difficult than they initially imagined. The North was no more welcoming than the South had been, either culturally or economically. This migration created enormous family strains and difficulties, but it also contributed to the strength of black mutual aid and adaptive strategies for family survival (Smith 1985).

Coping with Deprivation and Oppression

An extended definition of the family, with sharing of family members between various households, has provided needed flexibility and resourcefulness in the face of social oppression and deprivation. For example, Carol Stack studied life in an African-American ghetto in the 1960s and early 1970s (Stack 1974). She found that strategies for survival in severe economic deprivation included strong alliances of kin and nonkin, involving exchange of goods, resources and the care of children. Social and economic lives were so entwined that not to repay a "debt" meant that someone else's child would not eat. Stack reported the following principles for living: "You have to have help from everybody and anybody," and "The poorer you are, the more likely you are to pay back" (1974:28).

In the community she studied, Stack found that temporary child exchange represented mutual trust and provided a means of acquiring self-esteem. As she began allowing her own child to stay over in the homes of friends she made through her work, she learned that this communicated her trust and respect in her newly acquired community.

Similar to the findings of ethnographic studies in Africa, "household" was not a meaningful way of defining a family in the African-American community in which Stack lived. According to Stack, a person was sometimes a resident in three different households, eating in one, sleeping in another and contributing resources to yet another. She defined family in this community as follows: "the smallest, organized, durable network of kin and non-kin who interact daily, providing domestic needs of children and assuring their survival. The family network is diffused over several kin-based households, and fluctuations in household composition do not significantly affect cooperative familial arrangements" (Stack 1974:31). Informal and formal adoption of children continues to take place at much higher rates in African-American families; nearly 15 percent of all black children are informally adopted (Billingsley 1992).

The communal sharing Stack identified increased the survival potential of all members of the community. On the other hand, no one could "get ahead" either. Stack described one couple who inherited a sum of money, an amount that could have given them the boost they needed out of poverty. But neither resources nor needs could be kept secret in the poor community studied by Stack. "Members of the middle class in America can cherish privacy concerning their income and resources, but the daily intimacy created by exchange transactions in The Flats [the community she studied] insures that any change in a poor family's resources becomes 'news'" (Stack 1974:38). Information about the inheritance spread through the domestic network, and soon the inheritance was absorbed by demands and needs in the family network that could not be refused. More recent research has shown that middle-class African-American families are not insulated from the problems of poverty, even when they move to distant suburbs. Their culture still expects communal sharing of resources (Gilkes 1995).

This egalitarian expectation extends to relationships within the family as well. African-American couples have been more egalitarian in many respects than Euro-American couples. Dual-career marriages have been the norm far longer in African-American families, driven by the economic necessity for all able-bodied adults to be employed, just as the rise in dual-career marriages among Euro-American families is also in part a response to economic factors. Research indicates that African-American men are significantly more involved as partners in housework than their Euro-American counterparts. African-American men spend about seven hours a week on housework, whereas Euro-American men average only five hours. Yet to say they are *more* egalitarian does not mean that the work is divided equally. Both African-American and Euro-American working wives still average thirty to forty hours weekly on housework, far more than their husbands (Billingsley 1992).

Despite such flexibility and resourcefulness, social oppression and deprivation of economic resources have left their marks on African-American family
life. Sociologist Andrew Billingsley's research indicates that for the hundred
years between the end of slavery and the end of World War II, the structure of
African-American families was remarkably stable. Most families were nuclear
families at their core, with other relatives also frequently included in the household. Divorce was rare; 78 percent of all African-American families with children were headed by married couples. As late as 1960, African-American men
could find well-paying blue-collar jobs in industry (Billingsley 1992).

Such employment opportunities have become scarce in the past few decades,
making it increasingly difficult for high-school educated African-American men
to fulfill the provider role for their families. In 1993, 46 percent of African-
American men between the ages of sixteen and sixty-two were not active participants in the American labor force. This figure relates closely to the 48 percent of
African-American families headed by women (Staples and Johnson 1993:235).
Unemployed men often do not marry, since they are unable to contribute to,
much less support, a family. The frustration and despair associated with unemployment are also associated with crime and drug usage, and all of these factors
are exacerbated by societal racism that expects and provides little to strengthen
the ability of African-American men to participate as contributing family members. By 1990, one out of four African-American males aged twenty to twenty-
five was in the custody of the criminal justice system, and homicide had become
the leading cause of death for this age group. More young African-American
males go to jail than to college, and the costs to keep each of them there exceed
tuition, room and board at Harvard or Yale (Billingsley 1992; Staples and
Johnson 1993).

As a consequence, a large segment of the African-American male population
is missing from many poor African-American communities. Women represent
75 percent of African-American church membership. More affluent churches
have larger male memberships, but holiness and Pentecostal congregations,
which are often poorer, have congregations sometimes over 90 percent female
(Gilkes 1995:185).

Those African-American men who "make it" still face the inequality of the
U.S. system. Depending on the occupation, African-American men in the
same occupations and with the same responsibilities make an average of
between $60 and $87 for every $100 white men make. The salaries for Afri-

can-American men in industry and service occupations are more comparable to those of white men than they are for college-educated black males, who earn 77 percent of comparable white male earnings (Bennett 1992:2). Because of this inequality, 30 percent of African-American families are poor, compared with 9 percent of white families. African-Americans are more than twice as likely as whites to be working poor—that is, holding a full-time job that provides an income below the poverty level. Fifteen percent of African-American persons are considered "working poor," compared to 6 percent of whites (Bennett 1992:3).

Since 1960, the incidence of female-headed single-parent African-American families has risen significantly. Under half (43 percent) of African-American adults age eighteen and older were currently married in 1993, a considerable decrease from 64 percent in 1970 (Saluter 1994:2). Beginning in 1980, for the first time since slavery, a majority of African-American children lived in single-parent families. Billingsley observes, however, that this is a shift more in the role of marriage than in the role of family in the lives of African-Americans.

> The allegiance to family is still so strong that on any given day the overwhelming majority of African-American people will be found living in families of one type or another. In 1990, for example, 70% of the 10.5 million African-American households were family households with persons related by blood, marriage, or adoption. Contrary to popular belief, this is about the same as the proportion of whites who live in families. (Billingsley 1992:371)

Billingsley goes on to point out that all the types of family structures found in African-American family life are also found in Euro-American families. For example, numerically there are more Euro-American female-headed households than there are African-American female-headed households. Single-parent families result from of an interplay of economic, political and social circumstances that discourage the formation and duration of nuclear family systems. Some families are more protected from these forces than others.

In fact, what distinguishes African-American families from Euro-American families is the significance of the extended family, both in the household and as a larger network of relationship. There is much less of the "every nuclear family for itself" mentality among African-American families than there is in Euro-American culture, even though Euro-American families also depend on the extended family in times of crisis.

These cultural distinctives are crucial for churches considering how they can minister effectively with African-American families. In the mid-1980s, Wallace C. Smith pointed out that to focus mainly on small group discussions and educational seminars or on counseling with African-American families is "to attempt a white strategy, based on white cultural and economic attainments, upon a people who are facing much different cultural and economic issues" (Smith 1985:80).

Church in African-American Community Life

Robert Staples and Leanor Johnson (1993) have suggested that the church is the modern-day tribe. Through its worship, teaching, benevolence, belief systems, morals and values, and rituals, the church welds unrelated families to one another and to the community. "Each member is literally referred to as 'sister' or 'brother,' elders receive high respect, the minister is venerated as the earthly spiritual chief, and a host of unseen heavenly angels and a supreme Father are believed to be governing the living and the dead" (Staples and Johnson 1993:211).

Historically, black churches have provided connection and legitimization of family relationships when recognition was not available in the larger society. After emancipation from slavery, it was through the black church that people made appeals for information about kinfolk who had been separated by slavery. It was through the black church that dependent children were informally adopted and cared for (Gilkes 1995). The black church also legitimized the informal marriages of many former slaves, demanded marital fidelity and designed programs to foster male leadership in the family (Staples and Johnson 1993).

The black church continues to serve as a buffer against the racism and oppression of African-Americans. Historically, it has been the only institution operating independently of the white power structure. As a consequence, the black church has provided many opportunities for leadership and affirmation not available to African-American people in American society.

While visiting a National Baptist church, I entered the rest room before the worship service. A young teenage girl was standing before the mirror, practicing reading the morning announcements aloud, oblivious to the women coming and going. They and she recognized that her responsibility was important and she needed to prepare. Later in the worship service, when she had completed reading the announcements with strength and enthusiasm, there was a round of "Amens." But even if she had faltered, the congregation would have responded with "Amens" and "Go on, child; it's all right."

In church, African-American children also see African-American adults in status roles not available in white society. The head deacon might be a janitor, the head usher a medical doctor, and the Sunday-school teacher a domestic worker. "Regardless of their station in the larger society, all receive recognition and status in the church" (Staples and Johnson 1993:214).

Families also receive tangible assistance from their congregation. One study showed that one out of five members of African-American congregations receives either financial assistance or needed goods and services from their church (Staples and Johnson 1993). There might be a special offering to help the Jones family with medical bills, or to turn the lights on in Sister Smith's home. Another study found that 67 percent of black churches sponsor at least one family support program targeted to the wider community (Caldwell, Greene and Billingsley 1994). They support such programs as family counseling, aid to the incarcerated, emergency food and financial assistance, homeless shelter, home care, meals on wheels, academic tutoring, child care, African-American culture classes, college financial aid, performing and visual arts classes, Head Start, mentoring, life skills training, recreation, low-income housing, financial services and counseling, youth employment, substance abuse counseling, and general health services. Many African-American churches are actively involved today in community and economic development efforts—efforts that have a significant effect on the culture of their community and the families who live there (Caldwell, Greene and Billingsly 1994; Freedman 1993; Gilkes 1990).

SUGGESTIONS FOR CULTURALLY RELEVANT FAMILY MINISTRY

As this very brief introduction to African-American family and church life illustrates, the cultural overlays that define families, along with families' current ecological context and historic factors, have great relevance for determining how the church can effectively care for families. If our ministry is to be relevant to the families in our congregations and communities, we must understand who those families are culturally. Our programs must relate to their life strategies, their values and their enduring assumptions about family life. The following guidelines will help family ministry leaders understand and be relevant to the families they are attempting to serve.

1. Recognize the importance of cultural differences, even subtle ones. There is nothing more disrespectful of a family than to ignore cultural differences and thus imply that they are insignificant. Ignoring a family's culture implies that the family's experiences, history and values are not important. For example, for a Euro-American person to be "color-blind" with African-American families implies that the experiences of being African-American in our white-dominated culture are not important. They *are* important. Why should we ignore *anything* about a family? But culture is rarely overt—it is implicit. For that reason we feel embarrassed to comment on it, to make the implicit explicit. Overt discussion, however, is often a powerful way to communicate interest and care.

More subtle cultural differences may go unnoticed, let alone acknowledged. Perhaps that is why I so appreciate Margaret Blackburn's narrative about her family. On the face of things, her family and mine are much alike. Both are white, with Southern roots, traditional in structure. She is only a decade younger than I am; we both have husbands and children. Yet her narrative points to significant and profound cultural meanings for her family that differ from my own. These differences show that even when we think we share the culture of the families with whom we are ministering, there may be subtle but very significant differences.

2. Read about one or more of the cultural overlays relevant to the families with whom you are ministering. There are many resources that describe the historic experiences, life strategies, values and beliefs of particular ethnic and people groups, such as McGoldrick, Giordano and Pearce's *Ethnicity and Family Therapy* (McGoldrick, Giordano and Pearce 1996). But reading about cultural groups should be accompanied by caution in applying what is read. Such materials by definition are generalizations about a group's characteristics. Generalizations are true only "in general" and must always be nuanced in a particular community or with a particular family. Remember that whatever you read is only *one* overlay of several that define a family, and another overlay may actually cancel out the characteristic you just read about. Readings provide *hypotheses*, not facts about family life in that cultural group. Hypotheses need to be tested by observation.

3. Learn from families themselves. After you have gained some general knowledge about a cultural group, the best place to learn about the cultures of families is within those cultures. Sometimes families can provide windows into their life together that bring what you have read and observed from the outside to life, such as Blackburn's description of her family. Immerse yourself in the life experiences of families. Visit them in their homes, visit where they work and play and go to school. Talk with them about what you see or read but do not understand.

Most families are delighted to find out that church leaders want to understand their daily lives. Asking them to tell you the stories of their family, the dreams and goals they have, will tell you much about their values and beliefs.

4. *Become aware of the cultural overlays that define your own family.* This is perhaps the hardest part of developing cultural sensitivity. To open oneself to understanding other cultures means seeing an understanding of reality that often does not match your own. It creates an uncomfortable awareness that our definitions of what is real and what is important, which we have held to be self-evident and universal, may instead be culturally relative. Becoming aware of cultural differences makes us vulnerable to questioning our family's assumptions and strategies for life. A significant cultural overlay for many church leaders' families is the dominant American culture. That culture shapes how we see the world and our relationships in it in significant ways. Understanding this cultural overlay is particularly significant when relating to families who have different national and ethnic heritages. It is too easy to label families who differ from us culturally as "dysfunctional." Indeed they may be dysfunctional when viewed from within our own cultural framework. But their adaptive life strategies currently or historically are or were functional, and understanding how they functioned is important.

Here are some of the characteristics of American culture that serve as a lens through which we see and evaluate the culture of families like and different from our own.

Optimism and efficacy. Americans believe that if we just work hard enough and smart enough, we can get what is important to us. No goal is too remote for the individual who has the will and determination. Americans believe in being decisive and not simply allowing events to take their course. Persons should set goals and pursue them. Not to do so is seen as laziness or excessive dependence on others. In the face of circumstances beyond their control, however, Americans may feel their core values shaken.

Supremacy of the individual. Americans believe that the self-determination and self-fulfillment of individuals is more important than the welfare of the community or the clan. To choose a career or marriage partner based on what parents need or want is virtually inconceivable to the American mind. This value of self-determination has enabled many Americans to launch out on paths very different from what their families might have chosen or wanted for them. It has created a love of freedom and a keen sense that one must take responsibility for oneself. On the other hand, the individualism of our society can lead to a self-centeredness and loss of community that can leave us feeling isolated and alone.

Belief in science and rationality as the routes to truth. Americans are invested in the scientific method and believe that there is one truth and it can be discovered. They are much less trusting of truth defined by tradition or "feelings." Emotions are important primarily because if they are not understood and reckoned with, they can distort rational/cognitive processing of information. Emotions are thus not routes to truth but possible barriers that must be addressed. They are considered "irrational" and thus secondary to science and rationality. Yet science is a value system; it is not value-free. It may even be a barrier to other truths available only through intuition, relationships and emotion.

Informality. Americans are "democratic" in speech. Persons frequently address one another using first names rather than the more formal "Mr." or "Ms." and last name. Restaurant staff and receptionists address strangers who may be twice their age by their first name or as "honey." These language patterns communicate the American value of equality. In some ethnic groups that have experienced unequal treatment at the hands of dominant American culture, however, more formal address is used to communicate the respect not offered by mainstream society. In African-American churches, for example, adults—even friends—address one another in public as "Sister" or "Brother" and the family name.

Significance of material success. Americans tend to measure their own success and the success of others in economic terms. Churches measure their success, for example, in terms of "church growth," both in members and in budget. It is not surprising that families, too, may evaluate their success based on material possessions or ability to provide financial support for children's education. The emphasis on materialism, however, has resulted in a widening gap between rich and poor and an impoverishment even of the rich, who have undervalued other forms of life "success."

5. Be prepared for the conflicts created by crosscultural experiences. You may find yourself responding emotionally to families of cultures different from your own. Perhaps you feel defensive, as I did with the three German women. Perhaps you feel impatient and exasperated, wondering how these people can believe or value what they do, and wanting to help them change. For example, I find myself feeling exasperation with parents who smack their preschoolers for what I consider normal and developmentally appropriate behavior (dropping spaghetti off a highchair tray and watching it fall, or wiggling in church).

6. *Changes in families almost always involve changes in family culture.* The evolving changes in gender roles in Margaret Blackburn's story illustrate this. Before attempting to make a change, however, we must really understand the meaning and place of the life strategy within the culture. The dropping of spaghetti by a preschooler may be fine in my middle-class home. In the home of a family living in poverty, however, learning not to waste a very precious item—food—may be more significant than learning that dropped objects fall to the floor. The wiggling toddler who is a member of an oppressed racial minority group may be learning a very important lesson—not to call attention to oneself—that may help him or her survive in a racist, hostile world. Or perhaps these family behaviors are carryovers from previous times when food was scarce or minority children who called attention to themselves could wind up in major trouble. It may be time for a change in these family behaviors, but change efforts should be carried out with respect for the significance that family strategies almost always have had for survival and adaptation.

If I find myself uneasy, frustrated or impatient with a family's culture, it's likely that the family feels the same way toward me and my behavior. My parenting may look permissive and even neglectful. So I need to be careful, if I truly want to understand a family or group of families, to keep my own ways from being inadvertently offensive or disrespectful.

7. *Plan ministry that is culturally relevant, in both its goals and its processes.* As we consider how to minister with families, we must begin with goals that are relevant to them culturally and experientially. Wallace Smith points out that parent education seminars for African-American families are "white strategies based on white culture" (Smith 1985). Of course educational seminars may be helpful, but an emphasis on parental responsibility for children inadvertently discounts the significance of the extended family in African-American cultural experience. If parenting seminars are the *only* ministry provided to help families with childrearing, we are implying that what African-American children need most is more effective parenting. We have not addressed factors such as community violence, racism and economic deprivation, and these may be highly relevant factors in the lives of African-American children in a particular community. A more relevant goal, then, might be organization of the African-American community to mobilize in behalf of the needs of its children. The community itself could then determine what needs to be done.

Second, to be effective, the *processes* of ministry must be culturally sensitive. Seminars may be much less effective in a community that has had conflicted relationships with the educational system. Bible studies that apply Scripture to family life and the raising of children will be more congruent, particularly in a church culture where doing Bible study together as a community is highly valued. The content itself may be similar to that of a seminar, but the process of delivery is more culturally relevant.

Imagine that you would like to help spouses communicate with one another more effectively regarding their values and beliefs about sexuality. In a conservative white Southern congregation, a relevant goal might be to have spouses to put their thoughts and feelings into words and to listen empathically to each other's thoughts and feelings. In white American culture, including conservative Southern congregations, sharing thoughts and feelings about intimate aspects of life is considered appropriate for husbands and wives. Having them talk about thoughts and feelings about sexuality in front of other couples, however, would not be culturally appropriate. Instead it might be appropriate to teach skills of listening, empathy and self-disclosure using other topics, especially if those topics are humorous. Humor is appropriate to share among couples; conversation about sexuality is not. Couples could then be given three questions concerning their values and beliefs about sexuality, and a scripture passage to read together—alone—and discuss. To ensure that these discussions take place, they could be structured into the group time rather than given as "homework" assignments, but couples should be allowed to scatter through the building for a specified time for their private conversation. This process honors the privacy that is valued in this cultural context, and at the same time it provides a structured environment and the implicit blessing of the church community for holding such a discussion.

8. *Whenever possible, introduce change to family culture from within the culture.* Most people are more amenable to change when it is introduced by persons whom they trust to understand their situation and the implications of the proposed change. Indeed, all other things being equal, an insider is more likely to understand the implications of a change than someone from the cultural "outside." In the above scenario, for example, a white Southern couple who are members of the congregation are much more likely to be able to influence couples to take the discussion seriously and follow through than a young, single congregational staff member.

Sometimes we are members of one or more of the cultural overlays that define the context of families with whom we are ministering. Other times we are able to "join" the cultural context; over time we earn honorary or actual membership in the culture. We may then be able to support and challenge families by coming alongside them.

There are other circumstances in which we will always be outsiders. In those circumstances it is much better to serve as a consultant to culture members, who in turn can minister directly with families. Consultation implies partnership rather than supervision. It implies that each brings specific expertise to the situation.

When I spent a year as a family ministry consultant in Australia, I was asked to lead parenting courses for Christian Chinese-Australian families. Many of these families were first-generation immigrants experiencing the collision of two very different cultures. In addition, many Euro-Australians were extremely opposed to the influx of Chinese families into their communities, so these families were experiencing overt prejudice and racism. I pondered what basis I had from which to speak to these families and found very little common cultural ground beyond our shared Christian faith. So I decided to consult with church leaders who were themselves Chinese-Australians. I worked with them as they developed a parenting course that would be relevant to the experiences of Christian Chinese-Australian families. They led the courses. As I worked with church leaders, I was careful to be very tentative in any contribution I made to their work, repeatedly stating that my experience was American and thus very different from their own. They should determine what was relevant to their experience and what was not.

A family's culture is their own. It is their identity, and it is theirs to change, in their own time and way. Ultimately we are always consultants, even to persons who share some cultural overlays with us. We bring our own experiences and the knowledge that we share; the community and its families must determine what to use and how to shape it for their own life together.

Section Two

The Processes
of Family Life

WE HAVE LOOKED AT THE ECOLOGICAL, SOCIOLOGICAL AND cultural contexts for family life in the United States. This section looks at the *inside* of family life—how families develop and change over time and the phases of life; the processes of family life that influence their development (attachment and caregiving, communication and conflict, and intimacy); how power is distributed and managed in family life; the processes of shaping a sense of family identity; and the characteristics of strong families.

None of these processes take place only within some protected interior of the family. They are shaped by all the other processes of family life, and by the larger contexts of community, culture and historic time in which the family is living. Together with the earlier section of the book, these chapters provide a broad understanding of family life in the United States today.

Chapter 4

Stages & Phases
of Family Life

F AMILIES CHANGE OVER TIME: MEMBERS ARE BORN AND DIE, GET mad and leave, fall in love and get married, or simply move in. Members change their roles: a dependent infant cared for by adults becomes a relatively autonomous teen who presents the family with new challenges but also helps with the cooking. Teenagers face the developmental tasks of establishing their own identity and launching their own career and, sooner or later, their own adult family. Their parents must provide them with a shifting combination of security, freedom and responsibility. At the same time, parents are dealing with their own developmental issues—midlife career and marital changes and the beginning signs of aging. In addition, their own parents may be increasingly in need of social support and, if they are frail, caregiving or other forms of assistance.

The family itself grows and changes in response to these developmental tasks of its members, adapting and reacting to the complex interplay among the developmental issues of family members at different stages of the life cycle. Authority shifts and is remolded to fit changing relationships. Families are, finally, not the structures of relationships that last but processes that link one generational expression of family to the next. Family history is a product of family developmental processes over time (White 1991).

People do better with the changes and stresses of life when they know what to expect. It certainly helps to know that it is "normal" for the intoxicating sexualized intimacy that characterizes courtship to change into a more stable (but perhaps less exciting) attachment and sexual bonding during the early years of marriage. It helps parents of teens to understand that the teen's oscillating expectations for parental presence and care one moment and noninterference the next are normal. This oscillation is simply part of the process of redefining the family relationship that must happen as child becomes adult. The church community can be a significant support to families as they navigate the various channels of family development.

DEVELOPMENTAL STAGE THEORY

How families develop over time has been the subject of considerable social-science theory and research, beginning with the publication in 1948 of Duvall and Hill's *Report of the Committee on the Dynamics of Family Interaction* (Duvall and Hill 1948; see also Hill and Rodgers 1964; Rodgers 1973). Early family developmental theory centered on marriage and the birth and raising of children as the events that mark the stages of family life. Duvall and Miller posited eight stages.

☐ Stage 1: Beginning families (marital couple with no children)
☐ Stage 2: Childbearing families
☐ Stage 3: Families with preschool children
☐ Stage 4: Families with school-age children
☐ Stage 5: Families with adolescents
☐ Stage 6: Families as launching centers
☐ Stage 7: Families in the middle years
☐ Stage 8: Aging families (Duvall and Miller 1985)

A quick look at these stages reveals the importance of the ages and stages of children as definers of family life. Five of the eight stages relate directly to the birth, growth and launching of children. The first stage is clearly simply a preparatory phase; children have not yet been born. Even more recent theorists have posited the presence and growth of children as the foundation for family development. In fact, James White argues that the tie between parent and child is the fundamental requirement of family life. Families must include two or more generations, and human groups are not families unless they include children (White 1991).

Other family-stage theorists have divided the family life cycle somewhat differently. For example, Betty Carter and Monica McGoldrick posited six stages instead of eight: (1) leaving home (single young adults); (2) the joining of families through marriage; (3) families with young children; (4) families with adolescents; (5) launching children and moving on; and (6) families in later life (Carter and McGoldrick 1989).

These stage models emphasize that family development occurs in the linear dimension of time, a result of at least two generations of kin growing up and growing old in interaction with one another. Joan Aldous has suggested modifying the concept of the "family life cycle," which implies that families cycle through the same or similar stages at different times (Aldous 1978). According to Aldous, the concept of "family career" more accurately captures the linear nature of family life stages. The concept of family career also leaves open the possibility that different families have different career paths. Divorce, remarriage, cohabitation and singleness are careers divergent from that of the nuclear family.

The structure of the family, and what is appropriate and expected given that structure, determines the stages in these models of development (White 1991). For example, American culture expects preschool-stage families to be structured in many ways by the biological needs and rhythms of the preschool child. Bedtimes, nap times and elaborate rituals structure the family's life together.

Because the stages are sequential, this model of family development suggests what stage will come next and how the family's life will be different in that stage. The demands of the preschool family will ease some as children enter school. Parents will have more free time and can expect fewer sleep interruptions and more ability to invest in activities that are independent of parenting responsibilities. By contrast, the family of a child who has severe learning or physical challenges and cannot care for self may well experience the move into the school-age years as particularly stressful. Their continuation of caregiving does not fit what is expected according to the socially recognized stages of family life.

A social norm is a rule, an expectation of how things are "supposed" to occur or be done. Families are constructed with social norms of who is *allowed* to do what, who is *required* to do what and who is *forbidden* to do what (White 1991). These norms change over time. For example, who is allowed to drive the family car changes as adolescents reach driving age. For the family with a senior adult with failing eyesight and increased reaction time, a marker event defining a new family life stage may be the adult child's *forbidding* the parent to drive. In return, the adult child is *required* to drive the parent to the doctor and run other errands, or at least to make sure that someone does.

Norms, then, are the building blocks of relationships, and changes in norms often mark the changes from one stage of family life to another. There are norms about every stage of family life, both norms that develop within the family and cultural/social norms from without. For example, there are norms about responsibility for frail elderly parents. Imagine the social response to a middle-aged person who fails to act on knowledge that her elderly parent's driving has become hazardous to self and others, or who does not see it as her responsibility to provide or arrange for needed transportation to doctors and the grocery store.

Of course, not every change in norms marks a change of family stage. A preschooler may learn to dress herself. First she is encouraged ("allowed"), with applause from the parent, to pull up jeans that the parent has placed over her feet. Later she is expected ("required") to go to the closet, select what she is to wear and put it on alone. Putting one's clothes on alone does not by itself signal a change in stage. When it is put with the whole class of behaviors called self-care, however, it does mark the shift from dependent infant/preschooler family to the more autonomous school-age child family. This shift involves norms about grooming, going somewhere without supervision (to the schoolbus stop or a friend's house in the neighborhood) and being trusted with money.

Stage shifts tend to be accompanied by disruption in the family's structure of role relationships. Families feel themselves floundering about, searching for new ways of relating to one another and the world around them, before settling into new behavior patterns. Of course, change in families is relatively constant, with roles evolving over time. Stage shifts, however, are disruptions even of the expected rate of change, the change the family is "used to." For example, over time adult children may gradually experience a shift to greater mutuality with their older parents. As parents age, the mutuality evolves gradually into more responsibility on the part of adult children. The stage shift, however, may come when the parent is diagnosed with advanced Parkinson's disease or breaks a hip and faces an extended and perhaps incomplete recovery. The change is no longer subtle; for the first time the adult child must take on the responsibility for learning about and taking care of the details of the parent's finances, self-care and household management.

Often families experience these changes as "points of no return" (Aldous 1996). Once the parent has moved into the child's household or an assisted-living apartment and the parent's home is sold, there is no going back. Once one has married, one cannot go back to the never-married status, even through divorce. Once the child is born, there is no going back to being childless. Once a teenager-turned-young-adult's curfew is lifted, it is hard to return to parental oversight.

Research has confirmed that movement from one stage to another creates stress or adds to any stress the family is already experiencing. Even stage changes marked by happy events create stress. For example, the newly married couple must form a family unit that incorporates the partners' often conflicting expectations. The birth of children and the launching of adolescents create major realignments of roles and responsibilities within the family. Families also experience stress when the stages of development are disrupted in some way or family events occur outside of what the culture considers the normal sequence of development. Unplanned pregnancy is always a crisis, but it is probably a much greater crisis for an unmarried adolescent or the woman approaching midlife than for a married couple in their early thirties, everything else being equal (which it never is).

Stage theory is helpful in showing that families in the same stages or stage transitions experience similar challenges and can be expected to respond to those challenges in some predictable ways. Stage theory also points out that the roles and norms of family life do not remain static but change over time. The role of mother and father is continuous, but it also changes in content from birth through childhood and adolescence and on through the stages of adulthood and aging. Aldous has talked about *role sequences*, or the changing roles that evolve over time (Aldous 1996). She also has pointed out that family members usually are in *positions* composed of a cluster of roles that fit together, such as son-brother-grandson, or wife-mother-daughter. Consequently, the role sequences each member experiences make up what Aldous calls the *positional career*. The content of the various roles shifts over time, and the ways each role is lived influence the other roles. The mothering of children has a significant impact, for example, on the role of wife. As children grow and need less parenting involvement, the roles of spouses with one another change in various ways.

Stress and Coping Across the Developmental Stages

David Olson and his colleagues have studied the coping and stress of nuclear families over the life stages (Olson 1989). They surveyed one thousand families (husbands and wives and their children, if any) from every region of the United States, although the heaviest concentration of families came from the upper Midwest. An overview of their findings suggests the importance of these stages for understanding and caring for families throughout life.

First, they found that children create stress and strain in families, and that mothers and fathers experience that stress and strain differently. Wives' satisfaction with their family life began declining with the birth of children and reached its lowest point at the time of launching children. Husbands had a similar pattern, but the husbands' satisfaction scores began increasing sooner, when the adolescents were still in the home. Consequently, marital and family satisfaction was higher at early and later stages of the family life cycle, when couples were living without children. Couples were least satisfied with their families during the adolescent stage, when family stress was highest. When families were very satisfied, potentially stressful experiences had minimal impact on them. This suggests that perceiving one's family to be satisfying and healthy in some ways protects the family from the negative effects of stress.

The researchers found that having children in the home actually *lowered* stress for families providing care for frail elderly relatives, especially for women who were also employed outside the home. For these women, work provided a helpful respite from caregiving. And the presence of young family members helps lower stress from the multiple demands they are experiencing rather than compounding it.

Olson and his colleagues studied how families use various coping strategies throughout the life cycle. These researchers identified the most important coping strategy for families overall as *seeking spiritual support* (Olson 1989:152). The next most-used strategy for coping with stress was *redefining* the demanding situation in a way that would make the situation seem more manageable. Husbands consistently use redefining as the coping strategy of choice throughout the life stages. Wives use redefining more selectively, employing it less during the years they are parenting adolescents and more during the retirement stage of the family cycle (Olson 1989:144).

The researchers found that husbands and wives did not evaluate their families in the same way. Parents and adolescent children agreed even less in how they assessed their families. That is, different persons in the family have a quite different perception of the family's strength and challenges. One family member cannot be presumed to be able to speak for the entire family.

The Limitations of Developmental Stage Theory

As helpful as stage theory is for understanding family development, it also has limitations as a guide for congregational family ministry.

1. Stage theory posits the nuclear family as the family. Even with the introduction of the concept of family careers and divergent paths, developmental stage theory posits the nuclear family as the norm. Requiring groups to have dependent children in order to be called families further limits the applicability of stage theory. In fact, the stages do not even apply to many nuclear families. Couples launching teenagers may find themselves faced with a pregnancy (either their own or their child's); launched young adults often come back home, bringing with them children as the fruit of relationships ended in divorce; older adults may find themselves raising grandchildren.

2. Marriage and parenting are increasingly detached from one another in our society.

> Love and marriage,
> Love and marriage,
> Go together like a horse and carriage.
> First comes love,
> Then comes marriage,
> Then comes Suzie with a baby carriage.

I jumped rope to this singsong rhyme in elementary school in the 1950s. It expresses norms about the progressive stages of courtship, marriage and parenting. When there was a "mistake" resulting in a pregnancy before marriage, a quick and quiet ceremony made sure that the right ordering of marriage and baby carriage was maintained, even though community members knowingly raised eyebrows as they counted only six or seven months between marriage and carriage.

But today the processes of parenting and the processes of marriage are increasingly independent of one another. Marriage is no longer a requisite, much less a prerequisite, for pregnancy and parenting. At the same time, increasing numbers of couples are voluntarily and involuntarily remaining childless, or at least delaying parenting until much later in life.

For some, cohabitation has replaced marriage as the family form into which children are being born. Births outside of marriage are much more likely to take place in cohabiting relationships than they are as the consequence of casual unions (Loomis and Landale 1994). Because cohabiting relationships do not have the social sanction and benefits of marriage, however, and because many cohabiting couples are poor, these relationships face daunting challenges to their endurance as families. Cohabiting living arrangements do not last long—an average of 1.3 years. More than half (60 percent) actually end in marriage. However, unions begun with cohabitation are almost twice as likely to dissolve within ten years compared to all first marriages—57 percent compared to 30 percent. About 56 percent of the children of cohabiting couples who marry will experience the disruption of their parents' marriage—versus about 31 percent of children born to married parents who did not live together before marriage (O'Brien 1989).

Even more fundamental changes are taking place in parenting roles as they relate to marriage. When fathers began leaving home with their lunchboxes during the Industrial Revolution, a quiet revolution was launched in fathers' roles in the lives of their children. Prior to that time, children had been considered the property of their fathers. In a nineteenth-century divorce, fathers almost always received custody of the children. When fathers went to work outside the home and the role of homemaker/mother became glorified, however, children rather quickly became the property of mothers.

Today many fathers are no longer even resident members of their families. More than half of all children born today will spend part or all of their childhood in a one-parent home, usually the home of their mother (Children's Defense Fund 1996). In addition to pregnancy outside of marriage, divorce is a major contributor to the disengagement of fathers from parenting. With marital separation and divorce, some fathers also disengage from their children, painful reminders as they are of past hopes and disappointments. Some fathers try to stay involved in their children's lives but are unsuccessful. Hostility with the ex-spouse makes it extraordinarily difficult for them to cooperate for the sake of mutually caring for children. Occasionally a mother deliberately creates obstacles to the children's continued involvement with the father. Often more than one of these factors are at work.

3. *The life span of family units is growing longer.* The stages are relatively unbalanced. For example, Duvall's theory of the family life cycle apportions six stages to the first forty years of life, with the last forty years of family life holding only two stages. With the lengthening of life, this imbalance is increasing. An age marker of eighty-five years is now being used to identify "the oldest old."

This age group is growing faster than any other segment of the U.S. population. Between 1960 and 1980, the oldest old increased by 141 percent (Johnson 1993).

Older adults are maintaining family households much longer. In 1900, 75 percent of men over sixty-five were householders; by 1981, the proportion had increased to 91 percent (O'Brien 1989). A surprising number of the oldest old, 46 percent, still live in a single-family dwelling rather than an apartment or more protected senior housing (Johnson 1993:322).

The oldest old have more depleted family resources than the general population over age sixty-five. Of those living on their own, most women and many men have been widowed. Also, women in advanced old age today have fewer children than did their counterparts in 1900. They have an average of only one daughter, compared to 3.3 daughters in 1900 (Johnson 1993:318). Their children are likely to be senior adults themselves and may be dealing with their own health problems or impairments.

Sara Qualls's study of family care for frail elders has suggested a series of stages that characterize families by the level of care they provide to one another (Qualls 1997). Qualls notes that not only do families provide care for elders, but elders provide a rich array of reciprocal services such as childcare and financial assistance.

Caregiving for elders differs in major ways from caregiving for children. Caregiving for infants is a major task that involves physical and emotional involvement twenty-four hours a day. Over the years of a child's development, however, the level of care needed decreases and consumes less time, until a child's adulthood when parents provide emotional support and occasional assistance. In contrast, caregiving for elders moves in the opposite direction, from support and occasional assistance to greater levels of monitoring and physical care.

The stages at the end of the life cycle are not the only place where change is taking place in family-life norms. Significant variations are also taking place in the middle stages. American adult children remain longer in their parents' households, and are more likely to return after leaving, than ever before. From 1970 to 1983, the number of twenty- to twenty-four-year-olds living with parents increased 42 percent, while the number of twenty-five- to twenty-nine-year-olds increased 24 percent. In 1984, 37 percent of all eighteen- to twenty-nine-year-olds lived in their parents' household (O'Brien 1989). The stage called "launching" may thus span more than a decade, and even longer when there is more than one child in the family.

4. In stage theory, the family is a context for individual development. A close examination of the stages of family development reveals that focus lies on the development and careers of individual family members, with the family cast simply as the context for that development. The only stages that focus on the development of family rather than the development of individuals are courtship and marriage.

Nevertheless, family development appears to be defined as the *interplay of the dynamics of individual development.* Somehow family development is the process of working out in one family group the sometimes conflicting developmental tasks of individual members—the adolescent's developing autonomy and the parent's midlife crisis and the grandparent's increasing frailty.

Glen Elder has called this a "life-course approach." This approach views the individual as the elementary unit of the family, and the focus is on the ages and stages of individual family members (Elder 1983). The aging process, therefore, is the real focus. Aging is a complex process that involves three dimensions: chronological age, social age and historical age. Obviously, "chronological age" simply refers to the number of years a person has lived. But chronological age is not the same thing as social age or historical age. Social age concerns the social timing and structure of lives: a mother of young children is a "social age," even though chronologically she may be anywhere from fifteen to forty-five years old, or older. Historical age places people in historical context through membership in specific birth cohorts: baby boomers, baby busters, Generation X. All three dimensions locate people, and through them their families (Elder 1983).

Understanding these dimensions of ages and stages is important for working with families; but family development is more than the interaction of individual development in the family group. There are also processes of *family* development that occur in interaction with the development processes of individuals.

The Significance of Stage Theory

Stage theory has been extremely helpful in its description of stress that occurs at the transition between life stages, and especially when those transitions occur at times society deems inappropriate. Stage theory has also been particularly useful in articulating the developmental issues of both parents and children that form the backdrop for parenting. Much good has come for families through family-life education programs built on these stages. Stage theory is most helpful, however, when it is not considered universally applicable for all families, but when its application is more carefully defined as the stages of life for nuclear families—married couples with children.

Churches need to take an active role in creating and nurturing family relationships that include but go beyond the marital and parenting roles of the nuclear family. Thus we need a model of family development that fits all families, not just the nuclear family during the first half of life. Within such a framework, more narrowly defined theories for different kinds of families, such as the developmental stages for nuclear families, can be useful. Then the specific processes of development in adoptive families, blending families, families of adult children and elderly parents can be studied as the processes of nuclear families have been.

PHASES AND CYCLES OF FAMILY DEVELOPMENT

Interestingly, only a few theorists have used interpersonal processes to describe the development of families over time.[1] The work of Lyman Wynne and Kenneth Terkelson, as well as study of biblical covenants, has been foundational for my own understanding of the processes of family development.

Lyman Wynne: Relational processes. Lyman Wynne describes four processes that unfold in relational systems: (1) attachment/caregiving, (2) communicating, (3) joint problem-solving and (4) mutuality (Wynne 1984). "Attachment and caregiving" refers to the bond of affection that develops between family members over time and circumstances. "Communication" refers to sharing interests and exchanging meaning and messages with one another. "Joint problem-solving" refers to sharing and collaborating in tasks, interests and activities. "Mutuality" is the renewing and deepening of the relationship through the previous three processes as the family changes over time.

Each of these processes builds on and assumes those that precede it. Joint problem-solving, for example, must be preceded by attachment. A family will not stick it out through a difficult problem if they are not attached to one another. Evidence for this can be found in higher divorce rates during the early years of marriage (Peck and Manocherian 1989) and higher rates of adoption disruption in the first year after placement (Festinger 1986). Joint problem-solving must also be preceded by a communication system in which people understand one

---

[1]Material in this section has been adapted from content previously published in Garland and Pancoast 1990.

another. Many families embroiled in chronic conflict may not have developed effective communication that allows them to solve problems.

Wynne names each of these processes by its positive side, but he makes it clear that the negative side of the process is important for family development too. For example, the negative side of attachment/caregiving is separation. Short separations—such as a child's occasional evening with a friend while the parents have time alone—actually strengthen a healthy attachment between child and parents. The child learns that parents do come back, that relationships endure separations. On the other hand, when a child is separated from parents for long periods of time, such as during placement in foster care or while a parent serves in the military overseas, the family system may not develop further. The long separation impairs the process of attachment. In the same way, occasional failures to communicate effectively or solve problems that confront the family may be challenges that, when overcome, strengthen the family. But if the family fails repeatedly in these relational processes, the relationships themselves may deteriorate.

Kenneth Terkelson: Meeting needs. Kenneth Terkelson has suggested that sequences of behavior in which family members meet one another's needs are the most important processes that control the development of the family (Terkelson 1980). As family members provide care for one another, they become attached. As they solve problems and communicate with one another, they develop intimacy and mutuality. As members meet each other's needs, from changing an infant's diaper to listening to a distressed adolescent or accompanying a frightened spouse to the hospital for medical tests, families develop a sense of cohesion and create a sense of "resource sufficiency"—that together they have the resources to do what individual members could not do on their own (Terkelson 1980:31). They develop the assurance that "together we can face anything." Family members feel secure in one another. By contrast, families that fail to meet members' needs typically generate a sense of "resource scarcity" and family fragmentation.

Members' needs change over time. The infant son grows into a young child and no longer needs diapers changed. Instead he now needs a parent to take time to listen to and encourage his new reading skills. The adolescent girl now needs support and encouragement in taking responsibility for her own finances. New needs emerging from growth and aging in family members lead to a period of instability in the family's structures, and then gradually to new structures.

Thus new structures mark a new developmental phase. The meeting of an infant's physical needs, which occurred in frequent bursts of activity interspersed throughout the adult's other activities, has given way to rituals of sitting on the couch for a half-hour with a shared book. Care becomes less behavioral (dressing the infant) and more verbal ("Johnny, get dressed; breakfast is almost ready!"). Although these changes seem relatively small, they bring a period of family instability. Children who are used to parents' doing for them must learn to do for themselves, and parents must let them, with all the mismatches of clothing that this will mean. Gradually the relationship between Johnny and his parents changes from an emphasis on physical caregiving to an emphasis on communicating. Wynne suggests that attachment/caregiving is succeeded by communication. Terkelson's emphasis on need-meeting and Wynne's relational processes are thus both illustrated in this example.

Contracts and Covenants

Like the meeting of needs that Terkelson describes, making and living covenants is another process that overarches the four that Wynne articulates. A covenant is a commitment to love and care unconditionally. Covenants can be contrasted with contracts; contracts are relationships that exist *because* each fulfills the expectations of the other. Contracts have "if" clauses: if you will love me and take care of me, I will love you and take care of you.

Relationships between people often begin as contracts. Each of the parties enters the relationship because it offers certain rewards (companionship, enjoyment, affection, help with a difficult task). We can certainly see this in the courtship of potential marital partners. It is also true in the initial relationship between an infant and parents. Parents expect the infant to provide love and affection, and perhaps companionship and a sense of meaning in life. In return, the infant needs total care.

The initial contract depends on at least some evidence that the other will fulfill their side of an exchange of benefits. As persons meet one another's needs, however, loyalty and commitment grow (Sakenfeld 1985). The relationship becomes more a covenant and less a contract. A covenant is an unconditional relationship; it depends on a "leap of faith" in which members choose the relationship whether or not the other will or is able to deliver what is hoped for (Kaplan, Schwartz and Markus-Kaplan 1984).

As the covenant deepens, the rewards may still be important and expected, but the rewards no longer serve as an essential condition for the relationship to continue. Family is still family, even when there is disappointment in one another and perhaps a crisis of unfulfilled expectations. For example, when a child is found to have autism or developmental challenges that compromise her ability to show affection or fulfill parents' expectations, the family is faced with a major crisis. Nevertheless, the basic family relationship and commitment to the child are not usually questioned. Marital partner, sibling and adult child-parent relationships all carry expectations that are sometimes not met, yet the relationship itself usually continues.

Few relationships are purely contracts or covenants. Like the necessary negative counterparts of Wynne's processes, covenants require contracts, although the covenant itself is larger than any of the contracts that occur between covenant members. Contracts such as "if you'll do the cooking, I'll do the cleaning" ease family members through a maze of shared responsibilities. They serve as tools of problem-solving, however, rather than as the foundations for the relationship. A breach in such a contract does not signal the end of the family, just as our sin does not end our relationship with God. To be a family implies that there is commitment beyond a quid pro quo arrangement; we have a covenant together. Like the processes of family development described by Wynne, a family's growth from a contractual to a covenantal relationship is nurtured as family members respond day in and day out to one another's needs.

Family Developmental Phases: A Framework for Family Ministry

These relationship processes suggest that family development takes place in phases, which I have called courtship, formation, partnership, consolidation and transformation. Phases differ from stages in that the boundaries between one phase in a family's life and another may not be clearly defined. Phases tend to overlap with one another and do not necessarily always occur in sequential order. As we will see, as new family members are added through birth or consolidation, a family may in some respects return to the earliest phases of family development. Nevertheless, that return does not mean that the family regresses to an early "stage"; it is moving forward, even as it revisits developmental processes that it has experienced before.

Development thus takes place more as a spiral than as a circle or a linear path. Each time the family enters a phase of family life, it does so in a different way, bringing with it all of its history and changing culture. It is in a different place, although some of the themes of the phase will be similar. A cycle implies that the family comes *back* to the same place, while a spiral pictures the family returning to the same issues by going *forward;* the phase may be the same, but the family's place in it is different.

1. Courtship. Family development begins with a phase of courtship. Whether intentional or unintentional, individuals go through a period of courting each other as they either choose or feel compelled to form a family unit. *Courtship* may be a confusing term for this stage, because its connotations are generally limited to dating, romance and sexual attraction. I would like to broaden the definition of courtship, however, to include a wide variety of other kinds of relationships between persons who are in the process of becoming family with one another. For example, courtship includes the process of considering adoption or pregnancy as a means of adding family members. Prospective parents look with new interest at the infants of others. They shop for or admire baby clothes and baby furniture. They talk about possible names for future sons and daughters. There is an element of the romantic, of idealization, in this fantasizing about taking on the role of parents. In essence, it is a time of courtship with the fantasized infant. This may take place before or after pregnancy after occurs. The pregnancy does not have to be "planned" for the prospective parents to go through a period of courtship, preparing themselves for this new relationship.

Courtship may also be a time of selecting a specific other person as a family member, such as the decision to adopt a specific child with special needs or to form a relationship with a mentally ill adult who is "familyless." Long-term friends may implicitly explore the options of committing themselves more fully to one another by sharing more of their resources and making choices as a family unit.

Sometimes courtship is a time of defining whether and how persons compelled to be in relationship will be family to one another. A new stepparent and stepchild try to figure out how they will relate to one another in a newly formed household. The stepchild may have had little choice at all, except in trying to thwart or encourage the developing relationship between the parent and potential stepparent. Stepparents, stepchildren and in-laws have to "court" one another; families do not happen instantly when marriage occurs. The option exists for the relationship *not* to be defined as family. The child may refuse to accept the stepparent as a family member, even though they live in the same house and may even become friends.

Courtship is a time of contractual relating, not covenant making. *In essence, it is a prefamily phase.* The underlying issue is whether each will fulfill the other's expectations and needs for family. Will adoption of this person bring me opportunities for caregiving and love that will fulfill my need for purposefulness? Would another type of relationship or another person be a better match between what I can give and what I want in return? Such language is jarring because it smacks of calculation, and consequently these contracts are rarely spoken openly; often they are not even allowed into conscious thought. Also, what is exchanged between persons may not be in any sense equivalent. Although each expects some return from investment in the relationship, the expectation may be quite different for each. One may expect intimacy and companionship; the other, security and protection.

During the courtship process, then, the relationship is conditional, although none of the potential family members may be consciously aware of what those conditions are unless they are breached in some way. The conditions may also be relational more than structural. The stepchild and stepparent may not feel they had much choice about each other, but they do make choices about the extent to which they will *relate* to each other as family within the new family structure in which they find themselves. A teenager may, for example, largely ignore the presence of a new stepfather and lash out in indignation at any attempt at discipline with "You're not my father, so stop trying to act like you are!"

How family ministry can help. Ministry with families in this phase of development can take a number of shapes. The church can provide a context in which potential family members can develop relationships that can become familylike, especially persons who are family-deprived. Crossgenerational programs in which persons of different ages interact meaningfully with one another can become fertile ground for the development of relationships. House churches and home cell groups are seedbeds for familylike relationships. Ministries may also actively recruit familylike relationships for the familyless. Some churches encourage members to tutor and mentor children in the community. Other churches provide a means for individuals or families to make friendly visits to frail elderly adults who do not have family. This visiting may be a time of "courtship" that occasionally turns into a more long-term familylike commitment.

2. Formation. Just as all first dates do not lead inevitably to engagement and marriage, not all crossgenerational and family ministry programs aimed at developing relationships lead to the development of familylike relationships, nor should they. But if persons traverse the courtship with an increasing commitment to one another and a decision, either implicitly or explicitly, to become a family, then they enter the family formation phase. During the formation phase, the process of moving from a contract to a covenant relationship begins.

The wedding, with its "for richer, for poorer, in sickness and in health, until death do us part" vows, symbolizes the covenant making of the formation phase. A wedding is followed by a honeymoon, a time for the new family to develop intimacy and establish their new life together. Although a weeklong honeymoon is too short to accomplish all the relational tasks of the formation phase, there is at least societal recognition that this is a turning point, a formative period that will give shape to the relationship's future. Marriage represents the *beginning*, not the conclusion, of the formation of a family.

We also ritualize the advent of children with baby showers and birth announcements. The birth event is followed by a parental leave that in some respects serves the same function as the honeymoon. We recognize that this early period of bonding lays the foundation for the family's continuing development.

Walter Wangerin has written about the formation of family that takes place in marriage, *after* the courtship phase:

> Love does not make a marriage. At [the wedding] each may feel an intense commitment to the other, but that commitment is not independent of feelings. Rather, it's founded on nothing *but* feelings—and feelings are as unstable as water, while marriage is the establishment of stability itself in a relationship. Feelings come and go. Marriage is meant to endure *in spite of* them. . . . Nor does marriage begin when two people set up housekeeping together. . . . If that occurs before a public wedding, it's like starting a job without a contract: there are no secure assurances, and one might be fired on a whim, at a change in the economy, for spite, or for expedience. . . . Marriage begins when two people make the clear, unqualified promise to be faithful, each to the other, until the end of their days. That spoken promise makes the difference. . . . A promise made, a promise witnessed, a promise heard, remembered, and trusted—this is the groundwork of marriage. (Wangerin 1987:18)

The formation stage of family development presents opportunities and needs for ministry. Clearly, preparation for marriage is a pivotal ministry with families. The congregation's public recognition and celebration of weddings undergirds and supports this significant milestone in family development. Marriage education in the first year after the wedding also can have major significance in the formation of the marriage. Likewise, parents can benefit from classes, courses and support groups that celebrate, support and guide them in their care for new family members.

There are few rituals for the formation of other kinds of family relationships. Although some creative families invent their own means of celebrating and ritualizing their formation, they rarely receive the benefits of societal or community recognition. Churches can help families celebrate new family bonds and in so doing help members develop a sense of entitlement and belonging to one another. A ceremony of adoption or joining gives family members a chance to *name* their relationship with one another and *claim* their identity as a family unit. They announce the rights, obligations, connections and commitment that now and henceforth exist between them. As they describe their relationship with one another, members underscore their mutual understanding of what they are entitled to expect from each other.

A foster father and child wrote together their pledges to one another and read them in a small ceremony in the church sanctuary with their community gathered around. The father read the words they had prepared together—"I will love you and support you from now on. I will not try to take the place of your birth father, but I will be your friend, and I will discipline and care for you the very best way that I know how to help you grow into all that God intends for you to be."

The child responded with a pledge he had written himself: "You will be my foster dad. I will love you and respect you. I will try to follow the rules. I will call you Dad, but we both know that I have a father that I still love, too. Loving you won't take away any love for my father. We will be one another's family from now on." Not only did they define their relationship for themselves, but they also publicly recognized their family relatedness and sought and obtained the support of their faith community.

Although such events mark this formative phase of family development, the phase itself extends before and after the marker event and is characterized by the following developments.

Persons feel intimate with one another. Intimacy is the sense of attachment and closeness one experiences with a child because one is primarily responsible for the child's welfare. Intimacy also develops when persons share meals or other resources, and when persons see one another's private selves not generally shared with others, as happens when family members care for one another during sickness or personal crisis. Wangerin points out that our idealized images of each other come off in three rooms of a house—the kitchen, the bedroom and the bathroom (Wangerin 1987). These are the rooms where true intimacy takes place, where we are ourselves—bodily, humanly ourselves.

Persons feel a sense of entitlement with one another. They feel that they have a right to be in each other's lives and to claim each other as family. Persons in this stage feel freer than during courtship to offer advice or express their own opinions, even though doing so may lead to disagreement. Stepparents and foster parents become entitled to the right to discipline, and stepchildren and foster children test the relationship until they feel secure that they will not be deserted even when they show anger or break the family's rules.

Frequently a sign that foster or adoptive children are bonding with their new family comes in the form of misbehavior. The child is seldom consciously aware of this, but her behavior tests the strengths of the new bond, almost as if to say, "If I break the rules—the contract you gave me for being a part of this family—will you keep me and still love me?" In essence, the child is testing to see whether the contract has become covenant, whether the conditional care has become unconditional love. Similar testing often happens with stepparents. Understanding the meaning of children's misbehavior often helps parents to "hang in" and continue to love the child. In fact, foster and adoptive parents can quietly congratulate themselves that the child trusts them enough to put weight on the relationship and see if it will hold. The child, in a curious way, is signaling through her misbehavior her willingness to enter into family covenant.

In other families, the sense of entitlement may show when persons feel free to use one another's personal belongings, with or without asking permission first. They may be willing to share food, drink from the same glass or use the same towel when they would never do so with anyone else. There is a growing sense of "what is mine is yours." Obviously, the sense of entitlement sometimes creates serious family conflict, but the conflict is not only about the use of belongings but also about the meaning of being a family with one another.

In studies of adoption, entitlement is defined as the legal and emotional right parents have with regard to their children. The legal right is conferred in court; the emotional right grows out of the parents' increasing comfort with their roles as parent to the child (Cohen, Coyne and Duvall 1996). When a sense of entitlement does not develop adequately, parents often have problems with their children. They may feel unsuccessful in disciplining the child or getting him or her to take responsibility (being overly strict or overly permissive). Parents may be overly sensitive to rejection by the child and may need the child's reassurance of love. Entitlement is thus different from attachment. Attachment deals more with comfort and protection; entitlement is about rights and responsibilities (Cohen, Coyne and Duvall 1996).

Legal entitlement also marks the other legally recognized family relationship—marriage. On the negative side, it has only been in the last few years that rape has become illegal in marriage in the United States. Before that time, it was assumed that men were "entitled" to their wives sexually, even if that sexual right was exercised violently. Obviously, spouses also are entitled by law to one another's economic resources, and inheritance in the event of death is legally protected.

The issue of entitlement is particularly significant, of course, in family relationships that are *not* legally recognized. For these families, emotional entitlement must be strong enough to maintain their bond.

Persons feel that they belong to one another and that their relationship has permanence. A breach of contract is far less likely to break the relationship as a family completes the formation phase than when courtship has just been completed. When the family is formed, members feel like family with each other and have difficulty imagining dissolving this commitment. Sometimes this is demonstrated as divisions between individuals' economic resources become blurred. Family members may share checking accounts or make purchases together (an automobile, a house or furniture).

Two women who had lived together in an apartment for a number of years decided to pool their resources and purchase a home. Their decision characterized the permanence they felt in their family bond and also communicated that permanence to others.

How family ministry can help. Family ministry can take several shapes with families in the formation phase. Families benefit from educational programs that help them understand the relational processes they are experiencing. Attachment, entitlement, permanency, and the relationship between contracts and covenants are all concepts that lend themselves to educational programs. Family members may need guidance in developing functional family roles; in deciding how much of their time, financial resources and physical living space they will share and how much they will retain privately; and in negotiating relationships with one another's other relatives.

For example, foster and adoptive families need to work out relationships with the child's biological parents and siblings that are the most functional for all the persons involved. Discussions defining such family relationships are not always comfortable. Adoptive parents may feel threatened by and uncertain of how to respond to their children's need to discuss their biological background.

Roommates and couples may feel uncomfortable and embarrassed to speak explicitly about their need for privacy as well as their desire to share more fully in one another's lives. Adult children and their dependent aging parents may balk at the thought of discussing their relationship openly. Family ministry services of the church can provide education about the importance of such communication and can provide settings and experiences that encourage this kind of family talk. Trust and strengthened family bonds develop out of such discussions.

Family ministry may also need to include crisis intervention as families flounder in the formation phase.

A stepfather stormed out of the house and stayed gone several days when his adolescent stepson defied the house rules he had established. The mother had come to her son's defense, and the stepfather consequently felt cut out of the family and showed his anger and hurt by leaving. The stepfather was testing his new parenting wings and his role in the family. The son was testing the limits of his entitlement to challenge the rules and still be accepted by the stepfather.

And the mother felt caught between the two men she loved. She had wanted her new husband to help her with the tasks of parenting, but it seemed to be backfiring badly. They had not realized that she was still a "single parent." Her husband and son were "courting" each other but did not yet have the attachment, intimacy, cohesion and entitlement with one another that would be needed for the stepfather to function as parent.

When this family was helped to see the developmental issues at work, they could begin to work constructively rather than blaming their conflict on the stepfather's "poor parenting skills," the boy's inappropriate "hostility and defiance" or the mother's "overinvolvement" with her son.

3. Partnership. When the family has developed intimacy, cohesion, entitlement and a sense of permanency, it moves into the phase of partnership. In addition to caring for one another, families in the partnership phase are working together in relation to the physical and social world around them. This phase of family living corresponds to the phase of generativity in Erik Erikson's phases of adult development (Erikson 1968).

Note, however, that this phase is not limited to midlife adults but character-izes families with members of different generations working together in the tasks of living as a family. Working through the shared life tasks and commitments that were undertaken in the formation phase, often before the meaning of those commitments was fully understood, characterizes this phase. The term *partner-ship* often brings to mind the relationship between two persons who are more or less equal. But multiple persons who have differing power and authority, such as adults and children, may also be in the partnership phase.

Families in the partnership phase often confront two major issues. First, the family's boundaries may be opening and closing as members are added and leave. Many families define their task as nurture; they are partners in the work of parenting (biological parenting, adoptive parenting, foster parenting or informal parenting of children and adolescents in the extended family and friendship net-work). They may also center their work on nurture by extending hospitality to others beyond their household. A "family" of unmarried adults (roommates, a religious order, grown unmarried siblings) may give hospitality to others, either adults or children, the same significance in defining their relationship as parent-ing takes on for nuclear families.

For many families, then, the partnership phase actually includes periods of reworking the stages of courtship and formation as members are added and fam-ily relationships reshuffle to incorporate new members. In an old television series, *The Golden Girls*, three unmarried retired women live together in a subur-ban home and essentially become family for one another. When one's aging mother needs a place to live, they incorporate her into their family unit, with the requisite role shifts and adjustments. It is obvious that the new family member's biological daughter bears primary responsibility for "Ma" and that, in turn, this daughter is entitled to the nurture that children of all ages often want from their parents. But the sharp divisions of responsibility and entitlement soften over time. The other two roommates also come to treat her as "Ma" and to be treated as adult daughters.

In fact, care for aging parents often is the most profound example of the fam-ily caring for itself. It may actually be a time of bonding between family mem-bers, renewing or deepening their earlier covenant with one another (parent and child) or perhaps for the first time experiencing family intimacy with persons who have been within the boundaries of family but not a part of the inner circle. Adult children and parents have time to talk about the important and not-so-important aspects of their lives as they make trips to the doctor or the grocery store or experience myriad other moments of caregiving. Adult children may provide the most intimate of bodily care in an increasingly exhausting, but also potentially highly meaningful, drama of family caregiving.

Although processes of communication have obviously been important throughout the family formation process, communication becomes fundamental during the partnership phase. Communication means "to share meaning." It is not only being good listeners and talkers but achieving mutual understanding.

During the earlier family life phases, good listening and talking might have been sufficient. If family members have been attentive and caring, they may have experienced feelings of intimacy even though they did not always understand one another. During the family formation process, the fundamental issues were primarily feelings (intimacy, entitlement, belonging). Thus feeling cared for and listened to might have been adequate for moving the family through the formation phase.

During the partnership phase, however, family members must focus more collaboratively on their work together. Feelings of being loved and listened to may unravel when it becomes apparent that attentiveness has not led to understanding and agreement. Understanding and conflict resolution are necessary if the family is to move forward into the tasks they face.

It is one thing for an aging parent and adult child to chat on the phone a couple of times each week. It is another thing for them to try to work out the best living arrangement when the parent's poor health makes independent living no longer possible. It is one thing for a young, dual-career couple to talk with one another about the demands of their jobs and their stress. It is a much greater challenge for them to work out who will stay home for five days with a child who has chickenpox.

How family ministry can help. Educational programs on communication, conflict management, values clarification and family problem-solving all are relevant to families in the courtship and formation phases, but especially in the partnership phase. For the most part, churches have offered family life education in marriage enrichment and parent education programs. Yet members of other kinds of families face these same relationship challenges and can benefit from educational programs and self-help literature that recognizes the relational processes of communication and problem-solving in all kinds of families. All people who live together, whether roommates, spouses or older adults living with their grandchildren, must come to terms with the daily tasks of sharing a household, must face anger and conflict generated when people share space and resources, and must wrestle with differing values for guiding the family's life. When families of all stripes participate together in church seminars and family life workshops designed to address these issues and build relational skills, the result is often creativity and mutual learning.

4. Consolidation. The consolidation phase is characterized by processes of closure and the completion of life tasks and commitments that were central during the partnership phase. The major issues of this phase are (1) altered exchanges with the environment (unemployment or retirement) and (2) threats of loss or transformation of core family relationships (the terminal illness of a spouse or other primary life partner). In contrast with the open boundaries of the partnership phase, which pushed the family toward a reworking of formation processes, this phase moves the family toward some sense of closure on at least some aspects of their life together.

Some members may be leaving to start new family units of their own. Remaining members feel dramatic changes in family roles and processes. Although core relationships may remain intact, they are altered by the changing family membership. When families define their task as the nurture of family members (such as parenting or caregiving for an aging parent), the loss of the target of care involves not only an alteration in the family's boundaries and structure but a crisis of function. The task is completed. When adults have centered their work together in the raising of children, how do they redefine their relationship when the children no longer need the same level of involvement?

Other shared tasks may also end during this phase. Retirement or career changes may signal the end of a mutual commitment to some of the family's purposes beyond its own maintenance. The family's boundaries change, then, not only because of changes within but also because of changed relationships with the family's environment.

How family ministry can help. Families in the consolidation phase often have just experienced or are in the midst of a crisis, whether that crisis be death of a family member, divorce or separation, unemployment, retirement or another change in family membership or in the family's relationship with other social systems. Crises such as a retirement or a grown child's leaving home may not necessarily be experienced as negative events, but there is still significant upheaval. Programs that provide information about survival strategies for families in crisis or transition can be extremely helpful in normalizing what families are experiencing and giving them guidance for developing coping strategies to fit their particular situation.

Family life reviews can guide remaining family members in reminiscing about the paths they have traveled together. They can strengthen their roots in their past shared experiences to support them in their future development together.

5. Transformation. The next phase of family development is transformation. Core family relationships end, and the remaining members no longer constitute a "family." For example, a spouse or lifelong roommate dies. This is not the final phase of family development but actually the beginning of the next cycle. As core relationships end, family members may be gradually absorbed into other intimate social networks and families. These "remnants" of previous family systems serve as carriers of the family's values and norms into the new family they join, re-creating some of the patterns and lifeways of the family system from which they have come.

The phases are thus a spiral: transformation is courtship for a new or altered family system. A surviving spouse may assume a more central role in the family of an adult child. Or the surviving member may develop or strengthen peer or neighborhood relationships that become the next "family."

The aging adult who has lost a lifelong partner is redefining relationships with close friends or grown children who are open to more close-knit bonds of relationship. The unmarried foster parent watches the adolescent boy whom he has provided with a home return to his biological parents, and having dealt with the sense of loss and willing to risk attachment again, he is considering adoption of a special-needs child.

How family ministry can help. This is often a time of grief, not only for individuals but for whole families. Understanding and living with grief that will never be totally resolved happens best in a community that supports and acknowledges the grief, whose members know the family well enough to keep caring long after the funeral or the other loss is past. Family ministry can encourage family members to live through this period by reviewing their family history with each other, by preparing histories and resources for family members who will come after them. The community can also be a significant resource for transformation, a place where persons who find themselves alone can gradually be absorbed into other families in the faith.

FAMILY DEVELOPMENT AND FAMILY CRISIS

Times of developmental transition, as families move from one phase to another, are key points of family upheaval and crisis. Family members find themselves in unfamiliar roles, with expectations they may or may not fully understand or have the skills to meet. Parenting a teenager is different from parenting school-age children. Living with a new spouse and sharing a checkbook is different from dating or living with a roommate. Taking over the financial and decision-making functions for a frail parent is different from having dinner with that parent every Sunday. Living with a partner who has just been diagnosed with Alzheimer's disease presents a whole new panorama of responsibilities and griefs to a midlife adult and grown children.

Obviously, all of these changes create crisis. They are times when family members are less certain than usual about what to do and how to do it. And times of crisis and certainty are times that people are more open than usual to new learning, to receiving help, to making changes. They may seek a community of support. At such times, ministry can make a real difference in the lives of families.

Chapter 5

The Processes
of Family Development

THE LAST CHAPTER INTRODUCED THE PROCESSES THAT UNDERLIE family development: attachment and caregiving, communication, problem-solving, and intimacy (mutuality). These processes occur in every family, regardless of structure, and they provide a helpful framework for ministry with families.

ATTACHMENT AND CAREGIVING

Being family to one another is not simply being even closer than the closest friends; there is a different dimension of relationship that distinguishes friendship from family relationships. That dimension is called *attachment*. Attachment is demonstrated (1) when family members experience a need to be with one another when experiencing distress, (2) when the presence of other family members brings a sense of comfort and diminished anxiety and (3) when separation from the other and an inability to be reunited create anxiety (Bowlby 1969; 1975; Weiss 1993). Even the threat of separation is enough to create anxiety and lead to behaviors aimed at reuniting the person with attachment figures. Threats to the attachment relationship generate so much emotional intensity that it is difficult for persons to think rationally and solve problems (Pistole 1994).

Research indicates that attachment relationships differ in the amount of security they provide to attachment partners. In a *secure* attachment, the partner is esteemed and is expected to be responsive to attachment needs. The child learns to play in the backyard knowing that the parent is in the kitchen and will be there to help if the child calls. Adults can trust each other; they expect the partner to be there when needed, to be faithful. Secure attachments allow family members to be away from each other without worrying that the family will forget them or will not be there for them when they return. They can trust the covenant; they feel assured of being loved no matter what.

Insecure attachments often result from experiences in which attachment figures have turned out not to be dependable and trustworthy. Neglected children, for example, often have problems forming secure attachments, both with the neglectful parent and with subsequent attachment figures, even into adulthood. They may be jealous of family members' love for others, or worry that family members *will* love others. Insecure attachments take several forms. In a *preoccupied attachment* relationship, a person clings, trying to keep available a partner whose responsiveness is uncertain. The clinging person has low self-worth but high esteem for the partner. In an *avoidant* attachment, the person tries to avoid needing anyone. These are the persons who, when in distress, bury themselves in their work or attempt to soothe themselves, perhaps with alcohol or drugs (Pistole 1994). Both adults and children can experience these insecure attachments.

Attachment theorists have studied the difference between the role of a child's attachment figure (parent or other primary caregiver) and a friend or playmate. The child seeks out the attachment figure when the child is frightened, tired, hungry or sick. By contrast, the child seeks out a playmate when in good spirits and feeling confident, with the desire to engage in playful interaction. For adults, friends and romantic dates usually function as "playmates"; spouses, over time, become attachment figures. John Bowlby points out that although the roles are distinct, they are not incompatible. Mother can sometimes be principally an attachment figure and other times a playmate (Bowlby 1969). Similarly, spouses often are friends and playmates as well as comforters in times of distress. In other words, attachment figures can also be playmates, but playmates are not necessarily attachment figures, although they may become so.

Attachment lasts throughout life and is especially salient in times of stress or distress, even though it may become a less central force in adult life. Attachment is not the same thing as dependence. Dependence refers to ties to *groups* of others, such as mothers or fathers or teachers, who are virtually interchangeable. Children *depend* on adults, and many adults can meet their needs for feeding, comfort and interpersonal interaction. Yet all the adults who meet their needs do not become attachment figures. The child who brings an untied shoe to a nursery worker at church is probably exhibiting dependence, not attachment. *Any* known and trusted adult figure, thinks the child, can help with the shoe.

Adults too have dependency needs. When going through a difficult life experience, adults may share their thoughts and concerns with relative strangers on a bus, or may seek attention from any number of potential caregivers—neighbors, a pastor, the receptionist in the doctor's office, acquaintances, friends. In contrast, attachment is relationship with a *very particular* other, one on whom there may be dependence, but more than that, who cannot be replaced or for whom there is no substitute. The difference between attachment and dependency is most keenly experienced in the loss of an attachment figure. When a spouse of thirty years dies, no amount of time with other people can replace the lost partner or soothe the grief. Over time, other attachments may form and the grief may ease, but the attachment figure is never actually *replaced*.

The meeting of attachment needs among family members, particularly in adults in relationships of long duration, often takes place below the level of consciousness. Family members may not be aware of their depth of attachment to one another until the relationship is threatened in some way. In the language of the family, this is the very natural process of "taking each other for granted." Paul describes the spouse as being like one's own body (Eph 5:28-29). We often do not think much about our body, especially if it is functioning well. When was the last time you felt gratitude for your toes and how well they help you maintain your balance, or for how well your neck allows you to turn your head? Those body parts get our undivided attention only when they hurt or are injured. Otherwise we have to be deliberate in giving our attention to the gift of a healthy, functioning body. Our attachment to one another functions similarly; we are often not even aware of it unless the attachment relationship is threatened in some way.

David Schnarch says that "loving is not for the weak" (Schnarch 1991). In the process of loving someone, something both wondrous and terrible happens. The partner becomes unlike any other, and thus irreplaceable. Ultimately every attachment relationship ends, resulting in profound grief that cannot be alleviated by friends and acquaintances and "keeping busy." The other has been a part

of the self. Just as persons can learn to adapt and function well without an ampu-
tated arm or leg, partners learn to go on without a beloved who has died. But the
arm does not grow back. In some sense grief is never totally resolved, although
functioning returns over time. Adult children who no longer need their parents
for survival nevertheless are surprised by how long they mourn after a parent's
death. No one else can take the place of the one who is lost. Other bonds form,
but the events and experiences shared with the lost one cannot be duplicated.
Divorcing spouses are often surprised at the depth of their attachment to one
another and the mourning they experience, even though the relationship was
destructive and painful.

A Word About Codependency

A word is needed here about the current fascination with the phenomenon of
"codependency." This term was originally used to describe the coping strategies
of family members of persons addicted to alcohol. Those behaviors often inadvertently seem to contribute to the addiction rather than helping to overcome it.
For example, a spouse destroys the alcoholic's hidden liquor supplies, tries to
cover up the alcoholic's hangover by calling the office to report that he or she is
"sick," or tries to monitor the alcoholic's every move to keep him or her from
drinking. These behaviors actually underscore the alcoholic's continued lack of
responsibility for the addiction. The spouse is called "codependent" because his
or her life too has become dependent on or organized by alcohol. The partner
"depends" on the caregiving or monitoring role as assurance of the attachment of
the addicted person.

Unfortunately, codependency became a catchy label for *anyone* who met their
own needs by caring for others. Some have even talked about an "addiction to
people," thus pathologizing people's care for one another. Of course, some people
do seem to get their sense of self entirely from caring for others and do not care
adequately for themselves. They evaluate their own self-worth based on their
ability to influence the lives of others. But as Mary Pipher says, "We have confused people about the healthiness of loving their own families" (Pipher
1996:119). It says much about our social values that we have not pathologized
those who do too little for others and needed to learn to do more. Consequently,
some have confused attachment and caregiving with, of all things, family dysfunction. Attachment and caregiving are healthy foundations for family life; they
are not signs of family pathology.

COMMUNICATION

Communication can be defined most simply as the process persons use to provide information to one another. It is not at all a simple process, though; communication requires constantly learning to read and understand the complexity of information that is relevant in family life. Parents learn the subtleties of messages communicated by an infant's different kinds of crying; both adults and children learn the meaning of fleeting facial expressions, gestures and tones of voice. Paul Watzlawick, J. H. Beavin and Don D. Jackson's book *Pragmatics of Human Communication,* published in 1967, brought attention to the significance of communication as not so much a set of skills that apply in every interpersonal situation as a process of relating that is unique in every family system.

Communication occurs when we create symbols and put them in some medium through which others can perceive them and make sense of them. Thus communication involves (1) the creation of symbols, (2) the medium for symbols, (3) the cognitive processes by which they are created and interpreted, and (4) the relationship between symbols and the reality to which they refer (Fitzpatrick and Ritchie 1993). The symbol and medium may be integral to one another, or the symbol may be entirely independent of the medium. For example, the meaning of the words (symbols) "Aren't you a piece of work!" depends a great deal on the medium through which they are communicated. If said by a parent in a lilting voice, accompanied a broad smile, when opening a child's straight-A report card, it means something quite different than with a scowling face accompanied by parental hands on hips in a living room cluttered with toys. The words "I love you" may be spoken or written, said in person or on the telephone, but still carry the same general meaning. Even so, the context contributes to the meaning, strengthening or weakening it, if not altering it entirely. "I love you" whispered in a moment of sexual intimacy carries a different connotation than "I love you" said as the opening words of forgiveness when one has hurt the other.

Types of Communication

There are basically two types of information: having to do with the environment and having to do with the relationship. Communication about the environment usually takes places through words, whether spoken or written, such as "We're out of milk; can you stop and get some?" or "I have to work overtime tonight; go ahead and eat without me." Communication about the relationship can also take place through words, such as "I love you so much" or "I am so angry," but the words are often given significance by accompanying nonverbal behaviors. Some of these are vocal, such as tone and inflection. Words can be shouted or whispered, shrill or carefully and evenly spoken, drawn out in a whine or punched out in staccato. Often words are accompanied by physical behaviors as well—hugs, a shaking head, shrugged shoulders, hands held in control behind the back, facial muscles contracted in a frown or a smile or clenched jaws, with a multitude of variations that all have meaning. Relationship information may be communicated without words at all, simply by the use (or lack of use) of physical behaviors. For example, a silent stare at a television, avoiding eye contact with an irate spouse, is communication about the relationship. It may be interpreted as "I don't care about what you are saying," or its opposite, "I am too overwhelmed by you to allow myself to respond."

Communication often involves both kinds of messages at the same time. Even the seemingly innocuous "We're out of milk; can you stop and get some?" can be said with thinly disguised anger or frustration. The relationship message, if it were put into words, might be "I am so angry; you *said* you would take responsibility for the grocery shopping, but you let us run out of the basics. You've let me down once again; I just can't trust you." The message about working late might be offered with a grimace, sinking shoulders and tone that sounds tired. If put in words, the message in words might be, "I'm really tired of this overtime work. I would much rather be home with you. I hope you understand that. It's something I just have to do."

Over time, families develop their own languages of both verbal and nonverbal behaviors. Certain words take on unique family meanings, as do the intricacies of nonverbal behavior. These become part of and express the family culture. Family communication often uses private symbols as means of recognition (for example, a special whistle to locate one another in a crowded store) or as means of marking the family relationship as special (such as pet names for one another). As we saw in chapter four, these special symbols become significant elements of the family's culture.

An outsider may misunderstand the meaning of such behaviors. Unfortunately, sometimes family members do as well. Because nonverbal behavior has to be interpreted, it may be interpreted by the receiver in a way the sender did not intend. The partner staring at the television to avoid contact may be interpreted as not caring when in fact his or her feelings are too intense and frightening to be allowed expression.

Conflicts sometime erupt in families because information is sent unintentionally. Family members become experts at "reading" one another, even when the senders of communication do not intend to be communicating at all. An adult who comes in from work to prepare dinner in a kitchen still in shambles from the morning rush hour may feel frustrated and angry. The anger represents a culmination of the day's hassles, fatigue and a sense of being overwhelmed at the work left to do at home. It is expressed with little awareness in sighs, or the banging of cabinet doors, or simply silence. Family members, keenly tuned in to one another, may read this as anger directed at them. The family cook, however, did not mean to communicate with others and may become defensive and feel invaded if others respond defensively with "What are *you* angry about?"

The development of a shared language and signal system in family members communicates shared identity. Over time, this system of communication becomes ever more nuanced. When families experience significant changes from without or within, members often have to move back to a more explicit, verbal form of communication. Words and behaviors also change their meaning and purpose in relationships over time and can symbolize far more than their immediate message.

When our son was fifteen, he often brought friends to our home. Once I gave in to the temptation to join a group of them in watching a movie, just because I enjoyed their company. But soon my son looked over at me and said, "You need to go to bed, Mom." The words were said in jest, a funny turnabout for a son to say to a mother who just a few years before had been saying those words to him. He knew them well. As a young child, he had heard every evening, "You need to go to bed, John." They were words with a complex message, spoken by parents who were expressing care for him but also were ready for him to be "filed away" for the night so they could have some peaceful time together. The underlying message seemed to be "I really wish you would give us some privacy, but the way I say this will make it sound as if I'm imposing bedtime for your own good." I had naively believed that John simply heard the care for him and did not "get" that we wanted him in bed for our own sakes as well.

Thus these simple words said by adolescent to parent carried a powerful message. They were certainly more culturally acceptable than a more direct "Mother, please leave," because they were said with humor and at least feigned care. They made us laugh. The words also carried a much more basic message, a message about the change in the relationship between us. John was telling me what to do—a sign of new equality between adult and almost-adult. He was asserting his right to be alone with his friends without his mother. An equally significant message was the reassurance of affection and care, implied by his humorous tone. Seven words can carry a lot of meaning about relationships when accompanied not only by nonverbal behaviors but also by a history of family communication.

Communication Styles

John Gottman, a family science researcher, has studied videotaped conversations of two thousand married couples and provided us with the best understanding to date of marital communication (Gottman 1994a; 1994b). Although his research has been confined to interaction between spouses, his findings are helpful for understanding communication in other family relationships as well.

Gottman discovered that there is no *one* way to be happily married. Instead his research identifies three styles of marriage that work. *Validating* marriages involve very compatible couples. These couples deal with their differences calmly, openly and honestly. *Volatile* spouses, on the other hand, argue dramatically and vehemently, often attempting to steamroll each other into their point of view. But volatile marriages can also be very satisfying and positive, characterized by expressions of love and romance. In other words, volatile couples both fight and love with passion. Finally, *conflict-avoiding* couples are less passionate, both in conflict and in love. Successful conflict-avoiding couples have developed a solid bond that allows them to overlook disagreements. To others, conflict-avoiding couples may seem to lack passion. These spouses experience themselves primarily as very much alike and compatible, like matching bookends.

Although all three styles of marriage can be satisfying, partners whose individual styles differ can face some difficult challenges. The families in which we grow up teach us their communication style, and communication style is a major component of family culture. When persons from different family cultures seek to form family with one another, they may run into significant challenges. For example, a conflict-avoiding partner may feel overwhelmed and attacked by a volatile partner. In turn, the volatile partner feels ignored by and unimportant to the conflict-avoiding partner, who does not respond energetically to the overture for a good, air-cleansing argument. What seems to the volatile partner to be healthy discussion, of course, seems like a conflagration that threatens to destroy the marriage to the partner who has learned a style of conflict avoidance. It helps if a couple can identify their style differences so that each is not devastated by the other's apparently "unloving" style of relating. Identifying and learning about differences in style can be very helpful content for family life education programs.

Despite the dramatic differences, all three kinds of couples who are happy in marriage share one characteristic, according to Gottman's research. All of them exchange positive care and expressions of love five times as often as they engage in conflict or take verbal swipes. In other words, the style is not as important as the balance between negative and positive emotions expressed. Marriages with lots of conflict, then, need *lots and lots* of positive, loving interaction to balance the conflict. When conflict increases, so does the need for care. Volatile couples are particularly susceptible to allowing difficult times to move them to a dangerously high level of conflict that cannot be balanced by positive interaction.

This research suggests some ways to strengthen family relationships. Ephesians 4:25-29 encourages us to "speak the truth," saying "only what is useful for building up, as there is need." Truth, especially when it leads to conflict, must be wrapped in words and actions that build rather than tear down love for one another. Angry words can be loud or soft, frequent or seldom, passionate or quiet. However an angry word is expressed, it needs to be preceded or followed by *five* words of appreciation, love and care.

PROBLEM-SOLVING

Whatever a family's style of communication, conflict and anger are inevitable. Siblings who have less cause than Cain did may have murderous thoughts about one another. Simply the way a little brother chews his food, walks or stares at an older sibling can elicit rage. Spouses find themselves controlling (or not controlling) impulses to do harm to each other. An infant who will not be comforted at 3:00 a.m. can evoke in a parent an overwhelming sense of helplessness and powerlessness that leads to frustration and anger.

Sometimes family members do not have the understanding and skills for handling conflict and anger constructively. About 20 percent of all homicides involve one family member killing another. One out of three or four American wives has been physically harmed by her husband. A person in the United States is three times more likely to be killed because of an argument with a family member or a friend than to be killed in a robbery (Blackburn 1995; Straus,

Gelles and Steinmetz 1980). Family members who have not experienced physical violence in the family may still have come close enough that the anger in self or another has frightened them.

Why Families Generate Conflict and Anger

Why is it that families can generate so much anger? First, the issues that generate anger in families may be small, but they are ubiquitous. Like pebbles in our shoes, many conflicts are with us with every step we take, day after day—irritating personal habits, how we share space and resources such as checkbook registers, limited hot-water tanks, thermostats that family members want to adjust differently, and on and on. Many of these are simply the result of personal differences. What is a "comfortable" temperature for a living space? What is the definition of "cleaning up the kitchen"? Are the contents of one's pockets left on the dresser a "mess" or "my-stuff-and-I-have-a-right-to-put-it-there"? Does a teen's twenty-minute shower use "too much" hot water, or is the complaint one more unwelcome parental attempt to control?

Even family members who do not live together experience conflict over coordination and sharing of time, resources and space. A frequent area of conflict between young couples and parents, for example, is decisions about whose family the young couple will join for the holidays. Families sometimes are rent asunder over how to use time and finances to provide for a frail elderly parent, how to share living space in times of crisis, or how to divide an inheritance.

Limited resources. Anger in family life increases proportionately to the stress of demands and constraint on resources to meet those demands. For example, research has found that parenthood significantly increases anger. With each additional child in the household anger increases, and children increase anger more for mothers than for fathers. Parenthood introduces two types of stressors to family life: economic strains and the strains associated with childcare (Ross and Van Willigen 1996).

Limited space. Personal differences between friends or acquaintances not sharing a living space do not make much difference. Who cares if one's friend takes long showers, or lives in a messy apartment, if one does not have to share hot water and living space with that friend? Differences with a friend versus a family member can be compared to the degree of irritation created by a mosquito in one's backyard versus in one's tent. In a limited space, differences become disagreements.

Implicit Relationship Issues

It is sometimes mystifying how seemingly mundane decisions can generate so much emotion and be so difficult. After all, how hard can it be to make plans such as "If you cook, I'll clean up," or "I'll try to keep my mess out of the living room and dining room, if I can have one place where I can leave my stuff spread out like I want it"? If it were just a matter of developing a reasonable plan, it would not be so hard. When families are planning their daily patterns, however, more is happening than meets the eye.

Power and autonomy. Almost every issue involves the autonomy and power of individual family members, and often these are defined in relationship with other family members. For example, the partner who says, "If you cook, I'll clean up the kitchen" may be giving the message "I get to sit down and read the paper while you cook, and I'll clean up the kitchen when I feel like it. I will not give you the power to make me feel bad for not helping you with dinner." The partner who habitually and irritatingly piles papers in the middle of the dining table may be saying, "You are in control of most of our life together, but there are still corners of my life that are mine over which you have no power."

Family members often feel anger rise when a partner's actions make them feel robbed of autonomy. Few people have more power over us than our family. By spending too long in the shower, one partner can keep the other from having hot water for a bath. By leaving the scissors in a strange place, one partner can keep the other hunting in exasperation for thirty minutes.

Affection and commitment. In addition to power and autonomy, communication over seemingly innocuous, straightforward issues often involves latent communication about basic affection and commitment between family members. Because relationship communication often occurs nonverbally, it may be less clear to family observers, and even to family members themselves.

Working out patterns for living together in a family is not like negotiating a business deal. In business relationships, each person drives a hard bargain and tries to get all they can out of the other. Both parties are expected to look out for themselves. When the hard bargaining is over, they let one another know with a smile, a pat on the back or a handshake that it was nothing personal, just good business.

But in families it *is* personal. We are not supposed to try to get everything we can out of each other. Thus when family members think another member is acting selfishly or ignoring their needs, they may feel used and unloved. Of all the people in the world, one's family is supposed to act in ways that are supportive and even self-sacrificial. So when a husband leaves the car for a wife to drive with an empty gas tank, she not only feels a loss of power over her life—she had planned just enough time to get to work, and now she will be late—she may also feel unloved. *If he loved me, he would have been thoughtful enough to gas up the car after his trip.*

The more upset or anxious a family member's response to the actions of the other, the more that family member interprets those actions as carrying emotional/relational meaning, even if the acting member had no intention of communicating that message. Because emotional/relationship meanings are often communicated nonverbally, they are subject to being read into others' behavior.

Understanding Anger and Its Expression

Anger is the meaning persons give to changes they experience in their bodies when they sense danger. We sense danger when we think we may lose something important, or when we feel out of control of our lives. When driving, we may experience a flash of anger at another driver who threatens—invading our space, blocking our way, ignoring our need to be able to change lanes. These three possibilities suggest three ways of feeling threatened—physical threat (invasion of our protective space makes us vulnerable to an accident), threat of loss of power over one's own life (blocking our path may make us miss that next traffic light, which is about to turn red, so we'll be late for work) and threat to self-esteem (the other treats me as if I'm not important).

The same kinds of threats are experienced in family life. Occasionally our physical well-being is threatened by a family member's actions—we trip over tools the partner has left scattered on the floor. More often, our sense of power and control over our lives is threatened. Imagine that you have settled into your comfortable chair with a cup of coffee and the Sunday paper in the late afternoon, only to find that somebody else has read the paper first and cut out several sections that included what you want to read. You had planned this relaxing moment, and it has been taken from you.

Finally, family members can threaten one another's self-esteem. In fact, because we have such intimate knowledge of one another, we often carry more potential threat of harm to family members' self-esteem than anyone else in their lives, friend or foe. Imagine sitting with friends having a good time when your parent or partner launches into a story about something embarrassing you did. Everyone laughs, but you feel exposed.

The experience of threat easily translates either as fear or as anger, depend-ing on one's personal state. If we feel relatively safe, the emotion will be anger. A loud sound in the night, if unrecognized, may evoke fear—is someone break-ing in? If I hear the same sound but recognize it as a family member carelessly slamming a door and disrupting my sleep, the feeling is likely to be anger. Fear can also rapidly turn to anger; these two feelings are very much related, with the only difference being our interpretation of events. Think about how quickly worry and fear turn to anger when a teenager uncharacteristically comes in an hour after curfew. The parent has been worrying about all the things that might have happened, and the simple sound of the teenager's car in the driveway sig-nals that she hasn't been in some terrible accident but seems simply to have ignored her parent's need to know where she is. The fear dissipates and the emotion becomes anger.

Anger involves three connected elements. First, some new information reaches the person. Perhaps something happens, someone says something, or something expected does *not* happen (e.g., a family member is not at an appointed meeting place). Second, one interprets that information as a threat. If the partner is not at the appointed place, one may interpret the absence as result-ing from anything from absent-mindedness and thoughtlessness to abandonment or a serious accident. Finally, one's body goes through changes to prepare to respond to the threat, depending on which interpretation of events seems most likely. The heart pounds, muscles tighten, blood flowing to the digestive system is restricted and goes instead to lungs and limbs. These physiological changes prepare us for meeting the threat, whatever it may be: we are prepared to express our anger at the partner or to race to the hospital where the partner has been taken from an accident scene.

Anger is at root the process of physiological arousal that prepares us to defend against or escape from threats. But our bodies, and even our minds, do not always distinguish between the various *causes* of physiological arousal. Anytime we are cold, hot, hungry, tired, exercising or bombarded by noise, the body is in a state of arousal to defend itself or seek relief from whatever prompted the aroused physiological state.

Often the times families have together involve such physiological stress. On weekdays most families have only the tail end of the day together. People are tired and hungry, frustrated and still concerned over events of the day at school or work. They are already in a state of some physiological stress, so that it takes little more to evoke an anger response, often heightened by events unrelated to the trigger.

---

physiological stress → → → → → → →
                  ↘   ↘

trigger event ⇨ interpretation ⇨ body changes (fear/anger) ⇨ anger/fear response
(not anger arousing in itself)

Obviously, anger expressed in a family setting is not always the result of what a family member has or has not done or said. Sometimes family members *blame* each other for experiences originating outside the family. If a family has created an atmosphere of safety, where members feel accepted whatever their feelings may be, the family may become the place where feelings about the threats of life can be expressed. A bad day at work results in crabby, angry behavior at home. A best friend humiliates a child, and that child comes home to dissolve in a temper tantrum over something that would normally be readily accepted. A very minor event, word or gesture that normally would simply be overlooked or even evoke laughter may trigger anger in a family member already stressed—physiologically aroused—by other experiences.

Sometimes it is not that family members are blamed for what happened elsewhere but that telling about frustrating or stressful experiences reawakens the experience of anger. If the listening person then says or does the wrong thing, the anger initially generated elsewhere may become channeled toward him or her.

Imagine, for example, that a boss has been unfair, and the employee is telling her husband about it. As the husband listens, he becomes upset and angry at the boss. After all, when someone has hurt or been unfair to a beloved, we become anxious, concerned or angry. Because we care, we want to make things better for the beloved. So the husband responds from his own escalating feelings of anger at the boss with "You just need to tell him what he can do with that job. Nobody's going to treat you that way."

The wife may then say, "Look, I didn't ask you to tell me what to do, and we're certainly not in any position for me to simply quit. All I asked was for you to understand what I'm going through."

He may feel rebuffed and say in turn, "Well, I *was* trying to understand. If you don't want to know what I think, then why bother to tell me about it?"

Suddenly they are angry with each other, feeling misunderstood and unappreciated. The physiological arousal created by their anger at the situation made it all too easy for them to turn on each other. Under other circumstances the wife might have ignored her husband's words, or even interpreted them as expressing his loving care. She is feeling threatened by her experiences at work, though, and it is easy for her to add those feelings onto the much smaller threat she feels from her husband's challenging her sense of autonomy and ability to manage her professional difficulties. He, meanwhile, is also tense and angry at the situation. Normally he would understand her sharp response to his perhaps ill-worded attempt to express concern and support. Given his own state, however, he interprets her response as a rejection of his care and concern, rather than a reaction to his attempt to solve her problem.

CREATIVE USES OF ANGER

A family's style has much to do with what is considered appropriate or inappropriate in expressing anger. Those who avoid conflict may use quiet, indirect methods, whereas volatile families may ignore anything less than raised voices and slammed doors as messages of anger. The family's style is influenced, of course, by its own culture, the broader culture of its community and the society to which it belongs. There are three basic ways anger can be expressed—ventilation, withdrawal and reporting.

Venting
American culture supports the belief that anger is a physiological pressure that needs to be discharged, else it will do physical damage to the person experiencing it. This view pictures people like pressure cookers or steamy bathrooms that need vents. If we do not "let it out," we will explode like a pressure cooker with a clogged valve, or the linings of our stomach will peel into ulcers the way wallpaper peels off the wall of an unvented steamy bathroom. So some people rant and rave and say things they "don't mean"—they just need to "vent."

Unfortunately, this free-speaking approach often has an opposite effect. The more anger is expressed, the more physiological arousal is generated. That is, family members become more and more agitated and angry, sometimes until they reach a point of exhaustion and then feel relief or, tragically, until they physically strike out at each other.

But not all loud and emotional communication is venting. What makes communication venting is its focus, which is catharsis, not problem-solving. Venting aims to gain the relief that can come when we give expression to our anger. If the anger is at someone outside the family or an event or reality that cannot be changed, venting may be one of the few ways the anger can be discharged. Unfortunately, if venting is used to express anger over a recurring family problem, the problem itself remains unchanged.

Vented anger is discussed often by biblical authors, since it is the expression of anger that most often develops into physical assault or verbal hostility (Gen 34:18-31; Ex 2:11-15; 2 Sam 13; Prov 14:17). Obviously, anger expressed in physical or emotional attack on an other is intent on doing harm, not on problem-solving. Anger expressed in venting becomes the first step toward murder, not toward reconciliation (Mt 5:22). Social science research indicates that expressing negative emotions actually tends to keep families from being able to resolve difficulties (Forgatch 1989).

Feelings do need to be expressed, but they need to be expressed *as a means of helping define the problem so the problem can be addressed.* Then angry feelings need to be controlled, even inhibited, so they do not obstruct problem-solving.

Withdrawal

For fear of the consequences of expressing anger, or perhaps simply because it is the way a family's culture has taught, some persons withdraw from others when they are angry. The withdrawal may be communicated nonverbally, through pained and softened speech or silence, or through physical distance or absence. Some people ruminate over the events that evoked the anger, nursing hurt and rage over what has been done to them by others. Suppressing differences and feelings about those differences means family members share less and less of themselves. Trust erodes (Rausch et al. 1974:31). Although the storm may blow over, the problem remains, and family members give it an inflated meaning. The negative feelings can overwhelm all positive feelings about the other and grow into a wish to destroy rather than protect and nurture the beloved.

According to John Gottman's research (Gottman 1994a), the most lethal pattern for a marriage is one where the husband stonewalls his wife's attempts to have a "meaningful discussion." The pattern develops more or less like this: When there is conflict, the husband feels anxious, upset and angry. He tries to handle his feelings by allowing his eyes to glaze over and fix on a point just over her shoulder, looking toward her but obviously not at her. Then he withdraws, hiding in television viewing or going to his study or shop or out to the golf course or the pub. The more frustration there is, the more overwhelmed he feels by his wife's demands, and the more he tries to avoid the conflict by avoiding her.

She becomes more upset. She tries harder, perhaps becoming more insistent and intense in her requests that he listen to her. When this does not work (and it does not—he simply retreats further), she becomes critical and disgusted. Her disgust is not only with him but with herself; she hears herself nagging but does not know how else to reach him.

More and more they live parallel lives, separated from each other by resentment. Both feel increasingly hurt and hopeless. The wife may not recognize that the husband's distance is not an indication that he does not care but that he cares so much that conflict makes him anxious.

He may need to tell her when he begins to feel overwhelmed and practice openness to hearing her. She, in turn, may need to learn that, paradoxically, lowering the intensity of her conversation may enable him to hear her better.

Though Gottman's research was only with married couples, these processes are not limited to marriage; they can take place in almost any family relationship.

Conflict and anger are instruments of truth. The Bible straightforwardly condemns the practice of pretending everything is all right instead of honestly facing rifts in relationship. Jeremiah and Ezekiel both excoriate prophets who said that all was well with Israel, ignoring the rift between the people and God (Jer 6:14; 8:11; Ezek 13:10-11, 14-16). When there is something wrong in a relationship, God pursues it and exposes it. Then the wrong can be healed and made right again. In the same way, Christians need to take anger and conflict seriously in their relationships, not ignoring them or pretending they do not exist.

On the other hand, not all absenting of self from others is "withdrawal." There are times when family members *need* to retreat into privacy for functional anger management. Some people need time alone when they are angry or edgy. This is often true when the anger was generated outside the family. "I had a bad day and I just need you to stay out of my way" can be a loving way of explaining the occasional need to retreat.

When the anger is generated within the family itself, the physiological arousal may swamp the person's ability to think rationally and creatively about the problems that elicited the anger. Healthy families operate on the principle that people cannot say anything they feel anytime they feel it. One or more members of the family learn to "back off" or say something to soften the intensity (Stanley et al. 1998).

Retreat to regain calm and a clear head may be very helpful before family members gather to try to solve the problems in discussion. Retreat can be used as time to pray for God's guidance in tackling issues in ways that "give grace" and "build up" rather than tear up the family relationship (Eph 4:29). "Time out" is a right that can be claimed by anyone. It is a time to go to a quiet place alone and collect oneself. It is a time for prayer, for saying to God, "Help me see myself as my family sees me. Help me respond to this situation with patience and love and skill." It is not a time to rehearse how wrong everyone else is. Rather, it is a time to let stress drain away so that actions can come from love, not self-justification. "Time out" is always time-limited. One must come back, when refreshed, to deal with whatever the problem was that created the anger and stress.

Some persons who have habitually withdrawn from conflict and denied their feelings of anger may need to use retreat time to rehearse mentally the importance of the issue and remind themselves that love for their family should motivate them to deal constructively with the conflict. They may need to think through their perspective on the issues and remind themselves that to share their perspective, even if it creates conflict, is more loving than to hide it and harbor resentment and hurt.

Reporting

Anger is a God-given emotional signaling device, designed to alert us that something is wrong. It is to relationships with others what pain is to the physical body. Pain beginning in the chest and running down the arm is an important signal of a problem that needs to be attended to as soon as possible. Even if the pain dissolves for a time, to ignore it is to put the body in peril.

Anger is "family pain." It indicates that there is a problem somewhere that needs to be corrected, if possible. It needs to named truthfully and reported in ways that do not lead to sin against one another and that build up rather than tear down the relationship (Eph 4:25-29). Truthfully naming the problem means reporting one's experience and feelings—for example, "I am upset because you have not done your chores"—not tearing the other down and thus sinning: "You are such a slob; I can never depend on you for anything."

The teachings of Jesus make clear that no matter where the problem originates, we have a responsibility to tackle it. In Matthew 5:23, self is the offending party. In Matthew 18:15, the other person is the offending party. In both situations the instruction is the same: to go and establish a communication link (Buttry 1997).

The expression of anger, both our own and that of our beloveds, protects us and the relationships that are dear to us. When a family member is doing something dangerous, an angry protest may deter them—a shout at a child heading for the street, an angry protest from a child being ignored while parents are tending a new baby. In both of these cases the expression of anger aims to protect the special relationship, in one case physically and the other emotionally. Anger indicates when there is a problem that needs to be addressed in a relationship; one family member feels others are not doing their fair share of the chores, or a difference in values has created a clash in parenting styles or in managing finances. Reporting anger in ways that encourage problem-solving and creative tackling of differences is an act of love. According to Gottman's research (Gottman 1994a; 1994b), frequent complaining actually makes for healthy relationships. Only when partners air complaints can they work together to deal with troublesome spots in their relationship.

Ephesians 4:26 says, "Be angry but do not sin; do not let the sun go down on your anger." Here Paul recognizes the importance of anger but also cautions that it can easily lead to sin. Unfortunately, this verse has often been paraphrased "Don't go to bed angry." For some families that is a helpful watchword. Many people, however, have assumed the verse means that quarrels must be completed before sleep. Thus families stay up half the night trying to solve problems when they are tired and furious. It would be more constructive to agree that a retreat for a night of rest is needed and a return to the problem when they can be more creative and constructive is the best way to avoid sinning against each other.

The new day for Jews began at sunset, not at bedtime. Paul is thus saying that anger should not be allowed to go on and on; it should not infect our tomorrows with one another. Register the problem that created the anger, and then make plans to deal with the problem later. The problem does not have to be solved in the nighttime. What we must do is avoid allowing anger to take up permanent residence in our hearts.

Reporting anger, then, means saying or doing what needs to be said or done according to the need of the moment, that it "may give grace to those who hear" (Eph 4:29). That is, the anger is *used* in behalf of the relationship. Anger is used to strengthen ("edify") the relationship when we tackle issues and problems together. The point is not to prove we are right, wonderful and long-suffering while others are wrong, terrible and mean-spirited. Anger is not used to bolster one's self-esteem at the expense of other family members.

When we express anger to build up ourselves, we have not really taken to heart the good news of the gospel. We do not have to be right or faultless to be accepted by God. We do not have to be perfect to be loved by God. If a family is modeled after God's love and acceptance, they will love us even if we are wrong.

I-Messages

Many family life education programs teach family members to use "I-messages" to report anger and conflict constructively. I-messages contain three components: a statement of what the sender is feeling, a statement of what the recipient is doing to contribute to that feeling, and a statement of what the sender would like to see happen to improve the situation (Gordon 1975; Miller, Nunnally and Wackman 1975). For example:

☐ *what the sender is feeling:* I am angry because . . .
☐ *what the recipient is doing:* you are just sitting there watching television when I told you to clean your room;
☐ *what the sender wants:* I want you to turn off the television and do what I asked.

I-messages should describe people's behavior, not their personality. For example, "You have left your clothes all over the bathroom" describes the behavior, whereas "You are such a slob" describes the personality. It is easier for us to modify our behavior than it is to change our personality, so describing problems in terms of behavior is more productive for problem resolution.

I-messages also avoid "all or none" statements. For example, "You have left me waiting for you three times this week" is more accurate and is more likely to lead to problem-solving than the generalization "You are always late."

I-messages also report what the sender observes, not what the sender infers about what is observed. For example, "I am upset because you slammed the door and haven't said a word since you came home" reports the sender's feelings and what the recipient has done. On the other hand, "I am upset because you are so angry at me—again" reports what the sender infers the recipient's behavior to mean. There is more likely to be agreement on what the observable behavior is—slammed door and lack of verbal exchange—than on what the behavior means.

The first message can be followed with a message about what the sender *infers* the behavior to mean, but this is more tentative and appropriately recognizes that the meaning of the behavior may be different from what is inferred: "When you slam doors and don't speak to me, I think that means you are angry." The recipient is thus invited to confirm or disconfirm the inference and is less likely to give a defensive response.

Clearly, I-messages do not aim simply to express feelings but to express them in a way that helps family members work together to resolve problems. The point is not "why I'm right and you're wrong," but rather "I have a problem and I need your help in addressing it." Rather than expressing and justifying self, the goal is constructively addressing threats to the relationship.

We-Statements

Building on the concept of I-messages, Wesley Burr suggests that family conflict management is better served by "we-statements." He points out that I-messages emphasize the individuality, autonomy, separateness and independence of the people involved. They assume problems are "owned" and solved by individuals on their own. "When you _____, I feel _____, because _____ " is a very powerful message. It implies that there is a problem *between* you and me. We-statements, on the other hand, suggest that we are together, and together we have a problem. "I'm bringing up a problem, but it is something we need to deal with rather than a situation where I have already figured out what the problems and solutions are" (Burr 1990).

Combining I-messages and we-statements is a powerful strategy for conflict management: "We seem really unhappy with one another: we both are upset because our bank account is overdrawn. We seem to not be communicating well enough about our finances. I'd like us to see what we can work out together to keep this from happening again."

The goal of this discussion is not to provide families with sentence formulas into which they can stick their feelings, observations and desires, and magically come up with solutions. These conflict management strategies serve to help family members think through how to move from nursing their anger and thoughts of "everybody's done me wrong" to using their anger lovingly to tackle barriers and construct a more loving and caring family environment.

In essence, I-messages and we-statements are simply means to complain to one another about problems—the kind of complaining Gottman notes is healthy for marriages and, presumably, for other family relationships as well.

As anyone who lives in a family knows, the exact wording of messages is not nearly as important as the underlying feelings and intentions. Learning to spout I-messages and we-statements is relatively easy. Learning to sort through one's feelings and use them in behalf of those one loves is a spiritual discipline that requires vigilance, prayer and self-control.

DESTRUCTIVE USES OF ANGER

If a family member does not report anger and complaints in such a way that the family or partner can respond, or if we ignore one another's complaints, they turn into what John Gottman has called "complaining's evil twin"—criticism (Gottman 1994b). To complain is to describe one incident that one wishes were different: "I waited to clean out the garage so we could do it together as we planned today, and now I have to do it alone because you have to work." A complaint slips into criticism when we blame or attack the other: "You put your work before me again and leave me to handle everything by myself."

The difference may not seem significant, but the recipient experiences these messages quite differently. Criticism tends to be a generalization that attacks the other's sense of self and leads to defensiveness. It is not an "I-message"; it is a "you-message." There is a subtle but important distinction between speaking about one's own feelings and observations and speaking a judgment about the other's personality or values. We could say that it is the difference between speaking the truth (Eph 4:25) and the judging of others that Jesus warned us against (Mt 7:1). A practical disadvantage is that the partner's defensiveness means that attention of both partners turns toward self rather than the problem.

The complaint can be answered with something like "I'm sorry I let you down. I don't want you to have to do it alone. Could we do it a little at a time this week, in the evenings after supper?" The complainer feels heard, and a first attempt at solving the problem has been made. In contrast, partners often answer criticism with something like "Why do you always make a such a big deal out of nothing? There'll be another Saturday; the garage isn't going anywhere!" Here the complainer not only does not feel heard but also experiences a counterattack—"you're making a big deal of nothing." The feelings of disappointment over not having the day together, or not getting a necessary chore done, are lost in the mounting anger, further alienating the partners.

Good complaints are essentially I-messages; they state the facts and one's own feelings. "You are going to work instead of cleaning out the garage with me. I'm disappointed." They don't, however, label the person—either by calling them a name ("you are a workaholic") or by naming their character ("you are so thought-less"). Good complaints also deal with *this* situation and avoid words like *never* ("you never keep your promises to me") and *always* ("you always find ways to avoid responsibility"). Sometimes it may seem that such an "always" or "never" statement is justified. Even so, these words do not help solve the problem; they just cause a bigger problem. Family members need to learn to listen to and work through complaints together, so that they do not degenerate into criticism.

Obviously, learning to express anger and complaints is important in relationships between the generations and in sibling relationships and faith-families, not just in adult partnerships. Children learn as they experience parents' anger and are disciplined when they do not meet parents' expectations. Children also need help in learning to express their anger and resolve their differences. Siblings do not necessarily develop creative ways of handling problems when adults simply leave them to "work it out on their own." They learn by watching adults work through their own feelings and complaints with one another and with them.

Distinguishing Between Anger and Contempt

Contempt is a feeling of loathing of the partner, as though the partner were worthless and hopeless. Contempt is the opposite of respect. Respect values the other despite and beyond any conflict or problem. Contempt is not the same thing as anger. Instead contempt *uses* anger to communicate that the partner is worthless.

When criticism has wormed its way into family relationships, contempt often follows. Partners find it more and more difficult to act lovingly toward each other. It is hard to be loving toward someone who considers one worthless (Gottman 1994b).

Most people have felt and even expressed criticism and contempt for a family member at one time or another. When we have done so, we have sinned. Jesus made it clear that we are neither to judge (criticize) one another nor to hold one another in contempt (calling one another a fool; Mt 5:22; 7:1-2). We each are responsible for disciplining ourselves to respect and love the other. Anger should be used to strengthen our relationship, not diminish the partner.

When Anger Becomes Violent

Sometimes anger is expressed violently: someone strikes out at another or throws something at the other or against the wall. Sometimes people strike out in frustration, sensing that words have failed to express the depth of frustration and hurt. A wet dishcloth is thrown to slap the other on the back of the head, hands reach out in a shove, or a pan is thrown to the floor with a loud clatter.

Such expressions signal danger. Family members need to recognize the need for distance and allowing emotion to dissipate until it is manageable. When the anger has subsided and both can talk calmly, it is time to face the failed communication together. What is keeping us from feeling heard and understood? How can we keep from lashing out again? A helpful family rule is to use only voices to communicate anger, never hands or objects. If partners cannot find more effective and safe ways to communicate, it is time to seek help from someone outside the family.

There is a second and more virulent form of violence—violent action that tries to force or punish the other. One slaps or hits the other to stop words of anger or to emphasize a command. The goal is not communicating one's own anger but controlling the other.

Talking it over usually will not keep this kind of violence from occurring again, even if the violent partner expresses sorrow and vows never to repeat the hurt. This kind of violence is not about communication; it is about power. One partner feels the need to control and dominate others. Often that person has problems trusting others to love and remain loyal. This can be construed as a fundamental problem in forming secure attachments. Violent persons become violent out of a need to maintain power over family members they fear they cannot trust otherwise.

It is critical to distinguish this kind of violence from the first kind, that which arises out of frustrated communication, because this violence does not respond to improved communication or family members' attempts to be more or do more to please the violent one. These families need help from outside, and usually the violent person must be separated from the family to protect members from further harm, at least temporarily. If members cannot build safe relationships with one another, the separation may have to continue; the covenant of care of the other as a member of the self either was never formed or has been broken. In chapter twenty-three we will look in more depth at ministry in the presence of family violence.

Families, particularly church families, tend to avoid admitting that they need help. As Christians, however, their love for one another should move them to "speak the truth" (Eph 4:25) and name the sin. Love "rejoices in the truth" (1 Cor 13:6); only when truth is spoken can trouble be confronted and changes be made. Above all, we must not assume that to forgive means to forget or excuse the sin of violent anger. Love insists that sin be confessed and that repentance bring true change.

INTIMACY

One of the major themes of the Bible is intimacy. God wants to be known by us; God knows our innermost being. Jesus instructs us to stay connected, to be intimate with him by abiding in his love (Jn 15:4-7). Before the Fall, Adam and Eve were "naked" and "not ashamed" before each other and before God (Gen 2:25). At the culmination of Jesus' life, he was stripped naked and held up for all to see, God with us (Jn 1:14-18), allowing us to know and see who God is.

Intimacy is not a feeling or an act of romantic endearment. Intimacy is "a fundamental bonding between persons' innermost senses of identity" (Heyward 1982:44). It is the outcome of attachment, communication and problem-solving. Intimacy is a sense of knowing and being known by the intimate other, which grows out of a generalized sense of closeness between persons. It is often characterized by self-disclosure, feelings of cohesion, physical acts exchanged (changing diapers or nursing an infant, bathing a frail elderly parent, caring for an ill family member, rubbing a tired back, rocking and soothing, sexual intercourse) or communication of thoughts and feelings (Moss and Schwebel 1993).

Intimacy makes us vulnerable. Will I be rejected because of my physical self or my thoughts and feelings? Will the other find me beautiful or repugnant? Will others still love me when they have to wash me and feed me because I cannot care for myself? This vulnerability is most significant where we differ from one another, whether bodily differences or differences in ideas, feelings or needs. In the vulnerability Adam and Eve felt after they sinned, they covered up the parts of their bodies with which intimacy can be expressed most wonderfully, and also the parts of their bodies that were most obviously *different*. When we feel threatened, our first reaction is often to cover up thoughts, bodies, feelings that differ from the other's, for fear of being rejected (Stanley et al. 1998).

Intimacy is not always conscious. The child whose bottom is being wiped and who is mesmerized by the face of an animated caregiver voicing affection and delight may be much less aware of the intimacy of that encounter than the caregiver is. Even adults may not be fully aware of the intimacy between them as they wait by the bed of a desperately ill child, or sort through piles of paper preparing their tax forms, or experience all the other moments of profound togetherness involved in living as family. Evidently Adam and Eve were in this state of unawareness; only when their intimacy was destroyed and they sought to cover up did they seem to be aware that they were naked together.

Nevertheless, there are times when family members are suddenly aware of the intimacy they have. David Schnarch defines intimacy as the ability to experience being *me* and *I*, at the same time, in relation to another person. That is, *I* am aware of being *me* in relation with the other who loves *me* and is loved by *me*. Being close to another involves knowing the other. Being intimate with another involves knowing the self. Usually we know ourselves only in our personal thoughts and dreams. But to feel and know the self in the presence of another is joyful and freeing (Schnarch 1991).

Intimacy can grow only out of closeness, however, and persons have different levels of tolerance for closeness and distance.

> One cold winter night, two porcupines were trying to sleep together. They wanted to be as close as possible to share their warmth; but when they moved too close, they stuck each other with their quills. When they moved too far away, they became chilled. It took quite a long time of adjusting themselves to one another to find just the right position for the greatest amount of warmth and the least amount of pain. (Adapted from Maxwell 1979)

Most families are groups of porcupines trying to adjust to each other's needs for closeness and distance. We do not want to be known all the time. There are aspects of other family members that we wish they would keep to themselves. There are some thoughts and feelings we do not want to share. There are times we desperately want solitude and silence. The need for privacy and solitude is not a judgment on the relationship; it is simply part of how we are created. Jesus needed time away from his "family" of disciples and took frequent solitary retreats.

We differ in the balance between togetherness and solitude, sharing and privacy, closeness and distance that makes us most comfortable. One spouse would really like to sleep in a double bed, tucked up against the partner. The other feels guilty for wanting a king-size bed and fights the urge to tuck a pillow between self and other to preserve some space. An infant wants to be in physical contact, or at least sight, with the parent all the time, while the parent longs simply to be able to go to the bathroom alone and shut the door for five minutes. Only a seemingly few years later, that same parent may long for just five minutes of conversation with a teenager about what he or she is really thinking and feeling, while the teenager feels suffocated by the parent's concern.

Intimacy and distance are continuing issues in families. Family members have different visceral senses of personal space and needs for privacy. These visceral senses change with individual development and life circumstances. Intimacy involves such seemingly different issues as sleeping patterns, physical arrangement of space, use of time, shared and separate activities, locked or open bathroom doors. There are no established rules all families can follow to resolve these issues; each family develops its own ways of addressing its members' needs for intimacy and privacy.

Boundaries

Families have boundaries, and intimacy takes place in distinctive ways within these boundaries. One of these is a sense of privacy of family life. The old warning about hanging out one's dirty linen in public expresses this graphically. Family members need to feel safe with one another, that their private lives will not be shared outside the family. There is a difference between family secrets (such as violence or incest or alcoholism) that keep a family from getting the help it needs and family privacy (not sharing intimate details of family life with friends and colleagues). When a child naively shares what others might consider private, teens and adults may find it funny but also embarrassing.

The development of family boundaries. Boundaries of privacy are not automatic; they are learned over time. We define these with one another. The formation phase of family life often includes some conflict over boundaries. What was acceptable to share with one's friends about a date is no longer acceptable to share about one's spouse.

Boundaries shift throughout a family's career. For example, the bowel habits of infants may be the subject of conversation among new parents wrestling with what is healthy and what should cause worry. Such conversation among parents about their adolescent children, on the other hand, would be a serious breach of family privacy. Boundaries are almost always inferred and seldom overtly named, except when they have been violated.

Boundaries do need to be overtly delineated, however, when family members for some reason have difficulty knowing where they are and what they mean. Adults who experienced breaches of healthy boundaries as children may need guidance in where these boundaries are and how they function. Often children who have been abused and neglected need to be explicitly taught appropriate and inappropriate boundaries, both as children and as adults.

Infringements on family boundaries. A generation ago, for many families the most troublesome infringements on boundaries involved neighbor children coming to the door to seek play partners during the dinner hour, an office insisting that a family member work overtime, a relative or friend often dropping by unannounced and staying too long, a relative assuming more entitlement in the family's life than the family wanted to allow.

All these infringements on family boundaries must still be negotiated. In addition, however, a whole new and much more sophisticated set of intruders threaten by means of technological wizardry. Our lives, even in the heights and depths of family intimacy, are in a continual state of interruption. Cellular phones, beepers and call-waiting features on telephones carry the expectation that we are always available, that whatever we are doing can be interrupted. Consequently, our time together sometimes becomes fragmented, and the world pulling at us from outside the family may be louder and more insistent than the quieter need for completing mundane chores together or a having a conversation about the day's events.

Sexuality

Sexuality is one dimension of family intimacy. In our society it is taboo to consider sexual intimacy to have a role in any family relationship other than between adult partners. Nevertheless, often family members do relate to one another in implicitly sexual ways that do not involve adult sexual partnerships. Nursing mothers know there is sometimes a sexual dimension to nursing an infant. The physical comfort of an infant's emptying a full breast and the pleasure of suckling are powerful bonding experiences for the dyad often referred to as the "nursing couple."

As children grow, they sometimes flirt with the parent of the opposite sex and fantasize about marrying that parent when they grow up. The parent plays a special role in affirming and strengthening the growing sexual identity and self-esteem of the child. The parent's admiration of the child's growth into a beautiful young man or woman, accompanied by respect for the child's growing need for privacy and autonomy, lays the groundwork for healthy adult sexuality. Parents comfortable with their own sexuality can affirm their children's developing sexuality without feeling threatened and without violating appropriate boundaries. Similarly, adult children and grandchildren recognize that an elderly family member who has lost a spouse has an increased need for physical touch that communicates intimacy—hugs, held hands, kisses at greeting and departure. The full sexual intimacy of adult partners is a significant arena of family intimacy that will be addressed in chapter twenty.

Emotion Work

Family sociologists have long been telling us that wives find family life more satisfying when the work of the family is shared by their husbands than when the majority of the work falls on wives' shoulders. That sharing translates into a constant juggling of household chores, cooking, shopping, car maintenance, family correspondence, financial management and childcare. But simply balancing the chore lists is not enough. According to the research of sociologist Rebecca Erickson, though the sharing of family chores is important, the sharing of "emotion work" is even more significant (Erickson 1993).

"Emotion work" means providing other family members with emotional support by listening sympathetically, talking things over and confiding in each other. Handling the emotions of family members is just as much a job that needs doing to keep a family afloat from day to day as is paying the bills or doing the laundry. Even more important, it needs to be shared. One partner cannot do all the work of handling the emotions of a family without feeling overwhelmed and even unhappy. Here are some of the "chores" involved in emotion work:

☐ confiding innermost thoughts and feelings
☐ initiating talking things over
☐ trying to bring a family member out of restlessness or depression
☐ expressing faith in a family member
☐ sensing when one's partner is disturbed about something
☐ offering encouragement
☐ giving compliments
☐ staying close during troubled times
☐ offering advice

☐ respecting other family members' points of view
☐ giving affection
☐ expressing concern for the partner
☐ being a good friend
☐ doing favors without being asked

The significance of emotion work has been indicated by research with families dealing with highly stressful situations. Most of us would imagine a stress-free, orderly existence with lots of shared leisure time would create more intimate family life. We assume that heavy demands on family members' time, such as those involved in caring for small children or frail elderly parents, create risks for marital unhappiness. Yet a study by sociologists Jill Suitor and Karl Pillemer (Suitor and Pillemer 1994) found that over the course of a year of caring for an elderly parent, some marriages actually became more satisfying than they were before. Other couples, however, found their satisfaction with their marriages significantly lower as time wore on.

Why did some marriages thrive and others suffer? One would guess that sharing the caregiving tasks equally rather than one spouse doing all the caregiving would make the difference, but in fact, the researchers found that these families really did not share equitably in caregiving. The wife was still doing most of it, even when the frail parent was her in-law. The key to increased marital happiness in the midst of stressful time demands was the emotional support spouses provided one another. In marriages that thrived, the husband supplied major doses of appreciation and admiration, rather than resentment, of his wife's service. As one wife expressed it, "He just stood by me." Of course, it might have been even more satisfying if partners had worked together in caregiving and shared the load.

Whether one member carries more than their share or the caregiving responsibilities are shared, families can thrive when external demands are heavy. Families do not need to be carefully tended in hothouses, protected from stress. In fact, they grow best when they are about their calling to care for one another and for their neighbors and communities, supporting each other, recognizing the value of each other's work, blessing and standing with each other.

Support for Family Intimacy from Others
Sharing intimate concerns and fun activities certainly puts pizzazz in family life. Paradoxically, however, support from friendships and acquaintances *outside* the

family also supports intimacy within it, so long as family members recognize and honor the differences between family life and friendship.

For the most part, families are working partnerships with fun thrown in for spice. We do not pledge to stay family as long as it is fun. We pledge to be family to one another no matter what, with only our loyalty to God as a condition. Friendship is the opposite; friends are play partners. The joy of intimate conversation and shared interests is the stuff of friendship. Although sometimes friendships endure rocky periods, we expect friends to continue being friends because we *really enjoy* one another. When the joy stops, most friendships gradually fade. That may not be right, but it seems to be true.

The differences between family and friendship are certainly not absolute, but one thing we do know. People who feel they have great marriages and families also feel they have great friends—*in addition to* their family members. It is wonderful when family members are friends, but ideally they are never the *only* friends. Family members need friends with whom they can laugh and share concerns. Most important, good friendships provide a sound reality check. Are the issues my family is dealing with a lot like what everyone else is dealing with? Is the grass greener in other pastures—or does it just look that way? Good friends are an antidote to limited vision and the sense that one's problems and concerns are unique. Time with good friends helps family members gain a fresh perspective on the joys and struggles of family life. It helps a partner or parent to know that other partners or children bring on the same kinds of frustration that hers do. It helps an adolescent to know that friends also love and are exasperated by younger siblings. They can then turn to family members refreshed, a little more comfortable with self and family.

We need to give attention in our churches to the development of Christian friendships. We need others whom we can call "friend," those to whom we can "make all things known" (Jn 15:15), those with whom we can keep "pleasant company" (Ps 55:14). We can then love our families with the richness and strength we gain from walking with others who share our lives but not our living space, who help us laugh at ourselves and cry over troubles.

IMPLICATIONS FOR FAMILY MINISTRY

All these processes of family development lend themselves to education for Christian living, regardless of the age of persons or structure of the family in which they live. Processes of attachment, communication, conflict and intimacy affect every person in a congregation and every family in a community. They involve not only learning skills but learning why these skills are important to Christians, how they help us live faithfully and lovingly as witnesses of God's love.

Such education does not take place best alone but in interaction, practice and support from a whole community of people trying to live into the attachment, communication, conflict and intimacy demands of family life. Sometimes we learn best when we see that we are not alone, that the struggles and joys we experience are not all that different from those of others, even others who live in situations that *look* quite different from ours. The community of faith itself can be a place where attachment, communication, problem-solving and intimacy take place among family members. Following are a few examples.

□ Teach and preach about these processes as the context for Christian discipleship. Help *all* families learn skills that strengthen these processes in their lives.

□ Provide rituals that symbolize and thus strengthen attachments, particularly between those who are not recognized as "family" by our society. The dedication of a small circle of family friends to be the "faith-family" for a new child, for example, provides social support and sanction for these people to take responsibility for this child as aunts and uncles and grandparents in the faith. Rituals for all kinds of new relationships such as adoption and fostering serve as important symbols for families and for the community of faith.

□ Plan for ways that families stressed by separations can be family at church rather than being separated, so that their attachment to one another is not stressed even further. For example, children who spend much of their week in childcare and adult partners whose work keeps them separated for long hours may need to be *together* in Christian education, worship and fellowship.

□ Recognize that the grief of lost attachment figures is long term. Providing ways that ritualize and communicate respect for the loss can be enormously supportive for family members—bereavement services during holiday seasons, opportunities to memorialize lost ones by lighting candles or giving flowers, sending remembrances or phoning family members on key days such as birthdays or anniversaries.

□ Recognize that as we live as a community of faith, we model covenant living for families. Keep congregational communication balanced in positive and negative exchanges. For each criticism or problem that is or needs to be voiced, be sure that five messages of affirmation and appreciation are also spoken.

☐ Model in congregational interaction good skills of communication and conflict management. Teach families by example, and be explicit about the work this takes in Christian discipleship. This may mean *learning* these skills as a congregation, as a part of Christian education for congregational *and* family life. Given the level of unresolved conflict in congregational life today, this may be significant for church leaders as well as for family ministry.

☐ Provide time for family members not only to be together but also to be with others, *apart* from the family, where Christians peer friendships can be nurtured.

☐ Provide additional help for families through counseling, either by qualified professional staff in the congregations or by referral to trusted professionals in the community. Frame help-seeking as responsible and faithful behavior in the face of significant life challenges. Continue to offer support, encouragement and ministries that challenge the family to faithful living within the congregation. Counseling is not a replacement but a supplement to discipleship within the congregational context.

Chapter 6

Power in Family Life

P OWER MANIFESTS ITSELF IN MYRIAD WAYS IN FAMILY RELATION-
ships.[1]

The accepted sociological definition of power is *the probability that one person is able to exert his or her will despite resistance from others* (Weber 1947). In families, resistance from others may be latent or overt. Power may be so subtle that it is not even recognized by family members—including the one exerting power. "Exert will" sounds like something that is done with intention and forethought—and family interaction often seems unmarked by such intentionality. It may be more helpful, then, to think of power as the *influence* of one family member on the behavior of other family members, regardless of whether that influence is resisted or even recognized by any of the actors. For example, a cranky infant can be a very powerful individual, controlling the sleep and time of one or more adults; but the baby lacks any awareness of "power."

A Dynamic of All Family Relationships

Power—or "influence"—is not a characteristic of one individual; rather, it is a

---

[1]Much of the material in this chapter was first published in Garland and Garland 1986. It has been updated and revised.

characteristic of the relationship between persons. An infant crying has power only if parents are tuned in, listening and responsive. That same infant is powerless if closed doors and loud music keep parents from hearing the crying. In hierarchical family relationships, someone holds the most powerful position to the extent that other family members grant that person power, whether out of fear or out of belief that the power is appropriate.

Power is a dynamic that infuses all family relationships. We are always attempting to influence one another; we are always attempting to exercise power. Families must make decisions about who does which chores, how to budget and save money, where to go on vacation, and many other matters of daily or major negotiation. To the extent that family members depend on one another, they give power to one another. Family members also powerfully influence one another's moods and feelings.

Culture Shapes Family Power Dynamics

The surrounding community and culture give shape to power dynamics in family life. Thus cultural changes often bring changes in the balance of power in the family. Historically, for example, men have had greater power in marriage than women. Much of this power is derived from the economic arrangements of family life. Where men are the primary earners, they have greater independence and control over the means for family economic survival than women. Women have historically been less able to exert power in the family, or even to have the power to leave abusive family relationships, because of their economic dependence. As women have entered the work force, they have gained negotiating leverage in the family that some theorists have regarded as a threat to the stability of families. At the very least, many women who in previous generations could not consider divorce as a solution to their marital miseries now can, because they have or can obtain the economic means for survival.

Two generations ago it was common for American husbands to give wives allowances for groceries and household management. Many wives had no knowledge of their family's income and financial status. That was never true of all families, but it certainly was true of many more than it is today. At the same time, women tended to have power over the less tangible resources of the family, such as interpersonal relationships. In the 1960s, pioneering family therapist Virginia Satir pointed out that many mothers operated as "family switchboards," controlling all the communication in the family. Women translated between father and children, with some fathers seldom having one-to-one relationships with their children apart from their wives. Again, such a communication pattern did not characterize all families, but it certainly was more common than it is today.

Other aspects of the larger culture, such as social and technological changes, also influence power dynamics within family life. For example, the remote-control device (RCD) for televisions has created an interesting power dynamic. Twenty years ago, changing the television channel required getting up, walking across the room and changing a dial from one number to another. That action was available to virtually anyone in the room who was willing to move, even the smallest child. There was also not a large selection of channels nor the technological ease to "channel surf." Today, however, the RCD has become a new scepter of family power. Researchers have found that men control the RCD more than women and are much more likely to engage in "unnegotiated channel switching"—that is, changing channels when they want to without consulting others who are also watching. Children fight with one another—and with their parents—to get control of the scepter. Of course, some families avoid the ensuing conflict over the imbalance of power by buying additional televisions, so that each person can watch television in isolation from the others. This solution may defuse the power battle, but it does not necessarily resolve it.

Gender as a Factor in Family Power
The power relationship between husbands and wives receives more attention in the New Testament than any other aspect of family life. The church, too, has also given major attention to the ordering of power in marriage. In many respects, as power in marriage goes, so goes power in other family relationships. Norms that give men authority and power over women and expect women's submission to that authority and power also emphasize adults' authority and power over children. These norms order family life hierarchically. By contrast, norms of equality and shared power between men and women also emphasize the empowering of children and increasing equality in the adult-child relationship as the child grows.

Thus relationships between family members tend to be shaped by either a hierarchical and authoritative ordering of persons or by an egalitarian and collaborative negotiation of power. Because of the significance the Bible gives to power issues in marriage, and the continuing debate in some sectors of the church today, the following discussion will examine relevant biblical texts and current research concerning power and marriage at some length.

HUSBANDS AND WIVES IN BIBLICAL TEXTS

Did God ordain that men outrank women, and that wives are to submit to their husband's authority? Or is the relationship between husband and wife to be a partnership, so that they not only stand together on an equal footing before God but also relate to each other as equals?

Some twenty years ago, when many of today's middle-aged American adults were forming marriages, over a million people attended Bill Gothard's seminars on family life (Bayly 1977). Using a military analogy, Gothard contended that the family ought to be ordered by a "chain of command." Everyone in the home is under authority, he said, and God deals with family members through these channels of authority. This authority is not considered domination so much as protection. When persons get out from under this "authoritative umbrella," they expose themselves to unnecessary temptations that they are too weak to overcome. In other words, the husband's authority protects the woman from Satan (Howell 1979).

> "Before the fall," says Gothard, "Eve had a different relationship. Satan came directly to Eve instead of through Adam. When the woman was beguiled, God put a restriction on her. 'Thy desire shall be to thy husband, and he shall rule over thee' (Genesis 3:16). But this restriction was for her own protection. Now Satan can no longer get through to her unless he goes through the husband." (Bockelman 1976:74)

In the 1970s, the decade following the cultural angst of the 1960s, a revision of powered relationships was occurring in many aspects of social life. Women were asserting their rights; the civil rights movement challenged a racist order of society; adolescent and young adult children were openly claiming the right to dress and live according to values differing from those of their parents. The cultural changes reverberated through families too. For many, new claims of the rights of all to live in egalitarian family relationships were threatening, and reactions often cited the biblical texts that form the foundation of Christians' understanding of how persons ought to live with one another. Both men and women authors argued that God ordained marriage to be a hierarchical relationship. Maxine Hancock wrote that the husband's judgment was the absolute norm for the wife: wives do not submit to their husbands because they are gentle and kind, or good, or godly, but simply because they are the husbands (Hancock 1975). Judith Miles stated that women are "in-carnate models of submission and loyalty" (Miles 1975:151); she argued that it is through the woman's submission that the man learns how to submit himself to God. In a revealing passage, Miles described how this view influenced her own marriage:

> One day this familiar verse acquired a heightened meaning for me, "Wives be subject to your husbands, as to the Lord" (Eph 5:22). It could not mean *that!* Not as to *the Lord!* But here it was. I was to treat my own human husband as though *he* were the Lord, resident in our own humble home. This was truly revelatory to me. Would I ask Jesus a basically maternal question such as "how are things at the office?" Would I suggest to Jesus that he finish some task around the house? Would I remind the Lord that he was not driving prudently? Would I ever be in judgment over my Lord, over His taste, His opinions, or His actions? I was stunned—stunned into a new kind of submission. (Miles 1975:44)

Marabel Morgan's bestseller published in 1975, *The Total Woman,* included these words: "It is only when a woman surrenders her life to her husband, reveres and worships him, and is willing to serve him, that she becomes really beautiful to him" (Morgan 1975:96-97).

Others who viewed submission of the wife and headship of the husband as divinely ordained found some of the popularized statements of the position extreme; they made more moderate applications from the same theological presuppositions (Foh 1979; Hurley 1981).

The position of these authors is not new; it has been taken for granted for centuries. Biblical texts have been bandied about to support both the traditional and the emerging egalitarian perspective on gender relationships. So simply compiling an arsenal of Scripture passages does not clinch the argument. Scholars of equal ability and piety have appealed to the same Scriptures to defend incompatible positions (Hull 1975). Some have tried to take a mediating approach:

> Both [views] have worked well for Christians at different periods of history. So instead of arguing about one being right and the other wrong the best conclusion probably is that a Christian couple may take their choice; but they had better make quite sure, from the beginning, that they are both making the same choice! (Mace and Mace 1976:30)

But is it simply a matter of a couple's choosing a pattern of marriage as they would choose wallpaper? If we recognize that a variety of patterns of marriage can be found in Scripture, on what basis do we claim that one pattern is more right than another?

Male and Female He Created Them

The creation account in Genesis 2 provides the primary foundation for a hierarchical understanding of husband-wife relationships. M. F. Stitzinger provides a representative example of this view (Stitzinger 1981). He has outlined eight points from Genesis 2 that he thinks prescribe "definitely" and "clearly" a hierarchical role relationship. First, he notes that God created the man before the woman (Gen 2:7). Second, God designated the man as "Adam," the term used also to describe all of humankind. Because God gave this name to the man rather than the woman suggests to Stitzinger that the man occupies the position of head. Third, God gave Adam a position of leadership and authority before Eve's creation (Gen 2:15). He was cultivator and keeper of the Garden, and he was the one restricted from eating of the tree (Gen 2:16-17). Fourth, Adam exercised his authority without Eve's involvement in the naming of the animals (Gen 2:10). To give a name is to have authority over that which is named. Fifth, his leadership role is clear since it was he who needed a "helper" (Gen 2:18, 20). God met this need by custom-designing a subordinate who would assist him in carrying out God's commands. Sixth, he again exercised authority in designating his helper's name, his first act of rule over her (Gen 2:23). Seventh, that he is to leave his mother and father and cleave to his new wife (Gen 2:24) means that he is the one to act, to take initiative, to lead. Finally, the man is the spokesperson for the relationship, since it is he whom the Lord addresses in the Garden (Gen 3:9, 11). Stitzinger concludes that subordination of the woman was a divinely intended part of the created order, because it preceded the fall from grace.

Others have interpreted the creation narrative differently. Even if one uses the kind of exegesis that Stitzinger uses, it is not difficult to reach other conclusions. That man was created prior to woman proves nothing. If we look at creation proceeding in an ascending order with man as the crowning touch, as in Genesis 1:26, it would follow that woman, created after man, would be foremost. The order of the creation of the man and the woman, however, has nothing to do with male authority and female submission. Nor does the fact that the woman was built from the rib of the man. The man was created of "the dust from the ground"

(Gen 2:7), but that does not make him subordinate to the earth. On the contrary, he was created with power over the earth to till it (Gen 3:23). Following this logic, the woman should have power over the man from whom she was taken (Trible 1978).

The arguments about the leadership priority of the man totally ignore Genesis 1:26-31. The use of the plural in these verses indicates that God did not design a hierarchical relationship between the male and female when he created them: "So God created man in his own image, in the image of God he created him; male and female he created them" (Gen 1:27). He creates *them;* he blesses *them* and gives *them* dominion (Gen 1:28); and in Genesis 5:1-2 he also names *them.* They were created as equals. The man and the woman were intended by God to correspond to each other. The woman was not created simply to be a "helpmeet," as a corruption of the venerable King James Version has it. The English term *helper* connotes an assistant and subordinate. The text, however, does not connote inferiority. *Helper* is a term the Old Testament uses elsewhere for God who creates and saves Israel (Trible 1978:90). The key for understanding the meaning of the woman as "helper" is the phrase "as his partner" (Gen 2:20), literally "opposite to him" or "corresponding to him." What the man needed was a soulmate and not a servant. This is why the animals, although also helpers, failed to pass muster. He established his supremacy over the animals but failed to find a partner in them. The woman is a bone-and-flesh mirror image of the man, who remains incomplete without her. It is not insignificant that she was taken from man's side, for she was to be his partner. She is therefore no mere appendage to the man; as one flesh they are a part of each other's being.

Those who see marriage as a chain of command have also argued that the Tempter approached the woman because she was the weaker and more vulnerable. Eve's encouragement to her husband to partake of the fruit is interpreted as an act of insubordination. Her sin of disobedience to God is in part her self-assumed position of leadership over her husband. Adam listens to his wife, and by allowing her to have authority over him, he sins in distorting the natural hierarchy. When God comes, he calls to the man, not the woman, thus placing primary responsibility on him (Gen 3:9).

This kind of psychological exegesis could also argue, however, that the woman is tempted first because she is more sensitive and thoughtful than the man. She at least engages in theological dialogue with the serpent; Adam dumbly accepts the offered fruit ("she also gave some to her husband, who was with her, and he ate";

Gen 3:6). She is beguiled by a creature more subtle than any other (Gen 3:1, 13); what is Adam's excuse? The order of the temptations does not suggest anything about the vulnerability of the woman or the natural superiority of the man. Both were equally guilty of disobedience to God, and it had nothing to do with violating supposed role assignments.

The key passage for our concerns, however, is Genesis 3:16. The actions of both the man and the woman have corrupted the "very good" of God's creation. Their sin results in dire consequences for their relationship: the husband now shall rule over the wife. This new development implies that it was *not* what God had originally determined for their relationship. Trible points out that the dominance of the husband in 3:16 is *de*scribed, not *pre*scribed (Trible 1978:41). It is the upshot of their joint disobedience. Walter Brueggemann comments: "In God's garden, as God wills it, there is *mutuality and equality*. In God's garden now, permeated by distrust, there is *control and distortion*. But that distortion is not for one moment accepted as the will of the Gardener" (Brueggemann 1982:51).

When the rule of man over woman is understood as a result of sin, the hierarchical pattern of marriage becomes something less than God's intention for humanity. For this reason one can hardly appeal to Genesis 2—3 as the biblical warrant for it. If anything, the hierarchical pattern is a perversion of God's intention in creation. The partnership has been destroyed. Walter Wangerin suggests that the significance of the words "he shall rule over you" lies not in the word *he* but in the word *rule*. Whereas there should be collaboration and agreement—a humble care in which each empties self for the sake of the other—a code of law is now imposed on the relationship. Law will rule instead of grace. Thus sin disfigures the good God offered us. We were meant to be his image in the world, an image of love and self-giving, not of law. Through Jesus, however, we can experience redemption (Wangerin 1987).

The Household Rules of the New Testament
The pivotal New Testament passages for the argument that God has ordained hierarchy in the husband-wife relationship are Ephesians 5:22-33, Colossians 3:18-19, Titus 2:4-5 and 1 Peter 3:1-7. Each of these injunctions is embedded in a larger unit that Martin Luther christened *Haustafel*, a list of rules for the household. Generally, such a passage consists of a string of admonitions to household members—wives and husbands, children and parents, slaves and masters. Parallels

to these lists of duties have been noted in Stoic moral philosophy, Hellenistic Judaism and Aristotelian political thought, showing how household rules were formulated in conformity to the conventional ideals of the ancient world.

In Hellenistic Judaism the conventional household code is exemplified by Philo of Alexandria: "Wives must be in servitude to their husbands, a servitude not imposed by violent ill-treatment but promoting obedience in all things" (Philo *Hypothetica* 7.3). In the same vein, Josephus wrote: "The woman, it [the Law] says, is in all things inferior to the man. Let her accordingly be obedient, not for her humiliation, but that she may be directed; for the authority has been given by God to the man" (Josephus *Against Apion* 2.201).

Family role assignments were modified by Christian perceptions and recast to speak to particular needs in the Christian communities. They were influenced by the Old Testament and qualified by a distinctive Christian motivation. These things were to be done "in the Lord" (Eph 5:22; 6:1, 5-7; Col 3:18, 20, 22-23; 1 Pet 3:4). The New Testament does not assign rights to certain members and duties to others. The lists of duties normally occur in pairs and are considered reciprocal. Consequently, when we examine these passages we can expect to find reflections of the way things were between husbands and wives in the ancient world from centuries of cultural conditioning. But we also can expect to find flashes of a distinctively Christian vision of the way things ought to be between husbands and wives.

The question of why domestic codes are found in the New Testament at all is another issue. They were not designed to provide a Christian theological justification for the existing social order. Instead the New Testament authors aimed to induce Christians to lead irreproachable lives as a witness to heathens. For example, when they see the reverent and chaste behavior of their wives, unbelieving husbands may be won to the Lord (1 Pet 3:1-2). The early Christians were trying to avoid being maligned as political or social revolutionaries, which would limit their opportunity to spread the gospel. Apparently some fanatics were being swept away by their newfound freedom and equality in Christ and were breaching social conventions in such ways as to bring discredit to the name of Christ (Hoskyns and Davey 1981). Some tried to bring change too fast and went too far in upsetting the conventions of the social order. Marriage relationships were undermined. The duties of family life were being disregarded, and responsibility for mutual care was being shirked in a mistaken zeal. Sexual decorum was ignored in public settings (1 Cor 11:2-16).

The early Christians were concerned with being well thought of by outsiders (see 1 Cor 10:32; 14:23; 2 Cor 8:21; 1 Thess 4:12; 1 Tim 3:7). The patriarchal order of the household was widely believed to underpin the stability of society. Thus New Testament household codes are attempts to rein in the enthusiasts so that Christianity would not be lumped together with other religions of the time that were blamed for undermining the foundations of social order. This can be seen clearly from Titus 2:5: wives are to be "submissive to their husbands, so that the word of God may not be discredited."

Colossians 3:18 represents a rejoinder to Christians' impatience with the restraints that seemed to curb their newfound freedom and equality in Christ. The wife's submission to her husband was something "fitting," proper not only according to society's expectations but also "in the Lord." It would be dangerous, however, to think that this state of affairs was intended to be permanent.

Ideas about what is "fitting" have changed across the centuries as the gospel has moved across lands and cultures. As societal pressures changed, the leaven of the gospel permeated and changed—slowly, to be sure—Christians' attitudes toward the institution of slavery. The same thing should be said for expectations regarding the hierarchical subordination of the wife. We can see this leaven already beginning to transform the attitude toward the relationship of husband and wife in the New Testament. Even though the wife is exhorted to be submissive to her husband, when the commands to the husband are carefully studied, we see that his role is not that of overlord. The call to love his wife as his body and as Christ loves his church, and to bestow honor on her as a coheir of the grace of life, entails submission on the part of the husband.

Ephesians 5:22-33. *Instructions to wives.* In Ephesians 5:22 the wife is instructed to be subject to her husband as to the Lord. Actually, no verb occurs in the Greek text of verse 22. It reads literally: "wives to your own husbands as to the Lord." The verb *be subject* must then be supplied from 5:21: "Be subject to one another out of reverence for Christ." This verb is also found in 5:24: "Just as the church is subject to Christ, so wives ought to be, in everything, to their husbands." The verb *be subject (hypotassō)* is never used specifically with *wives* as the subject. Although it is possible grammatically for verse 21 to begin the new section with the domestic code, it is more probable that it completes the thought of verses 18-20. There readers are challenged to "be filled with the Spirit, as you sing psalms and hymns and spiritual songs among yourselves, singing and making melody to the Lord in your hearts, giving thanks to God the Father at all times and for everything in the name of our Lord Jesus Christ." Since verse 22 must be read in light of verse 21, the notion of wives' subjection is transformed. It is not a demand for the wife to assume a divinely ordained role of underling. Her submission to the husband must be viewed as part and parcel of the Christian calling. Mutual submission is evidence of being filled with the Spirit and is expected of *everyone* regardless of age, station or gender. All Christians are to be subject to one another in the fear of Christ (see also 1 Pet 5:5).

This exhortation to be subject to one another reiterates a theme found throughout the teaching of both Jesus and Paul that Christians are called to serve others and not to assert their own rights (see Mt 23:11-12; Mk 10:42-45; Jn 13:14-15; Rom 12:18; 15:1-3; 1 Cor 10:33—11:1; Gal 5:13; Phil 2:3-4). Subordinating personal interests for the sake of others does not make a person a subordinate in the kingdom of God. Those in Christ are to seek first the welfare and interests of others and to do nothing from selfishness (Phil 2:3-4). The call to be submissive to others is therefore similar to the call to be humble (Eph 4:1-3). This basic truth must color how one interprets the subjection of the wife in Ephesians 5:22. If all Christians are to be subject to one another, the wife's subjection to her husband is not some role unique only to her in God's scheme of things.

A second point about verse 22 is that the word *obey* is *not* used; its introduction in the King James Version was based on error. In the continuation of the household rules, children are instructed to obey their parents (6:1) and slaves are told to obey their masters (6:5), but wives are not commanded to obey their husbands. Wives do not serve as husbands' vassals.

Third, the passage directs wives to be subject to their husbands *as to the Lord.* This does not mean they are to be subject as if their husbands were their lords, for this would require the plural, "as to their lords." The husband is not the wife's lord or savior (5:23), nor is the husband somehow representing Christ for her, nor is her submission to him an occasion for demonstrating her allegiance to Christ, as is the case with the slaves' submission to their masters (Eph 6:7; Col 3:23; see Barth 1974). "As you are to the Lord" has to do instead with the motivation of her submission. We are responsible to Christ in all aspects of life, including the intimacy of marriage, and the wife's commitment to Christ is therefore to be the ground of her commitment to her husband. What is interesting is that nothing is said about the wife complying with the natural order of things in the universe, which was an argument used by other writers in the ancient world (see Schweizer 1975:216). The wife's voluntary submission to her husband simply reflects her calling (and every Christian's calling) to relate to others by Christ's standard of love and humility.

Instructions to husbands. Far more is demanded of the husband as "the head" of his spouse in Ephesians 5:25-33, no doubt because the husband had far greater power and autonomy in the culture of the day. The commands directed to the husband are clear, but what it means for him to be designated as "head" is less clear. The headship of the man is mentioned also in 1 Corinthians 11:3, "But I want you to understand that Christ is the head of every man, and the husband is the head of his wife, and God is the head of Christ." The meaning of *head* in this passage is not "chief" or "ruler" but "source" or "origin" (Bedale 1954; Bruce 1971). That Christ is head of every man means that he was the source of every man's existence as the agent of creation (see 1 Cor 8:6; Col 1:16). By the same token, according to the creation account in Genesis 2 (alluded to in 1 Cor 11:8, 12), man was the source of the woman's existence. She was called *wo-man* because she was made from man. Now, Paul points out, men and women are interdependent, since "man comes through [is born of] woman" (1 Cor 11:11-12).

Finally, the source of Christ is God, since all things are from God. This concept of headship as source is therefore not a real parallel to Ephesians 5:23. In 1 Corinthians Paul is not dealing with marriage and the relationship between husband and wife but with problems that had emerged in the community's worship surrounding issues of differences between male and female. For this reason, Paul appeals to the creation accounts, which affirm that man was created male and female.

To understand what is meant by the phrase in Ephesians 5:23, "the head of the wife just as Christ is the head of the church," we must turn to Ephesians itself. It carefully qualifies the headship of the husband. He is the head of the wife *in the same way* that Christ is the head of the church. The term *head* was used earlier, in 1:22 and 4:15, to describe Christ. It was asserted in 1:22 that Christ is head over all things, but he is head over all things *for* the church. The headship of Christ is a source of life and vitality for the church. The head is the source of the body's development and growth (4:15-16); in Colossians 2:19 the head is said to nourish the body.

In Ephesians 5:23, Christ as head of the church saves his body. This is where the analogy between the husband as head of his wife and Christ as head of his church breaks down, since the husband is no more able to save his wife than himself. The husband as head of his wife, however, *is* able to nurture his wife, his body (5:28). This idea is pursued in verse 29. The husband as head is to nourish and cherish his wife, his body, just as Christ does the church, his body.

The passage as a whole was therefore not intended to set out an order of pre-eminence in the marriage relationship but to show how the husband was supposed to relate to his wife. Christ does not relate to his church as an ancient potentate tyrannizing his subject or as a five-star general domineering a buck private. Instead he nourishes, cherishes and loves.

In our culture, in which marriage is idealized as care for and emotional nurturing of one another, this expectation seems unnecessary. In the cultural context of Ephesians, however, Paul's teaching was revolutionary. Marriage for Paul's audience was not centered on mutual emotional and spiritual nurturing; many considered wives to be property, inferiors with whom some husbands would rarely even converse.

If the husband was to be the head of his wife as Christ is head of his church, he was to love his wife *just as* Christ loves his church (see Eph 5:2). It was certainly nothing new to tell husbands to love their wives, but this love is given a new dimension when the standard is Christ's love for his people. The husband was to learn to love his wife from the concrete expression of Christ's love. Christ gave himself up in behalf of his church (see Gal 2:20; Phil 2:6-11), which was precisely how he became its head. He did this, according to Ephesians 5:26-27, that he might sanctify the church and present it spotless and glorious, holy and blameless, before his throne. This love aspires to what is best for the beloved, even when the loved one is unworthy of such love (Rom 5:8). Christ loved without conditions. This is the kind of love that the husband is expected to have for his wife. It is an awesome demand, without parallel in the ancient world. This kind of love revolutionized power relationships in the family.

The conclusion is reached in 5:28: "In the same way, husbands should love their wives as they do their own bodies." Again, the example is Christ. *Just as* Christ nourishes and cherishes the church, his body (vv. 29-30), so must the husband nourish and cherish his wife. It is not that the husband is to love his wife as much as he loves his own body, but he is to love her *as* his body. She *is* his body. As one flesh (v. 31), the two have become a part of each other. With this statement the dichotomy of superior-inferior is erased completely. This is not subordination but identification (Caird 1976). Any chain-of-command authority is destroyed.

Since the emphasis on one flesh is the climax of the argument, it deserves attention. The first thing to clarify is that becoming one flesh does not imply that in marriage the husband and wife become an amalgam in which individuals lose their identity (Bailey 1952). The quotation comes from Genesis 2:24 and thereby refers back to the original state of things between man and woman. After the Fall, sin disfigured the relationship between the husband and wife. Christ, however, has reversed the consequences of the Fall (see Rom 5:1-21). Those who were dead in their sin have been made alive in Christ (Eph 2:5). We are new creations, created in Christ Jesus for new works (Eph 2:10). As Christ's death and resurrection made possible the reconciliation of Jew and Gentile, begetting in himself one new humanity and putting to death enmity and effecting peace, so it is also the case between husband and wife. In Christ, the old tensions are resolved and the marriage relationship acquires a new norm—no longer antagonism and rule but union and equality as God intended from the beginning. The dominance-subservience pattern has passed away; a new order has come into being. The touchstone of the husband's relationship to his wife is now to be Christ's sacrificial, nurturing love for his people.

The pagans lord it over one another; but it is not to be so among you, Jesus warned (Mt 20:25-26). The husband's own example of sacrificial, *submissive* love is to elicit whatever submission the wife entrusts to him. That love is to be inspired, never demanded. Ephesians 5 therefore characterizes marriage as "an experience of surrender without absorption, of service without compulsion, of love without conditions" (Richardson 1958:258). The Christian marriage is to be distinguished by partnership.

1 Peter 3:1-6. The injunctions to wives in 1 Peter 3:1-6 need to be understood within their context in the epistle as well as the historical context. The passage appears in the midst of a series of exhortations beginning in 2:11. A basic premise of the exhortations is that by "doing good" (see 2:14-15, 20; 3:6, 13, 17; 4:19) and by enduring suffering quietly (see 2:20, 3:14, 17; 4:16, 19; 5:10), Christians will be able to "silence the ignorance of the foolish" (2:12, 15). The household code beginning in 2:18 is modified in light of this premise and employed to address the problem of how Christians should handle themselves in a situation of persecution (see Lohse 1954; Schrage 1974). Slaves and wives, especially those married to non-Christian husbands, are singled out for instruction because, as D. P. Senior notes, they "had to endure the most painful conflict between their Christian freedom and their efforts to live a good life in the world"

(Senior 1980:48). The counsel, however, is not applicable only to slaves and wives. Christian slaves and wives married to non-Christians become a model of how Christians of all stations are to behave in the face of verbal abuse, scorn and bitter opposition.

When compared to other household exhortations in Ephesians, Colossians and the Pastorals, 1 Peter 2:18-25 has noteworthy distinguishing features. First, servants are identified as "household servants" (*oiketai*, a word used only three times elsewhere in the New Testament) instead of the more frequent term *slaves (douloi)* which appears in the other exhortations to slaves (Eph 6:5; Col 3:22; 1 Tim 6:1; Tit 2:9). Second, in contrast to all other household codes in the New Testament, the servants' duties are mentioned first. Elsewhere slaves and masters are considered last. Third, no mention whatsoever is made of masters and their responsibilities to the slaves. Fourth, the commands to servants in 1 Peter 2:18-20 are buttressed by a reflection on the suffering of Christ in verses 21-25. Thus the exhortation is given a unique and extensive christological foundation (Elliott 1981).

The best explanation for these unique features is that household servants become exemplars for all the members of the household of God, since "all the members are in a certain sense *oiketai*, like *oikonomoi* (4:10), servants of one another" (Elliott 1981:207). Their vulnerability typifies the vulnerability of all Christians. Their possible suffering under callous masters squares with the potential suffering of all Christians in a hostile environment (see 1:6; 3:14, 17; 4:1, 13, 16, 19; 5:9-10). What is required of them—fear (2:18), endurance (2:20), a clear conscience (2:19) and doing good (2:20)—is required of all Christians (fear, 1:17 and 2:17; endurance, 1:6 and 5:10; a clear conscience, 3:16, 21; doing good, 2:14-15; 3:13, 17). Can it be that slaves alone are called to suffer and follow in the footsteps of Jesus (2:21)? Surely the writer understands this as the calling of all Christians; and because the slaves serve as models for all Christians, no mention is made of the owners' responsibilities. Elliott concludes: "The focus is reserved for those alone whose condition and calling most clearly represent the situation and vocation of the entire household of God" (Elliott 1981:207).

The New Testament uses the humbler rather than dominating parties as models of true Christian believers (Lillie 1975:182). The church is identified as the bride of Christ (1 Cor 11:2; Eph 5:23-24; Rev 21:2, 9; 22:17). Jesus instructs his disciples to turn and to become as little children (Mt 18:1-4). Paul and others identify themselves as slaves of Christ (Rom 1:1; Gal 1:10; Phil 1:1; 2 Tim 2:24;

Tit 1:1; Jas 1:1; 2 Pet 1:1; Jude 1; Rev 1:1; also Mk 10:44). Using those whom society considered of the lowest estate as role models for all Christians turns gradations of rank or value upside down.

Instructions to wives. Recognizing the paradigmatic function of the household rules in 1 Peter helps clarify the instructions to wives. First Peter 3:1-6 does not make wives the focus of attention because they were prone to rebelliousness and needed to be bridled. They were addressed because their conversions created potentially grievous discord in their families if their husbands remained unconverted. Those counseled were wives married to non-Christians, for their husbands are described as not obeying the Word, and consequently needing to be won (compare 1 Cor 9:19-22 for the idea of "winning"). These men were not simply unresponsive to the Word; the other occurrences of the word *disobey* in 1 Peter (2:8; 3:20; 4:17) suggest that it refers to active hostility. The husbands were antagonistic to Christianity and highly displeased when their wives became Christians.

The lot of a wife who had, from the husband's perspective, been ensnared by a suspect superstition could be perilous. This was especially the case where the wife was expected to adhere to the religious beliefs of her husband. The situation was not so delicate when a husband became a Christian, since his wife would normally follow suit (see Acts 16:31-34) and since he had unquestioned freedom of action. For wives it was otherwise.

The strain resulting from a mixed marriage can be detected in 1 Corinthians 7:12-16. Some Christians in Corinth apparently felt obliged to separate from or divorce their pagan partners. First Peter recommends neither course. The Christian wife instead was to live out her commitment to Christ within the marriage and in submission to her husband. This meant that she was to be the best wife she could possibly be. For many it must have been like walking on eggshells. The woman had already breached patriarchal domination by becoming a Christian and disowning the gods of her husband and nation. Like the slave addressed in 1 Peter 2:18-20, she was to accept any suffering that might come from her situation in the same way Christ did (2:21-25). Living day in and day out with an embittered and all-powerful husband could easily evoke terror, but the wife is counseled to do right and to let nothing terrify her (3:6). It was advice applicable to all Christians: "But even if you do suffer for doing what is right, you are blessed. Do not fear what they fear, and do not be intimidated, but in your hearts sanctify Christ as Lord" (1 Pet 3:14-15).

This means that 1 Peter 3:1-6 is not intended to set forth the divinely sanctioned pattern for all marriage relationships. No word at all is addressed to a wife married to a Christian husband. It presents both a stratagem for evangelizing an unbelieving husband and a model of behavior for all Christians—all, at this time, were virtually powerless in their world and surrounded by hostile forces (see 3:8—4:6). It is not advice on how the wife might win the affection of her husband, or even advice about marriage at all. Instead it advised how a wife might win her husband for Christ without a word (3:1-2).

What is required of the wife in 1 Peter 3 is required of *all* members of the household of God. They too are to be submissive (2:13; 5:5-6). The emphasis on the good conduct or behavior *(anastrophē)* of the wife that is to be observed by her non-Christian husband ("when they see the purity and reverence of your lives," 3:2) is no different from the appeal made to all Christians: "Conduct yourselves honorably among the Gentiles, so that, though they malign you as evildoers, they may see your honorable deeds and glorify God when he comes to judge" (2:12). The phrase translated "reverence" in 3:2 literally reads "in fear." That does not mean the wife was to live in fear of her husband (see 3:6) or in reverence of him. "Fear" is used here, as throughout 1 Peter, as an abbreviation for the fear of God required of all Christians (1:17; 2:17; 3:14-15) as the basis of their conduct in the world. These wives are also encouraged to nurture a gentle and quiet spirit (3:4), but it should not be thought that a quiet demeanor befits only wives. *Gentle* is the same word used in the third beatitude, "Blessed are the meek" (Mt 5:5), and to describe Jesus (Mt 11:29; 21:5).

The admonition to adopt an attitude of quietness needs to be read in the context of hostility experienced by the wife married to the pagan and by the entire community. Quietness reflects the spirit of Jesus, who when he was reviled did not revile back (1 Pet 2:23). This is the ideal for all Christians, who are not to return reviling for reviling but to hold their tongues except to bless (3:8-11). The early church encouraged modesty in outward demeanor as a means of commanding respect from outsiders and because they believed that a quiet, peaceable life would have evangelistic effects in a predominantly pagan society (see 1 Thess 4:11-12; 2 Thess 3:12; 1 Tim 2:1-4). It should not be surprising that this attitude is commended to the wife married to an unbeliever.

A brief word should be said regarding the writer's concern about feminine adornment. Those who insist on interpreting the Bible literally should follow the path of early church fathers who understood verses 3-5 (see also 1 Tim 2:9-

10) as a ban on all finery and beautification aids. The emphasis, however, is on true beauty as something that is spirit deep, not skin deep. Admonitions against outward ornamentation were widespread in the ancient world. First Peter is by no means so cynical; but in keeping with the contemporary appraisal of true beauty, the wife was encouraged to inculcate a gentle and quiet spirit. By so doing she would be numbered among the daughters of Sarah. It was Sarah's character and supposed submission to her husband that are counted as true beauty in 1 Peter 3:5-6.

This picture of Sarah's submissive obedience to her husband is certainly idealized. At times it was actually Abraham who was obedient to her. For example, his barren wife demanded that he cohabit with her slave Hagar so that she might be able to reproduce through her (Gen 16:2), and later Sarah gave him an ultimatum, confirmed by none other than God, to cast out the slave with her son (Gen 21:10-12). Nor was she always meekly quiet. She lashed out at her husband after Hagar conceived (Gen 16:5). On the only occasion that she called her husband "lord"—just as well translated "husband"—she was laughing derisively upon overhearing the news that she and Abraham were to become parents: "My lord is too old" (see Gen 18:12 NIV). She then lied to God about having laughed (Gen 18:15).

That Sarah is presented as a model for Christian wives married to unbelievers is probably attributable to how she was portrayed in later tradition. According to the rabbis, she was the mother of proselytes. According to Philo (*Allegorical Interpretation* 3.244-45), she pointed Abraham on the way to virtue (Balch 1981:105). By imitating Sarah, Peter believed, the Christian wife might also win her husband to virtue and to Christ.

Instructions to husbands. A short, concluding word is directed to the Christian husband married to a Christian wife. He is told to live with her showing consideration or, literally, "according to knowledge" (1 Pet 3:7). What is this knowledge? Apparently it is a distinctively Christian perception that stands over against what has already been labeled as "the desires that you formerly had in ignorance" (1:14). The Christian has come to know God (see Gal 4:9) and consequently can no longer operate with the same value system of his pagan past or surroundings (1 Pet 1:18; 4:2-4; see also 1 Thess 4:3-5). The Christian husband is expected to relate to his wife in holiness and honor because she is a partner in the grace God has bestowed on all humanity.

The husband and wife were therefore to "cohabit as coheirs" (Elliott 1981:201). Treating the wife as a coheir destroys any hierarchical concept of their relationship. To treat her as anything less than an equal directly impinges on the husband's relationship to God. The phrase "so that nothing may hinder your prayers" implies that if the husband mistreats or debases his wife, he will soon begin to pray like a noisy gong (see 1 Cor 13:1). Christian wives may have to endure ill-will from their non-Christian husbands (1 Pet 3:6), but the Christian husband is never to aggrieve his wife if he wishes to bear the name Christian.

One last word should be said about the description of the wife as the "weaker sex." It was common in Greco-Roman society to describe woman in a derogatory sense as weaker (see Selwyn 1947). This is not the connotation of "weaker sex" in 1 Peter. Nor is the writer referring to a psychological weakness, for a Christian wife was expected to be able to bear up under intense pressure (3:6). She is not spiritually weaker, since she is designated a coheir of the grace of life. Perhaps the phrase refers to her physical weakness in comparison to (most) men. It is more meaningful, however, to consider this as a reference to the subjugation of women by the male-dominated culture. Although women were coheirs in God's kingdom, they were disenfranchised in the male kingdoms of this world. They were vulnerable, powerless and considered by some to be expendable. This powerlessness, or political "weakness," was not a characteristic inherent in being female but a role prescribed for her by a male-dominated society. She was not weaker because of any personal shortcoming but because she was a woman—a lesser class of persons—in a man's world. The wife was not one of the mighty of the world, and therefore the husband was to bestow honor on her (Best 1971). He was not to regard her or treat her as his world did, and Christian marriage was not to be governed by the law of the strongest.

The Pastoral Epistles

The instructions to wives found in the Pastoral Epistles can be understood only when the problems they were meant to address are clarified. A careful reading reveals that problems concerning marriage had surfaced in the churches. According to the Gospels, commitment to Christ can cause estrangement from the natural family (see Mt 10:37-39; Mk 3:31-35), but some early Christians seemed to have gone out of their way to create tension. Some rejected their family ties and encouraged others to do so as a sign of devotion to Christ. They left houses, spouses and children, assuming that they were supposed to do this for the sake of the kingdom (see Lk 18:29). They viewed marriage as a hindrance that could exclude a person from the kingdom (see Lk 14:20). If the various apocryphal acts of the apostles are any indication, this disdain of marriage gained an even greater foothold in the second century.

The Acts of Paul and Thecla serves as a notorious example. According to this work, Paul proclaimed blessed those who keep the flesh chaste, for they shall become the temple of God (2:5). He was said to preach that one has no resurrection unless one continues to be chaste and not defile the flesh (2:12). Thecla, a virgin engaged to Thamyris, was quite captured by this teaching. She wanted to be counted worthy to stand before Paul along with other virgins, and as a consequence she refused to marry. This naturally provoked Thamyris as well as Thecla's mother. Charges were brought against Paul for alienation of affections because of this new doctrine of the Christians (2:14). An attempt, encouraged by her mother, was made to burn Thecla for rebelling against the law of the Iconians. One might think that the canonical advice of Paul, "It is better to marry than to burn" (1 Cor 7:9), would apply; but Thecla was miraculously saved by rain and continued preaching the gospel of sexual abstinence to the end of her life.

A similar pattern where a woman, incited by the preaching of an apostle, withdraws from a marriage to live an ascetic life is repeated in *Acts of Thomas* 12—13, *Acts of Peter* 33—34 and *Acts of Andrew* (see also Irenaeus *Against Heresy* 1.24.2). This negative attitude toward marriage and sexuality must have infected the church at the time the Pastoral Epistles were written (see also 1 Cor 7). When a marriage partner became caught up in this enthusiastic asceticism, serious problems ensued not only for the marriage but also for Christians' reputation in the community (Balch 1981).

From 2 Timothy 3:1-9, we can detect that the heretics had made particular headway among impressionable women. Verses 6-7 reads: "For among them are those who make their way into households and captivate silly women, overwhelmed by their sins and swayed by all kinds of desires, who are always being instructed and can never arrive at a knowledge of the truth."

The instructions to wives in the Pastoral Epistles must be understood as a response to these problems. The epistles affirm that God created sexuality and marriage and therefore they are good. They were not to be rejected but to be received with thanksgiving by those who believe and *know the truth* (1 Tim 4:3-4). Hebrews 13:4, "Let marriage be held in honor by all," is a similar response to the negative appraisal of marriage.

The difficult passage in 1 Timothy 2:15 should be seen in this light. To say that woman will be saved through childbearing was to affirm childbearing. It was not to suggest that the path of salvation was different for men and women. This counsel reappears in 5:14: "I would have younger widows remarry, *bear children, and manage their households.*" One of the qualifications of the "real" widow was that she had *brought up her children* (1 Tim 5:10). In Titus 2:4-5 the elder women are asked to train younger women to love their husbands and children, to be sensible, chaste, domestic, kind and submissive to their husbands. It seems that these instructions were given because some were influencing wives to do otherwise in the name of God. The women were being dissuaded from living out any marital role because marriage and bearing and rearing children were seen as impediments to salvation.

An overriding concern in the Pastorals is "that the word of God may not be discredited" (Tit 2:5). The writer wished to avoid giving the enemy any opportunity to malign the Christian community for antisocial behavior, particularly when it came to obligations to family and marriage conventions (1 Tim 5:14). In writing to the Corinthians, Paul was concerned that "all things should be done decently and in order" (1 Cor 14:40). The Pastorals' stress on the wife's subordination to her husband and her role of domesticity was intended to counter heretics who encouraged wives to eschew their marriages in order to pursue some higher calling. It was meant for a particular situation where marriage bonds were being disdained.

1 Corinthians 7

First Corinthians 7 provides a glimpse of Paul's view of the relationship between man and wife in everyday matters of hearth and home. In dealing with problems that were emerging in Corinth between husbands and wives, not once does Paul call for or even hint that the wife should submit to her husband. Quite the contrary—marriage, as portrayed here by Paul, was to operate on the principle of mutuality and equality. Everything said of the husband is said also of the wife (1 Cor 7:2, 3-4, 12-13, 14-16, 33-34). She does not need to be instructed on these matters by the husband (see 1 Cor 14:35) but is addressed directly as an equally responsible party.

The first section (7:1-5) deals with the sticky subject of conjugal relations. Some couples in Corinth were abstaining from sexual intercourse in a misguided attempt to attain a fancied spiritual perfection. Paul opposes asceticism for marriage partners. Marriage is to be a fully sexual relationship. The husband and wife owe each other sexual intimacy (vv. 2-3); it is neither defiling nor optional. The explanation Paul gives for this opinion was that the wife does not rule (have authority) over her own body, but the husband does. This would have met with husbands' hearty assent in the first-century world. Paul, however, continues with a statement most atypical of the Greco-Roman world (Cartlidge 1975): the husband does not rule over his own body but the wife does (v. 4). There is no trace of any idea here about the husband's rights and the wife's duties. In sexual matters the wife is not expected to submit passively as a docile bed partner. She is an equal partner. *Both* husband *and* wife are to recognize that their spouse has a greater claim on them than they have on themselves. Paul's application to the Corinthian situation is that one partner may not unilaterally decide to abstain from coitus to pursue some private spiritual discipline (v. 5).

What is new here, when compared for example with Judaism, is that withdrawal from one another for spiritual purposes must be a mutual decision. In Judaism the husband had an inalienable right to absent himself from his wife for study or prayer. The wife need not be consulted, only informed. Paul argued, however, that one may abstain only by mutual consent. Regardless of what kind of head the husband is, he may not head off on spiritual retreat without consulting his wife, who has every right to say no. What is also new from a Jewish perspective is Paul's implication that a wife may also wish to retreat for prayer. This passage is the only one in the New Testament that specifically describes husbands and wives making decisions, and the emphasis is on arriving at a solution by mutual agreement and not by husbandly decree.

Another striking passage is 1 Corinthians 7:12-14. Paul contends here that Christians yoked to unbelievers need not feel defiled in some way by this union, as if they were joining a member of Christ to a demon, as some seem to have believed (see 1 Cor 6:16; 2 Cor 6:14—7:1). The Christian was never to initiate a divorce simply because the spouse was an unbeliever; and if the unbelieving spouse wished to continue the marriage, the Christian could rest assured that the partner had been "sanctified" by the Christian wife or husband.

What Paul means here by "sanctify" is most difficult to unravel. Surely he is not referring to some kind of sanctification by proxy. This is not an argument about sanctification but an argument against divorce. In 7:16, Paul recognizes that the spouse has not yet been saved and may never be converted: "Wife/husband, for all you know, you *might* save your husband/wife." Neither can it refer to the Christian witness and influence of the believing spouse on the unbelieving; the perfect tense of the verb is used, not the present or future. The perfect tense refers to some action completed in the past with continuing results—the spouse *has been* sanctified.

The answer to what Paul meant by "sanctify" is to be found in the vocabulary of Jewish marriage laws. The verb *sanctify* means "to set apart" or "to consecrate." In the Mishnah, *Qiddušin* (sanctifications, from the verb *to sanctify*) is the title of a tractate that discusses betrothals (see b. *Qiddušin* 2b). To betroth a wife is to sanctify her; she is set apart from all other men by her husband-to-be through money, document or intercourse (*m. Qiddušin* 1:1; see *b. Qiddušin* 2b). The husband thereby renders the wife a consecrated object. In Jewish thinking of the day, only husbands could do this. In fact, in all areas of life, women could be sanctified only through the deeds of men (Neusner 1979). In 1 Corinthians 7:14, however, Paul maintains that the wife also sanctifies her husband, sets him apart from all other women. Both a husband and a wife have the same sanctifying power.

The last passage in 1 Corinthians 7 that underscores the mutuality of marriage is verses 32-34. Paul assumes that the married man is anxious about worldly affairs, or how to please his wife; and the married woman is also anxious about worldly affairs, or how to please her husband. Paul does not scorn this concern. He recognizes that marriage brings anxieties and troubles in the flesh (7:28) and would prefer that men and women be free from this to give undivided devotion to the Lord (7:35). A person who has a spouse and children to care for would not be as free to travel hither and yon across the Mediterranean world as Paul was in his missionary travels. Paul could focus his anxiety on his churches (2 Cor 11:28), where married persons must also be anxious for the welfare of family.

Paul assumed that being married involved being concerned with pleasing the spouse. It would have been taken for granted, of course, that this was the task of a wife; but according to Paul, the husband has the same goal. He was not to be anxious about how to rule his wife or how to make her submit to his authority, but about how to please her. Marriage for Paul entailed mutual dedication.

In 7:25-26 Paul makes it clear that he was offering his opinions: "I think." It is the opinion of one who has been counted by the Lord's mercy to be trustworthy, but it is still *his* opinion. He "thinks" he has the Spirit of God on these matters (7:40). Paul based his opinions not on divine laws of the universe but on what he believed would be to the Corinthians' advantage and would promote good order or seemliness (7:35) in their world and situation. Nevertheless, each individual may decide for himself or herself how to live in obedience to God's call when it comes to marriage. Paul would not throw a noose on anyone (7:35). Each is considered able to make responsible choices. Wives are not viewed as underlings required to submit to the authority of their husbands. The relationship between husband and wife was to be based on equality and mutuality, not authority and dominance.

Conclusions

Man and woman were created by God to be equal partners in marriage. A hierarchical relationship in which the husband rules is not the will of God but a distortion of the relationship between man and woman. Although the forced repression of wives into submissive roles became an almost universal custom and was normative in the first century, we find in the New Testament the winds of change. Husbands are to love their wives in the same way that Christ demonstrated his love for his people. They are not to put themselves first but their wives first. Wives are to be honored by their husbands as coheirs of God's grace and therefore equals. Wives and husbands mutually rule over each other's body. The principle that is to govern the marriage relationship of those in Christ is therefore to be mutuality and partnership under the lordship of Christ.

POWER IN MARRIAGE TODAY

Despite these biblical foundations for mutuality and partnership in marriage, social norms continued to support the powered male position in families and the submissive role for women. The change toward egalitarian marital roles has been extremely gradual and marked by regression as well as progression.

That change has gained great speed, however, during the twentieth century. In the mid-twentieth century Ernest W. Burgess and Harvey J. Locke concluded in the seminal work *The Family: From Institution to Companionship* that major changes were materializing in American families (Burgess and Locke 1945). The institutional (traditional) form based on culturally prescribed gender roles had been useful in maintaining the order of society in a closed and hierarchical culture. In an open, democratic society, however, the importance of social order was being replaced by an emphasis on the quality of relationships between persons. Marriage was therefore going to be more defined by companionship and assignment of roles through interaction than by prescribed cultural expectations. In subsequent years, every respected textbook on sociology of the family discussed institutional versus companionship marriage, with the assumption that companionship marriage was more fitted to our cultural context. Nevertheless, many Christian communities still emphasize a hierarchical, man-as-head-of-household ordering of the family.

The Traditional Family

How does the traditional model look in modern American society? In traditional marriages the husband is dominant. The husband's position is like the presidency in a democracy; he may delegate certain powers and decision-making, but he has the final responsibility (Scanzoni and Scanzoni 1976). He controls the purse strings, and the wife may have no idea about the family's finances, debts and assets. The roles of husband and wife are based on what is expected in the specific cultural group rather than something worked out through negotiation between the individual spouses. Certain tasks considered "women's work" are not undertaken by men except through kindness or necessity (the wife is ill or pregnant or has increased demands because of her employment outside the home); in this case the husband "helps out." The wife's role is to care for the home and children. The husband's primary role is breadwinner.

The differences between the roles of husband and wife result in different assumptions spouses make as they structure their lives and juggle responsibilities. The wife operates out of a basic philosophy that "if the family does well, I do too," whereas the husband reasons, "If I do well, the family does too" (Scanzoni 1978). The woman is therefore primarily invested in her home and family, and the man in his career and self-development.

In the traditional family, leisure activities tend to be pursued with same-sex friends rather than with one another. Women talk with women; men participate in or watch sports together. Social gatherings find the men congregated separately from the women. Because of their different interests, a husband and wife may have little to talk about together (Peplau 1983).

Traditional marriages have existed in all social classes and taken many different forms. R. H. Turner (1970) identifies three based on the role of the wife, because her role is traditionally pivotal for home and family. In the homemaker role, the wife is an expert in home management and childrearing, spheres in which she influences her husband. In the role of companion, the wife develops her personal attractiveness and grace and her skills as a hostess for her husband and his friends. She is concerned with providing her husband with a haven from the world of employment. In the role of "humanist," the wife is active in her church or community as a volunteer. Often a wife in a traditional marriage will perform all three roles to a greater or lesser extent.

In actuality, many American couples are somewhere between a hierarchical pattern of relating and more egalitarian attitudes, struggling with behavior patterns they learned from the traditional families in which they grew up that do not fit their current family realities. To speak of traditional marriage patterns therefore is to speak about a whole continuum of relationships that are really united only by an emphasis on order and defined expectations. In the 1980s, Letite Ann Peplau dubbed the modifications of traditional marriage patterns "modern marriage" (Peplau 1983). In modern marriage, the male is still dominant but not as strongly; roles are still specialized but not in all areas; and more responsibility is shared. Togetherness and companionship are often important.

The Egalitarian Family

"Companionship marriage" and "egalitarian marriage" are terms used interchangeably to refer to marriage based on equality of the partners. Spouses are companions to each other and share both power and responsibility. Gender-based role specialization is absent both inside and outside the marriage. M. Young and P. Willmott (1973) have called this phenomenon "symmetrical marriage," because partners match each other rather than complement each other. Partners divide their family work according to the situation and the spouses' needs and abilities rather than according to gender. Both may be employed or only one; they may share a job or both have part-time careers. They may do housekeeping chores together, take turns or divide tasks according to skill and interest. No matter who does what, the critical issues are that partners consider themselves equals, that expectations are worked out together rather than assumed because of gender. Both expect to grow as individuals, whatever that growth may mean for each.

Because each couple must work out their own pattern, this model requires a great deal of interpersonal skill in expressing needs and wishes, understanding the partner and negotiating differences. Issues that are not issues in traditional marriages have to be dealt with. Who gets up with the baby at 2:00 a.m.? Who stays home from work to let the plumber in? Who addresses Christmas cards? It is virtually impossible to keep things in perfect balance, to keep things "equal."

A favorite *Sesame Street* episode when my children were small involved Bert eyeing Ernie's piece of pie. Bert complains that his piece is smaller than Ernie's, so Ernie eats part of his to make them equal. Then Bert's is larger, so Ernie takes a bite of Bert's to even things up. On it goes, until two empty plates and Bert's empty stomach remain. It is hard enough to cut even pieces of pie; to divide a constantly changing list of household responsibilities and such amorphous concepts as power or dominance, or even time, into equal units is virtually impossible (Bernard 1982).

Who Does the Housework?
For this reason, although many couples are egalitarian in attitude, truly egalitarian relationships are rarely achieved. In fact, relationships that are devoid of gender-based stereotypes appear to be extremely difficult to establish. Research concerning household responsibilities show that in two-career marriages, wives still spend *at least* twice as much time on household chores as husbands, regardless of the women's employment status (Condran and Bode 1982; Demo and Acock 1993; Ferber 1982; Hochschild 1989). A Gallup survey in 1990 with a sample size of 1,234 individuals asked persons who was responsible for doing "all or most" of each of nine common household chores. Men had responsibility for only two of the nine areas. Seventy-four percent of the respondents identified men as the "most likely spouse" to handle minor home repairs, and 63 percent as the one to do yard work. Women were the "most likely spouses" to do the laundry (79 percent), care for children when they are sick (78 percent), care for children on a daily basis (72 percent), clean the house (69 percent), wash the dishes (68 percent) and pay the bills (65 percent; Barna 1993:103).

Cultural variations in companionship marriage have also been discovered in research, suggesting that the egalitarian ideal is more apparent in some groups than others. In the United States, role relationships in African-American families on the whole are far more egalitarian and less gender-related than in white families; and rigid gender-based role prescriptions are most common in middle-class white families, even those who would most emphasize companionship in their marriages (Willie and Greenblatt 1978).

The gendered assignment of roles is not limited to husbands and wives. There are also significant differences in expectations for children based on gender. After the age of five, girls do more household work than their brothers, on the average, and the difference is especially accentuated among older teens. Older boys continue to do about the same amount of work as younger children, but older girls substantially increase their contribution (Goldscheiter and Waite 1991).

Through interviews, Arlie Hochschild (1989) learned that "men's jobs" and "women's jobs" could be identified by three characteristics. First, women do the jobs that must be done daily and have time prescriptions, such as cooking. In contrast, men's jobs are less often daily and do not have specific time requirements: changing the oil in the family car, doing household repairs. Second, women more often do two or three things at one time—cooking, doing laundry, cleaning. By contrast, men's tasks tend to be done one at a time, such as mowing the lawn. Finally, women are the managers of time and motion; they hustle children through their daily routines, manage shopping lists, organize transportation arrangements, repair visits, appointments with the pediatrician. As a consequence, women often become family "tyrants"—pushing people to do their chores and stick with the family schedule.

What is more, women's work is often not simply mechanical; it is often highly interactional and significant in weaving the life of the family. For example, daily cooking and feeding a family involves ongoing construction of family relationships. It involves coordinating persons and bringing the family together, knowing the family schedule and ideally even being able to control it (Devault 1987). The cook has power over potentially the most significant time of the family's life together: the daily shared meal. Thus the feeder of the family often has the responsibility for weaving and preserving a significant aspect of the family's culture. How food is shared, the actual foods that are eaten, and the norms for eating together all communicate to the members the family's identity and values. Family work is the essential labor of life, the activity of nurturing and caring. It is not like other forms of work, because the economic outputs are clearly secondary to the relationships, affection and obligation among family members that can be nurtured through the work itself (Ahlander and Bahr 1995).

As the example of cooking shows, who bears responsibility for family chores may or may not indicate who has less power in a family. Many sociologists and popular opinion makers have assumed that it is more desirable to have someone else in the family do the housework and cook the meals and care for the children than it is to do it oneself, and thus the person who carries the least responsibility for these chores has the most power. Nevertheless, there is power vested in responsibility, as we have seen in the role of family cook. Likewise, the person who cares for children often has the most intimate and enduring relationship with the children as they grow. The person who pays the bills has a much clearer sense of the family's financial status than others. Even housework carries with it the power to determine how *clean* is defined and how the physical furnishings and belongings of the family are ordered.

It is interesting that social sciences studies of housework tend to *assume* that the person bearing these responsibilities have less family power. This is more an indication of the lack of value attached to housework and family maintenance than of the power attached to them.

Traditional Versus Companionship-Based Relationships

A significant amount of research has explored the outcomes of these two ways of structuring power in marriage. The differences have obvious implications for daily family life.

1. Traditional relationships are less overtly conflictual. Decisions are made together in a companionship marriage; by definition, nothing is "given" except the commitment to one another to work things through. The potential for conflict is therefore enormous.

Interpersonal conflict may not be obvious to the observer of a traditional relationship, but it *is* present. Often the power struggles in a traditional marriage take place in nonverbal ways. Anyone who grew up with traditionally oriented parents can usually attest to the fact that wives are not necessarily powerless just because they are not the family heads. Tears, silence and "headaches" may be indirect ways of expressing anger and balancing power differentials. To have power (or powerlessness) prescribed as a legitimate part of one's role is not the same thing as exercising or not exercising power in given situations. The quiet of a traditional marriage, then, should not always be mistaken for harmony. Reviews of the research conducted in the mid-twentieth century found that wives in traditional marriages tended to be significantly more depressed and to suffer more from other mental health disorders than men, working married women and unmarried women (Bernard 1982).

2. Egalitarian relationships are more personally satisfying. Research since the mid-twentieth century has consistently pointed out that couples in companionship relationships are more satisfied with their marriages than those in traditional relationships (see Bean, Curtis and Marcum 1977; Blood and Wolfe 1960; Centers, Raven and Rodrigues 1971; Locke and Karlsson 1952; Michel 1967).

3. Egalitarian relationships are less likely to be violent. Violence is more likely to occur in homes where the husband has all the power and makes all the decisions than in homes where spouses share decision-making. L. Walker (1979) found that spouse abusers and their abused partners typically believe in and live out a traditional model of marriage. In their revealing research, Murray A. Straus, J. Richard Gelles and Suzanne K. Steinmetz found that under 3 percent of wives in egalitarian marriages had been beaten by their husbands in the previous year. In traditional marriages where the husband was dominant, 10.7 percent of wives had been beaten—a rate of violence more than 300 percent higher than for egalitarian marriages (Straus, Gelles and Steinmetz 1980). One explanation for this sobering statistic is that men in hierarchical relationships tie their identity to the submission of their wives. When a wife is not submissive, or at least when he perceives her not to be, he has the need to "show her who's the boss around here." He must not only restore the order of the relationship but also restore his damaged male identity. His identity is linked to the amount of power he wields over others.

    4. Egalitarian relationships are more flexible in the face of crisis. Because roles in traditional relationships are gender defined rather than interpersonally defined, no mechanism enables change when change is necessary. After all, gender is not readily changeable; interpersonal relationships are. When a wife who heretofore has been at home goes to work, a dramatic change must take place in household management. In a traditional marriage, the only response possible is her absorption of the new demands through a delicate juggling act. The husband may "help out," but the responsibility for the home remains hers.

    Other crises experienced by the couple may create even larger demands and add stress to the marriage: the birth of a seriously ill child, the demands of aging parents, the illness or unemployment of a spouse. Partners in egalitarian relationships tackle the crisis by struggling through changes in their patterns of doing things—not a simple matter, but not necessarily relationship-threatening either. In traditional relationships, such a change in patterns is a challenge to the very contract on which the relationship was formulated.

From Companionship to Partnership

In American culture, the goal of the companionship model for family life is the individual growth and self-actualization of the partners and the growth and enrichment of the family relationship. Particularly in marital relationships, there is major emphasis on achieving deeper intimacy with one another—the process is the goal. Wife and husband are to develop their gifts as individuals in the larger world outside the marriage and to use this greater maturity to deepen the intimacy and sharing of the marriage. The marriage has no major function except to meet the spouses' interpersonal needs and enable the individuals to accomplish their own tasks and personal goals. Other functions of marriage, even procreation, are less significant than the emotional nurture of the partners.

The major obstacle to the success of companionship, therefore, is often identified as a lack of interpersonal skill (Mace 1982). It is through our interpersonal relating, after all, that intimacy develops. As important as interpersonal skills are, however, they do not guarantee "success" in marriage. Skillful communication cannot give meaning to life or provide fulfillment. It is here that companionship marriage and *partnership marriage,* a model of marriage for Christians, most clearly diverge.

The goal of partnership marriage is the pursuit of the purposes of the marriage as the couple has identified them in the will of God. Those purposes may include nurture of children or others, hospitality and service to community, care for the physical world, or a combination of these and other shared purposes. Partnership marriage does not focus on itself, an earthly institution, but strives to transcend itself. In the companionship model, authority and responsibility are to be divided; in partnership, they may take many different shapes depending on the context and tasks of the couple. Structure, decision-making processes and prominence of careers cannot be prescribed by the partnership model. It proposes no particular way of doing things but instead focuses on a vision and a purpose that go beyond the marriage itself.

The difference between companionship and partnership. Companionship marriage is like *Roberts' Rules of Order;* the concern is how to do things so that each is treated fairly and equitably. It coordinates the partners' activity but says nothing about the purpose of the activity. The purpose of relating, however, is central to partnership marriage. The partnership transcends rules and patterns of working together.

In summary, *companionship marriage is organized by the process of power distribution; partnership marriage is organized by the relationship's purpose.* Companionship marriage is primarily a focus on structure and process; partnership marriage is primarily a focus on the content and intention of marriage. Yet companionship is prerequisite to partnership. Partnership can develop only from a base of equality between persons.

Equality must be the basis from which partnership can grow. A Christian wife finds herself trying to act on her faith by being lovingly submissive and serving—

doing the dishes or laundry or whatever else has been the expectation; but she wants to do these tasks as an act of love, not simply because it is her job. All the while, however, she is seething inside, or depressed, because her service is taken for granted, expected of her as a wife. Occasionally she may erupt, angry at her partner for what appears to be his complacency in the face of her self-giving service. She may then regard her anger as a sign of how far she is from achieving the will of God, which deepens her frustration as she attempts once again to be more loving. It is only when the couple can break out of the old role expectations that she can choose submission. One cannot *choose* to submit when no other choice is available.

Martha and Matt had been married for five years and both had been pursuing their own careers when they had their first child. Martha chose to work only part time while their son Tim was an infant, and their daughter Susan was born when Tim was two years old. During the years they were both working full time, Matt and Martha had fairly evenly divided the housework and other home responsibilities, although Martha did most of the cooking. After the birth of the children, Martha began taking on more of the housework responsibilities, since she was there to do it.

During the five years she worked part time, this pattern worked well; but Martha began to feel rising resentment. Jobs she and Matt had once shared had become her responsibility; even parenting the children seemed to be more her responsibility than Matt's. He was always eager to help out, and she appreciated his pitching in on the dishes or giving the children baths or reading stories. But why was she always saying "thank you" when he did things that he ought to be doing anyway? She was firm in her desire to be Christlike in her relationship with her family; she wanted to be loving and to place the needs of her husband and family foremost, as she believed was important.

It was only as they sorted through their expectations that Matt and Martha began to understand what was happening to them. Martha could not change her feelings about caring for her family simply by chiding herself that she needed to do what she was doing in love. Nor could Matt communicate his appreciation for her by "helping out." It took a major reordering of responsibilities to establish a mutually felt equality from which they could serve one another and work together in their mutual parenting task. They had to work out in their own lives the understanding that love means acceptance of the other—and oneself—as an equal, with neither partner being more important despite society's greater valuing of the income earner.

What characterized the process of change for this young couple was not necessarily a division of chores on a more equitable basis so that all was equal, nor even a modification of this ideal. Instead it was the recognition that they were not simply roommates who loved one another while each pursued their own goals and dreams. They committed themselves to a joint task—parenting—and worked toward a relationship that furthered their work on that task and other tasks together. They became partners; mutual respect and equality were implicit in their decisions and in the approaches to change that they chose.

The basis of partnership marriage is the mutual respect, equality and intimacy found in companionship marriage, but it involves still more. It is a partnership in a joint calling from God. The egalitarian relationship is a cultural pattern leading couples toward the vision of partnership in the Bible. It provides a starting point and makes partnership a possibility. When families reach that point, they can put away the scales that measure how much power and responsibility each has and how fair and equal family roles are. The *ultimate* goal is not order, nor equality, but fulfilling the purpose of family relationships intended by God for each couple. Hierarchical and companionship patterns are concerned with the structure (roles and power relationship) and the processes (intimacy and conflict management) of families. The ideal of partnership addresses the overarching purpose of the family and thus transcends concerns about roles even while assuming equality.

Development from companionship to partnership. In many ways, moving from companionship to partnership is like the moral growth of a child. During the elementary school years, fairness becomes the child's criterion for "right." If another got two pieces of candy, then I should too. How many times does the parent of an eight-year-old hear "But that's not fair!" Most companionship marriages—or hierarchical marriages becoming companionship-oriented—begin here, with a sense of the injustice of traditional gender roles. The objective is to even things up. This concern for fairness is actually a process of defining one's self through which the child learns that both self and others are persons with worth. The child obtains "identity." A similar process occurs in marriage. The companionship marriage has in view fairness, equity and identity.

From the development of self-identity and worth the child is able to move beyond ensuring fairness and into maturity. Maturity comes when persons are ready to use themselves in some purpose larger than themselves—a career, a social change effort, the care of others. When one has experienced justice and has learned to deal justly with others as persons as valuable as oneself, one can give oneself over to a cause. Similarly, when couples have experienced justice and equality in their relating with one another, they can give themselves over to goals larger than treating one another equally and furthering one another's personal growth. Then companionship can become partnership, because role structures do not matter. Wife may cook and husband may mow the lawn, but these activities have an entirely different meaning than they do in the hierarchical relationship.

IMPLICATIONS FOR FAMILY MINISTRY

Theorists of human relationships have identified two basic patterns of interaction, based on equality and difference (Watzlawick, Beavin and Jackson 1967). Equality is the basis for symmetrical relating: partners focus on their alikeness and emphasize sharing. On the other hand, difference is the basis for complementary relationships: one partner is more powerful than the other. Complementary relationships are characterized by one partner caring for or being responsible for the other. We identify symmetrical partners as "two peas in a pod"; complementary partners are Jack Sprat and his fat wife—"opposites attract." The results of these two kinds of relating are quite different. Symmetrical relating often results in conflict and change; complementary relating results in less intense interaction and stability.

Traditional marriage emphasizes complementary relating, and companionship marriage emphasizes symmetrical relating. It is apparent, however, that neither pattern alone is ideal, and only rare relationships would be wholly characterized by one or the other. In most relationships there are areas in which one partner exercises primary responsibility and "cares for" the spouse (complementary relating) and areas in which they are equal companions, working together and tackling differences (symmetrical relating). Relationships that become stuck in a consistently symmetrical pattern risk flying apart when changes occur too rapidly or when conflict is too intense. Relationships that are stuck in a consistently complementary pattern at best tend to be boring and distant and at worst may disintegrate when the same patterns of relating do not adapt to the changing needs of the partners and their tasks.

Couple relationships, of course, are not the only relationships characterized by these patterns of power distribution. Parenting begins in a highly complementary pattern that becomes more and more balanced by symmetrical power over time; it may shift back toward complementarity as the parent ages, becomes frail and is cared for by the child. Sibling and other family relationships too are based on some balance between the two patterns of power distribution.

Working out the dance of complementary and symmetrical relating, of power and submission, and of equality takes time. And it takes place best in a supportive community in which families can see models of growth into family partners with a life purpose for which they were created and brought together. Here are some suggestions for helping congregations be that kind of community.

☐ The biblical texts concerning power and submission and men and women are difficult to understand without the historical/cultural context of the authors. Christian education and sermons that give families this context and that teach and apply these texts to marriage and other family relationships can be enormously helpful to family members working out for themselves what it means to be Christian.

☐ Congregations need to be communities that not only talk about but also *model* egalitarian, consensus-building approaches to life together. Congregations can teach families how to make decisions, how to share the work and how to work through conflict by how they do these things as a community of faith. When we use power to override one another, we are essentially modeling that whoever has the most power can control. When we instead work harder at building consensus and at including everyone in decision-making, we model partnership for family life.

☐ If marriage and family life has a *purpose* beyond the meeting of family members' needs, families can benefit from programs that help them to identify and live out those purposes.

Chapter 7

Family Identity

P EOPLE ARE KNOWN BY THEIR NAMES, AND NAMES IDENTIFY PEOPLE as members of families. We thus carry our families with us as significant parts of our personal identity wherever we go and are called by name. Although others may not understand the meaning of that identity, it grounds us in our own minds as members of a particular family, even when we are far from them or anyone who knows them. Family is thus a very important part of how we are known as individuals and, perhaps most important, how we know ourselves.

The importance of family identity carried in the name is illustrated in the considerable thought and energy people often give today to the changing of names with a change of marital status. Does a woman keep the name of her family of origin, or does she hyphenate her last name and add her husband's family name, or does she simply take her husband's last name and treat her family name as a "middle" name—or drop it altogether? If she takes his full name and then is widowed, does she continue to be known by his name? If she takes his last name and they divorce, does she keep his name or change her name back to her family-of-origin name?

I could continue to list issues of identity presented by names, including those of children whose last names differ from their parents'—parents divorced or never married, parents with hyphenated last names, stepparents who want to adopt children and change their names. All these issues have subtle but profound implications for family life in our culture. Those who do not share a name may be family for one another, but that family relationship is less socially recognizable and thus less supported by the community. For example, when a child's last name is not the same as that of the parents, it raises questions about who "belongs" to whom.

Sometimes a name locates a family in a particular cultural or ethnic group—McReynolds, García, Oladipo, Chang. Historically, such cultural identifiers have been so important in American society that persons have changed their family names, or immigration officials have perfunctorily changed them, to bring about better "blending in" to a culture which saw itself as a "melting pot" for diverse ethnic identities. Often Schmidt, for example, became Smith.

But names are not simply cultural identifiers. They also identify us as members of a family group that includes certain other persons. In my own community, it matters if my name attaches me in the minds of others to the mayor, the president of a large company, the church pastor or the town rabble rouser. To a child in school or Sunday school, it matters deeply if the family name communicates the identity of "Sarah's little brother," because that carries certain expectations. This community identification may bring with it certain privileges, or it may bring negative responses from those who are prejudiced by experiences with others in the family. We are expected in some way to be "like" other members of our families. A teacher may register surprise when "Sarah's little brother" proves to be a troublemaker and she was not, or vice versa.

Besides locating us culturally and tying us to particular other persons, names communicate a group identity that overarches the individual members. That group identity is especially salient to family members themselves. To others, the family name Garland may be most significant because of known individual members of that family. But to the Garland family itself, there is something more about "being a Garland." There is a cultural identity *internal* to the family—how this family does things—that is more than the simple cultural/ethnic origins communicated by the name itself. As we saw in chapter four, families develop their own languages and patterns of living together, which are a part of their family identity.

When we alter the ways families live together by helping them develop more constructive patterns for communicating and managing conflict, distributing and managing power, or forming strong attachments with vulnerable family members, we have in essence changed a family's culture and thus, at least to some degree, its identity. The processes of family life are key components of family identity. In addition to *how* we live together, what our life together *means* is a significant aspect of family identity. Families recognize and deepen the meaning of their shared lives through family rituals and family stories.

FAMILY RITUALS

Every family has rituals. Rituals are the habitual ways we do both the everyday and the special tasks of life. Doing things the same way communicates to family members that they belong. Small children, in particular, love rituals; rituals provide security and a sense of meaning and purpose that may be hard to communicate in any other way. Rituals can be as simple as the time supper is eaten each evening, distribution of the morning paper by sections to family members to read over breakfast, or how children and adults prepare for the night's sleep. Family rituals are to family life what rules about punctuation and grammar are to writing. In and of themselves, they may not have much meaning, but they organize life such that the meaning of shared experiences comes through. That meaning may or may not be overtly stated or even recognized.

Many of the norms of hospitality, for example, become ritualized—always offering visitors something to eat or drink, leaving what one is doing to come and greet a guest, serving guests with the family's best dishes, sitting in the living room rather than a more casual family gathering place. These rituals carry multiple meanings. First, they remind the family of the importance of hospitality as a purpose of its life. Second, they also emphasize to family members their own status as "insiders"; guests are treated differently.

A dear, lifelong friend frequently hosts large, wonderful parties for an extended network of church folks and other friends. I always feel special when she sends me on an errand at the last minute, or gives me a kitchen job to do, or perhaps asks me to use a plate that does not match because her good china will not go around for everyone. Her requests communicate to me that I am an "insider," at least a quasi family member.

We can identify a family's rituals most readily during family celebrations. They carry a strong sense that there is a right and a wrong way of doing things. For example, a family that "always" opens Christmas presents on Christmas morning may have strong emotional reactions to the suggestion that they be opened on Christmas Eve instead. A family that shakes hands in greeting may be taken aback by a new son-in-law who greets his new family members with embraces and kisses. Certain foods served at certain times—pancakes on Saturday morning, turkey on Thanksgiving, watermelon on the Fourth of July—carry significance far beyond the nutrition they offer.

Rituals Communicate Identity and Solidarity

Rituals communicate in symbolic ways the family's sense of identity and solidarity. As I experience at my friend's parties, rituals invoke the family's boundaries. The family's identity says who this family *is* and, by implication, also who the family is not. "Who the family is" includes both *membership* and *values*.

My gladness at being sent on errands or assigned to wash pots in the kitchen during my friend's party illustrates the issue of family membership. She treats me like a family member. Membership issues are often most clearly seen at special celebrations. A member's absence, for example, is more keenly felt during a holiday than at other times. Even when a death is far in the past, the holiday season evokes memories of the lost beloved. In the same way, a new family member experiences his or her "newness," an on-the-boundary status in the family, most keenly during holiday seasons. The newly adopted older child or foster child may long intensely for a previous family relationship, or at least may feel and act out of a sense that new family ties are fragile. Being expected to participate in unfamiliar family rituals that can be carried out with little thought by family members with a longer history accentuates the sense of newness, of being not-yet-a-full-member.

Rituals also communicate values. The annual July trek to a hot city park for the family reunion obviously communicates who is and is not family, but it also communicates the value of staying connected. Some family members do not really care about staying connected, but they are saying to themselves and to their children, "It's important to Grandma that we be there; that's why we're going." Thus they emphasize the value of honoring and respecting older family members.

A family's values are communicated in everyday rituals as well. How a family shares meals, the newspaper and the television remote-control device develops elements of ritual. Obviously, through such rituals the distribution of power and role expectations in a family are reaffirmed. In that sense, rituals are "conservative": they conserve the status quo of power and role distributions.

Rituals also change over time, and new rituals are added to reflect changes within the family and its context. A new middle-class family ritual can be observed in video stores on Friday afternoon or evening: families go together to select their videos for the weekend. Video selection and viewing lead to new experiences of getting in touch with one another and sharing opinions, values and meaning (Roberto 1992). This ritual much resembles the family ritual of television watching in the 1960s, when no family had more than one television set and shows could not be video-recorded for viewing at individuals' discretion. Before that, the family gathered around the radio, and before that, for stories or the reading aloud of books.

Channels for a Range of Family Experiences

We often think of traditions and rituals sentimentally. In the Norman Rockwell Thanksgiving dinner scene, the family is gathered and everyone is smiling and feeling close. Family identity, however, includes distance as well as closeness, irritation as well as affection. Family conflicts are ritualized just as expressions of family affection are. A family may experience conflicts as ruts in which they are stuck. Ruts, too, communicate family identity and mark family boundaries, although not necessarily in comfortable ways.

For example, in three decades of marriage to my husband, we have developed certain "pet" marital conflicts that provide ready material for arguments. One of these is what I call the "surface conflict." I like the surfaces of our household—kitchen countertops, tables, bedroom dressers—cleared of what I call clutter. My husband, on the other hand, views such surfaces as functional for holding the contents of pockets and for keeping important papers in view until they can be attended to. When I am stressed by other events, his papers and other "clutter" become especially irritating. At such times I have been known to gather the clutter in stacks and deposit it in one place, such as the middle of his desk. Obviously, that irritates him because of the disruption to his filing system.

These behaviors and the animated conversation that often follows constitute a ritualized way we negotiate for control of our shared living space, an issue that takes on heightened significance when we are stressed (feeling a lack of control) in other areas of life. Although the process and outcome vary, our surface conflict has elements of ritual. Certainly we become infuriated with each other. Yet this conflict also reminds us of our roles as household comanagers and perhaps brings an odd sense of comfort that we have not changed all that much even though the world is changing around us.

The processes of conflict management also develop into rituals. Far more typical than Rockwell's idealized family at its Thanksgiving feast is a family gathered around a meal and engaged in an argument. Research based on audiotaped and videotaped family dinners shows that American family meals range in length from fifteen minutes to more than an hour and include an average of 3.3 conflict episodes per meal. There is a roughly even split between parents and children in the initiation of family conflicts (Vuchinich 1987). The family dinner, then, provides structure for the family not only to share conversation and information but also to air conflict. Of course, how successful the family is in resolving those conflicts is another matter.

Continuity That Can Transcend Changes

The marking of the boundaries of a family's life is particularly important during significant transitions. In many ways, rituals provide comfort to the family by reminding them of who they are. Young adults off for the first time to college or career want the household menus, the furniture arrangement and their own space to remain just as they left them. When change is swirling all about a family, there is great comfort in having the same foods we have always had, or hearing the familiar phrases and cadences of the family's mealtime prayer.

The reinforcement of family identity that rituals provide is also especially significant in a social context that is indifferent or even hostile, as in a move to a new community. Families may work hard to maintain their traditional ways, traveling to inconvenient markets to purchase ingredients for ethnic dishes and weathering considerable conflict with growing children over cultural values.

Rituals do change, however, albeit perhaps more gradually and often with more overt protest than other aspects of a family's life. Modifying and adding rituals are ways of folding the new into the old. The blending family or the new couple that combines two sets of holiday rituals, for example, is communicating to itself, "We are making something new but not leaving behind the histories we bring to this relationship." The adopted child who is encouraged to start a new family ritual is being given the message, "You are a part of this family too."

James Fowler has pointed out that family boundaries need to have the ability both to open and to close (Fowler 1991). They are like windows: Windows are useless when they are stuck either in an open position or in a closed position. The value of a window is in its ability to be shut during inclement weather but opened when fresh air is needed. Rituals, similarly, need to be "closed" when they provide protection to the family's solidarity and identity, but "opened" when newness needs to be incorporated into the family.

Revealing Transcendent Meaning in Daily Experiences

Through everyday experiences—eating together, greeting one another, talking through the day's events around the supper table—family members may glimpse ways in which family life transcends the routine and partakes of the sacred. Such transcendence, often experienced at odd moments, comes in our recognition that there is more to what we are doing than the overt acts themselves. In the routine of a goodbye kiss, a family member may have a flash of recognition of the ritual's meaning: that return is never guaranteed and thus this moment is as precious as it is routine. Or the person may sense that the trust in one another to keep returning is a covenant gift. Even when the "kiss is just a kiss," the transcendent is there, a part of the underlying form and substance of family life.

FAMILY STORIES

A house is a place furnished by furniture.
A home is a place furnished by memories.

We remember and celebrate who we are by telling *family stories* that usually get "better"—both more polished and more embellished—with each telling. Family stories are often told during ritualized occasions—at family reunions, during holidays, at birthday or graduation celebrations, on the annual family vacation. Family stories provide us with our own shared history, remind us of moments of joy and sorrow, and communicate "We are family to one another."

"Remember the time we went camping and it poured rain for two days?" The rest of the story may not even be told; everyone laughs together in memory. Children need and want to be told the special stories that surround their birth, the funny things they did as infants and toddlers, their parents' feelings about them. These stories say, "Your coming into this family was very significant. You are a very important member."

Family Stories Belong to the Family

A family story is usually not new information for the hearers. Everyone in the family knows the story, and that is just the point. The story belongs to the family.

If the story is being told for the first time to someone, it is often because that person is being initiated as a new family member, or because a family member wants the "outsider" to understand some characteristic of the family that can be illustrated best with this story. A family is a "community of memory." A family is more than a current group of people; it is a continued story, with earlier and later chapters. "To be a family is to keep memories alive" (Smedes 1990:249).

Telling a family story is like reading the same book to a small child for the fiftieth time. She corrects you when you miss a word or an inflection. Of course she knows the story; she listens not to learn something new but to be comforted and enjoy the familiar, and to confirm her relationship with you. Often during the telling of a family story, family members jump in and tell the story together. It is easy to distinguish a story that is truly a "family story"; its telling is quite different from an individual's story *about* the family that has no real family meaning. When a family story is being told, family members are clearly listening and engaged and sometimes contributing verbally or nonverbally; the story has meaning for them. An individual's story may be met instead with detached interest, boredom or polite disengagement. Although the story may have meaning for the teller and may even be interesting to the family, it is not a *meaningful family story*.

Stories are remembered not because they are entertaining, although they may be. They endure because they speak about things that matter. Facts can be fashioned into a multitude of meanings, of course, and the congruence of meaning families give their shared stories points to the significance of the stories' meaning for them as a collective. When family stories no longer serve that purpose, they disappear (Stone 1988).

As families live in and through all the phases and processes of family life, they contribute to the ongoing development of their life story. Stories include the ups and downs of family life. The most significant stories may be those that surround the addition of family members. Both children and adults want to hear and tell again and again of the day a child was born or adopted, or the first meeting of a couple and their falling in love. In our culture, family pictures are significant artifacts of those stories. They tell us who we were then and who we are now. The family story, too, figures prominently as a boundary marker. Birth and wedding stories mark new family relationships.

Using the Past to Tell About the Present

Stories are not simply "facts" about past events, as though there were a file of family minutes that could be retrieved for review. Instead stories are selected and told because they relate to a present concern or event. Often stories take on nuances and emphases, and sometimes even new elements that heighten their meaning for the current teller and hearers.

Every family has stories that have been embellished into powerful myths about who the family was and, by implication, who the family is. When family members argue about what "really happened," it is an argument about facts, but it is also usually an argument about meaning. For example, a mother telling her child the story about her labor and delivery may exaggerate the length of the labor and the danger of the delivery, with the story climax being her joy at first seeing the new baby. The meaning of the story may be "You've been wonderfully troublesome since the beginning, and I still delight in you"; or "I've suffered for you, and you were worth it." If another family member corrects the mother by saying, "Now honey, you were in labor twelve hours, not eighteen," the conflict is probably significant because the meaning of the story has been discounted, not because the fact has been corrected.

New Story Meanings Evolve over Time

Stories take on new meaning for new times in a family's life. That is the value of family stories; they are richly layered, with multiple meanings all directly related to *us*, the family. An example from the life of my own family, which I recounted in an earlier chapter, has been dubbed "The Night Mom Lost John." Here it is again, told here as a family story rather than a factual account.

My husband was out of town. It was a cool weekday evening in early November, and the schedule was a typical middle-class family headache. John, age eleven, had soccer practice at a field a twenty-five-minute-drive away. Sarah, age thirteen, had a violin lesson about twenty minutes from John's soccer field, and I needed to make a quick visit to a client family in their home not far from Sarah's music school. I quickly strategized with the children. I would drop John at soccer practice first. He would probably finish before I could get back, but I told him to walk to the nearby store, which had a snack bar, get something to eat and wait for me there. I would drop Sarah at her lesson, visit the client family, come back to pick up Sarah and then circle back for John. It should work.

An hour later, when I went to the grocery-store snack bar to pick up John, he was not there. Sarah and I searched the store, then drove the half-block to the soccer field. John was nowhere. I went back to the store and had him paged. I alerted the store clerks to watch out for him, and left Sarah in the storefront to wait in case he showed up. I quickly checked a couple of other nearby stores, but he was not there either. Then I drove four blocks to the home of one of John's friends, to see if he might have walked home with his friend. The friend's father immediately pulled on his coat and went to walk the streets around the soccer field.

By now John had been missing more than an hour; I hurried back to the store. Learning that he was still not there, I called the police. The police responded quickly. I gave them John's description and told what he was wearing—blue soccer shorts and a T-shirt. It was now dark, and the evening had turned cold. I was sobbing uncontrollably, frightened and overwhelmed with guilt for not planning more carefully and being more protective. Sarah was trying to comfort me as we sat in our car in the dark parking lot, patting me and saying, "It's not your fault, Momma; he's just stupid."

The police organized search teams and concentrated on the nearby railroad track; a child had been abducted from our city just the week before. A search helicopter was brought in and began to comb the area with spotlights. A colleague from work happened into the parking lot, saw me and two police cars, and hurried over. I wept on his shoulder, and he waited with me. He slipped away for a moment and made a phone call to his wife. She in turn called my colleagues and my church. Word then spread quickly. Within thirty minutes, several other friends had gathered to wait with me. Prayer chains and groups gathered. I found out later that the soccer coach was contacted by the police to see if he had any information about John, and the coach called the team's parents. They got back in their cars and gathered in the home of one family who had a citizen's band radio, where they listened to the police search and prayed. A nearby store owner brought me a cup of hot cocoa.

Back in the parking lot, the neighbor volunteered to take Sarah home, to wait by the phone should John try to call. Everyone was hoping he would escape from his supposed abductors. AJ, the police bloodhound, was given one of my son's dirty socks from the back seat to sniff. As many families can testify, children often use the back seat as a clothes closet and changing room in their rush from school to sports and music lessons. With the whiff of John's sock, AJ tracked John all over the soccer field and to another store, a discount store a block away.

There was John. When I first began my search, I had gone to that store looking for him, but he had evidently been in the restroom when I hurriedly walked through the store. So there he sat, waiting for me now almost three hours, more and more frightened. He had seen the police cars go by and the search helicopter floodlights. At first he had tried to call home, but that was before Sarah got home. Now it was 10:00 and the store was closing.

The police and AJ brought John to me. After we hugged each other and thanked everyone, John said, "Please, Mom, don't tell anyone what happened." But there was no keeping it a secret, I told him, so he might as well begin to plan a really good story to tell at school the next day. His soccer teammates would know, and they would probably tell others. We went home. Sitting on our front steps in the dark and cold was the minister from our church. He listened to the story and hugged John.

This story first served as a cautionary tale in our family. We need to be careful; just one slip and we will lose one another. It is still a story that makes my throat tighten. It is every parent's nightmare, to make a mistake that puts a child at terrible risk. I also wrote an article about chronic family stress and used this story to illustrate my theory (Garland 1994b).

Over time, however, as I have told the story to others and relived the experience in the telling, the story has taken on other meanings. It is not just a story of stress; it is also a story of how supportive community can be. It shows that community is not always apparent and is not necessarily geographic but becomes activated in crisis. Work colleagues, friends, church members, the church leader sitting on my front porch, parents of my son's teammates, the police, and the kind store manager who brought me hot cocoa sprang into concerted action in less than two hours, each doing what they could do. All these people had activities that they simply dropped to come to my aid. Even though I was out of my own neighborhood, I was quickly surrounded by a community of neighbors. So over time the layers of this story become richer, evolving from "The Night I Lost John" to "The Night I Found Our Community."

Kinds of Family Stories

Stories reveal what a family wants to believe about itself. They say something about the family, about its character, its history and its virtues.

Humorous stories of survival. One genre of family stories is the vacation or holiday disaster. These are usually told and retold with more zest than stories of disaster-free vacations. They include, for us, the Maine vacation with friends when every day was so rainy and foggy that we could see none of the scenery we had driven more than a thousand miles to enjoy. With those same friends we journeyed one very hot August to the Florida Everglades; the climax of that trip was shared seasickness on a miserable boat outing. These stories are important because they say that not only can this family (and friendship) survive adversity, but we can laugh at it and keep on loving each other.

Family founders and heroes. Other family stories are about adventures, awards and good deeds. These stories announce that this is an important family, a smart family or a beautiful family. Some stories are about founders or heroes. For example, researcher Elizabeth Stone recounts a powerful family story from the life of Paulette Berry (Stone 1988). Paulette was eight years old when she was among the first black children to attend a formerly all-white elementary school in Topeka, Kansas, as a result of the 1954 Supreme Court declaration that segregated schools are inherently unequal, the case of *Brown* v. *Board of Education of Topeka.*

> Her grandmother took her and her brother to school that first morning, and on the way Paulette Berry remembers hearing a story she had heard from her grandmother many times before. "She would tell me and my brother about my great-great-grandfather Dodge, who was a slave in Tennessee. He was an organizer, and to make an example of him, they cut his stomach open, just cut it right open. The last they ever saw of him, he was running up the road holding his guts in. He still kept his dignity." (Stone 1988:144-45)

This ancestral slave was a hero the Berry family sought to emulate. The word *guts* is the key to the story. It suggests courage and the power to contain oneself with dignity even when mortally wounded. The story is not a story of safety, or even of survival. It is a story of power and victory transcending life itself, of not being *emotionally* conquered even by the gravest of physical danger. Paulette Berry's great-great-grandfather did not spill his guts; he turned his back on the enemy and held himself together. This powerful image helped an eight-year-old girl cope with virulent racism. Paulette said, "When something came up where they didn't want me and my brother to waver, or where they were afraid we would waver, they'd tell us that story" (Stone 1988:145). If this ancestor could maintain such dignity, the family story communicates, then his descendants can do whatever is required of them.

Cautionary and hardship tales. Other stories are cautionary tales. They tell of the cousin who was badly injured in a motorcycle accident, or the uncle who became an alcoholic.

Finally, families have hardship stories. These are the "I had to walk five miles uphill in two feet of snow every day to go to school" tales. Older family members want the young to hear these stories so they know that families do not survive without hard work. They teach that family does not come easily but is hard won and therefore should be valued (Pipher 1996). Sometimes these stories locate the family in historical events—surviving the Dust Bowl days in Oklahoma during the Depression, the Trail of Tears, the Holocaust, internment camps for Japanese-American families during World War II, or the riots of the 1960s.

WEAVING A HISTORY TOGETHER

The rituals, traditions and stories of family life are most often not the product of deliberate planning; they just happen as a part of living together. Sometimes family rituals need to change. In some families, rituals have become rigid and maintain ways that are no longer useful. Rituals also protect particular balances of authority and power that may need to change with changing circumstances.

In this time of rapid cultural and social change, however, many families experience the need to develop rituals and new traditions in a deliberate way. Other families, particularly those that are depleted by stressful life circumstances or multiple crises, may have lost their sense of identity. Changes outside and inside the family may have disrupted its rituals. One family found that the father's new job in church leadership meant he was away many evenings at the dinner hour. The preschool children were showing signs of distress over their father's absence at a time they had come to expect his presence. So the parents very intentionally reversed their day. The children were always up early, so Dad stayed home with them for breakfast and a couple of hours of family time each morning before going to the office (Briggs and Briggs 1988). It helps families to develop simple, patterned daily rituals that strengthen their cohesion and reaffirm their identity and esteem (Laird 1990).

Family stories need to be told and retold in a context that values a family's history. Children and new adult members need to learn anew the roots of the family, and long-term members confirm their membership and identity and the meaning of their life together in the telling. Sometimes, as with "The Night I Lost John," a family's story needs to be recast, so that its meaning is changed from how a family has failed to a story of family survival.

In many ways, families are constantly re-creating themselves and their world through their changing stories and rituals. The church can help families appreciate the importance of rituals and stories and can give some guidance in developing rituals and stories that carry meaning.

Daily Experiences as the Stuff of Family Traditions

The most significant rituals and traditions are not holiday experiences, as important as these may be, but the daily and weekly occasions that mark our lives. We often think back with nostalgia to the experiences that were made special simply because they were common and repeated and gave meaningful punctuation to our days. Making school lunches, hugging in greeting and farewell, walking the dog, watching the news and talking over events together—any act can become a family ritual. A ritual sanctifies ordinary time, pointing to the sacred that underlies everyday experiences (Pipher 1996).

Mealtime. Throughout the Bible, sharing a meal has special significance. Much more happens than the satisfaction of physical hunger. Intimacy develops between people who share food together. Jesus used his last meal with his disciples to symbolize his continuing relationship with them, even after his death. He fed them after his resurrection, and with the bread and fish came an opportunity to talk together (Jn 21:9-23). It was only when Jesus fed the two disciples in Emmaus that they finally recognized him—"their eyes were opened" (Lk 24:30-31).

Eating together has great significance in the lives of many families. For many, it is the only time the family assembles in one place. If there is no time for family worship, there is often at least time for prayer before the food is shared. This prayer often follows a familiar formula, or it may be sung, the joining of voices symbolizing the union of the family.

Many families find it difficult to make time to eat together. Breakfast may be a catch-as-catch-can affair on the way out the door, and lunches are usually eaten at work or at school. The only shared meal for many families is the evening meal. Even then, schedules conflict: someone is at ball practice, or an adult has to work. Even if the family does assemble, the television may be turned on for the evening news, or someone has their nose in the newspaper, or the phone rings just after the "amen" of the blessing. Or perhaps the neighborhood children are waiting impatiently in the backyard for Joey to come back and join them, so he bolts his supper down and is gone.

If families choose to make mealtime a shared priority, it can be an enriching experience, a time to nourish not only physical bodies but also the family body. To share a meal says that we care for one another, that we want to have our "eyes opened" (Lk. 24:31) to know one another anew. Enabling this to happen takes considerable planning, compromise and continuing adjustment. Here are some suggestions that can be shared with families.

□ *Make a realistic plan.* To plan a family dinner every night may be unrealistic. Chart out the schedule of each member and look for what can be juggled and rearranged so that the family has a shared time. Set a specific time, even though that time may be different on Tuesday than it is on Thursday. Begin with realistic goals.

□ *Agree on rules for family dinners.* Is this a time to talk about the day's activities? to plan joint activities? to negotiate who has the car when? to handle problems? Decide what you as a family want for that time—then stick to it. My husband and I were employed by the same institution during the years our children were in our home. We found it tempting to talk about work—a conversation that excluded (and bored) our children and did not help us to put boundaries between work and home. We made a rule that we would not talk about work at dinnertime. We often slipped, but the children were excellent monitors and let us know when we had violated the rule.

□ *Mark the beginning of the meal.* Many families begin with prayer. Recited or sung prayers can include everyone. Or one person can lead in prayer, or there can be a time of short prayers by everyone. Be sure that it is a meaningful time for everyone. You have not accomplished your purpose if a family member is miserably and hungrily eyeing the mashed potatoes during a twenty-minute devotional reading.

□ *Set a reasonable time during which everyone agrees to stay at the table, regardless of when they finish eating.* This eliminates the rush to get back to other activities.

□ *Eliminate distractions.* Turn the television off, take the phone off the hook or turn on the answering machine, ask the teenager to take the headphones off. On special occasions, mealtime can be planned to coincide with a favorite television show to be watched together. On a regular basis, however, VCRs are wonderful inventions; tape the news and watch it later, not during supper.

□ *Use small touches to make dinner together special.* A lighted candle, a fresh flower from the yard, a table set with the good dishes says to your family, "We are special. We don't have to have guests to make eating together a special event."

☐ *Expect problems and conflict; they are a part of living together.* As noted earlier, family mealtimes are frequently characterized by conflict—an average of more than three per meal, to be exact. There may be times that mealtime can be cordoned off from ongoing conflicts and problem-solving, especially "special meals." On the other hand, since conflict and problem-solving are so much a part of family process, and mealtime is often one of the few times a family is together, it is unreasonable to expect total protection of this time from family conflict. Instead, attempt to live the rule that positive interchanges need to outnumber negative interchanges by five to one. If mealtime is regularly consumed by conflict, it may be a sign that the family does not have enough time together and all the conflict is being channeled into this time.

Television. Family television viewing also figures into some family's rituals and traditions in meaningful ways. I remember sprawling on the floor with my sister and watching shows like *I Love Lucy* and *The Andy Griffith Show* while my parents sat on the couch behind us. I can still hear the sound of my father's laughter. My husband and I think back nostalgically to the first year of our marriage, when we lived in the genteel poverty of students. The highlight of the week was Friday night, when we bought carryout fried chicken and took it to our apartment to share while we watched *Fright Night*—old scary movies—on television.

Television can actually be good for family life, depending of course on how much and what is watched, and whether it is shared. One researcher found that talking coincided with 21 percent of television viewing (Daly 1996:78). Watching television together may give the family a way to relax and laugh and talk. Choosing what to watch together, and developing rules about what and how much family members are allowed to watch alone are not only about what we do and do not want our family exposed to but also, and perhaps even more important, what we want our family to weave into its traditions and memories about life together.

Shared recreation. Families today must be vigilant and creative in making and protecting time for rest and fun together. Many families put family time on the calendar so that other events and activities are not allowed to take precedence. Couples may schedule a "date night" on a regular basis. Some families schedule a Saturday or an evening for family time and allow nothing to interfere. Of course, this may sometimes generate interpersonal conflict—an adult believes a work assignment must take priority, or children have something to do that, from their perspective, would be a lot more fun.

Shared work. As important as shared recreational times are, times to do work together may be even more significant and are especially important for children. As much as children may gripe about chores, for example, they need the sense of belonging that comes from being contributing members of the family. Feeling competent and knowing that others depend on them teaches responsibility and significance.

Teaching children to do family chores or including them in adult work takes time. It is much easier to whip through preparing a meal oneself than it is to include a child in the preparation. Children also are busy and tired, and their complaints about not having time to help are often accurate. Consequently, parents often do not involve their children in the work of family living—cleaning house, cooking, washing dishes, doing laundry, grocery shopping and so on. In fact, children of parents who work outside the home are *less* likely to help with household work than children of a full-time homemaker (Cogle and Tasker 1982). Parents who do include their children in chores do so primarily in order to teach responsibility (White and Brinkerhoof 1987).

Children do not need to be swamped with housework any more than adults do. They need time to play, to do homework, to be with friends. But they also need time to participate as productive members of the family. Their responsibilities can be structured as time to share with one another and with parents. Getting the job done *together* takes on importance. The seven-year-old standing on a stool washing dishes while Dad brings them to him from the table feels like— and is—an important member of the family. He and Dad may have a chance to talk that they might otherwise not have taken.

Responsibilities need to fit the age and capabilities of the child. Even a three-year-old can match socks while Mom folds laundry, or can help stir ingredients in a bowl. Giving a child responsibility expresses the adult's confidence in the child. It says, "I know you can do this."

In the same way, adults can share in their children's work. Developing shared interests can demonstrate support and esteem. This may be as simple as carefully going over papers from school. Or it may mean developing a shared hobby, or learning together about a topic of shared interest for a child's science project.

Of course, adults too need to work with one another as family. Making contributions to the family's life together is important for *every* member. Older adults who have physical limitations or a degree of dementia can also be included in meaningful ways in different aspects of the family's work.

The greater the time demands on a family, the greater the temptation and often necessity of dividing up the list of responsibilities so that each takes care of a separate list—you fold the clothes while I cut the lawn; you run the kids to soccer practice while I go to the grocery store. Families often need to think carefully about what each needs to do separately in order to manage everything that must be done, and what they can name a "family chore" to be done together. Housecleaning, yardwork and cooking are regular responsibilities that lend themselves to cooperative effort.

Finally, families can and need to share responsibilities for ministry beyond their own boundaries. As important as caring for one another is, families also need to be about the work of caring for neighbors and caring for God's created world. Even small children experience what it means to live the demands of the Christian faith by watching their parents and by being included in ministry themselves. Such ministry might include

☐ supporting a mission activity financially, or preparing simple meals so that the saved money can be sent to hunger relief

☐ including an elderly, isolated neighbor or friend of a grandparent in family outings or festivities

☐ participating in ecology organizations, recycling waste products, participating in a neighborhood or park cleanup effort

☐ forming a caring relationship with a family with special needs

☐ regularly setting an extra place at the table and inviting a child's friend, a newcomer to the community, a lonely college student or any neighbor to share a meal.

When a family works together and people have opportunity to relate to one another around their shared responsibility, it has a different way of being together from verbal discussion and problem-solving. Sometimes the work provides opportunity for some of the most profoundly meaningful conversation in family life. Even when the conversation is just chat, a subtle but significant reorientation and re-creation of family relationships takes place in the shared work. Old conflicts probably do not get resolved, but they tend to take on a little less significance, or at least are put into the context of the whole relationship.

Marking Special Events

In the press of hectic schedules, many families are tempted to skip over holidays and potentially special events. In some American subcultures such as my own, work takes precedence over celebration, and indeed a celebration feels like just one more chore to be checked off. Someone must bake or decorate the birthday cake, or at least order and pick up one from the bakery. Wrapping a present and hanging decorations become items on the to-do list. A holiday may almost be dreaded because other work will pile up and catching up will be hard. Families with this constellation of values often need to be challenged to keep holidays and celebrate.

Other subcultures have rich traditions of setting time aside for celebration. Celebrations are welcomed because they are perceived as giving respite from work rather than adding to it. Often these families need no help in making opportunity to celebrate.

In general, because of the predominance of the work ethic and individualism of mainline American culture, many families are rather poor in meaningful rituals. American businesses recognize far fewer holidays than in European countries. Both kinds of families may therefore need to be more intentional in celebrating events that are not recognized holidays but are nevertheless special: new driver's license, first tooth, toilet training, an adult's promotion at work, the first day of spring, payday. Parents need to find quiet but meaningful ways to celebrate a child's significant rites of passage that may not be appropriately celebrated with the entire family: the advent of puberty, a girl's first brassiere, a boy's first razor, the conquering of a fear.

Families need to mourn together when mourning is called for. Times that families need to mourn that may not be socially recognized include the death of a pet, a miscarriage, the anniversary of the death of a beloved friend or relative. Funerals for pets are often important, especially for children who are confronting death for the first time. The anniversary of a family member's death can be marked by a candle or an extra chair at the table, and perhaps reminiscences of family events that included the lost member. Flowers can be given to a widow or widower on the wedding anniversary date.

Other periodic unholidays also deserve celebration. Hot cocoa and popcorn can celebrate the first snowfall of the year. One family I know celebrates the advent of summer by taking a hike up a nearby mountain and singing "God Bless America" at the top. Special or particularly loved foods can be used to celebrate a diversity of family events—good grade cards, special awards, even the cleaning of a teenager's room. All of these celebrate our life together; the milestones and half-milestones of life deserve to be marked.

Keeping Family Archives

Organizations often keep archives of historical information—minutes of meetings and all the other records and items that are significant to the organization. Families, too, keep archives—photographs, baby books, the family calendar, old letters and cards, children's artwork, programs and newspaper clippings recounting family members' activities and accomplishments. All of these items say "This is us."

Some families ritualize the keeping of the family archives. On New Year's Day members collect and put the family pictures into albums, reviewing the year past.

Keeping a written or taped record of family stories can also be meaningful. Many older adults welcome younger members' invitation to put their life stories into writing. Tape recorders taken to family reunions can be powerful tools for family story-collecting.

Some families have suffered the loss of family records. A child moved from foster home to foster home before being placed in an adoptive home may be bereft of stories about her childhood, or even baby pictures. A house fire or other natural disaster may mean a loss of all the family photo albums. Refugee families and others who have been homeless or have fled their homes may have also lost tangible records of memories.

Children who have lived in multiple foster homes and other placements can be helped to develop a sense of identity and history by composing a "life book." The social worker helps the child to put together an album of memories, going with the child to take pictures of homes and families and institutions where the child has lived, contacting extended family to seek out stories and photos, recording the events and experiences of the child's life. Families who have lost their tangible memories can be helped to reconstruct their own past using similar processes.

Honoring Daily Rites of Passage

Rites of passage are rituals that mark changes in our lives. In American society, getting a driver's license is a rite of passage from the dependence of childhood to the independence of adulthood. Our life is marked by these rites of passage—going to school for the first time, the first day on a new job, marriage, retirement. One church pastor has a "blessing of the driver" ceremony that recognizes teenagers' new driver's licenses. The pastor leads teenagers and their families in prayers of thanksgiving for the youths' maturity and their families' nurture, and prayers of petition for the new drivers' safety. With this rite of passage, the church recognizes and encourages both teenager and family as their relationship changes, signified by a car key being placed in the teenager's possession for the first time.

In the same way, our days can be marked by small but meaningful rituals that are rites of passage. Coming home and leaving home can be marked by the hug and kiss, the dropping of other activities to talk for a moment with all our attention on one another. A ride in the car back and forth to school can be a special time to talk with a young teen who might rarely sit down and talk elsewhere. With small children—and not so small children—quiet sharing with a parent sitting on the edge of the bed as they settle in for the night, along with prayers said together, is often a special time of communion.

RITUALS OF REDEMPTION

Putting a family back together after a divorce or death resembles putting a city back together after an earthquake has leveled it. It is still the same city, with many, but not all, of the same people. But the way those people organize their life together has changed dramatically. Sometimes family members try to put the structures back, stone by stone, just as they were before, but they find that no matter how hard they try, they cannot. Sometimes they say to themselves, in effect, *Since everything is flattened anyway, we might as well make some changes.* Yet not everyone will agree on what ought to be changed.

One of the hardest parts of losing a family member is the disruption of the family's traditions and rituals. Other family members may not even have been aware these traditions and rituals existed, but they now are conspicuous by their absence. After a marital separation, for example, children may have particular difficulty with the daily rituals. Ears still strain, listening for the front door to open, around the time Dad used to come home from work. Janie has a sick stomach at bedtime every evening; it used to be her special time with Dad, when he would read to her and tuck her in with some whispered words of affection.

Marker events and celebrations also make difficult hurdles. Christmas is a notoriously difficult holiday to endure when a family has lost a member. Of all the holidays, it is the most likely to be full of special family rituals, which now seem empty or "not the same" without the child who has died or the parent who is living elsewhere. Anticipating how hard it will be, families sometimes attempt to do something completely different, hoping to slide through the occasion with as little pain as possible. Birthdays, graduations, family reunions—all of them are painful reminders that the family will never be the same. A new family culture has to be created from what is left.

The addition of a new member who seems to be a "replacement" provides an even more difficult hurdle for children than coping with the loss of a member. Children cope far better with parents' divorce than they do with their remarriage. The remarriage of a parent after the death of a partner may also create as much difficulty for children as the death itself—or more. Perhaps the difficulty comes because the family is no longer rebuilding the "old city"—the family as it was before it was disrupted. Instead an interloper has come in with new architectural plans. Nothing seems stable. Parents may find it particularly hard to be understanding of their children's difficulty when they are themselves swept up in the joy and growth of the new relationship.

Recognizing the loss of rituals and being intentional about creating new structures of meaning for the family can be helpful, particularly when the new structures weave in elements of the old.

IMPLICATIONS FOR FAMILY MINISTRY

Some families have vigorous rituals and stories that ground family members solidly in their identity, rituals and stories that also evolve with the family's needs and purposes over time. Other families have not learned to value rituals and stories and thus have not developed these resources of family identity as fully as they could. Still other families may be so ritualized that they oppress and stifle needed family change, and their stories limit rather than nourish family adaptation and resilience.

Like the processes of family life, these aspects of family life lend themselves to education for Christian living. Families can learn to develop simple, powerful rituals that communicate experientially what it means to be Christian and to belong to one another and to Christ. The congregation can be a place where they learn to tell their stories, and to draw strength for today's living from those stories. And as with the processes of family life, families learn the significance of rituals and stories by participating in the congregation's rituals and stories. The community of faith, too, has powerful rituals and stories that tell us who we are because of who we have been and who we are becoming. During difficult times, the rituals and stories of our life as a people of faith sustain us, just as they sustain families.

Here are some of the ways we can help congregations develop rich rituals and stories that undergird meaningful, joyful life together.

☐ Recognize and live the importance of rituals in our life together as a congregation, and the importance that subtle changes can have. The order of worship and who leads it, the kinds of music, the involvement of all kinds and ages of members, how we greet one another, who sits where are all rituals that tell us who we are and how we are related to one another. These can be subtly modified to bring about more meaningful and inclusive participation in congregational life.

☐ Find ways to tell the story of the congregation's life together on anniversaries or other special days, through the display of pictures and brief accounts of the congregation's history on walls and in church publications, or in storytelling sessions in which church members recount their own history of life in the congregation.

☐ Provide ways families can make congregational activities part of their family rituals. Christmas caroling in family groups is only one example of seasonal ways all kinds of families can participate in worship, service and recreation together. Intentionally including all kinds of families communicates who the congregation is as well as who the families are.

☐ Find ways to bring new families into the congregation through rituals, by teaching them the stories of the congregation and by inviting them to share and listen to family stories that communicate concern to know who they "really" are and who their new community "really" is. The community of faith needs to know not only its own stories but also the stories of its people. The telling of these stories in turn undergirds and strengthens family identity. Encourage families in the congregations to tell their family stories as a way to deepen relationships of understanding in small groups and in times of informal worship.

Chapter 8

The Characteristics
of Strong Families

IN THESE FIRST TWO SECTIONS WE HAVE EXPLORED THE RESEARCH
and theory concerning family development, family processes, the distribution of
power in families, family rituals, and the cultural and sociological context for
family life. None of this exploration has been out of disinterested curiosity; we
are looking for what makes strong families that effectively nurture family members. If we can identify these characteristics, perhaps we can instill them in families through programs and services and the ways we structure our communities.

A set of characteristics of strong families has, in fact, begun to emerge from
the social sciences. An important arena for research in recent decades has been
identifying a core set of characteristics of families that are able to endure the
inevitable crises and stresses of life. This chapter will summarize this research.
First, however, some cautions are in order.

FAMILY STRENGTHS: A CAUTIONARY TALE

In a city near mine, a very dangerous junction of three major highways occurs in a
very congested area. The snarl of roadways includes sharp curves and lanes that
merge with one another without warning, resulting in a high number of traffic

deaths each year. The city attempted to address the problem by installing flashing lights to warn people before they approached the intersection. The police department published a flyer about driving in that area and included suggested driving speeds. They distributed the flyer in driver's education classes and printed it in the local newspaper. Finally, the fire department bought two new ambulances equipped with all the latest technology, so that accident victims could receive quicker and more effective care.

All these attempts to lower traffic fatalities helped, but only marginally. The number of accidents decreased, but it was still high. It seemed that the major outcome was that more people were surviving accidents—though sometimes with serious injuries—rather than being killed. It became clear that the engineering of the intersection would have to be revised before there could be any significant decrease in the number and seriousness of accidents at this dangerous junction. Roads would have to be widened and routes changed to make the curves more gradual.

But the community did not find this proposal as appealing as the other strategies that had been tried. Reengineering the road would be very costly; it would disrupt traffic flow for everyone; and it would take several years to implement. It would not bring any immediate solution to the problem. The community is still undecided, and no action has been taken.

In a time when 50 percent of marriages end in divorce, when increasing numbers of people are not marrying at all, and when the well-being of our children is clearly declining, the dangerous intersection and the community's attempts to respond are a parable for our attempts to build strong families. The warning lights and guidance provided by family-life education programs can certainly help, but they do not tackle the systemic issues in our culture that make family life so hazardous and difficult to navigate well. Crisis intervention and counseling may lower the family "fatality rate" and reduce the permanent emotional (and sometimes physical) injuries that families inflict on their members, but counseling cannot solve the major problems that confront *all* families. If we are really going to help families navigate safely the passages of family life, then we will have to tackle the basic engineering of our social system—the focus on individual freedom and self-actualization without a balancing focus on individual responsibility and commitment to others; the emphasis on privacy and mobility without a balancing emphasis on community and rootedness; the emphasis on individual and corporate profit as the means to a healthy economy without a balancing emphasis on social justice and kindness that contribute to economic and social stability; the investment in technology without a balancing investment in persons and their ecology.

Sigmund Freud and subsequent theorists of mental health and mental illness explained pathology purely in terms of family dysfunction. Mother was controlling or rejecting or smothering; father was distant or authoritarian. Those hurt by this dysfunction needed individual treatment. The problem was in the family, and the consequences were individual pain and pathology.

Of course, theories and theorists of mental health and mental illness are very much products of their society. Just as the community preferred to blame careless driving rather than a dangerous intersection for its traffic accident rates, our society believes that individuals and families are responsible for their own suffering. The problem is located in the family—at least on that point we still agree with Freud. Consequently, bookstore shelves are loaded with paperbacks of popular psychology that blame our families of origin for all our neuroses and interpersonal problems.

This literature has added pressure to already beleaguered families and encouraged more introspection than social action. In effect, we keep buying ambulances and studying our driving techniques. But Mary Pipher warns that the family pathology approach is worse than useless. "One of the reasons our culture is falling apart is that intelligent people are going into the therapy instead of becoming social activists" (Pipher 1996:127). The Freudian approach blames the drivers without fixing the road.

Any discussion of strong families, then, must be placed in this context. We will always need to teach defensive driving, and we will always need to have a few ambulances, no matter how safe we can make the roadways. It will help to understand those who navigate safely and well—the strong families. They have much to teach other families, and even to suggest with regard to how the road should be engineered. Ultimately, however, learning their defensive-driving strategies will not substitute for finding answers to engineering problems.

FACTORS THAT INFLUENCE HOW FAMILY STRENGTH IS DEFINED

Yet another set of cautions is needed before we look at the characteristics of strong families. What makes a family strong depends on several factors: what our definition of "strong" is, what kinds of families are being studied, their experience with stress, and where they are in the developmental life spiral.

What Is Family Strength?

Is a strong family one in which there is no mental illness, no infidelity, no divorce, no problems with the children? Or is a strong family one that copes well with mental illness, with infidelity, with divorce, with problems with the children? Is a strong family one that does not show up on the appointment roster of any counseling center? Or is a strong family one that seeks professional help when it is needed? Is a strong family one that a helping professional determines is "strong," or one that family members themselves say can cope with anything and be stronger for it?

Clearly there is no "right" answer to these questions. Yet almost all family-strengths research has been based on families that have none of the problems listed above, families that have not sought counseling, families that a social scientist has labeled "strong" using observational criteria. Indeed, the families that have been studied *are* strong. But there are also strong families that have problems, that have sought professional help, that feel strong to their members because of what they have endured even though others might call them "broken." In fact, perhaps the characteristics of *these* strong families are even more important for us to study, but studies of these families are much less common.

In 1977 George Vaillant published a longitudinal study of ninety-four white men that had begun when the men were college students in the 1940s (Vaillant 1977). Each of the men had been interviewed in depth and their physical and mental health monitored at the beginning of the study and throughout their lives. The study focused on how the men adapted to life, the factors that contributed to their mental and physical health, and how successful they were in their careers and in their families. Determining how mental health should be evaluated was one of the major challenges of the study. Should it be based on the individual's assessment of self? Or should others make judgments based on observations of the individual? If evaluation was by others, then who should make this judgment? Vaillant points out that terms like *health* and *sickness* are merely useful abstractions.

> On the one hand, imaginary physical illness may lead to real hypochondriacal invalidism. Is such an individual sick or well? On the other hand, as in the case of Teddy Roosevelt's real asthma, John Kennedy's tangible back injury, and Franklin Roosevelt's crippling polio, serious physical illness may contribute to mastery of life. Thus, inner processes can either erase or magnify the effects of external illness. (Vaillant 1977:14)

If defining physical health and illness is so difficult in individuals, then defining family health and strength is an even greater challenge. Determining which families are strong and which are "dysfunctional" is a value judgment that implies some objective set of criteria for evaluating families. But there are no objective criteria that apply to all families. The absence of problems does not necessarily indicate family strength; in fact, the presence of problems may actually contribute to strength. Like asthma, back injury and polio, family troubles—infidelity, problems with children, illness—may be the impetus for developing a family's resilience and creative coping.

Vaillant learned in his study that most of the symptoms we call "mental illness" are actually functional adaptations to emotional or psychic injury. "Most mental illness is more like the red tender swelling around a fracture that immobilizes it so that it may heal and less like the tangible biochemical defect of diabetes" (Vaillant 1977:369). Many forms of anxiety and depression, like blisters and fractures, are the logical outcomes of life experiences.

In the same way, much of what we call family dysfunction is actually the adaptation of families to their life circumstances—the personal histories and experiences members bring with them, the interaction of members, the social and physical context in which they live. Assessing family strength therefore needs to be a complex process that includes not only external observations of families but also the family's internal experiences. Assessment needs to include not only a current look at family functioning but also an in-depth historical examination of a family's experiences over time, a tracing of how they came to be who they are.

What Kinds of Families Are We Studying?

Most of the empirical research concerning what makes for strong families has been conducted with family systems composed of middle-class Euro-American couples in their first marriage, living with their own biological children. Typically, social scientists have identified "strong" families by their reputation in the community, or by exhibition of characteristics considered signs of health in our society, such as children who are successful and happy in school. These families are then compared and contrasted with families who have been defined as "dysfunctional," perhaps because there has been a divorce, or unhappiness leading to requests for social service, or mental illness, or family violence.

Can these research studies be applied to families other than relatively trouble-free Euro-American middle-class suburban families? Are the characteristics that lead to a Euro-American middle-class suburban family's being identified as "strong" and "healthy" the characteristics that a family would need to survive and thrive in an inner-city ghetto or a refugee camp, or to endure the experience of schizophrenia or drug abuse in a teenage child, or to cope with the chronic unemployment of a male adult family member or the dementia of an elderly parent? Are the characteristics of these "strong" families applicable to single-parent families, or blending families, or the families of single adults?

Family characteristics that enable a family to survive and thrive are ecologically, socially and culturally specific. Any list of the internal characteristics of strong families that does not spell out the environmental, cultural and experiential limitations of families from which the list was drawn thus needs to be viewed cautiously. Research indicates that strong families look somewhat different from culture to culture. For example, chapter nine's historical review of African-American family life shows that strong African-American families have strong networks of extended kinship; this has not been found to be a significant characteristic of strong Euro-American families. Social class also seems to be an important variable in defining family strength.

There do seem to be some similarities in strong families in American society that transcend cultural differences (Stinnett and Stinnett 1995), even though the importance of various characteristics may vary among cultural groups. For example, strong networks of extended kinship may be less important to the strength of Euro-American families than to African American families simply because Euro-American families typically do not *have* such strong networks.

What Has Been Their Experience with Stress?

Family scientists have assumed that a decline in family functioning is inevitable in the face of stress. Studies of family stress have been directed at determining how deep and how long the decline might be and what is involved in recovery. Recent research has demonstrated, however, that family functioning can remain constant or even improve in response to severely stressful experiences (Burr and Klein 1994). Families, then, may become stronger not only as a consequence of coming out on the other side of stressful experiences, but even during the time in which they are attempting to cope. Studies of strong families therefore need to examine the experiences of families that are enduring or have endured a variety of stressful experiences, not just families that have been protected from such experiences.

Some interesting parallels can be drawn to the study of children who grow up in adverse circumstances and nevertheless become successful adults. These children were physically abused, lived with a parent with chronic mental illness, struggled with learning disabilities, or lived in debilitating poverty (Anthony and Cohler 1987; Fisher et al. 1987; Garbarino 1979; Garbarino 1995; Garbarino and Kostelny 1994; Guttman 1989; Lugtig and Fuchs 1992). Those who grow up seemingly unscathed by the adversity they experienced seem to have a number of characteristics in common. These characteristics parallel some of the characteristics of families that survive and grow stronger in the midst of adversity.

First, these children learned to define themselves more by their multiple talents than by their problems. They saw themselves as competent because of what they could do rather than incompetent because of the challenges they faced. Second, they had opportunities to learn about and share with others who had overcome similar adversities. Not only did this give them new ways of thinking about their experience, but seeing others like themselves who had been successful also instilled hope that they too could overcome adversity. Third, talking about the adversity or trauma gave them opportunity to master the experience by putting it into language that communicates surviving and thriving rather than being victimized. The right words can validate the pain and difficulty and also suggest ways to manage more constructively. Finally, they found and used sources of protection from the adversity. Sometimes the buffering came from within the family: a brother or sister or an extended family member protected the child from at least some of the adversity. Or protection came from the surrounding community, which provided meaningful and valued relationships that affirmed and protected the child at least some of the time (Katz 1997).

Brian Raymond grew up in Bangor, Maine, the child of divorced parents. His father is manic-depressive, and his mother was also hospitalized with mental illness when Brian was a sophomore in high school. From that point on, Brian lived on his own. For awhile he took care of his sister, but she was then placed in foster care. His mother, now out of the hospital, moved in with a male friend and occasionally called to check on her children. But she provided inadequate financial support. Many nights there was no food in the apartment. Brian took a parttime job after school to support himself. He never asked for help, but he did spend a lot of time at the home of friends, and he worked hard in school. Good people helped him out in the worst times. His girlfriend's family took him in for short stays and made sure he had food and clothes and gifts on his birthday. A businessman helped him start his computer repair service, with which he supported himself. During his junior year, Brian's best friend, Zach Woodward, asked his parents if Brian could come live with them. The Woodward family converted a small study into a room for Brian. Brian graduated from high school. He wrote the computer program the drafting teacher uses in all his classes. He is planning to go on to college as an engineering major. (Winerip 1998)

Strong families that have overcome stressful circumstances and debilitating crises seem to have had parallel experiences to those of children who, like Brian, survived adversity. These families hold themselves in esteem for who they are and what they have been able to do; they do not define themselves only by their problems. Second, they have had opportunity to talk with others who have had similar experiences. Third, they talk about their experience in ways that encourage their management rather than being overwhelmed. Finally, like Brian, they have been nurtured by a supportive community that affirmed their strength and gave them respite from handling their burdens alone.

A longitudinal study was done of 216 families who faced the terrible adversity of having a member missing. Their husbands and fathers served in the military in the Vietnam War and had been absent for an average of 6.6 years, or remained missing in action (McCubbin and McCubbin 1986). The researchers concluded that the following were important ways by which families survived this ordeal:

1. Families maintained their integrity, doing things to keep the family unit together as a cohesive unit.

2. Families worked to develop and maintain meaningful relationships outside the family unit that gave the family a sense of being valued and appreciated.

3. Families encouraged self-reliance in members by encouraging the development of personal skills and abilities, personal strengths, and independence.

4. Families banded together with other families in the same circumstance to support one another and to advocate for supportive social policies and programs.

5. Families developed a shared understanding, trust, and acceptance of what they were experiencing, usually with the assistance of their spiritual beliefs, thus making the difficulties comprehensible and meaningful (McCubbin and McCubbin 1986:71).

Are these characteristics that all families need to develop to help them cope with everyday stresses, or are they characteristics that emerge in families under the extreme stress of losing a member in wartime? Do families have these characteristics already as part of their repertoire for life, or do these characteristics emerge as families respond to the challenges before them? These questions remain unanswered. However, studying the strengths of families that have survived extreme stress clearly gives important insights into how we might build communities that encourage the development of these strengths—or potential strengths—in all families.

Where Are Families in the Developmental Spiral?
Hamilton McCubbin and his colleagues have studied family types and how they cope with stressful life events, both those stresses that come from inside as well as outside the family (McCubbin et al. 1988). They defined *enduring families* as those that are resilient and able to develop and to survive stress over time. Enduring families they studied appeared to have some characteristics in common, but each also had characteristics that were particular to its stage in the developmental life cycle. The families they studied were nuclear families at various stages of marriage and parenting.

The researchers found that enduring families in the *couple stage* (before the birth of children) adopt an orientation toward one another characterized by loyalty, self-control and independence—"being your own person." They share a belief in the meaningfulness of life and in God. They trust that things will work out in the future, and they believe that their family is basically strong and will endure. They have the skills for developing intimacy, expressing caring, and understanding one another (McCubbin et al. 1988).

The researchers found that enduring families at the *preschool and school-age stage* of the family life cycle are also characterized by a broad range of strengths that share some similarities with those in the "couple stage." These include family loyalty, the ability to depend on one another, a sense of meaningfulness and interest in the family, and a feeling of being in control of their lives. These families emphasize and are able to provide stability and predictability for one another through such means as regular times for shared meals and children's homework, bedtime routines, regular communication with extended family, and members checking in or out with one another as they come and go from home. Celebrations gain importance at this stage, with much attention devoted to children's and spouse's birthdays (McCubbin et al. 1988).

Enduring families at the *adolescent and launching stage* of the family cycle also manifest meaningful patterns of skills and strengths. This stage is marked by the greatest vulnerability families experience, a time in which the percentage of fragile families (those that may fall apart) peaks. Enduring families at this stage underscore loyalty, pride in the family, faith in God, a sense of needing to gain control over what happens in the family, and having similar values and beliefs. Family routines continue to be important, including contact with extended family, consistently sharing meals, predictable discipline, parents' taking time for one another, and regular chores for family members. Family rituals are not as important during this time of transition, however, and may even need to be set aside for a while. These families need to shape their routines and time together according to the immediate demands of family life and the need for greater individualism, particularly for adolescents. These families emphasize working together as a family to solve problems, including children and adolescents in decision-making, not keeping problems to themselves, expressing caring and affection, and trusting and confiding in each other. Family celebrations continue to be important (McCubbin et al. 1988).

Enduring families at the *empty nest and retirement stage* of the family cycle are marked by a strong emphasis on faith in God, believing in shaping their own future, counting on each other in times of need, and the meaningfulness of life. Family routines become important again: regular communication with extended family, regular family meals, checking in and out with one another, and expressions of affection in greeting one another. They emphasize maintaining family traditions (McCubbin et al. 1988).

The researchers point out that in some respects their findings confirm what families have known to be their strengths. Yet in a time of rapid cultural change, there is also surprise in finding the great significance accorded to family routines and stability. Although there are common threads, different family strengths take on added significance at the various stages of family life. What makes for strong families for preschool children differs from what makes for strong families of adolescents. We can also imagine that different kinds of family structures would also vary in those characteristics important to their strength.

THEORETICAL PERSPECTIVES ON FAMILY STRENGTH

A discussion of family strengths would not be complete without at least a brief overview of some of the theoretical issues that have shaped family strengths research. A review of the theoretical literature concerning family strengths reveals considerable debate about the characteristics that make for family strength and whether those characteristics are *linear* or *curvilinear*. In a linear variable, the amount of health or strength in the family increases as the variable increases. For example, the more communication skills a family demonstrates, the stronger it is. Or the more members are able to shift power and responsibility among themselves as their situation changes, the stronger they are.

David Olson's Circumplex Model

By contrast, David Olson and others (Olson 1989) have suggested that there are two major variables for determining family strength and well-being—cohesion and adaptability—and that these variables are *curvilinear*, not linear. A curvilinear variable is one in which the midpoint is the "healthy" point and the extreme ends of the continuum are considered dysfunctional. For example, human body weight is a curvilinear variable; one can weigh too much and one can weigh too little for what is considered "healthy." Health is defined by a fairly broad range in the middle.

According to Olson, cohesion, like body weight, is best for families when there is neither too much nor too little, but families are *moderately* cohesive. Cohesion is family members' connection to one another. Olson calls the most extremely cohesive end of the continuum "enmeshment." In families that are enmeshed with one another, there is little room for independence. Family members cannot think independent thoughts, have little or no privacy, and are overly involved in one another's lives outside the family. At the other end of the continuum is what Olson calls "disengaged" families. These families have so little cohesion that the family barely hangs together. Family members are out of touch and not very involved in one another's lives. As a consequence, family members may not hear or see distress in other members and are thus not responsive to each other's needs.

Enmeshment————————**COHESION**————————Disengagement

Olson also argues that *adaptability* is a curvilinear variable for strong families. Adaptability is the family's ability to change in the face of changing internal and external needs. Most would agree that the extremely unadaptive end of the continuum—what Olson calls "rigid"—is dysfunctional in an environment that is constantly changing. But Olson also argues that extreme adaptability is also dysfunctional. He calls families that are extremely adaptive "chaotic." They are so adaptable that they are unpredictable. They are constantly changing and as a consequence have little or no enduring structure and identity.

Chaos————————————**ADAPTABILITY**————————————Rigidity

Olson posits that strong families change their location along these continuums throughout the family life cycle, although they usually stay within the broad middle range and rarely stray to the extremes. For example, strong families with preschoolers are likely to have leanings toward enmeshment. A preschooler's parents need to be aware of the child's moment-by-moment activities, bodily functions and needs for parental intervention. By contrast, the strong families of young adults are likely to have leanings toward disengagement. Parents may be very unaware of and uninvolved in the moment-by-moment thoughts and actions of the young adult. Olson posits that communication is the family variable that allows change to occur over time on these dimensions. Together, the two dimensions form what Olson has called the "Circumplex Model" (Olson 1986; 1989; 1991; Olson, Russell and Sprenkle 1988).

Questions About the Circumplex Model
Recent research, however, has called into question Olson's curvilinear hypothesis. For example, Richard Cluff and his colleagues have argued that the concept of adaptability really includes two different family dynamics—the ability to change and the maintenance of family stability (Cluff, Hicks and Madsen 1994). A great deal of change may be thrust upon a family by outside forces, and the family may be unable to adapt. Or a family may change, but not in effective ways. Adaptability therefore should be considered *ability to make effective* change, not just change for the sake of change (see also Lee 1988; Walker 1988).

I would suggest, too, that families' contexts call for different kinds of adaptability. Sometimes adaptability is a temporary state of flux and change before the family returns to previous processes and structures. They are *resilient*, or flexible, in that they are able to bend and stretch with demands and then return, or "bounce back," to their former ways of being together. On the other hand, if the demands and stresses are permanent, then the family's adaptation needs to *restructure* its life together. The members bend and reshape themselves. Adaptation can include either or both resilience and restructuring. Sometimes families bounce back, but other times they bounce or bend forward into new ways.

I have always been fascinated by the trees that grow at timberline height in the mountains. They often grow more horizontal—across the ground—than vertical. Their limbs grow down and away from the relentless prevailing winds. They have adapted to their harsh environment and give shelter to other creatures. Like trees growing in austere conditions at high altitudes, some families develop structures and processes that are structurally adaptive to the strong and continuous winds of their lives. They are *structurally adaptive.*

Treeline evergreens are quite different from palm trees, which are also adaptive. Palm trees grow tall, but they have great flexibility that allows them to bend and bounce in tropical storms with high winds that can sharply reverse in direction. Palm trees are *resilient.* Of course, some storms are strong enough to break palm trees, just as treeline evergreens also sometimes succumb to particularly harsh, sustained conditions.

Some circumstances call for families to be palm trees more than evergreens. A tropical storm may be violent, but it is much more time-limited and varied than the almost constant harsh conditions in alpine regions. It also may blow from any and all directions, making any structure vulnerable and flexibility the only adaptation. The death of a family member, economic catastrophe or a teenager's involvement with drugs is like a tropical storm. Chronic poverty, racism and community violence are like alpine winds. One can perhaps bounce back after a hurricane. Bouncing back is impossible, though, if the prevailing winds are continuous. The only adaptation is to structure the family in ways that enable it to survive in its harsh circumstances.

To the extent that this metaphor applies to families, it seems that some analysis of the conditions to which families are adapting is needed. Adaptation includes both being *structurally adaptive* to the environment and being *resilient* in the face of periodic and changing needs. For example, it is one thing to adapt to the needs of a child seriously injured in an automobile accident who will require months of constant care but who will recover. This calls for flexibility, or *resilience.* A parent may have to take a leave of absence from a job, or a grandparent may temporarily move in to help out. This resilience is different, however, from adapting to a child's major head injuries resulting in permanent handicaps that mean she needs constant care for the rest of her life. Here flexibility is still important, but it does not go far enough. This family must *adapt structurally*, finding ways to make permanent changes in response to this new, unrelenting need.

The concept of cohesion also seems to be more complex than the circumplex model suggests. In research with families of adolescents, Michael Farrell and Grace Barnes found that cohesion has a direct linear relationship to positive outcomes for families with adolescents. In other words, "the more cohesive a family, the better the individual family members function, the better the communication between parents and children, the greater the marital consensus, and the better the behavioral outcomes for adolescents" (Farrell and Barnes 1993:129-30). They and others are suggesting that the concept of cohesion needs to be carefully separated from the concept of control.

Other research has supported Farrell and Barnes's conclusions (Barber and Buehler 1996). Cohesion is support, affection, helpfulness and caring among family members. Cohesion is measured on questionnaires by items like "Family members really help and support one another." In contrast, *enmeshment* is defined as family patterns that keep family members from developing independence and a sense of identity apart from the family. Enmeshment is measured on questionnaires by items such as "Family members feel guilty if they want to spend some time alone." Barber and Buehler found no evidence that families can be too cohesive, but they did find that psychologically controlling parental techniques are related positively with youth problems of anxiety, depression and aggression (Barber and Buehler 1996; see also Dundas 1994; Meijer and Oppenheimer 1995). In short, it appears that cohesion and enmeshment are two separate variables, as are adaptability and change. Both cohesion and adaptability are important sources of family strength, and they seem to be linear, not curvilinear.

Much empirical research and theoretical discussion and debate have gone into the development of Olson's model and its critiques, as well as other models of family strength, such as the model Jeanette Beavers and Robert Beavers developed in their study of the families of children with disabilities (Beavers et al. 1986; Beavers 1989) and the model developed by McMaster to study families with members with mental illness (Byles et al. 1988; Fristad 1989; Miller et al. 1985). Although significant debates and disagreements continue, including disagreement over the empirical definitions of some family variables, there does seems to be some basic consensus about what strong families in U.S. society look like. In summary, discussion of the family strengths about which most scholars agree must take place with several cautions:

☐ The most effective strategy for nurturing strength in families is to make social changes to build a society that truly supports family life. Teaching families the knowledge, values and skills that are believed to contribute to strong family life cannot substitute for making social changes.

☐ There is no consensus about what defines family strength, whether it is observed by experts from the outside or felt by family members.

☐ Almost all the research on family strengths has been conducted with middle-class Euro-American nuclear families. We do not know the extent to which this research applies to other kinds of families.

☐ Most of the research on strong families has examined families who have no mental illness, no involvement with the helping professions, no significant problems with children. This implies that strength leads to protection from these experiences. It is not at all clear, however, that family strength is to be found in the absence of difficulties; possibly it is best studied in families that have demonstrated an ability to survive and thrive in difficult circumstances, with help from the professional community and other community resources when necessary.

☐ One of the few areas of agreement in the research is that family strengths demonstrate themselves in different configurations at different times in the life cycle, but that families across the life cycle are more alike than different.

THEMES OF FAMILY STRENGTH

With all these cautions in mind, I have identified themes that appear repeatedly in the research on strong families. I have added some studies and expanded an earlier list developed by Nick and Nancy Stinnett (Stinnett and Stinnett 1995). In many respects, this list summarizes the discussion of earlier chapters. These themes suggest goals for family ministry programs and services.

1. Commitment to one another and a sense of connectedness. A sense of commitment is the foundation of family strength. When family members are committed to one another, they can endure significant challenges. Many people verbalize a commitment to family, but strong families put that commitment into action, making investment of time and energy in family life a priority. Many express their family commitment as an extension of their commitment to God (Barber and Buehler 1996; Curran 1983; Hill 1971; Kersten 1990; Lewis et al. 1976; Stinnett and DeFrain 1985; Stinnett and Stinnett 1995).

2. *Adequate time together, which is spent effectively in meeting family needs, working together and enjoying recreation.* Strong families have established family routines and spend significant amounts of time together. They eat meals together, do household chores together, go camping or engage in other forms of recreation together, attend worship together and celebrate special events (McCubbin et al. 1988; Olson 1989; Stinnett and Stinnett 1995). They recognize that *quality* time is not possible without a significant *quantity* of time together. At the same time, strong families recognize that individuals need to have time alone and time in activities outside of family life (Curran 1983; Daly 1996; Eisenman 1996; Gergen 1991; Israeloff 1989; Lee 1988; Lewis et al. 1976; Olson 1989; Plionis 1990; Stinnett and DeFrain 1985).

3. *Effective communication and conflict management.* John Gottman has demonstrated that strong families know how to complain well and how to listen and work through conflict effectively (Gottman 1994a; 1994b). Strong families also know how to use humor that is kind and nonhurtful as an antidote to stress and as a way of enjoying one another (Wuerffel 1990). Compared to strong families, distressed families are less confident problem solvers, tend to avoid problem-solving attempts and express resignation to the family distress (see also Burr 1990; Curran 1983; Fitzpatrick 1988; Forgatch 1989; Greene 1985; Hawkins and Roberts 1992; James 1991; Lee 1988; Lewis et al. 1976; Rausch et al. 1974; Sabourin, Laporte and Wright 1990; Stanley et al. 1998; Vangelisti and Banski 1993).

4. *Sufficient expression of appreciation and encouragement.* Strong families not only commit themselves to loving one another; they also like each other and let each other know it. They keep the rate of appreciation and expressed positive regard much higher than the rate of complaining and criticism (Gottman 1994a and 1994b; Stanley et al. 1998). As Nick and Nancy Stinnett write: "South African diamond miners move and sift thousands of tons of rock and dirt looking for a few tiny diamonds. Too often we do the opposite in our relationships; we sift through the diamonds eagerly searching for dirt" (Stinnett and Stinnett 1995:172). Strong families keep focused on the diamonds; they value the good and the delightful in each other (Curran 1983; Stinnett and DeFrain 1985).

5. *Agreement on and competence in the fulfillment of the roles and responsibilities of family life.* Strong families have clearly defined roles that are both flexible

and just, as defined in their social context. Increasingly, strong families are egalitarian families, but they also can transcend short-term imbalances in roles and responsibilities in order to work toward family goals (Ahlander and Bahr 1995; Bird and Ross 1993; Curran 1983; Dornbusch and Strober 1988; Erickson 1993; Gerstel and Gross 1987; Gottman 1991; Hill 1988; Hochschild 1989; Rexroat and Shehan 1987; Shamir 1986; Skolnick and Skolnick 1989; Spitze 1988; Stinnett and Stinnett 1995; Suitor and Pillemer 1994; Wright et al. 1992). For example, Gene Brody and his research colleagues (1994) studied ninety African-American youths and their married parents who lived in the rural South. They found that the quality of the father-youth relationship is linked to the amount of support for his role as father that the father receives from the mother. That is, families are stronger when they support one another in the fulfillment of their family roles.

   6. Shared spiritual life that gives meaning and purpose. In studying how families cope with stress, researchers have consistently found that involvement in religious groups and activities and a shared religious worldview that gives meaning and purpose to life experiences are among the most significant characteristics of strong families (Bahr and Bahr 1996; Brody, Stoneman and McCrary 1994; Burr and Klein 1994; Curran 1983; Deveaux 1996; Hatch, James and Schumm 1986; Stinnett and DeFrain 1985).

   7. Involvement in, support from and contribution to their community and larger world. Families can be strong when they have communities of people who care about them, and for whom they can care in return. The ability to be nurtured by and contribute to a community is expressed in part through employment in the work world. The family makes its contribution through the work of its members and in return receives the economic resources it needs (Everett and Everett 1995; Moorehouse 1993; Ulrich and Dunne 1986). Perhaps for this reason, economic distress—whether employment instability or inadequate economic resources, or both—has been found to weaken family relationships (Voydanoff 1990). Beyond paid work, children and youths learn to be caring and responsible members of the community when they see their family adults model caring and involvement and when they work alongside them in informal, unpaid services to others and to the community (Burr and Klein 1994; Curran 1983; Gerstel and Gross 1987; Lazzari, Ford and Haughey 1996; Roehlkepartain 1993; Wuthnow 1995).

   8. Positive family identity and shared life story. Strong families have daily and special rituals that affirm their commitments to one another, their respect and love for one another, and their patterns of relating. They have a rich heritage of stories that relate the meaning and purpose of their life together and what it means to be a family member. Their rituals and stories evolve over time in response to changing needs and experiences of family life, folding in new members and honoring those who have gone before (Boss et al. 1993; Fiese et al. 1995; Holland and Kilpatrick 1993; Hopper 1993; Karpel 1986; Lichtenstein and Baruch 1996; Orbuch and Veroff 1993; Shammas 1983; Ziegler and Ziegler 1992).

9. Ability to cope with crises and developmental changes. Families teach their members to manage crisis and suffering. Not all crises can be mastered; some simply have to be suffered through. Strong families provide a context in which their members can model for one another the effective management of crisis and how to "suffer well." Strong families know that no experience is worthless if it teaches lessons. They help their members become more tolerant, empathic and emotionally complex through crises and suffering. Families become more resilient *through* adversity, not despite it. What distinguishes strong, resilient families is a sense of coherence and a worldview and congruent values that give meaning to the family's experiences (Bigbee 1992; Boss 1988; Burr and Klein 1994; Figley 1989; Hawley and DeHaan 1996; Kasl and Cooper 1987; Lavee and Olson 1991; McCubbin and McCubbin 1989; Olson 1989; Pipher 1996; Reiss and Oliveri 1991; Walsh 1996).

Section Three

The History of Families & the Church

FOR TWO THOUSAND YEARS, THE CHURCH HAS INTERPRETED THE teachings of its Scriptures through the frameworks of knowledge, experiences and the sociocultural realities in which it found itself. As Stephen Barton has pointed out, "the history of the church *is* the history of the interpretation of the Bible" (Barton 1996a:5). The church's teachings about and policies concerning family life have resulted from the interaction of changing sociocultural realities with scriptural interpretation and church traditions and law. Consequently, ideals concerning family structuring and family functioning taught by the church and striven for to a greater or lesser extent by Christians have changed over the history of the church. Concurrently, families have been shaped not only by economic, social, cultural, ecological and biological factors, but also by prevailing religious teachings of their era.

Some may wonder why a book on family ministry takes a whole section to look at the history of the church and Western families. Couldn't we compare our knowledge about family structures and functioning today with this scriptural framework and determine where families need help? Wouldn't this be an adequate foundation for shaping a family ministry?

Perhaps, if we could stand outside history, outside our own place and time and experiences, a historical examination of the relationship between church and family would be unnecessary. The framework I bring for studying families and for studying Scripture, however, is fundamentally a product of my own place and time and experiences. History keeps us humble. It reminds us that we are always contextual. Seeing how others' views and concerns have been shaped by their time and their culture helps us to know, if we cannot really see, the limitations of our own perspectives.

History also provides windows on how others at different times and places, who have lived through experiences similar to or different from our own, have integrated Christian teachings with family living. We can learn from their experiences.

Finally, a historical look at churches and families can also help us understand how our current family structures and processes have developed over time. If we want to preserve or change family structures, our congregational life, and/or the processes of our society, it will help to understand the factors that have, over time, created, sustained and changed them.

Therefore, chapter nine will look at some of the major sociological and economic forces that have influenced the institution of the family in Western societies. Chapter ten will then examine the interaction and response of the church to these realities and the major impact Christianity has had in the shaping of Western families.

Chapter 9

A Socioeconomic History
of the American Family

THE SOCIOLOGICAL CONCEPT OF "FAMILY" IS A RELATIVELY RECENT development in the history of humanity. According to Frances and Joseph Gies, no European language had a term specifically for the mother-father-children group before the eighteenth century (Gies and Gies 1987). Kinship and households have been important social structures through all of recorded history, but throughout Western history, the meanings attached to those structures were different from those we now attach to the term *family*. In particular, that families are held together by affection, not by economic/social necessity, and that families have boundaries that lend them a certain privacy are both aspects of family life possible only in the last few centuries. People have always had kinfolk—mother, father, children, siblings—but the cultural *meanings* attached to these relationships are new. Marital love and the special relationship between parents and children—what we now call "nuclear families"—have existed since ancient times (Guichard and Cuvillier 1996). But spouses and their children were simply not considered the basic family unit as they are today.

In the Roman world, *familia* referred to a household, not a family in the modern sense. Among the wealthy and powerful, the *familia* consisted of hundreds of persons—children, servants, slaves; even livestock were numbered in the household. The household belonged to the *paterfamilias*, the head of the household (Brundage 1987). The *paterfamilias* was not actually considered a member of the *familia*, although his wife and children, like the servants and slaves and oxen and geese, were. The primary descent group of parents and children was known as one's "lineage." A lineage was a group that could actually trace their biological relationship with one another. A lineage was somewhat smaller and more closely knit than the "clan"—a group of persons who claimed a common ancestor. The identity of the Israelites as "sons of Abraham" and their division into tribes reflect this clan structure. A clan existed independently of its members and could own land and exert political power. In many ancient cultures, including Roman society, ancestors figured prominently in religious observances (Gies and Gies 1987).

THE HOUSEHOLD

Most members of the early Christian churches probably lived with persons we would consider "family," but those families were subunits embedded in a larger household. Thus there is no name for the nuclear family unit (husband, wife and children) in the New Testament. Instead the New Testament refers to the *household* when addressing personal/domestic life. In order to understand the context of New Testament teachings concerning relationships with children, parents, spouses and other household members, we need to understand what ancient households were like.

The Household/Family as Economic Unit

The household was the primary place of economic production in ancient society. In early Christian history and on for centuries, the house was not the place to escape from work but the place where much of the work was done; it was not the place to be free of a public role but the place where that role was carried out. For most people, work and home, family and work colleagues, religious expression, and the ebb and flow of daily life were intertwined in the same world of existence—the household. Whether the household's function in production was farming or home industry, the home had very open boundaries. Employees, slaves and outsiders doing business with the household were in and out of the household, sometimes living there as well as doing business there. Thus boundaries between the family unit and business relationships were fuzzy and relatively insignificant (Skolnick 1993).

The Role of Women

Women were subordinate to men, but they were colleagues in the economic support of the household rather than "dependents." The work of husband and wife, though defined by different tasks, was economically integrated and interdependent. Similarly, in ancient Israel the model Hebrew wife was not only mother and housekeeper but also an economic contributor, a manager of domestic industry. According to Proverbs 31:16-18, a good wife was one who purchased real estate for the family's economic production, planted and tended a vineyard, and sold her merchandise profitably, thereby leaving her husband free to sit and converse wisely among the elders of the land (Prov 31:23; see also Jer 31:22).

The roles of women in both of these societies were characteristically much more economically necessary to the family than the current domestic role of homemaker. As important as the role of homemaker is in many families today, it does not contribute significantly to the family's economic well-being, except in the arena of care for preschool children. Families that must purchase child care for one or more children bear a significant economic burden that would be relieved if a full-time adult could remain in the home. In previous centuries, many women were able to weave child care into their involvement in economically productive work, which took place in the household, although they sometimes used the assistance of older children or a wet nurse. It was not until the twentieth century that housekeeping and child care were considered a full-time occupation for women (Melville 1980). And it was primarily only with the Industrial Revolution that economic production was separated from family households, therefore making it difficult for adults to combine the world of work with child care.

The Autonomy of the Household

Many of the functions we now look to the community to fulfill were the responsibility of each individual household in ancient times. Today we put letters in a mailbox, but in the Roman Empire a household slave would be sent out to deliver the household's letters. Of course, that meant that rich households—those that had slaves—could more easily take care of themselves and their business than poor ones. Social services such as nursing homes, hospitals, orphanages, schools or systematic poor relief were not provided by the government either; households fulfilled these roles. Children who were unwanted or could not be cared for in their own household either died from exposure or were taken in by another household. Sick persons died if their household did not care for them; large households employed their own physicians and established their own sick rooms. Even education took place in the household; whether or not a child was educated was up to the family (Lampe 1992).

The Household and Religion

Households were also autonomous when it came to religion. Much worship took place in the household. Roman households had their own gods and their own altars. Christians used this household model of religious faith in developing the early churches. Churches did not have land and buildings; they met in private houses. In the third century, special rooms in large households began to be dedicated to worship.

The early house churches were composed of people who worshiped together where they lived. These house churches could function autonomously, presumably under the leadership of the household head. Households invited others to join them in worship and fellowship meals. Several house churches coexisted in large cities, because not all Christians could fit into one private home. This household pattern of congregating led to theological pluralism and a delay in the development of any central church government (Lampe 1992).

The mission of the early Christian movement therefore depended on households. The earliest missionaries, as they arrived in a new city, aimed to win over one household, which then became the base for reaching out to other households in the community (ibid.). Acceptance of new members into the church happened in two different ways: by entire households and by individuals. When large households joined the Christian movement, they did so on the authority of the householder, as in the case of the household of Stephanas (1 Cor 1:16), Cornelius's household at Caesarea (Acts 10:24, 44-48), and Lydia's and the jailer's households at Philippi (Acts 16:15, 33). We do not have any way of knowing the extent to which all members of the household understood the faith they were embracing. In each case, all were baptized together (Osiek 1996).

THE INSTITUTIONALIZATION OF THE CHURCH

Given the significant autonomy of households in the ancient world, there may have been considerable diversity from one household to another in theology and patterns of worship. By the seventh and eighth centuries, however, the increasing influence of the centralized church and its interpretation of Scriptures was having a significant homogenizing influence on households. The Scriptures of the church supported monogamous, permanent marriage and respect and honor of parents. No longer did a father have absolute power (Quale 1988). The church gave precedence to the family of marriage over the family of origin. Children could leave parents to marry and establish separate households. Consequently, the powerful patriarchal system of the Roman Empire was tempered. In addition, the same rules of family conduct applied to both rich and poor (Herlihy 1985).

Still, though the church would play an important role in defining family life by the Middle Ages, this role was slow in developing in the early centuries of the church. For three centuries there appears to have been no Christian wedding ceremony. In the East, crowns were simply placed on the heads of bride and groom. In the West, a priest was called in to bless the marriage; in some communities a blessing was said over the couple while they lay in their marriage bed. No community celebration was required (Herlihy 1985). Over time, however, the medieval church placed the family under its control by assuming jurisdiction over its formation, maintenance and even dissolution (Witte 1996). The church built an extensive system of canon law governing marriage and family life that was enforced by church courts. The influence of the church on family life will be explored more fully in the next chapter.

THE DEVELOPMENT OF THE NUCLEAR FAMILY

Economic and social forces have been powerful shapers of the family throughout history. Whenever economic or political conditions have encouraged production by relatively smaller groups, the nuclear family has tended to emerge as the living unit. The nuclear family fits economic conditions where accumulation and investment are necessary but production does not require large amounts of capital (Coontz 1988). Nuclear families are also relatively mobile, which suits situations where persons need to move in search of land, work and opportunity (Skolnick 1993).

Europe
Between the sixth and the ninth centuries, Germanic invasions led to the disappearance of large-scale slavery, and peasant agriculture replaced the large

household unit as the basic unit of economic production. As a consequence, monogamous nuclear families (husband, wife and their children), defined by paternal lineage, became the basic social unit, distinct from the clan or lineage (Brundage 1987). The basic unit of father, mother and unmarried children was sometimes enlarged by the inclusion of older generations, unmarried adult children and widowed or unmarried siblings of the couple. Peasant households (or "hearths") averaged five persons, and marriage provided the essential structure for the family group (Toubert 1996). Twenty to 35 percent of all newborns succumbed to infant mortality, and a third of marriages were barren or had no living heirs (Fossier 1996:411).

During this feudal period, the household continued to be the primary economic unit. Everyone worked together to produce what was needed and to provide a surplus to meet the demands of the lord in exchange for policing and protection. There were no salaries, profits or division of labor; "in the household, everybody did everything" (ibid. 413). Men and women were on equal standing, at least within the family. Sometimes babies were sent out for care because the mother had to work in the trade. This practice of putting babies out to a wet nurse sometimes led to neglect and abuse. Babies raised outside their own home had a much higher level of infant mortality than babies breastfed by their own mothers (Burguiere and Lebrun 1996).

Households of the nobility continued to be very large. In thirteenth-century England, for example, Thomas of Berkeley's household consisted of more than two hundred people. The patron's rule kept this large group together. Other men in the group pledged themselves to the patron in exchange for provision of food, shelter, clothing and protection. The patron, in turn, had responsibility to provide care for those who had thus committed themselves, but also had the right to beat them (Duby, Barthelemy and de La Ronciere 1988). The household head was duty-bound to perpetuate its existence by producing offspring and by providing allied houses with women "to secure their allegiance and ensure procreation" (ibid. 68). A wife who did not produce heirs was readily put away. Reproduction meant expansion of power; every noble household constantly sought to add more relatives, allies and servants.

> The castle of Ardres contained at its heart a nursery, where governesses took care of the mistress' offspring so that the lady herself could get on as quickly as possible with the business of conceiving the next child. As soon as children attained the age

of reason they were strictly segregated: girls were carefully watched to protect their virginity until the moment when they were conveyed in solemn cortege to the castle of their future spouse. (ibid. 69)

Marriages took place only after much deliberation by kindred on both sides. Each evaluated the other's degree of honor, and the decision was made in negotiations between the household heads. The young man and woman were simply asked for their consent (ibid.).

By the twelfth century it was common practice to allow only one son in a noble lineage to marry. At the same time, nobles tried to marry off all the daughters they could, in order to form alliances (Quale 1988). So powerful was the lineage during this period that children were perceived to belong to the lineage, not to their mother. For example, in the 1400s young widows in Tuscany could not keep their children if they remarried; the children were given over to their father's family (de La Ronciere 1988).

True friends were "friends by blood" and could be acquired only through kinship or marriage. In addition, the concept of "blood brotherhood" developed. Partners drank each other's blood, resulting in a covenant considered stronger than that of siblings. This practice did not continue on a widespread basis; whether this was because of or in spite of the analogous connection to Jesus' last supper with the disciples is not clear. Other practices of sealing allegiances between friends were much more common. Friends commonly signed contracts of mutual support. Godparentage established spiritual kinship between unrelated families; members of the child's family were not allowed to marry members of the godparent's family or even the family of the priest who celebrated the baptism (Aymard 1989).

During this period, the kinship group strongly resisted the independence of married couples and individuals; people needed one another to survive (Fossier 1996). Nevertheless, the meaning of "family" was shifting from an extended household to a nuclear family. One of the strongest unwritten norms of Western culture became the expectation that couples after marriage should set up their own residence. Few elderly parents lived long enough to make the three-generation household a common long-term arrangement (Collomp 1989; Skolnick 1993).

The shift to the nuclear family household had dramatic implications. Particularly striking was the dawning consciousness of emotional bonding among members. These bonds were more apparent and significant in the smaller household unit defined predominantly by the marriage and procreation of husband and wife than they had been in the larger household of centuries past. Children became clearly the responsibility of parents rather than of a whole household of adults. Spouses had privacy with each other, and with that privacy came increased expectations for spouses to meet each other's emotional and social needs, which before had been met by the much larger household. Instead of a number of adults—servants, relatives and business partners—with whom a woman or man could talk over the daily interests and concerns of life, in the nuclear household there was only the marital partner.

It should be noted that even during this early period of the nuclear family, many persons lived in other kinds of arrangements, whether due to early deaths of partners or late marriage. For example, records from fifteenth-century Italy reveal that nuclear families constituted a bare majority of a city's households. Some of these families included one or more relations—mother, nephew, niece, brother-in-law, widowed daughter. Providing housing for relatives was somewhat more common where a household was headed by a single person. Women with children but no husband (widows) and single adults living alone (not yet married) constituted a large number of households. Slightly under half of the men ages twenty-eight to thirty-two were married. Many men delayed marriage until they were thirty or older, and many never married at all. More often than not, the ability to marry was controlled predominantly by the man's economic resources (Bresc 1996; Brundage 1987).

Colonial America
From this historical socioeconomic background for family life, European settlers came to colonial America. In the seventeenth and eighteenth centuries, households in the colonies often were much larger than the nuclear family, including servants and apprentices as well as numerous children. The membership of the household was quite fluid. Death frequently removed members, both children and adults. Only slightly over half of all children born lived to become adults. More women died in childbirth than for all other reasons combined; one birth in thirty resulted in the death of the mother (Beales 1991:43). The woman who survived her childbearing years bore eight children on the average, though it was probably relatively rare for as many as six of the eight to survive to adulthood. A marriage often ended early in the death of one spouse; only half of adults reached

the age of fifty. Only one out of three marriages endured more than ten years. Unlike today, the death of a spouse was not something to be expected as one approached "old age" but a part of what we now regard as the prime of life. Those who survived often married two or more times (Scott and Wishy 1982:2).

Birth order was therefore much more important to one's life experiences in colonial America than it is now. First-born children were much more likely to spend some or all of their childhood with biological parents. Younger children were more likely to experience the death of one or both parents and to be members of stepfamilies or raised by older siblings (ibid.).

The frequent remarriage of widows and widowers meant that households often included stepchildren. A man who married at age twenty-five might lose his wife when he was thirty-five after she had borne him four or five children. He might then marry a young widow with one or two children, and together they would have several more children. If he then died, she might remarry and have still more children.

> One such "chain of marriage and remarriage" in Virginia from about 1655 to 1693, made up of "six marriages among seven people," yielded at least twenty-five children. A visit to this household in 1680 would have found the presence of children (ranging from infancy to the early twenties) from four of the marriages, some of whom did not have any parents in common. (ibid. 4)

Households also took in orphaned cousins or other more distant relatives. In the South, almost 20 percent of children were orphaned before their thirteenth birthday, and more than 30 percent were orphaned before the age of eighteen (Coontz 1988:84). Families also often brought in older children and young adults as servants and apprentices and, if they were not needed at home, sent out their own children to work in other households. The most important change in American family life has not been the breakdown of the three-generation family but, rather, the loss of flexibility with regard to taking in various children and strangers (Skolnick 1993).

Male property owners ruled in colonial America, both their own homes and the homes of servants. Although children usually moved into their own household upon marriage, it was often on nearby land that the man's father owned, thus continuing his paternal authority.

Only those who owned or were given property in this way were allowed to marry, and parents often chose the children's marital partners in the early colonial period (see also Beales 1991; Hawes and Nybakken 1991). Marriage was forbidden to servants, slaves, apprentices and minor youths (Scott and Wishy 1982).

Fathers clearly wielded considerable power. Fathers usually received custody of children in the rare case of divorce. Courts enforced household members' obedience to the householder. On the other hand, the community also had considerable say over the way householders managed their households. Household heads could be informally shamed and even formally punished for failing to exercise authority over wives, servants and children. "In seventeenth-century New England special public officers (tithingmen) were charged with maintaining family order and reporting household heads who were negligent in enforcement of their authority and duties" (Coontz 1988). Economic changes in the country brought changes to this tight patriarchy. Free land enabled young men to escape dependence on their fathers. Increasingly, individuals and families resisted community constraints on family life (Skolnick 1993).

Frontier America
By the late eighteenth century, American society had changed dramatically, and with it the structure and values of family life. Americans were on the move—and those moves were frequent. Nuclear families frequently moved far from kin, able to maintain only sporadic contact. For centuries families had been bound to place, but no longer. "American families changed locations, dwellings, crafts and callings, and churches with astonishing frequency" (Scott and Wishy 1982:181). The idea of family reunions grew during this era, a concept much less familiar—because it was not needed—in Europe (ibid.). The patriarchal, hierarchical worlds that immigrants from other continents and colonial Americans had known disappeared. Young people, not their parents, were choosing their own mates, and that choice was based on personal attraction rather than family property and connections (Hawes and Nybakken 1991; Quale 1988).

African-Americans
Family life was quite different for those who immigrated or were abducted from Africa. Not all Africans came to the colonies as slaves. Initially, colonial society was not divided by race but by class. White indentured servants were often treated as harshly as slaves (Coontz 1988). Nevertheless, societal division became increasingly racial, and slavery became the economic system that shaped African-American family life.

Slaves often courted without their owner's knowledge or approval, but they had to obtain his consent to set up a household. No Southern state recognized the legality of slave marriages or the legitimacy of slave offspring, but some owners allowed ministers or priests to perform slave marriage ceremonies. By the 1850s most owners were allowing slaves to have a "Scripture wedding" rather than a simple broom-jumping ritual. Nevertheless, recognition from the owner and the slave community was the only legitimacy given slave family life (Malone 1992).

During the first part of the nineteenth century (1810-1864), records show the following kinds of families among Louisiana slaves (Malone 1992:17):

married with children, 48.7%

single female with children, 14.5%

males alone, 12.9%

married with no children, 8.1%

multiple families, 5.6%

females alone, 5.4%

extended family, 1.9%

single male with children, 1.8%

nonnuclear family, 1.2%

Nearly three-quarters lived in households with blood relatives—parents, children, cousins or siblings. Researchers have concluded that these family households met the needs for family of a majority of slaves. Although the parent-child unit was the vital core, the real strength of the slave community was its acceptance of all types of families and households as functional and contributing. These families were neither matriarchal nor patriarchal. In slave families having both husband and wife present, wives had equal or near-equal status with their husbands. The family was matrilineal only as defined by the white society; that is, a child born to a slave mother was a slave regardless of whether the father was a slave (see also Cody 1983; Malone 1992).

THE INDUSTRIAL REVOLUTION AND BEYOND

With the Industrial Revolution of the nineteenth century, economic productivity became separated from the household for the first time. Newly built factories employed men, women and children. Initially the work unit was actually the family, growing out of the historic understanding of the family as the production unit of society (Perrot 1990; Scott and Wishy 1982). Factories hired entire families as part of one contract and would pay the family wages and provide a house for them to live in. For example, this contract was recorded in December 1814:

> Dennis Rier of Newbury Port has this day engaged to come with his family to work in our factory on the following conditions. He is to be here about the 20th of next month and is to have the following wages per week:

Himself:	5.00
His son Robert Rier 10 years of age:	.83
Daughter Mary 12 years of age:	1.25
Son William 13 years of age:	1.50
Son Michael 16 years of age:	2.00
His sister, Abigail Smith:	2.33
Her daughter Sally, 8 years of age:	.75
Son Samuel 13 years of age:	1.50

> House rent to be from $20 to $30. Wood cut up $2 per cord. (Scott and Wishy 1982:219)

Thus instead of working in their homes, entire families went together to work in factories. They were no longer working as partners with one another in the front-room shop or in nearby fields, nor did they have control over the work environment as when they were self-employed.

Over time, work increasingly became an *individual*, not a household or family, pursuit. Of course individuals had always been sent out to work; for example, children who could not be supported in the household had been sent out as servants or apprentices. But previously those who were sent out were subsequently attached to other households in which they served or were employed.

Before the Industrial Revolution, farming had been the economic support for many families, and farming was the prototype of the household industry. It was an "all hands on deck" operation, with schooling, church worship and other outside involvements scheduled to fit the family's work. School met during the winter months, when the family's work was less demanding and the children could be spared. Church met in the late morning, so that the family could complete its farm chores first. The sacred eleven o'clock worship hour in many American congregations is a remnant of this era, when families had to milk the cows and do other daily farm tasks before going to church. In 1850, 46 percent of the U.S.

labor force was involved in agriculture. A century later, in 1950, only 12 percent of American workers were involved in agriculture, and by 1980 it had dropped to 3 percent (Kain 1990:34).

Individual Career Instead of Family Production

The individual's career gradually replaced the family's business or farm. Household members were now productive only as employees selling their labor in the workplace. A person's work had little relationship to that of family members except in spare-time hobbies (e.g., gardening and other economically useful part-time pursuits) and in the pooling of earnings. The paycheck deposited into the family's bank account replaced work in tandem with other family members as the individual's contribution to the economic welfare of the family.

At first this move from the household to employment outside the home was mostly made only by men and the poorest of women and children. Those women who could afford at all to do so stayed behind in the home, continuing alone those gendered tasks that had heretofore been interdependent with the gendered tasks of men as the economic support for the family. Women continued to garden, educate children, sew and cook. Nevertheless, their economic contribution to the household gradually began to shrink. Homemade candles were replaced by purchased electricity, medical care by the medical professions, schooling of children by public schools, production of clothing and food products by garment and farming industries, and so on.

The concept of "breadwinner" resulted from this shift. No longer did the family grow and make or earn their daily bread together; one member was supposed to go outside the family and earn enough to support the rest. The "family wage," the idea that a man working full time should be paid enough to support a wife and children, is a concept that developed—and dissipated—in the twentieth century (Goldscheiter and Waite 1991). Before that time, women and children had worked alongside men. The purpose of the family wage was to put an end to child labor and to ensure that children had mothers at home to tend them (Quale 1988). By the end of the twentieth century, however, there were laws to ensure equality of pay, regardless of family circumstances, so that women and men received "equal pay for equal work."

The world of work and the world of the family had gradually been separated. The home was recast as a haven from the work world rather than the place where work took place. The division between household and work became not only a reality but a model of the way things are "supposed to be" (Lasch 1980). This separation carried moral overtones; the marketplace was considered dangerously corrupting. The men who spent their days in that world were saved by constant contact with the world of the home, where women acted as carriers of the religious values that could counteract the destructive tendencies of the market (Hall 1990).

The advantages of the extended household thus were transformed into liabilities. The household consequently became smaller. Fewer households could afford servants, because their service was no longer economically productive. Families could afford fewer children, because their presence was now cost producing rather than income producing. Not only did they not make an economic contribution to the household, but they kept an adult caretaker from doing so as well. The mutual interdependence of the family in shared work was lost. This was not true for everyone, of course; many rural families and small businesses retained the old interdependence. The ideal, however, had been changed.

Children as Economic Liabilities
The child labor laws passed early in the twentieth century were symbols of these economic shifts. These laws were good for many children, particularly poor children who before had worked incredibly long hours, often in dangerous and debilitating positions in factories and mines, in order to help support their families. Now their economic contribution had to come second to their schooling. Indirectly, this shift in economic status was one more factor leading to declining birth rates. Children were no longer economic contributors to the household. Now children were economic liabilities, "dependents" rather than two more hands to work in the family business or another paycheck to contribute to the family's support.

This shift in the role of children was accompanied by an increased sense that caring for these dependent members was what gave meaning and purpose to family life. At the same time, however, the number of years families were committed to this task was also diminishing. In previous centuries, most parents died before their youngest children reached adulthood; childrearing was a lifetime task. Today most adults spend less than one-third of their adult years—from age twenty to age seventy-five or beyond—in childbearing and childrearing. For the first time in history, today's average married couple has more living parents than it has children. Ours is also the first era when the longest stretch of a parent-child relationship comes after the child is an adult; we live more years as adults with older parents than we do as children in the households of those parents (Skolnick 1993).

Childbearing and childrearing have increasingly become a very expensive leisure-time activity rather than an economic contribution to the family. Increasingly, our society expects the parenting of children to be undertaken only in households that can afford them. That is, a family must have the economic resources for one adult to be absent from economically productive work to rear children or, alternatively, must earn enough to pay someone else to provide childcare.

Family as Unit of Consumption
As a consequence primarily of economic forces, the large economic unit of the household was replaced with the small, emotionally tied unit of the family. The family has been defined in Western cultures and by American norms as persons related to one another by marriage, birth or formal adoption, almost always consisting of married couples and their dependent children.

This unit's functions are far less expansive than those of the household it has replaced. The family unit retains two major functions not served by other social institutions. The first of these is a vestige of the household economic function. The family is still a primary economic unit, but the function of economic production has been replaced by economic consumption. For the most part, family members pool their income and draw from the common pot for making purchases. Big-ticket items—cars, refrigerators, houses—are bought to serve the family unit. Family members have to integrate and coordinate their spending, if not their work, in order to function effectively. Family members are responsible for one another economically and for one another's consumption.

The loss of economic production as a function of family life is not just a functional loss for spouses. It is also a loss of an economic tie between generations. Adult children no longer depend on parents to provide them with a trade or a family farm (although they may hope for help with the expenses of their own or their children's college education). The lengthening life span has meant that children are unlikely to inherit their parents' resources until they themselves are approaching retirement age. At the same time, senior adults no longer depend on their adult children to support them; they are expected to accumulate enough savings to support themselves until death. Thus the reciprocal economic relationship between the generations has been weakened (Goody 1996).

With productiveness removed from the family and consumption a primary family function, what sense of purpose many families feel comes from their joint consumption—taking the boat out on weekends, buying and furnishing a house, traveling or entertaining. When I have asked families to describe what gives their family a sense of meaning or purpose, many tell me about a special family vacation, or their plans to travel, or the retirement from employment they are anticipating. But a remembered vacation and the anticipated pleasures of travel or retirement are experiences that are relatively isolated and segregated from day-in and day-out living. Instead of providing a guiding purpose for all of a family's activities, they further segregate the meaningful moment from the round of daily activities. Monday through Friday is endured because it brings the promise of a weekend or because it provides the financial means to pursue activities or possessions deemed important. Family members remain isolated from each other in their work and school activities and share primarily in periodic leisure pursuits.

The Family Focus on Nurture and Attachment

The other remaining function of the family is providing family members with nurture, love and attachment to one another. The family is the place where individuals can express and meet needs, where acceptance and belonging are available for each member simply for being a member, where members take care of each other in times of need. They also provide "wrap-around" services to supplement what is available to family members elsewhere. Education no longer takes place under Mother's supervision but in a community school, although the growing homeschooling movement is an exception. Even the child in a community school, however, may need a little extra supervision or tutoring to make best use of that schooling, and the family is expected to provide that help. Medical care is dominated by professional healthcare providers. But it is the family that provides daily nursing through an illness.

All people are perceived as needing the consistent nurture and love of a family to whom they feel attached. Families are supposed to "be there" for one another in a crisis. The recent development of family leave policies constitute recognition of this important function of family life. As important as consumerism has become, few families hold together for the sake of the house, let alone the refrigerator. The most significant function of marriage, and the family of which it is perceived as the center, is to meet interpersonal needs.

The Household as Private Enclave

The move of economic production outside the household has gradually resulted in increasing privacy for the family unit. No longer is there an array of clients, servants and employees, apprentices, and extended family in and out of the household as a part of daily work. In fact, even the core family of many households is absent for a majority of most working days.

An interesting way of following the changing functions of marriage and the family over time is to trace changes in the structure of physical living and working space for households and families. Until the eighteenth century, privacy was not a concern in the design of houses. All family activities took place in shared space, without today's walls of privacy. For example, in colonial America most homes consisted of one or two rooms, with perhaps a sleeping loft upstairs (Shammas 1983). The largest room was called the hall, and members of the household spent most of their indoor waking hours here. A huge fireplace provided heat and was used for cooking. Cloth production, carpentry, food preparation, business dealings, farm management, schooling, eating, entertaining, recreation, conversation, sleeping and sexual relations all took place there (Cherlin and Calhoun 1996).

Larger houses lacked privacy because the corridor, a key feature of home architecture, had not yet been invented. In England and in the colonies before the late 1600s, homes were built so that the only way to get from one room to another was to walk through the rooms in between. Consequently, no room could be "private." By the 1700s, however, the homes of the wealthy began to include a central hallway (ibid.).

By the eighteenth century, the boundaries between family and neighbors had become more sharply drawn, and family relationships became more significant and exclusive (Melville 1980). With the Industrial Revolution, the glorification of motherhood and the notion that "women's place is in the home" were born. "With men leaving home to work, the contrast between home and the outside world became a contrast between woman and man" (Skolnick 1993:54). The concept of the "home" was developed, and invested with all kinds of new meanings—intimacy, love, privacy, comfort, protection from the larger world. The number of rooms in the household increased, and private sleeping space for married couples was expected. Although living this way was actually possible only for the middle class, it became the ideal dominating American culture.

The desire for increased privacy from the surrounding community continued and was buttressed by architectural and technological advances. During the first half of the twentieth century, most middle-class American houses were built with front porches. Before the development of climate-control technology, weather permitting or compelling, the family spent its time together on the porch during an afternoon rest or during the evening hours before bedtime. I remember as a child in the early 1950s playing in the Missouri summertime across the neighborhood yards with other children until after dark. It was too hot to be indoors. Summer family time was public; other neighbors also spent a good bit of time on their porches and could see and hear much of one another's doings. Friends called and joked back and forth from one porch or yard to another or sauntered over to visit for a while. The community could see each family.

This family-community interface was augmented in other ways. Clothes were dried on lines in the backyard, where the family laundress would come and go periodically on laundry day, chatting with her counterparts in other yards. People walked more—to schools, to stores, even to church; this too meant seeing and being seen in the community. At least one member in the family, usually a woman, worked in the household. These women often congregated for conversation or aided one another with work—swapping child care, cups of sugar, transportation. In many respects this community aid to household work carried over from rural areas, where the community would build barns and harvest crops together.

In recent decades, new architectural conventions have reflected changing social ideals (Melville 1980). In middle-class America, the public front porch has given way to the enclosed patio or deck in the backyard. Air conditioning has encouraged those who can afford it to stay indoors, which means they are less visible. The front yard is now a carefully manicured "face," only inhabited once weekly during the growing season by the pilot of a mower whose roar makes conversation with or even awareness of others almost impossible. Garage-door openers allow family members to drive into the family home; laundry is dried inside in dryers rather than on lines in the backyard. We might conjecture that one of the reasons poorer families in American culture have strong community networks is that the lack of these comforts and conveniences encourages them to live outside their homes more—relaxing and playing, walking, drying clothes, conducting family relationships in sight of the neighbors.

Going back even further to contrast with the community involvement in family life in ancient times, food today is cooked in climate-controlled kitchens rather than outdoors; water comes into the house in pipes rather than having to be carried from a community well; communication takes place via the home's telephone, television and computer rather than by physically visiting others. All these developments allow the family's life to take place privately—out of view of the community.

Symbols of Household/Family Change

One of the most significant historic functions of family life has been obtaining and sharing food. Obtaining food, whether through family agriculture or by earning the means to purchase it from others, is, after all, a fundamental function of any economy. The way food is shared reflects the nature of household/family life. In American society there is dramatic variation in the ways families share (or do not share) food. At one extreme is the hour-long Sunday dinner served on the good dishes, often with guests or extended family present. At the other is the freezer stocked with quick-fix foods that each family member can microwave and eat on their own schedule out of the container in which it was bought. Here the focus is on coordination and provision of resources rather than actual sharing.

Eating together was a significant event in the life of the early church, which met in households. The church meals we read about in Paul's letters were actually household dinners. In the Greco-Roman world, only those with spacious houses could afford the luxury of kitchens. The rest prepared food on portable grills or ate regularly at the "fast food" shop in the neighborhood. At that time the rich ate in and the poor ate out—quite a different arrangement from today. Eating in was a household event, and eating out was often the lot of individuals. The poor ate formal meals only on special occasions and when they were sponsored by a benefactor (Osiek 1996). Thus the regular Christian community meal had tremendous significance for poor members of the church.

Traditionally, men and women dined separately on formal occasions. At less formal occasions, women and children sat on chairs by the couches on which the men reclined (ibid.). Interestingly, vestiges of this pattern remained in Western society even until recent history. Commonly in rural America, the women served the men first and waited on them. After the men had finished eating and the table was cleared, the women and children would sit down to eat. Alternatively, sometimes the children would be fed in the kitchen, or the women and children ate in a separate place (such as the kitchen) from the men, who ate in the dining room.

Before the Industrial Revolution, a large breakfast after morning chores and a large midday "dinner" were the most significant meals of the day, fueling the manual labor that supported the family and including the family's employees, such as farmhands. Early in the Industrial Revolution in France, workers refused to carry their lunch or eat in the factory cafeteria; they preferred to have their wives bring hot lunches to the plant at noontime (Perrot 1990). In other communities, an extended break at noon enabled wage earners to return home for lunch. In some places this tradition has continued. In the 1980s my family and I spent a year in a small town in Germany and found this arrangement still existed there. Stores, businesses and schools closed for an hour and a half in the middle of the day so that everyone could go home for the midday meal.

In the United States this was only a transitional arrangement. It was not many years until the preparation of the noonday meal dwindled into the packing of a metal lunchbox. Until the 1960s many schoolchildren still returned home for lunch, a much smaller meal than the "dinner" of an earlier era. Increasingly, however, with the employment of women outside the home, there was no one there to prepare the noonday meal. Schools added cafeterias, and home kitchens were closed from breakfast until the evening meal, which became "dinner," the large meal of the day.

The hour of this last meal of the day has also gradually shifted later and later. Farm families were typically up with morning light or before; the last meal of the day, consequently, would be scheduled in the late afternoon, before evening chores. Employment outside the home often meant long hours away from home, however, and the meal had to be prepared after returning from the job. Thus the time for this meal has shifted from late afternoon (3:30 to 5:00) to early evening (6:30 to 8:00). Today many families are fighting to hold on to this daily time for eating together, as the scheduling of work and leisure increasingly impinges on the "traditional" dinner hour.

It is interesting too to reflect on changing menus and cooking methods of family meals. Although the long, slow cooking of meat roasts and the baking of bread still take place in some families, it is often done with slow cookers, ovens with timers, and bread machines, all of which can be set to "run themselves" while the family is away. It has become even more typical for families to use quick cooking methods—stir frying, broiling, microwaving—and convenience and prepared foods. Slow cooking methods were much more feasible when economic production took place in the household itself.

THE AMERICAN FAMILY AT THE TURN OF THE MILLENNIUM

The majority of American families, especially young families, have been under economic stress in recent decades. This economic stress is one reason that there are increasing numbers of families in which all adults are working full time outside the household, even parents of infants and preschoolers. Arlene Skolnick has called the late twentieth century a "quiet depression" masked by a conspicuous but highly uneven prosperity (Skolnick 1993:63). Changes in the wage and salary structure have been pushing the United States toward a two-class society. The upper fifth of the population enjoyed great prosperity during the last two decades of the twentieth century. Meanwhile, many families endured severe economic loss, and many others struggled simply to maintain a middle-class standard of living.

These economic shifts have had a strong effect on young families. The results have been a significant increase in the number of persons delaying marriage or choosing not to marry at all, in postponement of childbearing, and in numbers of families with all adults employed outside the home. Increasingly, adults are expected to continue working beyond the retirement age of sixty-five established in the first half of the twentieth century; families and society simply cannot afford to support a large proportion of the senior adult population in retirement.

These economic changes have contributed, along with other social changes, to a reshaping of family life. Women have increasingly been seen as equal partners in family life, as their economic roles become less and less differentiated from those of men. With the increase in women's economic contribution to the family has come a change from the status of "dependent" to equal partner. That has made remaining single or obtaining a divorce easier; women can support themselves without husbands, although it is often difficult when they have children for whom they are primarily economically responsible. Children have gone from being the property of fathers to being the property of mothers, until today both parents are thought of as having equal rights and responsibilities for their children. More and more families have no children, whether because they have not yet borne them, have already borne and launched them, or will never have children. And as we saw in chapter two, parenting and marriage are increasingly becoming independent of one another as family structures.

CONCLUSIONS

This brief review of the socioeconomic history of the Western family provides food for thought concerning ministry with families in our communities today.

☐ The first churches reached persons by reaching the groups of persons who lived and worked together. Church life was integrated into the mainstream of daily existence, not set apart.

☐ Families have taken many different shapes and forms in societies where Christianity dominated religious life. Economic and social forces, including mortality rates, have been most significant in determining family structures. The church has related to those realities, sometimes influencing them but not really determining them.

☐ The structure of the "traditional family"—breadwinning father and homemaker mother and their dependent children—developed as the ideal only in the twentieth century. It has not been a historical reality for more than 5 percent of the history of Christianity. However, family roles—parent, spouse, child, sibling, godparent, "blood brother," adoptive kin—have held great importance throughout history, even though the nature of the roles may have changed in changing times.

☐ The role of children has changed dramatically: where once they were contributing members of the family, they are now in the paradoxical position of being economic liabilities and at the same time the focus of the family's purpose and meaning. Yet many households no longer include children.

☐ Historically, the household or family's welfare was paramount, with individual's needs subordinated to those of the household/family. This contrasts sharply with the focus on the individual's welfare in our current social climate.

☐ One of the most enduring features of family life, across the diversity of structures families have assumed, has been the family meal. Eating daily meals together profoundly symbolizes family life.

Even in this brief overview of the history and development of the family in the West, it is clear that economic factors have had a pervasive influence on everything from who lives together in a household to what families eat and when and with whom. Undoubtedly the economic and social influences on family life today are just as pervasive. To understand families, we have to understand the social and economic forces that shape them, whether directly or indirectly. Today's families are just as much a product of today's economic systems as were the households of the Greco-Roman and early Christian era and the farm families of the nine-teenth century.

But families are not shaped by economic forces alone. The values of a society as reflected in its religious institutions and ideologies interact with economic and other social forces to shape families. In Western civilization, the Christian church has had a profound impact on defining and shaping families. Not only Christian families but also families immigrating into or brought in enslavement into Western civilizations have been influenced by Christianity. The Christian church has also exported its teachings and policies about family life through its missionary endeavors in other civilizations. We turn now to a look at what those influences have meant, both intentionally and unintentionally, for family life.

Chapter 10

The Church's Influence
on Family Life

THE GRADUAL SOCIAL AND ECONOMIC TRANSFORMATION FROM
extended household to conjugal family, and from unit of economic production to
intimate group defined by emotional attachment, had a profound influence on
the church's perceptions of and teachings about families. At the same time,
Christianity itself drove some of these changes in the Western world and has had
a profound impact on the development of the norms and realities of family life.
The church has never been a passive recipient of social trends but also has actively
shaped its culture.

New Testament writings define the function of marriage and family clearly.
According to the teachings of Paul, marriage is to be a relationship of mutual
love, analogous to that which exists between Christ and the church (Eph 5:22-
31). Marriage was not to be instituted primarily on the basis of what was good
for the economic and social well-being of the larger household. This view
diverged significantly from that of the culture in which the early church found
itself (Pannenberg 1985). Historically, marriage had functioned as a way to
strengthen and protect the larger family unit. For example, a simple way for a
family to protect itself was to turn an enemy into family through a marital alliance (Lévi-Strauss 1996). One of the best ways to strengthen a family was to ally

it with a stronger family through marriage. The feelings of the individuals involved were virtually irrelevant.

Social changes do not take place overnight; there is often a time lag of decades—or more—between a change in social thought and a change in social practice. Nevertheless, over time the church's definition of marriage, emphasizing free consent as it did, successfully replaced a cultural practice of arranging marriages based on the economic and political concerns of the larger family (Brundage 1987; 1993). Long before the Industrial Revolution removed from families the function of economic production, the church was redefining the central purpose and essence of family life. Centuries passed, however, before the shift from patrilineal household to marriage-centered family that began in the early centuries of Christendom was actually completed in Western cultures.

THE EARLY CHURCH

Many early Christians had the conviction that the church itself was their true family. Undoubtedly for widows, orphans, and the destitute, the church did function as a family, providing the physical necessities of life. On a more fundamental level, however, all who had become brothers and sisters in Christ shared the belief that this new spiritual bond should take precedence over all others, including that of husband and wife or parent and child. These early Christians did not necessarily reject biological or societal connections with their attendant responsibilities, but they believed these obligations were less important than the spiritual commitment they shared with fellow believers.

In some respects this shift in priorities genuinely threatened family life. Rebecca Weaver recounts the experience of Perpetua, a young Carthaginian mother, as recorded in *The Martyrdom of Perpetua*. Her father was not a Christian and implored her to abandon her life-threatening religious convictions. Christians were being sentenced to death, and Perpetua's commitment was bringing shame on the family—and didn't she realize that her still-nursing infant son needed her? But Perpetua refused to recant and was sentenced, along with other Christians, to be thrown to the beasts. In her diary, prior to her martyrdom, Perpetua wrote that miraculously her child no longer needed to be nursed and her milk dried up spontaneously without any discomfort. She interpreted these events as clear confirmation of God's blessing on her faithfulness (Weaver 1992). Faithfulness to God was more important even than maternal care of an infant son.

The placing of family life secondary to dedication to the church would continue for centuries. In the Middle Ages, nobles who sensed death's approach took vows of celibacy, donned the habit of St. Benedict and divorced their spouses so that in the last hours of life they might dedicate themselves to a "higher calling." "It was also common to break the marital bond in favor of one more pure: this was the only form of 'divorce' permitted by the church, and it required the consent of one's spouse" (Duby, Barthelemy and de La Ronciere 1988:143).

Christianity not only required willingness to sacrifice family; it also provided an escape desired by some from family obligations. Other than going off to war, joining the parish clergy or a religious order constituted the only lifestyle alternative to one's inherited family station and from marriage and parenting. During the early centuries of Christianity, marriage meant submission to heavy expectations and demands. Roman girls married young—at puberty—and were immediately caught in the life-threatening cycle of childbearing. An ascetic lifestyle meant liberation.

On the other hand, the ascetic lifestyle replaced the family of origin with the new "family" of the religious order. A monastery or convent was also an *oikos:* not just a place of residence but also a "family." It consisted of a spiritual single-sex brotherhood or sisterhood under the authority of a parental figure who was both superior and confessor. New members entered by a ritual birth, symbolized by assuming the tonsure and habit, and received a new name from the spiritual parent (Patlagean 1996).

Families sometimes used monasteries and convents as places to which they could send their "problem members"—sons without inheritance and daughters without dowry—although many convents required a gift upon admission. Entering a religious order was not always done voluntarily; the household head determined the life path for sons and daughters. Thus the church's religious orders also inadvertently supported the patriarchal household structure.

Sexuality

In the ascetical literature of the second through fifth centuries, it is clear that sexual renunciation was considered the primary path to divine favor and spiritual gifts. Other virtues paled in comparison; even vows of poverty were considered optional. Keeping the body pure was considered necessary for a spiritual marriage with Christ. Tertullian even went so far as to maintain that sexual expression, including marital intercourse, did not belong in the Christian life. Writers such as Augustine (354-430) and Jerome (c. 347-419/420) questioned whether sex had been a part of God's original creation. Origen (c. 185-253/255) and the anonymous author of the Gnostic *Gospel According to the Egyptians*, as well as others, stated that Adam and Eve were originally created free from sexual feelings. It was their sin that introduced sex, lust and death into the world (Brundage 1993).

Augustine, Tertullian, Jerome and others concluded that even in marriage, even when husband and wife have intercourse in order to conceive children, sexual expression always leads at least to venial sin. Many theologians thus placed restrictions on marital sex. Thomas Aquinas stated that intercourse must be engaged in only out of a sense of duty to conceive children or to render one's debt to a spouse. Motivation by duty was meritorious; motivation by pleasure or desire for one's partner was sinful (Price 1996). Obviously, if the only appropriate function of sexual intercourse was the conception of children, then any efforts at contraception were sinful.

At the fourth Council of Carthage in A.D. 398, it was declared that newlyweds should abstain from intercourse on the wedding night out of respect for the benediction. They could, however, pay a fee to the church to avoid this proscription. The church subsequently forbade sexual relations during menstruation, pregnancy and lactation; during seasons of fasting and on certain festival days; for forty days before Easter, Pentecost and Christmas; and for three to seven days before Communion. Abstinence was also recommended on Thursday in memory of Christ's arrest, on Friday in memory of his death, on Saturday in honor of the Virgin Mary, on Sunday in honor of the resurrection and on Monday in commemoration of the departed (Doriani 1996:48). In short, good Christians could have sex on Tuesday and Wednesday during limited weeks of the month and seasons of the year.

Marriage as Legal and Social Entity

For the first nine centuries of the church, marriage remained a legal and social entity, not an especially sacred one, even though it was considered to be a channel of grace. It was possible for a marriage to be contracted privately, even secretly, without involvement of either clergy or community, provided that both partners were old enough to marry (age fourteen for boys and twelve for girls) and otherwise complied with the rules for the formation of a marriage (Witte 1996). After intercourse had taken place, the two were considered joined together by God in a union that could not be dissolved. The government of a relationship required to be mutual but undertaken secretly was, of course, fraught with abuse. If the woman was overpowered and forced to have intercourse, was she subsequently married to her rapist based on his actions and her inability to repel him? Some taught that she was (Duby, Barthelemy and de La Ronciere 1988). Indeed, basis for this teaching can be found in Deuteronomy:

> If a man meets a virgin who is not engaged, and seizes her and lies with her, and they are caught in the act, the man who lay with her shall give fifty shekels of silver to the young woman's father, and she shall become his wife. Because he violated her he shall not be permitted to divorce her as long as he lives. (Deut 22:28-29)

By the fourth century, couples were required to obtain a priest's blessing on their marriage (Price 1996). In Gaul, the blessing was given while the couple lay in the marriage bed; in Italy, it was given in or at the door of the church. For Italians, mutual consent and the role of the church in marriage were most significant. The French emphasized the domestic nature of marriage and its sexual consummation. The blessing of the priest, however, heightened the role of the church in the formation of marriages. By the ninth century, marriage was firmly established as a function of the church.

One example of the lengths to which the church became involved with formation and dissolution of families comes from 1206. Evidently Pope Innocent III ruled a marriage null because the couple had not been able to consummate their relationship due to a gross disparity in the size of their genital organs. Innocent stated that if surgery or intercourse with a second husband enlarged the woman's vagina so as to make it possible for her to have intercourse with her first husband, then she must leave her second husband and reconstitute her prior marriage (Brundage 1993).

THE CATHOLIC CHURCH: MARRIAGE AS SACRAMENT

By the twelfth century, theologians of the Roman Catholic Church had begun developing a systematic theology and law concerning marriage and family life. From this period forward, three definitions of marriage and the family shaped church teachings.

First, theologians viewed marriage as a *natural association* that God had created as the appropriate channel for sexuality and the means for producing and raising children in the service and love of God. After the fall into sin, marriage became the remedy for lust, and a less worthy state than celibacy. Marriage was "a remedy for sin, not a recipe for righteousness" (Witte 1996:1109). Virginity continued to be idealized.

From another theological viewpoint, marriage was considered to be a *contractual unit* that two parties voluntarily and freely entered for a lifetime of love and service.

Finally, another group of theologies defined marriage as a *sacrament*. The union of body, soul and mind symbolized the eternal union between Christ and the church, bringing sanctifying grace to the couple, the church and the community. This sacramental definition integrated the other two definitions of marriage and family, giving the natural acts of sex and parenting spiritual significance. This view placed marriage and family life in the hierarchy of the church's institutions, although still not as elevated as celibacy (Witte 1997).

The sacramental definition of marriage crystallized in the thirteenth century and thereafter. Although the early church fathers had described marriage as a sacrament, thirteenth-century writers went beyond those teachings:

> Augustine called marriage a sacrament in order to demonstrate its symbolic stability. Thirteenth-century writers called marriage a sacrament to demonstrate its spiritual efficacy. Augustine said that marriage as a symbol of Christ's bond to the church *should* not be dissolved; thirteenth-century writers said that marriage as a permanent channel of sacramental grace *could* not be dissolved. (Witte 1997:29-30)

Although modified and adapted through the centuries, this sacramental model of marriage lies at the heart of Catholic theology still today and has made marriage and family life a central concern of the church throughout the centuries.

Monogamy

For those who married, monogamy in its strictest sense was obviously the ideal. Monogamy meant having only one spouse in a lifetime, not just having only one spouse at a time. Some church leaders forbade remarriage even after the death of one's spouse. This was not so as to preserve the monogamous relationship for the world to come, because Christ clearly taught that there is no marriage in heaven (Lk 20:35). Rather, church leaders simply valued the single state over marriage.

> To have married in one's youth, when blood was strong and family pressure irresistible, was unimpeachable. But for a mature and independent widower or widow to

seek a second marriage was evidence of less than Christian priorities. The Church called widows in particular to a special ministry of intercession, as a spiritual "altar of God." To prefer remarriage was to reject an important ecclesial role. (Price 1996:27).

As the church spread its influence, it encountered cultures in which monogamy was clearly not the ideal. For example, monogamy was not the norm for the Germanic invaders of the Roman Empire. Many of the wealthy had a number of wives and an entourage of concubines. Ultimately the church prevailed, but it was a long struggle that was successful, at least in part, due to economic and social conditions, not just religious teaching.

Who Could Marry

Consistent with the contractual perspective, which predicated marriage on the voluntary consent of both parties, the canon law of the Roman Catholic Church dissolved marriages formed through duress, deceit and coercion. In addition, the church dissolved unions considered invalid because of various preexisting legal, spiritual or familial ties. Clandestine marriages were also forbidden, although they evidently continued to take place. Marriage was under exclusive control of the church; the right to marry was restricted to baptized Christians (Brundage 1993; Schillebeeckx 1965). Once persons were married and their marriage had been undertaken voluntarily, however, the sacramental perspective underscored that the marriage could not be dissolved. The canon law of marriage was formalized by the Council of Trent in 1563 and has continued to strongly influence marriage laws in Western cultures ever since (Witte 1997).

In the eleventh century, leaders abolished marriage and sexual behavior for clergy. This effort was driven not only by the church's abhorrence of sexuality but also by practical considerations. It cost the church more to maintain clergy with families. The church also feared that clerics would use their office to accumulate an inheritance for their children rather than single-mindedly serving the church. This new policy was not simply a prohibition of marriage for new clergy, but also involved the expectation that the current clergy put away their wives and concubines.

The new rule of priestly celibacy resulted in suffering for women and children. Not only did wives lose their social positions, but they were driven from their homes and their honor was ruined when their marriages were labeled immoral.

The new policy branded children of clergy illegitimate and withdrew their right to inherit from their fathers. They were "reviled as the 'cursed seed' of their fathers' lust" (Brundage 1987:217; see also Quale 1988).

Not all clergy families accepted this policy without protest. Archbishop John of Rouen was stoned by indignant clergy when he ordered them to abandon their concubines. In 1077 a proponent of clerical celibacy was burned alive in Cambrai by outraged clergy (Brundage 1987). Over time, however, the church's policy was enforced and obeyed, though occasional protest and even open disregard for it have continued to the present. In 1996 a Roman Catholic priest was suspended from the priesthood when it was discovered that he had been secretly married for fifteen years. The bishop ruled that the priest "could resume his vocation if he decides to end his marriage" (Religion News Service 1996:1006). In other words, divorce would be the better choice, presumably because it would end the sexual relationship and the duality of commitment to a family and to God.

Equality in Marriage

Equality, not hierarchical power, was considered the governing principle for relationships between spouses. Gratian, the twelfth-century Bolognese scholar who has been called the father of canon law, repeatedly affirmed the equality of husbands and wives. He derived this principle from 1 Corinthians 7:4, which he paraphrased "A man does not have power over his body; rather, his wife does" (Brundage 1993:67). This equality held not only in rights but also in obligations; men were penalized just as severely as women for adultery and other sexual offenses. The canon law maintained the "clean-hands rule": only the man with "clean hands" (i.e., not himself guilty of adultery) could legally charge his wife with adultery.

This equality within marriage is quite remarkable in a social order that otherwise was based on rigid hierarchical structures. Women were assumed to be inferior to every male of the same social rank and generally incapable of handling power. For example, Bernard of Parma (d. 1266) proclaimed that a woman should not have power "because she is not made in the image of God; rather man is the image and glory of God and woman ought to be subject to man and, as it were, like his servant" (Brundage 1993:250).

Nevertheless, gender equality within the family seems to have been a critical factor in the growing recognition that marriage should be more than a physical union of a man and a woman in order to produce children and pass on property.

It was indeed the foundation for conceptualizing the potential for an emotional relationship in marriage. Although church leaders borrowed the phrase "marital affection" from the Romans, they gave it a quite different meaning. By the late medieval period, canonists were stating that society ought not to sanction union without love by recognizing it as marriage (Brundage 1993).

Church Teaching Versus Actual Family Life
Throughout history, what the church has taught and what was practiced by families of the church have often diverged. For example, the Catholic Church was deeply concerned about the morality of sexual activity and limited it to marriage. But families had different concerns. They were often more con-cerned about alliances which sexual activity could establish that would either hurt or help the family. "Institutionalizing a degree of permissiveness in the relations between young people was sometimes perceived as the best means of retaining a hold on an age group, which was by nature unstable, and making it co-operate with family strategies" (Burguiere and Lebrun 1996:126). Young men were expected to "sow wild oats"—that is, have sexual relationships with compromised young women who could not expect marriage. This was believed to be a means of controlling the sexual behavior of young men until an appro-priate marriage alliance could be formed. In some places, young people could meet and even live together while their families negotiated the nuptials. The marriage was celebrated once the girl had become pregnant, when the husband and his parents were assured that the girl could provide them with descendants (ibid.).

THE PROTESTANT REFORMATION

The Protestant Reformation was by no means a united effort, nor was it without precedent. Criticisms of the Roman Church's practices and beliefs had been com-mon. What was different about the sixteenth-century Reformers was their ability to secure a hearing and the Roman Church's inability to silence them. They had many different agendas and priorities, but at the core was their theology of mar-riage and the family. A number of early Reformers faced persecution by the Catholic Church and its political allies for violating the canon law of marriage. A number of the earliest leaders were ex-priests and ex-monastics who left their orders, denounced their vows of celibacy and married (Witte 1997).

According to the Protestants, one's primary Christian duty was not to church, tradition and family but directly to God, recalling the early church's emphasis on the duty to God taking precedence above all else. Individuals were responsible before God for themselves; one's family ties were neither protection nor limitation when it came to God's demands. The Protestant emphasis on conversion was largely responsible for a shift in priorities even further from family. Conversion carried the expectation, or at least the potential, of burning bridges between one's former life and a new loyalty to follow wherever God led. This emphasis reinforced individualism over family loyalty and relationships. Such a direct challenge of the family's authority complemented the Reformation's concurrent elevating of family life as a legitimate and worthy choice for Christians.

Protestant Models of Marriage and Family

Protestants held on to the naturalist understanding of marriage as an association created by God for procreation and caregiving. They also kept the contractual perspective, which posits that marriage is a voluntary association entered into by mutual consent. But they rejected the view of marriage as a sacrament. Marriage for the Reformers was a social institution independent of the church. "Participation in marriage required no prerequisite faith or purity and conferred no sanctifying grace, as did true sacraments" (Witte 1997:5). The nature of this social institution was seen somewhat differently by Lutherans, Calvinists and Anglicans.

Lutherans. Martin Luther emphasized the social dimension of marriage: oversight of marriage belonged principally to the government, not to the church. According to Luther, God has ordained two kingdoms in which persons live simultaneously. The earthly, political kingdom is the realm of creation and of civic life; it operates by reason, law and passion. The heavenly kingdom is the realm of redemption, of spiritual and eternal life; it operates by faith, hope and love. The earthly kingdom has been distorted by sin, but the heavenly kingdom is saved and renewed by grace. Luther taught that marriage belongs to the earthly, created kingdom and, although divinely ordained, functions primarily to fulfill human ends. Marriage is the present community for a couple, not a sacramental union for eternal life. If one broke that community—whether by adultery or desertion or another such violation of the contract—the couple could sue for divorce. And because marriage was a social contract, marriage had to be public, involving parental consent, witnesses, church consecration and registration, and priestly instruction.

Parents were given a more significant role in the marriage of their children than they had previously enjoyed. Their will was to reflect the will of God for the couple, and they had God-given authority to judge the maturity and readiness of the couple for marriage, as well as the legality of their prospective relationship (Witte 1997).

Calvinists. In the mid-sixteenth century in Geneva, John Calvin embraced many of the Lutheran theological and legal reforms, recasting and reshaping them. According to Calvin and his followers, marriage was not a sacrament, yet it was more than Luther's social contract. Marriage was a covenant that involved not only the couple but the entire community. Like Luther, Calvin insisted that marriage include the couple's parents, two witnesses, the minister and the magistrate.

> This Calvinist covenantal model mediated both sacramental and contractual understandings of marriage. On the one hand, this covenantal model confirmed the sacred and sanctifying qualities of marriage without ascribing to it sacramental functions. Marriage was regarded as a holy and loving fellowship, a compelling image of the bond between Yahweh and His elect, between Christ and His church. But marriage was no sacrament, for it confirmed no divine promise. On the other hand, this covenantal model confirmed the contractual and consensual qualities of marriage without subjecting it to the personal preferences of the parties. But marriage was more than a contract, for God was a third party to every marriage covenant, and God set its basic terms in the order and law of creation. Freedom of contract was thus effectively limited to choosing maturely which party to marry—with no real choice about the form, forum, or function of marriage once a fit spouse was chosen. (Witte 1997:8)

Calvin's early theology pictured marriage as an institution of the earthly kingdom alone that functioned primarily to keep persons free from the sins of lust, fornication and adultery. As his theology matured, however, Calvin developed a far more spiritual view of marriage.

> Conjugal love is "holy" when "husband and wife are joined in one body and one soul. God reigns in a little household, even one in dire poverty, when the husband and the wife dedicate themselves to their duties to each other. Here there is a holiness greater and nearer the kingdom of God than there is even in a cloister." (Witte 1997:110)

Anglicans. Particularly during the later Tudor and Stuart periods from about 1540 to 1640, Anglicanism developed a "commonwealth model of marriage"

(Witte 1997:8). This model built on the Catholic sacramental model, the Lutheran social model and the Calvinist covenant model. Marriage was certainly a symbol of Christ's love of the church, a social contract and a covenant, but more than these, marriage and the family served and symbolized the common good—the good of the couple, their children, the church and the state.

Initially this model rationalized the traditional hierarchies of husband over wife, parents over children, church over family, and state over church. England had rejected many of the Protestant reforms and had returned to medieval canon law, but under the headship of the English crown. The "little commonwealth" concept placed the family squarely in the hierarchy of social institutions of the great English Commonwealth (Witte 1997).

Principles for Marriage and Family Life

The reforms brought about by Calvinists and Lutherans in Protestant Europe and by Anglicans in England resulted in a number of changes that had profound impacts on family life: (1) an emphasis on the goodness of marital sexuality, (2) the rightness of marriage even and especially for clergy, (3) respect for women, (4) the possibility of divorce and (5) the vocation of parenting.

Emphasis on the goodness of marital sexuality. The Reformers were concerned with teaching and discipline in sexual matters. Both Luther and Calvin rejected the teaching that marital sex must be limited to attempts to conceive offspring. The virtue of sex was its expression and increase of a couple's love for one another, not whether it resulted in children. It was a normal part of marriage, a sign of love that needed no procreative function to justify it. Affection and love lay at the heart of the good of marriage. Calvin did worry that married couples who had sex simply for pleasure might be falling short of Christian perfection, but he also offered the comfort that God pardons any consequent sin because of the value of marriage. In fact, Calvin turned the Roman Church's view upside down: for Calvin, marriage was the greater good and led to holiness. He was suspicious of celibacy, which he considered morally suspect and a path to unhappiness and sin (Brundage 1987).

Nevertheless, the belief that sexuality was sinful still competed with and sometimes dominated the belief that sexuality is inherently good. For example, the Puritans built on the beliefs of Reformers and taught that within marriage, sex is pure. Robert Cleaver and other later Puritans, however, developed a Puritan sexual ethic more fully, calling for moderation, even in wedlock, and occasional abstinence, such as during fasts and menstruation. They advocated beginning sexual interaction with prayer for God's blessing of the couple's seed—an indirect indication that the primary purpose of sex is procreation. Over time they formulated so many warnings and restrictions that their pronouncements regarding the goodness and purity of sexuality lost meaning. Some warned that a plague would fall on children begotten during uncontrolled marital sexual activity. For example, in 1603 Cleaver wrote:

> Christians therefore must know that when men and women raging with boiling lust meet together as brute beasts, having no other respect than to satisfy their carnal concupiscence, when they make no conscience to sanctify the marriage bed with prayer, when they have no care to increase the church of Christ . . . it is the just judgment of God to send them either monsters or fools, or else such as . . . most wicked, graceless and profane persons. (Quoted in Doriani 1996:42)

One can imagine the shame and grief experienced by parents who bore children with disabilities or who died in infancy in a context of teachings such as this.

The rightness of marriage and family even and especially for clergy. Opening marriage as a possibility for the clergy was one of the most significant planks in the Reformers' platform. They pointed out that the requirement of celibacy had not promoted sexual purity at all. Because marriage had been forbidden to them, Roman Catholic clergy evidently had frequently established concubinage relationships. Bishops simply fined priests for "whoring." Those clerics living with concubines were required to pay annual penitential fees and "cradle taxes" when children were born to them (Ozment 1983:5).

These abuses were eliminated when the Reformers made clergy marriage a possibility. They offered priests who were living with concubines the opportunity to marry, which many chose to do. The Reformers believed that the clergy should set an example of Christian life for the laity in domestic as well as spiritual matters—and to do so, they should be married.

Of all the Reformation's applications of theology to everyday life, nothing affected clergy more than this. Protestant clerics became self-styled and sometimes dogmatic counselors and speakers with regard to marriage and childrearing. Piety in families became ever more important. The Reformers expected fathers to lead their families in daily prayer and Bible reading (Burguiere and Lebrun 1996).

Family life also put the religious thinking of church leaders to tests that celibate clergy had been able to avoid. For example, Martin Luther, husband and father of six children, discovered that life within a family has a profound way of influencing one's theology. It was within his own family that Luther met the greatest challenge to his theology and faith—the death of his thirteen-year-old daughter left him battling with anger at God (Ozment 1992).

Respect for women. For the Reformers, the appropriate foundation for a marriage was the love of husband and wife and their mutual willingness to make sacrifices for one another. Marriage was to be based on respect and trust. Although physical attraction and emotional love were important, they were not the conditions for marriage. Indirectly, this emphasis on mutual affection resulted in an elevation of the status of women. A drawing by Peter Lombard, originating in the Middle Ages and often referred to by writers of the sixteenth century, pointed out that woman was created neither from Adam's head nor from his foot, but rather from his "middle" or "side." "She had not been set above him to rule over him as his lord, nor was she placed beneath him as a 'footstool' or 'footrag' for him to abuse as he pleased; rather she had been created to be his 'co-worker' and 'companion' " (Ozment 1983:64).

Both Roman Catholic and Reformed church leaders recognized a woman's right to put her conscience above what had been preached as her marital duty to obey her husband. For example, she could rely on her pastor's rather than her husband's instructions if the two conflicted (Quale 1988).

The possibility of divorce. The Roman Catholic view of marriage as sacrament, an eternal enduring bond, had made divorce impossible, although annulments were possible for unconsummated marriages. Initially the Protestants also defined the marital contract as irrevocable; even escapes earlier provided by the Roman Catholic annulments were no longer available. Luther stated that the community formed by a husband and a wife was the most fundamental building block of society. Consent, companionship and mutual respect became the watchwords of marriage.

Because the foundation of marriage was changed from sacrament for procreation to contract for companionship, however, the door was opened for divorce. Luther himself believed that the marriage bond was too important to be allowed to stand if all communication, affection and respect between spouses were irrevocably destroyed. At the same time, that bond was too important to allow a marriage to end without every attempt being made to save it.

Most of the Reformers agreed that divorce could be granted on grounds of adultery, desertion, cruelty or unwillingness or inability to engage in sexual intercourse. Luther considered it a right and even a duty to remarry after divorce. For Calvin, the right to remarry following divorce was a matter of freedom of conscience: religious authorities should not impose limitations on conduct that are not based in Scripture (Brundage 1987:559). Thus the Reformers granted the right to remarry, at least to the innocent party (Witte 1996).

The Reformers' emphasis on mutual commitment and communion fed the concept of romantic love. The secularization of this teaching led to the concept of "marriage for love." That has devolved in our own society to a belief in the centrality of romantic love and intimacy for marriage and, consequently, the legitimacy of dissolving a marriage in which feelings of romantic attraction and affection wane. Although there has been a long journey from the early church and Reformation teachings of the significance of mutual, self-submissive love as the ideal of marriage, current divorce statistics are a result not only of sociological, cultural and economic factors but also at least to some extent to centuries of church teaching about the importance of love as the bond of marriage.

The vocation of parenting. Luther saw fatherhood, even the care of infants, as a divine vocation. Parenting was a responsibility too important to be left to one parent; it should be shared by mother and father. The maternal role was perceived as being more important during infancy and early childhood. The father's role became increasingly important after age six or seven, when regular discipline was considered to be critical to the formation of the maturing child. The Reformers believed that the bond between father and child was just as intimate and enduring as the maternal bond (Ozment 1983).

The significance of the parent-child bond was increased with the elimination of the practice of godparenting. Luther rejected such "spiritual relations" as "superstitions" that limited Christian freedom. The concept of godparenting had been expanded in unwieldy ways that precluded the possibility of marriage among even distant kin of the godchild and godparent (Aymard 1989). Unintentionally, however, the elimination of this practice decreased the role of the community in family life; parenting now was virtually the exclusive responsibility of the biological parents.

In the early seventeenth century, English Puritan church leaders wrote "conduct books" to model family for Christians. Diverging from the Lutherans and Calvinists, and more in concert with the Anglicans, their model was hierarchical.

For the Puritans, the absolute authority of the man, the subordination of women and the (often harsh) disciplined upbringing of children provided the "bedrock of evangelisation" (Fletcher 1996). Robert Schnucker has analyzed materials published at the turn of the sixteenth century that laid down rules about the beating of children, for which both parents bore equal responsibility and which was delivered equally to both genders. Parents were strongly advised to use physical discipline only when verbal reproof had failed, and then without excessive violence and never in anger (Schnucker 1990).

THE ENLIGHTENMENT

Beginning in the eighteenth century, both in Europe and in the New World, changes in social structures had a significant impact on the relationship between the church and families. Over the next century, the mother became recognized as the parent primarily responsible for children's upbringing; after all, the mother was increasingly the default parent in the home as men began to leave home for work as the Industrial Revolution gathered steam. During the time that home increasingly became a haven from the amoral world of work, stress was increasingly placed on the innocence rather than the inherent depravity of children, who were the fruit of that haven. Popular advice books instructed parents in ways to teach children responsibility, thrift, industry, delayed gratification and sexual restraint (Brady 1991). As medicine emerged as a profession, physicians began replacing ministers as the voice of male authority about family life (ibid.).

Enlightenment thinkers increasingly emphasized that marriage was a contract rather than sacrament, covenant or commonwealth. It was defined as a bargain struck between two persons who thus voluntarily entered a private, intimate association. The terms of that association were up to the persons themselves. This private contract model clearly paved the way for much of the transformation of marriage and family life in the twentieth century (Witte 1997).

Nevertheless, the church still strongly influenced the sphere of the family. Protestant families engaged in daily prayer and Bible reading, usually as a family group. Family Bible reading was an extension of the practice of reading to one another as a form of entertainment. The father usually presided over the family Bible reading, which consisted of reading a few verses, singing and reciting the Lord's Prayer or other written prayers. Bibles were expensive, and few families owned more than one, which was preserved and passed from generation to generation, often with vital information (such as dates of births, weddings and deaths) recorded in them. Many family members still could not read; the family Bible study time made the Scriptures accessible to illiterate family members on a daily basis (Lebrun 1989).

Evangelicalism, a reform movement within the Anglican Church, emerged in the late eighteenth century. Evangelicals assumed that woman's godliness was linked to her maternal and wifely duties. Eve had fallen because of her unabashed sensuality. But Mary, the mother of Christ, had given new hope to womanhood by bearing Jesus. Woman could shine at home, "the gentle moon to her husband's sun, the modest violet showing its beauties only to those with time and patience" (Hall 1990:58). Men had power in the world, but women could influence men. Indeed, this was a woman's special skill. It was women's particular responsibility to care for men in such a way that men would listen to them and heed their advice. The evangelical portrayal of family roles gave middle-class men and women a way to make sense of the rapidly changing world (ibid.).

THE CHURCH AND NON-EUROPEAN CULTURES

With the invasion of the New World by Europeans, missionaries came to evangelize the indigenous population. It was in Mexico, conquered at the end of the 1520s, that the church first attempted to enforce Christian marriage on a large scale as the most effective means of Christianizing the Indians (Bernand and Gruzinski 1996). The missionaries stressed the nuclear family—husband, wife and children—as the Christian family and attempted to eliminate the more extended household system of the indigenous culture. The church discriminated between legitimate children and bastards. "The children of polygamous and 'incestuous' couples who had been removed from their paternal homes by zealous monks were the first of those abandoned creatures who constituted one of the running sores of colonial society and a reservoir of cheap labour for the Spaniards" (ibid. 183).

Redemption and conversion meant more than religious teaching; it meant that the Indian civilization, including family and tribal structures, had to be destroyed and replaced by European Christian culture. Native American children were forced to attend school—frequently boarding schools, since their parents were considered to be a bad influence (Shoemaker 1991). Such thinking continued into the nineteenth century (Carey 1993) and also was reflected in Western colonization and enslavement of other civilizations. African slaves were stripped of family names and relationships and given new "Christian" names.

Because the church in Europe controlled writing, the clergy were able to impose a collection of rules not only on European but also on colonized societies, developing a certain homogeneity between cultures. At the same time, however, in many places the gulf widened between church norms and actual family life (Goody 1996).

THE CHURCH AND FAMILIES IN RECENT HISTORY

Until the twentieth century, the Catholic and Protestant models of marriage and family life crafted in medieval and Reformed Europe continued to be the foundation of family law and social norms in Western society. Many of the characteristics of the so-called modern family—nuclear structure, free choice of marriage partner, and the ideal of conjugal bonding based on mutual affection—have been in place, or at least in the works, since A.D. 800.

In interaction with the forces of modernity, marriage as a social institution has increasingly devolved into a simple contract between persons, to be formed, maintained or dissolved as the couple sees fit. John Witte points out, however, that this is not necessarily a movement from sacred to secular:

> The medieval Catholic model was every bit as secular in its theology and law of marriage as the Enlightenment contractarian model. The modern contractarian construction of marital equality was every bit as religious in inspiration as earlier Christian constructions of marital hierarchy. Each model has struck its own balances between church and state, clergy and laity, rights and duties, order and liberty, dogma and adiaphora in matters of marriage and sexuality. These balances were struck on the basis of deep religious convictions. (Witte 1997:12)

In most recent church history, both Catholics and Protestants have continued to develop theological understandings of family life.

Family as Domestic Church

The Roman Catholic Church has referred to the family as the "domestic church." The church officially declared at Vatican II that "the family is not merely like the Church, but is truly Church" (Carey 1993:115). The United States Catholic bishops proclaim this vision: "A family is our first community and most basic way in which the Lord gathers us, forms us and acts in the world. The early church expressed this truth by calling the Christian family a domestic church or church of the home" (Lynch, Preister and Ad Hoc Committee on Marriage and Family Life 1988:70). And in a homily in Perth, Australia, Pope John Paul II made the following statement:

> The family is the domestic church. The meaning of the traditional Christian idea is that the home is the Church in miniature. The Church is the sacrament of God's love. She is a communion of faith and love. She is a mother and teacher. She is at the service of the whole human family as it goes forward towards its ultimate destiny. In the same way the family is a community of life and love. It educates and leads its members to their full human maturity and it serves the good of all along the road of life. In its own way it is a living image and historical representation of the mystery of the Church. The future of the world and of the Church pass the way of the family. (November 30, 1986; in Lynch, Preister and Ad Hoc Committee on Marriage and Family Life 1988)

According to the Catholic Church, the mission of the family encompasses four distinct but interdependent tasks:

1. The family is to form an intimate community of persons;

2. The family is to serve life in its transmission, both physically by bringing children into the world, and spiritually by handing on values and traditions as well as developing the potential of each member to serve life at every age;

3. The family is to participate in the development of society by becoming a community of social training and hospitality, as well as a community of political involvement and activity; and

4. The family is to share in the life and mission of the Church by becoming a believing and evangelizing community, a community in dialogue with God, and a community at the serve of humanity. (Lynch, Preister and Ad Hoc Committee on Marriage and Family Life 1988:8)

The significance of this portrayal of families is twofold. First, families serve as significant "feeder" systems for the church, providing it with members and leaders nurtured in the bosom of faithful families. Second, the family serves as an *example* to the church. If family is the most basic church, then the church, to be effective, should emulate the characteristics of family life at its best and most faithful. Wendy Wright points to the difference it would make if churches were modeled more carefully after family:

> This way of viewing family as domestic church could have profound consequences for the larger gathered Church if the wider body truly began to learn from families what it means to be Christian community. Perhaps church as "the professionals doing for the nonprofessionals" or church as "committees that direct programs," or church as "fix-it shop for crises" or church as "social club" might give way to a renewed vision of Christian community. (Wright 1990:25)

Roman Catholic leaders have advocated taking a family perspective in planning, implementing and evaluating policies, programs, ministries and services of the church. This has meant relating to individuals in the context of their family relationships and evaluating the impact of everything the church does—its policies, programs and ministries—as they affect families. At every level of Roman Catholic organization—both diocese and parish—a family advocate is supposed to be appointed to take responsibility for the family dimension of the work and life of that organizational group (Lynch, Preister and Ad Hoc Committee on Marriage and Family Life 1988). The "Family Impact Questions" that follow guide the family advocate's continuing assessment of new policies and programs:

1. How does it state a vision of family life that is faithful to Christian tradition?

2. In what ways does it develop within the family both a greater appreciation of family activities as sacred and also a better understanding of the family's ecclesial mission?

3. How does it promote the unique ministry of the family?

4. How does it promote the tasks of the family without overburdening families?

5. How does it help spouses to remain faithful to the Church's teaching regarding their responsibilities for the transmission of life?

6. In what ways does it promote the knowledge and skills that can enable a participating family to become a more effective community of persons?

7. How does it promote the development of family prayer, ritual and celebration?

8. In what concrete ways does it promote the organization of families into small faith communities and help them to be more politically active in protecting the rights of all families?

9. How does it enable families to be more effective in handing on their values and traditions? (ibid. 22)

This significant support for families, however, extends only to families formed by first marriages. Divorce and remarriage clearly remain outside of what is acceptable for full participation in Roman Catholic life, as represented by the following statement by the International Theological Commission as part of the church renewal that followed Vatican II:

> The incompatibility of the state of remarried divorced persons with the precept and mystery of the paschal love of the Lord makes it impossible for these people to receive the sign of unity with Christ in the Eucharist. Access to eucharistic communion can only come through penance, which implies detestation of the sin committed and the firm purpose of not sinning again. . . . While this illegitimate situation does not permit a life of full communion with the Church, Christians who find themselves in this state yet are not excluded from the action of divine grace and form a link with the Church. Therefore they must not be deprived of pastoral assistance. (Delhaye 1984:32)

Family as Foundation for the Church

Although Protestant leaders have not articulated the role of the family as "church," they agree that family is integral to and an essential foundation for the church. Church leaders have not simply been concerned about the daily lives of their members but also have perceived that what happens in the home profoundly affects the church. For example, in *How to Have a Family Altar*, published in 1951 and widely circulated in evangelical circles, Norman Williams envisioned the role of the family as quite similar to the Roman Catholic "domestic church." Williams quotes Jesus' teaching that he would be present wherever two or three are gathered in his name (Mt 18:18-20): "I think Jesus had in mind the little praying families. He was looking down the vista of time at all those families that would daily gather together in prayer" (Williams 1951:7). Williams and many others taught that the way to revival in the church was daily family prayer and worship in the home.

When church leaders have described the family as the foundation for the church or as a church itself, they have often tied this definition to the nuclear family. The place of other kinds of families and of those who choose celibacy is not addressed.

Efforts to Strengthen Families

Out of alarm over rising divorce rates, the twentieth century brought a flurry of attempts to strengthen marriages and families among the various Christian

denominations. Articles and books on family life were augmented with a pleth-
ora of church programs and parachurch organizations designed to help families;
one example of the latter is Presbyterian Mariners. In the 1920s in Wilmington,
California, Presbyterian pastor Louis Evans and his wife perceived the need for
an intentional ministry with married couples and founded the Mariners. The
Mariners "ship" is a congregational group of couples and individuals that shares
in gatherings and celebrations and becomes a family for one another. Each Mariners ship takes on a "cargo," an area of outreach to or involvement with the
needs of others for which they share responsibility. The idea spread among other
congregations, and Mariners had become a national organization by the mid-
1930s (Trout 1993). The emphasis on families serving as a unit responding to
the needs beyond themselves is unusual in programs designed to strengthen
families, as is the inclusion of persons living in situations other than nuclear
families.

Another effort, the Christian Family Movement, began in Chicago in the
1940s, during World War II. Its emphasis was less on strengthening family life
and more on Bible study and the living out of faith together. Pat Crowley, an
attorney, began a men's group called Catholic Action, which was modeled on the
methods of Young Christian Workers in Belgium. His wife started a group for
wives that met at the same time. Describing the beginnings of the movement,
Patty Crowley said, "We met separately because in those days the church never
heard of husbands and wives meeting together. We often wondered why we
weren't meeting together. Pat and I decided to invite a few of these couples to
join us for a weekend. And that was the start of the Christian Family Movement"
(D'Antonio 1995:251). No longer were individuals just being instructed by the
church about how to live with their families in the privacy of their homes; the
family relationships were now being lived out in the presence of other members
of the congregation.

Marriage Encounter began in 1948 in the Roman Catholic Church. Catholic
leaders had been reconsidering teachings about marital sexuality, giving much
more consideration to the emotional bonds of married couples and laying less
emphasis on procreation as the central function of marriage. The Marriage
Encounter movement, one of the first marriage-enrichment programs, was born
out of this concern and has continued to the present (National Marriage
Encounter 1978).

Finally, one of the most influential organizations for shaping the relationship of churches with families has been Focus on the Family, a parachurch organization developed by psychologist James Dobson that produces educational literature and a diversity of media resources for families and congregations. In many churches with a diversity of theological persuasions, literature from the Dobson organization is used for shaping family ministry programs more than literature from the church's own denomination. Dobson's approach mixes "traditional" parenting, biblical insights and basic psychology. Dobson is currently *the* central figure in conservative Christianity. His television and radio broadcasts have a weekly audience of twenty-eight million people, and a core of four million listen to his radio show *Focus on the Family* daily. The video series he developed has been seen by over seventy million persons, most of them within their own congregation. His most popular books have sold more than sixteen million copies (Gerson 1998:23).

Focus on the Family represents a major shift in the relationship of church and family. Many of the programs of the church have wed the social sciences with theology and biblical teaching. Coupled with effective use of mass media, accessible and attractive practical resources for families and congregations, and an overt national political agenda, however, Focus on the Family has demonstrated the influence parachurch organizations can have.

CONCLUSIONS

Anyone tempted to despair over the church's ability to have an impact on family life need only review the history of the family over the past two thousand years to realize that the church can be a powerful shaper of family life not only among its own members but indeed in the society in which it is embedded.

The church is a human institution, however, with a potential for hurt that sometimes offsets the potential for good. Spelling out what is ideal and the "best" has the potential for oppressing those who are not able to achieve that ideal or who feel called to walk a different path. A sexual relationship between husband and wife that is embedded in reverence for the Creator and prayers for blessing on their love is ideal. However, the Puritan teaching that any less than this could result in the malformation of a child no doubt created undue hardship and unwarranted shame. The teaching that celibacy is virtuous led to a denigration of marriage and sexuality, and to overt injustice in the case of wives and children cast aside when celibacy became a requirement for priesthood. The teaching of monogamy led to the abandonment and enslavement of children and wives of indigenous peoples in the New World. More recently, the teaching that marriage is best has led to a marginalization of single persons and a paradoxical treatment of celibacy as a second-best life commitment within many Protestant communities of faith.

This brief review of the church's influence on family life suggests several principles for family ministry.

☐ Any teaching about what is ideal should be firmly grounded in grace and love and inclusion for all those who might otherwise inadvertently be drawn out of the circle of concern. Jesus kept folding in those who were socially unacceptable in his day, and he challenged his followers to think beyond their usual categories of inclusion. A doctrine of family life fueled by judging who is "in" and who is "out" based on their family situations needs to be carefully scrutinized. Rather than seeing the ourselves as sieves controlling what comes into the boat called the church, it seems better to see ourselves as nets cast out to gather in all kinds (Mt 13:47).

☐ The church's teachings constitute one of several shapers of family life, including economic, social and cultural realities. Thus teachings and programs should be sensitive to the intended and unintended interactions with other forces in family life.

☐ Different Christian traditions have defined the relationship between family and church differently, based on their theological premises and cultural traditions. Knowledge of different traditions and approaches, however, can be important ground for creative ministry in one's own context. For example, the Family Impact Questions developed for use in Roman Catholic organizations can be modified for use in other settings to evaluate the impact of programs and processes on families.

☐ Although the influence of the church on family life has evolved over time, there have been watershed points when this change outpaced other social and cultural changes—the Reformation, the Christianization of indigenous peoples, even today's parachurch movements. In short, the church can be a powerful force for dramatic social change.

Section Four

Biblical Foundations
for Family Ministry Today

S INCE PAUL WROTE LETTERS TO THE EARLY CHURCHES, CHRISTIAN leaders have recognized that Christians living with and loving one another demonstrate what it means to be a follower of Christ. The Roman Catholic Church, the Reformers, the Puritans and certainly church leaders in diverse traditions today have had much to say about what a family is, its importance in the life of Christians, how it should be ordered and how family members should relate to one another. The family is a particularly significant proving ground for Christian discipleship and a vineyard for the fruits of the Spirit. It is in families that love, forgiveness, grace, long-suffering, patience, kindness and self-sacrifice are often learned and lived most profoundly. The term "family ministry" may itself be relatively new in the long history of the church, but care for, exhortation about and attempts to intervene in family life have been present since the beginning.

As we saw in sections one and two, what makes for strong families in American society has been a topic of considerable research in family sociology and psychology over the past few decades, and family ministry has inadvertently been shaped according to the community mental-health model which evolved in the 1960s and 1970s in the social service professions. The primary goal, according to this model, is to prevent problems by providing support services and educational programs. When family problems still occur, programs of crisis intervention are needed to limit the damage. Although the dream of community mental-health centers was only partially realized, it was an ambitious and exciting plan. With a strong network of educational programs and counseling services, much mental illness and family dysfunction would be averted.

Many of those who are shaping church programs today came of age in graduate school during the 1960s and 1970s, and they have translated this model to the church. "Family ministry" is the church version of community mental-health services. Indeed these programs have done much good. Many families have benefited enormously from their congregation's marital preparation courses, marriage enrichment retreats, parent education seminars, support groups for adults caring for frail elderly parents, and the many other real services congregations render families. The needs for ministry with families are myriad, however, and seem to be increasing exponentially year by year. No church can meet all the needs, even for educational services and counseling within its own membership, much less in the larger community. It also seems that these programs, as beneficial as they may be, are often too little too late. They do not cut to the heart of the social forces that besiege families today. This is where the community mental health model fails the church. Community mental health centers were mandated as government-funded agencies to meet the mental health needs of the population in their assigned geographic area. That was their mission. Consequently, assessing community needs and responding effectively to them was their reason for existence and the means for evaluating their effectiveness.

Churches are not community mental health centers, however. As important as ministry is to their mission, their *primary* reason for existence is not to prevent mental illness or family breakdown whenever possible and provide help when prevention has not been possible. Therefore the community mental-health model, with its community needs assessment, cannot be the *starting point* for family ministry. Instead, understanding the church's mission, and a particular congregation's contribution to that mission, is the place to begin. A story from Jesus' life illustrates how congregations need to begin their thinking about ministry priorities.

Jesus Teaches About Ministry Priorities

As the Jewish leaders plotted to kill Jesus, a woman entered the room where he reclined at the table for dinner, broke a jar of costly ointment, and poured it on his head—a gesture recognized in that culture as conveying great honor and respect. The disciples were dismayed, perceiving this to be a waste when there was so much need around them. The ointment could have been sold and the money used to feed the poor. Jesus responded by demanding that they straighten out their priorities: "Why do you trouble the woman? She has performed a good service for me. For you always have the poor with you, but you will not always have me" (Mt 26:10-11).

This rebuke to the disciples seems unfair, especially since it immediately follows Jesus' teaching that those who will inherit the kingdom prepared for them will be those who feed the hungry, give drink to the thirsty, welcome the stranger, clothe the naked and visit the prisoner (Mt 25:31-46). He had just said that serving needs is the way disciples show their care for him: "Truly I tell you, just as you did not do it to one of the least of these, you did not do it to me" (Mt 25:45). Aren't the disciples responding appropriately to the woman's wastefulness in face of all the need around them? Wouldn't a follower of Jesus be expected to use such a resource to care for the needs of others?

Jesus' teaching about the costly ointment points us again to why we serve. We serve not just because the need is there, but because we love Jesus and want to communicate that love. Our service is to be motivated by our love of Christ, not just by the needs of our communities. The disciples had missed the point. They could serve Jesus directly as a sign of their ultimate loyalty and love. Later, they would serve the poor and the powerless as *signs of their commitment to Christ.* We serve through ministry with those who represent him in our midst—hurting and oppressed people. We are driven to serve by our mission, not simply by their needs. If we start with a focus on the need, then like the disciples, we will miss the point. If we serve only because the need is there, we will become discouraged and burn out, because the needs are so extensive. There will *always* be family violence and divorce and inadequate parenting in this world; no matter how hard and effectively we work, we will not make it all go away. We must stay connected to the source of our service, the vine of which we are branches (Jn 15:1-11). We serve because we love Jesus, and if we stay connected to that loving relationship, then we will not be overwhelmed by the enormous needs around us.

Jesus' description of himself as the vine, God as the vine-grower and us as branches captures what happens if we forget that we are merely branches of Christ, expressions of Christ's love. We must "abide in the vine," otherwise we cannot bear fruit. When we lose focus on our connection to Christ and our service as expressions of that connection, we become disconnected: "Whoever does not abide in me is thrown away like a branch and withers; such branches are gathered, thrown into the fire, and burned" (Jn 15:6). What a picture of burnout!

Where Should We Begin?

What does Jesus' teaching about priorities have to do with family ministry? Like the disciples, we find ourselves overwhelmed by all the need. How should we use our limited resources? The catalog of family needs and problems in our society seems to be growing. Government leaders turn hopeful eyes to churches as key resources in caring for families. The governor of Mississippi asked every church in his state to "adopt" a welfare family and do whatever it took to help them. The governor of Texas has called for new church-state partnerships to meet human needs. A special task force proclaimed, "People in distress are not exclusively (or even primarily) government's responsibility, and the faith community should—as prescribed by both the Old and New Testaments—tend to people's temporal as well as heavenly needs" (Governor's Advisory Task Force on Faith-Based Community Service Groups 1996:vii).

Should the church become a combination welfare service and community mental health center of a new era? The more fundamental question, of course, is, what is the church's mission with regard to families? Before responding to concerns about the institution of the family in general and to the needs of specific families in our communities, churches need to consider carefully what family ministry *should be* according to the church's definition of itself and its mission. How can we best serve Christ through our ministry with families? Ultimately, that question must shape what we do.

Perhaps the unease about families reflects problems in our society's definition and expectations of family life. Leaders are calling for the church to help shore up the American family. If our society's understanding of family is flawed, however, then jumping to respond to needs without first examining our priority of being servants of Jesus Christ is the wrong thing to do.

I suggest that the church's ministry with families should begin not only with an understanding of families in our society but also with an understanding of who we are as a community of faith and what the role of the family should be in the lives of Christians. We can imagine that the resources we have for honoring Christ through service are like the costly ointment. Those resources include our budget, staffing and church programming. Before we run out to sell our costly ointment and distribute the proceeds as far as they will go to assuage family needs, we need to ponder what honors Christ the most. What can we do that will truly reflect the message of Christ?

In the first chapter of this section, I present my understanding of family relationships as God intended them to be, based on biblical themes and texts. I make no pretense of examining all the texts that relate to families; instead I look for themes that suggest whether and where and how the church should pour itself out in ministry with families.

It is appropriate that we give attention to families in our congregational ministries. The apostle Paul included guidance for family living in his letters of instruction and encouragement to the early churches. Christianity is a faith that deals with the fundamental, nitty-gritty issues of life: how to handle anger with a brother or sister (Mt 5:21-24; Gal 4:26), how husbands and wives are to relate to one another sexually (1 Cor 7:3-5), how parents are to discipline their children (Eph 6:4). Stephen Barton has pointed out that the Bible provides foundations for our understanding of family by giving us

1. a rich repository of narratives about tribes, clans, households, and family relationships for Christian reflection. Many of these are not "ideals" but instead serve as correctives of any false sentimentality about family life;

2. law, custom, poetry, and proverbial wisdom pertaining to family life (e.g., "honor your father and your mother");

3. prototypes—Ruth and Naomi, the extravagant love of the father for the prodigal son, the friendship of Jesus with his followers; and

4. powerful correctives to any tendency to give the family an inflated importance, with its abhorrence of idolatry and advocacy of the headship of Christ (Barton 1996a).

Before I examine biblical teachings about how we are to live in families and the meaning of family life for Christians, however, I want to be clear about the limitations of my understanding. This survey of biblical teachings is an examination of how the Bible is speaking to me about family relationships at the turn of the twenty-first century, in my place of living and loving in one corner of American society and one niche in a modern church rich with diversity. I have chosen passages of Scripture that have been significant to me as I wrestle with the meaning of family in the life of Christians and of congregations. As Rodney Clapp has noted, "To create and live in a truly Christian family, the church in every generation and culture must read the biblical story anew" (Clapp 1993:15). We cannot simply try to go back to the way families have been in the past; instead we must plunge forward with the truths we find in Scripture as they apply to the challenges and opportunities of our own place and time.

The examination of biblical teachings related to family life which follows should be read as "gleanings," not an attempt to draw out the central themes and intentions of the biblical writers in each passage. I will focus on what I think the texts tell us and imply about family life then and now. What place should family have in the lives of Christians, and how should they live in those family places?

Chapter 11

Biblical Definitions
of Family

ANY DISCUSSION OF BIBLICAL TEACHINGS ABOUT FAMILY LIFE
must begin with biblical definitions of the family. Definitions of family create
expectations about what families can or should be or do. Among American
Christians, definitions of family life that are enjoying popularity today seem to be
based as much on American culture as on attempts to understand biblical texts
about human relationships and God's intention for them. Unfortunately, when
unexamined, some of these definitions tend to erode and diminish rather than
strengthen and celebrate the reality and potential of families. Yet it is impossible
to read Scripture from outside our own experiences and concerns. My own concerns and experiences of ministry with families and communities have shaped the
following exploration of biblical definitions of family.

With that qualification, a good place to start in attempting to understand
what God intends families to be is the beginning.

IN THE BEGINNING . . .

In the creation account of Genesis 2, God creates the man for a reason—to nurture and protect God's good creation. Yet something is missing. The only aspect

of creation that God declares "not good" is the aloneness of the man (Gen 2:18). Therefore God decides to fashion for the man a work partner. Thus the animals are created. Each one God makes is brought to the man, and the man names them all, but none of them is quite right. Many of them could be good servants for the man. The horse, the ox, the donkey, the dog—all have great potential. But they each lack something. The man does not just need someone to help him; he needs a partner, someone who can share in all aspects of the work God has called him to do. Although the animals can serve, they cannot be true partners.

Therefore, the Scripture tells us, God puts Adam to sleep and takes a rib from his side. From that bit of bone, God makes a woman. God makes her not from the dust, as Adam was made, but from Adam himself, symbolizing their similarity. Here is someone who can truly share in the good work God has given him to do.

The goodness of God's creation, when it comes to people, is found in our potential and need for relationship with one another. It is "not good" for us to be alone. God created in us a need for intimate relationships, a need that draws us to leave the persons from whose bodies we came—our parents—to form a new "body" with a new partner (Gen 2:23-24). Being family means sharing the same ribs, the same flesh. The old saying that you cannot know another until you have "walked a mile in his moccasins" gets taken a step further in families. We become family when we feel as if we are walking with the same feet. Family has a place, then, from the very beginning of God's intention for humanity before the Fall, and even before the advent of children. Jesus' life and teaching transformed and fulfilled that intention, both as he came into the world as a baby in a family and as he then lived and taught about family relationships.

JESUS' LIFE: A TRANSFORMATION OF "FAMILY"

The stories of Jesus' own conception, birth and childhood tell of very human events shot through with the surprises of direct divine intervention. The surprise begins in the family tree of Matthew 1: "An account of the genealogy of Jesus the Messiah, the son of David, the son of Abraham. Abraham was the father of Isaac, and Isaac the father of Jacob, and Jacob the father of Judah . . ." On and on, for fifteen verses, the writer lists fathers. The series of fathers in the genealogy lead the reader to expect at the climax "and Joseph the father of Jesus." Instead the pattern changes abruptly: "And Jacob the father of Joseph the husband of Mary of whom Jesus was born." Joseph did not father Jesus as Jacob, his father, fathered him. This genealogy explains how Jesus, who had no biological, human father, could be the son of David: Joseph claimed him as his own, named him and "grafted" him into the lineage of David.

The passage that follows, which describes the events surrounding Jesus' conception (Mt 1:18-25), does not aim to prove that Jesus was born of a virgin; the passage simply takes that for granted. Instead the passage focuses on Joseph's naming of the son in obedience to the instructions of the angel. Scripture's intention is not to spotlight the virginal conception so much as to narrate how Jesus is the son of David *in spite of* the virginal conception (D. E. Garland 1993). Jesus was adopted by Joseph.

What does this mean about families? Just as Adam was created by the direct hand of God, so Jesus was formed directly by God, then grafted into the old line of descent. Jesus is the fulfillment of the promise of God when God *adopted* David as his son (2 Sam 7:14). All along, God has not been constrained by biological descent. The conception and birth of Jesus fulfilled the ancient promise to the ancestors and at the same time break through our usual definition of the "ideal" family. Americans usually think of the "model" family as a husband and wife with their own biological children. Jesus' birth and teachings challenge this. Family, according to Jesus' own lineage, family now means adoption, not simply biological relationship.

Indeed, the adoption of Jesus by Joseph points to the good news that Jesus will develop later in his teachings (Mt 12:46-50): from this point forward, no one must be without family because wombs are barren, marriages are broken or never formed, or loved ones die. The human experiences of conception, birth and marriage are transformed by the in-breaking Spirit of God, reforming family. In God's kingdom, "God sets the lonely in families" (Ps 68:5-6). In less spectacular but no less significant ways, the experience of family living takes on new meaning with the conception and birth of Jesus.

FAMILY AS VOCATION

Ernest Boyer has pointed out that the twelve disciples were not the only ones called to serve Jesus (Boyer 1984). Before Jesus was born, God called Mary and Joseph. In some ways less free choice was involved in their calling than when Jesus called the disciples from mending their fishing nets—though perhaps Mary and Joseph could have fled like Jonah, refusing the commission offered them. But how could either of them have graciously said to the angelic visitors, "Well, thanks for the opportunity, but I'm not interested"? The callings of Mary and Joseph were initially not to leave all behind and put their lives on the line, although only a few months later they did make the decision to leave all behind, fleeing to Egypt to protect their infant son from the wrath of the king (Mt 2:13-15). Initially they were simply called to be family—always a calling of total self for the sake of others.

The disciples were called to follow Jesus; Mary and Joseph were called to feed him. The disciples were called to learn from Jesus, Mary and Joseph to teach him to speak; the disciples to stand beside him, Mary and Joseph to help him stand. The disciples were called to suffer with Jesus the pain of his death so that he might give the gift of life. Mary and Joseph were called to suffer for him the pain of birth so that he might give the gift of love (Boyer 1984:17). God chose to do it this way. God could have chosen to bring Jesus to earth full grown, walking in across Lake Galilee. Instead Jesus was born as a helpless infant, to young parents divinely called to nurture him toward his calling.

The call to live faithfully as family to those we find in our care is just as much a response to the call of God as the response to leave everything behind to take up Jesus' cross.

THE ROLE OF COMMUNITY IN FAMILY SUPPORT

Living out their calling was far from easy for Mary and Joseph. Yet they were not alone. Each of the four major events of Jesus' birth and childhood recorded in the Gospel of Luke shows God's presence transforming the family's experience—a leaping babe-in-the-womb, angelic visitations, the filling of prophets with the Holy Spirit, and the astonishing wisdom of the young Jesus. These are stories not simply of two parents raising their special child with God providing unusual evidence of blessing. More than that, they are stories of God at work blessing them *through a community* that participated in significant ways in Jesus' care and preparation for ministry.

A Leaping Babe
As soon as Mary learned from the angel about the conception that was about to take place within her, she went "with haste" to the home of Zechariah and Eliza-

beth, her cousin. At the sound of Mary's voice, the babe within Elizabeth "leaped" in recognition; Elizabeth was filled with the Holy Spirit and shouted, "Blessed are you among women, and blessed is the fruit of your womb" (Lk 1:42). Elizabeth continued with words of hope and promise about the child growing within Mary, until Mary herself burst out with a song of praise.

We can only imagine how this young girl must have felt, hastily running away to her cousin's home, away from her own family and community. She has seen an angel; she is pregnant and not married. We do not know if she told her parents about these disturbing events, or anyone else for that matter; but her hasty trip seems to signify an attempt to run and hide to collect herself for what may be coming. How comforting Elizabeth's greeting must have been! Here was someone who understood and confirmed her strange experience, *before* she even tried to recount it.

Running outside the confines of Mary's parental family to the larger family was thus divinely affirmed. God caused Elizabeth's babe-in-the-womb to leap, which led to Elizabeth's blessing. As Mary faced the daunting task before her, she was nurtured and blessed by extended family.

We are told that her needs for nurture and support during this critical time were met most significantly not by her parents or even by her husband-to-be, but by the larger family system. In response to Elizabeth's divinely inspired affirmation and support, Mary praised God.

Angelic Visitations

Late in the pregnancy, Joseph and Mary's lives were again interrupted, this time by a government mandate to travel to Bethlehem. This would be no home birth. Bethlehem may have been home to some of Joseph's relatives, since this was his family's home territory. But here we do not hear of anyone coming forward to support this young girl having her first baby. This was his family, not hers, and evidently no one in the family made a place for the couple or gave them welcome (Lk 2:1-7).

Conception and birth are to be celebrated, and when Mary had fled to her cousin Elizabeth, God prompted celebration with the leaps of a babe-in-the-womb. Now with no one in Bethlehem celebrating this very significant birth, God intervened, sending angels to shepherds in the fields. The angels told the shepherds the good news of Jesus' birth and sent them to see him and to make over him the way new babies should be made over, especially this baby (Lk 2:8-20).

Imagine what it must have been like for Mary and Joseph, young and far from home, to have this group of rough shepherds show up in the night to see their new baby and talk about how wonderful he was. This group was a significantly different crowd from the usual grandparents and aunts and women friends of the new mother whom we would expect to gather at such a time. These were men, and rough, low-class ones at that. They were a very unlikely group to be making a huge fuss over this new baby. Yet their words of adoration were the kinds of words that a mother stores in memory to draw from when times are difficult; Mary "treasured" their words to "ponder in her heart."

This story introduces a new understanding of family that later gains full expression in the teaching of Jesus. Sometimes following Jesus requires physical separation or emotional distance from our families. Mary and Joseph were far from the community Mary had known she could find with Elizabeth and Zechariah. We must be willing to leave our families, Jesus said in his teachings, to follow him (Mt 4:22; 8:21-22). Nevertheless, when we follow God's call, whoever does the will of God becomes our brother and sister and mother (Mt 12:50). When Joseph and Mary follow their calling, giving birth to this baby—who was God's plan and not theirs—God miraculously surrounds them with a rough lot of shepherds who are likewise following God's instructions. These men take the celebrative place normally reserved for family because they have believed.

Jesus' birth was evidently not particularly noteworthy, except that the young couple could not find shelter and welcome, so that Jesus was placed in a manger. There is no word in the canonical Gospels about whether Joseph found a midwife or a helpful relative to aid in the delivery. What the Gospel writer finds significant is that God broke into this young couple's aloneness. God's child needs to be celebrated and welcomed into a larger family and community, and in a lonely world God provides that family and community. Later Jesus would teach his followers that every child is his ambassador, his representative with us. Thus every child deserves community recognition and celebration.

Spirit-Filled Prophets

Jesus' parents took him to the temple in Jerusalem for the rites of purification when he was forty days old, as prescribed. Imagine how this young couple felt;

perhaps people were whispering about the child and about them. Even if they had not heard the unusual circumstances of his conception, they probably had heard the shepherds' tales about angelic visitations.

As the little family walked into the temple, Mary and Joseph were greeted by two prophets, each of them faithful in prayer and waiting for the "consolation of Israel." Each in turn took the child out of the arms of his parents and praised God. Each of them blessed Mary and Joseph, telling them how wonderful their child was, how important he would be, but how hard it would be for them to love and care for him (Lk 2:21-38).

Like the previous passage, this story tells us nothing about Mary and Joseph's parenting skills. Instead it tells of a community blessing. God intervenes, filling these two old prophets with the Holy Spirit, and they turn and bless the child and the parents.

Their words carry not comfort but challenge. Parenting is difficult, and parenting this child will be especially painful—"and a sword will pierce your own soul too," says Simeon to Mary (Lk 2:35). This appears to constitute a forewarning that Jesus' life will be controversial—"this child is destined for the falling and the rising of many"—and will end in an untimely and torturous death.

Nevertheless, the words contain blessing, if not reassurance that it will be easy. Anna and Simeon in essence are saying to Mary and Joseph, "You are doing important work in raising this child." These are words every parent needs to hear, of course. It is not as though Mary and Joseph did not know their son was special, but the prophets' words must have been added to those Mary stored up for pondering through the difficult times ahead.

Once again, here God is surrounding this young family with a community that blesses and challenges them. These words are about the importance of community, not just about family. The role of the community becomes even more significant in the following passage, the last we hear of Jesus' childhood.

Astonishing Wisdom in a Child

The final story in Luke of Jesus' birth and childhood reveals even more fully the significance of the community in the life of this family. When Jesus is twelve years old, Joseph and Mary's family walk to Jerusalem for the holidays with an array of friends and relatives.

As they make their the way home, we might imagine this conversation: Joseph says to Mary, "How long did you tell Jesus he could stay with Levi and his folks?"

Mary replies, "I didn't tell him he could stay with Levi. I thought you had given him permission to go with Uncle Eleazer!"

A whole day had passed before either of them missed Jesus. In their world, the care of children was shared by the community of friends, neighbors and relatives. They may have been alone at the birth event, but they are alone no longer. They have just assumed Jesus was traveling with someone else in the clan.

Today we would charge them with child neglect. Mary and Joseph's community, however, made no such accusation. Jesus was not in a children's shelter alone and frightened and wondering when his parents would come for him. Instead he was surrounded by a community of faith, where he was both learning and teaching.

In Luke 2:49 we hear from Jesus for the first time: "Why were you searching for me? Didn't you know I had to be in my Father's house?" What he says foreshadows a familiar theme in his teaching: the way Jesus defines family is different from how we are used to defining it. When his mother frantically wails, "Your father and I have been searching for you in great anxiety," he replies with a public announcement of who his father really is. Jesus points to the fact that more than Joseph's son, he is God's son. At the same time he redefines his relationship with Mary and Joseph, he is redefining who his followers can trust to be family. He has named God's house as his home. Later he will tell his followers, too, that they find home in God's house (Jn 14:2).

These stories of Jesus' childhood recorded in Luke's Gospel are enriched by Matthew's account of the visit of the wise men, the subsequent massacre of the infants by Herod's soldiers, Joseph's divinely inspired escape to Egypt with Jesus and Mary, and their return from Egypt after the death of Herod (Mt 2:13-10). These events also reveal God's support and care for this new child and family. Following the stars, the wise men provide this baby and family with a baby shower fit for a king. Then, when an angel reveals the king's plan to destroy the newborn, Joseph and Mary follow God's call into a frightening unknown. One can imagine the drama when Joseph awakens from a dream in the middle of the night. Not even waiting for dawn, he scoops up the sleeping infant and his tired young wife to take off on yet another journey. Mary evidently trusts her young husband's words that God has spoken to him in another dream, and off they go.

Following God's plan does not just call for personal sacrifice; it also involves families sacrificing together, taking risks and trusting one another.

Emerging Themes: God's Intention for Family Life

Two themes about family life can be drawn from these stories of Jesus' childhood. First, we note that they are not entirely happy stories. They are stories of Mary and Joseph struggling and pondering what is only partly understood, and sometimes not understood at all (Lk 2:50). Even divine visitations do not answer all their questions and uncertainties. The family lives of those who follow the Lord are not any easier than those of others. Mary and Joseph probably did not plan for a life together that would involve visits from shepherds and kings, midnight escapes to foreign countries or a precocious preteen who disappears in a big city for three days with no apparent remorse for the anxiety visited upon his parents. The newlyweds Mary and Joseph had no time to develop their relationship with each other before they were called to follow God's leading into all these challenging circumstances.

Second, these stories reveal that Mary and Joseph certainly were committed and willing to follow where parenting this child would lead them, but they did so with the support and involvement of the community. Jesus learned and began to teach himself and others in the nurturing community he found in the temple. His and his parents' understanding of themselves and their relationships with one another were affirmed and blessed by Cousin Elizabeth and prophets and shepherds and kings and the teachers in the temple. Undoubtedly the stories of Jesus' birth that Mary had pondered in her heart were told to him; they were stories of his parents' faithfulness, but they were also stories of a family rooted in and nurtured by a much wider community that God provided.

JESUS' TEACHINGS BY WORD AND EXAMPLE

The unusual and miraculous events of Jesus' conception, birth and childhood have dramatic implications for our understanding of the significance and role of families. Jesus' adult ministry likewise has much to say about families.

Conflict in Family Life

Although Jesus did not include much instruction for family life in his teaching, much can be gleaned from the examples of his relationship with his mother. The wedding feast at Cana provides us with a glimpse of their relationship. Mary pushes him to do something about the wine shortage (Jn 2:1-12). Jesus responds by telling her that the timing is wrong for him to intervene. But she does not take no for an answer; instead she turns to the servants and tells them to follow his instructions. She assumes that he will do as she wishes. In fact, Jesus responds with a miracle.

The conflict was open between them, not hidden. Their relationship obviously endured and perhaps was strengthened by this conflict; the very next verse tells us that Jesus went with his mother, brothers and disciples on a trip to Capernaum for a few days (Jn 2:12).

There were other times of misunderstanding and conflict (Mt 12:46-50; Lk 2:48-51), yet Jesus and his mother's faithfulness to one another lasted all the way to Jesus' death (Jn 19:25-28).

As we note the openness of Jesus' clash with his mother, we must also pay attention to its context and meaning. In Jesus' culture, children of all ages were expected to be obedient and respectful to parents. This is not a twentieth-century child arguing with parents in order to get his way, nor a grown son saying, "It's my life and I'll live it the way I want." Instead Jesus' words are spoken out of his recognition that there is One who claims more loyalty and deference even than his mother. He is not defiant but rather is showing who has his ultimate allegiance.

According to C. S. Lewis, the image of Jesus' conflict with his mother is edifying only if "we are quite sure that he has been a good son and that, in his rebuke, spiritual zeal is triumphing, not without agony, over strong natural affection" (Lewis 1970:191). This picture can be helpful and not a stumbling block for us only when we find it hard. If we take any secret delight in Jesus' stand with his mother, we have missed the significance of this passage. In the end, of course, this is the only point at which the adult Jesus responds acquiescently to his mother's control.

If we can draw principles from this incident for application in our own lives, then a family relationship is one in which we need to
□ speak honestly and forthrightly
□ submit to one another when it is right and good to do so (Jesus did turn the water to wine, just as he had gone home with Mary and Joseph from the temple and "was obedient" [Lk 2:51])
□ not submit to the other when our faithfulness to God would be compromised (although Jesus did obey his mother this time, he was not obedient to his mother when she came seeking to talk with him presumably to take him home [Mt 12:46-50], nor did he obey his brothers when they wanted him to go to Judea [Jn 7:3])

☐ remain steadfastly faithful with one another despite the differences, the mis-understandings and the personal cost (Mary did not always understand, but she was faithful to the end, standing near the cross to watch her child suffer extended torture and death; in return, Jesus' last act before death was caring for his mother [Jn 19:25-28])

As Jesus provided us an example through his own family relationships, he also taught specifically about the appropriate meaning and place of family for his followers.

The Meaning and Place of Family

Jesus used family relationships in his teachings to illustrate that discipleship costs everything—even one's family and one's own self. Discipleship should not be entered lightly. Commitment to God is to be greater even than the most important human commitments—those between family members: "Whoever comes to me and does not hate father and mother, wife and children, brothers and sisters, yes, and even life itself, cannot be my disciple" (Lk 14:26).

Jesus' statement that to be his disciple you must hate your family makes use of a Semitic idiom that means essentially "to love less." "I love this and I hate that" meant "I prefer this to that." For example, the Old Testament says that Jacob loved Rachel and hated Leah (Gen 29:30-31) and that God loved Jacob and hated Esau (Mal 1:2-3). This does not mean Jacob actually hated Leah or that God literally hated Esau, but that they preferred one over the other. Jesus was simply saying that families were not to be preferred over God. One is to love one's family, but one is to love God more (D. E. Garland 1990).

Jesus' teaching echoes the Old Testament's repeated theme that the love of Yahweh must precede all else. The stories that we find most troubling in the Old Testament sound this theme, such as God's command to Abraham to sacrifice Isaac in Genesis 22. We ache for Abraham as he travels with his young son to the place God has appointed for sacrifice. God stops Abraham at the last moment, as he raises his arm, knife in hand. Abraham has proved his willingness to go to this extreme in obedience.

Ezekiel 20 contains a startling reversal of the injunction to honor one's parents:

I said to their children in the wilderness. Do not follow the statutes of your parents, nor observe their ordinances, nor defile yourselves with their idols. I the LORD am your God; follow my statutes, and be careful to observe my ordinances, and hallow my Sabbaths that they may be a sign between me and you, so that you may know that I the LORD am your God. (Ezek 20:18-20)

Faithfulness to God must take precedence over obedience to wrong-headed parents. On a slightly different note but sounding the same theme, Deuteronomy 21:18-21 commands the death of a stubborn and rebellious son in order to purge evil from the midst of Israel, in obedience to Yahweh. Love and obedience to God always must take precedence, even when it means betraying family loyalties.

It is in fulfillment of this expectation, then, that Jesus said he had come to bring a sword to divide families (Mt 10:34-36). Allegiance to God sometimes brings conflict and division in one's family; this cannot be avoided if there are family members who "love darkness rather than light" (Jn 3:19). In saying he had brought a sword, Jesus was emphasizing the high cost of being a disciple, not calling family strife desirable.

In fact, Jesus is clear that obedience to God is virtually the *only* justification for family disloyalty. For example, consider his parable of the rich fool (Lk 12:13-21). A brother, presumably a younger brother, interrupted Jesus' teaching with a demand that Jesus force his elder brother to share his inheritance. Jesus responded, "Man, who made me a judge or divider over you?" Jesus was saying indirectly that this man should have felt shame for arguing with his brother over their inheritance. There is much more to be gained than property, and something much greater can be lost. For Jesus, the brother was more important than the money.

Are Jesus' followers whose families choose the darkness, who are divided by conflict over faith, left to face life alone, bereft of family? Jesus uses his own family, both in these teaching episodes and then, finally, in the moments before his death, to illustrate that losing one's family because of loyalty to God leads to a whole new family for the faithful.

The Faithful Will Not Be Deprived of Family

Matthew 12:46-50 shows us Jesus' mother and brothers coming to speak with him. When told that his mother and brothers were outside, Jesus replied: "Who is my mother, and who are my brothers?" And pointing to his disciples, he said, "Here are my mother and my brothers! For whoever does the will of my Father in heaven is my brother and sister and mother."

Mothers who read this passage feel ready sympathy for Mary and her sons, for it almost sounds as though Jesus is saying, "That woman is not my mother, and they are not my brothers—these followers and believers are my *real* family." But look again—Jesus was not denying his relationship with his mother and brothers; he was *widening the circle*. In John 19 it is clear that Jesus recognized his mother as his mother (vv. 26-27). His mother was with him to the very end of his life.

Actually Jesus' teaching about family in Matthew 12 echoes his explanation of the relationship of his teaching to the Scriptures: "Do not think that I have come to abolish the law or the prophets; I have come not to abolish but to fulfill" (Mt 5:17).

Similarly, during another of Jesus' teaching sessions, a woman in the crowd apparently is overcome with adoration and yells out, in effect, "Bless your mother!" (Lk 11:27-28). Jesus responds, "Blessed rather are those who hear the word of God and obey it!" Once again, family loyalty is second to our loyalty and obedience to the Word of God. The physical fact of motherhood gives Jesus' mother no special status. According to Jesus, our status is defined by our volitional loyalties and actions, not by biological and cultural roles and relationships over which we have little control. So Jesus is not doing away with family loyalty but transforming its meaning and putting it in its rightful place.

In our culture, family most often means a spouse and biological children and parents. Jesus has come not to do away with these relationships but to fulfill God's promises to "set the lonely in families" (Ps 68:5-6). Families are now defined by a common purpose—to live out the will of the Father. Bill Leonard equates the terms *church* and *new family*. "Through Jesus Christ, the church represents a new family bound together, not by flesh and blood, but by faith" (Leonard 1996). It is faith in Jesus Christ that is the "proof of kinship" in God's new family.

We can appreciate the significance of this teaching only when we understand how central the kin-defined family was for Jesus' hearers, just as Jesus' rebuke of his mother must be held in front of a cultural background of filial deference. Jesus' sayings about the family were hard for his followers to hear because of how highly families and family loyalty were prized in their culture. Although love and loyalty still characterize many families today, in our culture there is an element of choice in the forming and dissolution of families that was not present in Jesus' day. The radical nature of his teaching therefore has lost some of its sharpness for us. Jesus "may call upon us to transcend the family, but we must first know and value the thing we are transcending if our action is to have religious significance" (Meilaender 1990:135).

This is not the last time Jesus' relationship with his mother provides the canvas on which he will portray the good news about family for the faithful.

The Scene at the Cross

John 19:25-27 records that Mary stood at the foot of the cross with other women, watching her son die. She had presumably followed behind and watched as he bled from the untreated wounds from the scourging, struggled and fell under the weight of the cross beam he was forced to drag to Golgotha. She watched helplessly as the soldiers beat him, as they stripped him, as they drove spikes into his hands and lifted him up on the cross. She loyally stood there all day, suffering indescribable grief. Beside her was Jesus' beloved disciple.

Then Jesus looked at her and said, "Woman, here is your son." And to the disciple he said, "Here is your mother." And from that hour the disciple took her into his own home.

When he spoke these words, Jesus knew that "all was finished" (Jn 19:28). Thus his last action was arranging for family ties between these two people he loved dearly. He said only two more things after speaking to the beloved disciple and his mother—"I'm thirsty" and "It is finished."

Throughout this passage, the writer states that events happened "in order to fulfill scripture" (e.g., vv. 24, 28, 36). Each of the events of the crucifixion, including this family-making scene, fulfills the intention of God recorded in Scripture. Jesus' words to his mother and his disciple are part of the grand plan. What can this mean for us?

Jesus' words from the cross sound like a marriage ceremony—"I now pronounce you mother and son." Perhaps the beloved disciple and Mary would have cared for each other regardless of Jesus' words. Nevertheless, Scripture indicates that there was a transforming power in Jesus' words: *"And from that hour* the disciple took her into his own home" (Jn 19:27). He had not done so before, nor did he wait to check it out with the folks back home. The words were transformative.

There is power in being named and recognized as family. We do this in the marriage ceremony—we *adopt* one another as family, "for better or for worse."

My husband and I have dear friends who have two children the same ages as our own young adult children. Their children have been in our home often through the years. Almost two decades ago, when the children were preschoolers, our friends asked David and me if we would be willing to be their children's godparents. In our culture that is a sort of social insurance, a promise to raise these children as our own should some unforeseen tragedy leave them orphans. We said yes. In essence, we and our friends said to each other, "Yes, we want to be your family." And from that moment my relationship with those boys changed. I no longer treat them as visitors in my home. Now they are *mine* in a very real sense. I expect them to live by our rules at our house, and when they are hungry they feel free to scrounge something to eat in our kitchen. I feel a strong attachment and love for them.

Speaking my commitment, and having our friends speak their commitment and need for us to be family, was a transformation of our relationship. It had power. Our relationship has lasted even though we moved more than a thousand miles away. As I write this, I am thinking about the fact that I will trek to the airport next week to pick up the older son, now almost twenty, who is coming to spend a week of his vacation with us.

Many languages have terms for people who are part of a family but are not biological kin. We need such family language in the church. Family bonds need to be spoken even more than the kinship bonds. There is power in being named and recognized—"we are a family." Naming one another as family is part of making family happen.

This family is different from simply loving one's neighbor, or even from the community of the faithful called the church. The record of the crucifixion found in Luke, when put alongside John's account, makes a contrast between the love of neighbor and the love for family. Love for neighbor does not depend on reciprocity or even mutuality. When Jesus said, "Father, forgive them" (Lk 23:34), his love for those who crucified him did not depend on their response. They did not have to respond to him at all for him to love them. We are to love our enemies and to expect nothing in return for our love.

Family love, however, is based on mutual commitment. Family relationships are two-way. In the Gospel of John, Jesus did not speak only to the beloved disciple, telling him to take care of his mother. He spoke to Mary too. He gave them to one another. We can be a neighbor to another who has no commitment to or even expectation of us. But we can only be in a family with other people who in return see us as family. Family relationships are covenants between persons. And covenants require commitment on both sides.

Mary is now only secondarily Jesus' biological mother; she now is to be primarily defined as "mother" in a family that includes this new son, her son by faith. This family defines those who follow Jesus as her closest relatives. "Now for those who follow Jesus, the critical blood, the blood that most significantly determines their identity and character, is not the blood of the biological family. It is the blood of the Lamb" (Clapp 1993:78).

The genealogy with which Matthew begins and the final scene at the cross in John serve as bookends to the gospel; they are the beginning and the end of Jesus' earthly ministry. From beginning to end, the ideal of family has been transformed, just as Jesus transformed water into wine at the wedding in Cana. Marriage is a form of adoption: a man and a woman leave their biological families to adopt each other as "one flesh." Those words from the very beginning of Scripture, undoubtedly spoken at the wedding in Cana, have found fulfillment at the foot of the cross. The new model of family is not biological kinship but adoption.

Sometimes our biological kinfolk desert and betray us. Sometimes our own life journeys take us far from kinfolk, or death separates us. Some Christians have been abandoned by their families because of their decision to follow Christ. The Gospel of John records that the last act of Jesus' earthly ministry enacts an adoptive model, now not limited to marriage and parenting but available to all who would have mothers and brothers and sisters and children created by bonds of shared faith and commitment.

The church must follow Christ by ensuring that no one in the family of faith is familyless—that everyone is adopted into family. This is not to be a second-rate way of being family for one another, a way to take care of strays who missed out when families were being formed, or who suffered some loss that left them familyless. Instead, the adoptive family has become the ideal, the model, the witness that there are no limits to God's ability to create goodness, not even the limits of biology. Even families formed by biological links, when transformed by this good news, become adoptive families, choosing and covenanting with one another by giving themselves to following Christ.

A person's biological birth is no longer enough. There must be a second birth based on one's relationship with God, and the results are more profoundly influential in shaping the person even than the first birth (Rom 8:15-17; Gal 3:26—4:6).

We get a glimpse of this in the voices of persons—children and parents—who live in adoptive families. Their relationships provide a metaphor for the significance of this transformation:

> What I have learned about myself as a result of being adopted has helped me grow
> . . . and continues to affect the decisions that I make every day. . . . I have

learned that a family is not a group of people sharing last names, eye color, and inheritable diseases. *All families* are about giving understanding and love by choice, not requirement. My parents love me as much as they love my brother, their biological child. They *chose* to love both of us. . . . Never refer to a person's "real" parents when you mean "biological." My parents are more real to me than anything I've ever known. (Cora Mulder, age seventeen, speech to her high-school class)

The Ethiopian Eunuch

The early church discovered the full meaning of Jesus' radical message in Philip's encounter with the Ethiopian eunuch, recorded in Acts 8. The eunuch lacked family and thus lacked hope for a future. Because of his physical disability, he was not even allowed to participate in worship in the temple (Deut 23:1). The very label by which he was known defined him as an excluded one. He was not a person with a limitation; he *was* the limitation—a "eunuch."

Nevertheless, the good news of Jesus Christ is that he now has a place in God's new family. He is not simply allowed to participate. He is now *equal*. God's new family is not simply a way to include those who are otherwise unacceptable or unwanted. Jesus' point was that all persons who put their faith in him are acceptable and wanted in his new family. "According to the *gospel*, family begins with baptism. . . . Here is a whole new family birthed in the waters of baptism, a family that knows that we are related by hope, not biology, a family that remembers that our true home is not the biological family, but the church" (Erdman 1995:92).

The beautiful promise in Isaiah 56 resonates through Jesus' teaching, a promise that the eunuch who holds fast to the covenant has an everlasting place in God's family, a place even more secure than that of the father of sons and daughters:

> Do not let the foreigner joined to the LORD say,
>   "The LORD will surely separate me from his people";
> and do not let the eunuch say,
>   "I am just a dry tree."
> For thus says the LORD:
> To the eunuchs who keep my sabbaths,
>   who choose the things that please me
>   and hold fast my covenant,
> I will give, in my house and within my walls,
>   a monument and a name
>   better than sons and daughters;

I will give them an everlasting name
    that shall not be cut off. (Is 56:3-5)

Indeed, in Christ the eunuch has not only an everlasting name but the embodiment of that name in the promise of family—children—in the community of faith.

SUMMARY

Jesus' teaching is not a departure from but the fulfillment of Old Testament messages about the meaning and place of family. The story of God's command to sacrifice Isaac (Gen 22) foreshadows Jesus's teaching. The highly troubling account of Ezra's restoration of the purity of God's people by commanding them to put away their foreign wives and children (Ezra 9—10) speaks powerfully and painfully of our first loyalty to God, above all else. Imagery of family is important in the Bible, but it points us to the family composed by God, not by human alliances or even biological relationships. Jesus' hard sayings about family point out that there are times when following the will of God means leaving family behind, as when he called the disciples away from their families. Sometimes it even means severing family ties (see Mt 10:34-37; Lk 11:57-62; 12:51-53; 14:26), which will be replaced by bonds with a promised new family in God's kingdom.

Our church culture has flipped the understanding of the early Christians. Instead of honoring singleness and denigrating marriage as a second-best choice, we honor marriage and treat singles as though they were second-class citizens in the church, a population group to be "ministered to" rather than key figures in the community. As Rodney Clapp has pointed out, however, singleness is important because of the vision it provides to all of us of what it means to truly trust God:

> The married Christian ultimately should trust that his or her survival is guaranteed in the resurrection; the single Christian ultimately *must* trust in the resurrection. The married, after all, can fall back on the passage of the family name to children, and on being remembered by children. But singles mount the high wire of faith without the net of children and their memory. If singles live on, it will be because there is a resurrection. And if they are remembered, they will be remembered by the family called church. Christian singles are thus radical witnesses to the resurrection. (Clapp 1993:101)

Family and community of faith: Different and both important. Some Christians assume that the family Jesus promises us is the entire community of faith—that we are to relate to one another equally, without partiality, as one very enormous, intimate family. A careful examination of Jesus' own relationships, however, suggests otherwise.

For example, the account of Lazarus's illness, death and raising back to life provides an interesting glimpse of Jesus' love for Mary, Martha and Lazarus: "Accordingly, though Jesus loved Martha and her sister and Lazarus, after having heard that Lazarus was ill, he stayed two days longer in the place where he was" (Jn 11:5-6). Why did Jesus procrastinate? When we love someone, we are expected to go with haste if their life is endangered. Lazarus was terminally ill.

Obviously, Jesus was once again using his own relationships to teach; a miracle was on the horizon. But for our purposes, the interesting feature of this story is not the central focus—the raising of Lazarus from death—but Jesus' relationship with the brother and two sisters. He *loved* them. This is interesting, because we assume Jesus loved every follower equally. Do we detect some partiality? Mary, Martha and Lazarus were *special* to Jesus.

The Gospels also reveal that Jesus had an inner circle of disciples, those with whom he was especially close (Mt 26:37; Lk 9:28; Jn 13:23). He called on these persons when he was especially troubled; he loved them with a special love.

In fact, it appears that these people were like family to him. When Jesus saw Mary's sorrow over Lazarus' death, he cried with her. And as with Mary his mother, perhaps it is the displays of conflicting expectations that show best the family role these people played in Jesus' life.

Jesus was teaching some distance away, and the women sent for him, saying, "Come as soon as possible; Lazarus is dying." But Jesus did not come right away as they expected and wanted. He arrived too late, at least from their perspective: Lazarus had already died.

Neither Martha nor Mary minced any words: they told Jesus just what they thought. Both of them, at different times, said, "If you had been here, my brother would not have died." They spoke their mind. This sounds much more like family members speaking with appropriate boldness to one another than followers speaking to a revered teacher.

Remember, at the wedding feast Jesus responded to his mother's expectations with a miracle. He does so again here.

This account of Jesus' relationship with Mary, Martha and Lazarus raises the somewhat uncomfortable suggestion that Jesus loved differentially, and so does God. The theme that certain people are special to God sounds throughout the Bible, from the story of Esau and Jacob on. Ray Anderson and Dennis Guernsey comment that if God loved everyone equally, then God would love no one particularly; this idea, they say, is scandalous. Love has its value in being uniquely chosen by another. The basis for love, then, is not equality or inclusivity but rather "being chosen" particularly for a unique relationship with the other (Anderson and Guernsey 1985).

Jesus taught us to love our neighbors as ourselves, and he made it clear that we are to minister to the needs of all of God's children. There is no limit on God's love, and there is to be no limit on our love. But that does not cancel our need for special people in our lives, a family of folks who have chosen one another, who support and are committed to one another.

Neighborly love is universal; it calls us beyond our loyalties and special relationships. But it does not replace the family. Jesus showed us the importance of both neighborly love and family commitment. From the cross he spoke forgiveness for those who were killing him—"Father, forgive them; for they do not know what they are doing" (Lk 23:34)—a demonstration of love. He also was concerned for his mother and his beloved disciple—his family (Jn 19:25-27).

Followers of Christ too need special relationships—families—within the larger community of faith, and within the ever-widening circle of neighbors for whom we are to show love. This special love was given more meaning in the last words of Christ from the cross.

IMPLICATIONS FOR FAMILY MINISTRY

The following guidelines for family ministry can be drawn from Jesus' own life and teaching.

☐ From Jesus' conception and adoption by Joseph into David's line to his last act from the cross, God provides us with the hope and reality of adoption as a way of forming families when we follow Christ. All followers of Christ belong in a family, and it is the work of Christ's church to turn this hope into reality.

☐ The call to live faithfully as family with those we find in our care is just as much a response to the call of God as the response to leave everything behind to take up Jesus' cross. Living faithfully in this calling is a part of God's divine purpose, and it often requires commitment and faithfulness in difficult times. The family lives of the faithful are not any easier than the solitary following of those who leave all.

☐ Family ties, especially those formed by faith and commitment rather than by kinship, need to be spoken.

☐ Family ties need to be mutual. One person's devotion cannot create a family.

☐ Families face conflict together. Families of the faithful need to learn how to do this.

☐ Family relationships are always relative; our faithfulness to follow Christ comes first, even when it requires the ultimate sacrifice of leaving family.

☐ There is a difference between a community of faith and a family. A congregation of a thousand people—or even two hundred—cannot really be family to one another except in the sense of extended family. Within that large group there need to be intimate family relationships, just as Jesus had with his disciples and friends. At the same time, families need to be embedded in these larger communities that support and share in the responsibilities of family care. Jesus' own childhood gives ample illustrations of the importance of such a community.

Chapter 12

Biblical Roles
for the Family

J ESUS' TEACHINGS ABOUT FAMILY LIFE SUGGEST THAT FAMILY IS TO play two significant roles in the lives of his followers. First, families are to serve as the channel through which ministry takes place in the name of Christ. Second, families provide the world with graphic portrayals of who God is.

GOING HOME VERSUS LEAVING HOME

According to the Gospels, following Christ often means leaving everything, including one's family (Mt 10:34-37; Lk 11:57-62; 12:51-53; 14:26). But not always. Sometimes following Christ means returning with a sense of calling and renewed purpose to the responsibilities of family and community membership. Jesus frequently sent new followers back to their homes, to be his emissaries there. For example, when the man with the legion of demons experienced healing and release from his torment, he begged Jesus to allow him to follow. Instead Jesus told him to go home and tell others what God had done for him (Lk 8:39).

Jesus never said that those who stayed at home—such as Mary, Martha and Lazarus—were less worthy disciples than those who shared in his traveling ministry. Derek Tidball has concluded that Jesus provided a twofold structure of discipleship, (1) leaving all behind and following Christ and (2) returning to home and family to live out one's calling there. Neither is spiritually superior (Tidball 1983). Jesus gave both messages—"go home" and "follow me"—depending, perhaps, on the needs of the movement as well as on the gifts and circumstances of each individual. This foreshadows Paul's later teaching that within the body of Christ are many members with different functions, all equally important (1 Cor 12:12-13).

Clearly, Jesus sometimes did call people to leave their families. Interestingly, however, in each case in which a family relationship of the would-be disciple is standing in the way of following Christ, and that family relationship is identified, it is the relationship with the father. For example, in Luke 9:60 a would-be disciple pleads, "Lord, first let me go and bury my father." Another would-be disciple wants to say farewell to "those at my home" (Lk 9:61). As we saw in chapter ten, the father in the culture of Jesus' day represented much more than the individual's relationship with "Dad"; he symbolized the patriarchal household's lifetime responsibilities to and expectations for its members. Jesus calls followers instead to responsibility and loyalty to the heavenly Father.

Nowhere do we find an account where a would-be disciple is specifically called away from children or even spouse. Nevertheless, Jesus makes it clear that his followers must be *willing* to sacrifice even these most intimate of relationships. Some of the disciples were married, and following Jesus probably did involve some travel away from spouses. Yet evidently this did not involve a severance of these ties. We know that the disciples and Jesus were in the disciples' homes, because on one occasion Jesus healed Peter's mother-in-law in Peter's home (Mk 1:30-31). This is not the same as the later practice of those would use Jesus' teaching as a pretext to abandon family commitments. In fact, Jesus castigated those who tacitly sanctioned overriding the command to honor parents with a legal loophole favoring religious vows (Mk 7:10-13).

It seems, then, that Jesus was concerned more with *priorities of loyalty*. He did not call his disciples to sever relationships simply as a means of showing their ultimate commitment to God.

In calling the disciples away from their nets and from their parental families, Jesus used the imagery of fishing—a symbol that proves rich for the church in our modern culture. Referring to this passage, I have asked members of several congregations what one needs to go fishing. Inevitably people speak of a line and a pole, bait and a hook. In our culture, fishing means catching fish one by one; we even sometimes talk about church programs as "bait" to bring in people.

But Jesus' calling to his followers was based on a very different picture of fishing. Simon and Andrew fished with nets, great nets of strong ropes that were thrown out into the water and used to gather in many fish at one time (Mk 1:16). James and John were mending their nets when Jesus called them (Mk 1:19); broken and frayed nets were not as effective in the task of fishing. The church is Jesus' net—a large web of relationships that folds people in, gathering them into the net, into the community of faith.

We do not fish in isolation, as lone fishers in hip boots wading into swift water. In fact, in our me-centered world, it is the relationships among us—the network of families and community—that draw others into the community that is the body of Christ. Jesus said that the world would know us by our love one for the other (Jn 13:35). This is the good news for our world: God intends none of us to be alone, but to be part of a loving family.

This fishing-with-nets image suggests the basic tasks of family ministry. First, everyone in the community must be woven into family relationships, even those who are isolated and without family as the world sees family. Second, we have to mend the frays and tears in the net. We have to work on relationships in the community, young and old, keeping the connections strong and repairing damage when it happens. Finally, we are not satisfied simply to display a strong and well-woven net; it is meant to be used for fishing. The purpose of our net-working is not simply to satisfy ourselves that we have a good net; the net is to be tossed into the sea to draw in others. As God's people we have to toss our relationships into the sea, taking them into a society where people feel as if they are swimming alone in deep waters and need to be folded in.

The image brings us full circle and shows that calling away from and calling into families are only different facets of the same calling. We are called to use ourselves and our relationships with others—including and especially our families—to serve God and to point to God's kingdom. In that kingdom everyone has a place in the family. The role of the church is to equip the saints for their roles in the body of Christ. Sometimes that means calling them forth into new relationships, when their response to Christ demands that they put hand to the plow and not look back (Lk 9:62). Other times the church helps persons live more faithfully and lovingly within the families in which they find themselves. One of the functions of our family lives is to serve a world desperate for the good news that in Christ we are never alone. One of the ways we do this is by living as witnesses to the love of God.

FAMILY IMAGES FOR CHRIST, GOD AND GOD'S PEOPLE

When Old and New Testament writers wanted to describe the love of God for people, they often used family images. God is variously described as mother, father and husband; Jesus is described as brother and bridegroom (see table 12.1 for references). These family images bring visceral responses based on our own family experiences. For example, the writer of Deuteronomy assures us that we do not have to rely on our own strength; God carries us the way a father picks up a child who is too tired to keep walking (Deut 1:31). For those of us who can remember being scooped up and carried in strong arms, this is a powerful image. We almost physically relax into God's presence as we read this Scripture passage. For those of us who have gently lifted a tired child and felt them cuddle into our arms and lay their head on our shoulder, we know from experience the kind of care God feels for us.

Invoking a different feeling, Paul used the relationship between husband and wife to picture Christ's love for and relationship with the church (Eph 5:32). Marriage is an image of commitment freely chosen and then lived into day after

Is 49:15; 66:12-13; Hos 11:1-4	God as nursing, nurturing mother
Ex 4:22-23; Jer 31:9	Israel as "son"
2 Sam 7:14; Ps 2:7	the king as God's son/adoptive son
Mt 5:9; Rom 8:14-16; Gal 4:1-7	believers as children/adopted children of God
Hos 1—4	God as faithful husband of wayward wife Israel
Rom 8:29	Christ as "first-born among many brethren"
1 Cor 4:15	Paul as "father" through the gospel
Rom 15:14; 1 Cor 16:20; 2 Cor 9:3-5; Phil 3:1; 4:1; Col 1:2; 4:15	Christians as brothers and sisters
Rev 21:1-2	Jesus as bridegroom for the new Jerusalem

Table 12.1. Family images for Christ, God and God's people

day, through frustrations and disappointments as well as in joy and intimacy. Whether the marriage is one's own, one's parents' or grandparents', or that of friends, we all have experienced marriage emotively as well as cognitively.

Family also provides images for the relationships Christians are to have with one another in the community of faith, not just our relationships with God. Paul's favorite way of referring to the members of the communities to whom he wrote in the epistles was as "brothers" and "sisters" (Rom 15:14; 1 Cor 16:20; 2 Cor 9:3-5; Phil 3:1; 4:1; Col 1:2; 4:15). He clearly expected Christians to enter into the same kinds of loving relationships with each other that he modeled for them (Rom 12:9-10).

No set of human experiences has more potential for evoking depth of emotion and breadth of commitment than family relationships. Over and over, then, biblical texts draw upon these images. These images are most significant, however, if they are lived out in the faith community. Those who can best relate to them have themselves been carried when they were tired, have been loved when they felt unlovable, and have been cherished by a beloved. Thus the use of family metaphors indirectly calls the people of God to live in these ways with one another, pointing to a God who loves us even beyond the love that we have experienced with one another. The more effective we are in loving one another, the clearer is the image of God we provide for others.

In the next chapter we will examine more of what it means to live in family relationships that give witness to who God is. Before we do so, however, there are two concepts that deserve exploration because they relate directly to how the Bible defines families and because they have implications for how churches minister with families today. These concepts are "household" and "covenant."

The Household

In the Old Testament, Israel was often referred to as a "household" (e.g., Amos 5:25). In the New Testament, the concept of household carries meaning from the prevailing culture of the day. A description of ancient households can be found in chapter nine. It is important to remember that the household was more like a small community than the intimate structure we think of today as family. Hebrew households might have between fifty and one hundred people—quite different from the 2.6 people of today's average American household (Barton 1996a:11). It included a number of families, and sometimes individuals, under the absolute authority of the senior male. Households were economic units; members often worked together to earn their shared livelihood, perhaps through agriculture or some form of business. The only limit to the size of the household was the ability of the householder to support the members (Tidball 1983). Paul draws the term *steward* or *commission (oikonomos)* from well-known household roles in household economics and applies this term to himself and the other apostles (1 Cor 4:1-2; 9:17; Eph 3:2; Col 1:25).

One's very identity and even survival depended on membership in a household. Thus those without a household—widows, orphans, sojourners (and those who left households to follow Jesus)—found themselves in perilous situations. There was no one to care for them, and there was no social security. The Old Testament equates righteousness with incorporating these "hopeless" ones into the family/household (Zech 7:9-10) and unrighteousness with neglecting them (Job 31:16-32; Gowan 1987). Defining righteousness by the extension of family boundaries thus foreshadowed the radical and inclusive definition Jesus would give to family.

Characteristics of ancient households. Several characteristics of households are thus significant for our understanding of New Testament teachings about families.

1. The role of adoption. Having a male heir was of great importance in Roman culture; it was the means for ensuring the continuation of the household and care of its members. If no son had been born, a householder could choose to adopt a son and make him his heir. Adoption was thus familiar in the New Testament world and was considered a valuable status (Tidball 1983:80). To be adopted meant to become an heir to rule the household. Paul used this image, so powerful in his world, to communicate the new relationship a person can have with God through Christ (Rom 8:12-25; 9:4; Gal 3:26-4:4; Eph 1:5). According to Paul, adoption by God gives us the status of joint heirs with Christ (Rom 8:17). Adoption by a householder brought with it important privileges in the present as well as the future. Paul wrote that adoption by God similarly brings us significant privileges now and in the life to come—freedom (Gal 4:7-8), glorification with Christ (Rom 8:17) and the redemption of our bodies (Rom 8:23). Just as Jesus' life and teaching gave hope that through him every follower could have a new family, Paul's explicit language of adoption made clear that in Christ every follower could claim the treasured status of adoption.

2. The place of slaves and freed slaves. Slavery was widespread in the Roman Empire. A third or more of those living in major cities were slaves, and they were owned not only by the wealthy but also by persons of more modest means. Slavery was simply the means of organizing labor at the bottom end of the economic continuum. Slaves were often better off, if they had good masters, than were free persons in a society without social systems of care for the poor (Dunn 1996).

In addition to slaves, households included former slaves who had been freed. When a slave was freed, the freedperson's relationship with the master did not come to an end. The former slave promised loyalty to the household and its well-being. The householder promised to care for the social and economic needs of the freedperson and the freedperson's family (Tidball 1983).

According to Derek Tidball (1983), the relationship between a freed slave and the master may have been what Jesus was referring to when he told the disciples that they were no longer servants but friends: "I do not call you servants any longer, because the servant does not know what the master is doing; but I have called you friends, because I have made known to you everything that I have heard from my Father" (Jn 15:15). Possibly Jesus was calling up this household image, not the casual relationship of limited shared interests that people often mean by "friends" in our society. Similarly, Tidball points out that this was the meaning inherent in the Jewish leaders' warning to Pilate that if he released Jesus, he would be "no friend of the emperor" (Jn 19:12). Releasing Jesus could be construed as disloyalty in Pilate's relationship with the emperor.

3. Shared religion. The household expressed its solidarity by sharing in a common religion, that of the head of the household. Not only did this bind them together, but it also differentiated them from households that worshiped other gods. In Roman society, worship took place primarily within the household. It is in this context that we read of the conversion and baptism of households such as those of Cornelius (Acts 10), Lydia (Acts 16:13-15), the Philippian jailer (Acts 16:31-34), Crispus (Acts 18:8) and Stephanus (1 Cor 1:15).

Learning from ancient Palestinian households. Our cultural understandings of family and community are no more divinely ordained than were those of the Roman world, and that is, perhaps, a most important reminder. It is *how we live in* the structures of our culture that points to God's grace and love. Our families and communities are similar to those of ancient Palestine in at least one significant aspect: they provide us with experiences that equip us to understand God's relationship with us. We can imagine based on our own family experiences what it means to be adopted by God. We can imagine in our hearts what it would be like to have no family and then to be gathered in and placed in the most honored and loved family position, that of heir. Although we have not actually experienced slavery, our own heritage of slavery and slave ownership give us images of what it would be like to go from being a household slave to being a "friend." Families give us a grammar of emotional experiences through which we can experience and express God's love and care.

Finally, the description of ancient households in the New Testament also teaches us by the stark dissimilarity with our own culture. We struggle with the seeming lack of individual autonomy implied when whole households convert and are baptized, as did that of the Philippian jailer (Acts 16:33). Our culture's individualism, ingrained deeply within us because we are creatures of our place and time, conflicts with the thought that persons were folded into the community of faith without apparently deciding as individuals to take this step. We have trouble accepting our communal nature; we think of ourselves as individuals who make autonomous decisions and can make choices, particularly in the arena of religion. The fact that some of the ancients came to faith with their whole household confronts us with the fact that we come to faith and walk in faith as part of cultural units sharing daily life, not simply as isolated, autonomous individuals. The relationships persons have with the most intimate persons in their lives, whether in the household of 2000 years ago or in traditional or nontraditional families of today, determine and give shape to our faith. Obviously, then, the lives of families together must be of central concern to the larger community of faith.

GOD AS COVENANT PARTNER

A second biblical concept that is significant for our understanding of the role of families in the lives of Christians is *covenant*.[1]

The Bible records repeatedly that God's relationship with God's people takes the form of covenants (e.g., Deut 7:6-9; 2 Sam 7:11-16; Ps 98:3, 100:5, 136:1; Lk 22:20). A covenant *(bʿrit)* is a pact or agreement that binds two parties together with rights and responsibilities on both sides. The relationship between a freedman and a householder, as described above, is a covenant. The term *bʿrit* was often linked with the word *ḥeseḏ,* translated variously as "covenant," "stead-

---

[1]Portions of this material were developed in Diana R. Garland and Betty Hassler, 1987, *Covenant marriage* (Nashville: Family Ministry Department, Sunday School Board of the Southern Baptist Convention).

fast love," "loyalty" or "devotion" (Ps 42:8; Prov 3:3; Lam 3:22; Sakenfeld 1985). Steadfast love and faithfulness are thus at the heart of covenant relationships.

Covenants are freely offered. The only condition is the willingness of the other to enter into the relationship; the covenant does not depend on what each gets out of the relationship. By contrast, contracts spell out what each partner will do for the other in a mutual exchange. Contracts are quid pro quo, "something for something." Each person is in the relationship for what can be gained for the self.

Biblical writers often used family covenants to picture the relationship God offers us. Perhaps the most dramatic example is Hosea's relationship with his wife, Gomer. Their marriage, marked by her repeated infidelity and his loyalty, served as a living witness of Yahweh's steadfast love for Israel even in the face of Israel's unfaithfulness.

Characteristics of Covenants

Scripture often uses marriage as a dramatic metaphor for God's love (Prov 2:17; Jer 2:2; 3:1-8; Ezek 16:8-32; Hos; Mal 2:14; Mk 2:18-20; Eph 5; 2 Cor 11:2). But the significance of the concept of covenant is not limited to marriage; it informs how we live in all family relationships. Covenants should be the foundation for Christians as they relate to one another as brothers, sisters, parents, children and "friends," as Jesus used this important term for family/household relationships (Jn 15:15). Biblical examples of such family covenants include Naomi and Ruth, mother- and daughter-in-law (Ruth 1:4-7), and Jonathan and David, friends willing to share their inheritance with each other (1 Sam 18:1-4).

A common biblical theme is that our ways of relating with one another ought to reflect God's ways with us (Lev 19:2). The characteristics of covenants have implications, therefore, for how we live as family members, whatever the family roles may be (Sakenfeld 1985).

Covenants begin unilaterally. God offered covenant to Abraham and to Noah and effectively gave them little choice. God offered an unconditional covenant, just as a parent offers covenant unconditionally to a child. God's commitment was there whether they responded or not. There was no condition to the basic covenant, although if they were to benefit from the covenant, they had to fulfill their side.

Although covenants begin unilaterally, they can become bilateral. Jack Balswick and Judith Balswick (1989) call unilateral covenants "initial" covenants and bilateral covenants "mature" covenants. Parents form unconditional, initial covenants with an infant. Over time, the covenant matures as the infant grows up and the love and commitment become mutual.

Even in the mutuality and unity of a deepening covenant, partners retain their individuality. In many ways, covenants point to the biblical theme of unity in plurality. Once one looks, one finds this theme of unity *in* plurality repeating itself throughout Christian teaching. "From the Trinity in heaven to the marriage bond on earth, built into the structure of reality are forms of union that do not swallow up or confound the persons entering into them but even enhance their distinctiveness. . . . We need one another to be ourselves" (Oppenheimer 1989:106-7).

1. Covenants are the result, not the origin, of loving, faithful relationships. Covenants are marker events in a growing relationship. For the nine months of a baby's gestation, parents begin to imagine and fall in love with the child to be born. The unconditional love they offer the child expresses a growing relationship that intensifies in the agony and ecstasy of the birthing process and in the bonding that takes place afterward. For the adopted child and parents, a similar period of growing and deepening in relationship with one another precedes the formation of unconditional love and family covenant.

God established a covenant with "those who love him and keep his commandments" (Deut 7:9). God had been demonstrating love and commitment toward the Israelites long before the covenant-making that took place at Mt. Sinai. The covenant had not been established in Egypt, before they began their journey together. Instead it was a significant marker event, a defining moment, in a growing relationship of love and devotion. In the same way, the covenant God formed with Noah and his family came *after* they endured ridicule from neighbors for building an ark in the backyard and a harrowing experience through the worst storm ever. Only then did God offer the rainbow as a sign of covenant (Gen 9:12). Naomi and Ruth had lived together ten years and suffered together the deaths of husbands and sons before they established their covenant (Ruth 1:4-7). Jonathan and David were friends who had come to love each other deeply and risked everything for each other before they formalized their covenant (1 Sam 18:1-4).

Hesed, loving commitment, comes first and then is reinforced and sealed by the covenant. Self-sacrifice, loyalty and love may be demonstrated for an extended period before a covenant is formed. Wedding-day promises mark a commitment of spouses to one another, but their covenant develops out of their ongoing relationship with each other, the daily acts of loyalty and love and care on which their relationship has already been founded and out of which it will deepen in the future.

Persons legally or biologically related to one another may or may not establish covenants. Friends may come to a place that they covenant to be family for one another.

2. Covenants endure. Scriptures affirm that God's love "never ceases" (Lam 3:22) and that nothing can separate us from the love of God (Rom 8:38-39). God's love is patient and enduring, even through hurt and disappointment. In the same way, families are permanent relationships, single bodies that cannot be divided, "one flesh" (Eph 5:31). Covenants are intended to last a lifetime.

To say that covenants are permanent seems cruel toward those who have already suffered through the hurt of a breach in the family—a divorce, a child or adult who runs away, an unresolved feud. What did Jesus mean when he said, "What God has therefore joined together, let not a man put asunder" (Mt 19:6; Mk 10:9)—that folks should go on living in destructive relationships?

Jesus' teaching does not suggest that somehow an abusive marriage that stays intact is holier than one that does not. After all, God is said to have figuratively divorced Israel (Is 50:1). Instead Jesus was pointing to an emotional and interpersonal fact: family relationships do not end until life ends. Family members can stop living together, stop talking to one another and stop seeing one another; but each remains a part of the other simply because of their shared history.

A friend went through a painful separation and divorce after twenty years of marriage. He tried to remove every trace of the marriage from his life. One evening he built a fire and began throwing into the fire, one by one, the accumulated photographs from family vacations. It was then that the realization struck: to destroy everything that reminded him of his former spouse was to destroy his own past, many good memories and, in the end, his own identity. His ways of relating to others, his ideas, even his habits such as on which side of the bed to sleep had been shaped by the marriage with her. Even if he never saw or spoke with her again, she was part of his life. "Part of the power of the marriage metaphor lies in its capacity to convey the notion of a relationship never really undone, despite even the formalities of a divorce declaration" (Sakenfeld 1985:71).

3. Covenants cost. An advertisement in an American business magazine proclaimed our culture's truth: "In business, you don't get what you deserve. You get what you negotiate." Sometimes business norms leak into family relationships.

We negotiate over who has to do what chores or who gets which privileges; we wheedle for some advantage. Sometimes, of course, bargaining and "playing the game" with one another can help families try out new options in response to problems or a need for change, such as the discussion and compromising that take place around setting bedtimes for children, budgeting scarce family dollars or deciding on how to spend a few days of vacation together. Nevertheless, the fundamental commitment of family—the covenant—is the very opposite of business negotiation. The focus is not on what one deserves but on willingness to give to the other. It is on giving rather than on getting. There are also expectations for receiving, of course, but these do not control the basic commitment the way a contract controls a business commitment. And these expectations are not really about receiving what we deserve but about receiving what we need from the others in the family.

When Israel entered into covenant with God, it gave up other gods and followed Yahweh to wander in the wilderness. The Israelites were not shy about letting Moses and Yahweh know that they had given up bountiful tables in Egypt for the uncertainties of the desert (Ex 16:2-3). Family covenants too are risky and sometimes costly. They cost us the lives we know as we commit ourselves to live loyally and lovingly together into an unknown future. Every family has times of desert wandering—sickness, alienation, frustration, crisis, disappointment. The Bible identifies the condition of the one-flesh relationship as leaving behind father and mother to begin a new family. Such risky leavetaking marks all kinds of family relationships, not just marriage. Ruth gave up her father and mother and everything that was familiar to her to go with Naomi. Jonathan risked the wrath of his vengeful father and even his own significant inheritance as the king's first-born son for his friend David.

Families sometimes load up in a covered wagon (or rental truck) and strike out for new territory, as Sarah did with Abraham and Ruth did with Naomi. We choose paths together at the cost of other individual choices. Even if we remain in the same neighborhood in which we grew up, we must work out a lifestyle and make choices different from those we might have made had we only ourselves to think about. As my divorced friend experienced so poignantly, every aspect of life bears the mark of the covenant.

4. Covenants involve both freedom and responsibility. The Jewish people had a hard time recognizing that even though God had entered a covenant with them, God did not "owe" them. God's covenant was offered freely, and God stays in the covenant freely. Jesus made this clear when some were flaunting their specialness in God's eyes; he said that God could raise up a covenant people out of the stones of the earth (Lk 3:8). God *chooses* to be in covenant; there is no contract that forces God's loyalty and love. In the same way, we are free to accept or reject God's love and grace.

Although covenants are freely offered, they also include responsibilities. Christians live in the paradox of God's free grace paired with the expectation that they bear fruit. God loves us unconditionally, yet Jesus told us to "be perfect" (Mt 5:48). We too have expectations of God. We expect God's presence, God's sustenance, God's provision and even intervention on our behalf. The psalms are full of laments based on what the authors perceive to be appropriate expectations of God: "Where is God? God is supposed to be here when I am in need." Psalm 86 provides an example of such covenant expectations:

> Incline your ear, O LORD, and answer me,
> for I am poor and needy.
> Preserve my life, for I am devoted to you;
> save your servant who trusts in you.
> You are my God; be gracious to me, O Lord,
> for to you do I cry all day long.
> Gladden the soul of your servant,
> for to you, O Lord, I lift up my soul.
> For you, O Lord, are good and forgiving,
> abounding in steadfast love to all who call on you. (Ps 86:1-5)

There is a subtle but important difference between expecting that God will be with us and feeling that God owes us. Feeling that God owes us implies a contract, not a covenant—we have kept our end of the deal; now God should pay up. On the other hand, expectations are based on previous experience with God, not on what we have done in some kind of bargain. We expect God's grace because we have known it in the past, not because God owes us grace. We expect God's presence in times of trouble because we have experienced it in the past, not because God "has" to be there for us.

Family covenants do not mean that our families owe us. When we turn our attention to what we ought to be getting from the other, we have turned the relationship into a contract. The chief concern becomes *my* rights, what *I* am due. Nevertheless, it is easy to slip into thinking about what covenant partners "owe" one another, because covenants are based on our need for each other. Naomi and Ruth needed each other. They were alone in the world without means of support. David also needed Jonathan; his life depended on him. Jonathan later needed David's faithfulness to seek out and befriend Jonathan's son Mephibosheth (2 Sam 9:1-9). Asking for help and meeting each other's needs builds our relationship. Treating the other as a servant who owes us mistakes the covenant for a business contract. David took care of Jonathan's son "for the sake of your father Jonathan" (2 Sam 9:7), not just to pay back what Jonathan had done for him. In covenants, no tally sheets are kept. Covenants are not agreements designed to last only so long as each receives promised benefits.

There is also another aspect of responsibility significant in covenants, and that is that we remain responsible for our own actions even within the covenant. Covenants do not mean blind submission to one another. Naomi told Ruth to go back to her people, but Ruth *disobeyed* her and stayed with her. She knew full well that Naomi could not protect her or even take responsibility for her well-being (Ruth 1:15-18). Likewise, Jonathan did not blame David for the troubles that came as a result of his loyalty (1 Sam 20:30-34). He remained loyal even when it enraged his father and even when it became clear that David, not he, would become king.

Living in covenant with another does not suggest that we give up responsibility for our own behavior through blind submission or obedience or even loyalty. We retain our primary responsibility toward God, and that responsibility must come before any human covenants. Perhaps Ahab's experience provides us with the most graphic example. Ahab made a covenant with his "brother" Benhadad (1 Kings 20:34). Because of their covenant, Ahab released Benhadad, who was a war prisoner. This sounds like a merciful, loving act of one man in behalf of another. God, however, was not pleased; freeing Benhadad was not God's will, and this deed was added to the list of Ahab's many sins (1 Kings 20:35-43).

God's anger over mercy shown to a war prisoner disturbs us. Nevertheless, this story teaches a significant lesson about covenants: our actions of loyalty based on family covenants may be misdirected and out of line with God's purposes. When this happens, we sin. We are always responsible for our choices and behavior even when we think we are acting loyally and lovingly. We cannot blame our family when our good intentions lead to bad results. Nor can we allow our family covenants to become foremost, above our covenant with God.

The freedom and responsibility of covenants have been an issue of considerable theological import in the history of the church. For the church, baptism became the sign of the new covenant, just as circumcision was the sign of the old. According to the Reformed tradition, all children born into the Christian community can be presumed to have inherited the community of the new covenant and thus can be baptized as infants as the expression of this inheritance. The Anabaptists took a very different view and developed a quite distinct use of the term *covenant.* According to the Anabaptists, membership in the church cannot be inherited by birth into the Christian family or community (Roth and Ruether 1978).

Thus denominational and theological differences influence our understanding of family and community dramatically. Are we born into the community, as reflected in infant baptism? Or can we come into the community only through a personal choice to place ourselves for adoption? This is not an idle question; it raises the question of who is the family within the church. Is it the biological family? Or is it the faith family?

5. Covenants are defined by the participants, not by the expectations of others. The God we worship and with whom we live in covenant is the God who created the universe, who threw the stars into their places, who created the countless living creatures on the globe. This God we worship also is our Father, according to Jesus (Mt 6:9). This Holy Other is the One, we are told, who keeps track of how many hairs are on our head (Mt 10:30). Our God is the One to whom we are to "pray without ceasing" and with whom we are to share all our needs. God is in constant relationship with us. Jesus was clear that our relationship with God is one of intimacy. There are no special rules for how we are to relate to God; we do not have to perform washing rituals to approach God; we do not have to go to special places reserved for worship; we do not have to use special language to persuade God to listen to us.

The people of God have often lost sight of the importance of this personal relationship with God, focusing instead on rules and expectations about how to fulfill their end of the covenant relationship. It is, after all, less demanding to follow prescribed rules than it is to maintain a personal and intimate relationship. God made it clear in the beginning, however, that God's covenant meant Israel's and the Lord's fellowship with and devotion to one another.

The people broke the covenant when they stopped listening to God (Jer 7:21-26). To be in relationship with another, one must know the other, and knowing the other means being present to and listening to the other. Listening is key to covenant relationships among Christians. Every husband, wife, friend, child or grandparent is different from every other husband, wife, friend, child or grandparent. We cannot live in covenant with a family member by following rules someone else has set for family life; we must work it out with one another. Our needs and gifts differ. All of us carry expectations of how families "ought" to relate, perhaps from the families we lived in growing up, the families we see pictured in church literature or sitting in the pew next to us, or even those we see on television. But if it is truly a covenant in which we commit ourselves to caring for one another, we quickly learn that our family cannot follow someone else's blueprint.

The fact that covenant partners are free does not mean we can do what we please, but that we can choose how to live loyally and lovingly. There are some basic expectations of every family, such as fidelity and companionship, which we choose to make a part of our covenant. Some of the choices we make in our family covenant differ from those others choose because they reflect our commitment to meet one another's needs.

John grew up with parents who never talked about their problems, but John remembers the long cold silences between them. As a little boy, he was sometimes not able to eat because the quiet was so oppressive; he tried to stay away from the thick silence by playing alone in his room. When Beverly married John, she soon learned how painful silent anger is for him. Part of their covenant is to voice their anger, even if they cannot always work through their problems immediately.

Finally, just as God's covenant with us is personal and not simply a set of rules that have to be lived, family covenants are not defined by lines of authority and specific role expectations. How we are to relate to one another is not defined by rules about what is appropriate behavior for males and females but by our gifts and needs.

6. Covenants are intentional and have purpose. In the childhood of many who are middle-aged today, before the advent of HIV/AIDS, best buddies sometimes pricked their fingers and commingled their blood as a ritual of becoming "blood brothers"—a ritual that, as we saw in chapter nine, dates back hundreds of years. It was a graphic ritual of family-making, of covenant. The making of covenants is an intentional process of taking one another as family, with all the responsibilities and privileges that entails. This can be seen in Laban's covenant with Jacob; as a result of their covenant, the uneasy peace between them became a secure and clearly defined relationship (Gen 31:25-54, especially 44-54; Roth and Ruether 1978). Covenants do not "just happen"; they are choices made freely and intentionally.

Intentionality implies purposefulness. When we do something intentionally, we have a reason for it. As we read through the Old and New Testaments, we see God's purposes unfolding through a history of covenants. God's covenant with Israel was to be a means of redemption for all the nations. God's covenant with the church calls us to bear fruit in our ministry in the world. God expects us both to enjoy the freedom that our covenant with God brings and to serve one another through love: "For you were called to freedom, brothers and sisters; only do not use your freedom as an opportunity for self-indulgence, but through love become slaves to one another" (Gal 5:13).

Human covenants, too, have purpose. Christians should purpose that their families become clear witnesses to the grace and love of our Lord. We aim to demonstrate the transforming power of God's love in human relationships. These relationships transform the world around them. Israel was in covenant with God not just to have a cozy inside place compared with other nations. Quite the contrary: the covenant with Abraham was to bring a blessing to all nations (Gen 18:18). The families of Christians too have a mission to fulfill. Their communities should experience them as a transformative presence. God has a purpose for families; our covenants are to be expressed not just in our private lives with one another but also in our relationships in the world around us.

CONCLUSIONS

The place of family in the life of a Christian has obvious implications for family ministry. Leaving a patriarchal household to embrace the insecure life of becoming a prophet's follower and the dimensions of biblical covenants are in many ways ideas quite foreign to our own culture. Yet these concepts form the basis for biblical teachings and narratives about family life and therefore need to be part of the knowledge base all Christians. Exploration of this content needs always to conclude with reflection on what it means for us and for our commitments in our own historical moment and cultural place. The following, then, may be questions helpful for conversation in the community of faith.

☐ In what ways do we experience Christ's call to leave behind old responsibilities and constraints and follow him into a life that brings us new faith family relationships?

☐ In what ways do family relationships and community relationships offer a net for fishing in our world? Are there frays and tears to be mended? Into what deep waters do we need to be throwing our net of relationships, drawing others in?

☐ How are we providing experiences for one another that point to God's love and care for us? How can we help those who have been abused or neglected or rejected to learn in the community of faith what it means to be tenderly carried and nurtured and adopted as the chosen heir? Are we showing an accurate picture to our world of who God is in our relationships with one another?

☐ How are family and community covenants reflective of the biblical covenants between God and God's people? In what ways can we build our dedication to one another and to God even and especially as our obligations grow? How can we undergird one another's faithful covenant living?

Chapter 13

Biblical Words
for Family Life

Unless the LORD builds the house,
those who build it labor in vain.
PSALM 127:1

FAMILIES ARE TO BE GRAPHIC PORTRAYALS OF GOD'S COVENANT offer, a covenant characterized by intimacy, partnership and love. Families are also to be channels of God's love beyond their own boundaries to those who have not experienced it. We will begin this chapter by looking at the many kinds of families God has worked through to achieve these purposes. We will then turn to some of the central themes about God's intentions for family life.

GOD CAN USE ALL KINDS OF FAMILIES

The Old and New Testaments encompass quite a menagerie of family structures—husbands and wives (including husbands with more than one wife), adoptive families, single-parent families, friends who are family, and on and on (see table 13.1). Obviously, to say that a family structure occurs in Scripture does not mean it is an "ideal." Still, each of these categories does represent a family through which God chose to work. What is important is not being a member of the "right kind" of family, but rather living in "righteous ways" within whatever state of family relationships we find ourselves (1 Cor 7:10-24).

Gen 14:14	extended household
Deut 21:15; Esther 2:3	polygamous marriage
(see pp. 175-95 for extended listing)	marriage
Mt 8:14; Lk 8:1-3	marriage, couple separated by work (Peter was evidently married, since this is his "mother-in-law," but he has been following Jesus, so he must be separated from his wife. Later, she must have accompanied him; see 1 Cor 9:3)
Gen 27:46; Ex 2:15-21; Ruth 4:9-10; Esther 2:17; Acts 16:1-3	interracial/intercultural marriage
1 Cor 7:12-16	marriage between believers and unbelievers
Ruth 1—4	second marriage
2 Kings 4:1-7, Lk 7:11-12	single-parent (widowed) families
Ruth 1:8; 14-15; Rom 16:13	adult children and their parents, parents-in-law
Gen 48:6; Esther 2:14-15	adoptive family (adoption within the extended family)
Gen 15:2-3; Ex 2:10	adoptive family (adoption outside the family)
Gen 16:1-15; 30:1-7; 9-13	adoptive family (surrogate parent)
Ex 2	crosscultural adoption
Gen 19:31-38	incestuous family
Lk 18:15-16	unrelated adults as family
Acts 4:32	Christian community

Table 13.1.   Diverse family structures through which God has worked

Don Hebbard has asked why, if families are so important, God did not provide us with one perfect or near perfect model. He concludes, "There are no ideal families, just real families" (Hebbard 1995:59). The Scriptures record not only many kinds of family structures through which God has worked throughout history, but also that God has used families with all kinds of "dysfunctions," quirks and downright sinfulness. Despite all the family flaws listed in table 13.2, God used the families in which those flaws occurred. The family tree of the Messiah alone includes polygamists, adulterers, prostitutes, murderers and the unfaithful

Gen 3	blaming and lying
Gen 4; Judg 11:29; Sam 13:28-33	family violence and murder
Judg 19:16-30; 2 Sam 13:1-14	sexual abuse/incest
Gen 11	infidelity and murder
Gen 27; 37	parental favoritism, sibling rivalry, dishonesty, hurt
2 Sam 6:16-23	marital contempt
2 Sam 14:28-33; 18	alienation of children from parents

Table 13.2.   Flaws, sins and dysfunctions in families used by God

as well as kings, priests and prophets. If God can use these folks, then surely God can use our families too.

In summary, what *kind* of family one lives in is not as significant as how we allow God to work through us in whatever family state we find ourselves. The ideal is (1) living faithfully within the context God has placed us and (2) from that place—whatever it is—using our family relationships for the sake of God's purposes.

FAMILY LIVING AS A MEANS OF DISCIPLING

One of the primary ways God's purposes are achieved through family relation-ships is the discipling that takes place within them. More than anywhere else, family life has the potential for teaching what it means to love, and to love in ways that discipline—disciple—us in the ways of Christ. The thirteenth chapter of 1 Corinthians points to the challenges that living lovingly presents. Love is something to be "pursued" (1 Cor 14:1).

Helping Christians to live rightly—righteously—in families was an integral aim of Paul's teaching. Paul filled his letters to the churches with instructions for family living. The third chapter of Colossians points us to the significance of family living in the life of the community of faith. Verses 15-17 picture the wor-shiping church in almost sublime language:

> And let the peace of Christ rule in your hearts, to which indeed you were called in
> the one body. And be thankful. Let the word of Christ dwell in you richly; teach
> and admonish one another in all wisdom; and with gratitude in your hearts sing

psalms, hymns, and spiritual songs to God. And whatever you do, in word or deed, do everything in the name of the Lord Jesus, giving thanks to God the Father through him. (Col 3:15-17)

The very next verse begins the instructions for family living, with words for wives, husbands and children. Clearly, family life is an integral part of the Christian life. Christian discipleship involves not only singing hymns and "spiritual songs" but also living the nitty-gritty daily experiences of our most intimate relationships—handling anger, spouses relating to one another sexually, parents disciplining their children. Keeping up appearances on the outside is not enough. Christian living takes place in bedrooms and kitchens, in the hall waiting to get into the occupied bathroom, when a family member has all-night colic, or the stomach flu, or Alzheimer's disease. Living in families patiently, kindly and with self-control equips us for ministry to our neighbors by the roadside. The family is a "school of virtue" in which God places us, day after day, with persons we are to learn to love (Meilaender 1990:145).

Family Living Can Be Spiritual Discipline

The concept of spiritual disciplines has been wonderfully helpful for many Christians. Spiritual disciplines are for the spirit what physical exercise is for the body—a means of strengthening and conditioning. Spiritual disciplines are the ways we intentionally and regularly open ourselves to God's working in and through us. They are ways we seek to move beyond living mindlessly on the surface of our routines; we use spiritual disciplines to open ourselves to experiencing and celebrating God in our round of daily activities. The day begun and ended in a time of prayer and Bible study is experienced differently and with a greater awareness of God's abiding presence and transcendent purposes than the day begun and ended without thought for anything more than how all one's tasks can possibly be accomplished in the allotted time.

Recent attention to spirituality has been profoundly shaped by monastic practices such as silence, solitude, contemplation and centeredness (Foster 1978; Palmer 1990). The concept of spiritual discipline provides a helpful corrective to our Western preoccupation with the results of whatever we do. Westerners want, above all, to be effective. Too often we define the value of prayer, Bible study and tithing by their results. Prayers that are answered are "effective." Bible study is fruitful when it leads to a better understanding and answers to hard life questions. Tithing can provide resources for helping our global neighbors through mission endeavors.

It is harder for Westerners to grasp that these activities are valuable in and of themselves, regardless of their outcome. Christians grow as a result of prayer, Bible study and tithing, even if their prayers are not answered in the way they expect, or they have more questions than answers after studying their Bible, or the world continues to look ever more distant from God's kingdom. We are called to these spiritual disciplines because they are valuable in their own right, because we need to do them, because they make us aware both of God's presence and of God's transcendence.

Over the past two thousand years, some Christians have decided to devote themselves to a solitary life of prayer and contemplation. A dichotomy consequently developed between this ascetic life of prayer and devotion, considered the "spiritual" life, and a life in the mainstream of family and community. And if a spiritual life consists in the main of solitary prayer and Bible study, then family living does preclude this kind of lifestyle. People who try to live by monastic norms often suffer defeat under the pressure of family demands and responsibilities. Parents of preschoolers say, "I just can't find ten minutes to meditate when the children won't interrupt me, much less an hour." They feel guilty and "unspiritual." The world of contemplation is often pictured as the kernel of the spiritual life, whereas the busyness of an active family life seems its very opposite.

Without denigrating the importance of time alone for contemplation, study and prayer, it is important to recognize that family life can also be a significant source and context for spiritual growth. Wendy Wright points out that most of the language of spiritual life has imaged the individual's solitary pilgrimage or journey. Although we can imagine families "on journey" together, we more often think of families as "home," as a psychological space and place of habitation, the very opposite of journey. Wright says that the Christian life can be imagined not only as "journeying" but also as "dwelling." "We need to see that we need not always enter new landscapes in order to grow in God, that we can also cultivate a settled space and make it richer and more inhabited with meaning" (Wright 1990:12). The words of Jeremiah come to mind: "Build houses and live in them; plant gardens and eat what they produce. Take wives and have sons and daughters" (Jer 29:5-6). Defining spiritual discipline exclusively as withdrawal from relationships and activity is one-sided. Solitary prayer, contemplation and study are spiritual disciplines, but so is living lovingly and faithfully and justly in a family. In fact, perhaps such "active" disciplines are even more challenging.

Family living does not have to be done as a spiritual discipline, of course, any more than prayer, Bible study and tithing are always spiritual disciplines. Lots of people pray—when they are scared or in a tight situation, or have a difficult decision to make. "Please, God, if you'll just get me out of this, I'll be good for the rest of my life." Certainly that is prayer, and it is important, but it does not grow out of disciplining oneself to pray regardless of what one feels. People often study their Bible to seek an answer or to be inspired or comforted, not as an ongoing discipline of life. People often tithe because they have been told that God will bless them if they do so, or because they want to do something significant with their money, or even to get the tax deduction. These may all be good reasons to tithe, but they do not represent spiritual discipline.

Family living does not have to be a spiritual discipline either, but it certainly can be. In fact, it can be one of the most demanding of spiritual disciplines. It can be a part of our lives day in and day out, week in and week out, on our going to bed and our rising up. It is not easy to pray before responding to a grumpy partner or whining children first thing in the morning. It is not easy to discipline oneself at such times by thinking, *What would Christ have me do? How can I handle this in a way that edifies and imparts grace?* (Eph 4:29). It is hard to respond with love and grace to daily inconveniences and irritating habits that family members inevitably visit on one another. Family life is a spiritual discipline when we attempt to guide our thoughts, actions and words by the teachings of Christ.

Family Living Can Strengthen Our Faith

Just as consistent physical exercise results in a strengthened body, so spiritual discipline, over time, results in a strengthened faith. According to James 2:24-26, we are "justified by works." Our faith grows, is "brought to completion" (Jas 2:22), by the work we do, by our behavior day in and day out. Through faithful, sacrificial living we come to know God better. Justification means "being straightened up." We stand taller in faith, upright and straight, because of what we do, not just what we believe with our minds.

Justification is sometimes understood as God's excusing us, making us "just" or "straight" when we are in fact unjust or crooked. A better interpretation is that our working and living out our calling as Christians straightens out and completes our faith. We grow in faith as we put into practice the teachings of Christ.

No situation provides a better challenge for this kind of justification than family living. The Bible teaches us that caring for children and the helpless and loving one another are central to discipleship. Caretaking and nurture are significant at several levels. For one, they have the potential for increasing our sensitivity to injustice in the larger community and world.

> It is very difficult to stay up all night rocking a sick child, cooling her fevered brow, changing her soiled linen, rubbing her fragile body with ointments, praying unceasingly for her healing—and return to your corporate suite on the twenty-something floor and sign the order to lay off ten thousand workers. . . . After listening to the sound of your toddler's erratic breathing all night, it's pretty hard to sit in a senate chamber and vote for measures that threaten our environment and the health of our children's children. . . . We cannot survive with our hearts whole if we insist on liberating ourselves from the tasks of caregiving and nurturing. (Weems 1996)

Covenant-based family living provides the foundation for the individual discipleship that results not only in completion of our personal faith but also in our "doing justice" in the world (Mic 6:8).

Family Living Can Be the Ground for Encounter with God

Biblical stories indicate that God more often speaks to people in the midst of the mundane, routine, unspectacular chores of their lives than in those intentional moments when people seek revelation. Sometimes these revelations occurred within the daily life of being family. Brothers fishing together to provide for their families met Jesus (Mt 4:18-22). A starving widow was gathering sticks to make a fire on which to cook the last of her food for her son when Elijah found her and provided miraculously for her and her family (1 Kings 17). A Samaritan woman was found by Jesus as she made her daily trek to draw water for her household (Jn 4:17-26). Jesus' teaching was directed specifically to Martha in the midst of her kitchen work (Lk 10:38-42). The women who went to perform family duties of care for the dead found instead the good news of resurrection (Lk 24:1-9).

The story of Leah in Genesis 29 tells of God's finding the faithful in the midst of family life—and a very troubled family life at that. Leah was Jacob's unloved wife, the older sister Jacob was tricked into marrying when he really wanted the younger sister, Rachel. We hear the story of Jacob's love for Rachel and his faithful fourteen years of work to purchase her as a beautiful testimony to romantic love. But our heart aches for Leah. Her father pushed her off to a man who did not love or want her. Leah hoped bearing children would cause Jacob to love her. She bore him son after son, four in all. But her motherhood elicited resentment, competition and even hatred from Rachel, because Rachel could bear no children. It sounds like a recipe for a miserable existence for Leah: unloved by her husband, resented and hated by the other woman in the house.

Scriptures do not indicate that Jacob ever loved Leah, despite her longing for his affection. But although nothing changed outwardly in these strained family relationships, something happened to Leah. According to the text, Leah's attitude changed after the birth of her fourth son. She stopped waiting on Jacob to love her and said to herself, "This time I will praise the LORD" (Gen 29:35).

In her beautiful exposition of this text, Roberta Weems points out that Leah's story is "about the sacred, unestimated power in societally spurned tasks of caring, of tending to the needs of others" (Weems 1996:10). Leah's experience of God came through the din of small children and an oppressive family situation. Leah's story is not often explored because we have no traditions that elevate family life and caring for children as spiritual discipline. In fact, these are often seen as impediments to a spiritual life rather than a path of spiritual discipline.

> It is not coincidental that the Hebrew words for *womb* and for *compassion* are derived from the same root. Seeing Leah loveless, despised, and unwanted, God did not merely open her womb. God enlarged her compassion. Far from being a distraction from God, caregiving opened Leah to the very discipline that would teach her what it meant to be a creature, created, and creative. (Weems 1996:44)

It was not in silence or a life of contemplation, nor even in a fulfilling marriage, but rather through struggle and trying to make sense of life in a difficult family situation that Leah learned to praise God. In the end, perhaps even in some way as a consequence of this change in Leah's attitude, it seems that something also changed in her relationship with Jacob. His last command from his deathbed to his sons was to take him home and bury him next to Leah (Gen 49:32). Perhaps he learned to love and respect this woman who learned to praise God in the midst of it all.

FAMILY LIFE HAS FRUIT TO BEAR

"The fruit of the Spirit is love, joy, peace, patience, kindness, generosity, faithfulness, gentleness, and self-control" (Gal 5:22-23). This list points to the significant crucible family life can be for spiritual growth and fruit-bearing. None of the fruits of the Spirit listed in Galatians 5 are personal characteristics that we can exhibit in isolation from others. One cannot love or be kind or generous or faithful or gentle without an object of that love, kindness, generosity or faithfulness. Joyfulness, peacefulness, patience and self-control find no place of more effective challenge than in family life. Any parent of an active preschooler, any family member of a person with Alzheimer's disease, any teenager with a teasing younger sibling can testify to the challenge that putting these virtues into practice represents.

Other spiritual disciplines do not require the living-in-relationship through which these fruits can be made evident. One can tithe or study the Bible or pray or fast all alone. One can even serve others in ways that do not involve constant daily sharing of one's most private world. Of course, one does not have to live in a family to be in relationship with others who are the objects of one's kindness, goodness and faithfulness. But there is no greater challenge and discipline than to live in kindness, faithfulness and goodness with a family. To make an analogy with exercise, relationships with friends and acquaintances are afternoon strolls while family living is a triathlon. It is relatively easy to be kind and faithful and good to acquaintances and friends whom we encounter every now and then. Being kind and faithful and good to people who leave messes in the kitchen for us to clean up, or chew gum loudly when we are trying to read, or drive the car and leave it out of gas—these are daily challenges.

Family life thus carries the potential of nurturing the fruits of the Spirit in our individual lives. In addition, however, our relationships themselves have the potential of bearing fruit, encompassing and at the same time exceeding what any one of us can do by ourselves. Those fruits include love, hospitality, procreation, forgiveness, celebration, grace and hope.

Love

As we saw in the above sections, over and over the Bible uses family relationships as images for who God is. Perhaps no description of God is more fundamental and significant for our understanding than that God is love, and that our family and community relationships are to reflect that love (1 Jn 4:16-21).

No other description is more countercultural, either, in our society where individual rights and achievements are far more valued than community, where we want intimacy on our own terms with the ability to end relationships that become too demanding or stifling of our individual development. Family relationships smack of duty and responsibility rather than individual choice—of obligation as well as devotion. This is true even for marriage. As William Willimon points out, the major issue for Christians is not so simple as choosing the right person to marry. Instead it is sustaining one's commitment so that love develops. The wedding ceremony does not ask each whether they love one another now, but whether they *will* love one another in the future. Love is something we promise to do, the result of marriage rather than its cause.

> Stanley Hauerwas has argued that we always marry the wrong person. That is, we never marry the one we thought we were marrying—because marriage changes us. So you wake up one day and realize that the person next to you is not the person you committed your life to five years ago. Of course, you are not the same person either. . . . Nobody ever chose to marry a person who is addicted to alcohol, or who develops a terminal illness. But sometimes you wake up in a marriage and that is the person you've got. Being a parent is like that too. Parents never get the children they thought they were giving birth to. . . . What we need, when we marry or have a child, is some means of turning our fate into our destiny. As Christians, our faith provides us the means to live together as parents, children, husbands and wives. Just as we didn't choose Samson or Sarah to be our grandparents in faith, so we didn't choose Jesus to be our savior. He came to us, not the other way around (Jn 15:16). (Willimon 1996:173-74)

The culmination of Jesus' teaching is this, that we are to love one another (Jn 13:35). Even family relationships entered voluntarily, such as adoption and marriage, are not the culmination of love but rather its beginning. "Rather than 'falling in love and then marrying,' couples love each other just enough to marry and then begin a lifelong journey through which they learn the depths, extents, implications, and skills of loving another human being as unconditionally and completely as is humanly possible" (Hunt 1987:126). This is true in every relationship, whether chosen or not. It is this love that witnesses to our connection to the God of love.

The love Jesus is describing here is a mutual love. Although love certainly involves sacrifice of self, even to the point of giving one's life, such self-giving is not the ultimate aim but rather a means to the end of mutual love (Gudorf 1985).

Even Jesus' ultimate sacrifice of his life for unrepentant sinners was aimed at restoring us to relationship with God, to mutual love (see also Miller-McLemore 1994).

The significance of a relationship of mutual love is rooted deeply, in the very creation of humanity. In the first account of creation, God makes humans male *and* female, saying, "Let us make humankind in our image, according to our likeness" (Gen 1:26). It is the *and,* the relationship between "us," that is the image of God. It is not our noses, or our eyes, or our intelligence that is like God, but rather that we are in relationship with one another, a relationship that is to bear fruit and care for the created world. The importance of the relationship between the man and the woman is confirmed in the second creation account, found in Genesis 2. Although this account does not talk about the "image of God" as does the first, it makes a point of God's analysis that man's aloneness was the only aspect of creation to be judged "not good" (Gen 2:18).

What is it about the relationship between us that is image of God in the first account and completion of the good creation in the second account? Perhaps the first love song, recorded in Genesis 2:23, says it most eloquently: "This is at last bone of my bones and flesh of my flesh," a partner with whom each could be "naked, and not ashamed" (Gen 2:25). Having another with whom one can share everything down to the bones and flesh of life, one with whom one can be totally vulnerable and feel safe, pictures for us the relationship God offers not only with one another but also with God.

The partnership of a man and a woman has great significance as the image of God's love. Hosea loved Gomer, his wife who kept running off into prostitution. He kept taking her back, painting a picture of God's love for God's bride, the people of God, however unfaithful. In addition, however, Scripture uses other family relationships to portray God's love. For example, we have the image of the father's love for both his sons in Jesus' parable of the prodigal son. As the father takes the wayward son back and also loves the grumpy elder brother enough to go out and plead with him to join the party, so God folds us into his love. The endurance of family love points to the endurance of God's love: "love never ends" (1 Cor 13:8).

Hospitality

When Jesus sent out the Twelve, instructing them not to carry extra money or clothing, he was issuing not only a call to these disciples to proclaim the good news but also a call to the community of believers to extend hospitality. Disciples were to receive one another as they would receive Jesus (Mt 10:40-42). "The emphasis, then, is on the quality of love and compassion in the community more than upon sacrifice on the part of the individual disciple" (Russell 1994:28).

Christian hospitality is quite different from the connotation the term *hospitality* often carries in our culture. It is not synonymous with social occasions, with cooking fancy meals or using the good dishes in the dining room instead of eating in the kitchen. In fact, Christian hospitality is quite the opposite of our culture's sense of hospitality, which is often synonymous with "entertaining."

Entertaining refers to a break in a family's routine in order to take care of visitors in special ways, different from ordinary daily life. It often entails sprucing up the living quarters, changing to nicer clothing, serving fare that is fancier than the everyday, using all the special accouterments the household can muster. Sometimes we are right in doing these things, as a way of honoring the presence of a guest. More often, however, the motivation is impressing the visitor that this *is* our everyday behavior and fare and that the preparations are "no trouble." Too often such "special care" inadvertently communicates "otherness" rather than welcome. True hospitality means not hiding who the family really is but opening the family's boundaries to include the other. It means inviting another into the heart of the family as a valued representative of Christ's presence. That can be symbolized by pizza on the kitchen table or other ways we truly make others feel "at home."

My own experience of feeling most welcomed was with a friend, a mother of preschoolers. The general disarray that often characterizes the home of preschoolers did not embarrass her in the least, because she did not feel the need to impress me; she simply welcomed me in, mess and all, as one would a member of the family.

Hospitality is individual or family virtue extended to others. When it is met with receptiveness, it leads to fellowship/familyship. Thus being a foster parent is hospitality; and when the child meets this hospitality with openness, it leads to true parent-child relationship. Each shares their own "territory"—both physical and emotional—with the other. True hospitality welcomes the stranger to bring their strangeness with them and thus changes the home ground, not just melting into what is already. Both are changed. The stranger brings a new story that can become a part of the family's story. Each is "hospitable" to the other.

According to Robert Roberts, not only our relationships with others who are close to us but also our relationships with strangers are important to healthy functioning. True hospitality has several characteristics:

1. The others have to be outsiders. They cannot be our own children, for example. We can be generous to our children, but not hospitable, because it is their home too.

2. You must have some territory to share, even a hotel room, or the exhaust grate a homeless person shares with another homeless person.

3. You must provide outsiders with the benefits of one's home territory (food, friends, car, etc.). If I gave a thousand dollars to a homeless person on the street, I may be generous, but to be hospitable I have to welcome the person in my home. The hospitable person *fellowships* with the beneficiary in a way unnecessary for generosity. We treat them as members of the family. (Roberts 1993)

Hospitality inevitably makes us vulnerable to the stranger, whereas generosity does not. The opening of the family boundaries brings the risk that the one invited in will disrupt, and perhaps even harm, the family in some way. The person invited to supper may stay too long and keep us from other activities or from going to bed at our accustomed time. The visitor may actually steal from us, or in other ways abuse the privilege of being folded into the family. A foster child who has not resolved previous abusive experiences may in turn abuse the family in some way. The stranger might even bring total destruction on the family. For example, families that provided shelter for Jews during the Holocaust risked their very lives.

On the other hand, hospitality often brings unpredicted blessings. Over and over Scripture tells stories of blessings from strangers to whom hospitality was extended: the widow who fed a stranger her last bit of bread, only to be blessed by unfailing provisions and the restoration of life to her son (1 Kings 17:8-24); the prostitute Rahab who welcomed Hebrew spies into her house and gained protection for her whole family (Josh 2:1-21); the woman at the well who gave a strange rabbi a drink and received "living water" in return (Jn 4:7-30).

At its extreme, hospitality becomes a paradox. Hospitality's success makes hospitality impossible, since adoption of the guest as a family member makes the outsider an insider. The goal of all Christian hospitality is transformation into the perfect familial fellowship in the kingdom of God, where the distinction between insiders and outsiders, between those who belong and those who don't, is broken down. Hospitality thus points us to the New Testament ideal of adoption as God's good news. It is the beginning of the adoption process.

Forgiveness

Martin Luther King Jr. related how Abraham Lincoln spoke a kind word about the South at the height of the most bitter conflict of the Civil War. A shocked bystander asked how he could speak so, and he responded, "Do I not destroy my enemies when I make them my friends?" (King 1963:53). This is the power of the love of an enemy expressed in forgiveness.

There are times when the enemy is within our own family and forgiveness has the potential of strengthening covenant bonds. Forgiveness offers us the possibility of moving on from hurts and failures to a strengthened covenant with one another (Mt 5:38-39; Rom 12:17). It is one of the ways we show evidence of God's love for us (Eph 4:32).

Our first impulse when we are hurt by a beloved is to hurt back. Since covenant family is a "one-flesh" relationship, however, to hurt the partner is to hurt ourselves. When we strike back to hurt and punish the partner, we widen the gulf of hurt and anger between us rather than finding ways to heal the relationship.

Of course we need to communicate our hurt or anger as a first step and invitation to resolve the difference between us. But the focus is on invitation to restoration, not on punishment.

The focus of forgiveness is the future; the focus of punishment is the past. Punishment focuses on giving the other what they deserve; whether it helps them or hurts them is not the issue. Forgiveness, on the other hand, focuses on the needs of the other and of the relationship for the future (1 Pet 3:9-12). Forgiveness says, "I am hurt and angry, but it will not help either of us for me to try to get even. I want to see what we can do to make things right between us." It is an *invitation* to restoration. Forgiveness does not depend on the partner's making amends or swearing never to do whatever it is again. "I'll forgive you and forget the whole thing ever happened if you promise never to throw anything away that belongs to me" is not forgiveness; it is striking a deal. Forgiveness is not contractual. It does not say, "If you promise never to do that again, I will forgive you." It simply says, "I will not seek to make you pay for what you have done."

By itself, however, forgiveness does not restore the relationship. Restoration can take place only when there is confession and repentance *plus* forgiveness.

God invites us into relationship, but we must respond with repentance. Allowing for restoration of the relationship without repentance actually encourages the other to sin, and thus is the opposite of grace. God does not overlook or excuse our sin; we are responsible for what we do. In the same way, partners in covenant family hold one another responsible for what they do. In Jesus' parable of the unforgiving servant (Mt 18:21-35), a king forgives an enormous debt when his servant pleads for mercy. The same servant, however, then turns a deaf ear to a fellow servant who begs for forgiveness of a much smaller debt. When the king receives word, he becomes furious. He expected changed action.

Forgiveness frees the other from having to repay the debt, but it also carries the expectation that the future will be different. For example, to "forgive" infidelity or violence in a family relationship is one thing, but to restore the relationship based on forgiveness without repentance allows the other to continue in the sin of unfaithfulness or violence. Love holds the other accountable to repent. It is often necessary to say, "I love you and I forgive you—I will not seek to punish you for what you have done. But I will not go on living with you unless you change your ways, because to do so would be to encourage you to hurt me, and thus yourself, again and again. When you repent and change your ways, then the relationship can be restored."

On display in St. Patrick's cathedral in Dublin hangs an ancient door with a rough hewn, rectangular opening hacked in the center. The story of this "door of reconciliation" and the related Irish expression of "chancing one's arm" are remarkable and instructive.

Almost 500 years ago, in 1492, two prominent Irish families, the Ormonds and Kildares, were in the midst of a bitter feud. Besieged by Gerald Fitzgerald, Earl of Kildare, Sir James Butler, Earl of Ormond, and his followers took refuge in the chapter house of St. Patrick's Cathedral, bolting themselves in.

As the siege wore on the Earl of Kildare concluded that the feuding was foolish. Here were two families worshiping the same God, in the same church, living in the same country, trying to kill each other. So he called out to Sir James and, as an inscription in St. Patrick's says today, "undertoake on his honour that he should receive no villanie."

Afraid of "some further treachery," Ormond did not respond. So Kildare seized his spear, cut a hole in the door and thrust his hand through. It was grasped by another hand inside the church. The door was opened and the two men embraced, thus ending the family feud. From Kildare's noble gesture came the expression "chancing one's arm." (Honeycutt 1987)

Kildare could have lost an arm; instead he gained restored relationship. Forgiveness is risky, but when met with repentance and reciprocal forgiveness, it leads to celebration.

"Forgive and forget" is not a Christian concept, even when there has been true repentance. Forgetting what is forgiven means throwing away the very fruit of the covenant relationship. Our victory over the sin in our life together gives us cause to celebrate. Remembering the trials in our relationship, like the Israelites retelling the story of God's faithfulness through their sinfulness, gives us hope for the future. Remembering means saving the door with its hole and its story.

Remembering is the responsibility of the one who has been forgiven, not the forgiver (see Mt 6:12, 14-15). The past must be remembered if the future is to be different. Lewis Smedes suggests that the concept of "forgive and forget" should be replaced with "redemptive remembering" (Smedes 1990). In the exodus from Egypt, Moses told the people of Israel always to remember what they had experienced—their own sin, God's forgiveness and the miracle of renewed covenant. The prodigal son probably never forgot the pigsty, and his father never forgot the emotional and financial cost of his son's behavior. Because they remembered, they could celebrate the restoration of their relationship.

Of course, sometimes relationships are not restored. Forgiveness is offered, but there is no confession or repentance. Or there is repentance and confession, but the wronged family member seeks revenge instead, continuing to hold the sin against the other until he or she has "suffered enough." In the meantime, bitterness continues to wreak its damage. No matter how loving we may be, no one can make a relationship "work" on their own—not even God.

These three fruits of living in families—love, hospitality and forgiveness/repentance—involve relationship between two or more family members or potential family members. Mutuality is not required for hospitality and love to be proffered, but they lead to a family covenant only when mutuality exists. On the other hand, forgiveness takes place in a covenant that already exists but has been torn; forgiveness carries the potential for restoration. It too must be met by a response from the other, the response of repentance. Of course, sometimes both parties in a family need to forgive the other, but unless both are also repentant, the potential for reconciliation remains only that—potential. The virtue must be met with response for the relationship outcome to take place.

Virtue	Response of other	Potential relationship outcome
hospitality	mutual hospitality	fellowship/familyship
love	mutual love	covenant
forgiveness/ repentance	repentance/forgiveness	reconciliation

Procreation

Before the Fall, Adam and Eve were given responsibility for working with God in creation—caring for the Garden and multiplying their numbers. In both ways we participate in and support the work of the Creator—and thus we are *pro*creative. One of the most significant and profound experiences of procreation is conceiving and giving birth to children and nurturing them into adulthood. We will address this more fully in a later chapter. There are myriad other ways, however, in which families express their procreativity. We nurture not only our own biological children but also the children (including grown children) of others. We care for the community and help it to support and nurture all God's children. We continue to bear responsibility as stewards for the beautiful garden in which God has placed us and which is threatened by our sinful abuse.

In all these activities, the family engages the world beyond its own boundaries. Our acts of care for the garden do not aim simply at keeping our own nest unpolluted; we are called to care for every living thing (Gen 1:28). Even the raising of children is an act of providing for creation beyond the family, because they will someday launch out to begin new families and contribute in their own ways (or not) to the creative purposes of God.

Procreation actually is the other bookend to hospitality. If hospitality welcomes and enfolds others into the family, procreation blesses and sends out. It calls out the spiritual discipline of letting go. Wendy Wright speaks of the twin disciplines of welcoming and letting go. "Letting go does not consist of ceasing to love, or detaching oneself from the affection one feels, but in loving more. Letting go involves radical faith. It means entrusting what you most love to the expansive care and protection of God" (Wright 1990:37).

Celebration

A significant characteristic of Jesus' ministry was his participation in celebration. Jesus frequently ate and drank as a sign of the greatest of all banquets that was to come. The more pious folk of the day accused him, in fact, of being a "glutton and a drunkard" (Lk 7:34). But Jesus said, "I have come that they may have life, and have it to the full" (Jn 10:10). Tony Campolo has pointed out that tithing in the Old Testament served to subsidize parties, festivals honoring Yahweh's goodness and forgiveness. The people gathered for festivals to eat, drink, sing and laugh, to be with family and friends in worship to God as they offered their tithes. Care for the physical needs of others came from *beyond* the tithe (Campolo and Aeschliman 1993). Jesus taught that the kingdom of God is a party, a great celebration (Campolo 1990).

One of the ways families point to the good news is to celebrate our life as family together, as witness to the big party to come when the kingdom achieves its fullness. Many of us have had glimpses of that party at some point, when for some unexplainable reason we stay gathered around the supper table a little longer, talking and laughing; perhaps a dear friend is with us, or teenagers are in the mood to talk. The rituals and rhythms of family life offer frequent occasions for rejoicing and celebration; we do not have to bear the mundane alone, and because of that, the mundane takes on meaning. Housecleaning, cooking, raking leaves, even cleaning out the garage can be occasions for joy as well as work because we have others who share in this life with us.

Celebration should not be disguised smugness. Christian celebration does not focus on what we have accomplished, what we have become or been able to purchase. Instead we remember that what has been accomplished has been because of God's grace and presence, *in spite of* our weakness and limited vision. We celebrate the glimpse of the kingdom to come, not snug, well-insulated homes of complacency. Through our grief and struggles together, we have sipped or even drunk deeply of joy not of our own making.

Finally, celebration is important because it strengthens our faith and commitment to that which we celebrate. In the mid-twentieth century, Regina Wieman wrote about the significance of religious celebration for families. Celebration brings about a "purification of the heart," as we magnify that which we value supremely. "By celebrating it we put it into such perspective that it towers over all else and possesses us more completely" (Wieman 1941:207).

Grace and Hope

Grace means "unmerited favor" (Balswick and Balswick 1989). Basing family life on contracts leads to an atmosphere of law and a ledgering of past rights and wrongs. Basing family life on covenant leads to an atmosphere of grace and hope for the future.

Obviously, we need routines—agreements, assignments and family rules that help us navigate our daily life together. But these are always relative and temporary; they are not the foundation, nor the condition on which our continued relationship rests. The rules, assignments and expectations are there to impart grace, to help us care for and love one another, not to repress one another.

Living in a family teaches us how far we are from perfect. We can reflect with gratitude on God's grace that has sustained us as we have stumbled through life together, making mistakes, losing our tempers, becoming weary and sloppy in our relationships. We experience God's grace in grown children who turn out to be wonderful people, in spouses who stand by us even when we let them down, in parents who have become friends despite the hell we put them through as teenagers, in friends who have become family despite all our imperfections.

Not only do we experience grace ourselves, but we model hope for others. Others see in us the evidence of God's grace and of our hope that God can continue to work with us and through us even though we were once defeated or divorced or made an overall muck of things. We all need to be part of a community of real, honest people who are not ashamed to share their struggles, not in spite of their failings but because of their hope in God's grace and power. It takes courage to allow ourselves to be vulnerable in this way. "Our hearts learn the truth from honest strugglers who dare to open the windows of their lives to us" (Smedes 1988:80).

There is also another side. Families also teach us that we can be better than we thought, that God's work in our lives is a process of miracles. In the parent-child relationship, according to theologian Elizabeth Achtemeier, this learning is particularly concentrated:

> We parents also learn from our children that we can be better than we thought—we can sacrifice sleep, time, material goods, and plans for the sake of another; we can love someone unfailingly who is acting totally unlovable; we can give ourselves away for the sake of another person and then find joy returned to us a hundredfold. The experience of raising children does, in truth, confirm our Lord's promise that whoever loses his life shall find it. (Achtemeier 1987:59)

Indeed, we are surprised that we make these sacrifices willingly, without even thinking, or at least thinking very often, about the cost. Someone has estimated how much the "average" American family spends on the raising of children. It is a huge number, more than most of us ever imagine spending on anything. I love using that statistic because it has wonderful shock value, even among parents. The reason it shocks, of course, is the grace that parents practice. Few parents keep such a ledger or would have given much thought to how many dollars and cents they have spent through the years on their children. Despite all the talk of our culture's individualism, our love affair with self-actualization to the detriment of family commitments, there are still ample evidences of grace. We are sometimes graceful without realizing it.

For this reason, families give us the ground for understanding the grace of God and the reason to hope in that which we cannot see. Rodney Clapp writes poignantly of his own experiences of family faithfulness as demonstrated in the lives of parents and spouse and a host of others:

> It is a history, a personal story, that allows me to imagine that differences and adversity can be borne. It has bred into my bones the hope and courage that fidelity can last a lifetime, that people can be trusted enough for me to marry one of them. It answers the needs of my heart for assurance of continuing love and the opportunity, the possibility, to grow together in profound confidence and trust. (Clapp 1993:122)

Intentional, "grace-full" living in family covenants gives us hope. Covenant families partake of the kingdom of God that was established at the very foundation of the world (Mt 25:24) and is here now. By the grace of God we can be and are being transformed in our relationships to be in the likeness of God's image: "we all . . . . are being transformed into the same image from one degree of glory to another" (2 Cor 3:18). God will help us (Heb 4:16). In Christ the old is passed away, the new is possible and in fact is here (2 Cor 5:17).

A few years ago I wrote a reflection on my marriage that could be about any family relationship, not just marriage:

> Making a quilt seemed like a fun late-winter project. Our blank white kitchen wall begged for something, and to pick up the design of the area rug under the table in a quilt-hanging seemed like a great idea. It would be beautiful, unlike anything my foremothers had made. I borrowed the children's colored pencils and sketched out the design on the back of a large cardboard panel. I had never made a quilt before, but how hard can it be to cut out simple shapes and sew them together? I bought the fabric and plunged in.

As I worked, I soon realized that the quilt was going to be different from what I had planned. I mismeasured some of the middle pieces—little mistakes that multiplied as I added layer on layer to the edges. I had to patch in extra pieces and change the design to fit the mistakes.

Eight months later (not the two I had planned), the quilt was finished and hanging on the wall. It was a lot more work than I had ever dreamed. It only remotely resembled my original sketch. It refused to hang flat, and one side is slightly longer than the other. Nevertheless, I like it. No one will ever mistake it for factory-made. It is quite different from the work of art I dreamed I could create; all the mistakes and corrections have become a part of the design.

As I put the finishing rows of stitches on the quilt, hoping against hope that a few more stitches would perhaps persuade it to hang straight, it dawned on me how much my quilt is like a good marriage. We start out with a dream that we can make a marriage better than the imperfect and (from our perspectives) dull marriages of our parents. We sketch out our plans, and we begin to build our dream marriage, far underestimating the work of quilting together two lives into one pattern. As we busily shape and stitch our lives day by day, we make mistakes and cause hurts. The marriage quilt becomes flawed, quilted as it is by two sinful people. We become discouraged; the pieces don't fit together as well as we thought they would. Compromises and patching are essential if it is going to hang together at all. The design must be altered; otherwise, we give up and throw it away.

If we persevere, however, and allow God to work in and through us, our marriage quilt takes on a unique beauty as love and grace and forgiveness turn the flaws into redemption. The hurts and wrongs are not beautiful, but the love that shapes them into the larger design of God's work through our lives can turn them into pictures to the world of the healing power of God's love. (Garland 1993)

Part Two

Leading Family Ministry

Section Five

Planning & Leading Family Ministry

T HE FIRST TWO SECTIONS OF THIS BOOK EXPLORED IN CONSID-
erable depth the meaning of *family* and examined the experiences of families in
our own culture today, both the processes within family life and the community
context which shapes, supports and challenges family living. The third section
looked at how the concept and experience of family have developed over time
and how the church has influenced that development. Finally, the fourth section identified biblical themes that speak to how we define and live in families.
Defining what we mean by family ministry obviously depends on these understandings of families—what they are and what they ought to be. To summarize,
family ministry is helping persons live as they ought to in family life, according
to the purposes and promises of God. It includes not only working with families themselves, but also developing the congregational community as a support
for righteous family living. Family ministry also is prophetic, speaking to the
larger community and society in behalf of families. This section turns to the
very practical matters of how to plan, implement and lead family ministry in
congregational life.

Chapter 14

Defining Family Ministry

LITTLE CONSENSUS EXISTS ABOUT WHAT THE TERM "FAMILY MINistry" means.[1] Some churches use "family ministry" as a catch-all category of programs designed to support persons in their daily activities and relationships. Others may mean by "family ministry" all the programs and services carried out in a particular place; they have built a "Family Life Center," and family ministry is everything that happens there. Consequently, family ministry can include a wide assortment of programs and services: exercise and fitness, stress management, childcare, support groups for the variety of challenges people face, marriage enrichment, parenting classes, retirement seminars, emergency assistance for families in crisis, counseling, and on and on.

Some churches have used family ministry programs as marketing tools—a way of reaching out and bringing in community folks. People will come to a course that addresses the stresses of living when they won't come to a worship service. People will come to use the church gymnasium when they won't come to Bible

---

[1]Portions of this chapter were previously published in the following: Diana Garland, 1996, What is family ministry? *Christian Century* 113, no. 33: 1100-1101; and Diana Garland, 1992, The changing family, *Review and Expositor* 90, no. 4: 455-73.

study. There has been some sense that if we can hook people with resources *they* perceive they need—recreational and educational programs—we can hold on to them to give them the resources *we* perceive they need—Christian discipling and membership in the community of faith.

A second impetus for the flurry of programs called family ministry is that churches are seeking ways to strengthen and support congregational families. Since the 1940s, American church leaders have been sounding a warning that families are perishing. The Christian family magazine *Home Life* was first published in 1947 by the largest Protestant denomination in the United States, the Southern Baptist Convention. Introducing this new publication, Clifton J. Allen, executive secretary of the Southern Baptist Sunday School Board, wrote:

> Your heart beats with the conviction, "There's no place like home." But one out of five homes crashes on the rocks of divorce. Family life is being blighted by strong drink, lust, and worldly pleasure. Happiness is driven from literally millions of homes by misunderstanding, selfishness, irreligion, and ignorance. The home front is under siege. This peril is a call to action. Fathers and mother must awake to their God-given privilege and responsibility. Churches must grasp their supreme opportunity to help parents build virile Christian homes. . . . Our homes demand and deserve our best. They are at the center of God's plan. . . . They are the fountain of our nation's life. (Allen 1947:1)

Similar alarms were sounded in other denominations as well. In the mid-twentieth century, denominations and congregations began a number of initiatives to shore up family life: publications, marriage preparation, marriage enrichment, parent education and family counseling. Church leaders perceived that not only did families "out there" in the community need help, but families within the community of faith were also crumbling. Thus the target of family ministry programs became blurred. Many did not distinguish between helping church members live more effectively in families and reaching out to families in the community by addressing their needs.

At first blush, this dual target does not seem like a problem. It is glaringly obvious that church folks are not immune to the burgeoning family malaise. Both church folks and nonchurch folks seem to need the same thing—better education and preparation for family roles. Indeed, both groups could benefit from new understandings of what makes for strong families in American society, a topic of considerable research in family sociology and psychology.

As a consequence, family ministry programs have focused primarily on preventing family dysfunction through education (parent education, marriage education and enrichment), strengthening families through enjoyment of shared activities (activity evenings in the church facility, camping, sports) and counseling.

FAMILY MINISTRY AND THE COMMUNITY MENTAL HEALTH MOVEMENT

The community mental health center movement of the 1960s provided interesting parallels and opportunities for collaboration between church leaders developing family ministries and community social service professionals. Sometimes the same people were involved in both movements. Community mental health was a new government initiative supported by the social service professions. The federal government provided major funding to develop centers whose purpose was to lower the incidence of mental illness in a community through prevention programs and to treat those with mental illness and developmental disabilities in their own families and communities rather than in large state hospitals and institutions. Because theory of the day suggested that family processes cause or at least contribute to mental illness, developing healthy families was a significant focus of these centers. Both family ministry and the community mental health movement emphasized prevention of family problems when possible and crisis intervention to keep existing problems from escalating.

Because the government mandated that community mental health centers care for those suffering chronic mental illness and developmental disabilities, this responsibility often overshadowed prevention, education and crisis management services. In addition, government funding for community mental health centers was time limited and never fully adequate. As large state institutions were closed and persons with chronic mental illness and developmental disabilities returned to the community, community mental health centers found themselves dealing primarily with the pressing needs of these groups. And because the community stigmatized the centers as places that served the mentally ill and the developmentally disabled, other folks were less than excited about going there for educational programs and services.

Increasingly, social service professionals looked to other institutions to provide crisis prevention and family life education services. Both public schools and churches are located in virtually every community and touch the lives of many families. Consequently many community leaders, with the support of social service professionals, began to call on these institutions to provide prevention, education and counseling services for families.

The development of community mental health services has shaped church-based family ministry. During the 1960s and 1970s, research and theory in family sociology and psychology were mushrooming. Family therapy was developing into a profession. Seminary degree programs were increasingly providing content in pastoral care and family counseling, which drew directly from the social sciences and the professional literature of psychology, psychiatry, social work and family therapy. Larger seminaries began offering specialized degree programs in psychology, social work and family therapy. Pastoral care was also being recognized as a ministry specialization, and many came to seminary to prepare for church positions as pastoral counselors (D. R. Garland 1983). Grounded in the social science literature of research and professional practice, these new church leaders saw the significant role congregations could play in providing premarital preparation, educational programs and family counseling. In some respects, churches had historically been involved in these activities; now professionally educated social workers, psychologists and pastoral counselors were providing leadership (ibid.).

But these new church leaders had little to help them contextualize and adapt their professional education for the church. Many family ministry programs borrowed extensively from and thus bore a striking resemblance to professional theory and practice models from the social services. They often attempted to adapt these theories and models by substituting or adding language and concepts familiar in the church, but failed to consider the theories' basic premises and goals.

For example, one marriage enrichment curriculum for use in community mental health and other public settings was quickly followed by a "Christian" version. The curriculum drew heavily on exciting research being conducted at a large state university concerning communication patterns and their relationship with marital satisfaction and stability. The Christian version simply added Scripture verses to the beginning and end of each session. The goals, processes and content were otherwise identical.

Differences Between Mental Health Services and Family Ministry

Despite the parallels between mental health services and family ministry, there are fundamental differences between the goals of social service agencies and those of congregations. Educational programs in social service agencies evaluate outcomes by measuring marital and family satisfaction and well-being, often defined as the *absence of dysfunction*. In other words, these programs are successful if they prevent escalating conflict, family violence, mental illness, depression and the dissolution of family ties. That is what they are supposed to do.

Because of the influence of the mental health professions, family ministry has also been heavily invested in counseling and programs designed to prevent family problems. Counseling and the prevention of family problems are important objectives for congregational family ministry. Obviously, churches too want to prevent family violence, mental illness, depression and family breakup. It is wonderful when persons are happy and satisfied with their family life. But family life satisfaction should not necessarily be the *central* focus of ministry with families. Instead family ministry needs to focus on accomplishing the mission of the church.

How does that mission relate to families in the congregation and in the congregation's community? Public leaders express concern that if the foundation of a society is its families and families are crumbling, our society is in trouble. Is the mission of the church to preserve a particular society's stability? Or is the crumbling of families a symptom of societal problems requiring a more systemic response than family fix-it programs?

In fact, the call to shore up the family may be an attempt to preserve the status quo, a status quo that majors on individualism and self-actualization, that perceives families simply as the place where persons have their interpersonal and relational needs met. These are important functions, but by themselves they miss the meaning of family life for Christians.

As chapter thirteen made clear, families are one of the most significant contexts of Christian discipleship. For many of us, learning to live justly and lovingly with family members is one of the most difficult Christian disciplines. Many congregations also find it extremely difficult to reach beyond the bonds of blood and marriage, which our culture defines as family, to live the good news of the gospel. That good news says that when we choose to follow Christ, we will have all the mothers and brothers and sisters we need and, by implication, we must be that family for one another. Consequently, the church bears responsibility for ensuring that no one in the family of faith is familyless—that everyone is folded into the nurture of family. And finally, God created humanity with a purpose, a mission of care. God recognized that this was not for persons to carry out in isolation; they needed companions in the work, and so the partnership of family was created. The first man and woman were not created simply to be companions, but to be companions *in the work* (Gen 1:26-28). Families have a purpose, a calling from God, to be on mission together. Family ministry may thus need to be transformed in our minds into "families-in-ministry."

These three principles need to be the focus of family ministry for the church. Together they provide a core of goals for family ministry significantly different from and broader than community mental health's mandate to help families be less troubled and more satisfied.

A DEFINITION OF FAMILY MINISTRY

The church is a community on mission, a community that attempts to embody the characteristics of God and God's kingdom. That community on mission is the context for family ministry, which consists of *any activity of a church or church representative(s) that directly or indirectly (1) develops faith-families in the congregational community, (2) increases the Christlikeness of the family relationships of Christians and/or (3) equips and supports Christians who use their families as a channel of ministry to others.*

Family ministry is not just a set of programs that address family issues, although it certainly can include such programs. Family ministry includes everything a church and its representatives do that has an impact on the founding, development and ministry of families. Often congregations engage in family ministry indirectly and sometimes unintentionally, as part of their worship, ministry and life together.

Forming Faith-Families

According to this definition, the church has the responsibility to nurture the founding and growth of families, especially "faith-families," and especially for persons who are alone either because they have no family or their biological/legal family is not Christian. In addition, the church enriches the lives of all families by nurturing the development of ties to faith-family members. The church thus serves as a matchmaker, providing settings where potential faith-family members can meet and learn to care for one another. In many respects this is the most challenging of the three prongs of family ministry.

Faith-families are not the same thing as the "community of faith." The congregation serves as an extended family and community, but most congregations are much too large for members to be in primary, intimate relationship with everyone else. Families need community, and congregations can be a vital, supportive community for families. *Within* that community, everyone needs to be a part of a family unit, whether they are members of the same household or not. As we have seen, in our culture, family and household are not necessarily equivalent for everyone.

Often congregations already are serving as matchmakers. People do find each other and learn to love and care for each other. Future spouses meet in youth groups and single adult programs. Family ministry needs to include the formation of other kinds of faith-families, however, besides marriage. Adults need to be in faith-grandparenting or faith-aunting or faith-uncling relationships with children and younger adults; friends need to become faith-siblings for one another. Church programs cannot control the formation of these relationships; people cannot be "assigned" to family units any more than churches can select and assign marriage partners. But church programs can provide the context where people of all ages have interaction with one another, learn to care for one another and have the opportunity to adopt one another as family.

The most daunting challenge for congregations is finding ways to nurture the formation of relationships for which our culture has no name, those I call "faith-family" relationships. Perhaps this challenge is best met when we simply organize our life together such that the generations and people in different life situations can be with one another. A child has encounters with adults who can become the faith-uncle or faith-aunt. Adults who are not married can find faith-siblings, faith-nieces, faith-nephews. To the extent that a congregation provides a community for relationships to develop across the ages and family experiences of members, we are nurturing the formation of families. Age-graded programs need to be balanced with structures of congregational life that encourage meaningful conversation and activity across generations. Older adults, young adults, children, youths, singles, marrieds, parents and nonparents need to share together—at least some of the time—in congregational life.

Once faith-family relationships develop, they need to be named and celebrated, wrapped about with community recognition and blessing. For example, rather than celebrating our culture's Mother's Day and Father's Day—which exclude many—congregations can celebrate Faith-Mother's Day and Faith-Father's Day.

Here is an excerpt from an interview with a divorced twenty-four-year-old mother of a preschooler:

I know my son needs to be at church, but as for me, I've got to find somewhere that I feel like I'm learning something. They teach a lot about family values and marriage, and they don't realize that there's a lot of people who don't have that, not by their own choice. So I feel out of place. There are times like Father's Day, and as the preacher is preaching, I'm thinking that my son doesn't have that, and I just don't want to hear it. I just can't hear it. I want to hear something that relates to my experience and to others like me. A lot of people feel alone and they don't feel like they have anywhere to go, because they think that if they go to church all they're going to hear is family values, and a lot of people don't have that. I have it with my parents, but my son and I are a broken family. But I don't feel broken—I feel whole.

Perhaps this young mother would have felt she belonged if the church's emphasis had been on faith-parenting. Congregational members can find ways to recognize those who have mothered and fathered them in the faith.

Forming faith-families is sometimes easiest for those who already have significant family and familylike relationships. Some people are alone because they alienate others. They need special tutoring and guidance to succeed in forming and sustaining friendships and family relationships. And other people may need support if they are to learn to love these difficult persons.

A research project evaluating a parent education program for families at risk for child abuse found that although nurturing support systems for parents was a goal of the program, these parents did not become supportive friends for one another. The researchers conjectured that the parents may not have had adequate social skills to be friends and neighbors. But the program had not taught those skills; researchers had assumed that simply putting persons together would be enough for them to develop support relationships (Whipple and Wilson 1996).

Just putting persons in proximity is not always sufficient. Some persons need help learning how to give as well as to receive, how to listen as well as talk, how to care for others rather than drain others. They need tutoring in relating and caring.

In one congregation, a single young man with learning disabilities tried to hug everyone he encountered. Not only were his hugs sometimes unwelcome, but he often hugged too long, making the recipients of his hugs uncomfortable. Many persons in the congregation simply tried to avoid being near him.

An older man who served as the young man's Sunday school teacher was concerned not only about the discomfort the young man evoked but also the young man's isolation. He talked over his concerns with a church staff member, who encouraged him to boldly and lovingly tell the young man that his hugging made others uncomfortable. With the support of the staff member, the older man took on a mentoring relationship with the young man. He explained that one can hug only certain persons, and then only for five seconds or less. Together, he and the young man worked out a list of persons he could hug. The Sunday-school teacher then taught the young man to shake hands with others who were not on his hugging list. He provided the young man with hugs himself and made sure that several other adults understood what he was trying to do and also gave the young man hugs. The teacher gave the young man lots of praise for expressing affection more appropriately and fussed at him when he broke the new hugging rule. He took the role of "faith uncle" in giving good advice, loving support and firm boundaries. The young man now is being cared for and looked out for by several older adults, and other young adults his age are much friendlier and more accepting.

Increasing the Christlikeness of Family Relationships

Family ministry designed to help Christians live faithfully and lovingly in their families has at least two dimensions. First, the *focus* of family ministry ranges from developing a congregational life that supports and nurtures *all kinds* of families to more specialized ministry for *particular kinds* of families and family experiences. Second, the *goals* of family ministry range widely, from *building on the strengths* of families to *helping families cope* with difficult situations that cannot be changed.

Figure 14.1 shows how one area of content related to family life—forgiveness, repentance and reconciliation—can be addressed in four quadrants of ministry. The upper left quadrant provides content the whole congregation can apply in any family relationships. The lower left quadrant gives attention to the role of forgiveness and repentance in coping with many different kinds of life troubles; *many* families have one or more of these experiences at some point. The right quadrants address specific ministries for specific groups, not the entire congregation. For example, the upper right quadrant suggests ministry to build on the strengths of families that have experienced divorce, and the lower right quadrant suggests ministry to families within this group of divorced persons to cope with particular life troubles.

FOCUS OF FAMILY MINISTRY		
		All families	Specific family structures and issues
GOALS OF MINISTRY	Building strengths	Sermons, Bible study, small group discussions on the meaning of repentance, forgiveness and reconciliation in families; modeling these virtues in congregational life	Bible study and seminar discussion groups for families challenged by particular issues of forgiveness and repentance, e.g., helping divorced persons establish redefined continuing relationships with ex-spouses and their families
	Coping with life stressors	Sermons, Bible study, educational seminars dealing generally with family hurts that can be forgiven but cannot be reconciled (with many examples such as childhood abuse, family members who have cut off relationships because of life choices they have made, and so on)	Support groups and counseling services specifically for persons experiencing particular life stressors, e.g., divorced persons who have been abused or have abused others, those whose family members have committed suicide

Figure 14.1.   Dimensions of family ministry addressing forgiveness, repentance and reconciliation

The upper left quadrant, then, suggests family ministry that touches every family in the congregation. Movement both down and to the right results in ever more targeted ministries to specific groups.

Methods of Family Ministry

The focus dimension of family ministry—from all families to specific family structures and issues—is further defined by *methods* of ministry. Four methods of family ministry address increasingly specific family structures and issues: developing a congregational life that supports and nurtures all families, organizing and facilitating support groups and networks for families dealing with specific issues, providing these families with educational resources and programs, and counseling individual families.

1. Developing a congregational life that supports and nurtures all family relationships. When leaders have successfully taken a family-ministry perspective in shaping the life of their congregation, much of what happens in a church can help families live joyfully and faithfully and solve, or live creatively and redemptively with, the problems of life. In the church, families learn about and become

more skillful in the disciplines of family life—listening and communicating, for-
giving and repenting, handling anger and problem-solving, balancing intimacy
and autonomy, disciplining and loving one another, ministering inside and outside the family's boundaries.

The fundamental and essential method of family ministry is congregational
development as a supportive and nurturing community. The other three methods
of family ministry, which are more overtly focused on specific family issues,
depend on the existence of this supportive congregational life. Community life is
particularly important as a context for helping families deal with life stressors and
situations.

Intentional communities. Some faith groups become a haven, an "ecological
niche," a community that counters the values of mainstream society. They may
have ways of living designed to protect members from negative cultural influences. The Amish continue to live a lifestyle that sets them apart from the surrounding social world. Less radically, some congregations provide their children
with daycare and schools as a means of controlling what they are taught and protecting them from unwanted influences. Others provide support to parents who
choose to homeschool their children.

A few communities of faith may use communal principles, sharing cars and
other expensive items, making it less necessary for so many family members to
work outside their homes or allowing them choices about fewer work hours and
less demanding careers. In one congregation, a number of families have intentionally bought homes in the same block of an inner-city community, using their
presence to bring new stability and safety to the neighborhood. They share
evening meals, each household taking a turn feeding the others. A church may be
intentional in guiding and supporting families in making these choices and using
their presence as a means of bringing positive social change. Examples of such
family ministries are the Parenting for Peace and Justice support groups (McGinnis 1989).

Congregations that do not develop physical communities still often serve as a
significant community in families' lives. There they find others who share and
support their values and family culture, who provide advice and resources for
family living and who help them with life challenges.

Advocacy for families. Being an advocate for families is an essential part of
being a supportive and nurturing community. Congregations have voices that
need to be used in behalf of the needs of not only their own members but also

their neighbors, whoever and wherever they may be. No other institution is moved by a richer or more powerful vision of human community than the church. A congregation can be the leaven that raises the consciousness of the whole community about needs and vulnerabilities of families.

Advocacy can run the gamut from encouraging members to run for posts on the local school board to contacting national representatives concerning government policies that affect families. It can be as simple as writing letters to television stations applauding their family programming and discouraging the broadcasting of shows with violent content. Or it can be much more hands on, such as organizing families in a poor community to find ways to cleanse their neighborhood of gang violence and drugs.

In essence, the Christian church is to give witness to a whole new social order, the kingdom of God, not simply to repair the old. That can happen either by establishing an alternative community that strives to model that new order or by attempting to transform society—or both. Both choices communicate that it is clearly time for a new way, the way Jesus promised for those who are his followers.

For this reason, family ministry does not simply change the oil or tinker with the timing, so to speak, so families will run more smoothly. We are proposing a whole new transportation system for life. Families "transport" us from life to death. Family members are those with whom we share the journey.

Clearly, this perspective of family ministry is quite different from what might have grown as an offshoot of the community mental health movement. We are envisioning families quite differently from what our society means by family. We are making up the language with terms like *faith-families*. In a practical sense, perhaps language and envisioning do not change the tenacious realities with which people are currently struggling. Nevertheless, alternative realities begin with new vision and new rhetoric (Brueggemann 1978). The task of family ministry in our day may in essence be prophecy, evoking an alternative to the definitions of family and community of our society. Prophetic ministry seeks to penetrate despair so that new futures can be believed in and embraced (ibid. 111).

2. Organizing and facilitating support groups and networks. Supporting, nurturing and advocating for families is the foundation for family ministry. In addition, congregations may develop programs and services to address particular issues in family life. These programs and services can be conceptualized on a continuum from the most general to more specialized forms of family ministry. Families are helped by being with other families who share their life situation—parents of teenagers, caregivers for persons with Alzheimer's disease, mentors of single parents, faith-uncles and faith-aunts seeking to nurture faith-children whose parents are not a part of the congregation, parents of young adults who are troubled by substance addiction, grandparents raising their grandchildren. Together families learn from and support one another. This support may be formalized in a group, or it may be a more loosely structured network of families who keep in touch as they choose. The role of the church leader is primarily to help families find and link with one another and to help them identify useful resources. The families themselves provide any leadership needed for their group or network, although professional staff persons can help equip them and support them for this.

3. Providing educational programs and resources. Some families want or need to learn new information or skills that will help them with their particular situation. Educational groups or seminars—such as for parents or engaged couples—are common in congregations. Congregational leaders take a visible leadership role in this kind of ministry, either providing the educational content themselves or securing other knowledgeable educators. Congregational leaders may also supply educational resources such as books or videotapes for families to use individually.

4. Counseling. Finally, some families have barriers to learning information or skills they need. These barriers need to be addressed in individual, family or group counseling. For example, a married couple may be so angry and hurt with each other that they cannot learn in a group setting about anger and conflict management until they have been guided through their current crisis. Families face a variety of crises that need the individual attention of a counseling relationship. Congregational leaders may either provide this counseling or refer to community professionals.

Family counseling thus plays a supportive, not a central, role to the family ministries of congregations. Counseling is like tutoring—preparing people who need help in overcoming obstacles to full participation in the mutual relationships of a community. Some families are dealing with crises beyond the congregation's capacity to address. They need the loving support of the congregation, but they may also need a professional counselor to help them deal with posttraumatic stress syndrome after some devastating event, the death of a family member, a deep disappointment or another difficult life circumstance.

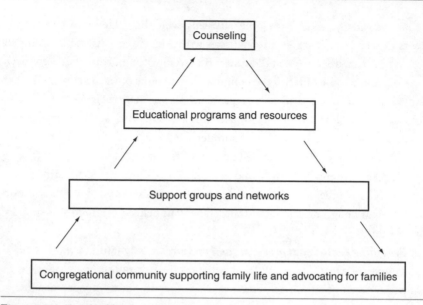

Figure 14.2.   Levels of family ministry

Figure 14.2 illustrates how each level of this continuum of care for families builds on the one below it. Only a congregation whose life together supports and nurtures families can effectively develop support groups and networks within the larger fellowship. Educational programs and resources can meet more specific needs. Finally, the effectiveness of family counseling depends on the presence of all these other elements of the community of faith. Once families have found their way through a particular crisis, they may be ready to benefit from educational programs and resources to help them continue to grow together. Often these programs become support groups and networks, such as parent education groups in which parents become friends and continue to provide informal support to one another long after the course has ended. As families receive the more specialized services of support groups, educational programs and counseling, they are prepared to participate more fully and mutually in the congregational community.

The Goal of Family Ministry

To complement the *methods* of family ministry, the *goals* of family ministry constitute a second dimension, ranging from the enhancement of strengths among diverse family structures and situations to helping families adapt to life stresses and challenges. The simple dichotomy of building family strengths and coping with life stressors is, of course, more complex, as shown in figure 14.3. The content of family ministry includes living with ongoing life challenges that will not change, tackling those problems in the family or community that can be changed, gaining knowledge and skills for family living, and building on family strengths. We can attempt to influence both processes inside the family and its community and environmental context. Most of the time, families can benefit from help from several quarters. This content can be provided in educational classes, seminars, ongoing support groups, and Sunday-school content and sermons.

The Dimensions Put Together: A Family Example

Figure 14.3 illustrates how we might conceptualize various approaches to ministry with a family consisting of a married couple, a senior parent with Alzheimer's disease, and two teenagers. The figure illustrates the variety of ways this family could be touched and supported by congregational family ministry.

Family ministry happens when caregivers feel welcome and supported in bringing their beloved[2] with dementia to participate in the life of the congregation as much as possible. It also happens when a congregational atmosphere encourages both peer relationships and cross-generational relationships that nurture teenagers' growing autonomy as well as family commitments. A congregation can provide a weekly evening of care for persons with dementia, giving regular caregivers the opportunity to be with friends for recreation and to put aside caregiving for a few hours. With this foundation of support and care, caregiving families may also benefit from a support group where they can share their burdens and joys. Caregiving families may also be helped by educational programs that address the nature and progress of the disease and provide practical guidance for living with Alzheimer's disease. Finally, individual or family counseling may be helpful at times as caregivers face all the difficulties involved in caring for a beloved with Alzheimer's disease.

Family ministry also seeks to change the community environment to make it more supportive of families. Sometimes this means making a change in the

---

[2]I use *beloveds* as a generic term for spouses, children, parents, faith-family members and any who function as family members.

The goals of family ministry					
		Living with ongoing life challenges	**Tackling problems in families and communities**	**Learning knowledge and skills for family living**	**Enhancing strengths**
The context of family ministry	within the family	educational seminars, resource materials, counseling and support group for caregivers of persons with Alzheimer's disease	educational seminars that help families work through conflict over roles such as caregiving and household management	parent educational seminars and support groups for parents of adolescents; family communication skills training	marriage enrichment for midlife couples; family recreation and faith-sharing programs; life review programs for adults with dementia and their parents
	within the community/environment	luncheon seminar for community police officers to educate them about caring for persons with dementia and their families in situations of violence or when the family member becomes lost	daycare and occasional respite evening care for senior adults with dementia; youth staff/parent networking that empowers adults to work together in behalf of teenagers	teaching friends how to provide respite care for caregivers; developing adult mentors and friends for teenagers	providing cross-generational family recreation; engaging parents and teenagers in Bible study and mission projects together; educating the congregation and community about relating supportively to persons with Alzheimer's disease and their families; overtly seeking to include these persons in worship and fellowship

Figure 14.3.   The relationship of family ministry goals to content: An example

congregation itself, such as adding a new program (adult daycare) or modifying existing practices (welcoming persons with disabilities to the worship service and promoting tolerance for the diversity of experiences this may bring). It also often involves programs designed to teach, strategize and/or advocate for some systemic change in the larger social world. For example, the congregation may join with caregiving families in sensitizing local police officers to the need for support and immediate help when a person with Alzheimer's disease becomes violent or wanders away from home. The church might sponsor a free luncheon for police officers with a brief presentation and discussion.

EQUIPPING AND SUPPORTING FAMILIES IN MINISTRY

The ultimate focus of family ministry is the support of families in their ministry with one another and in their community. A family's ministry may be simply centered in the activities of members as they live their Christian faith in work and play, at home and not at home. On the other hand, a family's ministry may also entail shared commitments and tasks. Family ministry equips, encourages and supports Christians to use their families as channels of ministry to others.

A congregation has the mission of reaching out with care to families in its own community and beyond. Ministry to families in the community can be service/ evangelism of the most meaningful kind—a ministry through families to families. Following our Lord, who reached out and physically healed families (the widow whose son had died, the father whose daughter was near death, the father with the demon-possessed son), congregational families can reach out with healing, with the good news that God loves us and has made the ultimate sacrifice so that we—and our families—can be redeemed. A divorce recovery workshop is a way of visiting those imprisoned by pain and loss; a childcare program is a cup of cold water to parents thirsty for help in caring for their children; a mentoring program for children growing up in risky situations communicates the good news that in the kingdom of God, we are surrounded by loving family who can help us with life challenges.

Three families of the Bible illustrate some of the diversity of callings that families experience.

Adam and Eve were the first family created. God did not create them and then send them off on an extended honeymoon. Their relationship had a purpose. They were called to be caretakers of the earth and all its creatures. Today's world is groaning under the abuse wrought by sinful humanity. Families are called to raise children and challenge adults to ecological responsibility and advocacy in behalf of God's good creation.

Abraham and Sarah were also given a specific task. They were called to parent a people who would live in covenant with God. Whether we are the biological parents or the spiritual parents of the children in our midst, we are called to raise up a people of God.

In my research I found the significance of raising children to be a major theme in the faith-life of families. This research covered all kinds of Christian families, those that included married couples as well as those with single adults, those with children as well as those composed only of adults. As part of a two-hour interview I asked these families, "What gives purpose and meaning to your life together as a family?"

I arrived just a bit early for one of these interviews, and Dan let me in. He is an imposing African-American young man who looks older than his sixteen years, standing six feet five inches. His mother was not yet home, and Dan was babysitting his four-year-old brother Joe. Dan offered to talk with me until his mother, Ms. Coper,[3] arrived, and we ended up conversing for almost an hour. Joe, I learned, is not really Dan's brother but Ms. Coper's cousin's baby. Joe's mother is mentally ill, so Ms. Coper has custody of Joe. Ms. Coper is a single mother with a clerical job. Dan told me a lot about his family, about his own near-scrapes with trouble, about how his mother dragged him to the pastor for a few little talks about his behavior and then started him in karate lessons to teach him self-discipline and how to channel his strength and energy in positive ways.

Later, my conversation with Ms. Coper filled out the family's story further. They really had endured some hard times. Money is tight. It is hard for a mother to raise sons by herself. But here is what Dan told me before his mother arrived, when I asked him about what role, if any, faith plays in their family life:

No matter what happens, my mom always pays her tithe, and we always try to go to church. We go to church mostly every Sunday. She might be on her last amount of money. I don't know if I could tithe, but she believes in God a whole lot. And I think that's why she's so comfortable with being single because I don't think anybody else could do it the way she does it. I think my brother and I are her social life. . . . She seems to like working with teenagers a lot. We used to have this youth ministry at church, and we always had teenagers over to the house talking about their problems and stuff. We talked about our problems, and about STDs and sex and AIDS and all kinds of stuff—gangs, violence and everything. I think it helped some of them out a lot. None of that really affected me because I always thought that, outside of my father being gone, I had the perfect home.

[3]Names have been changed to protect the family's privacy.

This mom has a house open to teenagers, open to helping them with their problems, and even folding into her family a preschooler who needs her mothering. In her daily life she models what it means to live by faith. She has made the kind of home for her sons that a teenager can rightly call "perfect."

Prisca and Aquila are one of the first families we read about in the early church. This was a busy family. They instructed others in the faith (Acts 18:26). They had a revolving-door guest room that wasn't a guest room at all—because people came and lived with them and became a part of their family. Paul lived with them for some time and worked in the family business as a tentmaker (Acts 18:3). Their home wasn't just a home—it was the church (1 Cor 16:9). Paul saluted them as his "fellow workers" who laid their lives on the line for him, and he said that not only he but all the Gentile churches gave thanks for them (Rom 16:3-4).

Prisca and Aquila's relationship with each other was the basis for a shared ministry that touched others far beyond themselves. The families of the New Testament were called to open their homes in hospitality to the community of faith and to strangers and to teach the good news to others (Rom 12:13).

A middle-aged married couple told me about the young married couples group of their church, which meets in their home each week. They see themselves as mentors for these young couples. They carefully prepare content for each Thursday night's session, which consists of Bible study and conversation about what it means to be a Christian family.

Congregations can play a significant role in supporting, encouraging and commissioning families for ministry, in all the diversity of ways families can minister. This happens in several ways.

Strengthening and Supporting Families

First, families need to be functioning well as a unit to be effective in ministry. They need to be able to receive care and support from one another. They need a shared attitude of thankfulness to God for each other, a shared positive identity, and a belief that with God's help the family can establish goals and work effectively toward them.

Family ministry aims at developing stronger family relationships *so that* families will be more effective witnesses and messengers of the love of Christ. But this is not a linear process. Families do not first become "strong" and then begin ministry. Instead it is transactional. Being in ministry together can strengthen families, as they experience efficacy and take on significant work as partners.

For Christians, an essential part of family life should be family worship and sharing of faith with one another. Simply exhorting families to do this, however, probably has little effect. Churches have been instructing families in family worship for decades (e.g., Williams 1951), yet if the families in my research are representative, few Christian families today have worship together. The common expressions of faith in the home are saying prayers at meals, reading Bible stories to young children, and talking about faith in times of crisis (a serious illness, a big decision that needs to be made, the death of a pet).

If there is to be meaningful prayer and family worship beyond these expressions, they will probably happen only when the congregation provides opportunities *at church* to pray and worship in family units. Families can be guided in doing this together and given resources to help them continue what they have learned.

Providing Opportunities for Service-Learning

Schools across the United States are taking up the strategy of "service-learning," which involves service as an educational method. When the experience of service is integrated into the classroom, course content becomes increasingly relevant to the real world. Students grow by being able to make a significant difference and by trying out new knowledge and skills. The community benefits by receiving their service and by having leaders trained for a future of community service (Roehlkepartain 1993).

Obviously, children and teenagers need such experiential connections to what is learned and discussed in church classrooms as well as school classrooms. In fact, however, many churches simply do not involve children and youth in service. Research by Search Institute indicates that only 29 percent of Protestant young people have spent eleven or more hours in a congregation-sponsored service project *in their lifetime* (ibid. 10).

Learning by doing is also important for adults, and it is important that adults and children and youths serve *together* in family groups, as well as in youth groups or adult mission organizations.

Service-learning combines methods of experiential education with the needs of the neighborhood or larger community. It involves families in learning about needs, studying what the Bible has to say about those needs and the church's response, gaining the knowledge and skills needed for service, engaging in service, and reflecting on these experiences. In short, service-learning occurs "when service and learning are intertwined in ways that express Christian love and commitment, while also deepening that commitment through reflection and study" (Roehlkepartain 1993:11). It is not a particular program or project; it is an approach to Christian education for the church and a lifestyle of discipleship for Christians.

Research by the Search Institute indicates that service involvement is a key factor in nurturing young people's growth in faith. In fact, it appears to be more powerful than Sunday school, Bible study or participation in worship. Young people who are involved in service are much more likely to be firmly bonded to their church and are much less likely to drop out. "The more time [a] youth gives in service to the community through the congregation, the greater the loyalty and bonding to the church" (ibid. 27).

Service encourages healthy lifestyle choices among teenagers. Young people who serve others develop positive self-esteem, self-confidence and social skills. They see themselves as significant in the lives of others. Consequently, they are less likely to engage in behaviors that put them at risk, such as using drugs and alcohol. The skills young people learn can be valuable as they seek out their vocational path. This can be particularly important for teens who have few other opportunities for skill development and contributions to society, such as young people growing up in resource-deprived, poverty-ridden communities. Service opportunities teach skills such as responsibility to complete a task, reliability, perseverance even when work is tough and frustrating, and getting along with others.

Finally, people involved in service as children and teens are much more likely to be involved in service when they become adults. The seeds planted in their lives bear fruit for a lifetime (ibid. 15-16).

There is no parallel research on the significance of service-learning for adults and families. We can hypothesize, however, that service-learning provides a significant context for deepening relationships among those serving together and for sharing faith across the generations. In other words, it strengthens the families in service as well as providing ministry to others. Service-learning can

□ encourage the development and strengthening of cross-generational relationships, both in the family and in the community of faith

□ provide life experiences that lead to spiritual growth

□ strengthen families as people who work and learn together, as well as synchronize their separate activities

☐ encourage the living out of Christian values and decision-making
☐ encourage a sense of responsibility and "response-ability" rather than power-lessness in the face of pressing needs in our community and world
☐ teach core biblical and theological concepts
☐ teach social and other skills and concern for others

Short-term projects. Service-learning in family ministry often begins with short-term projects in the community or on mission trips. For example, Linda Olson, minister of parish education at Our Father Lutheran Church in Littleton, Colorado, developed a program of "Servant Outings" to help persons of all ages learn to live their faith through ministry (Olson 1997). She believes church members need to know what the needs in their community are, how community services are responding to those needs, and how they can participate. Servant Outings involve whole families in such activities as

☐ preparing a monthly birthday party at a home for developmentally disabled adults
☐ serving a meal in a homeless shelter
☐ preparing lunch in a downtown parish for senior citizens who receive Meals on Wheels on weekdays but have no one to prepare food for them on Saturday
☐ working with an inner-city congregation to provide a Vacation Bible School for community children
☐ collecting supplies and delivering them to a day shelter for women and children
☐ conducting a cleanup day to help restore the beauty of a frail elderly member's yard

Servant Outings are planned at different times during the week and day, so that persons who have differing schedules can participate. Parents with small children bring them along; both participating church members and the recipients of service enjoy having children in their midst. Children, at the same time, experience the meaning of Christian faith by participating in ministry with adults. The number of persons for a single outing has varied from five to fifteen. The outings last about two and a half hours. When possible, the group convenes for discussion and debriefing before and after the outing.

Servant Outings may be more disruptive than helpful in many settings. A one-time Servant Outing to serve a meal at a homeless shelter means that regular volunteers must be alerted or dismissed, staff must be ready to assist those who are unfamiliar with the routine, and participating church members must be trained. Yet the goal is not simply to assist the agency in its service but to teach church members about community needs and to provide opportunities for further service. One member, as a consequence of involvement with the feeding program for senior citizens, became an ongoing volunteer for Meals on Wheels and organized drivers for an entire week each month. A mother became a regular volunteer at a shelter for runaway youths. Because church families have seen needs face to face, they have found tangible ways to help, such as by purchasing medical equipment for a person with multiple sclerosis and giving ongoing financial support for a single mother.

There are many such short-term ministry projects that can involve families as units. For example, one United Methodist church developed a bicycle ministry. Throughout much of the year the men of the church buy old used bicycles at yard sales and repair them; at Christmas they are given to children living in poverty. The father in one of the families I interviewed told me what their involvement in this ministry means for them.

> I think faith means serving others, doing things for your church, and showing faith to children—not just my children but all children. We have a bicycle ministry, and I spend a lot of time—my [preschool] son and I together—redoing a bicycle. We started with something that someone threw in the trash and ended up with something we felt good about giving for someone's child at Christmas. We go to garage sales and junk yards and buy old bicycles for five or ten dollars apiece, and then we put money into them. When my son and I were working on that bicycle, he wanted that bike. He would have liked to have had that bike. And I think it was very important for us to explain to him why he and Dad were spending all this time doing this. It was important to a five-year-old.

Such service is also important to adults; it gives expression and depth to their faith.

Ongoing service commitments. A sign of the effectiveness of short-term service projects is families' willingness to take on commitments to serve beyond a one-time event. A family may commit itself to any of a number of tasks: keeping a strip of the roadway nearby beautiful and litter-free, visiting and being family to a church member in a nursing home, providing foster care for a child who has been removed from parents because of neglect or abuse. Sometimes these commitments are taken on through the sponsorship of their congregation; at other times families may find these opportunities for service through other channels.

However it finds its way, a family benefits from the congregation's support and blessing for following its calling.

One family decided that they wanted to provide foster care for two young adults with significant learning and physical disabilities so that these young adults would not have to live in institutional environments. The father in the family worked with an organization for persons with mental disabilities and learned of the plight of the two young men through his work. The parents talked with their church about their sense of calling and their need for support and blessing. As a consequence, the church trained several member volunteers in how to care for these young adults so that the couple could go out one evening each week. The church also trained Sunday-school teachers to provide care for the two young men during Sunday school and worship services.

Blessing and encouraging families as ministers in everything they do. Many families seek opportunities to live out their faith where they work and play. Each family must work out for themselves who they are created to be and how God is calling them. That cannot be determined by any program or structure—it comes out of our individual and shared relationship with Jesus Christ. Family life illustrates the importance of what Dorothy Day has called the "little way," a phrase borrowed from Thérèse of Lisieux (Forest 1994:23). Ministry is not only the isolated dramatic gesture or the "special project"; in essence it is the ordinary actions of life. It is what we choose to notice and respond to, and the care and attention with which we listen and respond. It is how we prepare meals for one another, talk with neighbor children, offer to run an errand for the elderly person next door. These too are works of justice and mercy, of Christian service, even though they may seem mundane.

An Example of Family Ministry: The Chest of Drawers
JoAnn and her husband are active members of their congregation and have two young daughters. A mission group in their church was formed to sponsor a refugee family from Bosnia. JoAnn was so involved in other ministries that she did not volunteer to be part of the mission group, but she followed its activities with great interest, and she and her husband wrote a check to help with the expenses of the refugee family.

The committee was gathering furniture to furnish an apartment prior to the family's arrival. One of JoAnn's friends mentioned in Sunday school that they had everything they needed except a chest of drawers; the committee had nothing in which the family could put clothes.

After the worship service, JoAnn walked toward the parking lot chatting with her friend Marta, her daughters running ahead of her. Her husband had to work that day and was not at church. As the two friends walked down the sidewalk, they passed a yard sale across the street, and a chest of drawers was prominently displayed. Turning to JoAnn, Marta said, "I'll go half if you will put up the other half." They talked to the owner, haggling a bit and explaining the reason they wanted the chest. Satisfied that the price was reasonable, Marta asked if JoAnn could cover the cost until Marta could go to the bank on Monday. But JoAnn had no cash either.

John, another church friend, was walking by, and JoAnn hailed him and asked if he could lend them the price of the chest. He happened to have his checkbook and pulled it out.

Next came the issue of how to transport the chest. JoAnn called over her daughters and handed them a drawer to carry between them. Several other children and teenagers walking toward the parking lot were pressed into service. JoAnn and John carried the chest itself. The chest and drawers became quite a parade, with laughing and kidding among the carriers. The chest was placed in a Sunday-school classroom, and the committee was informed it was there to be transported to the refugee family's new apartment.

This event was family ministry on several levels. First, it addressed the concrete needs of the refugee family; the chest of drawers could help them organize their lives together in a new and unfamiliar setting. More was involved, though. Relationships in the community of faith were strengthened. Friends who work together often experience a strengthening of their bond, a new dimension of shared experience. Their relationship not only means something to them; it is also a channel of service to others. Sharing work that contributes to goodness gives purpose and meaning to relationships beyond simply the gratification of mutual affection. JoAnn told the story of the chest the next week in Sunday school with obvious appreciation for the sense of transcendence experienced as the friends and family shared this task.

Christian education took place. JoAnn and Marta demonstrated a spirit of "willing readiness" for ministry to the children and teenagers they involved in the chest parade. Ministry does not take place only through planned projects. It takes place as the saints walk through life sensitive to need and ready to respond. No one had to put these words to it, though; the three adults and the small parade of children experienced it. Each child and teenager had the opportunity to *experience* the meaning of Christian faith. Moreover, each child and teenager recognized their own significance in the project. They made it happen; the adults needed them, worked with them, laughed and talked with them as all struggled up the street and to the second floor of the church carrying the chest.

JoAnn reached out to a teenager walking out of the church building after the work was done, resting her hand on his arm, "Thanks, Ryan, we really needed your help." A small exchange, perhaps, but a significant one. Ryan's participation was recognized, his role in ministry emphasized, his name spoken with blessing by an adult in the fellowship. Similar exchanges took place throughout the small band of chest-transporters. Not only the adult relationships but the cross-generational relationships were strengthened in this brief shared experience of work. Everyone was a little less alone, a little more connected in the community of faith.

By its very nature, an experience of family ministry, family-in-ministry, such as this cannot be programmed. Yet a program of the church—resettlement of a refugee family—laid the groundwork. And a spirit of "willing readiness" had been instilled. The significance of cross-generational relationships in the community of faith had been emphasized, and adults and children alike had been helped to know and care for one another.

FAMILY MINISTRY AS PERSPECTIVE

Family ministry involves programs but is much more than programs. At its foundation it is a way of looking at persons anew. Family ministry sees persons not as monads but as fragments of families, parts of a larger whole. We cannot care for persons without understanding the families in which they live, just as islands cannot be defined without reference to the sea in which they are embedded. It is the relationship between family members, the pattern of their lives, that defines a family.

Many church programs have viewed families as a collection of individuals at different places in the developmental process—children, youths, young adults, middle adults, senior adults. As a consequence, age-graded programming has been labeled family ministry. And it is. By caring for individuals in the different age brackets, we are caring for the families they represent. Even more importantly, however, family ministry should also attend to the relationship *between* the individuals in a family group, to that which holds people together in human covenants that signify our covenant as a people with our God.

Family ministry therefore calls for us to look at how a congregation's activities have an impact on the relationships between family members and potential family members inside and outside the congregation. It means examining how a church worships, does its business, speaks out with a prophetic voice in society and cares for its members and its neighbors in the community. Family ministry intentionally seeks to influence every aspect of a congregation's life in ways that encourage the development and transformation of families so that all members of the community of faith have a family, strengthen families so that they can be more effective pictures of and witnesses to the love of God, and develop faithfulness in families as they minister within and beyond their own boundaries.

Families need the support of a community of faith that sustains them and to which they contribute. Everything the church does touches families in one way or another. Often the programs that have the greatest impact are not even thought of as "family ministry."

Family ministry is not just a set of programs; it is a perspective, a set of 3D glasses we put on to look at everything the church does. Ministering with families, then, does not mean simply developing a system of support services and programs but reviewing every aspect of congregational life to determine its impact on and support of families.

Some Family Ministry Principles

The following questions illustrate what it means to take a family ministry perspective. These will help you think about your own congregation as it nurtures the development, growth and ministry of families. The next chapter will discuss in much more depth how to assess a congregation's current ministry and possibilities for ministry.

1. Are you thinking about forming, strengthening and discipling families as one focus of everything you do as a church community? Much of families' quality time happens when they are just living their lives together, not when they plan "special" time together. In the same way, much of the family ministry that takes place in a congregation happens while we are doing something else. For example, the most important family enrichment that takes place may be as family members study the Bible together in Sunday school, hear sermons on Scripture passages related to anger management or intimacy or hospitality, pray for and with one another in congregational times of prayer, and talk with others and share life events around the church supper table. These have a much more pervasive impact on daily family life than an annual enrichment event, as helpful as such events may be. Thus we need to be intentional about the goals of family ministry in everything we do.

In many ways, taking a family perspective in everything the congregation does is more difficult than planning an annual event. It means that one staff member cannot be given the assignment of "family ministry"; *all* church leaders must take a family ministry perspective in planning and evaluating what they do. And they must be able to think about their leadership not just of traditional families but of *all* the families represented in their church and community.

2. Imagine your church programming is a covered wagon. How heavy is the load? As a child I was fascinated with the television show *Wagon Train* and with *Little House on the Prairie* and the other books of Laura Ingalls Wilder. They told stories of families who put all their belongings in covered wagons and took off on the grand adventure of homesteading in the American West. I remember the poignant portrayals of families abandoning precious pianos, pump organs and family chests in Western plains and deserts—beloved objects that were no longer considered essential and had to be left behind. The horses and oxen could only carry so much.

My friend Anne Davis has suggested that this image fits many family and church calendars today. Most families and congregations are carrying all the responsibilities and tasks they can handle; adding programs to support them must either *help* them with other responsibilities they are carrying or allow them to ditch something already being expected of them, dear though it may be.

If the church is starting home groups for worship or study, then families participating in the home group should not be expected also to participate in all the regular programs at the "big" church. There are losses in this decision, but the advantages are projected to be more significant than what is given up.

Church leaders need to communicate clearly what is essential and what is enrichment for church members—and themselves. Programs are simply means to accomplish some purpose. When keeping the program going has become the purpose, it is time to reevaluate. Church leaders who frequently evaluate all that is going on in attempts to simplify the church calendar model for the congregation's families the importance of regularly taking stock, of living by the principle that busyness is not a virtue. Living simply and with clear focus is virtuous for families and for congregations. Simple living helps us stay rooted and focused in our life and ministry together.

Any deletion of church programs needs to be done carefully, with the involvement of all in the church who are interested in and committed to the program; such a process will model the kind of problem-solving that should take place in families as well as in faith communities. Families and communities take much longer to reach decisions than businesses, and rightly so. They need to bring everyone along, not just make the "right" decision. The process of decision-making needs to be inclusive and, whenever possible, consensual. One can imagine this as a family conference held standing behind a covered wagon, looking together at what needs to be shifted or abandoned.

3. Can families be families at church? Programs that allow families to choose to be in church or church activities *as a part of family living,* rather than as an *alternative* to family living, are essential elements in family ministry. Families need to *be* together at church, not simply learn *about* families at church.

Small churches are often much better at this than large congregations. In small churches everyone—including babies and children—worship together, have church suppers together and sometimes even engage in Christian education together. The resources of large congregations allow them to provide programs that target age groups and life situations, such as ministries for "singles," "young marrieds" and so on. As useful as such programs can be, when most of church life is so structured, the opportunity for faith-families to form in the congregation is stunted, and families may be stressed by activities that pull them in different directions rather than weaving them together. Here are some ways to combine family life with congregational life:

Cross-generational Sunday-school classes. Parents of infants and young pre-schoolers who spend forty to sixty hours in group childcare during the week may be reluctant to place their children in a nursery for a sixth day. For these families, a cross-generational Sunday school can welcome parents to study the Bible with other parents while they rock and play with their children. Older children and youths and their families may benefit from a mix of age-graded with cross-generational programs. For example, families and faith-families can meet together for cross-age Sunday school once a month.

Congregational meals. Wednesday night church suppers continue to be a thriving program in many churches, and with good reason. When done from a family perspective, they invite people to share the events of the week in cross-generational groups, encouraging adults to relate as aunts, uncles and grandparents to children who may not have such extended family members in their daily lives. In other words, families do not have to choose *either* family time *or* church, but instead can experience church *as* family.

Many families rarely have time for extended conversation over a dinner table. Eating together at church, then, may have special meaning. Instead of quickly preparing a meal or grabbing fast food on the way to church activities, family members can eat together at church; the functions of church and family are both fulfilled and strengthened. This also happens informally in some congregations as faith-family groups go to the same cafeteria week after week to have Sunday dinner. On the other end of the spectrum, persons who live alone and eat many meals with only a television for companionship find in the church dinner a welcome opportunity for family reunion.

Combining Bible study and sharing with family chores. One congregation in a low-income community rents the local laundromat one evening a week for a "wash and Bible study" session. While feeding washers and dryers, waiting and folding clothes, with children playing about underfoot, the women and men in the community discuss the meaning of the Scripture passage for the week. Single parents, grandparents and married couples enjoy sharing the mundane tasks of weekly living and the daily application of ageless spiritual truths. One can imagine other "portable" family chores being done together as a part of church life rather than alone at home—ironing, mending clothes, changing the oil in cars, addressing Christmas cards and so on.

4. Does your congregational life major on informal, interactive programs and processes? If families with members of all ages and stages of life are encouraged to form and grow in the life of the church, that life has to provide opportunities for interaction and relationship building. Although formal worship services are an important part of the life and ritual of many congregations, they are less conducive to family formation and growth than informal, participatory worship that includes all ages. Such worship services take on the character of a family reunion of God's people. Similarly, pickup softball games that are cross-generational are more likely to build relationships across the generations than are competitive leagues. Cross-generational small group Bible studies—in response to or in place of a lecture—may help people live out Christian truths with one another more than simply hearing those truths expounded. As wonderful as a concert may be, it should be balanced by congregational music-making. One congregation has a musical instrument night in which everyone brings something to play—trumpets, spoons and their own voices. They make a joyful noise in hymn tunes, laugh and enjoy one another and God's gifts.

There is a place for formal decision-making, complete with Roberts' Rules of Order, but church committees and ordinary business meetings are probably not it. The formality of such processes tends to intimidate and exclude many. They also model that groups can make decisions by overruling 49 percent of the group, which is not good for either churches or families. Processes of consensus building honor and include everyone's contribution. Consensus building is not as efficient as voting but is far more effective in both families and congregations.

In short, congregations may value formal worship, concerts, maybe even a competitive sports team, and formal decision-making processes. But there should also be plenty of room for spontaneity, for family relationships to develop and grow, and for creative problem-solving and decision-making that are good models for family life. Whenever possible, it is better to lean toward the informal, the participatory and the relational rather than the formal, the performance- and the outcome-focused.

LEADERSHIP IN FAMILY MINISTRY

The premise that family ministry is a perspective taken on everything that happens in a congregation shapes the kind of leadership family ministry needs. It is not a specialization within the life of the congregation and therefore does not fit on an organizational chart as the responsibility of an assigned staff member or church committee. Instead it is a focus for collaboration across the life of the congregation. Family ministry leaders, then, are not primarily the ones *doing* family ministry; instead they are the ones who *remind, call to collaboration* and *orchestrate* the leadership of others in the diversity of the church's activities and programs. The family ministry leader is the staff member or church member or committee who always raises the question "What impact does what we are doing or planning to do have on each of the kinds of families in our congregation and community?" In short, family ministry leaders are family advocates.

To be effective family advocates, family ministry leaders must first have a good working knowledge of the families in the congregation and community—what kinds of families they are, what their strengths and resources are, what they are challenged and stressed by, how they are living their faith together. Next, they must know the congregation and the community as the environments in which families are embedded—the ways they nurture and the stresses and strains they create for different kinds of families. The next chapter will look at how leaders can develop this understanding of families, congregation and community.

Family ministry leaders must also have a voice that can be heard and can influence the life of the congregation. In some congregations that voice belongs to the pastor or other staff members. In other congregations that voice belongs to lay leaders. In most congregations, shared leadership in family ministry that includes both church staff and members is ideal.

The Family Ministry Team

Congregations may have standing committees or teams with assigned responsibility for family advocacy, for ensuring that the family-ministry perspective is used in planning and assessing all aspects of church life. A congregation may also assign a short-term task force to conduct a congregational assessment or develop a strategic plan for family ministry. But family ministry is not a short-term or annual emphasis. To be effective, the congregation needs a continuing watchdog group that is always asking, "What about families?"

This team should model what they are advocating. It should include persons from the various kinds of families represented in the congregation and from various age groups. Ideally, whole family groups can be included in the team, so that serving together on the team is a part of the family's life together. The team should also include representatives from across congregational life—the staff, the Christian education program, the worship committee, the recreational program and so on.

The responsibility of the team is to assess the life of the congregation and its impact on all kinds of families, and to make recommendations concerning how processes and programs can be altered to make them more supportive of family life and family ministry. On occasion the family ministry team may also suggest the addition of programs to respond to needs they have identified. To be most effective, the team needs to periodically review and revise their knowledge about families, the congregation and the community, all of which change over time.

The Professional Church Leader

Professional church leaders can be most effective as they facilitate and support the work of the family ministry team. A professional church leader may be a paid or volunteer staff member of the congregation. The staff member may represent the staff on the family ministry team. The staff member may also carry the responsibility for being a resource person for other church leaders.

The leader may also be an outside consultant who has been asked to help the family ministry team with particular assessment, planning or implementation tasks. Congregations often ask professionals to serve as consultants in assessing and developing ministries with families. Church staff members may be aware of lacking expertise in understanding families or in conducting an assessment and responding to the strengths, needs and resources of families, so they turn to other professionals for help. A consultant is "one who covenants with the leaders of a congregation to assist them in taking action to make their congregation more faithful and effective" (Furr 1997).

A consultation contract spells out what the consultant is being asked to do. It may be anything from an oral agreement to a formal written document. Consultants often need to help the congregation and its staff understand what can and cannot be done in a consultation process. The consultant may make a series of recommendations for the church to consider, but the consultant cannot tell them what they "should" do or not do, nor can the consultant determine what the mission of the congregation is. Only the congregation can make these decisions. Once the consultation is completed, the consultant will leave and not take part in living out the decisions that are made. Therefore the decisions need to belong to the congregation.

As many congregational leaders as possible need to be included in planning and responding to the consultation. This includes not only recognized leaders in official positions but also the informal leaders who help shape the life of the congregation. The more active they are throughout the process, the more committed they will be to ensuring that the process bears fruit in the congregation's life. For example, a consultant may be asked to lead the church through a congregational assessment. The process is far more likely to bear fruit if many church members are involved in conducting a survey and interviewing than if the consultant quietly carries out these tasks alone. The process is also far more likely to bear fruit if the results of the assessment are shared in a large committee or even with the whole congregation, complete with multiple copies of the report, than if a single copy of the report is given to a staff member.

Consultants occasionally must face conflict between their own values and beliefs and those of the congregation. The value system, assumptions, beliefs, prejudices, theological stance, life experiences, denominational background and other characteristics of the consultant constitute the most important dynamic in determining what happens in church consultation (Schaller 1983).

A very large church with a sizable budget and twenty full-time staff members is located on the edge of an impoverished community where large numbers of single working mothers live with their preschoolers and school-age children. There is not enough quality childcare available in the community.

The church wanted to expand its ministry to families of young children. Church leaders had stated that churches should not support daycare centers because they believe women should not be employed but should stay at home and care for their children. The church asked a denominational agency serving children and their families to help them establish a parent education program and a weekday morning play group program for children and their mothers in its well-furnished family life center.

The agency staff was in conflict about how to respond. On the one hand, staff members felt angry about the church's refusal to use its considerable resources to care for the families that had the greatest need—quality childcare for working parents on the brink of poverty. On the other hand, working with the church to pursue its stated objectives might well establish an agency-congregation relationship that could be used to shape and even alter the church's response to the poor single-parent families in its neighborhood (Garland 1994a:169-70).

Such dilemmas are not unusual in church consultation and require careful thought and self-examination on the part of the consultant. One does not have to agree with every aspect of a congregation's beliefs and values to find enough common ground on which constructive work can take place. The consultant may decide that although he or she would wish the church had chosen to develop the daycare program so desperately needed rather than the morning play group, the play group is still a program he or she can support and help the church develop. In the process of working together, the consultant may gain enough trust from and knowledge of the congregation to suggest that they find ways to respond to the needs in their surrounding community, even if not with a daycare program.

The first step in leading a congregation's family ministry, whether one is a church member, staff member or outside consultant, is to learn about the families in the congregation and the physical and social community in which they live. Chapter fifteen will look at the processes for assessing congregations and communities.

Chapter 15

Assessing Congregation & Community

T HERE ARE TWO BASIC DECISIONS THAT FACE CONGREGATIONS wanting to take a family perspective in their ministry. First, the congregation needs to decide which families it wants to attend to—the families in the congregation or the families in the community in which the congregation is located, or both. The definition of family ministry provided in chapter fourteen focuses on ministry with families in the congregation and then, through these families, to the larger community. Second, the congregation needs to decide whether it will base its ministry on knowledge it already has of families or whether it needs to know more about the specific families in its congregation and community.

CONGREGATIONAL OR COMMUNITY FAMILY MINISTRY?

Sometimes a church plans a program for its own families and then hopes that program can also reach families in the surrounding community. In other words, the program is supposed to serve both as Christian discipleship training and as evangelism. In essence, this approach assumes that there are few significant differences between church families and community families.

Of course in many ways all families in a community do have much in common: they deal with the same kinds of stresses and demands, they face the changing developmental issues of their members, they have conflict. Nevertheless, Christians and non-Christians face family life and its challenges with different perspectives and values. Service to families in the congregation and service to families in the community are both significant ministries of the church. Congregational families need ministries to help them grow as Christian disciples in their lives together. Community families may experience the congregation's offer to help them with the challenges of family life today to be the most effective invitation to taste and see what Christianity is all about.

Congregations can do both. But they must recognize that these two emphases may overlap only partially. Congregational families and community families may differ both in their demographic characteristics and in their goals and values.

Demographic Differences Between Congregation and Community
Sometimes differences between congregational families and the community are easy to spot. A large downtown congregation may be dominated by nuclear families with children and adolescents, couples whose children are grown, senior adult couples and widowed singles—all of them middle-class persons driving from urban and suburban areas of the city. Yet the congregation's most immediate neighborhood may be filled with high-rise apartments housing young and middle-aged career-oriented never-married and divorced adults, and with low-income housing populated by single parents and the elderly poor. It would be difficult to target church families and community families with the same programs, just by virtue of the differences in the kinds of families in each group.

These differences may be more subtle but nonetheless present in suburban congregations as well. Compared to their surrounding communities, the families of many congregations are older, with a much higher proportion of married couples with children, married couples whose children have grown, and senior adult couples and widows. Single-parent families, blending families and single adults without children are present in a much smaller proportion in the church membership than they are in the community (Yankeelov and Garland 1998).

Goals and Values of Congregational and Community Families
Even when congregational families are the same "types" as those in the surrounding community, the goals and values of families in the congregation and families

in the community are—or should be—different. For example, both the congregation and the community may be composed primarily of parents (both single and married) of children and adolescents. Both families in the congregation and unchurched families in the larger community may express need for support in the tasks of parenting. The goals for parental support and education for church families, however, would probably be at least subtly different from goals that would respond to the felt needs of community families.

The goals for congregational families would probably include helping parents live out their Christian values and beliefs in effective guidance and modeling for their children. Such a program would probably begin with and stay connected to biblical teachings and theological concepts.[1]

Christian families want to help their children to learn and apply the ways of Christian living. Other goals of Christian parents will overlap with goals of community parents—to teach their children to love and care for others, to be responsible for self, to speak the truth, to hold to principles and values even in the face of opposition, to be joyful. On the other hand, Christian parents may emphasize self-giving and self-sacrifice, stewardship of self and resources, hospitality and inclusion of strangers and those who are "different," and other Christian principles of living that may be less important to community parents. In turn, community parents may emphasize material success, individual autonomy and other values that, although not necessarily antithetical to Christian living, are not central.

The parenting program for community families would more likely begin with concepts such as self-esteem and building resilience in the face of life stressors, and would draw from the social sciences literature. Beginning such a program with an in-depth Bible study would probably not be an effective means for engaging community families.

Obviously, some congregational discipleship programs will draw in community families, and some of the participants who most benefit from community ministry programs may well be congregational families. Nevertheless, the primary focus needs to be clear, and these secondary benefits can then be celebrated but not mistaken for indicators that ministry can effectively target both congregational families and families in the community simultaneously. Don Hebbard has called this a question of "inreach" versus "outreach" (Hebbard 1995).

---

[1]See chapter eleven.

If either a congregational or a community focus must be chosen, recognize that this decision is made based on the values and commitments of the congregation rather than any objective set of facts. Both discipleship of Christians within the community of faith and evangelism to persons in the community are important. A congregation gives emphasis to one or the other based on numerous factors. These include the congregation's own development and current experiences, the interests and commitments of its leaders, and how it perceives its role in the community and into the future. Does the congregation really want to give more attention to the families in its midst, or is it itching to reach out to families in the surrounding community?

It is important also to consider which initial approach has the most potential for building rather than siphoning off the energies, commitments and resources of the congregation. Ministry with congregational families may build momentum for reaching out to the needs in the surrounding community. On the other hand, a discouraged, shrinking church may find that targeting the needs of community families with effective programs can generate new life for the congregation as it rediscovers its role of service. Ideally, of course, both emphases can be sustained.

WHAT IS KNOWN ABOUT CONGREGATIONAL AND COMMUNITY FAMILIES?

Congregational leaders must decide the extent to which they can minister with families in their congregation or community based on what they already know about those families' strengths, challenges and concerns. Sometimes church leaders have extensive knowledge of the inner workings of families, challenges they face and external resources available to them.

A congregation does not have to know everything there is to know about families to recognize a clear and present issue in family life that could benefit from focused attention. For example, a number of parents may be calling the youth minister with concerns about violence and gang activity in the high school. The youth minister probably does not need to conduct an extensive assessment at this point to determine how many parents are feeling these concerns. The youth minister probably simply needs to invite parents to a gathering to determine how best to address the concerns that have already been expressed.

Sometimes congregational leaders think they know the needs of congregational and community families because the congregation appears to reflect the larger society, and there is extensive documentation of the challenges that face families in society today. For example, a congregation and community with a large number of dual-career couples with dependent children probably does not need to take a survey to determine whether these families feel stressed by the multiple demands on their time, or whether there is at least occasional conflict over the division of household responsibilities. That congregation can conjecture with some measure of confidence that these families may be interested in finding ways to lessen their time stresses. A conversation with several families may be all that is needed to confirm or disconfirm that they feel stressed by multiple demands.

Church leaders who believe they know what the strengths and challenges are may simply move directly to devising a strategy for building on family strengths and helping families address the challenges in their lives. The congregation with time-stressed families may move directly into considering all the ways the congregation can address this need—a sermon series on Christian living in a time-oriented culture, a special workshop or Sunday-school focus on time and Christian family living, a revision of the monthly church calendar to lessen the church's stress on these families, and so on.

On the other hand, assuming that we know what is going on with families means we run the risk of being wrong, for several reasons.

1. Congregations and families may look like but not be like the standardized picture of congregations and families. Our risk of making wrong assumptions about what life is like for families is most acute if we have not bothered to ask the families themselves. For example, not all busy families experience the demands on them as negatively stressful. Some families enjoy and seek out what they see as significant activities that enrich their lives together, even though they sometimes feel tired. Many families with teenagers enjoy rich, delightful relationships between the generations, and although they have their moments of conflict, they do not see themselves as embattled in the way that our culture pictures the "typical" postmodern family of teenagers. Do not take for granted that you know what is stressing families.

2. Families may not be what they seem to be at church. Sometimes we simply don't know the needs of families because people consider church the last place they will let their concerns be known openly. Some families feel that they must hide who they really are from the church community, perhaps because they fear being shamed, judged or even ostracized. Their shame may be based on an aspect of their relationship they fear being discovered—marital infidelity, family violence, a child conceived prior to marriage. Or they may fear judgment of the family structure in which they live: the homosexual couple describes themselves as "roommates" and carefully guards against knowledge of their sexual orientation; a cohabiting couple who have never married do not correct those who assume they are married. In congregations in which divorced persons are stigmatized, a blending family may not make it known that this is a second marriage for one or both spouses.

Although some families may appear to "hide" who they really are, more often we simply see what we are looking for, expecting others' experiences to be like our own. The homosexual, cohabiting or blending families probably do not work at disguising their identity, but because church leaders themselves live in nuclear families and see the world through their own experiences, they may not look for or recognize other kinds of family situations. If we have never seen the child from a previous marriage who lives a thousand miles away, and have never considered asking about the possibility of previous marriages, we may suppose that a family is "nuclear" when it is in fact "blending." We consequently may never know that family's struggle with the grief and stress of separation from a child and the financial strain of supporting, at least in part, two families. We may not know that an adult drives across town every evening, seven days a week, to check on and help out a frail elderly parent who is tenaciously holding on to independent living. We may not know that another family is dealing with alcohol addiction in one member, or with family violence.

3. Less visible family characteristics may be more significant than those readily seen. The family characteristics we do see are usually "real," but they may not be as important as those that are hidden. And sometimes what we see seems to imply a response that is "given," yet may not be the only or even the most effective way of caring for families.

For example, the way the problem of time stress for families is expressed may suggest that families need help in managing their time more effectively or need to find ways to prune the commitments on their calendars. Perhaps a less visible characteristic of the family is its relative isolation with all the responsibilities of childrearing and household maintenance. Rather than offering a time management seminar, then, the church may determine that it needs to become a more family-supportive community. If the church provides a nourishing meal and brief Bible study for all ages on a weeknight, parents can come after work, picking up children on the way, to eat with members of their community, have thirty minutes of Bible study and prayer, and go home to a clean kitchen or be off to other activities. Paradoxically, adding a program may actually be supportive of time-stressed families.

4. There may be ascribed needs that are not felt. Finally, there are *ascribed* needs that may not be actually felt by families in the congregation and community. Ascribed needs are those that observers believe the family has, whether or not the family feels those needs. In contrast, *felt* needs are those concerns that families believe they have, whether they are willing to say so or not.

For example, I may not think I need to cut back on animal fats in my diet; I feel good and my weight is normal. But when the physician tests the level of cholesterol in my system and finds it far too high, the need for modification of my diet is *ascribed* to me by the physician. The ascribed need becomes a *felt* need if (1) she tells me about my high cholesterol and I believe her, (2) I also believe the research findings that high levels of cholesterol can lead to cardiovascular problems, and (3) I understand that levels of cholesterol can be controlled by diet.

Obviously, not all ascribed needs become felt needs. I may ignore the physician and keep slathering butter on my white toast. I might keel over tomorrow with a heart attack, or I might live to 103. The family that is busy may hear our suggestion that they need help with lowering stress, look at one another and agree that they are very, very busy, and then grin and say they don't want to change a thing.

It is important that families be allowed self-determination—to say what they need, what they can do, what they feel called to do. Families need to be given the opportunity to speak for themselves and to affirm or disconfirm what others might assume. In other words, as church leaders assess the needs to be addressed by a family ministry, at some point families themselves should be given opportunity to say who they are, what their strengths are, what challenges and stressors they are facing, and in what ways they would like to experience the church's help.

Ascribed needs are significant for Christian discipleship. Nevertheless, ascribed needs are important in family ministry assessment. The church does not wait for Christians to feel the need for discipleship training; we know Christians need to be in Bible study, prayer and worship together. Christians need a community of faith to which they are responsible and that cares for them; they need guidance in hearing God's word and calling in their own lives. Christians need discipleship training for family living, whether they recognize it or not.

We do not have to wait to be told that families need help in managing conflict in ways that strengthen and edify rather than destroy their fellowship, that families need a community to hold them responsible for their covenants and to support them through all kinds of life experiences. The divorced father with a child a thousand miles away may not feel the need to stay in contact with the former spouse to work on raising their child together, may not want the grief of disagreements with the former spouse and the chain of goodbyes and sadness over separation that a continuing relationship with the child will bring. The church nevertheless ascribes to that father the need to feel community expectation and support for being a faithful parent to the child and partner in parenting to the former spouse, even though this is much more demanding than simply cutting off relationship.

Congregations also ascribe to families the need for guidance in finding the meaning and purpose of their life together. Many Christians have only a vague sense that their family ought to be about something besides simply taking care of and providing for one another. The concept of "family calling," that families have a purpose beyond self-care, is not familiar in our culture. Family ministry, however, includes teaching this concept and stressing (thus even bringing an added—though necessary—stress for some families) that families need to be about more than taking care of themselves.

It is important to distinguish between felt needs and ascribed needs because families will not make the time and commitment to participate in programs designed for them unless they feel the need. Therefore we can begin with ascribed needs by attempting to turn them into felt needs. The physician begins by laying out all the dire consequences that may befall me if I do not lower the cholesterol in my diet. If I protest that I inherited high cholesterol from my mother and there is nothing I can do about it, the physician may present me with research findings showing that diet can modify cholesterol levels. To be effective in treating me medically, the physician cannot simply stop with identifying my needs; she must also help me feel those needs.

Churches are institutions that overtly attempt to shape people's values and beliefs. We expect the church to help us feel needs we might otherwise ignore—need for Bible study, need to be faithful in prayer and stewardship, need to exercise self-control, and so on. In the same way, the church needs not only to accept what families and society says the needs of families are but also, out of its own beliefs and values, to attempt to shape those needs and identify needs that might otherwise be ignored.

What Further Knowledge About Families Is Needed?

Doing family ministry begins as we seek the answers to several questions.

☐ Who is the primary target of our family ministry, at least to start with—congregational families or families in the community, or both? If we are attempting to minister with both, then we need to have two columns of planning paper, two plans and two ministries, with perhaps a middle column for collaboration and overlap.

☐ What do we know about these families? What kinds of families are they? What are their strengths and challenges?

☐ What are we basing our knowledge on—general social knowledge, our specific knowledge of these families, or a combination of both?

☐ Given what we know about these families, what do we think their needs are? Are the needs we know felt needs or ascribed needs or both? What are the possible gaps in our knowledge?

☐ Do we trust our knowledge enough to begin ministry with these families? Or do we need to learn more?

Sometimes the decision is that enough is known to begin. Someone in the congregation is just itching to lead a parenting workshop with a new curriculum available from a denominational publisher, several parents have expressed an interest, and that is enough. "Plug and play" is the approach of choice. Doing the parenting program may generate interest in conducting a more comprehensive planning process.

Unfortunately, however, congregational leaders sometimes assume that *enough* has been done because *something* has been done. Doing something that is needed is not the same as doing what is needed most, or what will really make a long-term impact in the lives of families. It may be, but it may not. "Plug and play" programs may be very helpful, but they should lead to or be a part of—and not substitute for—a more comprehensive planning process.

If ministry to and through families is to be a perspective taken by church leaders on the entire life and work of the congregation and its ministries in the community, often more knowledge is needed about those families. Congregational leaders need to ask those who know families, and they need to ask families themselves,

☐ who these families are demographically

☐ what they are doing well in their life together

☐ what challenges and stresses they face

☐ the extent to which their community supports them and provides opportunities for spiritual growth and shared service

☐ how the congregation can help

Seeking this information about congregational families is doing a congregational assessment. Seeking this information about community families is doing a community assessment.

PROCESSES OF CONGREGATIONAL AND COMMUNITY ASSESSMENT

We use the same processes for both congregational and community assessment, although the knowledge being sought and some of the methods used are sometimes different in the two kinds of assessment. We will first look at the processes of assessment, which are common to both kinds. Then we will turn to methods that are specific to each. The processes of assessment are

☐ planning—what (to learn), how (it will be learned), who (will do the learning), when (it will be learned)

☐ collecting information

☐ analyzing and interpreting information

☐ sharing with others who need to know and be involved

☐ deciding what to do in response to what has been learned

Planning the Assessment

A community or congregational assessment can be as much work as you allow it to be. Planning needs to take into account what you need to know and why you need to know it. Planning is usually undertaken when energy and commitment are high. Be careful not to take on an assessment process that is so ambitious that it exhausts everyone and then you can't do anything with what you learn because you have used all your resources! On the other hand, the assessment, if done well and clearly related to the action that will follow, can be a significant source of energy and growing commitment to the ministry.

Involve as many persons in the assessment process as possible. These persons will be the advocates for family ministry in the congregation. Knowledge about families gleaned in the assessment process will empower them for leadership in the ministries that will be built from it. Include those who most need to know what is being learned. It is important to involve those you think will be leaders in the action that will follow. The involvement of a family ministry team of church leaders and congregational representatives is essential.

If you are considering developing a specific kind of ministry, that focus will suggest who else needs to be involved in the assessment process. For example, if you are exploring the possibility of developing a resource center for families with children, then it is probably very important to involve members of the children's and youth committees, parents of children who are active in the congregation and supportive of the ministry you are considering, deacons and other church leaders who will ultimately determine the resources that will be given to this project, and church staff members who will oversee the ministry.

In summary, those who will be leading the congregation in ministry need to be involved in the very initial steps of planning what kind of assessment is needed and how it will be done.

Biblical foundation. Begin planning the assessment process by defining the reason you are gathered. What is it in Scripture and in the life of the community of faith that has led you to this interest in the families in your congregation and community? You may find section four of this book to be helpful as you choose Scripture passages that relate to family ministry. Pray together for vision and the presence of God in your work.

Goals. What is it that you want to learn, and why? Take time to state the goals of your assessment clearly in writing for all to see. Come back to these frequently. They can always be changed, particularly if your assessment process raises new issues worth pursuing. But changing the goals needs to be done intentionally, not just because you forgot what it was you were about.

Boundaries. Once you are clear about what you want to learn and why, it may be fairly clear what the boundaries of your assessment are, but it is still helpful to make them explicit. Since you may have different people gathering different portions of information, it is very helpful to agree how big your target is.

Within the congregation, you may target one kind of family about which you want to develop greater understanding so that you can minister to them more effectively—unmarried adults and their families, parents of adolescents or families of frail elderly persons. It may be relatively easy to limit the boundaries of your assessment, therefore, to those families that exhibit the characteristics you are looking for and who are members of your congregation.

The boundaries of your assessment may not always be this clear, though. One megachurch decided to do a random sample of its entire membership so that congregational leaders might have a profile of the kinds of families represented and understand better the processes of family life in their congregation. The mailing list of members was used to survey the church. Leaders were unhappy, however, that few single adults responded to the survey. It then became clear that most of the several hundred single adults who participated in the church's singles ministry were not members of the congregation and thus had not been included in the sample.

Is your assessment of the congregation limited to members only, or does it include visitors and others who have expressed interest in or participated in the congregation's activities? Are there other groups of members who might not be included in your assessment because of the methods you are using? For example, a survey conducted on Sunday morning may exclude those who are shut-in, or those who work on Sunday but participate in weekday worship.

Defining the community may be even more challenging. The church's community may be defined in any number of ways. One of the best is simply to ask representatives of the congregation to look at a map together and say what they consider the boundaries of their community to be. Or a map with pins or dots locating the various homes, workplaces and schools of members can provide a visual definition of the current extent of the community in which the church is embedded. Including the workplaces and schools of members, as well as their residences, gives a better picture of where the congregation is really interacting with the community daily.

This can be an instructive activity for the church as a whole. Put an enlarged map of the community on a wall in a high-traffic area of the church building and invite people to mark their home, school and work locations on it. A different color can be used for each (blue for home, red for work, orange for school). Pins, stickers or colored markers can be used. A facilitator stationed by the map can provide help to persons not familiar with maps and can discourage those who are tempted to move the markings as a prank. The facilitator may even have two or three interview questions to ask people as they add their markings, so that two kinds of data are gathered at once.

Such an activity has the advantage not only of helping the family task force define the boundaries of its assessment but also helping the whole congregation gain a clearer sense of identity. Simply drawing a line around all the markings says, "This is our community." Clusters of dots suggest places where programs and services can be located outside the church facilities. For example, a cluster of work dots may suggest a general area in which a brown-bag lunch program can be initiated.

Often the church has defined its community using natural boundaries: the river on one side, an expressway on another, an industrial area on another. Plotting the actual locations of congregational members identifies the extent to which those natural boundaries are actually definitive for the congregation. If the congregation seems concentrated in the surrounding community, then that community will probably become the target of the community assessment. If members live and work all over a metropolitan area, however, a larger focus may be helpful.

On the other hand, if the assessment is driven by a goal of reaching beyond the current geographic boundaries of the congregation, such as into an area of significant poverty and need, or an area of new development where no churches have yet located, then those goals need to drive the establishment of boundaries. The map will show the challenge: how can the congregation engage persons in the community in everyday interactions of living, working and playing?

Methods. Once the boundaries have been set, you can begin to determine what methods will help you learn what you want to learn. There are often multiple ways to approach questions. For example, if you want to know how many families with school-age children there are in your community, you can go to the library and look at census data, or you can call local elementary schools and find out how many children are enrolled. Methods of congregational and community ministry are simply tools for learning more, and they should be chosen with the crucial questions clearly in mind.

Gathering information from families is a subtle signal that the congregation cares about them and is hoping and planning to respond to what is learned. Asking families what they need implies that the congregation will try to respond to at least some expressed needs. Therefore be clear about why you are asking questions and be sure the congregation is willing to respond to what is learned.

Some methods are quick and relatively easy. For example, you can ask people to fill out a five-question survey during a Wednesday-night church supper or on a Sunday-morning bulletin insert. Others take more time and resources, such as an extensive survey of every member of a congregation.

There are times when congregations should consider conducting an extensive process of assessment. Such an assessment is important to a congregation wanting to launch into family ministry as a new perspective on everything it is doing. An extensive assessment has an added benefit of not only gleaning new understandings of families' lives but also generating concern and motivation within the congregation for ministry. For example, a family service professional could argue with considerable confidence that in almost any congregation in the United States today, there are significant numbers of families that struggle with anger and conflict management, and there is likely to be a significant minority that have experienced and may even now be living with violence. Congregational leaders, however, may not really believe that this could be true in their congregation and community. A survey in which congregational family members report in significant numbers their difficulties with anger and conflict and the presence of family violence will be compelling motivation to do something in response.

Some congregational assessment methods, especially those involving group discussions or reports to the church community, can have another added benefit: building a sense of congregational identity. That often happens as an outcome of the mapping process described above. A series of group discussions among members about their common identity as a community of families mirrors a family reunion where the stories of family identity are told and retold. At a family reunion, new members of the family hear old stories for the first time and begin to take on the family as their identity. Older members have their identities reaffirmed. In the telling of who they are, the family *becomes* more of who they are— a group of people with interwoven lives who, for better or for worse, are committed to continuing to be knit together as a people.

In the same way, a congregational assessment gives members of the congregation opportunity to hear and embrace the stories of their shared identity. They find persons who share similar life situations, and they find persons who are very different from themselves but who nevertheless are part of the community and thus part of their lives. As a consequence, informal processes of change may be launched. Fortunately, church members do not always wait for church leaders to launch a new program.

One church held a forum and invited members to talk about what they would like their congregation to do in response to the needs of families. A young divorced woman spoke of the stress she felt trying to raise her children alone, especially with her own parents living in another city, and her belief that other families with young children were so stressed that they did not feel they could take the time even to participate in such a forum. Afterward, an older woman hesitantly asked the young mother if she and her children would come to her home for dinner on Sunday and then said, "If the kids are comfortable, you can just let them stay with me for the afternoon, and I'll take them to the evening activities at church, and you can pick them up there later. My grandkids live a thousand miles away, and it would be a real treat for me."

At the same forum, a middle-aged woman said she was trying to decide about nursing care for her mother, who had Alzheimer's disease. None of her friends were dealing with this issue yet. She wondered if the church could offer a seminar or something to help families facing this issue. Later that afternoon, an older woman who attended the forum called her to say that her mother had Alzheimer's too, and perhaps they could get together for coffee and compare notes.

The goal of the assessment process should be primarily to learn what is needed for action. At the same time, however, choose methods of assessment that contribute to your overall objectives of building a family-supportive community of faith. Later this chapter will describe in more detail some of the methods and resources for congregational and community assessment.

In summary, as you consider which methods to use, the following questions can be helpful:

1. What methods or combination of methods would help us learn what we need to know?

2. Which of those methods identified by the first question can we afford, given our resources of time, energy and finances?

3. Which of the methods identified by the second question would provide a process that would build commitment and involvement in ministry with families and/or would strengthen the community of faith?

Needed financial resources and persons. Some methods are virtually cost-free; gathering census data usually means simply making a trip to the main library in town or accessing census data on the Internet. This data can provide a wealth of general information about the community. Community leaders are often willing and happy to share their opinions about families in the community over a cup of coffee or in their office. Surveys mean paying for photocopying and, depending on the sophistication of the information, having the responses entered into a computer and summarized so that the most information can be distilled. As methods are chosen, prepare cost estimates for gathering and analyzing the data and for preparing and distributing reports. Determine where the funds will come from before proceeding.

Conducting an assessment may not cost a lot of money, but it may take a great deal of time and energy commitment by members of the family ministry task force. Who knows how to read census data, or is willing to be taught by a reference librarian? Who would be comfortable interviewing the mayor, the school principal, counselors and others? Who will do the surveying? Who will analyze the findings and prepare a report for church leaders, and perhaps for the entire congregation? As you plan, make tentative assignments, with the agreement (enthusiastic, if possible) of those who will be responsible for each step of the process.

It helps to have a large calendar on which to chart the process of assessment. What needs to be done and when? How long will it take? What needs to be done before each step? Always allow about one-third more time than you can imagine it could possibly take to do each task. Also, deciding the best time to conduct an assessment has to take into account the rest of the church calendar. The weeks from Thanksgiving until after Christmas, during Holy Week and Easter, and the Sundays of Mother's Day and Father's Day are the worst times to try to involve a congregation in anything other than the celebrative events of the season. The summer months often are times of sporadic attendance and staff vacations. Consequently, most congregational assessment processes in American congregations need to take place between early September and mid-November, or between mid-January and mid-March.

Times for completing information-gathering. Talk together realistically about what people can do and the time it is realistic to expect for this project. Be sure everyone knows what they are to do and by when. Plan at the outset for times to come back together and share what is being learned as information is gathered, then analyzed and interpreted, and as a report is prepared for the church.

Collecting Information

This can be an exciting time, whatever methods are being used. Be sure that team members keep written records of interviews and experiences they have as they talk with or survey church and community members. The more persons involved in the assessment, the more important it is to develop a process for recording and sharing what each is learning. For example, in one community survey we conducted, we had sixteen different team members interviewing key informants.

Together we developed the questions they would ask each informant and agreed that each would write out a summary from each interview, with several key quotations, using the same word-processing program. The computer and program were available to the team in the church office. The team leader used the individual contributions as the beginning of a rough draft of a report to share with the congregation.

Analyzing and Interpreting Information

Once the information is collected, it needs to be organized in a way that makes it useful and points to elements that are most significant. Analyzing the information almost always means finding a way to reduce numbers and words to meaningful statistics and phrases. Instead of listing all the responses to an interview question, for example, it is important to look for themes and then tally all those related to each theme.

For example, the following family strengths were noted by community leaders in one survey:

☐ families have lived here a long time and often have lots of community connections

☐ even though people are poor, they seem to always have a friend who will help out

☐ neighbors seem to know one another

These were summarized as "strong social networks" followed by the tally "3" to denote this category of response by three leaders. Keep the original surveys, though, so you can refer back to the original responses if you need to.

Survey data often lends itself to summarizing by simple tallying, as above, or by figuring averages (e.g., average age, average length of time in the community). It is very helpful to have the original words and stories, though, for they give meaning to the summary. For example, the category "strong social networks" is much more meaningful if one or two of the original responses are given as illustration.

Interpreting information means to *apply values* to it. For example, to say that "one of the strengths in this community is that most families seem to have strong social networks" makes the value judgment that strong social networks is a strength, not a liability. Other meanings could be given to the same information. For example, imagine that a family ministry team has undertaken this assessment process in order to figure out why community families do not come to the events and programs the congregation is offering. They know that few congregation members are members of the community they are trying to reach. The finding of "strong social networks" in the community is therefore significant: it means that information and contact with persons outside the church community may travel much more effectively by informal contacts ("getting to know" people) than by formal contact (newsletters, community posters). Therefore ministry efforts will need to work through established community relationships more than through media advertising or publicity. What is more, community residents may be much more comfortable consulting informally with neighbors and friends about problems and issues than they would be in a congregational workshop or seminar. Thus an informal drop-in support program may be much more effective than a structured educational event. The finding of strong social networks presents a significant challenge to the way the congregation had imagined that it would involve community residents in its ministries. Somehow congregational members will need to meet and form relationships with community residents before residents will be interested in participating in the church's ministries.

In this example, the same piece of information was interpreted differently because of the different interests of the interpreters: one was interested in how families related to their community while the other was interested in identifying the most effective channel for involving community residents in congregational programs.

Here are some basic questions that many congregational and community assessments attempt to answer:

☐ What are the strengths of families in this congregation/community?
☐ What resources are available to families in this congregation/community?
☐ What resources are needed by families?
☐ What are some of the ways these resources could be provided?
☐ What would providing these resources cost us?
☐ What, if any, of these things *should* we do as a congregation?

Sharing with Others Who Need to Know and Be Involved

Keep the congregation informed throughout the assessment process, from the beginning—before the goals are set—all the way through to the final report. Invite participation and suggestions. You want the congregation to be involved so that the project genuinely reflects their calling and involves them in responsive action.

Share bits of information as it becomes available; do not wait for a final report. Tidbits and updates can be highlighted in the church newsletter or weekly bulletin. Keep the relevant committees and leaders of the church fully informed all along the way of what you are doing and what you are learning. Otherwise it may become your project and they will bless your doing something with whatever it is you learn, so long as you do it and don't expect much from them.

At the end, be sure to plan one or more sessions in which you can share what you learned with the whole congregation, as well as with decision-making committees and leaders. A written report is especially helpful. If you are presenting it to a large group, accompany it with overhead transparencies or slides drawn from the written report. Avoid highly technical or detailed information. Make it as simple and straightforward as possible. Begin with strengths and resources, then move to the needs you have discovered. Be sure to include in your report, or in its appendices,

☐ the mission statement and goals of the assessment
☐ the names of those participating in the assessment
☐ the methods you used, with a copy of all questionnaires and interview forms
☐ charts and graphs that make the information easy to visualize
☐ limitations of the study
☐ recommendations

Deciding What to Do with What Has Been Learned

Once the assessment is completed, be sure to take time to contemplate and celebrate what you have learned. Remember, though, that you have just begun. The assessment report should be a springboard to planning what you will do, now that you know more about the strengths, challenges and needs of families in your congregation and community. The next chapter will describe the planning of family ministry.

METHODS OF CONGREGATIONAL ASSESSMENT

A congregational assessment for family ministry really involves two dimensions. First, of course, the assessment should define who families in the congregation are. What kinds of families are there (blending, nuclear, three-generation, etc.)? What are the processes of family life like for these families (communication, conflict and so on)? What kinds of stresses are they experiencing? What are their felt and ascribed strengths, needs and challenges? How are they experiencing and growing in faith together? What are the central purposes and callings of their life? What do they and others perceive the church can do to help them?

Second, the assessment should look at the congregation itself. What kind of community is the congregation for all the types of families it encompasses? Are there some kinds of families that seem invisible to or ignored by the congregation? In what ways does the congregation support and challenge family life? In what ways does the congregation create stress for families? Is that stress encouraging family spiritual growth, or is it destructive? To what extent does the congregation take a family perspective? What programs are offered that provide direct and indirect discipleship for family living?

The assessment of the congregation may be somewhat threatening for church leaders, and it is important to proceed with care and solicit their involvement, especially if you are an outside consultant. After all, this may feel like an indirect assessment of the staff's competence and vision. If you are yourself the church's pastor or staff member, you can expect the assessment process to cause you to take some deep breaths. Recognize that there is much more that gives shape to a congregation than your own leadership, and remind yourself that conducting an assessment such as this helps develop vision.

Good leaders know their congregation; undoubtedly you will know much of what the assessment finds, although there will also be some new information. Even in the few cases where little actually new information is gained by the leader conducting the assessment, the process gives all the leaders involved an opportunity to share in defining who the congregation is, what its strengths are and what challenges it faces in ministry with families.

Finding Information Already Available

Some information is readily available to you. If the church has maintained an accurate database of members, it is often not difficult to pull up information such as ages and zip-codes for residences. An understanding of the congregation's identity and culture can be gleaned through a review of its covenant and historic records.

Other information may be gathered easily by talking with each other. A representative group from the congregation may be able to sit down with a list of church members and, name by name, indicate the kinds of families congregational members represent. But this assumes that this group really knows the families of members. Sometimes this is true; often it is not, particularly if the congregation is large or mobile. There may also have been other surveys done by the church or membership records that will provide information useful for family ministry planning.

Jackson Carroll and colleagues (Carroll, Dudley and McKinney 1986) have provided helpful resources for assessing the culture of a congregation. The congregation planning an extensive assessment will want to refer to the work of these researchers. They describe four dimensions for understanding a congregation:

☐ *Congregational identity*—that persistent set of beliefs, values, patterns, symbols, stories and styles that make a congregation distinctively itself. Like family identity, congregational identity is rarely verbalized, even by members to each other. Instead it can be distilled from gossip, unwritten rules, and tacit signs and symbols.

☐ *Social context*—the setting, local and global, in which a congregation finds itself and to which it responds. The context includes the institutions and social groups, as well as the social, political and economic forces operative in the setting.

☐ *Process*—the underlying flow and dynamics of a congregation that knit together its common life and affect its morale and climate. Process includes how leadership is exercised and shared, decisions are made, communication occurs, problems are solved, and conflicts are managed.

☐ *Program*—those organizational structures, plans and activities through which a congregation expresses its mission and ministry both to its own members and to those outside the membership. This is the "face" most often visible in the church's representation of itself to itself and to the outside world.

For family ministry planning purposes, the knowledge of the members of the family ministry task team will often provide ample information about these dimensions of the congregation without resorting to more formal assessment processes. For example, discussing the team's responses to the following questions will be helpful in translating understanding of families in the congregation and community into plans for family ministry:

☐ *Congregational identity.* How does the congregation define families? How does it see itself currently ministering to families? What is most important to the congregation in relating to families and to the community? What does the congregation perceive its mission to be? Does the congregation see itself as a neighborhood church, or does it serve a broader geographic region? Does the congregation perceive itself as including a diversity of peoples and family groups—and does it see this as its mission? Or does it see itself as a "special interest" congregation, serving a particular population niche?

☐ *Social context.* What denominational identity does the congregation have, and how important is it that the congregation use denominational literature and programs? How does the congregation relate to its community? Does it see itself as politically active or a haven in which members can withdraw from the surrounding society? How stable is the neighborhood and community in which the congregation is located, and what kind of relationship does the congregation have with its community?

☐ *Process.* Who leads, who provides vision, who makes decisions in the congregation? Does the committee include these leaders, or does it have the ability to influence them? How are decisions made and new ministry directions established? What happens when members do not agree on the vision and ministry of the congregation?

☐ *Program.* What current programs and services are being offered to families and through families? What kinds of families receive most of the focus of the congregation's energies? What kinds of families are ignored?

Obviously, much of this information will be highly relevant when the family ministry team tries to turn what it learns about families into a plan of action. That plan must be developed in the context of the congregation—who it is, how it decides what to do, what it perceives its mission to be. We will look at these implications in more detail in chapter sixteen.

Whom to Ask

Almost always, however, there is some information that is not readily available, or the information available is not entirely trustworthy for your purposes. There are two sources of additional information: key informants and families themselves.

Key informants. "Key informants" are persons who by virtue of their experience or position have information about families in the congregation. Some of the key informants in a congregation are

☐ staff persons who provide counseling and ministries with various age groups
☐ lay leaders who have responsibility for ministry with defined congregational groups
☐ teachers in the congregation's various programs

☐ "central figures," or persons who are a trusted friend or mentor to many and have a lot of informal relationships that keep them apprised of what is going on in the congregation

Families. Second, one can ask families themselves. In fact, there is no substitute for listening to families; often their felt needs are quite different from those ascribed to them by key informants.

Gary Hauk describes his own experience in trying to figure out how he could best care for his grandmother. He asked his father what his grandmother needed. His father said she needed health care and financial assistance. He also asked her minister. The minister said she needed someone to visit her. Finally, he asked his grandmother what she needed. She said she needed to be doing something for someone else (Hauk 1988).

Sometimes everyone in a congregation can be asked to share information about their family. A whole-congregation survey is certainly possible and can provide an extensive overview of a congregation at a particular point.

In doing congregational surveys or interviews, do not limit yourself to adults. Children and adolescents can be wonderful sources of information about family life and the congregation. Include them in surveys and discussion with family groups, and talk with them in groups of peers. I have found children and adolescents to take very seriously the responsibility to give accurate information about their families and congregation. They feel honored and appreciative of the interest shown in their views. Care should be taken, however, to obtain parents' permission for conversation with their children and to ensure children's safety in the process. If children participate in a survey being given to everyone in the congregation, and the survey does not have names attached, there should be little concern. On the other hand, in group settings or in individual conversations children should not be asked for information that might be confidential or damaging to the family, although they may sometimes volunteer such information anyway.

It is possible, although rare, that in a group discussion or written survey a child or teenager (or adult) will say or write something that indicates the presence of family violence or even potential for suicide. In our research project with thirty-two congregations, one teenager did write a response that indicated suicidal thoughts. If you receive such a clear indicator that there is abuse or a threat of suicide and you have access to the child and family's identity, the public agency responsible for child protection or local law enforcement officials need to be consulted about whether a report needs to be made and how best to provide protection for threatened family member(s). Of course, such information can be revealed in many other ways than in a congregational assessment. Sunday-school teachers and youth leaders are frequently the persons to learn first about family violence, because they are trusted adults in whom children confide. Every congregation's leaders need to know their state's laws about reporting such concerns and to have a policy about responding with care and a timely referral for professional services (Alsdurf and Alsdurf 1988; Eilts 1988; Horton and Williamson 1988).

Working with Congregational Samples

Often a family ministry task team chooses to use a sample of the congregation rather than the entire congregation, and then assumes that the sample represents the entire congregation.

Random sample. The most statistically reliable choice for drawing such conclusions is a random sample. A group of individuals chosen randomly from the church membership represents the entire congregation. "Random" means that every person has just as much a chance of being in the sample as every other person. Therefore any inaccuracies in conclusions extrapolated from the sample to the whole congregation are due simply to chance, and not to the selection process.

For example, in a congregation of one thousand members, the task force decided to use a sample of one hundred persons. The number 2 was pulled from a box in which ten slips of paper had been placed, each with one of the numbers 1-10. Corresponding to the randomly chosen number 2, the second name on the church mailing list became the first person selected for the sample. The team chose the next person by counting down the mailing list ten names from the first person selected, and so on through the mailing list until one hundred names were selected. A survey was then either mailed or carried to each of these persons. Those who did not respond to the survey were contacted by phone or a visit from the family ministry task force in an effort to obtain as many surveys from the randomly chosen sample as possible. The same process can be used for choosing a random sample of persons to interview, either by phone or in person.

Convenience sample. Another type of sample is the "convenience sample," a group selected because they are available or "convenient." For example, everyone attending Sunday school or morning worship one Sunday fills out a survey. Such a sample may tell you a great deal about active members who attend every Sunday, but it would be dangerous to generalize any conclusion from the survey to the entire congregation, including inactive and homebound members. On the other hand, a convenience sample may be adequate for drawing conclusions about the active members of the congregations, especially if cautions are noted about the limits of the survey. Because convenience samples are so much easier to work with than random samples, they are most often used for planning congregational assessments.

In working with a convenience sample, it is important to determine every conceivable factor that may limit the ability to generalize from the sample to the larger congregation. For example, a survey conducted during a morning worship service may inadvertently leave out the nursery workers, the adolescents who had an all-night fellowship the night before and slept in instead of going to worship, and a number of young adult couples who would normally be there but couldn't resist going to the lake together on this first warm, sunny spring morning after eight weeks of rainy weekends. You can correct for the absence of these persons simply by providing two survey times and asking people to fill out the survey only once.

Methods for Obtaining Information

There are four basic ways of obtaining information from key informants and families: interviews, brainstorming group sessions, informal surveys and formal surveys.

Interviews. Interviews with families and key informants can constitute a rich source of information about family and congregational life. Interviews can provide the assessment team with stories of families' lives and the congregation that give meaning to the numbers and statistics of a survey.

Interviews may be highly structured, almost like a survey instrument, only an interviewer asks the questions and records the responses rather than having persons fill out the instrument themselves. Or they may be very open-ended, with a few questions to guide discussion. The questions need to be clearly related to the purposes of your assessment and not simply fishing to learn more about families with no clear purpose in mind.

In many ways, interviews require more expertise to conduct than a simple survey. Developing the right questions to ask in an interview takes considerable practice. Then what the family shares must somehow be sifted for the information being sought by the assessment team.

Nevertheless, an interview can be a wonderful process, both for the interviewer and for the family. In the research project I am pursuing to study families and their faith, I had the privilege of interviewing more than one hundred families in their homes to learn about how they experience faith. I asked relatively simple questions, such as

☐ Whom do you consider to be your close family?

☐ How did this family get started?

☐ What have been some of the significant moments in this family's life?

☐ What gives you a sense of meaning and purpose together as a family?

☐ What does faith mean to you?

☐ How do you live your faith together as a family?

☐ What do you think the church could do to help your family?

Most families found this a very significant discussion; many had not talked about faith with one another. I often wished that the leaders of their congregation could hear what I was hearing.

Peter Steinglass reports an interesting, and unexpected, outcome of his research with the families of chronic alcoholics. He and his research associates conducted interviews in groups with families of chronic alcoholics. The interviewers were carefully instructed not to try to intervene in any way in family life. They were simply to facilitate the families' discussion with one another. Two years later, in a follow-up assessment, the researchers were surprised to find that in virtually every case, the families reported that the drinking had stopped either during or shortly after the first assessment and had not resumed. When families were asked about what they believed caused the change, they responded that it was the therapy groups they had participated in two years previously—the research assessment groups that were carefully designed *not* to be therapeutic! This research gives anecdotal evidence of the potential power that assessment itself has in making changes in family lives (Steinglass 1995).

Brainstorming group sessions. Gathering "listening groups" for the family ministry team can be a powerful assessment tool. Gather church members to talk about their experiences in the congregation. These groups can be composed of a diversity of persons in the congregations—different ages, different kinds of families, different lengths of membership and levels of participation in the congregation. Limit the size of the group to no more than eight or ten, so that everyone has ample opportunity to contribute. If you would like to hear from more people, schedule a series of such groups. Caution the family ministry team that they are only to listen, not to react or participate in the discussion except to encourage others.

In conducting such a group, church consultant Lyle Schaller suggests that the group facilitator be sure that everyone in the room has the chance to speak at least twice within the first fifteen minutes (Schaller 1997). Otherwise quiet people will stay quiet.

First go around the group and ask participants to state their name, how long they have been in the church, and why they picked this church. Begin the discussion by focusing on congregational strengths. Ask each participant to "brag" about the congregation; what is one thing this church does really well in caring for families? Then ask, "What is the one fork-in-the road question facing this church in its ministry with families?" Or "What is one aspect of this congregation's ministry with families you would like to see changed?" (ibid.).

Brainstorming sessions can also be used to gather much more specific information, such as how the congregation's current programs and processes affect different kinds of families. For example, call together representatives of the different kinds of families in the congregation—parents (married and single) of children of different ages; adolescents in single-parent, two-parent and other kinds of families; single adults; senior adults (single, married, widowed); and so on. Together, have the group evaluate the various member activities and programs of the church's "regular" weekly schedule, and then for holidays (including secular days that are celebrated in the church, such as Mother's Day, Father's Day and Fourth of July) and special times of the year (summer camps, shortened summer schedules and so on). You can begin by placing placards across the top of each wall listing side by side all the weekly activities and annual special emphases. Include both programs that are directly related to family ministry (e.g., the family supper, cross-generational recreation night) and those that are not (committee meetings, building maintenance workday, Advent worship services).

Below each placard, invite family representatives to write the way that activity or event is experienced as strengthening, neutral or negative by the families they represent. A different colored marker can be used for each: green for strengthening, blue for neutral, red for negative. Provide each representative with all the colors of markers being used. A representative may use more than one color for each activity. For example, under the Sunday-school placard, the single-parent family of preschoolers may write in green, "Helps to be with other persons my age to study the Bible," and in red, "I hate leaving the baby in the nursery after she's been in daycare all week while I work." Ask each representa-tive to note where the comment came from, such as by adding the initials SP (single parent).

When everyone has completed their comments, encourage others to ask ques-tions and add to what has been written. If the posters can be left undisturbed, ask representatives to take a week to talk about any questions that have arisen in the process with other families and then meet again to begin to see what ideas emerge from this exercise.

Talk together about the patterns that can be observed. Be sure to begin by looking for themes of strength: what activities of the church seem to be most sig-nificant to the nurture of families, whether they are intentionally family ministry or not? Then look for activities and programs that seem to be having a negative impact on family life and which kinds of families feel the least amount of support and nurture in the congregation. Do not attempt to come up with solutions at this point; simply note what can be observed.

This kind of assessment process moves the family ministry task force away from simply considering what new program or activity can be implemented for families and opens up the whole picture of the church's ministry with families.

Informal surveys. Informal surveys can be done as a part of a regular program of the congregation, such as Wednesday-night supper or Sunday school. This kind of survey will tell you about the persons who attend this activity and not necessarily about those who are not active. An informal survey can mean supply-ing blank paper and simply reading questions to the group and asking them to write their answers. Or you can provide a printed survey and ask them to fill in the blanks. Keep it simple, asking for only the information that is most important to your assessment. The short survey instrument on the next page can be used for this kind of assessment.

If you want to learn about the diversity of family structures in the congrega-tion, including faith-families, it is important to define and discuss what the term *family* means prior to asking people to tell you in a survey who their families are. Otherwise they will use American society's definition—the nuclear family. The following questions may help persons define their families:

☐ Who shares the same bank accounts with you, or at least knows where and about how much you have in the bank?

☐ If a tornado devastated our town, whom would you be absolutely desperate to locate and make sure they were safe?

My Close Family

1. What kind of family do you live in (such as single parent and children; live alone and have faith-family members nearby; husband and wife and children; me and my roommate, and so on)?

2. What do you like best about your family?

3. What do you wish you could change about your family?

4. What challenges is your family facing?

5. In what ways is this church helpful to your family?

6. How could this congregation help your family?

☐ Whom could you expect to take care of you, or at least take responsibility for making sure you were cared for, if you had an extended illness?

☐ If you had to move a thousand miles away, who would go with you, or would at least consider moving with you? For whom would you make special provisions for maintaining daily/weekly contact?

☐ Who are the persons you share your daily life with year in and year out?

Usually these questions will help people define who the members of their families are. In particular, single adults may need to be encouraged to think more broadly about who their family is, beyond their immediate household.

If the survey is being conducted where there are likely to be several members of the same family sitting together and the questions include items that may be rather sensitive, such as "what I want to change about my family," it may be useful to ask people to move about and not sit next to a family member. This will remove the temptation to look at one another's responses and will encourage frank answers. On the other hand, the survey may be conducted as a family activity, with family members answering the questions together and one family member serving as the family scribe. This will provide information with a very different character, and it will also give families an opportunity to talk over their responses together. More sensitive or difficult family issues, however, are not as likely to be communicated. Which approach to use depends upon which kind of information is most important to you and what you want participants to experience in the process.

After the surveys have been gathered, one or more members of the family ministry task team will then need to organize the survey information. If the group is not too large, it is often helpful to have the responses typed out, with all the answers to each question listed together.

Read through them all first, to gain a sense of the kinds of messages that are there. Then read back through and develop categories. If two responses are similar, put them in the same category. For example, the following two responses were given to question two:

☐ "We've been through some hard experiences but we always knew we could count on one another."

☐ "We always work through our problems together; we are determined not to split up."

These could both be tallied for a category called "commitment." Responses do not have to be assigned to only one category. You might also create another category for the second response, "problem-solving skills."

All the categories can then be listed (with a few or all of the responses that belong to that category), and the number of responses that fit that category can be tallied. These can become a report back to those persons who took the survey, as either a brief presentation or a written summary of findings. It is the responsibility of the family ministry team to ensure that those participating have some opportunity to know what was learned and what is being planned as a consequence.

I have used a similar assessment process as part of a larger Bible study of what it means to be family. In a meeting of the entire congregation during a cross-generational Sunday-school hour, I provide a very brief overview of several New Testament passages that have been most formative in my understanding of family. Then I ask everyone to gather in a group with the members of their family present. Persons by themselves are asked to gather in small groups. Each family group (or individual, if they are by themselves) is given a large sheet of blank newsprint and markers and asked to draw all the members of their family doing something.

This often turns into a happy chaos of activity. As families work on their drawing, I wander about admiring their work and encouraging those who are uncomfortable with drawing, telling them just to use stick figures or geometric shapes. It is critical that the activity include everyone, even single adults who say they have no family. A brief conversation with them sometimes helps clarify that they do have a dear friend who is "like a sister."

As families complete their drawings, a member is asked to turn their paper over and note on the back the family name(s) and the first names of other persons in the picture, how they are related and their ages. No names need to be put on the front of the picture. For example, a mother might turn her paper over and write:

Martha Smith (42)
Jon (Martha's son, 18)
Matt (Martha's son, 16)
Mattie (Martha's mother, 71)

This information can be gathered later by the family ministry team as a means of tabulating the different kinds of families in the congregation.

Family members are then asked to tape their pictures (picture side showing) around the walls of the meeting room or sanctuary. A few minutes is spent circulating, looking at the various kinds of families in the congregation. Of course the pictures illustrate not only the diversity of families in the congregation but also the various ways they see their lives together. Single persons may show themselves alone, and this says something to the congregation about its fellowship. On the other hand, many may depict themselves as part of families that had previously not been visible to a congregation that regards them only as "singles."

After participants have opportunity to look at a few of the others' pictures, call the group back together and ask them to discuss together:

☐ What did you learn about your family as you worked on this?

☐ Those of you who worked as a family group, did you all agree about who was a member of your family?

☐ What did you learn about the other families in this congregation?

Often I close these sessions with singing and prayers of thanksgiving for the families God has given, asking God's guidance for living the promises of God more faithfully as a congregation. The family ministry team later gathers to discuss what they learned from observing the congregation in this exercise. One or more people also retrieve the information from the backs of the pictures.

This activity illustrates that assessment can take place as a part of studying what it means for Christians to be family. The assessment process can be a significant experience of self-examination for participants as well as providing information that will help the family ministry team in its planning.

Another informal survey may grow out of a time of studying the role of family life for Christians. The sense of calling and purpose in family life is a matter of considerable import in Christian education. Just as congregations often write mission statements to give focus and direction to their life together, so families can engage in a process of writing a mission statement, with the following instructions:

Describe together what you feel God wants your family to be doing as a family in your relationships with one another and in caring for others and God's creation.

Such an activity gives family groups opportunity to think through what really does hold them together and give direction to their lives. They can take their statement home to post on the refrigerator or bulletin board as a reminder. If copies of these mission statements are made available to the family ministry team, they can be a significant source of information about the strengths and needs of families within the congregation.

Formal survey. The most comprehensive assessment approach is to conduct a formal survey of the congregation. A formal survey uses an instrument that has been carefully designed and tested to ensure that it will gather accurate data that will be reliable for the purposes for which it was designed. Such an instrument actually takes much less of the family ministry team's time than the informal survey. The surveys are already prepared, and in many cases the completed surveys are sent to the publisher for analysis, after which a report is sent to the church for use in family ministry planning.

The Church Census is one such formal survey instrument, developed as a part of the Family Ministry Research Project of Louisville Presbyterian Theological Seminary and now available from the Baylor Center for Family and Community Ministries (see appendix B). The Church Census is designed to develop a profile of a congregation's families—the kinds of families in the congregation and information about families such as ages, income, use of time, shared participation in the life of the congregation, length of time they have lived in the community, the distance they drive to church and so on. It also assesses the strengths and challenges families are experiencing, the stressors in their lives, and ways they are living out their faith together.

The Center for Family and Community Ministries provides the survey instruments to a church leader or a consultant who is working with the church. Once the survey has been conducted, the completed surveys are sent to the Center, where the responses are entered into a computer for analysis. The results of the analysis are returned to the congregational leaders in an extensive report (see Garland and Yankeelov 1998).

The Congregation's Mission and Sense of Identity

Undoubtedly the congregational assessment will identify plenty of needs and possibilities for ministry. No congregation can respond to every need and ministry opportunity that presents itself. In order to decide what to do in response to what is being learned, the family ministry team needs to assess the congregation's mission at the same time that they assess the congregation's and community's families.

The church's mission answers the question "Who are we and what do we feel called to do?" To answer that question, the team might find it helpful throughout the assessment process to talk about

☐ what they are learning and how it is affecting them as individuals and as a community of faith

☐ what gifts and strengths are being identified in the congregation and its families

☐ how those gifts and strengths might be used in response to needs being identified

METHODS OF COMMUNITY ASSESSMENT

Community assessment is a process for determining the resources, strengths and needs in a community—usually the geographic area or region surrounding a congregation. A community assessment involves seeking many of the same kinds of information as are sought in a congregational assessment.

First, the assessment attempts to define who families in the community are. What kinds of families are there (blending, nuclear, three-generation, etc.)? What are the processes of family life for these families (communication, conflict, etc.)? What kinds of stresses are they experiencing? What are their felt and ascribed strengths, needs and challenges? What do they and others perceive the church can do to help them?

Second, the assessment should look at the community itself, just as the congregational assessment looked at the congregation as a community in which families are embedded. What kind of community is this for all the family types identified as living there? Are there some kinds of families that seem invisible or ignored by the community? In what ways does the community support and challenge family life? In what ways does the community create stress for families? What community resources are available to nurture families? What can the congregation do to help the community be more sensitive to and supportive of families?

Finding Information Already Available

There is often a great deal of information readily available about the community from a variety of sources. Often the community assessment may involve no more than gaining access to and interpreting this information for the purposes of ministry.

Census data. Every ten years (e.g., 1980, 1990, 2000) the United States Census Bureau counts persons in a designated area, called a census tract, and gathers information from that area, such as number and sizes of households, ages, gender, race and ethnicity, and income. Census reports tell, for example, how many single-parent households there are, how many older adults are living alone, and how many families are living in poverty in a particular census tract. This information can be found in the government documents section of public libraries.

Of course this material does not document people's attitudes, or the strengths of their families, or the extent to which people in the community help one another. But it certainly provides the best foundation available for a basic definition of families in an area. Some of this data is updated more frequently than every ten years. Census data is also available on the Internet.

Other library sources. At the public library you can find all kinds of other public documents that will tell you about your community. State governments keep track of unemployment rates, child abuse statistics, numbers of persons receiving various forms of state assistance, and rates of various kinds of crime in the state and in local communities.

Much of this information will be statistical—numbers, percentages and charts. The statistics will mean more to the congregation if they are accompanied by stories of persons in the community. To say that 30 percent of families in the community surrounding the church live in poverty takes on meaning when we know a poor family and hear about the family's struggles and experience their resilience. Therefore it may be very helpful to supplement this information with contact with persons in the community who can flesh out the statistics with their own stories or the stories of other families.

Key Informants

Community leaders can provide information from their corner of the community that can help you better understand both the resources and the problems that will not be apparent in statistical information. A school principal or counselor can share valuable impressions about children and teenagers and about the needs and strengths of families with school-age children. Elected officials, mental health professionals, youth workers and business leaders all have informative perspectives.

By looking at what it is you want to learn, you should be able to come up with a number of key persons you could interview. Some of them may be members of your own church. Do not neglect persons who may not be obvious, such as an older adult who tutors in the schools, the owner of the local teen hang-out, a high-school teacher who is a favorite among many youths and so on. Many of these people will be happy to talk with you and share their ideas about what the church can do to minister with families.

Before meeting with a community leader or visiting an agency or organization that works with families, write out several key questions you want to answer. You may want to do this together as you plan your assessment, so that everyone who is interviewing community leaders is working with the same questions.

☐ What kinds of families are served by this agency/organization?

☐ What kinds of services and other resources for families are available?

☐ What kinds of families are they not able to serve?

☐ What kinds of strengths does this person see in families in this community?

☐ What kinds of challenges and stressors does this person see facing families in this community?

☐ What does this person wish the church could do for families in this community?

In asking the key informants how the church can help, frame the question with two prongs: what the congregation can do to help the agency in its work with families, and what the congregation can do in other ways. It helps to set forth both prongs initially, before the key informant has opportunity to respond. In that way the informant understands that the church is interested in helping families both through the agency and in other ways. (Otherwise the key informant may first respond with ways the church can help the informant's work with families. Then, when the next question from the interviewer is "What can the church do directly or in other ways with families in this community?" the key informant might assume that the response to the previous question did not interest the interviewer.)

Send questions to the key informant prior to the interview, so he or she can be thinking ahead about what to share with your team. During the interview, audiotaping may be possible. A few key informants may find this somewhat threatening and be less willing to talk candidly, but many will appreciate the seriousness you are giving to your task. If you choose to take notes instead, try to capture pithy quotations that will give life to the report you will prepare from your visit. Try to help the persons who will hear or read your report get a feeling for what you have heard and seen in your community assessment.

At the conclusion of the interview, you may want to ask if you can pray for the key informant. Many will be surprised and pleased, but some may seem uncomfortable or unwilling, and if so, these feelings should be respected. If they are willing for you to pray, give thanks for the calling on this person's life to serve families and for the service she or he is giving to families and the community. Pray for blessing and strength. The person may experience this prayer as a recognition and blessing of her or his ministry that carries tremendous power and significance, particularly if such recognition has not been received from the person's own faith community. It may be that continued prayer support for this person's ministry with families can be one aspect of the congregation's ministry in the community.

Some tangible expression of appreciation for the person's time and energy is certainly in order. A thank-you note is appropriate. You may also choose to bring or send a small token of appreciation; a specially painted coffee mug highlighting the person's community role or a gift certificate to a bookstore or ice-cream shop. Such gifts can carry a value that far outweighs their monetary cost. Letters of appreciation for a public servant's helpfulness can also be sent to that person's supervisor. You will also want to send each of the key informants a copy of any subsequent report you prepare out of your community assessment.

If task team members have not interviewed others before, it may help them to practice on one another. The following pointers will help:

☐ Ask open-ended, nonjudgmental questions that are easily understood.

☐ Ask one question at a time.

☐ Listen. Try to put yourself in the place of the person and imagine what the world is like from inside him or her, based on what you are hearing. Put your own thoughts and opinions away for now; there will be time after the interview to think about whether you agree or disagree with what you are hearing. Do not voice your evaluation of the informant's ideas and conclusions, even if your evaluation is positive; that assumes that you know more than the informant, or you are just listening to see if the informant agrees with your preformed position. It is appropriate to express appreciation for new insights and information ("Wow, I had no idea!" "I've learned so much from you," "You have been really helpful") but not to express agreement or disagreement ("You are so right; I'm glad you agree with us," or "That just can't be true; you must be biased from working with these folks all the time"). It goes without saying that you are there to listen to the informant rather than share your own ideas and thoughts.

☐ Give the interviewee time to organize thoughts and respond. Some questions, such as "What do you think our church could do that would really be helpful to families in this community?" require some time for thought. Refrain from making suggestions or leading the person to say what you hope to hear.

☐ Take notes during the interview, even if you are audiotaping, just in case the recorder malfunctions. After the interview, flesh out your notes with your observations, thoughts and feelings about what you have experienced.

☐ Send the person a thank-you note and perhaps share something of what you learned, if appropriate.

Community Residents

Another helpful method is to set up interviews with people who represent those about whom you are trying to learn. Again, begin by deciding what questions you want to answer. Then determine how you will locate those to be interviewed. You may simply knock on doors. Or a community leader may be able to put you in touch with a few families to interview. It often helps to have someone the person knows to vouch for you before you make your first contact, so that the family does not think you are selling something. A contact by phone may be sufficient, or if you would like a face-to-face interview, a phone call to make an appointment is more courteous and more likely to be warmly received than an unannounced visit.

Focus Groups

Invite a small group (five to twenty) to meet with you to generate information about families in your community. These can be community leaders or residents, or a combination. If the first group is helpful, you may decide to hold another one or two with a different set of people.

Providing a light meal as a part of the meeting often encourages involvement. These meetings are times for you to ask questions and listen. You may use a list of questions similar to those used for interviewing individual community leaders or residents. Be sure to have lots of poster paper and markers so you can record for all to see the responses to your questions about the resources and strengths, problems and stressors of families in the community. There are a number of helpful resources for planning effective focus groups (Krueger 1998a; 1998b; Krueger and King 1998b; Morgan 1998).

Community Surveys

Surveys are among the most costly processes in terms of time and energy, but they can provide information unavailable any other way. Surveying the community is an arduous task, often requiring door-to-door visits of community residents. You may try mailing questionnaires to individuals in the community, but mailed surveys typically have very low return rates. If you decide to do a community survey, be sure to include stamped return envelopes.

Sometimes you have only one or two questions, so that developing a survey questionnaire is relatively simple. If you want to learn a lot with a longer survey, it may be fruitful to contact someone at a local college or university who teaches research (in social work, education, psychology or sociology). That teacher may be able to suggest a student or group of students who can help design the survey instrument as a way to fulfill a class assignment. Also, you may consider inviting other congregations or community agencies to participate with you in surveying the community. You can pool resources and also benefit from the opportunity to collaborate.

Community Observation
One of the most important strategies to use in conjunction with one or more of the above methods is to send out a group either in small clusters or in pairs to drive slowly through the church's community and record their observations. Encourage them to stop and walk around, especially in the area immediately around the church or through a few other nearby neighborhoods. Give them a specific list of observations to make:

☐ the cleanliness and general appearance of the community
☐ the attitude of persons they meet
☐ where children, if any, are playing
☐ the general condition of homes and yards
☐ the types of businesses and their customers
☐ the level of activity in the community
☐ people's racial and ethnic identities
☐ the presence of public servants and services (police, buses)
☐ the location, state and use of recreation areas

Upon return, share observations. Put paper on the wall and have people map and illustrate what they have seen.

SUMMARY

Assessment methods are structured learning experiences. As the family ministry team conducts its congregational and/or community assessment, they are learning about themselves, about their congregation, about the community. The focus on the process of learning needs to be retained, not merely on the facts "out there." Assessing a congregation or community is not like catching facts as though they were butterflies to snag in a net and pin to a board. The end result of that is just a board decorated with dead bugs, however beautiful. Instead the process is more like watching and appreciating the flight and markings of a butterfly, and learning something not only about the butterflies we observe but about ourselves as observers. We are not simply learning about families, as though understanding of families and communities can be summarized as a set of facts in a report to be distributed in a church business meeting. Rather, we are learning about families by understanding how they move through their communities and how they live their lives day in and day out, and how this new understanding affects us.

I have found congregational assessments to be powerful learning tools for congregations, as they think not only about the information they glean about their families but also about how that information affects the family ministry team. Family ministry teams are often gratified and surprised to learn that there is so much strength, resilience and long-term commitment in congregational families. That very surprise is a significant part of the assessment process. It says that we approach congregational assessment believing that families are in trouble. On the other hand, some of those same family ministry teams have also found themselves shocked by the prevalence of violence reported in homes of church members. Again, the shock is also a significant piece of information. We assume that although we know that violence is a characteristic of our culture, it has not invaded the homes of "our" families.

Once the assessment process has been completed and the report prepared, the focus turns to deciding what it all means in the life of the church. Given what we know, what will we now do to care for families in our congregation and community?

Chapter 16

Planning & Evaluating Family Ministry

I N ONE SENSE, MINISTRY WITH FAMILIES BEGINS FROM THE MOMENT A family ministry team forms. As congregational leaders discuss what it means for Christians to live in families, as they study the issues of family life today, as they examine the strengths, challenges and stressors of families in their congregation and the wider community, changes take place. New ideas form; new sensitivities develop; and as a consequence, the language and relationships of congregational life subtly change. To the extent that the assessment process has included listening to families in the congregation and community, families have sensed that they are valued and that their concerns are important to congregational leaders.

Study of family issues in Scripture and culture combined with assessment of congregation and community thus provides a powerful catalyst for family ministry. But if nothing else happens, if the assessment results only in some new ideas and a report that gathers dust on a staff member's shelf, disillusionment can result. Family ministry team members experience dissonance between what they understand about the meaning of families for Christians and what their congregation is actually doing. Members of families may wonder why they answered survey questions or participated in focus group discussions, only to have the church go on with business as usual. Were their concerns and ideas not worth pursuing? Key informants may feel frustrated at the time and energy they expended talking with family ministry team representatives to no apparent purpose.

It takes time, of course, for a family ministry team to organize what they have learned, develop a plan of response and obtain congregational support for the plan. In fact, congregations move much more slowly from assessment to response than other organizations. They are, for the most part, composed of and led by volunteers. They operate best by making consensual decisions, involving not only leaders but various groups and constituencies in the congregation. A business organization might be able to take a community assessment and develop a comprehensive, powerful plan within a matter of a few weeks. Congregations, by contrast, may take months.

This is a problem only for those who expect churches to move much more quickly and decisively than they do—those working out of a business model rather than a community model. The slow rate of decision-making and action grows from the greatest asset of a congregation in the lives of families—it is a community of relationships. Processes of inclusion, of communication through a broad network of relationships, of informal rather than formal decision-making, are characteristic of a mostly egalitarian community of folks who have chosen to be in community with one another.

Several years ago, my congregation's minister of education asked me, because I was chair of the Christian education committee, to convene a task team to explore the possibility of changing our use of space for children's programs. The team's task was to recommend how space should be reallocated and renovated. Together, he and I convened a group consisting of parents, youth workers, children's workers, the after-school program director, the minister of youth and the church custodian.

One area of the building was currently being used by the after-school program for school-age children during the weekdays and by the youth group on Sunday. This meant that each week workers had to swap furniture, bringing larger tables and chairs for the youths in some classrooms for Sunday and then returning the children's furniture for the weekday program. The children's Sunday activities were held in another part of the building. As part of a building renovation, the staff recommended that the Sunday youth and children's programs trade space, so that the space used by the children's after-school program could be used by children of the same age on Sunday.

This seemed a rather straightforward, commonsense solution, and so I imagined that the decision process would require only one meeting, or perhaps two at most. Instead the process took eight weekly two-hour meetings. The group walked through the space and looked at all the changes—and costs—entailed in developing a high-quality space for both children and youth programs. They asked and listened to parents, Sunday-school teachers, after-school program staff, youth leaders and the youths themselves. They considered the role and status of the after-school program in the life of the congregation, and they pondered why the director of the after-school program was not a church staff member. They listened to emotions expressed by various members of the committee, concerns about what the assignment and updating of space should communicate about the value of children to the congregation. There was concern that if the church's children's programs shared space, furniture and resources with the after-school program, the after-school program's resources might be misused. There would have to be ways to separate supplies, have separate bulletin boards and so on. As the discussion progressed, the team decided that the church needed a mission statement concerning our children's ministries, since the after-school program and other children's programs were central to the concerns of the congregation. They developed one.

In the end, the committee recommended reallocating the space just as the church staff had originally suggested. In addition, however, they had responded to concerns raised by this decision by making major budget recommendations for renovating and furnishing the youth and children's spaces, successfully presenting a new mission statement to the congregation which included policy about the relationship of the after-school program to other church programs, and proposing that the director of the after-school program be named to the church staff. The entire committee—and the congregation—felt pleased with the outcome of our work, which took almost two months longer than I had expected.

It is important that church leaders recognize that churches are communities, not businesses. Their decision-making takes time. On the other hand, it is important not to mistake being bogged down for a careful, paced response. While the committee is working through decision-making processes, it is critical that others be informed of how things are moving and be assured that their contribution to the assessment was crucial and has not been discarded. The congregation can receive brief updates in the newsletter or bulletin. Brief notes updating key informants in the community can be powerful ways to keep them engaged with the congregation and can continue to encourage them in their work, reminding them that they are not alone in their concern for families.

This chapter will look at what to do after the initial assessment has been completed. The committee may be faced with a mountain of information about the congregation and its families and the community and its families. Members may be overwhelmed with the diversity of families and family needs that have been discovered. What should they do? How does the committee decide which needs are *most* important? Even after a particular need has been chosen as the focus of planning, which of several responses to that need is the *best* response for this congregation?

BEGIN WITH THE CONGREGATION'S MISSION AND IDENTITY

As hard as the team has worked in gathering information about families in the congregation and community, the process of deciding what to do should begin with a temporary sidelining of that new information. No doubt the committee's perceptions about the congregation, about families and about the community have been changed in the assessment process. With this new framework of understanding, the team needs to begin this phase of its work by reflecting again on the mission of this congregation, at this time and in this place. In other words, central attention needs to go to the congregational mission, with the assessment information in peripheral vision—still visible, but not currently the focus.

The fundamental question that the family ministry team must answer before going on to look at the various needs they have discovered is, *What is our congregation's mission with families?* How do we understand God's purpose for this congregation in its current context of time and place? A review of the discussion of the woman honoring Jesus with the costly ointment (Mt 26:10-11) in the introduction to section four of this book may help the committee shift from the congregational and community assessment to a discussion of congregational mission. Church consultant Lyle Schaller has stated that one of the most important tasks in planning for changes in a congregation is "to create widespread agreement on one coherent and internally consistent description of contemporary reality. This is important, first as a response to denial and, second, as an essential step in designing a strategy for creating a new future" (Schaller 1997:46). Defining the congregation's mission together establishes the most significant aspect of its current reality, which will provide perspective on all the other congregational and community realities the family ministry team has examined.

Obviously, congregations differ in size, culture, beliefs and mission. Just as individuals within a congregation have different gifts that contribute to the body of believers, so congregations have different gifts and strengths that they contribute to the work of the church. A congregation's history, heritage, worldview, context, processes and existing programs (Carroll, Dudley and McKinney 1986) significantly shape the kinds of ministry it can undertake with its own families and with other community families. Ideally a congregation's sense of mission grows out of its character and strengths, those qualities that distinguish it as a community. The congregational assessment that the team conducted should provide insights that can guide the process of defining the congregation's mission with families.

The following categories of questions were adapted from the work of Jackson Carroll, Carl Dudley and William McKinney (Carroll, Dudley and McKinney 1986). These can help the family ministry team discuss and define the congregation's mission, if that mission has not already been defined.

History and Heritage

What has this congregation done for and through families in the past? What is the current congregation's inheritance from past generations, and how has that heritage carried into the present? What theological premises have been most central? What has it stood for? In what ways has it experienced failure, and what has been done with those failures? How has this congregation known itself denominationally? How important has denominational affiliation been in the congregation's understanding of itself? How has the congregation viewed cross-denominational or ecumenical activities, and how willing has it been to participate in crossdenominational or ecumenical ministries? Finally, what do the answers to these questions say about how this congregation sees itself today and what it is willing and able and committed to do because of what it was willing and able and committed to doing in the past? With whom is it most used to working—other churches and agencies in its denomination, other congregations in ecumenical community efforts, parachurch organizations—or has it preferred to remain on its own?

Worldview

How does this congregation understand who God is? How does it define the purpose and meaning of family life? How should Christians live in families, and how should they as individuals and families care for the community and the larger world? What is the role of the church and what is the role of government in responding to families in need? What does the church see its role to be in the community and world? Which of the following most closely matches its self-perception?

☐ a haven, a protected environment in a hostile world

☐ a prophetic presence that uses its voice and position to bring social change

☐ a community of individuals, families and groups who are "on mission" in the world

☐ some combination of these

What do the answers to this question suggest about the kinds of ministries this congregation would be most comfortable with and motivated by?

One might guess that churches that are more theologically liberal would be more active on social issues than evangelistic churches, which emphasize personal salvation. Research has indicated, however, that this is not necessarily the case. Most active congregations are actually motivated by moderate and evangelical theological roots, not by liberal theological perspectives; they embrace both the importance of personal salvation and a passion for social justice (Dudley and Johnson 1993). For example, one large congregation located in an inner city emphasizes personal evangelism and concludes passionate preaching with long altar calls on Sunday mornings. Its Sunday worship is followed by weekday programs including respite care for children and persons with Alzheimer's disease; a free dental clinic; a shelter for homeless families; emergency assistance and financial counseling; tutoring for neighborhood children; and various support, educational and activity groups for children and adults living in the low-income neighborhood immediately surrounding the church.

Obviously, congregations are complex entities, and there is some danger in assuming that there is *a* worldview that represents the congregation. There may be a wide diversity of worldviews represented in the congregation. Defining the congregation's views about God, family and the role of the church in the world is thus best thought of as defining the congregation's *range* of views.

During a business meeting in a church whose members included many international families, a young adult made a motion that the United States flag, usually placed in the front corner of the sanctuary opposite the Christian flag, be removed. He suggested that the international members of the congregation should be able to worship and be a part of the community without having to be confronted with American patriotism. He suggested that the flag was hindering the church's ministry with international families. Several older members of the congregation, some of them war veterans, sprang to their feet in protest. A heated discussion followed; the issue was not resolved. A tug of war seems to have ensued. The American flag mysteriously is periodically moved to a closet and reappears in the front of the sanctuary the next week (Garland 1994a).

In many ways, this example seems to have parallels with an ongoing, unresolved family squabble over the "right" setting for the furnace thermostat. The control is adjusted up and down by two or more family members trying to make the house a place of comfort for themselves. In fact, there really is no "right" setting. The ongoing process of adjustment, compromise and lack of compromise illustrates a congregation's grappling with a range of not-always-compatible views. For the congregation, this particular difference in worldviews may not be a major stumbling block to its ministry with international families, so long as it is recognized. Instead of removing the American flag, the committee might recommend instead *adding* the flags of countries of origin of their members or of nations where the congregation is supporting missionaries. The family ministry team needs to consider the entire range of worldviews as it develops a family ministry plan, although its plan will probably build on what team members consider to be the major themes of the congregation's life together.

Context

Does the congregation see itself as a neighborhood church, a church that serves an entire region, or a "special interest" congregation? Is the congregation most oriented to its local neighborhood, to its metropolitan area, or more broadly to issues in its state, nation and world? To what issues in the local and wider community has this congregation felt compelled to respond? To what extent are congregational members and families involved in local issues, national politics, world concerns? What kinds of political and social issues most concern people in this congregation? To what extent is the congregation involved in denominational politics and concerns?

Every congregation is confronted with many possible directions for ministry. What kinds of causes have motivated this congregation to serve and to give, and what has it virtually ignored? What do the answers to these questions say about how this congregation relates to its community and world and the level of response it can be expected to make to concerns about families?

Processes

What are the rituals of the congregation that connect the church with the great traditions of the faith (baptism, Eucharist, footwashing) and those that reflect its own unique past and current identity (certain songs sung at certain times, established prayers and greetings, order of worship)? What can be changed, and what would be difficult to change? How does the congregation make decisions and solve problems? How does it handle diversity and conflict? To what extent is the congregation autonomous and free to set its own course in relation to any denominational ties? Who holds the power and authority in the congregation? What meaning does this have for the team's ability to envision an overarching family ministry plan?

Generally there are three main types of church polity: hierarchy, local autonomy and a combination of these two (Moberg 1984). In the hierarchical form, a group of superiors in a central church government appoints the church leader (pastor or priest), who continues to be subject to discipline from these superiors. As an officer in this central hierarchy, the church leader is constrained by the central church government but also freed from dependence on a local congregation. The congregation may protest the actions of the church leader but may not have the authority to initiate action against him or her. Hierarchical structures characterize Roman Catholic, Episcopal and Lutheran churches.

By contrast, in a locally autonomous church structure, such as Baptist, the congregation has the power both to choose and to exercise control over the church leader and the church organization. The central organization has minimal power. The church leader depends on the members of the congregation for financial and programmatic support.

Some churches, such as the Presbyterian and Methodist, combine these forms of polity, placing major control in the hands of a central body that endorses and therefore enhances the authority of the church leader. The congregation, however, is controlled by an indigenous board of elders that requests appointment of a particular leader and has considerable control over the life of the church community.

Denominational polity is significantly tempered by the leadership style and values of pastors and others who have power in a congregation. Some pastors govern churches with almost total power invested in their position. Others operate with a democratic, shared decision-making style. As to relationship to the denomination, some congregations choose to ignore the policies and positions of higher levels of church government and work informally—or formally—out of a different value base. As in any organization, a church's formal position statements and processes may be quite different from the values that pilot the organization and from the informal processes of operation.

Existing Programs

The final aspect of congregational identity brings us back to the assessment the team has conducted. What is the congregation currently doing in family ministry? What impact do current programs have on the diversity of families in the congregation and in the community? A congregation's programs reflect what it values enough to invest financial resources and energies in—and what it does not. What do current programs reflect about the values of the congregation?

Taken together, the answers to the questions in these five categories of congregational identity should give a clear depiction of the congregation and how it perceives its mission in the community and world. There is a richness of description that is important to retain, but it is also helpful to pull together in a few paragraphs a summary statement that describes the congregation at this point. From all it has learned, the family ministry team can pull together a vision statement that defines who the congregation is and describes its particular gifts and resources for ministry with its own families and the families in its community.

Finally, it is time to return to the assessment of those families and begin to define priorities for a family ministry plan. However, the mission statement that has been hammered out deserves to be kept in front of the family ministry team throughout this process.

DEFINING SALIENT MINISTRY POSSIBILITIES

During the focus on congregational identity and mission, the family assessment has probably been very much on the mind of the family ministry team, even though it has not been the central focus. As you have reflected on the congregation's history, its worldview and its relation to its community context, no doubt some of what you have learned about families has popped into awareness. Some of the needs and concerns you have discovered in the families in your congregation and community fit with how this congregation has cared for and responded to needs in the past and the kinds of concerns that drive its current ministry involvements.

So far you have conducted a family ministry assessment, with its two prongs: assessing the strengths and needs of families in the congregation and in the community, and defining the congregational identity and mission. The first prong is a "needs" assessment, the second is a "heart" assessment. Holding these two assessments together, in conversation with one another, will help you decide how to focus the ministry of the congregation in the most effective way.

Effectiveness in family ministry is judged both by (1) making a significant positive response to the needs and issues of target families and (2) making a significant positive impact on the spiritual growth of the congregation and members involved in the ministry (the congregational "heart"). Effectiveness depends on choosing the most appropriate focus(es) for your ministry as well as choosing the most effective program or service approach. We will look at each of these in turn.

Decide on Priority Concerns

Most often, the process of need and heart assessment has already led the congregation or team to a central concern they want to address in ministry. Indeed, the family ministry team may have been initially organized in response to a particular congregational concern. The need and heart assessment may have modified or nuanced that concern. Still, many family ministry teams need to spend little time deciding on their priority concerns. Even if priorities were not set in the beginning, they have likely evolved as the team has shared what they learned about families in the community and congregation, as they have listened to others and talked about who their congregation is and the mission that moves it.

If priorities have not emerged through the process, now is the time to establish them. Review together what has been learned in the need and heart assessment. This conversation needs to be launched with prayer and punctuated with pauses for prayer together. You are seeking God's leading not only for the committee but for the congregation. Here are some questions that can help guide your discussion.

What seem to be the most pressing needs of families in our congregation? in our community? Focus here on needs, not responses to needs. For example, "families need quality care for children in the after-school hours" is a need. "An after-school program in our church" is a response. There are often many responses to a need; for example, you might also join with other congregations in the community to offer a community after-school program, or you might advocate for schools in the area to offer after-school programs. Once you have identified priority needs, you can systematically review the possible responses.

What other needs may not seem to be as pressing but have in some way touched us in the congregational and community assessment? For example, say you have identified three families in your congregation and, based on school board statistics, learned that there are probably about fifty more in your community that have children with significant developmental disabilities; you have also learned that no church in the community is providing ministry that is sensitive to the strengths and needs of these families. At the same time, you have learned that there are more than nine hundred school-age children in your community who are unsupervised in the after-school hours, including thirty of the forty children in your own congregation. The number of families with children with developmental disabilities is not as striking, but your congregation has been particularly touched by their needs because of its direct connection with those three families.

Which of the needs we have identified are congregational needs, which are community needs, and which involve both congregational and community families? Do we believe our church is being called to inreach, outreach or both?

In looking at the list of needs we have identified, which do we think would be of most concern to our congregation? Which fit the mission that this church has had historically or that drives it today?

Given this list of needs which we think fit our church's mission, how many can we address realistically and faithfully? Which do we think are most important?

Effective and Appropriate Responses

Now that one or more needs have been established as the target of ministry, the planning process ahead may be clear. On the other hand, identifying the need(s) the congregation feels led to address does not necessarily mean knowing what to do in response. For example, does a high divorce rate in a community or congregation mean a counseling center is needed? Perhaps, but not necessarily. Two factors are involved. First, there are theory and research about what causes the need. Second, there are decisions about what responses are possible and "best" for the congregation to make, given its mission and identity.

What is it that causes divorce? Lack of skills—in communication, conflict management or financial management? Stress from the environment—interfering parents, unemployment, lack of adequate time together for bonding? A devaluing of marriage by our society—the media's glamorization of premarital and extramarital relationships, the multiple marriages of media stars, the valuing of individual autonomy and belittlement of self-sacrifice? Or is it an *over*valuing of marriage by our society—believing that one person can fulfill all our expectations for companionship? Or perhaps divorce results from a confluence of many factors. Our belief about what causes the target of our concern—what causes divorce—will indicate the direction, or multiple directions, ministry could take: retreats and seminars for teaching marital skills, counseling to address environmental stressors, sermons and educational programs to help establish appropriate expectations for marriage, support groups to sustain couples in their faithful life together.

For the sake of illustration, imagine that your family ministry team has decided to recommend to your congregation a ministry focusing on the strengths and needs of families with children with developmental disabilities, given that these families currently have no congregational resources for their children's spiritual nurture. You are interested first in addressing the needs of families in your congregation, and then in expanding to provide spiritual/faith community resources for *all* families of children with developmental disabilities.

First, list together what you think the causes are for this need. You will want to include input from these families themselves, perhaps from conversations you have already had with them, or by involving one or more family representatives in your committee's work. You might come up with a list such as this:

☐ Many people are uncomfortable around children with developmental disabilities because they do not know how to relate to them. Sunday-school teachers and other children's group leaders are not equipped to include these children, and there are no "special" classes for them.

☐ It is very difficult for these families to find baby sitters who will keep their children so that they can have time away together.

☐ The church is not equipped with accessible restrooms and classrooms for children who have physical challenges as well as developmental disabilities.

☐ Families themselves are stressed by the multiple demands of career and caring for their child with special needs as well as their other children. It is often much easier simply not to participate in congregational activities, especially when parents have to arrange care at home because their child's presence does not seem to be welcomed at church.

These factors suggest possible responses to the concerns of these families. In addition, the next chapter will explore several models of family ministry programs. Your group might come up with a list such as the following:

□ Train current teachers to include children with developmental disabilities in activity programs, and provide teachers with additional aides as needed. Modify *all* of the congregation's family programs so that these families will know that appropriate care will be provided for their children.

□ Plan three sessions of the regular Wednesday-night supper and community prayer service to focus on the gifts and needs these children bring to the fellowship, the place of persons with developmental disabilities in a Christian community, and how members can welcome them and their families.

□ Challenge the youth group to take on a special project of learning to provide quality baby-sitting for children with special needs. Plan an educational seminar to equip them for this care. Include interested adults, and ask parents to serve as consultants.

□ Undertake building modifications to make the building accessible.

□ Find ways the church can support a summer camp or weekend retreat for children with developmental disabilities, providing scholarships for the congregation's children if necessary. If such a program is not available, contact the appropriate denominational or ecumenical agency to see what it would take to organize it. During one or more days of the camp, provide a retreat for parents that gives them opportunity for rest, recreation and spiritual renewal.

□ Develop a support group for parents of children with developmental disabilities.

□ Because the concern that is being addressed is the spiritual nurture of these children and their families, recognize that the target of these programs and services is congregational families. Invite families from other congregations and from the community as well, however, recognizing that congregational families with special needs children may use these programs and services as outreach—ministering to others at the same time they are cared for by the congregation.

Now the task is deciding among the various possibilities for ministry. The congregation may be able to take on all of these. Or ministry approaches may be phased in over a period of months or even years. As you plan, take as much time as possible to build consensus. Cutting discussion short by taking a vote frequently works to lower the investment of those who are outvoted. Remember, again, that a congregation is not a business—it needs to model what it means to be family, and that means bringing everyone along.

"Best" Responses to Concerns

Several guidelines can help congregations that are uncertain about the best course of action.

Choose approaches to ministry that are congruent with the congregation's functions in the community. Jackson Carroll, Carl Dudley and William McKinney (1986) suggest that a church congregation serves six functions for the larger community. These functions point to what a congregation does *best*, at least from the community's perspective:

1. A congregation draws community residents out of their isolation and differences into relationships that may become mutually supportive. One young mother of two children, describing a family crisis when her husband was seriously ill but trying to continue working every day, said, "We have no social life except for our church. But church folks have been so good to ask after us, to pray for us, and to do what they can to help. I just hope I get the chance to give back some of the caring I've received."

2. A congregation provides programs that promote community solidarity and continuity. Although congregations often provide these services on their own, they also join with other congregations in their denomination or ecumenically in their community to serve this function.

An urban community was devastated by a tornado. Local churches joined forces in responding to the critical physical needs of their members and other residents. An ecumenical community ministry was born, with a part-time director and a staff funded by contributing churches. The ministry has continued in the twenty years that have passed since that time, turning its attention to other pressing family needs, offering emergency financial and food assistance, counseling, adult and child daycare, meals for homebound senior citizens, after-school care for children, and other services. In addition, the community ministry has become a rallying point of community solidarity. It sponsors gatherings to discuss political issues that affect the community, often inviting elected officials to speak to residents. It sponsors social events and community festivals. It also organized and facilitated a community pride and beautification project that has altered the town's earlier assessment of itself as a declining community.

3. A congregation socializes children and newcomers. In some communities, the activities a congregation sponsors for children and adolescents become the focal point for a peer group, often the only peer group other than the one in school that can challenge the influence of gangs and informal adolescent groups.

Churches also provide a powerful means for newcomers to meet other community residents. And they allow families who are "newcomers" to a particular life experience—like the birth a child with special needs—to connect with others who share that experience.

4. *A congregation sustains persons in need.* Congregations address the whole range of personal and family needs, from financial and material support to emotional and physical caregiving. Many churches, or the community ministries in which they participate, offer short-term emergency assistance to families in crisis. These programs have a range of volunteers and paid staff members. Their screening and record-keeping systems range from a shoebox with handwritten index cards to sophisticated computer systems linked to those of other community agencies. But churches do not limit their financial and other assistance to these formal programs. Needs are often communicated through the social network, so that a child in the youth group who wants to go to camp but whose family does not have the money for the registration fee learns that a scholarship is available, given informally by someone who heard of the need. A teenager in conflict with his single mother, who believes he is out of control and wants to place him in a residential care program, is offered a temporary home with a church family while the mother and teen sort out their relationship under the guidance of a professional counselor.

5. *A congregation provides rites of passage marking significant life transitions.* Even nonmembers often seek out the church for weddings and funerals. Churches that do not practice infant baptism have found other ways to celebrate the addition of family members, such as baby dedication or parent dedication services. Some churches have developed rituals for adoption, divorce, young persons leaving home, children returning from foster care, and other transitions, both common and unusual, that families face.

6. *A congregation both supports and challenges community values and institutions.* Sermons and Sunday-school discussions can address current issues in light of Christian teachings and beliefs. Churches also mediate between the private lives of individuals and families and the large social institutions of a community, thus protecting people from having to deal with these institutions alone. The church is one of the few institutions that can serve in this way. For example, pastors and their churches have been known to take on industries that were creating unsafe working conditions or school boards that were not providing equal education for all children.

In fulfilling these functions, congregations often are able to touch the lives of children and their families who are not accessible to other family services in the community. For example, a congregational support group for families with children with special needs might be much more appealing to many families than a similar program provided through a counseling center or a public agency.

Choose ministries that involve members. From the community's perspective, a congregation's particular contribution is the fact that it is itself a community. In that role it offers informal support networks and caregiving, informal and formal help in crisis, justice advocacy for all (with special attention to less powerful community members), and social and spiritual sustenance for daily living. Interestingly, these gifts in many ways delineate the mission of a congregation derived from biblical and historical truths. Above all, the fact that congregations are communities points to the need to emphasize ministries that use and build on interpersonal relationships that support and sustain and that strengthen informal resources whenever possible. Professional services cannot substitute for community and friendship.

In planning a ministry with families that have children with learning disabilities, a congregation's "best" choice would be doing whatever needs to be done to integrate these families into the life of the congregation. With this foundation in place, the ministry can then offer specialized programs and services such as support groups and retreats targeting these families' particular needs. As much as possible, the groups and retreats can be led by families themselves, perhaps with professional consultation.

Such an approach not only cares for parents and their children but also challenges and supports members of the congregation to grow spiritually by making a place for these families. It also challenges and supports congregational families to use their own gifts to reach out to families in the community. In other words, both prongs—the target families and the spiritual growth of the congregation—receive attention.

Choose professional ministries that grow out of the community ministries of the congregation. At times a congregation chooses to provide professional services. For example, because of its heart for families with special-needs children, a church may decide to support financially a community school for children with profound developmental disabilities. Or it may provide scholarships for counseling for families struggling with the ramifications of parenting a child with special needs. Or a large congregation may hire a professional staff member to lead the congregation in these ministries.

The decision to use the congregation's financial resources to provide professional services, whether inside or outside the congregation, grows out of the informal and integrative ministries that have already been put in place. Professional ministries are not the first response but a response that grows out of the deepening commitment of the congregation.

Choose ministries at the level of change for which the congregation is ready. In essence, planning family ministry means planning congregational change. Lyle Schaller suggests that there are three levels of change. First-level changes usually are a continuation of what the congregation has been or done in the past, perhaps with some minor modifications. This often means continuing to do what the congregation has been doing, only better (Schaller 1997). For example, a congregation whose Sunday-school curriculum is organized both by age levels and by life situations (sixth-grade class, single adult class, young parents class, middle-aged couples class and so on) might begin ministry with families with children with special needs by simply adding a class with trained teachers to teach children with disabilities.

Second-level changes involve some basic change in direction for the congregation, although they are modest in scale. Change takes place incrementally. Ideally this system of "change by addition" will not disrupt the ongoing current program or schedule. For example, the new class for children with developmental disabilities and their teachers begin to join the age-level class for part of the Sunday-school hour each week. Over time the collaboration is increased, so that *all* the teachers gain skills in leading all the children, and children gain knowledge of and comfort with one another.

Third-level changes represent radical departures from the status quo. Schaller suggests that decisions such as relocating the church to a different area of the city, replacing traditional music in worship with contemporary and changing pastors are third-level changes (Schaller 1997). This level of change is best approached with time and care to bring everyone along together, as much as possible.

For example, as a first step, bringing children with developmental disabilities into the worship service, if it is a very formal, performance-oriented service, is probably not fair to the children, their families or the congregation. After learning to love these children and value their participation, the congregation may be led to change its worship style to be much less formal and more participatory, with room for a variety of levels of participation—worship in which members with diverse gifts and capabilities can feel wanted and included. Third-level change has taken place—over time.

These levels of change are directly related to the depth of commitment the congregation is making to ministry. One-time ministry projects require little or no ongoing commitment and *no significant change*. Nevertheless, such projects are wonderful ways for a congregation to gain experiences that can be foundational in developing more significant ministries. Service-learning projects, for example, are useful experiences for the congregation that may lead to change. Providing a vacation Bible school class for children with special learning needs, or hosting a Special Olympics Saturday, would be such an activity. Awareness is raised. New interpersonal skills are developed. Relationships are formed. These are foundational in ongoing ministry commitments.

First-level changes are often short-term projects that have immediate, visible impact. The congregation may offer a four-week seminar for teens and adults interested in learning about caring for children with significant disabilities so that they can offer quality childcare. First-level changes may also be ongoing projects that involve very limited commitment from the congregation, such as the "special" Sunday-school class. The congregation may know about these programs but not really be changed by them in any significant way. *Second- and third-level changes* usually involve ongoing projects and commitments of the congregation— the integration of children with developmental disabilities into age-level Sunday school, and the change in worship style.

Choose ministries that church leaders, especially the pastor, will support. The support of the pastor can make or break any program of the church. The pastor's direct involvement in the ministry, as well as words from the pulpit and in other spoken and written messages, gives ongoing congregational visibility and ownership. If ministry is based on the mission of the congregation, then it needs to be woven into the teaching and prayer life and congregational identity.

SOME CHANGE PRINCIPLES

Some congregations adapt easily and quickly to change; others struggle even to make changes they need to make to survive, much less to minister more effectively and profoundly to the needs of families. Obviously, the level of change you introduce with your family ministry plan will need to take into account the congregation's willingness and ability to change. Below are several thoughts about introducing and implementing change.

1. Don't try to convince people that change will be easy. Anyone who has tried to make as simple a personal life change as cutting back on cholesterol or exercising thirty minutes a day knows that even small changes come with difficulty. The same is certainly true for congregations. Change, no matter how small, will cost something. This cost needs to be identified and noted to the extent possible. People are more willing to make a change if they believe their leaders understand the full weight of its meaning. Jesus made it clear, for example, that becoming a Christian is not an easy change; it costs us our very lives (Mt 10:38; Mk 8:34; Lk 9:23).

2. Change occurs more effectively when it is supported by personal relationships than when it is carried out by rational decision-making processes alone. Most people need opportunity to try out new ideas and possibilities with others. We sort out our thoughts and feelings in conversation. We often need others to walk into a change with us, or at least to offer ongoing encouragement. In a congregation, we need not only to present plans for change but to give people opportunity to ask questions and respond to those presenting the change and to have conversation with each other about what is happening.

3. Change needs to be introduced in language that relates to people's experiences. Jesus was a master at putting invitations to change into appropriate language. He offered fishermen the opportunity to "fish for people" (Mt 4:19). He offered the woman at the well "living water" (Jn 4:10), the blind man sight (Mk 10:52), the crippled man the ability to walk (Jn 5:8). The change being proposed needs to relate to the concerns of the congregation. And because there are many different concerns within a congregation, the same message may need to be delivered in different ways.

4. We change more easily when others can show us the way. It helps to know how others have made a similar change, done a similar thing. Stories of the experiences of others communicate powerfully.

5. Change sometimes requires leaps of faith. The Israelites quickly learned that what would make common sense—gathering up extra manna to put away for a little insurance—was not what God had planned. They learned to trust day by day for enough (and no more) of what they needed to keep on journeying (Ex 16:15-30). Most of us are much more comfortable if we know where we are going to end up, if we have a little stored away "just in case." Faith means trusting that God will remember, day by day, to provide us what we need for the journey, even if we cannot see all the way.

6. Change can be "catalyzed," but the results cannot always be predicted or controlled. It is not always possible to know where our decisions and actions will lead; we operate with what we know about ourselves, our God and our world at this time. One of the great comforts of the Christian faith is that we are called to be faithful with what we have at the moment; we trust God for outcomes (Lk 16:10).

PLANNING TO EVALUATE

A plan for evaluation needs to be formulated before a ministry is launched, as a necessary component of initial planning. Ministry evaluation can draw on the extensive methodological foundations of program evaluation used in family resource programs. An introduction to program evaluation is beyond the scope of this book; there are a number of resources that can be particularly useful for those not familiar with methods for evaluating programs (Kagan, Powell, Weissbourd and Zigler 1987; Levine 1988; Littell 1986; Pooley and Littell 1986; Weiss and Jacobs 1988; Whitmore 1991). However, some elements of ministry evaluation deserve special mention.

The evaluation should be as extensive as (and no more extensive than) the assessment process and ministry it is assessing. As a rule of thumb, the extent of the evaluation should match the extent of the assessment the congregation conducted. Many times the methods themselves will also match. For example, if the ministry with families of children with developmental disabilities was developed based on interviews with three families in the congregation and with a counselor at the local school, then evaluating the effectiveness of a new Sunday-school class and a support group for parents might also use interviews with participants and with the school counselor. A training program for baby sitters and childcare workers who want to care for children with developmental disabilities may evaluate its effectiveness using a questionnaire or survey at the end of the program, and a satisfaction survey among parents who subsequently allowed these trained persons to care for their children. Six months or a year later, a brief follow-up interview with both parents and childcare providers, to find out how the training was helpful and what could make it more effective, would also be valuable.

In other words, evaluation does not have to be an extensive process. Done well, however, it provides critical information for the congregation in deciding what it can and ought to do next in ministry.

The evaluation should provide information the congregation needs for its continuing ministry. This is, in fact, the only reason to do evaluation—to learn what you need to know for the next step. There are six questions that the congregation needs to have answered.

1. Are we meeting our objectives? Basically this seeks to discover whether or not you are doing what you set out to do. If the objective was to integrate children with special needs into the Sunday-school program, to what extent has that occurred? How many children are participating? Are increasing numbers of families with children with special needs participating in Sunday school?

Of course, the question is not simply whether we are doing it but *how well* we are doing it. How do parents feel about the spiritual nurture and care their children are receiving? Do the children like coming to Sunday school? Why or why not? How competent do teachers caring for these children feel? What impact has this new responsibility had on their faith and beliefs? How do other children feel about the inclusion of children with developmental disabilities in their Sunday school? What have they learned about faith and community as a consequence?

Notice the array of persons that often need to be involved in assessing whether objectives have been met—the families themselves, other congregation members (the other children) who are affected by the ministry, and the leaders who have taken on the spiritual nurture of these children as a part of their ministry.

2. Are there better ways we could meet our objectives? Should we modify what we are doing, or should we do something else? Beyond "how well" objectives are being met is whether there is an even better way. For example, parents may deeply appreciate the inclusion of their children in the age-graded Sunday-school program but may, if asked, suggest that their children would benefit more from a class designed specifically for their needs. Or the opposite might happen; parents of children in a special class may wish that their child could be a part of the "mainstream" of Sunday school, at least part of the time. Or parents may wish their children could be around other adults as well as children, and suggest that they would love to be included with their children in a periodic cross-generational Sunday-school learning experience. Teachers and others in the congregation may have similarly diverse ideas about what could be done, based on what has been learned through the experiences of ministry.

3. What impact has the ministry had on those who are serving? What might have helped that impact to be more significant? A ministry's impact on the congregation is a critical point of evaluation. To what extent are those who are serving—in this case, Sunday-school teachers and children themselves—growing in faith and deepening their understandings of themselves, of church and of God as a consequence of the ministry? Are they receiving the support and care they need for this sometimes difficult ministry? How else could the congregation and its staff support and empower them for service?

4. *What impact has the ministry had on the congregation? What might have helped that impact to be more positive?* How have others not directly involved in the ministry been affected by it? Have church budget dollars been allocated to the ministry? If so, how do church leaders and members feel about this use of their resources? From their perspective, what have been the most positive outcomes of the ministry? What suggestions do they have?

5. *How have the realities that started us in this direction changed, either because of what we are doing or because of other causes?* If the ministry was launched based on what an assessment revealed about the congregation and community, what changes have taken place there? For example, when the ministry with families of children with special needs was launched, no other local congregation was providing accessible church programs for these families, and there were no support groups for them. In the ensuing period, perhaps as a consequence of this congregation's example, other congregations have begun trying to include these families. This change may signal a possible change in the ministry. For example, perhaps the churches would like to combine efforts to offer a church camp for children with special needs, or perhaps a family camp for these children and their families.

6. *What changes, if any, should we make in our ministry?* Based on the answers to these questions, the family ministry team or other leaders continue to guide the development of the congregation's ministry.

The evaluation should use methods that can be woven into and be a part of the ministry. Most congregations have little patience with or inclination to engage in elaborate evaluation processes. Instead evaluation should simply be a part of the ministry. There are three basic approaches to evaluation, which are in most respects the same as the approaches to assessment explored in chapter fifteen.

Program statistics and community indicators. Congregations are most familiar with keeping records of attendance in programs. How many children with developmental disabilities have been added to the Sunday-school rolls? How many baby sitters and childcare providers have been trained? How many families have used their services?

There may be statistics available in the community that also relate indirectly to the ministry of the church. Has the school counselor made any referrals to the congregation? If so, how many?

Surveys and questionnaires. Almost everyone has filled out a survey or questionnaire at some point about what they learned, what they like and don't like about a particular program, and suggestions they have for improvement. Surveys can be used with participants and providers of ministry, with congregational members and leaders, and with key informants in the community. Surveys need to be kept short, asking only for information that is necessary. Don't ask for names, and provide a way participants can see that you will not know who wrote what, such as a box in which they can drop them rather than handing them to you.

Interviews and focus groups with targets of ministry and with those involved in ministry and with the congregation. Virtually every congregational ministry evaluation should include interviewing—talking with—ministry participants, ministry providers and the congregation. The responses given in a ten-minute interview with a parent will provide much more depth than the answers written by that parent on an anonymous questionnaire; on the other hand, many folks are more likely to give criticism on an anonymous survey than in discussion with a church leader. Thus a combination of anonymous survey questions and conversation works best. The value of interviews and focus groups is gleaning the stories of what has happened in people's lives, both the positive and the not-so-positive, as a result of the ministry. As important as program statistics are, it is the stories that share the heart of the ministry and that speak to the heart of the congregation's members, motivating them to continue or make changes in what they are doing to care for families.

Chapter 17

Congregational Life as Family Ministry

F AMILY MINISTRY CAN TAKE MANY FORMS. BECAUSE IT IS A PERSPEC-
tive on everything a congregation does, it can include everything from making
worship a family event to modifying how the church conducts its business meetings. This chapter describes some of the ways family ministry as a perspective can
reshape congregation life—its worship, its Christian education, it business, and
its missions and ministries.[1]

One of the most significant ways to help faith-families form and to undergird
existing family relationships in a community of faith is to encourage persons in
the same family and persons of different generations and life situations to participate in community life together, benefit from each other's gifts and care for each
other's needs. Family and cross-generational groupings are ideal for what we are
trying to accomplish in community life—caring for one another, ministering to
others, worshiping God. Both children and adults learn best about God's love by
being loved by God's people, about being a child of God by belonging in a faith-
family, about worship by worshiping with all God's people, about ministry by

---

[1]Some of the ideas in this chapter were previously published in Diana Garland, 1996, What is family
ministry? *Christian Century* 113, no. 33: 1100-1101.

serving in partnership with others.

There are times, of course, that age-graded, specialized groups work best for accomplishing particular objectives. But these peer groups need to be balanced by groups that bring together persons of different ages and life situations and that allow families to participate in congregational life together. Unlike the early Christian families, for whom church was for the most part an extension of family life, too many families today experience church as something that pulls the family in different directions. They may drive to church together but then not see one another again until the drive home. Yet worship, Christian education, Christian care, administration and ministry all lend themselves to family groups.

WORSHIP

Sometimes services of worship become so oriented toward the quality of performance—beautiful music, flawless liturgy, eloquent sermon—that the active participation of the congregation seems secondary. Yet everything leaders do in worship should guide participants in experiencing and giving glory to God. Worship therefore needs to engage everyone present, including the youngest of children, in active ways.

Instead, because children are sometimes bored by our worship and unable to sit quietly for an hour or more, many churches provide separate programming for children during worship, allowing parents and other adults to worship without being disturbed. Nevertheless, Jesus made it clear that welcoming children to participate with us is, in essence, welcoming God's presence with us: "Then he took a little child and put it among them; and taking it in his arms, he said to them, 'Whoever welcomes one such child in my name welcomes me, and whoever welcomes me welcomes not me but the one who sent me'" (Mk 9:36-37).

Children's presence in the church service represents the inclusion of *all* who want to worship, regardless of their ability to sit still or fully understand everything that we do together. More than that, however, their presence challenges us to *change our style of worship* so that everyone is a part. Worship should actively include the whole congregation. An active service encourages everyone to worship, and it also helps persons to recognize one another as members of the same community. For example, lay worship leaders, including children, youths, seniors and faith-family groups, can

☐ read Scripture, prayers or responsive readings

☐ write new words to traditional hymn melodies and teach them to the congregation

☐ create signs or banners, or arrange flowers and other objects from God's creation on a table in the sanctuary

☐ play a special part in the music—clapping hands, ringing bells

☐ use sign language as they sing

☐ play instruments (violin, recorder, etc.) along with piano and organ during hymns or during the prelude or postlude

☐ sing in a family choir composed of persons of all ages

☐ perform in a brief skit related to the Scripture reading

☐ greet persons at the door, be sure everyone has someone to sit with, and introduce visitors to members

☐ collect the offering

At Crescent Hill Baptist Church in Louisville, Kentucky, members are encouraged to bring bells on Easter—jingle bells, glass bells or whatever kind of bell they may have. Additional bells are available in baskets for those who forgot or are visiting. Every time the congregation sings "Alleluia!" everyone rings their bell in accompaniment. The sound is joyful noise. Everyone makes music; everyone has a part. Perhaps it seems like a long stretch from ringing Easter bells to strengthening family relationships, but those Easter bells are one small movement in the symphony of congregational identity and community. And strong communities nurture families.

There are many other ways to communicate inclusion and participation in worship. Weekly bulletins for younger children can explain the various worship activities, provide an outline of the sermon, ask questions that children can answer by listening, and include puzzles and games related to the worship theme. These worship aids give children an activity to do that relates to what they hear. Large-print bulletins for those with vision limitations and, in congregations that celebrate Communion by coming to the altar, delivery of the elements to those who cannot walk communicate inclusion.

During a baptismal service at First Baptist Church (NBC) in Waco, Texas, the choir leaves the loft in front of the baptistery, and the pastor invites the children to come up so they can see "up close" what is happening. Their curiosity is honored, and their rapt attention pulls adults in the congregation into the wonder of this event. The congregation participates through and with them. As persons come and go in the baptistery, the congregation sings a cappella "Wade in the water." What could be a "performance"—baptism—is instead a shared community activity of wonder, song and worship.

Prayers can name things that persons of all ages are concerned about or for which they are thankful. Instead of a children's sermon, which often simply uses children as an object lesson for adults and, at best, directs only a brief few moments of attention to children, the "adult" sermon can address all ages and invite participation through questions, stories and applications that relate to various age groups.

Whenever possible, interject joy into the worship of God's people—even laughter and fun. Children bring spontaneity, energy and often grins and chuckles into our midst. And when they permit themselves to, so do adults. One Easter at Crescent Hill Baptist Church, the very dignified interim pastor, an esteemed theology professor, brought a large Swiss cowbell to ring during the alleluias.

Being inclusive means being more flexible, being willing to let worship unfold and sometimes include the unexpected, and allowing God to work through persons of all ages and circumstances in the community. Practices that encourage children and youths to participate in worship also encourage greater participation and deeper worship among adults. Worship entails more than intellectual exercise. Adults too benefit from being encouraged to make concrete applications of the principles of our faith. They worship more deeply when they are included actively in the worship experience. Adults too can stay more focused in worship when there is variety that keeps their attention and encourages their participation.

It is appropriate and helpful for children to be separated from adults sometimes, just as parents and children in a family need time apart as well as together. Each congregation must find its own balance, built around the needs of persons of all ages. Being family oriented does not always mean keeping families together in clumps. Adolescents certainly may be much happier sitting with friends than with their parents. If the worship includes them, however, it is family oriented, encouraging the worship of families together in the same place, where they can see one another across the sanctuary and where they share experiences that can be talked over later. In my family interviews, I heard from many families that older children, youths and adults frequently talk in the car or over the Sunday meal about what they have all experienced together in worship.

CHRISTIAN EDUCATION

Faith is not cognitive knowledge—it is lived. We learn the knowledge and values and skills of Christian living—including family life—through a combination of hearing, conversing and experiencing. We need to *experience* the principles of Christian living as part of our discipleship training. That means we need to be educating whole families together. Intergenerational Christian education is vital to the ministry of the church because younger persons need to hear and learn from older persons (Deut 6:6-7) and older persons need to hear and learn from younger persons (Is 11:6).

Age-graded programming is limited in what it can do to help disciple Christians for faithful living in families. It is important—adult children of frail elderly parents need to be with peers to talk about the stresses and joys of their lives. But they also can learn and grow as Christians by being *with* elderly adults, even those who are not their own parents. Teens need a place to talk about their parents, but they need also to be *with their parents at church*, where in the safety of the church community they can learn to live patiently and lovingly with one another.

The fact that intergenerational learning is essential, however, does not mean that all programming should take place this way. There is value in traditional age groupings for some religious education. People of all ages learn certain things best from and with their peers. Personal and social issues and readiness for learning are different at different ages. Intergenerational educational experiences present a number of challenges to Christian educators. They take a lot of planning, and care needs to be taken that neither adults nor children dominate. It is difficult to address the wide range of knowledge, interests and motivations for learning.

Family-oriented Christian education is intergenerational, but there is more to it than that. It implies that at least some of the time we encourage families to participate in education together, as families and faith-families. Thus it does not simply throw the adults and the youth classes together; instead the youth class invites their parents and faith-parents to join them for educational experiences, or vice versa. It means providing a rocking-chair class so that parents of babies who have been in childcare all week can sit together with their babies for the Sunday-school hour, sharing the Bible lesson of the week while they rock and feed and play with their infants. For others, who desperately need the respite of an hour of Bible study with adults, it may mean having loving Sunday-school caregivers for young children.

In essence, family-oriented Christian education means studying the Bible in family groups and applying it to family life. It is a flexible approach to education that communicates sensitivity for family life experiences. The educational experience is built around and for family and faith-family relationships. In many respects, it takes what has been learned in congregations that use cell groups and home fellowships and applies it to the Christian education that takes place in the larger congregation. It develops the faith of families, not just the faith of individuals.

One of the best-known models of family-oriented Christian education is the family cluster, consisting of four or five families that meet weekly. Margaret Sawin developed clusters among Protestant congregations in the 1970s and is considered the founder of the "Family Cluster Movement" (Sawin 1979; Vance 1989). Participants are involved in a learning event designed for a cross-generational group, often with art materials or games, and then discuss their experience. Often the session is accompanied by a meal.

In another example, Elmbrook Church in Milwaukee coordinates forty-five "neighborhood home groups" spread over eight regions of the city and involving more than six hundred members. Each group is structured around a "core group" made up of two couples, or one couple and an individual. Other congregations that try this model might consider whether they want to make a marriage the core of the group; this depends on the congregation's understanding and definition of family. The coordinator of the groups describes the support of these groups:

> If you look at what happens in these groups, the family gets a lot of support in the sense that parents are finding resources . . . for dealing with the issues related to the family. At one level, we do programs and Bible studies that help parents with family problems: how to raise their kids, how to communicate and show love. And at a very informal level, you have a lot of support from others in the group. You may get a shoulder to cry on, some advice given from someone else who has been through the situation before, and, of course, people can pray for you (Wright 1995:274).

Many resources exist for thinking about and designing family-centered Christian education (D'Antonio 1995; Garland et al. 1995; Northrup and Bowan n.d.; Sawin 1979; Vance 1989; Vogt 1994; Wright 1995).

CHRISTIAN CARE

"Christian care" refers to the pastoral ministries carried out by church members: visiting the ill and the homebound, calling and caring for those in crisis or in life transitions, and welcoming people moving into the community. Some churches already use family groups to provide Christian care. Deacons take family members along on visits; parents and children are encouraged to take a Christmas gift basket to a homebound member together. It is also important to nurture faith-families by encouraging them to serve together. Children and youths benefit when loving adults in the congregation include them in visiting the homebound, celebrating the birth of babies, preparing food for families in crisis. Church leaders can pair up and each take a child or a youth on a visit to a church member who is in nursing care or homebound. Including children in Christian care ministry provides several benefits:

☐ Children feel valued and valuable as contributing members of the church community.

☐ Children learn to care for others and understand people and relationships better.

☐ Children and adults grow spiritually from serving.

☐ Adults learn to value the sensitive care children often bring.

☐ Adults recognize children's gifts, not just their needs.

☐ The adult and the child on the Christian care team develop a one-to-one relationship that may become significant to both of them.

Just as adults need help in learning to provide Christian care to people in the crisis of illness or the joy of a baby's birth, so do children. They need to be taught what is appropriate and how to communicate the concern and love they feel and represent on behalf of the church. Sometimes, of course, children should not be included. Situations of acute grief or crisis might frighten or overwhelm a child or require help beyond what a child can offer. In many more situations, however, those visited delight in and are helped by a child's presence.

There are other ways children can be included in the Christian care of the congregation. Even preschoolers can be involved in "disciple work." For example, one congregation's preschoolers, with their ministry partners, prepare and send letters to welcome newborns and adoptees into the congregation. The letters may well be the first a child ever receives. Because they are done in part by preschoolers, they contain more illustration than printed messages. One such letter to a new baby said, "You're going to like it here. These are the things we like." It contained drawings and cut-out magazine pictures of people, pizza, roses and animals.

Older children can prepare story tapes for sick children. Children select one or more of their outgrown picture storybooks and read the text onto an audiotape, using a bell to signal when to turn the page. Older children and young teens enjoy this activity, especially adding sound effects to go with the story. Homemade story tapes can be given to a younger child in the church or community, a "faith-sibling," as a way of weaving family relationships. Whenever possible, it helps for this care to be personal, so that the older child knows the younger and vice versa, rather than simply giving in some anonymous way.

Of course, child-adult relationships are not the only ones that are strengthened as Christian care is offered to and with one another. A cherished memory for me is the mid-December day after my mother-in-law died, when my two faith-sisters, Alice and Margaret, showed up at my front door, aprons already on under their coats. They knew out-of-town relatives were coming for the funeral, it was just days before Christmas, and we were exhausted from the long illness and final days of the hospital vigil. They ordered me out of the kitchen and simply took over the house and the children.

We had been close friends for several years, helping each other fill and unload moving trucks at various times, serving as godparents for each other's children, carrying food and advice from house to house and meeting frequently at fast-food restaurants. That December caregiving, however, showed me that we were truly sisters. Their commandeering of my kitchen and my household for three days, an act of "entitlement"—and responsibility that in our culture is reserved for mothers, daughters and sisters—was met with deep appreciation, not with the edge of resentment that I would have undoubtedly felt if they had overstepped role expectations. I never sent them a thank-you note; sisters in our culture do not normally use such formal expressions with each other.

ADMINISTRATION

Families can also participate as groups in the business of being church. Families can be asked to serve together on some committees. And children and youths can be included in the business meetings of the congregation.

Including children in the decisions and business of the church is probably the greatest challenge to family-oriented administration, but the challenge they present is also probably the most significant gift they offer to our shared work. Including them means we must do our work a little differently, less like a business and more like a community or family. Unfortunately, many parents consult and involve their children far more in family decisions than the church involves its children in church decisions.

Obviously, children need to be included in stages as they are developmentally ready. Preschoolers and young school-age children may be present for church committee meetings, but usually only because their parents serve on the committee. Even so, they can be included in meaningful ways in the committee's work, as members engage in projects or talk about the life of the church. A young child may be asked to draw a picture of the aspect of the church life the committee is addressing. The picture can be used on a poster or in the church newsletter to communicate the work of the committee to the rest of the church body.

Older school-age children and teens can take active roles as committee members, particularly on committees whose work directly affects them. They can help plan for the future as well as the present. Sometimes they can participate with older family members, and sometimes their participation provides opportunities for new and significant relationships to form with other adults.

Before including families with children—or children as individuals—on committees, take time with adult members to discuss the reasons children need to be included in the administration of the church. Talk over questions and concerns about what including children in the business of the church might mean. Help committee members, particularly those who may be uncomfortable working with children, learn how they can listen to and talk with children. Determine the ages of children and teens who could be expected to participate.

As a committee plans to include children in its work, some of the following suggestions may be helpful in working with children.

□ Plan a slower pace, with careful, concrete explanations. Suggest the following as a watchword for your work: "I will lead on slowly . . . according to the pace of the children" (Gen 33:14).

□ Listen to children and youth, and with your own attention and recognition, sensitize other committee members to the contributions of children.

□ Find ways to use at least a part of children's suggestions.

☐ Use games to learn one another's names, to learn more about one another, to generate ideas for the committee's work, and to break meetings into segments of thirty minutes or less.

☐ Plan some hands-on activities related to what the committee is doing (for example, the worship committee can make a banner or write a responsive reading; the social ministries committee can make an exhibit or poster about community opportunities for service; the building and grounds committee can plant a tree or paint nursery furniture together). Talk about the work of the committee while you *do* what the committee is all about.

☐ Use small working groups to avoid long committee meetings.

☐ Encourage children to make drawings or in other ways provide reports to the church community about the work of the committee that can be included in the church newsletter or bulletin.

☐ Sing together to begin or end meetings.

☐ Meet early in the evening, perhaps over a potluck or fast-food meal, to avoid conflict with bedtimes.

☐ Meet more often and for shorter periods.

☐ Be as sensitive to children's heavy homework nights and soccer team schedules as you are to adults' conflicting responsibilities when you choose meeting times.

These suggestions are not for children only; they will help adults become more active, creative committee members. For example, when children show signs of fatigue or boredom during a meeting, it may be a signal that the adults also would work more creatively if the meeting were adjourned or the discussion were continued over a shared activity.

Children can also help with other work in the church community—serving at a church meal or a reception, participating in work parties to repair hymnals or plant shrubbery. Children who are assigned age-appropriate chores at home have healthier self-esteem, particularly if those chores are done alongside adult members of the family and contribute to the family's life. The same is true of children who contribute to their church community. When they serve alongside adults, they have opportunities to deepen relationships and feel significant to the congregation. When those adults are family members, families are strengthened by serving together. When those adults are friends and mentors, networks of community support—so important both for children and for families—are woven more strongly. Either way, such service accomplishes much more than the completion of whatever task is the focus.

MINISTRY

Earlier chapters have talked about the importance mission and ministry need to have in the life of families in the congregation. For many families this is by no means a new concept. A research study published in 1994 reported that in more than one-third of American households (36 percent), volunteering together is part of family life. The most common partnership (60 percent) consists of a husband and wife, although in 22 percent of households, the adults volunteer with one or more of their own children who are younger than age twelve, and 17 percent with one or more of their children who are teens. The most broadly supported activities are helping older people (60 percent), children or youth programs (58 percent) and church or religious programs (57 percent). Nearly half of the families assist in sports or school programs (49 percent), and significant numbers are involved in environmental programs (31 percent) or aid to the homeless (25 percent). Family volunteering tends to become a tradition. Eighty percent of the volunteers had been serving with another family member for three years or more. Most frequently the decision to involve a family in community service comes from adults—30 percent say another adult became involved and got him or her involved, 27 percent say they themselves were the initiator. Among adults, however, 14 percent said that a child became involved and got him or her involved as well (George H. Gallup International Institute 1994).

Given the relative commonness of this feature of family life, it is surprising that more congregations have not focused specifically on how they can support and even collaborate with families in ministry and missions. Families that are already engaged in serving may need to relate what they are doing to their faith. Families that are so stressed by life experiences or absorbed in daily maintenance that they are doing little beyond caring for one another may need to be gently encouraged to reach beyond themselves, even if in limited ways. Below are some principles that can help in equipping, encouraging and sustaining families in ministry.

The connections between ministry and Christian knowledge and faith are not always immediately apparent. Help families talk about and explore the meaning of what they do. Families are often involved in ministry and service, but they may not have a way to talk about it. For example, I interviewed a married couple in their thirties with two young children. They mentioned several things they do as a family that I would consider "ministry": they have been in a parent-to-parent mentoring program with a younger family living in poverty; they volunteer with

Meals on Wheels once a week; he is a hunter and frequently gives meat to several poorer families in their community. One of the questions in my interview protocol is "Tell me a biblical character that you like a lot." The woman responded:

> I'd say the Good Samaritan because that is so typical of me; I always want to try to help someone if I see them hurting or down or whatever. And when there are people I can't help, I always feel guilty. I don't think I help so much because of my faith. I think I help because I feel like I've been so lucky and there have been people who have been so unlucky. And I guess it goes back to that I feel like God has blessed me. I don't know why he hasn't blessed them, but I feel like he calls on me to share my blessings with other people, so maybe it does come back to faith. But a lot of it's just guilt too.

Somehow her family's service both is and is not an expression of faith. Clearly, most people act sometimes for reasons they are not entirely able to put into words, or perhaps their reasons are so complex and the meanings so deep that they defy delineation. This couple went on to say that they had never talked about these kinds of things before or discussed why they do the things they do for others.

One of the values of family-oriented Christian education is that Bible study can be related by family members directly to their lives. They have opportunity, language and encouragement to discuss their faith and ministry in the sacred space of the congregation, when such conversation might never take place at home. The structured, sanctioned opportunity supplied by a church program can be a powerful catalyst for family conversation. Over and over, families I interviewed told me they had never talked about their faith together before, but they immensely enjoyed the interview.

Help families pray together about their mission and ministry. Many families have not learned to pray together at home; they need to learn how to pray together at church, and to be prayed for as a family on mission by others in their small group or even in the larger congregation.

Encourage families to share their stories with one another. Many families benefit by talking about their experiences and hearing the experiences of other families as they attempt to live their faith in daily life and in their community. As they talk, help them to connect what they have experienced with the great stories and themes of Christian faith. Ask questions and encourage observation. Encourage families to keep journals and take turns being the family "scribe." Consider sending a church leader to videotape various families in ministry and share it as a celebration of their work and an encouragement to others.

Teach families to celebrate either at the end of a time-limited project or along the way in an ongoing project. Celebrate commitment and perseverance, not just ministry effectiveness. Teach families to play as a part of the ministry. A stop for ice cream after visiting a faith-grandma in the nursing home or planting shrubs at church can serve as an important culmination and celebration of the work done together.

Recognize that families' ministries develop over time. In the beginning, allow the process to develop as families minister, play and grow together. Family ministry involvement does not necessarily follow a three-year plan. Allow involvement to evolve. Be ready, like the parent of a young child, to respond to "teachable moments" rather than constructing an elaborate curriculum. Listen and be sensitive to families' needs, gifts, challenges and sense of calling.

If you are involving families in a church-sponsored project, know when to "naturalize" what you are doing, expand it to another level or simply bring it to a close. There are times to begin things and times to bring them to a close. It may be that what begins as a church-sponsored project "naturalizes." That is, the formal support and structure of professional leaders is no longer needed; the informal network of families and community is enough. For example, a structured time for families to visit "adopted" grandparents in a nursing home may over time develop into relationships that are pursued outside planned visitation times. A skillful leader begins such a project with enthusiasm and helpful direction but, over time, encourages families to adapt the project according to their own ways of doing things and the needs to which they are responding. The leader may continue to provide healthy doses of encouragement and support, but this becomes much less formal.

Whenever possible, focus congregational efforts on supporting and deepening the ministries of individuals and families rather than reshaping them as congregational projects. Too often when we try to involve people in congregational ministry, we actually unravel their connections to social networks in which God has placed them. For example, an elderly woman may make frequent morning visits to several lifetime friends and community acquaintances who are now in nursing care. It would be ridiculous to encourage her instead to visit people she does not know as a part of the congregation's visitation program once a week on Thursday night.

Instead she can be encouraged to share with the congregation ways they can support her and those she visits. Much of what we do should support the places families already have in the neighborhood and community.

Call out the gifts and capabilities in families, and emphasize ways that they can connect personally with others and with God's created world. Ministries with particular others who are either known or will be known are preferable to ministries for anonymous others. Of course, this is not always possible. There is certainly a place in family life for giving money to serve persons they will never see or know. But financial giving means more if persons are also involved in ministry with persons they *do* know, rather than as a substitute for personal involvement. In the same way, a family picking up litter in a park together as a way of caring for God's created world is a helpful foundation for giving money to organizations who advocate for protection of the environment. Giving money is important, but it does not deepen faith and sense of calling as a family unless rooted also in personal action.

Help families to plan realistically. Some families jump into a new project with both feet but soon find they cannot sustain that level of activity. It is better to start with limited efforts than to experience a sense of failure. In the same way, emphasize that they do what they do because they are called by God to be faithful, not because they can single-handedly change the world. Often recipients of ministry are not as grateful as the ministers wish they were or do not make the life-changing decisions ministers think they should make. People still throw trash in the park a family has carefully cleaned up. Help families keep focused on why they serve, which is not just to get other people to change or to make the world a better place. Those are important and hoped-for outcomes of ministry, but ministry is primarily motivated by the desire to be faithful to live as Christ commands.

Continue to provide families with support even once their efforts seem to be self-sustaining. When a church leader asks how a ministry is going or offers words of appreciation and encouragement, it goes far to sustain the ministry. Finding and sharing resources that help families in their efforts communicate the importance of what they do. Resources include not only tangible supports (garden tools for families caring for a nearby park, use of the church van for families taking community children on an outing) but also information and encouragement (articles clipped out of newspapers or journals that relate to what a family is doing).

Families need a community of support among people who are trying to live out their own understanding of the gospel in visible commitments to ministry and social justice. As they tell stories of their work, of successes and disappointments and unanticipated learning, they move forward in their own spiritual journey and become more effective and sensitive caregivers. Alice Evans calls this process "transformative education" (Evans, Evans and Kennedy 1987).

Recognition and appreciation should be expressed in ways appropriate to the service. Churches typically recognize volunteers who fill organizational positions (deacons, Sunday-school teachers) by publishing their names in the church newsletter or having them stand in a meeting to receive words of appreciation. Sometimes families may be deeply touched by such formal recognition or by a handwritten note from the pastor or by a small symbolic gift. All of these can be called "tokens of appreciation," indicating that the family did not undertake the work in order to be praised by others. Such expressions also encourage others to consider their own calling.

At other times a family may be deeply embarrassed by public recognition. In these cases the privately spoken or written word communicates much more support.

Recognition obviously also needs to be sensitive to the situation. For example, the coach of a girls' softball team learned that one of the girls on his team lost her father to AIDS two years earlier. She seems to crave the coach's attention. After talking it over with his daughter, his wife and the girl's mother, he has often included this child in family outings, including a vacation trip. The inclusion has always been low-key, "because my daughter enjoys having another girl along." One would hardly mention from the pulpit this man's ministry of providing a needy child with a father figure. But a note from the pastor with a clipped article describing research that demonstrates the value of men in the lives of children communicates the significance of what he is doing. Writing a note to the coach's daughter, who is sharing her dad with others, also expresses appreciation for *her* ministry.

CONCLUSIONS

The heart of family ministry is living our life as a congregation such that we develop and nurture families and faith-families as they care for one another and minister in their community and world. In some ways this seems a simple way to do family ministry. Simplicity, however, is sometimes most difficult to achieve. It is often easier to add complexity—a family life emphasis for a month—than to consider how a congregation's style and processes of worship have an impact on family relationships.

Of course, a family ministry perspective and family ministry programming are not exclusive approaches to family ministry; they instead interact with each other. As a congregation takes a family perspective in its worship, Christian care, business and ministry, it identifies particular needs in its own families and in the families in the surrounding community. The following chapter explores some of the programmatic responses congregations are making and can make to these needs.

Chapter 18

Family Support Programs

THERE ARE MANY DIFFERENT PROGRAMS AND SERVICES THROUGH which congregations are helping to create new family relationships within the faith community, strengthening the faithful living of Christian families, and undergirding families as they reach out in ministry to the larger community. This chapter will examine two kinds of family support programs: programs that themselves provide resources to families, and programs that advocate for broader cultural supports for family life.

FAMILY RESOURCE PROGRAMS

Family resource programs are, as their name says, programs that provide resources—emotional support, information and practical help—to families. Many programs target families that are experiencing particular stressors— poverty, joblessness, poor health, young children. In many ways, family

---

[1]Some of the ideas in this chapter were previously published in Garland 1994a and Garland 1996.

resource programs offer many of the social supports that were once provided by a network of stable, extended families within a community (Zigler 1994). Bernice Weissbourd, one of the founders of what has been called the "family resource program movement," traces the roots of the movement to the Settlement House Movement in social work in the early 1900s (Weissbourd 1994). This movement gained major impetus from Urie Bronfenbrenner's groundbreaking research, which defined the significant interrelationship of child, family, community and the larger society in the development of children (Bronfenbrenner 1979).

As a consequence, many family resource programs have developed in organizations providing educational and health services to families of young children—schools, daycare centers, public libraries and churches (often those with daycare programs). Clearly, however, the programmatic focus on resources families need for strength and health apply more broadly than to the families of young children. Family resource programs build on four premises:

1. All families have strengths that are particular to their cultural background, beliefs and current situation.

2. Failures of a family or individual family member to handle life situations competently are, at the root, traceable to some failure of social systems and institutions. Families are doing the best they can, and their problems point to a lack of needed community resources and support.

3. The best care of families focuses and builds on their strengths and resources rather than perceiving them "as being 'broken' and needing to be 'fixed.' "

4. The goal of family services must be viewed "not as 'doing' for people" but rather as strengthening the functioning of families to help them become less dependent upon professionals for help" (Dunst 1995:2223).

Obviously, these premises fit the community-building focus and strengths perspective of family ministry. Of course some families do need professional services; sometimes families and people experience problems for reasons other than community deficits. Family resource programs therefore coordinate their work with specialized services for families that need them. Family support programs build on the premise that families benefit from having available a whole array of formal and informal community supports and resources.

In particular, families need to know and support one another. Therefore family resource programs emphasize programs and services for *groups* of families. All families have the capacity to support others as well as the need to receive support. For example, in a parent-to-parent program, *both* an older parent serving as a mentor and the younger parent receive as well as give. Support goes both ways. Family support programs are informal. They may be relatively unstructured times for people to drop in, such as a story hour in the church library or a Saturday-morning breakfast and play group for fathers and their preschoolers. The activity of a family resource program also is often dispersed; families and groups meet in one another's homes, or at a local playground, or at a fast-food restaurant. Flexibility is a key program aspect (Dunst 1995). The sections that follow describe some of the ways churches are providing family resource programs for their congregational and community families.

Activity and Drop-in Programs

Congregations can help strengthen and support families by encouraging them to spend time with other families at church. The church figuratively provides a "family room" where families and faith-families can gather. Sometimes this happens without any planning. Comfortable couches and chairs in a foyer may be filled with parents talking about their lives and their children—giving support to each other—while they wait for a children's program to dismiss. Senior adults gather early for the Wednesday-evening meal, just to visit. Encourage this kind of gathering by arranging comfortable furniture in ways that invite conversation.

In addition to these indirect ways congregations support family time, many programs more intentionally help people spend time with their families in the supportive environment of other congregational families.

Eating together. Meals prepared together in the church kitchen, brought in covered dishes from home, or catered and purchased by families all serve as opportunities to gather as families in community.

Celebrating and remembering. One congregation has a New Year's Eve fellowship at which individuals and families are invited to bring all their loose family snapshots for an evening of refreshments and organizing photos. Supplies are bought wholesale and made available at cost (albums, transparency pages, etc.), or people can bring their own. Children and youths love to look at the photos and remember, and can help with the task. A similar activity can take place at the end of the summer, in homes as well as the church hall. These occasions open up the possibility of families' sharing stories of their lives—just talking together in the ways that affirm family life and weave community.

Family chore party. People of all ages bring their sewing, mending and unpressed laundry for a time of repairing and ironing clothing. People can certainly do this at home, but a lot of conversation can take place when what might otherwise be onerous chores become an excuse to gather. Those who have ironing boards, irons and sewing machines bring them. Those with sewing and ironing skills teach those (both children and adults) who need a little tutoring. Some can offer to put together a pot of chili in the church kitchen and serve supper to the group in exchange for someone's doing their mending.

Playroom. A congregation can set up a family room at church for parents with small children. The room may have play centers with rotating learning activities geared to the developmental learning tasks of preschoolers (Louv 1994). Although a volunteer may supervise the room, parents stay with and play with their children—along with other parents and their children who drop in. Volunteers who supervise have knowledge about parenting and child development, perhaps themselves parents who can offer informal advice and support. The playroom can be open an hour or so on weekday mornings for unemployed and second-shift parents, one or two evenings a week, and Saturday mornings for noncustodial parents who need constructive activities to share with their children—and community support for their parental role.

Recreational Programs

Many churches make recreational and activity programs available to families and persons of all ages. For families with children there are after-school and weekend recreation, camps and retreats, clubs and organizations, and sports leagues. One church rents a large drive-in movie screen for summer evenings and shows movies on the church lawn. Families bring folding chairs and coolers and make an evening of it. Cross-generational sports, church picnics and the myriad ways the congregation is a community at play strengthen relationships and provide support to families.

Recreational programs and organizations that meet in the after-school hours and on weekends serve as important resources in the lives of all children and teenagers, but they are especially important for inner-city children growing up in the poorest and most violent communities. These programs provide significant buffering from surrounding risks. For example, Mark Katz quotes one gang member participating in such a program: "Kids can walk around trouble if there is some place to walk to, and someone to walk with" (Katz 1997:103). Church programs are especially important for many youngsters who have had negative experiences with school and agencies that offer "prevention" programs—such terms inadvertently label participants as possible problems (ibid.). Many young-sters who have had problems in school have no interest in spending more time there in after-school programs. Church programs can reach these youngsters simply because they do not call what they do "preventive" or "educational" but use terms like *club* or *hangout*.

It is not only youths that benefit from these programs. Volunteers involved in them have opportunity to develop significant faith-family relationships with chil-dren. And at another level, recreational programs open to all ages (such as sports leagues) give adults opportunity to participate as families in wholesome recre-ation that builds positive family memories and develops relationships with others in the community.

Retreats and Camps

Retreats and camps are popular and powerful ways to support families. Marriage enrichment retreats are annual events for many congregations. One church pas-tor takes all the couples in his congregation on a two-day retreat—Friday and Saturday—each fall. Members plan ahead, and many are able to arrange not to work these days. Others come and go as work schedules demand; the retreat center is only an hour away from the church building. The retreat balances Bible study, worship and teaching on family life issues with recreation and time to sit in rockers on the front porch of the lodge or hike through the woods.

Some congregations join forces with others for marriage and family retreats. Some denominations provide family retreats at convention centers and resorts on a regular basis all over the United States; congregations bring carloads and bus-loads of families for these experiences. Some congregations collaborate with oth-ers in their own region to offer retreats.

The Center for Youth Ministry Development has developed models of "self-care" retreats for parents and for "tired mothers." Time is set aside for medita-tion and prayer, and presentations focus on the importance of sustaining oneself as a parent—spiritually, physically, interpersonally, emotionally and intellectu-ally. The retreats try to make mothers feel pampered, offering massages, time alone and for journaling, time for naps, and time to worship together (Roberto 1995). Women's retreats and men's retreats give respite from family responsibili-ties and allow peers to strengthen and encourage one another in those responsi-bilities. Alternatively, these events may be cross-generational, such as a three-generational men's retreat for grandfathers, fathers and sons (Bowman 1993).

One congregation encourages families to organize their own camping outings. The church maintains a resource center of camping equipment that can be checked out. Other congregations organize a whole-church camping outing, reserving multiple sites for tents and trailers at a state park or another recreation area.

Clearly the variety of retreats and camps is limited only by a congregation's imagination. Many families and faith-families find that times away for recreation, learning and resting are high points in their lives together. Retreats and camps can also allow respite *from* family relationships and renewal of energy for the tasks of families—as in the retreat for tired mothers. One can imagine similar retreats for those who care for elderly family members, for parents of children with special needs, for mentors, for children of parents who suffer from mental illness.

Care Programs for Family Members

Most family resource programs are not a collection of unrelated programs but an array of integrated programs. Often these grow out of one major program. For example, many congregations offer daycare for dependent family members— childcare for preschoolers, after-school care for children, or care for adults with Alzheimer's disease and other forms of dementia. These programs are central in the life not only of the congregation but also of the families who are in and out of the church every day of the week. Congregations build family resource programs in and around these daycare programs. For example, those who care for persons with dementia often benefit greatly from information sessions, support groups and informal (and formal) counseling services.

Child and adult daycare. A study in the 1980s showed that churches are principal providers of daycare; one church in three houses such a program. At that time, churches housed at least one-third of the childcare programs in the United States; in 1986, 2.3 million children received daycare from the nation's churches (Freeman 1986). Since that time, the amount of childcare provided by congregations has undoubtedly increased.

However, the need for high-quality, affordable childcare remains acute. Almost everywhere in the country, childcare for a four-year-old costs more than the average cost of tuition at a public college. Two parents employed at minimum wage have to spend an average of more than 30 percent of their income to purchase childcare for two children (CDF Reports 1998). Congregations that have identified providing childcare and support for their families as a part of their mission are responding to the critical needs of families, particularly if they offer sliding-scale fees or scholarships for those in poverty, who have the hardest time finding good care for their children.

Similar needs exist for families who are caring for members with dementia. Middle-aged and older adults may be faced with the proverbial "rock and hard place" of either placing a parent or spouse in a nursing facility because they need twenty-four-hour care or quitting a job to stay home and give personal care for the family member. Both choices involve not only extraordinarily high financial costs but also high emotional costs. Adult daycare provides the family member with the stimulation of other adults' presence as well as programmed activities; it also allows the family to continue to provide care in the home and carry out other family and career responsibilities. Many of these adult daycare programs are located in churches or church-supported agencies.

Respite care. Not every church can offer full-service daycare for dependent family members. Some can offer respite care, however, either in the church facility or in the homes of families, as in the example in chapter sixteen of training baby sitters for children with developmental disabilities. Parents' Day Out and Parents' Night Out programs give respite to parents of young children. These programs are usually offered free or at a low cost one morning or one evening a week.

Telephone reassurance. "Reach out and touch," the advertising slogan for a large telephone company, symbolizes a primary way many family members care for one another. Adult children regularly call to check on elderly parents. Teens at college call home for sympathy when they are sick and for money when they are broke. Young parents call their mother or siblings when they are at their wits' end with small children.

Telephone support has also become a family resource program. Instead of "hotlines," telephone crisis intervention with professional counseling twenty-four hours a day, family resource programs set up "warmlines." Warmline volunteers talk with families that call for advice, or periodically place calls to check on persons who are isolated.

Some churches have developed telephone reassurance networks of latchkey children and senior citizens. The "phone friends" talk to each other each afternoon after school.

Another program has used a telephone warmline to support parents. Four churches in Austin, Texas, established the Parents' Warmline of Austin, a phone-in support, parenting information, referral and peer counseling service for parents. Volunteers answer the phone line either in the city crisis hotline office or by call-forwarding to their homes. The warmline was originally developed as the churches' response to child abuse and neglect; almost 20 percent of the calls received through the phone line deal with these problems. Most typical are "the tearful calls from single parents who feel hopeless and exhausted, from mothers of pre-schoolers who feel isolated and trapped, and from parents of 2-year-olds or teenagers who feel that yesterday's delight of their lives has suddenly turned into an uncontrollable enemy." The most commonly sought referral is a parent support group or parent-child play group. Less common but more serious are the calls from angry, panicky or grimly controlled parents, such as the twenty-five-year-old mother of five who said without emotion, "Where can I find a cheap baby sitter right now? I can't stay around these kids another minute. I don't need help, I don't want to talk, I've just got to escape" (Johns 1988:9).

Care for families of the incarcerated. Some congregations offer friendship, transportation, emotional support, links with other resources, and advocacy to families of incarcerated parents and youths (Adalist-Estrin 1994; Bayse, Allgood and Van Wyk 1991; Beckerman 1994; Carlson and Cervera 1991; Ferguson 1992; Hairston and Lockett 1987). Such support can be particularly critical for dependent children whose mothers are imprisoned. Churches who have been involved in providing worship services and visiting in jails and prisons often welcome consultation designed to extend their ministry to the families outside.

Family Networks and Support Groups

Families dealing with difficult life circumstances often gain important support, locate needed information or learn new skills simply in talking with other families that face similar challenges. For example, parents of emotionally disturbed, physically ill and developmentally handicapped children often value and nurture networks with one another. In some cases such a network of support, coupled with family counseling and respite care as needed, enables families to continue caregiving who would otherwise be forced to consider placing their children in a program outside the home (Lowe 1993).

Some support networks coalesce into groups. Support groups may also be created outright in response to a particular need. Support groups actually meet regularly, and everyone knows who the other members of the group are. Networks, on the other hand, may never actually meet and may have no real membership boundaries. Network members just meet for coffee, talk on the phone and connect others in an ever-expanding interpersonal web.

Support groups define themselves by the life situations members have in common: they are mothers whose children were killed by drivers under the influence of alcohol (Mothers Against Drunk Driving, or MADD); they are family members of persons with mental illness or a major disability; they are parents of teenagers; they are nursing mothers. Obviously, the formality of support groups differs widely, from national organizations such as MADD or AA to a group of mothers who get together for lunch once a week to talk about balancing career and motherhood. Whatever the level of formality, support group members are in charge of their group; these are not therapeutic groups run by a professional. Participants offer each other practical assistance, advice, a shoulder to cry on and shared laughter. Support groups are predicated on friendship, not on professional services.

Self-help groups offer those who feel isolated connection with others who can provide not only help but also affirmation and support. Group members serve as each other's models and mentors. They catch from one another the hope that problems can be coped with successfully. Support groups do not only deal with problems; they also help families prevent problems and face life challenges creatively.

A professional church leader may function as a resource for self-help groups, helping to initiate groups, serving as a consultant or occasional speaker, and linking new participants to appropriate groups. Often a church leader may serve as the catalyst for a self-help group but then becomes more and more peripheral as the group develops its own leadership (see Boukydis 1986).

Family Counseling
Some families need professional help for coping with life circumstances and stressors, and family resource programs need to have access to counseling services, whether within the congregation or in a trusted agency in the community. Don Hebbard calls counseling the "backstop" of family ministry (Hebbard 1995). A counselor to whom family ministry programs refer families should be licensed by the state and/or certified for practice by the appropriate professional organization as a social worker, psychologist, pastoral counselor or family therapist.

Professional practice in a church setting involves particular issues and concerns (Stedham 1989). Practice models need to be compatible not only with a Christian worldview but also with the church context of the client-professional relationship. Models that emphasize therapist neutrality or professional distance, or that depend on a professional mystique, may be not only inappropriate but impossible because of the less formal relationship that often exists between a church staff member and congregational or community members.

David Waters and Edith Lawrence's "competence" approach is a useful framework for clinical practice in a church setting, emphasizing the roll-up-your-sleeves, share-of-yourself partnership between therapist and client. They focus not on pathology but on vision—what does the client family really want? Or, in a church context, what is God's purpose for us in this? Waters and Lawrence talk about pathology and symptoms as misguided attempts at efficacy. People have a basic drive to be competent, to manage the world and "make it work," which is just as basic a drive as sex or aggression. One might think of this basic drive as the sense of purpose, the belief that God has a mission for each person and each family. The work of therapy is developing a vision (identifying God's purpose), encouraging the client family to take action, and beginning that action in the partnership of counseling (Waters and Lawrence 1993).

Adopt-a-Member and Befriending Programs

Some families benefit from having someone fill the role of an older family member or friend who gives advice, encouragement and informal instruction in family responsibilities. Concurrently, the person in the role of older relative or friend benefits from the mutual affection and care that can develop. One congregation makes sure that every elderly adult who is homebound has been "adopted" by a family in the church. Families visit and simply offer friendship.

One Methodist church in the Chicago area brings baskets of baby items to new mothers in the hospital who have been identified by the social services staff as high risk, such as single teenage parents. The baskets include coupons for one evening of in-home childcare by one of the women in the church, a monthly visit in which the church woman includes mother and baby in gamelike activities that support the baby's development, and on-loan toys for the new baby and mother to play with together.

Baptist Family and Children's Services in Columbia, Maryland, trains volunteers as "family advocates." The volunteers attend a three-hour session once a week for twelve weeks. In each session they learn and role-play new skills. The agency then pairs each family advocate with a troubled family that needs friendship, support and mentoring.

In a similar program in Texas, one volunteer regularly took an isolated and psychologically trapped young mother out for a chat at a nearby restaurant (Johns 1988:12). The most significant ingredient in effective support was the slow, non-specific process of relationship building. Mary Lee Johns also reports on a successful relationship between a volunteer team and a family consisting of a paraplegic and severely depressed father, a trouble-making six-year-old boy with learning disabilities stemming from a previously undiagnosed hearing loss, an exhausted and frustrated mother, and a nine-year-old boy whose behavior was beginning to reflect the family's crises:

> The team (with other church members) fixed up the house, arranged for physical therapy and day help for the father, found a hearing aid for the youngest and arranged to get him into special education, sent the children to camp (a pleasure for them and a respite for the parents), and supplied books and educational games for the youngsters. More important were the following activities: Volunteers played games with the children and took them for outings. The couples spent numerous weekend evenings playing cards or Scrabble. The women went window-shopping or lunched together. A special friend recorded the father's comments about being a paraplegic as a guide for other paraplegics. The father was helped to go to a ball game with the two boys. And hours were spent just talking about feelings, fears, hurts, hopes, and how to work through the family's many problems. Friendship and just-for-fun activities were reintroduced to this distressed family, enabling them to explore the world beyond their front door once again. (Johns 1988:12)

Teams participated in a fifteen-hour training program and consulted an hour each week with a professional program director hired by the council of churches in the metropolitan area.

Mentoring has become a particularly important service to provide to teens, and through them to their families. All teens need a trusted adult with whom they can talk in addition to their parents. Parents, after all, are parents, and other adults' opinions are valuable simply because they are outside the family. Youth leaders, Sunday-school teachers, grandparents and friends often become important in the lives of fortunate teens. As important as group activities and discussions are, special moments of sharing between an adult and a teen often come in the unprogrammed times—washing dishes at a retreat together, working together on a project or talking over a concern about a friend. In the best of circumstances, mentoring relationships develop naturally as adults and youths live and share in a community together.

One-on-one relationships with adults can be especially important for teens at risk for pregnancy, dropping out of school and drug abuse. These youths may not have significant adults other than their parents involved in their lives, however, and these relationships have to be developed more intentionally. Big Brothers and Big Sisters have been developing friendships between children and adult volunteers for many years. Schools, community centers and programs serving disadvantaged children and adolescents recognize how important adult-child friendships can be and are developing their own mentoring programs. The adult can be a friend and an informal tutor, someone a teenager can look up to and emulate.

"Mentoring" implies that one person serves as an example for the other, that the older and wiser person gives and the younger or novice person receives. A more appropriate term for family ministry is *befriending*. In biblical stories, God often chooses persons as guides who are full of flaws, perhaps, in fact, so that they will *not* be pointed to as exemplary. One example of an important adult-youth relationship in the Bible is Eli, the priest, raising Samuel. Clearly Eli's life was not exemplary; he did not encourage Samuel to follow his example but instead helped him to listen to God (1 Sam 3:1-19). Perhaps a more helpful concept for congregational programs than "mentor," therefore, is simply "friend." It frees and empowers both to receive as well as give, not to have the answers and sometimes to say, "Don't be like me; do better!"

Family resource programs that promote "befriending" for teens and others who can benefit from such a relationship begin by providing some structure for potential friends to become acquainted. Some mentoring programs for teens, for example, begin with overnight retreats or a recreation program. Or they pair adults and youths in community service projects. They focus on something besides the teenager's "neediness."

Befriending relationships do not have to match persons by race, gender or socioeconomic experiences; however, too much "social distance" can hamper relationship development and be too big a challenge. Some of the best modeling is gained from friends who have not necessarily had entirely successful lives but have endured struggles. Having survived difficulties is ground on which people can relate constructively to others who are struggling.

Whenever possible, allow persons in a befriending program to have some choice concerning who their partner will be. One program puts on a party inviting adults and youths. The kids then list three of the adults with whom they would like to be matched. Their choices are honored whenever possible (Walsh 1989).

Those who want to give of themselves in befriending programs often need some preparation for this role, and perhaps even a stint of training. The content of this preparation should include the personal skills required for befriending, as well as knowledge of the policies and expectations of the program. Effective befriending consists of four basic ingredients: listening, sharing of self, sensitivity and commitment.

First, an effective friend must listen and learn what the world looks like from the other's perspective. By listening and understanding, friends earn the right to share their own perspectives. Effective friends know how to give and take in communication, with an emphasis on listening.

Second, effective friends share themselves and their experiences rather than giving advice. A friend says, "This is who I am. This is what I have learned. I don't know if it will be useful to you or not; you will have to decide." Persons who need a friend, such as at-risk teenagers, often need an expanded view of the world, ways of connecting with the world, and the support to risk stepping into new opportunities. Friends give encouragement that can make all the difference: "Don't give up. Work hard. You've got so many gifts. Use them. There is no limit to what you can do." But this encouragement has to be based on a real knowledge of the one befriended. That means taking time to build a relationship. A friend can then say with feeling: "You can do what you decide to work for. Look how you brought that grade up in math." Without evidence (like knowing how she struggled with math), statements meant to be encouraging will sound empty and hollow. The one befriended will then be not only discouraged but also lonely—the friend has not understood how hopeless things seem.

A third requirement for effective befriending is respect for the other, including sensitivity as to when advice and instruction are and are not appropriate. For example, through a church program, my mother met two Chinese students who requested that she help them work on English skills. Her gentle correction of their English during conversation runs counter to what is normally comfortable in social discourse, but that was what was needed *and* mutually agreed upon. Friends need some kind of agreement before monkeying around in attempts to shape one another's social skills.

A fourth requirement is commitment. People—including at-risk teens—who most need friends are often not cute and cuddly. They may be challenging and distrustful. They may not keep appointments. An adult friend may spend a lot of energy just trying to make and keep contact. These youngsters' experiences with adults may have been too unpredictable for them to feel they can trust this new relationship. Whatever else, the adult friend must be dependable when nothing else seems to be.

Given the particular issues and challenges of befriending teens, the following guidelines can be helpful in developing a befriending program for youths and congregational members.

☐ Adult friends need to respect the parents' role and contact them before beginning a befriending relationship with the child. Parents should know what the program involves and with whom they can talk if they have concerns. Friends and parents both need to understand that friends are not trying to replace parents but reinforce what parents are already doing for their children. Parents should always be asked for permission to take their children on outings.

☐ Adult friends should plan to spend a minimum of a few hours every week with the child; nothing substitutes for spending consistent time together.

☐ The child should help drive the relationship, sharing in decisions about how to spend time together and what to talk about. Adult friends should not hurry conversation about "important" issues. They need the patience to build a relationship first and not to give up too soon. Children, especially those who have been knocked around by life, take time to learn to trust.

☐ Adult friends should respect a child's boundaries. Children and youths will have certain areas of their lives they do not want to talk about. Adults should respect their need for privacy. The adult should also be sensitive to how the child may feel about interpersonal differences. For example, the child may be embarrassed by the appearance of her home; if she wants to meet the adult friend at a fast-food restaurant instead, then that is the place to meet.

☐ The adult should look for opportunities to show a child a new image of himself, to give him opportunities to try new experiences, and to see what gifts and skills he can develop.

☐ Adult friends can let the child overhear positive comments about her and can directly remind her of her past achievements.

☐ Adults should take time to receive personal support from others. Befriending is hard work; adult friends need to encourage one another and learn from one another's experiences.

☐ Befriending programs need clear policies that protect both children and adults from accusations or actual inappropriate physical contact (e.g., Hammar 1995; Rifner 1997).

Basic Resources

Many families need help with basic resources. Food and clothing pantries are common family resource programs in congregations in or near poor neighborhoods. Some congregations help build family strengths in addition to responding to crises by developing food co-ops so that families can together buy food in bulk. One congregation has several community gardens. Families have assigned weeks for garden tending and then have the privilege of taking all the produce they can use.

Transportation is also a basic resource to which some families do not have access. A church in Little Rock, Arkansas, discovered in their community needs assessment that there were many agencies providing services for needy families but no reliable ways for them to get there. A church member donated a station wagon, the telephone company donated a mobile telephone unit, and a committee began looking for volunteers to serve on two-member teams consisting of a driver and rider. The church secretary agreed to make transportation appointments. The program LIFT (Laity Involved in Free Transportation) was born. Three days each week, church teams take residents of a shelter for abused women and their children to the doctor. Frequently they take pregnant teens to the clinic for prenatal care. People talk to one another while riding in an automobile, and friendships develop. The users of LIFT know that a church cares for them enough to be sure that their basic needs for medical care are met.

Enrichment Resources

Many churches have libraries that can take on new life as family resource centers. Some congregations print a list of titles that they would like to acquire, including prices, and encourage members to donate these to the church. The donor is given first opportunity to use what their donation has purchased. Churches do not need to duplicate, but they certainly can augment, what is available at a community's public library. Books, audiotapes and videotapes addressing family life issues, child development, health and spirituality in the home can be made available to the community through a church library.

Such a library requires someone knowledgeable regarding resources and families who can make it friendly and accessible to families. Some church libraries place a book cart in the church foyer before and after worship services, encouraging members to check books out and find additional resources in the library. Brief book reviews or listings of available resources in the church newsletter can encourage families to use the resource center (Roberto 1992; Sterner and Zukowski 1991).

Some churches make other family resources available for loan—sturdy educational toys, sports equipment, camping equipment, health aids (such as crutches in various sizes for children and adults who break bones or sprain ankles) or canners and other infrequently used cooking items. Some congregations even make vehicles available for loan to congregational families; the church van can be used for family cluster outings, or for a family daycare provider who wants to take children on a field trip.

Community Development Ministries

Some churches have identified their mission as the development of economic and social communities in which families can thrive.

Housing renovation and development. A number of churches have entered the housing industry in response to the loss of affordable and decent low-income housing in their communities. Third Shiloh Missionary Baptist Church in New Orleans is located near a public housing project that is home to eight thousand people. In 1988 drug traffickers set up crack houses across the street from the church; three times the church was burglarized. In response, the church took the funds it had been saving for a new building, along with some federal funds available for such endeavors, and bought the property across the street. On it they built ten new affordable apartments. The construction provided jobs for a number of people in a community where the unemployment rate is above 60 percent. The church then rented out the apartments and used the small profits to support tutoring and scholarship programs for community youth.

St. Paul Community Baptist Church in Brooklyn sponsors the Nehemiah Housing Project, which has provided hundreds of low-income families with homes, using funds from a variety of public and private sources (Billingsley 1992).

Immaculate Heart of Mary Catholic Church, located between two public housing projects, teamed up with a church agency, Catholic Charities, and obtained a $1.8 million grant from the U.S. Department of Housing and Urban Development to build and manage twenty-four apartments for the families of low-income senior citizens on land the church owns. The church established a nonprofit corporation to buy the land from the church and oversee the construction and housing management (Merk 1997).

Community safety. Some churches have declared war on drugs and crime in their communities in response to families' fears for their children's safety and future. Arsenio Hall, a late-night talk-show host, bought a crack house in Los Angeles in 1991 and donated it to his church, First African Methodist Episcopal Church, for its war against drugs. The house was turned into a youth center, and several other crack houses were put out of business by men of the church as part of regular church-sponsored neighborhood patrols. The patrols marched through the neighborhoods in groups of fifty to two hundred every weekend night, and as a consequence the neighborhood's crime rate has dropped 60 percent (Billingsley 1992).

Churches have also started businesses as a means to provide employment opportunities and stabilization, particularly in poor black communities. For example, Harvest Home Restaurant, sponsored by Bethany Baptist Church in Brooklyn, was built totally by contributions from church members and employs many church members (see also Garbarino and Kostelny 1994; Kretzmann and McKnight 1993; O'Hara 1996; Smith 1985; Tapia 1994).

FAMILY ADVOCACY

Community development ministries have broadened the focus of family ministry from supporting and caring for individuals to changing the community to be more supportive of family life. Some congregations involved in direct community development are also advocating broader social and cultural changes in behalf of families. "Advocacy is using love plus power to seek justice in society" (Bobo and Tom 1996:55). Congregations providing compassionate service to children and their families who are oppressed by intractable social problems such as poverty, poor education and unemployment find advocacy a logical outgrowth of their ministry.

In advocacy, the congregation uses its voice to speak in behalf of families when families are not being heard. An advocate is defined as one who pleads the cause of or intercedes for another, who is relatively powerless, with one who is relatively powerful. An advocate acts in others' behalf, to do for them what they cannot do for themselves. The range of issues that are the focus of family advocacy is wide and constantly changing. Advocacy is needed to address the needs of the poorest families in our communities, but sometimes middle-class families too are powerless by themselves to address problems such as community violence or workplace policies that make juggling family responsibilities difficult. The issues range from problems in the neighborhood and community and city to national and even international policies and decisions that have an effect on family life.

When faced with possibilities for action, groups within congregations often involve themselves willingly; they want to work in behalf of the needs of families. They may differ from each other politically and theologically, and the congregation's views may differ from those of other congregations in its denomination, but Christians can be brought together in their belief that support for strong families should be a priority.

Kimberly Bobo and Phil Tom report a project that developed advocacy ministries in thirty-two Illinois and Indiana congregations. By "advocacy ministries" they mean ministries that seek systemic solutions to problems, not simply individual solutions. For example, instead of establishing a tutoring ministry to help children who have trouble reading, advocacy takes on in some systemic fashion the school system's failure to teach children reading.

Bobo and Tom found that congregations that shy away from advocacy do so for at least five reasons:

1. They prefer to develop their ministries in terms of people they want to serve rather than issues or social problems. That is, they are focused on relationships with people rather than social institutions or problems.

2. Some congregations are out of touch with the community; they study the issues but do not include persons they want to serve in their attempt to address the issues.

3. They don't believe they can really make a difference.

4. They are uncomfortable discussing and using power.

5. They tend to be ignorant of biblical evidence of God's desire for justice.

Bobo and Tom conclude that the following principles can help congregations move to advocacy:

1. Seek to involve people directly affected by problems in the design and implementation of community services.

2. Design an extensive listening and discernment process to ensure that community problems are truly heard and understood.

3. Build in opportunities to help congregations reflect on their ministries.

4. Challenge Christians to understand and use their power.

5. Develop a long-term vision on a spiritual foundation (Bobo and Tom 1996).

Advocacy seeks to bring about some change; sometimes it is successful and sometimes it is not. An ethnographic study of successful child-advocacy efforts found that four ingredients were always present (Dicker 1990).

First, advocates must propose concrete solutions to the problems they take on. Simply railing against injustice does not bring about change. People need concrete suggestions about what they can do to make a difference. It is counterproductive to report statistics of child poverty, drug abuse, teen pregnancy and school failure without providing hope for change and avenues for action that promise to make a genuine difference. Each evening, television newscasts fill the homes of millions of Americans with stories of injustice, suffering and violence. People feel overwhelmed. Many shrug their shoulders in anger and frustration. They think: *How can we possibly respond to all that need?* Consequently, when the television is turned off, so is their sense of responsibility.

Problems are only the beginning point. In order to respond, people need to know that there are solutions. They need a sense not only of responsibility for suffering but also of *response-ability*. Effective advocacy moves from problem to solution; it shows people that they can make a difference. Nothing is better than a success story of real families being helped by a congregation's efforts.

Second, Sheryl Dicker's study of successful advocacy efforts found that they empowered families to make decisions affecting their lives. Proposed solutions to social problems need to be carefully thought through for both the negative and positive consequences they may have. No one can be more helpful in this process than those directly involved—the families themselves.

Even when others are giving voice to the needs of families, those giving voice need to consult with families. For example, many churches have taken on the challenge of providing affordable, high-quality childcare for children who need it. Nevertheless, parents need to have options about childcare so that they can make choices based on their children's needs. Some parents believe their children are better cared for if they can stay home and not work while their children are infants. How can we help parents who want to make this choice? Other parents need to have good choices for childcare that meets the needs of their children, whether an in-home baby sitter, a family daycare home or a childcare center.

Third, it helps to have partners inside the systems a congregation is seeking to change. Obviously, if one is advocating that a congregation become more inclusive of children in its worship and administration, it really helps to develop a partnership with the pastor, church staff members and other concerned church members. In the same way, find partners within community organizations and government policy-making systems that are the targets of a congregation's advocacy efforts. Most social workers, public school officials, government employees and policy-makers involved in social services care deeply about families. Many stay in difficult positions because they are trying to help in the face of enormous obstacles. Some are discouraged and frustrated, and a few lose sight of the motivation that called them into service in the first place. They need support just as much as the congregation needs their partnership in achieving the changes that are needed.

The community assessment can be a good time to nurture relationships with community leaders. If there is disagreement about some things, look for common ground where there can be mutual support. Common causes may lead to unlikely partnerships that can accomplish great things. For example, members of some denominational networks for child advocacy range across the spectrum of positions on the issue of abortion. Nevertheless, these networks are speaking in chorus on "pro-life" issues for children after birth— health care, adequate family income, hope-filled developmental and educational opportunities.

Finally, successful advocates use a variety of strategies over a prolonged period to achieve their goals (Dicker 1990). Strategies for bringing about change may include educating and involving church members, networking, writing and preaching about justice issues in the church, lobbying and writing to legislators. No one strategy is likely to be effective by itself.

Not all advocates have access to all these strategies, but they can partner with those who do. Advocates must be able to commit themselves to processes that sometimes take a long time, with repeated failures and disappointments, before change comes. Effective advocates keep dreaming, keep believing that what they stand for is right and that right will eventually prevail.

Most congregations and agencies should base their advocacy efforts in services to families and stay rooted in that service. The fire in the belly of advocates is fueled by knowing and caring for actual families, not simply tables of statistics about rising rates of teen pregnancy or divorce or child abuse. Firsthand experience arouses compassion and commitment; there is no substitute for it.

Congregations often wisely begin with low-profile issues and advocacy activities and proceed to higher-profile, more controversial issues and activities. After-school activity programs and tutoring for school-age children and teens are relatively low profile and noncontroversial. Writing to school board members advocating that an after-school program be housed in its facility is not likely to be particularly controversial either. Telling the same school board that the school ought to provide nursery care for infants and toddlers of teen parents who remain in school is more controversial. Doing so by picketing a school board meeting along with parents pushing their babies in strollers is even more likely to gain (or risk) a high and controversial profile for a church group among the general public, and perhaps more importantly, among church members who have been uninvolved—especially if advocates are using the name of the church.

Clearly, the group must seriously consider how appropriate the strategy is to its identity and preparation for an advocacy role. Compassion for families is nurtured through service programs. Congregational groups can then move from service to advocacy.

Inevitably, advocates face dark nights when they feel very small compared to the powers arrayed against them. The issues that confront families today are formidable. Congregations will not right all the wrongs that besiege families, nor do they have the power to transform society into the kingdom of God. They are called to be faithful, to be persistent in living justly and naming injustice, and to point others to the justice of God.

Chapter 19

Family Life
Education Programs

O NE OF THE MOST POPULAR FORMS OF FAMILY MINISTRY IN CON-
gregations is family life education. Family life education can be considered a category of family support programs, but it is also a primary goal for various kinds of
other family support programs. Directors of childcare centers may send home
leaflets that help parents understand the development of their children and how
families can facilitate that development, or they may offer a seminar on child discipline. Many church retreats combine recreation and worship with workshops
on communication and conflict management. The training of adults for befriending at-risk youths can be considered family life education.

Family life educational programs seek to provide families with knowledge, values and skills that will help members understand each other better and develop the
life patterns and processes that are associated with strong families (see chapter
eight) and with faithful family life (see chapters eleven to thirteen). Educational
programs may be offered for all kinds of families. For example, a seminar on understanding and handling anger and conflict would be pertinent to virtually every family and faith-family in a congregation or community. They may also be offered for
particular kinds of family structures and situations—divorce recovery and coparenting workshops, premarital seminars, workshops for adults with frail elderly parents.

Family life education can be offered in many formats. This chapter will look primarily at seminars, retreats and workshops specifically designed to address family issues. But family education can be infused in most of the other ways congregations structure their lives together, such as sermons and Bible study. Family life education can take place when audiotapes on relevant topics are made available for individuals and families to listen to in the car, or through television and video productions. Family life education is the major focus of a family resource center in a church library. This chapter cannot address the whole professional field of Christian education, but some of the most helpful principles for thinking about and designing congregation-based family life education programs will be summarized.

PLANNING FAMILY LIFE EDUCATION

Planning family life education programs begins with deciding what the objectives of the program are and designing the event itself, determining the format, and deciding the size of the group that is best suited to the program's objectives.

Objectives and Program Design

There are three interrelated domains of learning: (1) knowledge of facts and theories about family life, (2) values and attitudes, or what is important in family life, and (3) skills, or how people behave and interact to express what they know and value about family life. Most family life education needs to involve all three. For example, a workshop on anger and conflict in family life would include the following.

Knowledge. Families learn about different ways of handling anger and conflict. They may look at Scripture passages that address anger and conflict and derive a list of principles that can inform Christian living. The tools that most effectively teach new knowledge include reading material, presentations and lectures, and videotapes.

Values. The following values might be the focus of a family life education program on anger and conflict:

☐ Anger itself is good because it helps identify differences that need to be resolved.

☐ It is important that families learn to handle anger in ways that protect members from hurting one another and that encourage working together toward conflict resolution.

One can teach values most effectively by attaching new learning to a value already held. For example, exploration of a Scripture passage relevant to handling conflict ties values about anger and conflict to participants' values regarding the Bible and its teachings. Second, values are shaped by relationships with esteemed others who hold those values. For example, if an admired church leader advocates expressing anger in constructive ways and facing conflict together, participants are more likely to embrace those values. Finally, values are more likely to change if participants are able to talk them over with one another, reinforcing the importance of what they are learning and how it applies to their lives.

In summary, attitudes and values are likely to be successfully shaped by educational programs that tie new learning to what participants already believe and value, that are led by persons whom participants trust and respect, and that give plenty of opportunity for participants to talk through what they are learning and what it means for them.

Skills. Finally, handling anger and conflict requires skills in (1) listening, (2) speaking one's feelings in ways that do not elicit defensiveness and (3) problem-solving. Skills are learned most thoroughly when skills can be demonstrated and practiced repeatedly, with coaching as needed. That is, family life education is most effective when participants not only hear about skills they can use but also have opportunity and encouragement to try out new skills in the learning environment. Learning becomes particularly powerful when families participate in the educational event together and can thus try out what they are learning together.

The following principles are helpful for teaching family members new interaction skills in educational groups and seminars.

1. Provide positive response to people's attempts to use new skills: "That's it; that's good; you're right on target; keep it up." Encourage family members to respond positively to each other's attempts to use new skills at home, even when their performance is not perfect. The mood needs to be positive and playful, not serious and critical. Remember that people must *want* to use the skills—and this will not happen if they feel overly criticized and incompetent when they practice them.

2. As skills are introduced, be sure people know that they will be expected to practice them in the group or seminar. This will create a little anxiety, but it will help them listen actively to what is presented.

6. As skills are first modeled, help participants put labels on the specific behaviors they see demonstrated. Labels and names for the small behaviors that make up a skill help participants remember and use them. For example, "listening" when a family member is angry may be composed of the following behaviors: (a) eye contact, (b) nonverbal encouragement (nodding, occasional "uh-huhs"), (c) repeating back the essence of what the other has said, and (d) reserving one's own thoughts and feelings until the other feels understood.

7. Mix leaders modeling the skill with participants practicing them. Show them a piece and then have them practice it, instead of showing the whole skill sequence and expecting them to master it all at once. Learning interpersonal skills is not all that different from learning to ride a bicycle. You first learn to pedal while someone else runs alongside holding the bike steady. Only later do you learn to get on and push off at the same time you are pedaling and balancing.

8. If a skill is difficult or complex, it will require more demonstrations in different contexts and more practice by participants. The skills of forgiveness or of problem-solving require this kind of multiple demonstration and practice.

Without attention to all three components—knowledge, values and skills—lasting change is less likely to happen. Knowledge learning alone is like seed sown on a footpath. It may be the best seed around, but our patterns of living and habits of relationship are hardened from frequent use (Mk 4:3-9). Living patterns are unlikely to change unless the ground is tilled up and a new pattern gets at least a fighting chance amid our well-rooted styles of living. Learning that focuses only on attitudes and values leads to frustration; people *want* to make changes but are not given the skills and knowledge to do so. Finally, trying to teach only skills without the reasons the skills are valuable or the rationale for them can result in feet-planting opposition.

The best family life education embraces all three domains of learning. It presents new ideas and concepts. The person presenting those concepts is respected and trusted enough that participants find themselves valuing what is being said. Learners are given opportunity to share with one another, ask questions and make application to their own lives. And they are given opportunity to actually try it out, practicing new skills or ideas on each other, experimenting with applying them at home and coming back for support and encouragement.

Families will usually resist learning that involves changes in their values, cherished ideas and patterns of living. The more learning affects day-in and day-out life, the greater the resistance. When the new information itself is difficult, participants need more opportunity to turn it over in their minds and discuss it. For example, the concepts of forgiveness, repentance and reconciliation are complex, particularly when one attempts to apply them in daily life. Participants need plenty of opportunity to chew on these ideas and try them out. People need to go over the ideas more than once and think about them from different angles. Because these ideas also touch on deeply embedded values and attitudes, participants need plenty of opportunity to interact with trusted others in the group, to say, "What do you think of this?" and hear how others are grappling with and applying the ideas.

It helps to write out short objectives for a family life education program. What is it that you want people to know, to appreciate and value, and to be able to do differently because of this program? Once the objectives are clear, the kind of program, leadership and learning activities that are needed are readily apparent. Writing out the objectives keeps the program focused. It also circumvents the temptation simply to find a nifty speaker or piece of curriculum without really thinking about whether that speaker or curriculum can do what is most needed. Ideally, objectives for a program are established in dialogue with those for whom the program is designed, or based on a survey or other response from the target participants.

Format of the Program

Family life education programs can be scheduled as seminars, a weekly course or class, or an all-day or weekend retreat. Each has advantages.

A one-time seminar with a special speaker is a great way to introduce new ideas and kick off new emphases in a congregation. Neighbors of the congregation can be invited to participate in something designed with their interests and needs in mind. Such a seminar will probably not provide enough opportunity to make the applications to real life needed to bring significant changes. Nevertheless, they are a wonderful place to start.

Longer one-time events such as all-day and weekend retreats have the potential for an intense experience that generates real motivation for a new direction in family life, for rekindling hope, intimacy and affection, and for challenging attitudes and values. They also can cover a lot more ground than a series of classes taking the same number of hours, because they do not have to allow for multiple beginnings and endings.

New learning that takes place on retreats often needs the ongoing support that a weekly program can provide. Otherwise participants build up hopes and commitments to change and then have them dashed back home, when change proves much harder than they expected. New skills for family living—communication, conflict, child discipline and so on—are best learned when family members try out new ideas and behaviors in daily life, then come back to a supportive environment to talk about what they have learned and what they are struggling with. Educational leaders can make home assignments, encourage application in daily life, and keep working with families to make changes lasting. The major problem with a weekly class or seminar is the many interferences that challenge regular attendance. And the more sessions the course includes, the more attendance presents a challenge.

Size of the Group

Will the format be a lecture or presentation? Will there be opportunity for participants to ask questions, talk with the leader and each other, practice new skills? Based on the format being used, decide on the size of group that can be best accommodated. Large groups (more than ten or twelve) allow more room for people to "hide" and not participate, which is sometimes an advantage for reluctant attenders. On the other hand, in the climate of a large group participants need more assertiveness to ask questions and make comments. There is not as much opportunity to practice new skills, try out ideas and apply learning to life as there is in smaller groups.

If there is sufficient leadership in the group itself or there are multiple leaders, a large group can be divided into small work groups for discussion, practice and life application. These small groups can provide intimacy and mutuality, but a group leader must provide a high level of structuring. Members must be highly motivated to stay on task. Sometimes participants in small groups begin to digress, telling stories that are only peripherally related to the content. There is more pressure in small groups, too, for everyone to share of themselves and to agree with the values of others. Nevertheless, because of these characteristics, often more enduring relationships develop in small group experiences than in large groups.

Involving Congregation and Community

The formal channels of communicating about the program will reach many families—the church bulletin, letters, brochures and posters in the church facility or around the community. Others, however, will not participate unless someone contacts them personally, and often these are the families who have the most to gain from the program. The family ministry team can contact people themselves and can engage others to personally invite those families for whom they are preparing the program. Some families may need someone in the congregation to supply transportation, or simply to go with them so they do not feel alone.

Another way to facilitate involvement is to locate the program where the target participants are. Family ministry programs woven into the regular education programs of the church are often effective. Programs can also be placed where families with similar issues and challenges are: A brief parenting workshop can be provided along with a supper for parents who are picking up their children from daycare. A series of noon workshops on specific family topics can be held in a downtown or mall cafeteria. A discussion of the challenges of being a noncustodial parent can take place on Saturday mornings at a local playground or in the church's educational facility, while participating fathers play with their children.

Most families will not participate in family life education in their congregation unless it addresses needs they are experiencing currently. Family ministry leaders may ascribe needs and try to address those, but unless those ascribed needs fit what families are concerned about, they will have little interest in participating. At the same time, programs that focus on family strengths rather than problems will have more appeal and keep family members from feeling stigmatized as "troubled" if they choose to participate. Thus positive titles attract participation more than negative ones. For example, "Raising Responsible, Self-Disciplined Children" is more appealing than "Handling Child Discipline Problems."

Dolores Curran's excellent resource on parent education has wonderful practical suggestions on planning, communicating about and leading events that are broadly applicable to all kinds of family life education (Curran 1989). She suggests using the "3-W" principle for interesting persons in participating in educational events. The three *W*'s are the words *wonder, worry* and *wish:*

Do you wonder how you can help your children learn to take responsibility for themselves?

Do you worry that you'll have to call them every night at college to remind them to do their homework and brush their teeth?

Do you wish you knew how to help them to learn self-discipline?

Your program announcement and publicity should

☐ include all the kinds of people you are trying to reach. If it says the program is for families, be sure to indicate all the kinds of families that are welcome: two-parent and single-parent families, stepfamilies, grandparents and faith-families.

☐ use no language that will offend or discourage participation, such as *troubled, dysfunctional* or *hurting*.

☐ make it clear that this program will offer practical help and ideas.

☐ clearly indicate the content of the program.

☐ provide information on setting, date, time and cost.

☐ supply parking instructions.

☐ indicate whether childcare will be available (adapted from Curran 1989).

LEADING FAMILY LIFE EDUCATION

Obviously, there is a vast literature on planning and leading educational programs that cannot be addressed here. But some issues that are particularly germane to family life education in congregational settings deserve mention.

Should the leader be an expert or simply someone interested and willing to facilitate group learning? Family life education can benefit from the leadership of a professional with expertise in the content. A child development specialist, for example, can be invited to lead a parent education program. On the other hand, there are some excellent curriculum packages available that are designed for someone who has group leadership skills but no special expertise in the content area. The leader can simply be a church member who is excited about the content and willing to lead discussion. Often these groups call for participants to read material and come to weekly sessions to discuss what they have read.

Both of these approaches can be very effective, depending on the objectives. An expert leader may be able to present more new ideas and can more easily challenge attitudes and values. On the other hand, the group-based leadership may result in more mutual engagement among participants and enduring relationships of support for new learning.

Does the leader need to be someone with personal experience? Should the leader of a parent group be a parent? Should the leader of a marriage enrichment group be married? Should only couples lead marriage groups, or can one person be just as effective as a leader? If the learning objectives include changing attitudes and values, leaders who are respected because they have "been there" are ideal. A widow can use her own experiences to lead a workshop for the newly widowed. On the other hand, a skillful leader who does not have personal experience with the topic can draw on the experiences of the group, inviting them to share and thus create a climate for bonds to develop. Leaders with personal experience need to be careful, in fact, that their experiences do not become the only model for participants.

When a group is led by a family unit, such as a couple leading a marriage enrichment retreat, the leaders are not only sharing from their own experiences; they are modeling *as they lead with each other*. How they work together as leaders inadvertently models family relationships—how they handle conflicts, how they talk with and listen to each other, how they model either egalitarian leadership or one leading and the other supporting. This requires leaders to be acutely aware not only of the content they are presenting and the experiences and interactions of participants but also of how they are relating to one another.

For example, many marriage enrichment groups are led by a husband who is a helping professional and a wife who is a nonprofessional. As a consequence, the husband takes the major role in group leadership, and the wife supports him. Inadvertently such leadership communicates powerful messages about gender roles that may or may not be congruent with what the program is trying to teach.

On the other hand, if the marriage enrichment leaders are respected by others in the group and effectively use their relationship as a leadership tool, a couple can be a powerful leadership team.

Leaders working alone can still illustrate and model family interaction by involving participants in role-plays. When I am leading marriage enrichment groups alone, I often "borrow" a husband for role-plays about communication and conflict. This provides enormous potential for fun and a variety of issues to be discussed.

How can we make people feel secure and safe enough to risk learning? People learn best when they feel safe enough to experiment with new ideas, when they feel supported and when they know no one will laugh at their thoughts or their first attempts to try something new. They need to know the group understands how hard change is, that they are doing the best they can, that even the smallest changes in daily life are tremendous challenges. It is most important to keep people from feeling embarrassed by what they say or do, or from feeling shocked by what the leader communicates.

A man was stalled by the side of the road. His stick-shift car would not start. A helpful neighbor came along and asked if he could help. The stalled man said, "If you could just get behind me and get my car going about thirty miles per hour, I think I can pop the clutch and get it started." The neighbor agreed and walked back to his car. The stalled man got into his car and put it into neutral. He then looked in his rearview mirror and saw, to his horror, that the neighbor had backed down the highway and was now coming right at him at thirty miles per hour.

Clearly, we have to connect first with people, then nudge them gently into change.

Should the leader control or turn the group leadership over to participants? Many family ministry programs are one-time or short-term events in which a strong leader presents ideas and provides structured learning experiences. Leadership clearly and rightfully stays invested in the expert or facilitator. But in a program that meets over a period of weeks or months, there is real potential for enduring support relationships to develop. In this case a leader may be most effective by structuring and facilitating and then over time backing out of the leadership role as members become more active. Participants can be empowered to take leadership as they are given content they can read and react to, so that they have some access to the content directly rather than only through the leader's presentations. Also, methods that maximize participation and tap people's reservoir of life experiences will increase the potential for cohesive, enduring relationships to form.

In some ways group leadership is like parenting. Good parents try to guide their children into taking charge of their own lives. Children participate increasingly in family decision-making because parents have encouraged the development of responsibility and good decision-making skills. In the same way, an effective group facilitator encourages group members to take over the tasks of leadership and of demonstrating concern for one another.

In the ideal group (like the ideal family), if the leadership work is done well, most of the exhausting responsibility comes in the beginning. Later on the leader directs from the background and monitors but is not the one doing everything.

What kind of group rules should be established in church programs? It is much easier to set the rules in the beginning, so that should someone need a reminder, the issue does not seem so personal. The group can establish rules regarding such issues as starting and stopping on time, whether they will keep what is shared in the group confidential, what to do if a member cannot attend all the sessions.

One of the most important rules in family life education is that people should share their own experiences rather than telling others what to do. For example, in a parenting group it is better for one parent to say, "I don't know if this would work for you and your child, but this is what I did . . ." than to say, "You ought to . . ." This rule needs to be spelled out in the beginning, so that everyone understands. Every person is considered an expert on their own family, and no one else knows enough to tell that person what to do. But participants can be enormously helpful by offering their experiences, from which others can learn and develop applications for their own situation.

If the rule has been previously established, and a group member launches into giving another member advice, the group leader needs to interrupt, saying to the advice-giver, "It sounds like you have had some experience with this. Rather than telling Jim what to do with his son, I think it would be really helpful for all of us to hear your own experience with this, if you are willing." If a group has established rules, the leader is responsible for helping them live by those rules. Over time the group itself may take over this responsibility, but at least initially that is the function of the group leader. If the members agreed to start on time, the leader needs to start promptly, even if participants straggle in. If the group seems habitually not to be living up to its own rules, the leader may want to initiate a discussion of whether members want to change the rules.

Should a multisession group be encouraged to become less formal over time? Douglas Power conducted research with a support group for mothers. Leaders found that over a twelve-month period, there was a steady expansion of break time, which the group spent in the kitchen fixing and enjoying refreshments, and less time in the formal meeting. In the beginning of the year, the break took an average of eighteen minutes. By the end of the year, it took twenty-nine minutes. The leaders found that the break was used for exploring learning topics in detail, and mothers were more likely to talk about their individual children in the informal kitchen discussion than in the programmed time. Discussion also moved away from parenting and toward other concerns. The researchers concluded that groups, when left to develop naturally, will move toward informal support and away from the more formal meeting (Power 1987). If one of the objectives of a program is to develop enduring supportive relationships, allow this process to take place.

BEYOND FAMILY LIFE EDUCATION

This chapter began by saying that family life education often is woven in and around other programs of a congregation. At the same time, family life education programs often serve as a foundation for other programs and ministries of a congregation. For example, a parent education seminar series may lead, as Douglas Power's research indicated, into an ongoing support group. Or that same seminar series may be instrumental in identifying other family support programs that the congregation wants to launch—a library of educational toys for congregation members to check out, a monthly parents' night out, a Christmas-cookie decorating party for children and parents preparing baskets for homebound members.

The seminar series may move the group to broader issues; the group may decide to take an advocacy role for themselves or others. Parents may have shared their struggles with finding quality childcare and wondered together about what families with low incomes do. If the leader helps connect them to the broader social issues of childcare and child advocacy, they may begin to follow what is happening in state and national legislation addressing child care issues. Together they may stay informed, write letters to state and national representatives, and connect with other advocates. Many advocacy organizations publish newsletters and have Internet sites that provide up-to-date information and ideas of what congregational groups can do to encourage social changes that will provide greater support and justice for all families. Some of these are listed in appendix A.

Section Six

Ministry with Specific
Family Relationships

T HE EARLIER CHAPTERS AND SECTIONS OF THIS BOOK HAVE LAID
the foundaTion for an approach to congregational ministry that is inclusive of all
kinds of family relationships. Indeed, most of what a church does to support,
nurture and challenge families takes place in the daily and weekly life of the congregation—in its worship and educational programs, its ministry and its fellowship and business meetings.

Nevertheless, certain characteristics and issues of family relationships and circumstances require special attention. This section looks at some of the issues that
are distinctive to certain relationships in family life. The first chapter will explore
some of the issues of faith-families. In particular, it will examine how family ministries relate to persons who are not married. The second chapter will look at
some of the particular issues of marriage, as well as divorce and remarriage.

The third chapter will describe some of the issues parents face. Since discipline of children often receives central attention in churches' parenting programs,
and parents and their children are often a central focus of congregational family
ministries, some of the issues of child discipline will be discussed. In addition,
this chapter will explore the role of siblings in one another's lives and the relationship between adult children and their parents.

The final chapter in the section overviews some of the specific challenges that families face. In particular it explores what happens to families in situations of crisis and catastrophe and how the church can minister with them. Finally, the issue of family violence and the church's response is addressed.

Chapter 20

Faith-Families

I N MANY RESPECTS, THIS WHOLE BOOK HAS BEEN ABOUT FAITH-FAMily relationships. All our relationships are transformed by our commitment to God and, in turn, to one another in families and communities. We have received the "spirit of adoption" and are "joint heirs" together with Christ (Rom 8:16-17). As we saw in section two, many of the processes of family life—attachment and caregiving, communication and conflict, intimacy, the distribution and use of power, rituals and celebrations, weaving a family history—occur in all kinds of family relationships. Nevertheless, different kinds of family relationships have particular qualities. The relationships of spouses, siblings, and parents and children have unique characteristics. And there are also unique issues for those whose sole tie to one another is as "faith-family."

This chapter will look at *one subset* of faith-family relationships—those who are *not* related to one another by blood or marriage. In particular, it will look at faith-families formed by persons with no marriage or biological parenting relationship. These are not married couples and their children who adopt a senior adult in the congregation to be a "faith-grandparent." I have given attention to such relationships elsewhere. Marriage and parenting relationships tend to be the core of these families. This chapter will look at families in which no such core exists.

It will be a short chapter, some based on conjecture. Although a considerable amount has been written about single adults and single adult ministries, much of this literature works on the assumption that these are persons without family or, if they have children, that they are incomplete or "broken" families. Even the name "single adult" identifies unmarried persons as who they are *not* rather than as who they *are*. We do not have commonly accepted terms for the nonmarital, nonblood ties that bind persons to each other as family, and therefore these ties really have no social recognition. We have some terms that hint at faith-family relationships—*roommate, lifelong friend.* Yet these do not really capture the family commitment that may exist in these relationships.

I recently talked to a never-married middle-aged friend who was considering a job offer that would move her two thousand miles away. She named two women friends, who are also unmarried and who have functioned as family for her and each other for twenty years: "They are my family; how could I move?" Yet neither our society nor the church has a language to address the family crisis that the potential for employment relocation presents for these three women. In an age of increasing isolation and growing numbers of persons who are single for part or all of their adult lives, perhaps the church faces no greater challenge than to find ways to talk about and support family relationships not defined by marriage.

The role of the church is not just to try to understand and nurture the families of persons who are not married; the church is to help people make their faith commitments to God—and to one another—the defining characteristic of their bond (Mk 3:35).

SINGLE ADULTS: WHO THEY ARE

Singleness is no longer an exception but has become a significant portion of the lives of *most* adults and the entire life path for many people. Never-married adults now make up almost one-fourth of the U.S. adult population. When those who are divorced or widowed are added, unmarried adults represent 39 percent of the U.S. population over the age of eighteen. The proportion of men and women age thirty to thirty-four who have never married has tripled since 1970. From 1970 to 1993, the proportion of never-married women grew from 6 percent to 19 percent, and for men the proportion grew from 9 percent to 30 percent. These statistics disguise the fact that many of these adults are cohabiting, a choice rarely made in past generations. In 1993 there were six unmarried cohabiting couples for every one hundred married couples, compared with only one for every one hundred in 1970 (Saluter 1994:2).

Living Alone

For the first time in history, the United States has produced a society rich enough to enable many people to live by themselves. In 1993 one-third of all first-time home buyers were single (Taubman 1995). More than twenty-four million Americans—one out of four adults—live alone. Over fifteen million of them are women. Seventy-five percent of all people over age forty-five who live alone are women. Although in the movies singles living on their own are usually pictured as twentysomething, in real life most of them are over age thirty-five (ibid.). The statistics on adults living alone are skewed by large numbers of senior adults living alone after their spouses have died. Younger single adults often do *not* live alone; they cannot afford to support a household by themselves. They are usually sharing housing with parents, friends or a sexual partner. Older single adults, however, are increasingly choosing to live alone.

Sharing a Household

In the 1990 U.S. census, the relationship category "unmarried partner" was added for the first time. The definition of this category is "a person who is not related to the householder, who shares living quarters, and who has a close personal relationship with the householder." This category differs from the "roomer/boarder" and "housemate/roommate" categories, where the person is not related to the householder and shares the living quarters primarily to reduce housing expenses (Saluter 1994:4). It still does not clarify whether the adults are committed to one another or merely friends sharing a household for a period of time. Nor does it clarify whether the adults are sexual partners.

Many singles continue to live with or have returned home to live with their parents—29 percent of never-married and 13 percent of divorced adult children (White and Peterson 1995). The vast majority are staying or returning home because of their own financial and emotional needs, not to provide care for their parents.

Because cohabitation has become so pervasive, the rates of divorce and marriage no longer give an accurate picture of when families are formed and when they are dissolved. A national survey in 1987-1988 found that almost half of Americans in their thirties have lived with someone of the opposite sex outside of marriage. If this trend continues, cohabitation will soon become an experience in the lives of a majority of Americans, particularly since it has been on an increase at the same time that rates of marriage have been declining. Nevertheless, it appears that cohabitation has become another step in the process of family formation: more cohabiting relationships end in marriage (60 percent) than in separation (40 percent). Unions begun in cohabitation are relatively unstable, however, compared to all first marriages. Almost twice as many dissolve within ten years (57 percent) as do first marriages that end in divorce (30 percent). Cohabitation is more likely to occur among the poor and those who did not grow up in an intact family (O'Brien 1989).

The often-cited statistic that one out of four babies is born to an unmarried mother is tempered by the finding that approximately one out of three of these mothers lives with the father of her child. These children are raised in unmarried but not single-parent families. These relationships are far less stable than marriage. One out of three unmarried couples who have children do not marry one another (O'Brien 1989).

SINGLES IN THE CHURCH

Obviously, we cannot assume that the demography of American congregations mirrors the demography of American society. In fact, there are significant differences, both in proportions and in composition, between single adults in church and single adults in society.

Single adults in congregations are disproportionately older empty-nesters, retirees and widow(er)s. Young singles are significantly underrepresented. This characteristic of the single adult church population represents the broader trend in churches of becoming proportionately older and having fewer young adults than society in general. A survey of seventy-two Protestant congregations compared family demographics in congregations with the overall U.S. population; the statistical comparisons can be found in table 20.1.

Penny Marler concluded from her demographic study of congregations that "the family structure of the Protestant church is primarily comprised of two rather complementary cohorts: people who are in traditional families and those who used to be" (Marler 1995:50). Younger single adults and younger to middle-aged couples without children are simply not as well represented in U.S. churches as they are in U.S. society. In other words, church life seems to appeal primarily

Family structure	Percentage of adults in 72 churches	Percentage of U.S. adult population
Married, no children (including senior adults)	45%	33%
Single adults	29%	38%
Married with dependent children	26%	29%
Family structure	**Percentage of married adults in 72 churches**	**Percentage of U.S. married adult population**
Married with dependent children, adults under age 35	25%	42%
Married with dependent children, adults ages 35-54	69%	55%
Married with dependent children, adults ages 55 up	6%	3%
Married without dependent children, adults under ages 35	8%	17%
Married without dependent children, adults ages 35-54	22%	29%
Married without dependent children, adults ages 55 up	70%	54%
Family structure	**Percentage of single adults in 72 churches**	**Percentage of U.S. single adult population**
Single adults under age 35	28%	53%
Single adults ages 35-54	17%	21%
Single adults ages 55 up	55%	26%

Table 20.1. Families in congregations and families in the U.S. population (Marler 1995)

to families composed of married couples and their children, or of the remnants of the nuclear family—empty-nest couples and widows.

What It Means to Be Christian and Single

Many reasons exist for single adults to be underrepresented in our congregations. One reason that has major import for family ministry is the attitude of church communities toward single adults. Rodney Clapp has commented that most churches treat their singles ministries as "sanctified substitutes for singles bars" (Clapp 1993:89). There seems to be a pervasive attitude that "normal" people will sooner or later marry and that divorced persons are simply looking for the next mate. This is evidenced in the too-cute label given to some Sunday-school classes that mix single and married adults: "Pairs and Spares." As one woman told me, "I feel like a spare tire, something extra, just taking up space in the back of the car, as though I don't really matter since I don't have a man."

Perhaps one of the primary current contributors to this attitude toward single adults in Protestant congregations has been the preference for married adult males as church leaders. Leaders tend to be attitude-shapers among those they lead. If leaders consider their own lifestyle to be normal and "best," then inadvertently they communicate the attitude that singleness is less than the best.

This attitude is sadly unbiblical. The teachings of the New Testament clearly honor singleness (Mt 19:10-12), and Paul, without denigrating marriage, even holds it up as the *best* life choice (1 Cor 7:6-9). We turn biblical teaching upside down when we marginalize those who remain single. Paul was of the opinion that the one who was unmarried was less burdened by the anxieties of trying to please a spouse—by worldly affairs. The single person could be more devoted to pleasing the Lord (1 Cor 7:32-34). Paul simply thought— and he conceded that it was his opinion (7:25)—that singleness brought benefit. He encouraged any lifestyle that promoted "good order and undivided devotion to the Lord" (7:35).

Paul understood, however, that the choice to remain single may be a sacrificial choice. Stanley Hauerwas points out that the "sacrifice" singles make is not only the loss of the possibility of sexual partnership but the much more significant loss of children. In ancient Judaism, children were the hope for the future, the heritage that lives on. Hauerwas says that "there can be no more radical act than this [singleness], as it is the clearest institutional expression that one's future is not guaranteed by the family, but by the church. The church, that harbinger of the Kingdom of God, is now the source of our primary loyalty" (Hauerwas 1981:190).

Both singleness and marriage can be Christian callings. Both can testify to the truth of the gospel working itself out in the lives of individuals. For many adults who are single, remaining unmarried may not be an actual choice they make but a circumstance they learn to embrace. By the same token, many find themselves married in circumstances they did not choose. Few choose to be married to someone who will become an alcoholic, or develop Alzheimer's disease, or simply become unpleasant to live with. According to Paul, we are to live in the conditions in that we find ourselves as witnesses to something that transcends marital status (1 Cor 7:24).

ISSUES FOR FAITH-FAMILY RELATIONSHIPS

Of the processes of family life discussed earlier in this book, the three that seem most important when thinking about faith-families are adoption, the making of a family culture through rituals, and the processes of attachment and belonging.

Adoption

Adoption is a family term normally reserved for parents' legal adoption of dependent children. However, studies of the adoption of children provide a rich resource for thinking about the processes involved in forming family in ways other than marriage and birth. A recent study, the largest of its kind, examined the well-being of adolescents who were adopted as infants through adoption agencies. The study found that the adopted children did not differ in any significant way in their development of healthy self-esteem and identity and in their attachment to parents, compared to their nonadopted siblings and other adolescents in the United States (Benson, Sharma and Roehlkepartain 1994).

Even in the best of families and circumstances, some youths—both adopted and nonadopted—have problems. When this happens in adoptive families, the tendency is to blame adoption rather than examining the constellation of factors that can shape an adopted child's life. The researcher from the adoption study suggested that although adopted adolescents tend to do as well as adolescents in general, a more appropriate standard for evaluating the outcome of adoption is to compare each adopted child's experiences and well-being to what life could have been like had he or she not been adopted (Benson, Sharma and Roehlkepartain 1994).

This can be said for adults who "adopt" one another as family too. The issue is not whether faith-families are as strong or as intimate or as productive for their members and for the community as nuclear families. The issue is whether people who become faith-family for one another fare better than the alternatives, whatever they may be perceived to be.

Family Rituals

As we saw in chapter seven, rituals are important in establishing family boundaries; almost all rituals directly or indirectly clarify the family's boundaries and its relationship with the broader community. Rituals are particularly significant for faith-families, where the boundaries may be invisible to the outside community—others do not look at the family members and recognize them as family. Rituals can be anything from ways of greeting each other to things a family "always" does a certain way at a certain time. The ritual serves simultaneously to strengthen the bonds of the family and to demarcate the family from the broader friendship network and community (Reiss 1981:241).

Food is a critical factor in many family rituals. Weeknight meals, Sunday dinners and holiday gatherings mark the rhythms of family life (Devault 1987). Certain foods take on particular meaning. The meaning attached to chicken noodle soup or egg custard stems more from the caregiving relationship it connotes than from the actual nutritional value of the food. In my subculture, pot roast may bring on a wave of childhood memories of the hissing of a pressure cooker valve in the kitchen on Sunday and the gathered family. Serving pot roast, then, may signify for faith-family members "we are family." Pot roast is not usually something one serves to guests; it is a "family" meal. When we bring people together for meals we are not only nurturing the bodies of individuals; we are also producing family life itself (ibid.).

When a child is adopted, particularly an older child, the social worker often coaches the family to intentionally establish rituals that include the adopted child as a family member. Food often figures significantly into these rituals: a cake with candles that celebrates the adoption day; serving a particular food that the child likes and that signifies the inclusion of the child's tastes and cultural experiences as a part of the new family relationships. Taking pictures and putting them in an album or in frames supplies a visual representation of the new family. Rituals of adoption with gathered friends and the church community can be enormously significant. All of these approaches to strengthening adoptive bonds can be adapted, too, to faith-family relationships.

Attachment and Belonging

Both the process of adoption and the development of family rituals tie directly to the fundamental processes of attachment and belonging in all families, including faith-families. These are processes that occur over time and lead to a sense of security and rootedness. These are persons who give comfort by their presence and whose absence can create enormous anxiety and a sense of being lost. These are persons who have a right to give each other advice and opinions. These are persons whose identities are so intertwined that they cannot be pulled apart without doing fundamental damage to self and the other.

IMPLICATIONS FOR MINISTRY

Many of the principles of ministry with faith-families have already been named earlier in this book. Nevertheless, it may be helpful to reiterate some of the ways congregations can recognize and support faith-families, particularly those without a marital core.

First, we need to find ways to identify the families of all persons, including single adults, and begin to see them in that family context rather than as solitary units. The best means for finding out who the families of single adults are is to ask them. Single adults themselves have much to say about who their families are and how the congregation can help them live more faithfully as family members.

Once the congregation has a perspective that sees all persons as members of faith-families, the strengths and challenges of faith-families begin to be visible. Simply recognizing faith-family relationships provides support and strengthens the identity of families. Including faith-families as family groups in worship leadership and in educational programs and ministries communicates their significance.

Faith-families will benefit from programs and resources targeted to strengthening their bonds and providing them with community support. Few church curricula or other kinds of resources designed specifically for faith-families are currently available. In some ways this can be an advantage; programs and resources will have to grow out of listening to faith-families themselves and giving them leadership roles in family ministry.

WHY I HAVEN'T DISCUSSED "FAMILY VALUES"

I cannot leave a chapter that has addressed faith-families, and the families of single adults in particular, without touching on the current "family values" debate. The term "family values" as it is used politically today usually refers to *what kinds of families* are valued. "Family values" does not refer to ways we can "value families"; instead it seems to mean "which families deserve value."

Determining what kinds of family relationships should be valued—honored and supported—is obviously of great importance. In fact, much of the eleventh chapter of this book addressed just that concern: Who should the families of Christians be? What kinds of relationships ought to characterize the life of followers of Jesus? The problem with the current political debate is that it confuses the concept of "what families we ought to value" with "how we can value families by strengthening them." It assumes that if we can just reach some kind of consensus about what family type is "ideal" or the "model" and eschew other forms of family life, we will strengthen families. If we can agree that families ought to be composed of one husband and one wife and their children, then somehow we will have strengthened that family unit.

I am convinced, however, that most families will actually be stronger if we help them understand and live out biblical teachings about anger and conflict than if we try to define who is and is not family. Poor and middle-class traditional families will experience themselves as "valued" by social policies that ensure that wages are adequate for supporting their children and that they will receive health care and financial support for sending their children to college or job-training programs. Policies that focus on denying these kinds of resources to devalued nontraditional families will probably not really do much to strengthen traditional poor and middle-class families.

In the end, both of these matters—what is the model family and how do we strengthen families—are important to Christians and their congregations. One of the most significant issues at the heart of the family-values debate is how churches should think about and relate to persons living in homosexual relationships. Unfortunately we have allowed the debate to become a war of words, and sometimes of violence. The debate divides and hurts and diminishes the ability of the church to care for persons on both sides of the issue, who experience withdrawal of fellowship by those on the other side.

This book does not address whether or not congregations should recognize same-sex couples as families. Obviously, this debate is of critical importance to those families whose lifestyles are being debated. Same-sex couples will undoubtedly be dramatically affected by social policies that legislate recognition or denial of family status for them in arenas such as taxation, ability to visit one another in hospital intensive-care wards, adoption of children, and housing. Ethical issues such as these need discussing, but in a different setting than that where most of the discussion is now taking place. They need to be discussed in our communities of faith with our neighbors whose lives are affected by these policies, not just in the impersonal political arena. They need to be discussed with compassion and within covenants of care that will hold people together for continuing discussion, even when they passionately disagree with one another.

The hard issues that fragment the church today, such as abortion rights, sexual orientation and gender roles, have been so divisive because they have been debated by denominational committees and task forces rather than approached around kitchen tables and at church suppers. Whatever political conclusion we reach about these issues, there will still be unwanted pregnancies and persons with a homosexual orientation and conflict over gender roles. Legislation may have an impact on how public people can be with these issues of their lives, but the issues themselves will not be eliminated.

For that reason, discussion of these issues needs to be carried out within families and within our community. These kinds of ongoing life issues are best approached through primary relationships. They are not issues that can be resolved and disposed of by governing boards. Like other family issues, they are often not totally resolved but worked around and through for a time, until they warrant more attention. The issue is not only "Is abortion right or wrong?" but "What should Martha and Jim say to their fifteen-year-old daughter who is pregnant? She's hardly out of diapers herself, and the daddy is just a baby too," or "Your sister called in tears today. She's pregnant again, and the doctor thinks this one really has some problems. And they've already got three little ones. She is actually thinking about an abortion; she just doesn't know what to do."

We can help our congregations deal realistically and compassionately with these really hard issues of life where it is lived. Unless we begin by caring compassionately for persons wrestling with hard issues in our own caring circles, we have no business advocating for social policies and legislation. *Only when we have dealt compassionately* with issues as they touch us and others are we truly qualified to enter the debate over what governmental and church policies will truly lead to justice.

Political pronouncements and power politics do not strengthen families and communities. Working through issues together does. Learning to disagree lovingly and compassionately without severing fellowship with one another does. If we can do this in our families and congregations, then we will have the right foundation for engaging more compassionately in the larger social debate.

This discussion of the political term *family values* is intended to show that the ethical issues the term connotes are part of the context in which church leaders help congregations shape their ministry with families. It is almost inevitable that a church's family ministry team will begin its work with the question "What do we mean by family, anyway?"—and the debate is off and running. Some of my least effective work with congregations has been when I allowed that debate to swamp the work of the family ministry team. They could meet for hours and debate whether or not single adults are "families of one" or single-parent families are "not the biblical model" or whether gay and lesbian couples are "families." All of these are significant issues, but the problem is that a task force can debate these issues during meeting after meeting and never really do anything to minister with families. Or, because these issues are so difficult, they will simply stick with a "traditional" definition of the family. Or they will abandon their efforts at family ministry because the issues are too divisive.

Instead of talking *about* single adults, ask single adults in the congregation to talk about how they think of their families. Instead of talking *about* single parenting as being less-than, listen as Christian single parents talk about their family life and how the family ministry team's definition of family affects them. Instead of debating the meaning of sexual orientation for defining family, listen with as much openness and compassion as you can prayerfully muster to the life experiences of persons who are homosexual or parents whose children are homosexual. All of these might provide the ground for ministry.

This book is about the processes of family ministry, not solving the ethical debates of the day. In twenty-five years the issues will be different, but we will still be dealing with such questions as: How can we tackle the issues in ways that bind us together in compassionate care for one another and for those who need to be a part of our community of faith? How can we go after the lost sheep—those who have wandered and also those who feel excluded from the flock by our debates? How can we keep from using debate about principles as a means of avoiding the simple but very hard work of loving one another and providing our congregations and families with needed challenges and resources for faithful family living?

In her book *Traveling Mercies,* Anne Lamott describes her experience as a single adult who found herself pregnant. She had already had one abortion two years before; she had since become a Christian. She was now a member of St. Andrew

Presbyterian Church in Marin City, California, which she describes as "a funky little church filled with people who are working for peace and freedom." Lamott says, "When I was at the end of my rope the people at St. Andrew tied a knot in it for me and helped me hold on" (Lamott 1999:100).

> When I announced during worship that I was pregnant, people cheered. All these old people, raised in Bible-thumping homes in the Deep South, clapped. Even the women whose grown-up boys had been or were doing time in jails or prisons rejoiced for me. And then almost immediately they set about providing for us. They brought clothes, they brought me casseroles to keep in the freezer, thy brought me assurance that this baby was going to be a part of the family. And they began slipping me money. Now, a number of the older black women live pretty close to the bone financially on small Social Security checks. But routinely they sidled up to me and stuffed bills in my pocket—tens and twenties. It was always done so stealthily that you might have thought they were slipping me bundles of cocaine. (ibid. 101)

The church's affirmation and celebration of Lamott's pregnancy was not meant as an ethical affirmation of sexual relationships outside of marriage. It had much more to do with the gospel's ethical principles of compassion, expressed by wrapping love and support around this particular person. Lamott goes on to describe how the congregation's loving care has continued over the years of her son's childhood; he continues to be the recipient of hugs and affection and slipped packets of financial support. "The church became my home in the old meaning of *home*—that it's where, when you show up, they have to let you in. They let me in. They even said, 'You come back now' " (ibid. 100).

There will always be ethical issues that tempt us to talk without taking action. Doing something about real persons affected by the issues that confront us, however, often helps us gain clarity about the issues themselves. I have found it much more difficult to be dogmatic about certain issues after I have walked with a loved one facing that issue, or faced it myself.

On the other hand, I once heard a colleague preach a sermon entitled "Don't Just Do Something, Stand There." He had a point. Sometimes we do need to take stands and draw lines in the sand about what is right and wrong. That can be a risky action, however, because the lines we draw may exclude a brother or sister in Christ, even when we do not intend to do so.

Ultimately, compassionate care must be our primary focus. Jesus was very clear that the most important commandments were to love God and love neighbor, not to judge neighbor. The actions God looks for are compassionate seeking out and caring for those in need, not excluding them from our circle of fellowship. The most significant characteristic of our relationships will be the love we demonstrate, not whether those relationships are "family" as the world around us defines family. These are the deepest challenges of family ministry—to help Christians love neighbor and one another, thus showing our love for God. Simple, yet a tremendous lifelong challenge.

Chapter 21

Marriage & Divorce

MARRIAGE IS THE EXEMPLAR OF THE ADOPTIVE FAMILY, THE "faith-family." Two adults commit themselves to be family for each other for the rest of their lives. Marriage is somewhere in between the *obligation* relationship of kinship and the *choice* relationship of friendship. In marriage there is a public ritual, reminding the partners of the dimensions of obligation of their relationship and its confirmation by the community. But marriage is clearly distinguished from those other relationships by its active dimension; partners have actively chosen each other. Marriage thus epitomizes both the freedom of friendship and the obligations and permanence of kinship (Patton and Childs 1988).

MARRIAGE IN AMERICAN CULTURE

During the 1950s, the average age at first marriage in the United States reached an all-time low, with many people marrying in their late teens and early twenties. In 1960 the average age at first marriage was 22.8 for men and 20.3 for women. Since that time, the age at first marriage has continued to rise. In 1993 the median age was 26.5 years for men and 24.5 years for women (Saluter 1994:4).

Reason	Percent who mentioned
to have consistent companionship, someone who is there for you, some to share your life with	60%
to be loved and receive love, to be with someone who is concerned about you	24%
to have children	21%
for stability, security, to have deeper commitment in a relationship, having a long-term relationship	18%
to have a spouse or partner	5%
for financial security or benefit	5%
to have sexual intimacy; having a permanent partner; to have frequent sex	3%
to achieve happiness	2%

Table 21.1.   Reasons never-married adults give for wanting to marry (Barna 1993)

Those who marry today are concerned not just for marital stability but for marital happiness. Most Americans (other than statisticians) do not measure the strength of a marriage by the ability to ward off divorce. Consequently, the social science literature is filled with studies of the factors that contribute to marital satisfaction. Magazines and bestsellers popularize these findings and offer helpful hints on how to have a happy marriage. The Barna Research Group conducted a 1992 survey of families that included 172 never-married adults (Barna 1993). Those who said they would like to marry were asked to list one or more reasons. Table 21.1 indicates the expectations in U.S. culture for marriage: companionship tops the list.

In the same research study, 596 married adults described sources of satisfaction and frustration in their marriages. Table 21.2 indicates the percentage of respondents who named each source.

Marriage for Christians
Marriage in the lives of Christians presents special challenges.[1]

For Christians, there is more to marriage than being able to stick it out, or even being companions who are happy together for a lifetime. Christians face the

---

[1]Some of the material in this section was previously published (Garland and Garland 1986).

Sources of satisfaction	
companionship or friendship with the spouse	35%
the spouse's commendable qualities	29%
amounts of time and quality of shared experiences	18%
the children	17%
everything about the spouse	13%
the communication between husband and wife	12%
the things they have in common	10%
receiving such support from the spouse	7%
family life, in general	7%
the joint spiritual journey	4%
financial comfort and security	3%
Sources of frustration	
nothing, no frustration with marriage	25%
financial struggles, economic hardships	17%
conflict with spouse; constant disagreements	11%
job or career demands	9%
bad/annoying habits or qualities of the spouse	7%
difficulties related to raising the children	6%
not having enought time together	5%
expectations not being met (especially sexual)	4%
poor communication between husband and wife	4%

Table 21.2. Sources of marital satisfaction and frustration (Barna 1993)

challenge of living Christlike lives in and through their marriages. "Success" cannot be measured on scales of marital satisfaction or happiness alone but is dependent on the degree to which partners "lose their lives in order to save them." The challenge is not to find personal happiness but to give of oneself to another.

Biblical teachings on marriage. No biblical writer treats marriage systematically. In Old Testament writings, marriage is taken for granted as a secular reality that the prophets use as a poignant metaphor for the ups and downs in the relationship between God and Israel (Is 50:1; 54:6; Jer 3:1, 7-8, 20; Ezek 16; 23; Hos 2:19-20). Jesus' only lengthy discussion of the subject is precipitated by a test question from the Pharisees about the grounds for divorce (Mt 19:3-12; Mk 10:2-12). Combining texts from Genesis 1:27, 5:2 and 2:24, he argues that marriage has its basis in God's act of creation—"male and female he created them"—and that the two become a one-flesh unity. He asserts that God has joined the two together and therefore the bond should not be broken. Jesus says nothing, however, about the way this one-flesh unity is to be lived out. In fact, he says nothing about preparation for marriage, sexual relations in marriage, birth control, spouse roles, quality of the relationship, or how to strengthen a marriage—subjects that preoccupy many today.

Paul deals with the issue of marriage at length in 1 Corinthians 7 only because of the congregation's confusion over it, particularly concerning sex and the Christian, and because they had asked him to respond specifically to particular issues (1 Cor 7:1; see D. E. Garland 1983). Paul is responding to specific difficulties and aberrant attitudes in Corinth and is not trying to offer a complete systematic guide to married life. One cannot, therefore, heedlessly translate what Paul wrote here into a universally applicable marital code, although this text is profound and insightful.

The Bible also records many marital patterns and practices that would not only be socially unacceptable in America today but in some cases illegal—for example, the polygynous marriages of such biblical notables as Jacob (Gen 29:15-30), David (1 Sam 25:39-43; 2 Sam 5:13; 11:26-27) and Solomon (1 Kings 11:1-8). The number of wives and concubines was limited only by the resources required to maintain them. Even Yahweh's relationship to Northern and Southern Israel was likened to a marriage to two wives (Ezek 23), but this polygynous pattern can hardly be considered exemplary for us.

Most Christians today would also find levirate marriage unacceptable. This was the marriage, enjoined in Deuteronomy 25:5-10, between a woman whose husband has died without offspring and the husband's brother. Its purpose was to perpetuate the name of the deceased as well as to keep his property in the family. The failure to comply with this practice proved fatal to Onan and mortally embarrassing to Judah (Gen 38). Jesus seems to tacitly accept this marital practice when the Sadducees try to trip him up with their stock antiresurrection anecdote about the woman who married seven brothers in succession. Jesus rebukes them for knowing neither the Scriptures nor the power of God who raises the dead, not for endorsing levirate marriage (Mk 12:24-27).

These patterns of marriage, which would be considered strange if not aberrant today, indicate the importance of discerning the message of the Bible in its cultural setting. Marital customs and outlook change in the span of the Bible's writings and have continued to change throughout history. What we can find in Scripture is not a prescribed biblical pattern of marriage but resources for discussing how God's will is to be lived out in marriage in our time and place.

Marriage is a gift of grace. Much of the outcry about the high numbers of marriages ending in divorce today seems to carry the implication that people are just not working hard enough at marriage. The assumption is that spouses give up too soon on their marriage and put out too little effort to keep it alive. Some are even suggesting that we do away with no-fault divorce laws and make divorce much more legally difficult, thus forcing persons to "make it work." Notice the language—*make* it work.

This is what I have dubbed the "bent-arm hang" approach to marital relating. When I was in junior-high gym class, we had to go through the President's Physical Fitness tests. It involved proving mastery of several skills and tests of strength. I have little or no athletic skill and did not enjoy playing competitive sports. One of the tests required throwing a softball a certain distance. Despite my father's patient practice sessions with me, I flunked that test. To pass the tests—and the course—I had to do well on at least one of the remaining activities. Fortunately, at least in this case, I am a willful person; and one test called for just that quality—the bent-arm hang. The bent-arm hang requires no real skill, except the ability to hang one's chin above a chinning bar by the strength of one's bent arms (feet off the floor) for as long as possible. And I hung there, gritting my teeth and shaking all over from the exertion, until I had earned an A on that test and thus passed the course.

The purpose of the tests was to promote physical fitness and to involve children in athletics so that they might continue to be physically active and healthy. The result for me, however, was that I learned to hate athletics even more. It reinforced my belief that I was no good at sports.

The same false premise lies behind the belief that if people are given standards to meet and encouraged to try to meet them, they will learn to appreciate their marriage and will want to invest more of themselves with their spouse. The divorce rates are thought to signify that people "give up" too soon and that we have become "soft" on marriage and divorce. Some even imply that people get into marriage banking that if they are not happy, they can get out.

Despite this myth, it is a rare couple who marries thinking that the marriage is anything but permanent. But difficulties begin to mount, and the spouses feel the strain in their emotional muscles from doing the marital bent-arm hang. To call out to them, "Hang in there! Keep struggling and things will work out!" is like saying "Be warm and filled" to a cold, hungry person (Jas 2:16). Instead of helping, the community has added to their load of guilt and depression over their failure. The marriage may be legally intact—they passed the course. But the alienation and hurt are not what is implied in God's creation of the one-flesh unity of man and woman (Gen 1).

Working at marriage does not necessarily create a joyful, vital relationship. This is not to say that couples ought not to work at communicating with each other, to work through conflict and undertake all those other tasks that contribute to marital strength. It is dangerous, however, to promise marital happiness as a result of more skillful interacting. Often the marital enrichment programs and family ministries of the church unwittingly promote this very assumption. The words of the psalmist, "Unless the LORD builds the house, those who build it labor in vain" (Ps 127:1), might well be applied to the house and home of the married couple. We can busy ourselves working at our marriage, but labor alone will not ensure success.

There are three basic problems with the premise that hard work and commitment to hang in there will lead to a successful marriage. First, many people who have experienced marital failure have indeed struggled to hang on and have done everything they knew to do to salvage the relationship. Although little research has been conducted on the struggle of persons who are "hanging in there" in difficult marriages, what is available indicates that even their physical well-being is undermined by the struggle. Unhappily married people are less healthy than the divorced or happily married (Renne 1971). As these people go through the process of divorce and remarriage, health indicators improve—suggesting the real toll that an unhappy marriage exacts from persons while they are struggling to hang on. The experience of a failing marriage is rarely casual; it is a physical and emotional trauma.

Second, the belief that a good marriage can be achieved by hard work ignores the imperfection of persons, who can only rely on God's grace to lift them out of their unsuccessful attempts to perfect themselves and their relationships. No matter how hard spouses try, the maintenance of the marriage covenant cannot be guaranteed by their hard work. People who are flawed cannot form a perfect relationship. Madonna Kolbenschlag contends, "The permanence of the marriage bond is its fruit, not its root" (1979:138). A strong and satisfying relationship is not something people can assure; it is the fruit that comes in the process of relating to one another by the grace of God.

Of course spouses still must work at marriage. The merit of working at marriage shows in the success of marriage enrichment programs in improving the happiness of couples. The problem is when this is reversed and it is assumed that if enrichment programs and communication-skills training prevent problems, it is a lack of such training—insufficient work by the couple in exploring and utilizing all available resources—that causes the problems. To illustrate, people who get frequent headaches may learn that if they take aspirin at the first sign of the headache they can *prevent* the headache from developing. But this does not mean that lack of aspirin causes headaches (Markman, Floyd and Dickson-Markman 1982).

The third problem with the "bent-arm hang" myth is the implication that a marriage is the result solely of the actions and attitudes of the partners themselves. It assumes that a marriage is a "closed system," responding only to what the partners do or do not do. Actually many factors other than the personalities and behaviors of the two partners affect a marriage, such as children, extended family, neighborhood, employment, income, health or illness—even such factors as the physical space and privacy of the home or natural events and disasters. An examination of divorce statistics, for example, reveals that divorce rates are much higher among the poor and, in particular, the unemployed (Cherlin 1979; 1992; Cutright 1971; Ross and Sawhill 1975; Wilhelm and Ridley 1988). Poverty and economic uncertainty are usually beyond the control of the spouses, yet they create conditions that make marital survival more difficult. Of course, many poor people do not have troubled marriages; but they are certainly more vulnerable to chronic marital distress from the strain of not having enough in an affluent society. To tell them to "hang on" and "work harder" is to blame them for the stress with which they must live.

As significant as marriage is, it is not the most important relationship of life. A prevalent notion in U.S. culture is that nothing should come before work on one's marital relationship—not children (couples are told to keep the demands of parenting secondary to building their own relationship), not work (we are admonished not to bring work home but to recognize the need for "quality family time"), not even church (family ministry approaches often argue that church activities should not be allowed to detract from family/marital time). This relationship called marriage must be important indeed.

There are elements of truth in this, of course. It is true that parents need time with children and with each other and that the clutter of activities needs to be cleared away to allow this time together. For many, however, busyness is a way of filling time because they lack meaningful relationships with others beyond their spouse. In our mobile society, couples are often far removed from their families. Many churches are so large that they can no longer meet individual family members' needs for community, especially in a one-hour worship service spent in anonymity. As a result, the need for community and belonging, for family, must be met within the marital relationship itself. For many, the spouse is the only person with whom they can share lasting friendship and feelings of being a family. No one person, however, can meet all one's needs for intimacy and family relationships.

One might even argue that much of the current emphasis on family ministry may serve not to strengthen families but to raise the stakes even higher. Not only do Christians get the message that they are supposed to honor their marital commitments, but they are supposed to have increasingly enriched and fulfilling marriages. The Marriage Encounter movement within the Catholic Church advocates a process of daily dialogue: spouses write their private thoughts or feelings in a journal, share with each other what they have written and then discuss what they have read (National Marriage Encounter 1978). Although this kind of intimate sharing of thoughts, feelings and experiences can be of great benefit, advocating such a practice poses the danger—borne out in research on the effects of this approach—of couples becoming disillusioned and frustrated when they are unable to experience this intimacy in the press of daily life (DeYoung 1979; Doherty and Lester 1982; Doherty, McCabe and Ryder 1978). Couples are left with the heavy expectation that for their spiritual well-being they should have not only daily dialogue with God but also meaningful dialogue with the marital partner. Commitment is no longer enough; we are supposed to be on a perpetual interpersonal "high" in our marital relationship. Inevitably, doubts arise: *What's wrong with our marriage that we go for days without having a single intimate, meaningful, soul-searching conversation?* When these dry spells stretch into weeks or months, frustration or even despair is predictable.

Attempts to help strengthen marriage and family relationships sometimes inadvertently serve only to increase stress and at times precipitate crises in already overloaded relationships. One early research study reported that ten years after participating in Marriage Encounter, 19 percent of the couples reported more frustration because of awareness of unmet needs, 14 percent reported conflict over Marriage Encounter itself, and 9 percent reported greater discomfort in discussing feelings with their spouses (Doherty and Lester 1982). Similar results might be suspected from other such marriage enrichment programs, although the research examining these factors of disillusionment and frustration has not been conducted.

One problem, then, with all the attention given to marital relationships is that people begin to expect to live day in and day out in an emotional hothouse modeled on the empathic listening, sharing of self and collapse of individual boundaries that they experienced in a marriage retreat or similar program. Certainly these programs have been a great help to many couples, but they must be balanced with two guidelines. First, days will come—most days—when marriage partners will not experience this level of intimacy with each other; and these days may at times stretch into longer periods of relative distance—"dry spells." Second, this is to be expected because, as important as it is, one's marriage is not the most important relationship of life, and attention cannot always be primarily given to it.

In addition to the inevitable failure that results when marriage is made *the* relationship of life, the spiritual significance of elevating marriage to primary status needs to be examined. David Elkind perceptively writes:

> [People] want something permanent and beautiful to believe in. The current escalating divorce rate reflects, at least in part, this search. Just as the child gives up a succession of heroes because he or she discovers each of the heroes' faults, people today are willing to give up marriage if the partner is not perfect. In effect, therefore, the search for the God-like person who will be perfect in every way has shifted from the church to the family. Partners now seek in their mates the qualities once sought in God. . . . Among the stresses of contemporary marriages are the tremendous demands that were once fulfilled by a vital belief in God. (Elkind 1981:102)

The primary relationship of life is with God, not with a marital partner. Yet many couples enter marriage thinking that in this way they can escape their aloneness (Napier 1980) and implicitly that they can escape their need for God.

The Bible keeps marriage in proper perspective; it recognizes that marriage is an institution of this world that does not carry over to the next (Mk 12:25). It is not an end in itself. In marriage the two are to become one flesh, but flesh is one of those things that are passing away (1 Cor 15:50). Paul was not antimarriage, as some of his interpreters have unfairly labeled him, but he did recognize that devotion to a spouse is secondary to devotion to the Lord. Certainly the husband and wife are to be anxious to please each other (1 Cor 7:33-34), but what is primary is undivided loyalty to the Lord (1 Cor 7:35).

As a consequence, for Christians the marital relationship involves two dynamics, neither of which can be ignored. The vertical dynamic is each partner's individual relationship with God and their calling to ministry as partners. The horizontal dynamic is the relationship of partners with each other. It is their need to care and be cared for, to share joys and sorrows, to be intimate and to accept and feel acceptance. This dynamic enhances their ability to go out from a home base of acceptance and love into the service and sacrifice to which they are called.

Marriage for Christians is a partnership of mutual submission to the calling of the Christian journey, which transcends the marital relationship itself. If the union of Christ and the church is to be compared to the union of husband and wife, as it is in Ephesians 5, it would follow that the marriage relationship has a transcendent purpose in God's scheme of things. Not only is it a good in this transient life, but, according to Joe Leonard, it "reaches beyond itself toward participation in the creative/redemptive work of God" (Leonard 1984:9).

Sexuality

Marriage is the relationship in which Christians most fully express and enjoy their sexuality. Our culture, however, has the peculiar notion that "making love" is a skill that an individual can acquire, like playing the piano or violin, and that is transferable from partner to partner. A great pianist can apply musical skill to almost any piano. Similarly, we hear individuals described in movies or television, with obvious admiration, as being "good in bed." One can no more be an individually skilled sex partner than one can be a lover without a beloved. Sexual skill belongs to a particular relationship, not to individuals. And it develops over time.

Movies depict brief sexual encounters erotically, as though they bring partners to the height of pleasure, though risky and "sinful." The sin, however, is the treatment of persons as objects, instruments on which others can demonstrate their skill, rather than as an other whom one cherishes and lives in covenant with for a lifetime of intimacy. Being intimate with a lover is much more than "doing it." Married couples are often sex partners for twenty or thirty years before they are able to fully experience the intense intimacy and eroticism that come with abandonment of pretense in the safety of the trusted partner's presence (Schnarch 1991). Sadly, some spouses treat each other as objects, their marital intimacy stunted by our culture's view of sex as individual performance.

Over their lifetime together, however, a couple can increasingly be "naked and not ashamed," sharing their most intimate thoughts and feelings and exploring one another fully. Sexual intimacy deepens as partners learn to

☐ recognize vulnerability and greet it in each other with maximum tenderness and honor

☐ laugh at self often, but never at the partner

☐ be lovingly honest about what one wants and does not want

☐ give oneself permission to try new experiences with the other, recognizing that if experiences are disappointing, there will be another time—that is the joy of living in covenant

☐ appreciate intimacy in all its expressions—a simple look across a room; a talk long into the night; brief moments of sexual intimacy in the midst of hectic schedules and fatiguing demands; a long romantic evening of music and candlelight—for one is not more important than the other

☐ remember that sexual intimacy points to the joy of God's unconditional love; it is not a graded piano recital

Implications for Ministry

The definition of marriage for Christians needs to be clearly stated. Marriage is an opportunity to practice the teachings of Christ in our daily lives, living faithfully and lovingly, placing another's needs before our own. The challenge is more than two imperfect people can meet through skill and determination alone; it calls for recognition that God joins a couple together and it is through God's grace that love endures a lifetime. Thus marriage calls for ongoing prayer, by both partners together and by each of the partners alone, asking God to work through them as instruments of God's peace and love and faithfulness. Therefore, helping people to prepare for marriage and to care for each other as partners over a lifetime is discipleship training central to the mission of the church.

Marriage Savers, a standardized marriage policy being adopted by participating churches, is a proactive effort to reclaim the church's role as a disciplining body of believers rather than a wedding chapel for hire. Michael McManus, a Presbyterian layman, developed the concept. The minimal standards to which clergy agree involve some variation of the following:

□ A minimum period from an initial counseling session to the wedding. Some churches require six months, others even more time.

□ A minimum number of counseling sessions (e.g., at least four), with one devoted to a premarital inventory[2] and another to a biblical understanding of marriage and divorce.

□ A leader/mentor couple partnership, with the lead couple trained as role models and lay counselors.

□ Attendance at an engaged couples encounter or enrichment weekend or seminar.

□ A minimum number (e.g., at least two) of postmarital counseling sessions with the mentor couple during the year after the wedding (McManus 1993).

Marriage Savers also teaches children and youth what marriage means for Christians. Churches' work together in this program sends a clear statement to the community that Christians have a distinct vision for marriage.

Marriage enrichment seminars and retreats need to be perennial components of the church's ministry. They provide opportunity for couples to assess their relationship strengths, identify areas for growth, and feel the support of a community of faith that recognizes the import and challenge of their commitment. Research indicates that these can make a real difference in the lives of couples, promoting long-term change (Guerney and Maxson 1990).

Howard Markman and Scott Stanley at the University of Denver have developed the Prevention and Relationship Enhancement Program (PREP) for Christians (Stanley et al. 1998). In a study in Germany, sixty-four couples who took PREP are being tracked along with thirty-two members of a comparison group: eighteen who received standard premarital counseling and fourteen who received no counseling at all. Five years after the course, given in six weekly sessions of two hours, the PREP couples have a divorce rate of 4 percent. In com-

---

[2]PREPARE, developed by David Olson, is one of the best tools for this assessment. The inventory contains a form for each person to complete; these are then sent to the organization that publishes the tool, Life Innovations. Life Innovations conducts a computer analysis of the inventories and provides a printed profile to help the couple to examine their relationship. The content of the profile can also be used to provide information to the leader. Information about obtaining this and other similar resources is given in appendix B.

parison, 24 percent of the couples in the comparison group have divorced. Those who took PREP also reported half the incidence of physical aggression (Marano 1997).

DIVORCE AND POSTDIVORCE FAMILY RELATIONSHIPS

Divorce has become a growing reality in the church of today.[3]

About half of all those who currently marry can be predicted to divorce within seven years (Strong and DeVault 1995). Half of all recent marriages are remarriages for at least one partner (Ganong 1986). A majority of today's children will witness the disruption of either their parents' marriage or their own by divorce.

Perhaps the most alarming consequence of divorce is the long-term effects it has on children. Until recently, interpreters of the social sciences tended to say that living in a single-parent home is better for children than living in the hostile, tense environment of a conflicted family. New longitudinal research of adults and children in divorced families suggests, however, that divorce has its own set of negative consequences. According to data from a nationally representative sample of 17,110 children, children not living with both biological parents were more likely than those living with both biological parents to have repeated a grade of school, to have been expelled or to have been treated for emotional or behavioral problems. Compared to children living with both biological parents, children of divorce experienced an increased risk of accidental injury and poisoning. "The fact that there was no elevation in risk among children of never-married mothers suggests that the processes involved here are those relating to the conflict and crisis of divorce and remarriage rather than to the lack of supervision in one-parent households" (Dawson 1991:581). When the mother has custody, after a year or so older school-age and adolescent girls appear to have few problems traceable to the parental divorce. Boys, however, develop more problems in school, more acting out, and have a harder time in general. If the mother remarries, the picture reverses, with a change for the worse for the girls and an improvement for the boys, if they like the stepfather (Wallerstein and Blakeslee 1989). Most older children do not feel a part of the new family; they perceive it to be good for their parents, but not for them.

---

[3]Some of the material in this section draws from Garland and Garland 1986 and Garland 1995.

The long-range impact of parental divorce extends into the young adulthood of children. Parental divorce is associated with lower educational attainment and an earlier age at marriage for both sexes, although sons of divorced parents are less likely ever to marry. There is great anxiety and fear of being abandoned, unloved and betrayed. Many young adult daughters of divorced parents go through a series of broken relationships; it appears that they break off intimate relationships themselves so they are not left. The anxiety over infidelity can thus become a self-fulfilling prophecy. In a long-range study of divorced families, Judith Wallerstein found that two-thirds of the daughters, many of whom seem to adjust well to the initial crisis, later fear betrayal and are unable to make lasting commitments (Wallerstein and Blakeslee 1989). Daughters of divorced parents have a greater probability than daughters of married parents to experience divorce themselves (Keith and Finlay 1988). One-third of young adults whose parents divorced have little or no ambition and are underachievers. Twenty percent drink heavily. One-third of the young adult sons and 10 percent of the daughters have been convicted of theft, assault or some other serious crime (Wallerstein and Blakeslee 1989).

It is not only children who are negatively affected. Divorced partners find that divorce is not the solution to marital distress they had hoped. Only in one out of ten cases do both spouses report satisfaction with their lives after the divorce. Far more often the spouse who has initiated the divorce lives a happier life, while the other is left with feelings of chronic resentment and sadness (Wallerstein and Blakeslee 1989).

The Process of Divorce
Research into the processes of marital disaffection has uncovered three phases. The beginning is characterized by feelings of anger and hurt—emotions that continue throughout the process. Almost half of the subjects stated that they became disillusioned with their partners—that is, their partner's behavior was not what they expected. Thoughts during the beginning phase reviewed the negative traits of the partner and evaluated the reward and costs of the marriage. Nevertheless, hope for the marriage was also a frequent thought during this phase. Thus, although respondents were evaluating the relationship, they still retained optimism about the future. In this stage, the option of leaving is usually only a fleeting thought. Although problem-solving attempts are under way, there is also an attempt to please the partner, to be the perfect spouse (Kersten 1990).

During the middle phase, anger intensifies and becomes more pervasive. Apathy also begins to set in. Love for the partner is eroding. Thoughts continue to center on the negative evaluation of the partner and the assessment of costs and reward in the marriage. Thoughts about ending the marriage increase significantly. Problem-solving attempts continue but are more direct and assertive than in the previous phase, and attempts to please the spouse drop off. Some experience their first separation during this phase (Kersten 1990).

During the last phase, anger continues to be the prevalent feeling; hurt decreases and apathy increases. Most thoughts focus on ending the marriage; problem-solving attempts drop off significantly. Up to this point, counseling was rarely pursued by respondents, but now 27 percent of those studied were seeking counseling (compared to 12 percent during the middle phase). Thus the last phase was the most common time for marital therapy to be sought— when the partners were already settling on divorce as a probable outcome (Kersten 1990).

Approximately 40 percent of the subjects identified the first turning point as occurring during the first six months of the marriage, and another 20 percent had doubts between six months and one year. Thus 60 percent were experiencing dissatisfaction in their marriage during the first year (Kersten 1990). Of course it may be that *all* couples experience this but some are unable to resolve the dissatisfaction and move on. The finding does point out that the first year is critical, and perhaps also that the majority of those who end up divorcing never attach to each other during this early phase. They become married, but they do not become family.

These phases make it clear that the actual filing for divorce needs to be recognized not as an isolated event but as a marker in a long process of significant and painful family changes. It usually is preceded by months or years of conflict, indecision, separations and waffling that take their toll on parents' and children's security and sense of control. This process makes it hard for both adults and children to accept the fact that the divorce event is really final when there have been multiple separations and reunifications preceding the actual divorce. Many children struggle for years with painful fantasies of parental reunification.

After the divorce, emotional and material changes continue to create prolonged crisis. There is often a change in residence and, for many, a second marriage. In a national survey, a third of all children whose parents remarried experienced a parent's second divorce by the time they reached early adolescence.

That figure rose to nearly half by the time they reached their late teens (Fursten-berg 1991).

Recent changes in divorce laws brought with them unanticipated and unfortu-nate consequences. In an attempt to recognize the equality of women, no-fault divorce laws eliminated the issues of grounds, fault and consent from the legal process and instituted gender-neutral equal division of resources. Yet the circum-stances of men and women are not equal. Some women have been homemakers or have interrupted their career to stay home with small children. Nine out of ten divorced women also have the expense of caring for the children. Women and children experience an average drop in standard of living of 73 percent in the first year after divorce. Ex-husbands, in contrast, experience an average rise in their standard of living of 42 percent (Dornbusch and Strober 1988). Roughly two-fifths of all previously married fathers contribute nothing at all to their children's support. Among the other three-fifths, child support averaged about $235 a month in 1991. Child support from the noncustodial father amounts to only about 10 percent of the income of separated and single mothers and about 13 percent of the income of divorced mothers (Furstenberg 1991).

If the judge interprets the equal division of property to mean the family home must be sold so that its worth can be divided, the disruption and trauma for children and the economic vulnerability of their mother are significantly increased. There is a strong relationship between economic and psychological effects of divorce on chil-dren, in part, presumably, because of the distress it creates for their mother. "Income inadequacy" is the most influential factor in the anxiety and depression of preschool children in divorced families (Dornbusch and Strober 1988).

A final major outcome of divorce is that far too many children also experience the loss of their father. Over half of the children of recently separated couples do not see their father as much as once a week, and a third have not seen him at all in the past year. Among the children of marriages disrupted for ten or more years—that is, since early childhood—only one in ten had weekly contact with their father, and almost two-thirds had no contact in the past year. "Since the great majority of marriages break up while children are quite young, often in their pre-school years, these findings provide an especially bleak prognosis for long-term relations between fathers and children" (Furstenberg and Cherlin 1991:35-36). When the marriage ends with no further involvement by the departing parent (usually the father), all suffer. A noncustodial parent who attempts to completely sever the relationship with the former partner is more dissatisfied and depressed, the custodial parent is more overburdened and depressed, and the children suffer significant developmental and emotional distress (Ahrons and Rodgers 1987).

Clearly there is no easy solution to marital problems. Staying in a conflictual marriage with no resolution is damaging to children. So is divorce. Yet divorce itself is not the major stressor for children. Instead it is the extent to which divorce threatens their relationship with both parents, increases or decreases the tension in the home, and threatens their economic well-being. One research study found that children were having problems a decade before the actual divorce of parents; those problems were related to the poor quality of the parents' marriage and also may have contributed to it (Amato and Booth 1996). "If it is not marital conflict per se but parental conflict that hurts kids, then divorce is not necessarily the solution and may even be part of the problem. . . . For most couples the ideal divorce is no more likely than the ideal marriage" (Gallagher 1996:237).

Many adults who go through divorce experience it as more painful than the death of a partner. They undergo grief at the loss of one who has been a part of their life and memories, even if the choice to divorce was more or less voluntary. Partners often discover the full significance of their relationship only after divorce. They may have gone to great lengths to end the relationship because they believed they desperately wanted out, only to find that they miss the spouse and at times fervently wish they could restore the marriage.

During the process of deciding on separation and divorce, the conflictual interaction in the marriage and the individual's own internal thoughts center on what is wrong in the relationship. Thus spouses build up motivation and a rationale to take the final step of divorce. It is only afterward that the comfortable and familial aspects of the marital relationship are remembered. Like a tree on a mountainside that twists itself to fit around a boulder and retains that shape long after the boulder has been washed away by a torrential rain, each partner has been shaped by living *as a family* with the other.

Carl Whitaker, a renowned family therapist, has stated flatly that there is no such thing as divorce. Marriage involves an irrevocable investment of one's life. The trust of one's self to another can be disrupted or become destructive, but according to Whitaker, it can never cease to exist:

> The craziest thing about marriage is that one cannot get divorced. We just do not seem to make it out of intimate relationships. It is obviously possible to divide up property and to decide not to live together any more, but it is impossible to go back

to being single. Marriage is like a stew that has irreversible and irrevocable characteristics that the parts cannot be rid of. Divorce is leaving part of the self behind,
like the rabbit who escapes the trap by gnawing one leg off. (Whitaker and Keith
1977:71)

In addition to the irrevocable interpersonal bond between marriage partners,
those with children are irrevocably partners in parenting, viewed culturally as the
most fundamental of family relationships. Once a child is born, the marriage can be
dissolved, but not the family. "In their capacity as parents, neither ex-spouse can be
said to be single until one of them is dead" (Ahrons 1980:438). Spouses may no
longer be spouses, but they remain kin to each other as the parents of their children.

The legal term *dissolution* is often used as a synonym for the act of divorce.
But no marital relationship can be dissolved in the sense of elimination, especially when there are children, but even when there are not. The marriage relationship may no longer be visible to onlookers, but it still influences the lives of
the former partners through current interaction and/or memories of the past.

The permanence of marriage, even after legal divorce, is supported by social
research findings. In a study of divorced parents in the 1970s, Constance Ahrons
found that most divorced persons have and need to have a continuing relationship with the former spouse.

These relationships were predominantly kin or quasi-kin in nature, based on
the couple's shared history, including extended family and friendships formed
during the marriage. Some divorced parents considered their former spouses to
be friends, and like other friendships, these relationships were characterized by a
wide range of intimacy. (Ahrons 1980)

Most divorced persons are living out the reality, then, that legal action does
not end the interpersonal relationship. Those who have children and simply walk
away and never look back do irreparable harm, it appears, to their children thus
deprived of a parent.

Social research findings—that marriage is permanent, regardless of societal
beliefs and practices, and that trying to sever the bond of marriage creates
suffering—affirm the truth of biblical teachings about marriage and divorce.

Divorce and the Bible
In biblical times, divorce was not a court pronouncement but an independent
action taken by a husband against his wife. Deuteronomy 24:1-4 contains two
stipulations regarding divorce: first, the husband was to give his wife a bill of

divorce, and second, he could not remarry her after she had become the wife of another man who later divorced her or died. This law was intended to protect the wife. With a written certificate of divorce, a wife could not be charged with adultery should she remarry. Because divorce ended all rights of the husband over the wife forever, this stipulation also may have averted some rash decisions. And a former husband would be less tempted to interfere in his ex-wife's second marriage, should he decide he had made a mistake.

Deuteronomy 24:1-4 does not prescribe grounds for divorce. It impassively notes that if the wife finds no favor in her husband's eyes because she is guilty of some indecency (v. 1), or if he simply dislikes her (v. 3), he puts her away. The practice of divorce was simply taken for granted. The abomination was not divorce but remarrying the first wife. Divorce was so accepted as a part of life that even God is said figuratively to have divorced: "Thus says the LORD: 'Where is your mother's bill of divorce with which I put her away?'" (Is 50:1).

The rights of a husband over his wife were similar to his property rights; the wife was in effect a possession. The only restriction was that a husband could not divorce his wife if he had brought false charges of premarital fornication against her or had been forced to marry her because he had violated her virginity (Deut 22:13-19, 28-29).

In the New Testament, Jesus' teaching challenged accepted practice and turned from what was permissible to what God intends for marriage. Both Matthew and Mark record that the question about divorce was put to Jesus by the Pharisees to "test" him (Mt 19:3; Mk 10:2). The question of the legality of divorce and remarriage was politically dangerous; John the Baptist had been imprisoned and subsequently beheaded for publicly rebuking Herod Antipas for divorcing his wife to marry Herodias, the wife of his brother whom she had divorced (Mk 6:16-29). Jesus moved behind the implicit reference to political controversy to the ultimate issue, God's intention for marriage. God intended marriage to be an irreversible bond of two into one (Mk 10:6-9). It is to be characterized by a loyalty to the partner that is even greater than loyalty to one's parents. Jesus conclusion from this is the familiar words "What God has therefore joined together, let not a man put asunder" (see Mt 19:6; Mk 10:9). He attacked their assumption that God approved of divorce.

The correct starting point, according to Jesus, is not the concession to human sinfulness in Israel but what God intended from the beginning. Jesus implies that one does not find God's intention for marriage in Deuteronomy 24:1-4 but in

Genesis 1—2. In Matthew 19:7 the Pharisees ask Jesus, "Why then did Moses *command* us to give a certificate of dismissal and to divorce her?" Jesus clarifies for them that Moses only *permitted* this because of hardness of heart. It was a response of grace in response to sin, not a command for righteous living. According to Jesus, it is God who has joined the couple together.

We can also see Paul adapting the word of the Lord about divorce in 1 Corinthians 7:10-16, where he faces a situation not addressed by Jesus. Jesus' audience consisted of Jews married to Jews; Paul was confronted by a pluralistic society. He strictly forbids a Christian to divorce a Christian spouse, without exception, and he punctuates this with the word of the Lord (1 Cor 7:10-11). He relaxes the prohibition against divorce, however, when he addresses the problem of the Christian married to an unbeliever (1 Cor 7:12-16).

Mixed marriages—between Christians and nonbelievers—had apparently become a matter of concern for some of the Corinthians. They may have been worried that intimate connection with a pagan might defile them in some way. Was it similar to joining a member of Christ to that of a prostitute (1 Cor 6:15)? In keeping with the teaching of Jesus, Paul forbids Christians to initiate a divorce, reassuring them that the unbelieving partner is sanctified by the believing partner. Therefore they do not need to worry about being defiled by their spouse; if the unbeliever is willing to continue in the marriage, so should the believing partner. But Paul goes on to say that the Christian should not feel obligated to cling stubbornly to a marriage that the unbeliever wishes to dissolve. In this case the Christian is not bound (perhaps better translated "enslaved"). Christians have been called to peace (7:15). This means for Paul that they should not create strife by divorcing on religious grounds, nor should they obstinately attempt to salvage a marriage an unbeliever intends to end, in the fond hope that the unbeliever will eventually be saved (7:16).

In summary, if one asks "What is God's will?" the answer is, God wills that there be no divorce. God intended marriage to be permanent. When Jesus insisted that marriage should not be dissolved, he was not commenting on a particular marriage but uttering a moral challenge to perfection and correcting the injustice that was being wrought by the relatively powerful (men) against the powerless (women). In appealing to the creation account before the Fall, Jesus assumed that a new beginning was being inaugurated. In the kingdom of God there will be no "hard hearts" and no need for concessions, because God will put a new heart in the believer (see Ezek 11:19; 36:26).

God hates divorce (Mal 2:13-16), not the victim of divorce. God hates sin because of its destructive power in people's lives. In the same way, the church must unapologetically recognize the permanence and sanctity of marriage and hold to biblical principles as the measuring rod for Christian living, while at the same time loving and embracing divorcing and divorced persons.

It is not only those who end their marriages in divorce who fail to live up to Jesus' teaching about marriage, after all. All of us are sinners, and our sinfulness infects our marriages. In every marriage there are differences that flare into conflict. When that conflict is unresolved, a wedge of alienation—sin—is driven into the relationship. If the wedge is driven deeper through the accumulation of unresolved conflict, the process of emotional and spiritual separation—spiritual divorce—begins. A couple may live under the same roof with a legal marriage contract, but because of the poisonous anger and alienation that pervade their relationship, they are no less guilty of breaking their vows to love and cherish one another until death. They fail to treat each other with the tender care they would give their own body (Eph 5:28-29). God is more concerned with the hurt we inflict on each other than with legalities. Legal divorce is primarily a ritual of public recognition that the marital covenant has been rent; it is not in itself the rending.

Does Jesus' teaching require that Christians stay in unhappy, destructive marriages? The New Testament does not offer explicit answers. The church must give its counsel, recognizing that Jesus' words were intended to correct a serious misunderstanding that passed off divorce as God's will and caused many powerless wives untold suffering. He also challenged his disciples to the highest good. His church, then, should be cautious not to get bogged down in the same legal casuistry as his opponents by becoming preoccupied with defining terms and grounds.

Remarriage

Jesus' statements concerning remarriage may be broken down into two groups. The basic saying appears in Luke 16:18: "Anyone who divorces his wife and marries another commits adultery." Mark 10:11 has an additional phrase: he "commits adultery *against her*," and in Matthew 19:9 the exception clause is added. Only Mark 10:12 also mentions the wife: a wife who divorces her husband and remarries commits adultery. This was probably an expansion of the basic concept to make it pertinent for the Roman world, where wives could also initiate divorce. From these different accounts of the saying, it is clear that Jesus equates divorce and adultery.

A second group of statements concern the wife who has been put away. In Matthew 5:32 Jesus does not specifically accuse the divorcing husband of adultery but claims that by putting his wife away he makes her an adulteress (literally, "makes her to be adulterated"). He also adds, "Whoever marries a divorced woman commits adultery" (Mt 5:32 and also Lk 16:18). *Adultery* here connotes any violation of the marriage bond, which explains why an otherwise innocent man who marries a divorced woman is accused of adultery. He is considered guilty of violating another man's marriage, since the one flesh of the marriage, according to Jesus, continues to exist. Marriage is permanent, regardless of what human law says.

It would seem that with this judgment Jesus compounds the woes of the guiltless wife who has been put away by making her bear the added stigma of being an adulteress should she remarry—almost a necessity for her survival in the patriarchal society of biblical times, where women were totally dependent on men for shelter and sustenance. This was certainly not Jesus' intention. Instead his concern was to emphasize the permanence and sanctity of the marriage bond and the husband's guilt in putting away his wife—the husband is guilty of adultery and makes his wife an adulteress.

This would have met with a response of incredulity from a Jewish audience, since the essential words in a bill of divorce were that she was now permitted to marry any man. The whole point of the bill was to avoid the fear of adultery on anyone's part. It would be like saying to a modern audience, "Anyone who sells his car and buys another is guilty of theft; and anyone who buys the used car is guilty of theft" (Malina 1981:120).

Jesus' hearers also would have been surprised to learn that a man who divorces his wife and marries another commits adultery *against her* (Mk 10:11). By definition, adultery was something that a man committed against another married Israelite male by violating his property, or that a wife committed against her husband by violating the sanctity of his bed; but a husband could not commit adultery against his *wife*. Husbands could marry additional wives, have concubines and visit prostitutes without any qualms about committing adultery as long as they were not the wives of other Israelites. This was by no means encouraged or condoned, but it was not considered adultery.

In contrast, Jesus identified the lustful look as adultery (Mt 5:27-28). By claiming that a man commits adultery against his wife by divorcing her and marrying another, Jesus redressed the belittlement of the rights of wives in marriage. The wife is treated by Jesus as her husband's equal—as a person, not property.

Jesus clearly labels divorce a sin, but it is not the unpardonable sin that permits no second chance. Jesus' words were directed to those wrapped up in defining legalities. What would he have said to the divorced? The woman Jesus met at the well had had five husbands (Jn 4:16-19, 28-30, 39-42), but he did not tell her to return to her first husband. He did not label her an adulteress, nor did he tell her that she would be an unacceptable applicant for membership in the kingdom of God. Jesus also refused to join in the condemnation of the woman caught in adultery but told her simply to go and sin no more (Jn 7:53—8:11).

A broken marriage falls short of God's will, but this is true of any sin. Our approach to these questions should be governed by the principle of redemption that governed Jesus' ministry to people. Any moral superiority that the undivorced might feel toward the divorced who remarry is undermined by Jesus' claim that everyone who lusts after another is guilty of adultery (Mt 5:28). Every spouse has broken commitments to his or her partner, and every relationship undergoes alienation because of unresolved differences. We must be careful about passing judgments on others; we will be measured by the same standards (Mt 7:1-5).

Jesus' teaching recognizes that no matter what the laws do or do not allow, relationships between persons cannot be formed or destroyed by legal categories. Jesus did not concern himself with legal categories (single, married, divorced, remarried) or the rites for moving from one to the other, but with the will of God and the effects of interpersonal sin and alienation on God's children. All spouses fall short of God's intention for their relationship with each other. For some, the alienation and hurt continue until the radical measures of separation and legal divorce are the most appropriate step to take, and many then remarry.

Yet in spite of the principle of grace that should govern our attitudes toward those who experience a troubled marriage, we cannot simply dismiss the question and assume that with God's forgiveness the slate is wiped clean, so that remarriage is no different from a first marriage. We are creatures with a history, with roots in our past. The message of redemption is that we can be reconciled to God and transformed; our past failures need no longer control us and may have new meaning from the strength and growth that come as a result of those experiences—but they are not eliminated.

We still live with the realities of our past. Although new marital partners may welcome the chance to begin again, they often bring to their "new beginning" children, belongings from the former family, ex-in-laws who are still kinfolk to the children, and patterns of living that developed with a different partner. Wisdom is needed to untangle and live with the complex relationships and issues that are implicit in a second marriage. Remarriage often creates even more crisis and stress than the divorce for children, friends and extended family. Lives become more complicated, ex-spouses and grandparents fear being replaced by new relatives, and children's dreams of parents' reuniting are dashed. Children particularly feel torn by remarriage and are often more emotionally distressed by this than by the divorce (Visher and Visher 1989a). They feel split apart by the need to be loyal to two sets of parents. On top of this, they often experience the turmoil of adding stepsiblings that changes the age, sex and role structure of the family.

Implications for Ministry

Asking what the church needs to do in response to divorce and remarriage is much like asking how the church should respond to any of the myriad ways people suffer.

Offer loving discipline to Christians faced with divorce. In our day, the church that proposes to exercise discipline over its members raises eyebrows. Church discipline, however, can be just as vital in Christian growth as parental discipline is in the development of children. Discipline means guidance. Good discipline/ guidance helps people learn to take responsibility for their actions, make amends for wrong done and chart a course from repentance into righteous living. Discipline is essentially comforting. It assumes people's ability to make right what is wrong, with God's help and the help of a supportive community of faith. Discipline implies that the future needs to be different than the past, and thus implicitly that there is a future. Persons going through divorce need to be supported and challenged to heal, to redefine family relationships and to take responsibility in those relationships.

With regard to divorce, Christians need to understand that even though they legally divorce a mate, spiritually they still have responsibilities and obligations to that mate. "For Christians, a marital breakup does not mean a divorce from loving concern and service" (Campolo 1988). Even more important, Christians carry ongoing responsibility to parent their children, whether the relationship with the former spouse is functional or not. Earl Grollman, a rabbi, suggests that divorce ceremonies can give spouses a chance to say to each other, "Shalom, go in peace," and spell out in front of children, family and close friends what their relationship will be from here on. They can pledge forgiveness and commitment to work together as a mother and father and can pray with their community for God's help with these tasks (Grollman 1984).

Support parents in caring for the special needs of children. Divorce is a time of great insecurity for children. Preschoolers do not understand what is happening and exhibit distress through sleep disturbances and anxiety at each point of separation (e.g., mother going to work). School-age children experience fears of displacement ("Will my daddy get another mommy, another dog, another child?"), fantasies that the noncustodial parent will come back, depression and grief, fears that the absent parent is starving and not surviving outside the family, anger that parents are being very selfish and do not understand the child's needs. Children need contact with the absent parent, to see where he is living; they need comfort and reassurance, patience and encouragement to express feelings. Adolescents fear that their own relationships will fail and are very judgmental of their parents.

In summary, children need careful attention before, during and long after parental divorce. They need someone to listen to them and care about their needs. If parents are too wrapped up in their own loss and life disruption, that someone may well be a caring adult in the family of faith. Older children and adolescents are helped by knowing about the grief process and that they are not alone. They also need to be treated as participants in the process, not just observers. As one child said, "Nothing could be any worse than what you imagine, if you don't really know" (Troyer 1979). Recurring themes for children include anxiety, anger, sadness, a secret longing for parental reconciliation, diminished self-worth, self-blame for the nonresident parent's minimal contact or total absence, guilt because they believe they might have caused the divorce, divided loyalties, excitement and anxiety about a parent's dating, competition with parents' new partner(s), outrage when the new partner tries to take an active parental role, and confusion and role dislocation when there is a new marriage (Gottlieb 1988).

Caring adults and peers in the community of faith can provide a refuge, a place to express feelings, find support and put boundaries around the familial pain, so that play and normal child/youth activities can be restored. This support can come informally from friends or through participation in regular church programs with sensitive adult leaders. It can also be directive, through divorce support groups for children and adolescents. It is important to challenge parents—both as individuals and as parenting partners—to provide the parental presence, support and guidance that only they can give.

Provide divorcing persons with acceptance and support. For divorced spouses, developing a parenting partnership is a tall order; some experts have expressed doubt that it is even possible for many couples. Parents who cannot get along when they are married are unlikely to work out their differences when they are divorced. Remarriage often widens the emotional gulf even further.

Surrounding a couple with a community of people who believe in God's power to work with imperfect folks in difficult circumstances, and who love them enough to challenge them and walk with them in their effort, can make that which seems impossible possible. Friendship and the spiritual guidance that comes with participation in a community of faith are the most important ways this encircling support can be offered.

There are a number of structured ministries and programs through which churches can help parents take responsibility for reshaping their lives. Seminars and support groups can be immensely helpful (Richards and Hagemeyer 1986). Some families need more individualized guidance in making decisions about custody and parental responsibilities and in negotiating ongoing family relationships, which can be provided by professional counseling. But financial resources are typically at a low ebb in divorcing families. Congregations can provide professional help either directly by staff persons or by providing scholarships for services available in the community. The underlying focus of these ministries, although they may include mental health services, should be spiritual guidance—helping people find and live out God's will.

Perhaps the most pressing concern is the absent parent's (usually the father's) continued involvement in the lives of the children. Fathers who have infrequent contact with their children fall into four groups: those embroiled in conflict with their ex-wives, those with personal problems or barriers, those who live at a great distance, and those who have teenagers with busy lives (Arditti 1990). All may need help in developing effective bridges to their children.

Seek discernment with Christians about whether to remarry. Should divorced persons be required to live the rest of their lives single? Perhaps Tony Campolo has the best answer, if not the cleanest: it is too complex a question for a legalistic response; we must struggle with it as a church, not leaving the couple to struggle alone, and in each case we must hold in tension that our God is a God of second chances and forgiveness and that marriage is permanent. "Allowing remarriage for divorced persons only after prayerful deliberation and approval by the leaders of the church gives hope for remarriage without taking the whole process too lightly. This is a way of affirming people who need another chance while not accepting without question the belief that divorce and remarriage is a right of Christians" (Campolo 1988:201).

The church should not suggest guidance for the divorcing or remarrying congregant unless it takes place in an ongoing relationship of congregational love and support. Persons who have experienced divorce are grieving the loss of family—a spouse, in-laws, perhaps even daily contact with children. Finally, Christian discipline prepares people to hear the call of God. Divorced persons need to be challenged to find God's purpose for them in and through their experience.

Chapter 22

Parents & Children

I F MARRIAGE IS THE PRIMARY BIBLICAL METAPHOR FOR GOD'S RELA-
tionship with God's people and Christ's relationship with the church, then parenting is the primary biblical metaphor for God's relationship with each of us as
individuals. God is best understood as loving parent. Ken Chafin points out the
beautiful messages parents can draw from the parable of the prodigal son and loving father (Lk 15:11-24):

"You are free": Words of letting go
"I love you": Words of unconditional, uninterrupted bonds
"All is forgiven": Words of reconciliation
"I enjoy you": Words of celebration (Chafin 1991)

Parenting never ends in this lifetime, except in the most tragic of circumstances, when the death of children precedes the death of parents. Over time the
roles and the issues change, but the images endure—letting go and holding close,
unconditional and uninterrupted love, forgiveness, reconciliation and celebration.

PARENTING CHILDREN

Raising children is now considered a lifestyle choice; it is not necessarily a function of every family. Couples make intentional decisions about whether or not to

parent children. Even couples who do not actively make this decision but are surprised with a pregnancy still have the choice, in Western societies, of whether to allow the pregnancy to carry them into parenting or to abort. No longer is *bastard* the label evoking greatest sympathy for a child; now it is *unwanted.*

Parenting involves one of the largest economic obligations one can take on, with little expectation of any return in kind. Instead the return consists almost entirely of the deep emotional satisfaction that comes in myriad ways in relationships with growing children.

I relished watching my teenagers play team sports. I said to them, only half joking, "I feed and clothe you, and your job is to entertain me." They laughed, but they did not like it, and understandably so. How much entertainment or success does it take to return the commitment children know has gone into their care? Being a child is in too many cases an impoverishing experience. The only way to pay back is to be a success, in whatever currency is most pleasing to the parent—a sports star, high grades, social adeptness. The major way children contribute to their families today is emotional—pleasing parents.

Children have become an expensive hobby, something to be enjoyed in spare time if the family can afford it, like golf or another expensive pastime. As a glaring indicator of the belief that parenting is and should be a choice, Americans have about the same emotional reaction to poor folks having children as they do to welfare recipients driving fancy cars—you can only do that if you earned the money for it.

Issues for Parents in American Culture

Parents in our culture face a number of issues. First, parenting is a two- or more-person job, but many parents are raising children on their own. Second, many parents feel total responsibility for the well-being and development of their children yet feel their sense of competence eroding. Third, parenting requires a constant state of readiness and demands spiritual strength. Fourth, the role of father needs to be emphasized and supported. And finally, blending family life differs significantly from first-marriage families and presents particular challenges.

The best parenting requires a minimum of two adults working together. Parenting is a responsibility best carried by two persons; and even with two, there is need for a great deal of assistance and support, particularly when children are young.

Who those two persons are may vary. Of course they may be the biological parents, but they may also be a parent and a grandparent, or a parent and sibling. In many societies, and perhaps more often than we realize in our own, it is the mother and grandmother.

The combination of single parenting and employment creates an enormous challenge. Many single-parent families simply lack the resources to meet the new challenges they face: (1) financial security, (2) support for childcare and maintenance of the household, (3) relationships with family members, including the ex-partner's relatives, and (4) reorganizing and increasing their involvement with support systems to adjust for the lack of affirmation and nurturing received at home (Jung 1996).

On the other hand, single parents who have adequate financial resources and a supportive community can provide effective care and guidance for their children. Myina Olson and Judith Haynes explored the dynamics of single parenting through in-depth interviews with twenty-six single parents who had been identified as "successful" by qualified professionals. The following themes for successful single parenthood emerged.

☐ Acceptance of the responsibilities and challenges of single parenthood. A positive attitude toward life, acknowledging the difficult aspects of single parenting—lack of personal time, restricted social life, sole responsibility for multiple needs, financial stress.

☐ Resolution of anger toward the ex-partner, no detectable bitterness or self-pity, and a deep sense of satisfaction with their lives.

☐ Prioritization of the parental role. Warmth, pride and compassion for their children. Their goal in life was to be the best possible parent.

☐ Consistent, nonpunitive discipline.

☐ Emphasis on open communication.

☐ Ability to foster individuality within a supportive family unit.

☐ Recognition of their need for self-care.

☐ Dedication to rituals and traditions (Olson and Haynes 1993).

Awareness of the vulnerabilities and challenges of single parenting should not lead congregations to overlook that even two parents are really not enough adults for any child. Children need a network of adults with whom to relate: parents of peers, single persons, married persons without children, older adults, both kin and nonkin. Such a network provides a child with security, respite from parents and additional life models (Garland 1990b).

Many parents are under great stress: they feel total responsibility for the well-being and development of their children, yet they feel their sense of competence eroding. Parents feel responsible for the health, security, and intellectual and social development of their children. We live in an "accountable" society. If we become sick, it is assumed we did not handle the stress of work well, or we have neglected good nutrition and faithful exercise. If a child has problems, it must be due to "something going on" at home. State legislatures consider jailing parents for their children's delinquent behavior: if children transgress, parents are accountable. This attitude has long been embedded in our culture. For example, in the mid-twentieth century, Christian parents were admonished to look for their own failings when their children have problems:

> We believe any parent who has a lost, straying, and wandering child will find upon honest self-examination that he has failed in some basic way to bring his child in the way in which he should go. . . . Generally, the downfall of every character can be traced to some defect in the home life. (Williams 1951:17-18)

But if this is true, then God too has failed, because God's children certainly do wander. In fact, parents cannot be considered fully responsible for their children. The community, the ecological environment and the culture are multiple layers of influence on the lives of both children and parents.

Nevertheless, parents feel heavy responsibility for providing children with the experiences and opportunities they need to grow into healthy, happy, contributing adults. To help us with that responsibility an ever-expanding array of choices present themselves—choices of schools, extracurricular sports, music and other enrichment experiences, church programs. However rightly, schools and churches and other children's organizations increasingly expect parental involvement. Parents run faster and faster, trying to balance all these opportunities that quickly become expectations.

A new function has been added to the family of dependent children: command center for the deployment of wheels and parental presence. For one-parent families, the command center function presents almost insurmountable obstacles to a sense of competence. For two-parent families, this function is carried out in a complex planning process over the dinner table, or as parents communicate via telephone from work sites or through office voicemail systems. I recounted in two earlier chapters the terrible experience of being unable to find my son after soccer practice one fall evening years ago, when we had tried to cram too many activities into one evening. After the police search ended successfully, several friends said to me, "You need a phone in your car so your family can always reach you." My experience touches a raw nerve of family life today—the fear that with a misunderstanding or an unforeseen delay, our tight plans will come tumbling around us. Worse, parents sense that the very essence of their children's safety and well-being depends on their ability to maintain constant oversight and keep all the expectations juggled.

After that evening, I conducted a very simple research project. I asked people I encountered in my daily life, "How are you?" and categorized their responses. Not a single parent ever offered a response that fell in the category "bored." Besides the dominant nonanswer, "Fine," virtually everyone responded with something like "Busy," "Stretched," "Slammed," "Tired of rushing." Most people today seem to perceive the pace of their lives as speeding ever faster.

Coupled with an increasing sense of responsibility for virtually all aspects of family members' well-being, parents feel their ability to fulfill this responsibility eroding. Constant reports of crimes and violence create a sense of danger and inability to trust the wider social world for help and support. The immediate supposition that John had been abducted that fall evening illustrates this social climate. The questions then hound parents: Is it ever safe to allow a child to venture out in the community? How will they learn self-responsibility and independence if we are not able to let go?

The erosion of parents' sense of competence is occurring through the demise of communities and neighborhoods where people feel safe, cared for and able to rely on others. For many urban American families with children, few out-of-household activities are actually located in their neighborhood. School, church, work and soccer practice are widely flung, often far from the family's home.

The automobile is replacing the kitchen as the gathering place for the family unit. Conversation takes place in the car as it connects the dots of the family's social system, not at the kitchen table. The fastest-selling car in contemporary America is the sports utility vehicle—a vehicle large enough to live in and out of during a family's daily activities. Vehicles, unlike kitchen tables, are on wheels. Kitchen tables are often near the back door, a boundary permeable to neighbors and neighborhood. By contrast, autos are self-contained, moving through strange territory and more vulnerable to assault than accessible to support.

Chronic stress, as discussed in chapter two, most applies to parents with school-age children. One study of stress and strain in one thousand "average" American families found that "increase in the amount of 'outside activities' in which children are involved" was more frequently reported as a source of strain than any other source. A full 70 percent of families of school-age children and 68 percent of families of adolescents reported this source of strain. It was followed by "increase in the number of tasks or chores that do not get done" (50 percent and 48 percent, respectively). With the exception of "money for food, clothing, and shelter" (a source of strain for 62 percent of families of adolescents), all other sources of strain were present in less than 50 percent of families of school-age children and adolescents (e.g., money for education, parent's time away from the family, purchase of cars or other major items, changes or pressures in job or career; Olson 1989).

Parenting requires a constant state of readiness and demands spiritual strength. Parents need physical stamina, emotional strength and spiritual grounding for the daily rigors of raising children. Parenting is not like building a deck or hanging wallpaper. One cannot simply buy an instruction book, follow the directions, stake out a Saturday or two, and do it. It is a twenty-four-hour-a-day, seven-day-a-week responsibility for years and years. Sometimes the responsibility is a passive one, but even then parents are like napping firefighters, ready to jump and run.

I have been impressed with the freedom and joy that come when children grow into older teenagers. Even older teenagers, however, can call forth parental action at any moment, day or night. As a freshman in college, once I called home in tears over a problem now forgotten. The next day my father showed up on campus to take me out to lunch. He had called in sick, taking a "parental leave" day before there was such a concept, and drove to the small town an hour away where I was in college. Most parents just do that when their children need them.

Parenting brings with it distinctive opportunities for spiritual growth. In the Gospels, the child is presented as a model of discipleship for adults (Mt 18:4). And children also help parents begin to fathom the love of God: parents encounter their own irrational, unexplainable love and esteem for this one who, in the world's eyes, has no status or power—a child (Astley 1996). And yet this same child, who can move a parent to tears of gratitude and a new understanding of what love is, can also move the parent to violent impulses.

Recently as I looked out the window of a taxiing airplane, I read a sign directed to pilots who are moving their aircraft onto the runways: "Entering a controlled area. Tower clearance required." That phrase fits my own experience of parenting. It is much easier to be in the workplace, where there is only one central focus for my attention and energies. Parenting, on the other hand, takes place where there is lots of emotional traffic, not unlike the traffic on a busy airport runway system. Things come at a parent from all directions—including from the air above and behind and out of sight. In a family with more than one child and one parent, there is a multitude of interpersonal dynamics. In every family, parents are constantly responding to the demands of an insistent world of work and school and community, along with the changing needs and personalities of growing adults and children and the ubiquitous tasks of daily household life. Often the moments when parental wisdom is most needed come when parents are most tired, most stressed, least tuned in to their children's needs. Parents need "clearance"—help from "the tower," from One who can help give them direction. Prayer is an essential ingredient in parenting; it helps parents get the required "big picture" that is hard to see when they are on the ground and moving.

Fathers need encouragement and support. The overwhelming numbers of children who do not receive even financial support from their fathers provide a stark backdrop to a changing understanding of the role fathers need to have in their children's development. Being the breadwinner for one's children is no longer enough to put one in the category "good father," as it was a generation ago when mothers were the primary emotional caregivers. It is now understood that children need their fathers to be nurturing and functionally involved in their lives. Many fathers are trying to be Superdads—working at demanding jobs, attending PTSA meetings, assisting with homework, spending meaningful time with their children, going to their concerts and ball games, sharing in the housework and cooking, and maintaining a whirlwind, exciting romantic relationship with their wives.

In many ways this is the same shift that women experienced twenty years ago, with the new expectations that they could do it all—both career and mothering. Unlike women, however, men in our society typically have not gathered in groups for emotional support. One huge exception has been the Promise Keepers movement (Gilbreath 1995). This parachurch organization's tremendous success in bringing together men from a wide range of life experiences suggests how important it is that men receive encouragement, recognition and challenge from a faith community for the responsibility they carry for parenting children. Children need their fathers, and church communities can help fathers tackle the forces that keep them from being there for their children.

Single fathers, including teenagers, particularly need the ministry of the church. Although single mothers certainly need support and validation, fathers—whatever their marital status—need to be challenged and supported as significant caregivers for their children. Many of these young fathers want to parent their children, but they receive little encouragement either from their families or from the larger community. This is especially true if they are unemployed or in school and thus not able to provide significant financial support. The mother's parents, and often the mother herself, may not want the father around the baby. He may not have learned how to care for and relate to infants and young children, and if his awkward attempts are not encouraged by others, he may soon vanish from the scene. He is then written off as uncaring and irresponsible, thus fulfilling the stereotype of "the deadbeat dad" (Lindsay 1993).

Teenage unmarried men can be good fathers, but they need encouragement, support, and parenting knowledge and skills. A congregation's ministry of equipping and support for parenting can make a significant contribution in the lives of these vulnerable families. Many churches have virtually ignored the issues of unmarried parents in their own congregations and communities—and particularly the responsibilities of young unmarried fathers. It is a major challenge for the church to care for these families in ways that both extend love, grace and acceptance to them and teach them that God's plan is for children to be the fruit of a marriage covenant. An effective witness in our society to the loving Father requires us not to neglect ministering to needs and loving children—and their children—because we judge the choices they have made or represent to be wrong.

The noncustodial father—whether divorced or never married—also needs tender support as he attempts to be a caring, involved father yet does not share the daily lives of his children and must master an endless cycle of greetings and goodbyes. For example, one father, with encouragement from a supportive church leader, spends an hour each evening on the phone with his son a half-continent away, helping the boy with his homework. Many noncustodial fathers do remain very involved in the lives of their children and, in fact, have been found to be *more* involved than fathers living in first marriages with their children in traditional family settings (Cooksey and Fondell 1996:706).

Divorced and unmarried parents benefit from help in negotiating their relationships with each other so that they can help children maintain these vulnerable parental ties. The faith community can help articulate the spiritual significance of family covenants, unconditional love and steadfast faithfulness in the lives of parents and their children, even and especially in the face of the failure and the possibilities for redemption implicit in divorce and childbearing outside of marriage.

Blending family life differs significantly from first-marriage families and presents particular challenges. Blending families—those into which one or both spouses bring children from a previous relationship—differ significantly from families in which two people get married and have children that are biologically their own. It is particularly difficult when stepchildren visit but do not live in the home; it is hard to establish routines and rules, and the rhythm of family life is dominated by greetings and farewells. The following differences indicate the kinds of conflicts that frequently challenge blending families.

☐ The parent-child bond existed before the couple bond. There are deep loyalties and family history between the biological parent and child that do not include the spouse. When there is family conflict, it is easy for blending families to divide along the preexisting relationship bonds.

☐ Stepfamilies are born of loss—the loss of a husband or wife through death or divorce, the loss of the dream of the happily-ever-after family. There are old loyalties and ties—ghosts—that make living together challenging.

☐ Stepparents and stepchildren do not necessarily love one another and do not have a parent-child relationship. If a parent-child relationship does develop, it takes time and does not happen instantly, even if everyone wishes it would. A stepfather cannot immediately take on the role of disciplinarian, whether out of his own expectations or those of a child's mother who has wanted someone with whom to share this responsibility. He is not "entitled" to this role. Entitlement grows with attachment. Consequently, the role of the stepparent is poorly defined. Is he a parent, a friend, or neither? Even the legal relationship is quite fuzzy. With no bonds of affection and loyalty, it is particularly difficult for the stepparent and child to weather conflict.

☐ In most cases there is another biological parent elsewhere who has influence on the family. If children spend time in two households, continuing conflict between parents and different values and lifestyles create inevitable conflict for children, and often for the whole family.

☐ The blending parents' values may be different in various realms. Of course, this is true in any marriage, but in a first marriage, spouses often reach compromise and common ground on the important issues before and as their children grow. Stepfamilies face these conflicts not only between parents but also with children. A stepmother may think her husband's teenagers are rude and disrespectful, but their father and biological mother have encouraged them to say what they think and be free with their debate. How clean is clean, how neat is neat, rules about bedtimes and many other aspects of daily living are grounds not only for conflict but also for the hidden mines of "that's not the way my dad did it."

☐ Children may feel pushed out of a special relationship with the parent. They may actively (though not consciously) fight the growth of intimacy between the new spouses, particularly if they cling to the hope of parents' reuniting.

☐ Blending families take on a whole new set of extended kin who may put pressures on them to form coalitions and exclude prior extended-family members. The very number of people in a blending family can seem overwhelming (Ahrons and Rodgers 1987; Broderick 1993; Chapman 1991; Cherlin 1992; Coleman and Ganong 1990; Crosbie-Burnett 1989; Crosbie-Burnett and Giles-Sims 1994; Dinkmeyer, McKay and McKay 1987; Duncan and Brown 1992; Ellis 1991; Furstenberg and Cherlin 1991; Galvin 1991; Ganong and Coleman 1989; Giles-Sims and Crosbie-Burnett 1989; Kelly 1992; Pill 1990; Visher and Visher 1989a and b).

When parents live together, they modify each other's judgment. Each can depend on the other to moderate their mistakes and short-sightedness. Together parents can search for resolutions to the inevitable dilemmas of childrearing. Parents living in separate households, on the other hand, are much less likely to make joint decisions. In fact, each is more likely to hear of problems and issues after the other parent has responded rather than when response is being considered. As a consequence, each may tend to be critical of the other and defensive of oneself in a relationship already fraught with significant levels of defensiveness. Children are caught in the middle.

Parents who live in different households are likely to have only limited understandings of each other's experience. It might help to foster cooperation between such parents if each could learn the other's perspective and problems, and if they had ongoing access to a supportive professional to whom they can take the issues that baffle them or about which they cannot agree (Weiss 1996).

Obviously, living faithfully in blending families presents real challenges that call for the support and encouragement of the faith community. Blending families need the special challenges they face to be recognized, not ignored (Townsend 1998). Unfortunately, congregations often relate to blending families in the church like white people who tried to be "color-blind" in relating to persons of color. To ignore the color of a person's skin is to ignore an important and valuable part of that person. In the same way, if communities of faith try to ignore the differences of blending families from other kinds of families, significant aspects of blending family experiences are ignored. Blending families need

☐ to be listened to concerning the challenges of their lives

☐ to have available educational seminars, counseling and other experiences that give particular attention to their issues

☐ to be held accountable for dealing courageously with the challenges of coparenting with an ex-spouse

☐ to have their gifts recognized and used in the ministry and service of the church

Christians believe that God is making all things new (Rev 21:5), that in Christ we ourselves can be made new (Col 3:10). Congregations can challenge blending families to that new life of grace and service.

The Discipline of Children

Parenting involves a whole array of responsibilities—feeding, clothing, comforting, supervising, teaching, and communicating joy and enjoyment of the child. The responsibility that seems to undergird all of these responsibilities is *discipline*—the guidance of children into valued patterns of living and being. Family ministry with parents and faith-parents needs to equip them for disciplining—discipling—children. The previous section describes some of the issues that face parents in our society. It deals primarily with biological/legal parents who live in households with children. But parenting is not simply for biological/legal parents. John Westerhoff describes how infant baptism in some Christian traditions graphically symbolizes the community's shared responsibility for its children:

> By baptism we are made Christians. However, we often miss the radical nature of this symbolic action. In the case of children, godparents, who represent the "faith family" and act as sponsors for the child, bring the child before the community so that the child might be drowned (killed) and reborn and thereby begin life afresh, outside the bounds of biological kinship. The child is given up by its parents for adoption into a new family and acquires both a personal baptismal name and a new faith-family surname—Christian. (Westerhoff 1985:11)

When it comes to disciplining and loving children, therefore, the principles of parenting apply equally to faith-parents. In the following sections the term *parents* should be construed to apply to all those who bear responsibility for parenting—biological parents, stepparents, adoptive and foster parents, and faith-parents.

Parents are the experts on their own children. Parents need to experience themselves as competent. They gain vital information from others—including their church—that can help them in understanding and guiding their children. Ultimately, however, that information must be put in the context of their own special knowledge of each child. There are no "right" answers for all children—only an answer that may be right for their child. Parents develop a deep, intuitive knowledge of their child's physical, emotional and cognitive self. As we minister with and support parents, we need to respect that knowledge and offer ideas and empathy, without suggesting that we know better than they do what their child needs.

Parents need to know what they are aiming at—and so does the faith community. Because parenting and guidance of children takes place amid the everyday events of our lives, parents often find themselves responding to their children's actions moment by moment, without thinking about the overall aim of their discipline. Yet the most effective discipline aims beyond stopping unwanted behavior in children and focuses on qualities we want our children to develop—responsibility, courage, self-discipline, grace and joy. When parents are looking out for and encouraging these qualities in their children, they will find themselves spending less time and energy correcting misbehavior.

Encouraging these qualities means that parents must have enough emotional energy to actively express appreciation of their children when they are being "good," not just correct or punish when they are misbehaving. That emotional energy comes in part from a community that encourages and cares for parents, that knows what the *community* is seeking to shape in the lives of parents—love of others and of God, responsibility, courage, self-discipline, grace and joy. The faith community, then, is responsible for disciplining parents just as parents are responsible for disciplining children. The best, most effective discipline supports and celebrates responsibility, courage, self-discipline, grace and joy in parents as well as in children.

Parents are teaching about God as they discipline their children. For good or for ill, children take in an understanding of what love is and who God is as parents discipline them. Parents guide children's spiritual and moral growth in daily interaction, week by week and year by year, in far more profound ways than can be carried out in church school.

Walter Wangerin uses Jesus' relationship with Simon Peter to illustrate ways parents can seek to nurture children's growth into righteousness. First, Jesus anticipated Simon Peter's sin of denial. Jesus said, "You will deny me" (Mt 26:75; Mk 14:30). He prepared Peter to recognize the sin when it would occur. He could not have changed Peter's soul if the sin had never surfaced, or if the disciple had not seen and acknowledged the sin when it did.

Children do and will transgress. If parents anticipate this, they can plan to respond with grace rather than frustration. They can emotionally prepare themselves to use the opportunity for learning rather than explode in anger.

Second, Jesus personalized the sin. Peter hurt Jesus, and he needed to see the pain he had caused through Jesus' eyes. Children too need the wrongness of their actions, their responsibility for their behavior and the painful consequences for others to be spoken clearly. Any consequences for the behavior should come only after the wrong is named and the parent has thought through how best to use the opportunity to guide.

Third, Jesus healed the hurt. He clearly showed renewed confidence and trust in Peter in the command to "feed my sheep" (Jn 21:15-19). Children need to feel the parent's renewed confidence in their having learned, in their being worthy of trust, by being given responsibilities for self (Wangerin 1993).

Parenting that is based on God's grace ultimately raises children who are more graceful, faithful and responsible than parenting based on law and punishment (Garland, Chapman and Pounds 1991). Law looks to the past, to what the child has done and what the child deserves as a consequence. Grace looks to the future, to how this moment can be used to nurture a child's spiritual and moral growth. And Christians live under grace, not law (Rom 6:14). We receive from God what we need to grow, not what we deserve for what we have done. In the same way, parents can respond to children's behavior and misbehavior in ways that encourage them to grow and learn and act lovingly and faithfully.

Discipline based on grace therefore seeks understanding. It is not enough to know what a child has done; a parent must also understand the *reason* for the child's actions. The child's motivation indicates how discipline should be shaped in response. Understanding a child's motivation means putting self in the place of the child.

Often insights about child development are helpful. For example, an infant dropping food from a highchair tray to the floor may be experimenting with the principle that when one lets go of things, they fall—an important principle that children learn only by experimentation, however exasperating it can be for parents. Discipline based on grace recognizes the child's motivation to learn; the appropriate response may be removing the spaghetti and giving the child something else with which to experiment. In contrast, an eight-year-old pelting food across the table at a seven-year-old brother is motivated quite differently, and discipline needs to respond to *that* motivation.

Discipline based on grace means anticipating the potential for misbehavior. When possible, parents can guide children by clearing the way for them. Young preschoolers are not ready to learn that all the pretty things on the shelves are not to touch, that plugs are not to stick things in; therefore parents "babyproof" the household. Elementary children learn through making messes of paper and glue and paint, so we designate areas for such projects rather than waiting until an accident happens and there is glue on the living-room rug. Teenagers sometimes find themselves at gatherings in which drinking alcohol or using drugs is encouraged, so parents rehearse with them ahead of time what to do. Parents are like scouts on a wagon train, knowing what is ahead, preparing the way. They do not wait for misbehavior to happen. Parents set limits and tell children expectations ahead of time, and often children live up to those expectations.

Parents model grace in their own lives. Clearly, parents model for their children. Many parents wish the message "Do what I say, not what I do" would actually work. But parents hear their own voices in the voices of their children at play and in conflict.

One of the most significant ways parents model for children is the way they respond to their own sins and mistakes. No parent is perfect. Children learn from imperfect parents how to repent, how to discipline oneself to change, how to covenant to begin again. Of course, parents do not deliberately "sin in order that grace may abound" (Rom 6:1), but they do recognize that their struggles have an audience, that they are teaching their children by their example of leaning into God's grace and forgiveness. They model that repentance and forgiveness are the warp and woof of reconciliation, which is the underlying fabric of family covenant. They show that an error or a transgression is not the end of a relationship and that it can be overcome. What is more, when parents wrong children, their confession to being unfair or wrong confirms their children's sense of right and wrong and thus their moral judgments (Achtemeier 1976).

Parents help children experience the consequences of their misbehavior. There are times when children make mistakes and parents protect them from the consequences. That is grace. A parent who finds on the kitchen table a labored-over school project due that day gracefully takes the assignment to the child at school.

Families take care of one another in these ways. We teach that we look out for one another's needs.

On the other hand, if this is the third day in a row that the child has forgotten homework, the most graceful parental response may *not* be carrying the homework to school but allowing the child to experience the natural consequences of forgetting homework. *Natural consequences* are the most powerful teachers of children and are the best parental response—except when

☐ consequences are not necessary or helpful to learning (e.g., the big homework assignment accidentally left at home—the anxiety was lesson enough)

☐ consequences would create physical danger (e.g., a toddler running in the street) or too-high costs (e.g., a new bike left behind the parked family car)

☐ consequences are too far in the future for the child to learn from them (e.g., not brushing teeth results in dental caries)

☐ consequences are not discouraging (e.g., leaving lights on may raise the utility bill, but the child is not the one who has to pay it)

When one of these conditions exists but a child still needs to experience some consequence for the behavior, *logical consequences* are the parent's best choice. Logical consequences speed up the consequences of the behavior and/or are closely related to the offense. The child who runs into the street is no longer allowed to play outside except in the fenced backyard: "You are not big enough yet to remember not to run in the street." The child who habitually forgets to brush teeth loses out on the evening snack the following day, because there is no check mark on the chore list indicating that teeth were brushed. The school-age child who keeps leaving lights on must pay a quarter out of her weekly allowance to an "electricity fund" each time a parent turns off a neglected light.

Logical consequences often take the form of reparations—"making repairs" on what has been damaged. The most effective are those related to repairing damaged relationships, or what Mary Pipher calls "corrective emotional experiences" (Pipher 1996). A teenager who comes late or not at all to a family gathering can be asked to help the parent prepare and serve a nice family dinner. Financial costs of a child's behavior—repairs to a damaged car, broken window, muddied upholstery—can be made up in part by the child's work alongside the parent to make house repairs, paint or do yard work.

Good reparation gives the child a way to contribute to the family. Logical consequences are in some sense a form of punishment, but it is punishment based on the child's behavior and provides opportunity for restoration of what has been damaged. It is not simply a way of flaunting parental control.

Contrived consequences are the least effective response to misbehavior. Often these are stock parental responses to *any* form of misbehavior, regardless of its meaning or what the child needs to learn. Spanking is a contrived consequence. Grounding can be a logical consequence to a teenager's breaking curfew, but if it is used all the time whatever the offense, it becomes a contrived consequence. Contrived consequences often have immediate impact: the crying child who has been spanked for pelting a brother with food will not throw food, at least where a parent can observe. But the focus of contrived consequences is stopping the observable misbehavior—not learning for the future.

The use of punishment, particularly physical punishment, has the following consequences:

☐ When punishment is used too much, children associate it with the parent rather than with their behavior. As a consequence, children may seek to avoid the punishing parent.

☐ Children become more aggressive. Children who experience mostly negative discipline become frustrated and may act out toward others. When we feel hurt, we want to hurt someone else. In particular, one national survey found that the more frequently an adolescent was hit by a parent, the more likely that child was to become a spouse abuser as an adult (Straus and Yodanis 1996).

☐ The more punishment is used, the less effective it is. Punishment that is rare will be much more effective than constant spanking or denying of privileges.

☐ Punishment tends to lead to a reliance on external controls, not self-control. Children who are punished excessively often will act in ways the parent wants, but not necessarily when the parent is not supervising. The discipline is being provided by the parent, not by a self-disciplined child (Hughes 1988; Majonis 1991; Pieper and Pieper 1991; Rohner, Bourque and Elordi 1996; Rohner, Kean and Cournoyer 1991; Sehested 1994; Simons, Johnson and Conges 1994; Sinclair and Stewart 1992; Straus and Yodanis 1996; Wilmes 1988).

On the other hand, parenting with grace that uses natural and logical consequences requires considerable self-discipline and energy. Punishment and spanking are quick and easy. Children respond quickly, and parents consequently feel a sense of power just after a child's misbehavior made them feel incompetent or embarrassed. Indeed, physical punishment is used pervasively in American society. More than half of American parents continue using physical punishment with adolescent children, having hit them an average of eight times in the previous year (Straus and Yodanis 1996).

Parents may be confused by those who misquote Scripture, saying, "Spare the rod and spoil the child"—in other words, good Christian parents frequently spank their children. Proverbs 13:24 actually says, "Those who spare the rod hate their children, but those who love them are diligent to discipline them." This passage needs to be read along with Psalm 23:4: "Even though I walk through the darkest valley, I fear no evil; for you are with me; your rod and your staff—they comfort me." A shepherd's rod was used to guide sheep, keeping them on the path, not to hit them. Nevertheless, ancient Hebrews undoubtedly also used physical punishment with children. That was what they knew how to do. They had the right to *kill* children who were disrespectful (Lev 20:9). Obviously, what we know about providing guidance has changed dramatically, but the expectations of parents remain. The biblical teaching is not about methods of discipline but that it is the parent's responsibility to guide.

Parents teach self-discipline by empowering children. Parents often find it easier to make decisions than to share decision-making with children. The cook in the family decides what everyone else will eat and when. Parents decide when young children will go to bed, when they will get up and what they will do in between. Parents assign chores and determine how much television children can watch. This is autocratic decision-making—where one or a few people decide for the rest. Although autocratic decision-making works efficiently, it does not teach children self-discipline. They do not learn to take responsibility for decisions.

Some parents go to the other extreme, letting their children make all the decisions. But permissiveness does not teach self-discipline either. In fact, children learn to be *un*disciplined if they are simply allowed to do whatever they want with few expectations from others.

Shared decision-making allows a child to have some responsibility for making decisions within the limits of a parent's guidance. Those limits expand over time. The parent of a two-year-old shares decision-making by saying, "Do you want to wear the blue shirt or the red shirt today?" The parent of a sixteen-year-old says, "Here is the money for this fall's clothes. Let's plan together what you need to buy for school before you go shopping." Children can make choices within the limits of their parents' expectations. "You can practice the piano before school or after school" communicates both the expectation that the child will practice and the freedom to decide when.

Sharing decision-making is not practical or possible all the time. The family cook may decide what to buy at the store because of what is on sale. But even the shouted "Do you guys want the chicken fried or broiled tonight?" gives children some say in day-in and day-out decisions. And by sharing in the decisions, they take responsibility for what they choose. The child who called out "Broiled!" committed himself to eating broiled chicken for supper—it was his decision. The teenager who spent her clothing allowance on blue jeans and T-shirts has to take responsibility for her decision when no money is left for a new sweater. In these examples, children experience the natural consequences of their decisions. They learn to take responsibility for what they decide to do— they learn self-discipline.

Empowering children also includes teaching them how to manage their own lives. They have much to think about, just as adults do, and forget or put off doing things for which they are responsible—brushing teeth, making beds, putting clothes away, finishing homework. Parents often serve as reminders: "Did you brush your teeth?" When a one-time reminder becomes habitual and parents find themselves repeating themselves multiple times, reminding has become nagging. Parents have become their children's memory. Many parents then find ways children can remember for themselves: chore lists with stars to be pasted on when each job is completed, a note taped to the TV screen listing what needs to be done before the TV can be turned on; signs taped to the bathroom mirror; an alarm clock or kitchen timer a child can set for piano practice or to get up on time. When children themselves make the lists or tape notes to the front door to remind them what they need to take to school, they are mastering a key step in becoming self-disciplined.

Obviously, all parents want children who are responsible and self-disciplined. For Christian parents, however, teaching children self-control is discipling, preparing children for fruitful living that is aimed at "the prize" (1 Cor 9:24), a faith that is characterized by self-control, endurance and godliness (2 Pet 1:5-6). The community of faith can help parents make this connection between starred chore lists and Christian discipleship. Parents are not simply doing this to make their own lives easier; they are raising children in paths of righteousness.

Parents call out the gifts in children. Parents have a unique position for seeing and helping to shape not only a child's behavior but also the child's very personhood.

Parents see the gifts and abilities in children. By naming these, parents encourage children to develop the gifts God has given them.

Laurel Hughes (1988) has suggested that parents can do this by giving children positive personality labels rather than simply praising what a child has done. In other words, *in addition* to saying, "You were really kind to your little brother when I know you wished he would leave you and your friends alone," a parent says, "You are very kind and sensitive to the needs of others; that is a real gift." The message is not only "That was a kind thing to do" but also "You are a kind person." Research indicates that children who receive such positive labels perform many more acts of altruism than kids who are simply praised for their behavior. That altruism is also more likely to carry over to other kinds of behavior, not just kindness to the little brother when friends are around.

On the other hand, when a child misbehaves it is equally important to label the behavior, not the child. As with positive labels, children will tend to live into the negative labels they are given (Goddard and Miller 1993; Hughes 1988). If a child is told he is unkind, he is more likely to *be* unkind. Naming the negative *behavior* instead helps the child come to terms with the behavior and not be overwhelmed by the parent's negative opinion of his very personhood:

> You called your brother a brat and told him to get lost. I think that really hurt his feelings. I won't allow you to call him names; if you don't want him around, just tell him that and leave off the name-calling. If he keeps bothering you, let me know.

SIBLINGS

There is no relationship less defined by choice than that of sibling or stepsibling, with the possible exception of the child's side of the parent-child relationship. We are simply born into these relationships, with no opportunity before or after birth for making choices about who our brothers or sisters will be. This is also true of stepsibling relationships; few children have much if any role in making this decision. Yet these relationships have the potential of being the most enduring family ties of a lifetime. As we age and our parents and other first-generation relatives have died, only our siblings remember the details of our childhood from firsthand perspectives. Spouse, friends and children may remember the stories our parents told of our childhood, but they did not live it with us.

Child Siblings

Other than the spouse relationship, perhaps no other relationship entails the same level of intimacy as that of siblings. As children, we may have shared bath water, beds, drinking glasses and family secrets. Together we saw our parents' lives from a perspective not available to anyone else—including our parents themselves. We cared for one another, played with one another and fought with one another. Our life together prepared us for marriage—the sharing of space, stories, the affection and the irritation of a significant other.

The influence siblings have on one another is profound. Siblings set and maintain standards, provide models to emulate and advice to consider, and serve as confidants and sources of nonjudgmental support in times of stress. Siblings are more likely to confide in one another than in parents concerning romantic relationships, onset of puberty and pregnancy scares. Besides marital relationships, sibling relationships are often the only heterosexual relationships in which Western adults can express affection and closeness without eliciting disapproval and gossip (Lamb 1982).

One of the dreams parents have for their children is that brothers and sisters will be close, that they will provide love, support and loyalty to each other even after they have grown and parents have died. Certainly sisters and brothers have a powerful influence on one another. They can create misery, or they can be the closest of friends. As children find their place in a family with brothers and sisters, they can learn that shared love does not mean being loved less, that not being the best or the only does not mean being less important. Parents can help their child learn that the good qualities and gifts of a brother or sister do not take away from her own worth.

Parents can help their children shape strong, positive relationships with one another. Conflict is virtually inevitable in sibling relationships, but children often do not have the skills to handle conflict in constructive ways. It is not reasonable to expect children not to have conflict. It *is* reasonable to expect them to learn to express anger appropriately, to listen to each other and to develop skills in problem resolution. Sibling conflict provides the learning environment for interpersonal skills that apply throughout life. Rather than separating warring children, parents can coach them in communicating their feelings appropriately and managing their conflict constructively.

Children live in a competitive world, and unfortunately the home is too often no exception. In trying to guide children's behavior, parents inadvertently encourage competition with messages such as "Let's see who can clean up their room first," meaning that one will win. Instead parents can encourage cooperation with messages such as "As soon as you *both* have your rooms cleaned up, we can leave for swimming. Would you like to work together or each do your own room?" Of course, children compete without parental guidance, and one still may well be heard saying, "I beat you!" If parental attention goes to *shared* effort, however, cooperation becomes more prevalent.

Parents also can help children recognize how significant they are in one another's lives and the special responsibility that comes with being a sibling. Older siblings may need to have pointed out for them the special place they have in the hearts of younger siblings who look to them for guidance and affection. Children often need help in understanding what is going on with siblings developmentally—why a two-year-old brother says no so much, why a fourteen-year-old sister is moody, why a six-year-old wants others to be impressed by newly acquired and somewhat halting reading skills. In essence, parents include children as partners in providing a nurturing, supportive home for one another.

Adult Siblings

Siblings usually become more distant and have less contact after marriage. In turn, the arrival of children and the loss of family members through divorce, widowhood or death have the effect of opening up family subsystems to include more involvement with siblings, particularly through greater emotional closeness and support. Sibling ties have been called ties of "revocable detachment" (Connidis 1992:980). When support is needed or wanted, siblings are a potential source of it, particularly during and after crisis. These are ties that are taken for granted—ties of entitlement.

Most older adults have at least one living sibling, and compared to younger adults, older adult siblings report feelings of increased closeness and companionship. Nevertheless, it seems that these siblings are building on close relationships established as children and teens; closeness does not generally develop among siblings who have never been close. The strongest sibling relationship tends to be sister-sister. The next most potent tends to be sister-brother, followed by brother-brother. For childless older persons, assistance from siblings becomes more frequent and essential (Brubaker 1990).

ADULT CHILDREN AND PARENTS/GRANDPARENTS

Since the beginning of the twentieth century, the number of Americans over age sixty-five has tripled; average life expectancy has risen from forty-seven to seventy-eight years (Robb 1993). The part of the U.S. population that is growing most quickly is the "older old," those over age seventy-five. Many adults in their sixties and older are themselves providing care for frail (or not so frail) elderly parents. Their need for support, advocacy and help in living creatively and productively are just as significant as the needs of parents caring for children.

Children grow up in a fairly predictable number of years, becoming increasingly independent and less physically demanding over those years (except for the late-night vigils experienced by parents of driving adolescents). Senior children of older parents, on the other hand, have few guideposts in terms of the length of care that will be needed. In addition, the course of that care is likely to intensify rather than diminish over time.

At the same time the total years devoted to childrearing have decreased, the total years of elder care have increased significantly. Most of us spend the first twenty-five years growing up (being cared for), the next twenty years birthing and raising children (two children until they are age eighteen), and thirty to thirty-five years caring for increasingly dependent aging parents. In her research, Stephanie Coontz learned that more than twice as many impaired elderly are cared for at home as in institutions. Thirty percent of elderly Americans died at home, and 45 percent were transferred to the hospital shortly before dying, while only 25 percent died in a nursing home. These statistics indicate high levels of family involvement (Coontz 1992).

The middle generation is increasingly squeezed by demands for care from both the younger and the older generations, as well as by career demands. Many couples delayed childbearing and now find themselves increasingly sandwiched between the needs of dependent children and those of aging parents. Today's middle-aged married couples are the first generation to juggle these responsibilities at the same time that they try to maintain two careers. In most families there simply is no at-home adult to manage the caregiving for both children and elderly parents; most adults are working full time. In addition, families have fewer kin resources to draw on because of the shrinking size of the family. There are not as many siblings or aunts and uncles with whom to share the responsibilities as there were in past generations, and virtually all have careers that severely constrain time available for extended family care.

Negotiating relationships around issues of caregiving can be extremely emotionally taxing for both generations. What parents expect and want and what their adult children believe they need and are willing to do may conflict. These issues are often far more sensitive and difficult for families than conflict between parents and dependent children.

On the other hand, the relationship between adult children and their parents can be deeply rewarding for both generations. The role of grandparent can also be enormously important for all three generations. Grandparents can understand and affirm grandchildren's efforts to shape their identity in ways that simply worry parents. Grandparents can be "important guarantors and recognizers of adolescents as successful variants of the family's patterns and loyalties" (Fowler 1990:112). Grandparents can be comforting, reassuring both parents and children that what they are experiencing is part of a larger picture that they cannot see because they are embedded in the daily issues.

Finally, many grandparents carry primary responsibility for the care of their grandchildren. They may have custody of them, or they may care for them while parents are on the job. The three leading issues they deal with are (1) the altering of their routines and plans, (2) feeling more physically tired and (3) having a deepened sense of life purpose. These grandparents make great personal sacrifices, especially of plans for how they would spend these years, but they do so because what they have taken on is important and fulfilling (Jendrek 1993).

IMPLICATIONS FOR MINISTRY

Many a congregation's child care coordinator has asked an adult to care for the children, only to be told, "I did that when I had children in the nursery. Let those younger parents do that," or "I don't have any children myself. Why should I be expected to do that?" Such responses may sound selfish, but they reflect the lack of attention the church has given to the community's responsibility for children.

Teaching children the ways of the Lord is the responsibility of the entire people of God. Christians do that as parents, as grandparents, as faith-parents. Christians do that as they encourage and support all kinds of parents in the sacred task of caring for children.

In the same way, honoring and caring for parents is the responsibility of children, grandchildren and faith-children. Parent education seminars, parent support groups, and support groups for caregivers of frail elderly adults and for grandparents raising grandchildren are important programs that target the needs of particular groups of parents and adult children. These need to be supplements, however, to a program that calls out, equips and supports *all* adults as faith-parents and faith-children.

Chapter 23

Families Facing Challenges

Earlier chapters have explored the stresses and difficulties that are simply a part of family life in our culture. Some stresses and difficulties come as a consequence of the stages of life of family members: children grow through easy and not-so-easy stages, and so do adults. Other stresses and difficulties come through the family's interaction with social and ecological systems outside its own boundaries, such as employment demands, community expectations and economic pressures.

This chapter looks at some of the major crises and even catastrophes that can confront families. The first section looks particularly at crises—such as death and serious illness, or physical destruction of the home—that assail the family and may alter basic family structures and processes and even threaten the family's existence. The second section looks at the most destructive challenge that the family itself creates for its members: family violence.

CRISIS AND CATASTROPHE IN FAMILY LIFE

Congregations care for families in times of crisis and catastrophe with prayer, tangible support and sustenance, emotional support, and presence. Over and over in my interviews with families, they told me how significant their church was in helping them during times of trauma. A young mother described her church's response to the extended critical illness of their newborn son, now a toddler:

> A lot of people at prayer meeting wrote what our baby meant to them and how they were praying. I will keep what they wrote forever and ever. Our church was incredible. They brought us meals. For five weeks, every night, seven nights a week, somebody from that church brought us supper to the hospital. And it wasn't a casual thing to drop by the hospital. We lived thirty miles out of the city, and they had to fix something, drive it in, find somewhere to park, pay parking. . . . If you've ever had a long hospital stay, you know it will financially drain you, eating meals, meals, meals out. But they brought us supper, and I'm talking T-bone steaks, baked potatoes, salad, dessert. It was unreal. They would fix two individual plates and bring us more food than we could ever eat. For five weeks. Not only was it a godsend to us, but the people in the waiting room of the intensive care unit were saying, "Where do these people come from? Would you get your church people to come to our church and do a seminar on how to be good Samaritans?" It was such a witness to the other people. There are so many non-Christians sitting there day in and day out, and I wonder how they survive.
>
> We didn't have to worry about anything. They kept our yard cut, because it was summertime. My mother was so wonderful. I would bring my dirty clothes to her, and she would wash them and bring them back to me. She'd go buy groceries and stock my refrigerator. She kept us in breakfast food. I learned so much about what you need in a crisis.

Later she described the long months during which they could not take the baby anywhere because he could not be exposed to the risks of infectious disease. During this time, friends from the church frequently came and stayed with the baby so the parents could get out, or would call when they were going to the store and offer to pick up needed items. For the baby's first Christmas at home, a church member rented a Santa suit and came to visit so the parents could take pictures, since they could not take the baby out to the mall for this American family ritual.

The church provides a context for dealing with family crises, a context that emphasizes that these crises are transitions within that which abides before and after the terrible moments. Funerals are marked by the gathering of the family, at which the young children and young adults bear unspoken witness that the deceased lives on in those who follow and have been influenced by his or her life and love. We talk about what we will remember, memories that abide. When a job is lost or illness threatens a family's livelihood and coping strategies, the church's delivered meals, offers to care for children, and other tangible support emphasize that this crisis should be seen in the much larger context of the community's resources—resources that will help sustain when the small family unit, if left to its own devices, might flounder.

Crises and catastrophes: Some definitions. There is a difference between an emergency and a crisis. *Emergencies* are experiences in which some major stress comes from within the family—a child becoming seriously ill—or from outside the family—a tornado warning. The experience calls for an immediate response that supersedes any other activity or agenda. An emergency calls on the strengths and competencies of the family and its community. The goal of the response—an emergency run to the hospital or sheltering the family in the basement—is to resolve or protect the family from the stressor and return life to normal.

Sometimes emergencies become crises: the child's illness proves to be a chronic, life-threatening disease, or the tornado destroys the surrounding community. *Crises* involve some disruption in the family's basic structures and patterns of living. There can be no resolution or protection from the stress, because it has altered the internal family dynamics. Instead it must be adjusted to and aligned with in ways that change the family itself. There is no returning life to "normal."

Catastrophes are experiences that overwhelm people, making any semblance of normal life virtually impossible. The total destruction of the home by natural disaster, the sudden and unexpected death of a member, sudden financial ruin or the incarceration of a parent which sends children into foster care are all examples of catastrophes. In contrast with crises, catastrophes

☐ are unanticipated, with little or no time to prepare

☐ offer little guidance to the family as to how to respond

☐ isolate the family in an experience unfamiliar to others in the community

☐ place the family in what feels like a permanent crisis

☐ prevent the family from having any sense of control over what is happening to them

☐ create major disruption/destruction

☐ place the family in significant physical or emotional danger

☐ evoke emotional and physical responses that make coping difficult: sleep and eating disturbances, social isolation, depression, distorted perceptions, paranoia and so on (McCubbin and Figley 1983)

Family Responses to Crisis and Catastrophe

Crises and catastrophes evoke responses from family members that differ from their usual ways of functioning. They also create an environment in which even usual ways of acting and interacting take on a different quality.

Crisis and catastrophe fundamentally disrupt normal family functioning. In a crisis, family members often feel as if they are operating on "automatic pilot," using habitual patterns of behavior to get them through the moments and hours. Sometimes even automatic pilot fails to work for some family members. They have difficulty sleeping or eating and feel disoriented. The simplest tasks may be enormously difficult; a family member may start to drive home and end up at work, or forget how to make a bank deposit, or not be able to remember a commonly dialed phone number. Because of the high level of stress and anxiety, often accompanied by physical exhaustion (up all night at the hospital, or sifting through the remains of a household decimated by a tornado), creative problem-solving is virtually impossible. This disruption is the reason the tangible, concrete ministries of a church community can be so enormously meaningful to a family in crisis.

Crisis begets crisis. The old myth that troubles come in threes has some basis in fact. The enormous stress and disruption of a family crisis reverberates through the family and through the community. A teenage suicide is often followed by a rash of other teen suicides. Tornadoes usually hit more than one home, and the community itself may be in crisis. The crisis experience also lowers a family's coping capacity and competence for daily tasks. A parent distracted by worry over a desperately ill child and exhausted from nightlong vigils is more likely to have a traffic accident. The physical stress leaves family members more vulnerable to short tempers and destructive conflict, as well as physical illness. The mortality rate for men between fifty-five and sixty-five who have lost a spouse in the last year is four hundred times higher than for married men of the same age. The general rate of serious illness each year is 2 percent; for those who have lost a family member in the previous year, the rate jumps to 8 percent. The interpersonal toll is also high; the divorce rate for couples whose child has died is 80 percent (Labyak 1990).

Family members, together or individually, may deny the significance of the crisis. Denial can sometimes be very helpful. The reality may be too much to process at once. The child's serious illness is overwhelming, and parents insist that she will be better soon, that the doctors are mistaken. It is hard to deny the reality of a house leveled by a tornado, but the first couple of times a family returns to the home site from the shelter they have taken with friends or family, they round the corner with the "crazy" thought that maybe the house will be there as it always was. When a beloved family member dies, kin find themselves expecting the ringing phone or the footsteps at the door to be those of the lost one.

Denial can give families time to wrap their hearts and minds around the major change in their lives without being totally overwhelmed. Functional denial allows family members to look at the reality and then put it out of their minds for a while, giving themselves a chance to escape and emotionally rest before returning to the reality. This kind of denial is especially helpful when the crisis is "not yet"—waiting for medical tests, or waiting to see if a family member is going to be laid off in an upcoming downsizing. Functional denial is not *total* but periodic—taking off a few hours in the midst of tornado cleanup to go to a movie in a nearby town and rest and escape in the cool theater. Total denial is an unwillingness to look at the reality at all. The family member refuses to have the medical tests, despite ominous symptoms; the family decides to buy a new car a week before the downsizing announcement will be made. They act as though they can make the crisis disappear or not happen by ignoring it.

Families need "safe," controlled ways of confronting the crisis in the presence of others who give emotional support. The gentle presence of church community members gives the family others to listen as they talk over what is happening and help them process the new reality they are facing. The family is not alone in this; the faith community is and will be with them. Special rituals can help. A special congregational prayer for the family means a great deal to the family and communicates powerfully that they are not alone. A time of worship and prayer with the family itself may help pull its members together emotionally in the presence of God and trusted others; this may be especially helpful when the crisis seems to be pulling them apart.

Family members often blame themselves or each other for the crisis. A child hit by a car probably has a parent devastated by guilt at not being more protective. Children blame themselves for the illness or emotional pain in parents' lives, and perhaps even for a sibling's illness or accident, although this self-blame seems totally irrational from an adult perspective. Alternatively, and often wreaking major destruction in families, one family member blames another.

The human tendency is to look for someone to blame–if not self, then another. The Bible is full of illustrations of the destructive power of blaming— Adam and Eve blaming one another and the serpent (Gen 3:12-13), the disciples asking Jesus, "Who sinned?" (Jn 9:2).

Families often need help in recognizing that even though they could not stop the crisis from happening, they can do something about living into it. Even if someone was at fault, dwelling on blame does not move the family to constructive response.

Coping with crisis. According to research in family adaptation to crisis, how well a family copes depends on the interplay of a complexity of factors:

□ the pile-up of demands on or in the family created by the crisis itself, by other changes and by ongoing strains in their life

□ the family's characteristic ways of responding to stress and crisis

□ the family's strengths, capabilities and resources

□ the meaning the family gives to what they are experiencing (for example, whether it is an opportunity to learn and grow or it is terribly unfair and meaningless suffering)

□ support from friends, extended family and community

□ the family's problem-solving and coping responses to the total situation (McCubbin and McCubbin 1989)

Families cope with crises using any combination of four strategies: (1) taking actions that reduce the intensity of what is being demanded of them, if possible (e.g., deciding only to stay at the hospital during the day and go home to sleep at night, with a promise from the nursing staff that any change will result in an immediate phone call), (2) obtaining additional resources (e.g., having friends come to help with a hospital vigil or the cleanup after a tornado), (3) managing tensions and emotional exhaustion by taking time out for play, humor and other forms of escape, and (4) rethinking the meaning of a situation to make it more manageable (e.g., seeing the family as capable and competent; McCubbin and McCubbin 1989).

Related to the rethinking of a situation's meaning, faith can be key in defining the meaning of what a family is experiencing. Faith provides a sense of security and peace in the midst of turbulence. Claiming that security, while at the same time remaining active in addressing the challenges, is a process of balancing. It means balancing action and problem-solving with the recognition that only so much can be done and some problems are not solvable; they must be lived with and around. Families need to lean forward into action as well as back into the assurance that there are everlasting arms that will hold them.

Families often need to hear that their reactions to crisis are "normal." Courage is walking boldly into action with quivering knees and pounding hearts.

Only fools are not frightened by fearsome circumstances. Courageous families are also families that are afraid, that worry, that doubt themselves and sometimes flirt with blaming one another, but face their circumstances anyway because to love one another and to be faithful to their life together requires that they do so.

When a Family Member Is Lost

The worst catastrophe to befall families is to lose a member. In the midst of a natural disaster, sometimes we see a person standing in front of television cameras with a devastated neighborhood as a backdrop, proclaiming thankfulness if no one was hurt. Families can lose houses and fortunes, but the loss of a member cuts to the heart of the family's attachments and sense of itself. In addition to death, causes of family member loss include involuntary separations such as kidnapping and hostage-taking, imprisonment, extended military service overseas or being missing in action during war.

As noted in chapter seven, putting a family back together after it has lost a member resembles putting a city back together after an earthquake has leveled it. Sometimes family members try to put the structure back, stone by stone, just as it was before, but they find that no matter how hard they try, they cannot.

Families must alter and reconstruct traditions and rituals. One of the hardest parts of losing a family member is the disruption of the family's traditions and rituals. They may not even have been aware these traditions and rituals existed, but they now are conspicuous by their absence. Birthdays, graduations, family reunions—all of them are painful reminders that the family will never be the same. A new family culture has to be created from what is left.

The family needs to formalize memories of the lost beloved. Some families develop shrinelike areas in the home; the child's room is left undisturbed, just as it was the day the child went to the hospital. Stories of the beloved are important, and families want to tell and be told tales of the beloved. The stories provide some sense of connection to the lost member. Children are often terrified that they will forget what a mother or father looked like; they need pictures of the lost parent. One of the horrors of natural disasters is the loss of photographs, home movies and other irreplaceable props for family stories and memories.

The family loses connections to the part of their social network mediated by the lost member. Family members often tend different aspects of the family's social network. When a husband dies, the wife may suddenly realize that he was their connection to a whole array of friends and associates in his workplace. She now has lost not only him but her connection to these friends and acquaintances, who may come around for a time but quickly fade out of sight. Or a woman who dies may have been the family connector, keeping her siblings and their spouses and children tied together in a web of concern. Unless someone takes her role, the family may drift apart.

The family itself must restructure roles to fill the gaps left by the lost member. Some of these roles are obvious; if the lost family member was the bill payer, cook or child disciplinarian, someone else has to fulfill these functions. Interpersonal roles may be less obvious but are just as critical to the functioning of the family. If the lost family member was the one who facilitated communication, who nurtured, who created or underscored the humor in family life, or who refused to let conflict go unresolved into resentment, the family needs someone else to step into these functions.

When the Family Member Is Physically Present but Lost

Some of the most difficult losses of family members come as the consequence of disease or accidents that rob the family of the person they have known and loved, although the person is still physically alive and present. Brain injury or disease commonly robs families of the relationships they have known with a beloved. It is estimated that 15 percent of the U.S. population aged sixty-five and older has some type of dementia (multiple cognitive deficits, including memory impairment), with Alzheimer's disease the most prevalent disorder causing it. The incidence of clinically diagnosed Alzheimer's disease among those sixty-five and older is more than 10 percent. The numbers increase with age, rising to 47 percent for those age eighty-five and older.

Families provide about 80 percent of the care persons with dementia require. Because of the chronic and progressive course of most diseases causing dementia, sometimes lasting up to twenty years, many families providing care for these persons experience emotional, physical and financial exhaustion, on top of a pervasive grief that is unresolvable because the object of their grief is still present. It is not unusual for elderly caregivers to die before the person for whom they are providing care, in many cases partly because they have neglected their own health problems and physical and emotional limits (Kaplan 1996:13).

Ministry in Family Crisis and Catastrophe

Ministry with families in the midst of crises and catastrophes presents major challenges for congregations. As the young mother with a critically ill infant testified, congregations can be major sustainers for family members during these times. But congregations do better with some kinds of crises than others. Congregations do best in situations with which they have some familiarity. Although life-threatening illness and death visit families, particularly young families, far less frequently than in generations past, congregations have significant experience with serious illness and loss of life. At least some families in every congregation have been touched by the loss of a family member; they can imagine from their own experience what the suffering family is experiencing. Congregations do especially well at organizing meals, helping with chores, sustaining the family through the early weeks of crisis, and providing ongoing concern and attention to grieving family members.

Sometimes congregations must deal with crises and catastrophes affecting several families at the same time, or even the entire community. In one community, a church bus full of children returning from an out-of-town trip was hit by a drunken driver and subsequently caught fire. Many of the children—all from one congregation—died, and virtually all the survivors were seriously injured. This was not only catastrophic for the families that lost children but also for the congregation and community. Congregations provide needed care for multiple families as they cling to one another in the midst of such a tragedy. Often this care is augmented by sister congregations in the community or denomination, which come alongside and supplement what the congregation itself is able to do.

Whatever the crisis or catastrophe, however, there are some key ways congregations can minister.

One or more trusted congregational representatives can be present, providing a witness to the church's concern and an opportunity, if the family chooses to use it, for them to talk about they are experiencing. Families need to relate their story to begin to let the reality sink in, to express feelings in a safe relationship, and to begin to sort out what to do next.

Congregations can seek ways to provide concrete care, particularly by taking over family responsibilities or chores to allow family members to attend to the crisis. This includes all the services the young mother named—meals, housecleaning, shopping, childcare, transportation, laundry. The meaning of this support is not just the logistics of helping the family survive but the nurture that the family experiences as a consequence.

It is important that this care be offered in concert with the family's expressed needs, giving the family *more* sense of control over what is happening to them rather than less. For example, a young mother dealing with her husband's serious accident and critical hospital care may need someone to take her children for a few days. On the other hand, this may make her feel even more powerless, and she may prefer that someone sit with her husband for a while so *she* can spend time with the children. Families in crisis feel powerless; if the church can help them gain some sense of control, it helps. Sometimes that means asking them what would be most helpful. On other occasions, intuitive caregivers simply step in, because the family is in too much crisis to think clearly about what they need. For example, the world was astonished by the care Ken and Bobbi McCaughey experienced from their Missionary Baptist Church in Carlisle, Iowa, when their septuplets were born in 1997. "Seventy volunteers organized by the church help care for the babies in shifts around the clock. 'This is just the normal, everyday way this body of believers works,' Craig Milligan, an area cattle farmer, told ABC" (Walsh 1998:9).

Congregations can link families with information and support they need concerning the specific issues they face. Helping interpret medical information, talking with others or finding books or other resources that provide some guideposts for their experience may be enormously helpful. For example, a friend can visit the library or bookstore, read through self-help literature on coping with Alzheimer's disease, and then bring a caregiver what look like the three best resources.

Trusted congregational members can keep a watchful eye out for the family. This is a role to be taken only if there is a preexisting relationship of deep trust and mutual care between the congregational caregiver and the family. Helping monitor their self-care and decision-making, a congregational caregiver can be extra eyes and ears for stressed family members who may not see one another's needs. A congregational member can see the panic in the face of a child in the aftermath of a father's heart attack, when adult family members are distracted by their own worry and the crisis itself. That congregational member can either help the family see the need to talk to the child or, if there is sufficient relationship to warrant it, take the role of a faith-relative and talk with the child about her concerns and what is happening.

Real communities do have a level of entitlement to offer advice to members. A trusted congregational member can suggest to parents of a critically ill children that they really do need to go home and sleep away from the hospital and have a normal dinner with their other children, while a trusted friend takes the hospital vigil for them.

WHEN THE CRISIS IS FAMILY VIOLENCE

One of the most frightening family crises for congregations is family violence. Violence is the distortion of anger. As discussed in chapter five, anger serves as an emotional warning signal that something is wrong in a relationship, just as pain is a physical symptom of something amiss in the body. Violence uses the anger in ways that destroy, however, rather than ways that constructively address problems.

The Most Common Form of Violence in Our Culture

More than three million children are reported abused or neglected in the United States each year. The rates of child abuse and neglect have increased *more than fourfold* in the past two decades (U.S. General Accounting Office 1995). Neglect can be just as damaging to children's physical and emotional development as overt abuse. In the United States, an average of three children die each day of some form of maltreatment or neglect (Children's Defense Fund 1996).

Persons in our culture are far more likely to experience violence at the hands of a family member than a stranger. A person is three times more likely to be killed because of an argument with a family member or a friend than to be killed in a robbery. Most children who are killed die at the hands of family members (54 percent); only 6 percent die at the hands of strangers (U.S. Department of Justice 1995; see figure 23.1). A gun in the home is forty-three times more likely to be used to commit homicide, suicide or an accidental killing of a family member than to kill an intruder in self-defense (CDF Reports 1995).

During the Vietnam era, fifty-eight thousand American service persons died in combat-related deaths. During those same years, fifty-four thousand women in the United States were killed by their husband, ex-husband or boyfriend (Blackburn 1995). It is impossible to know the full number of children exposed to family violence. Researchers estimate that at least 30 percent of American wives are the victims of some act of physical aggression by their husbands, and 10-15 percent are repeatedly and seriously beaten or otherwise physically harmed (Straus, Gelles and Steinmetz 1980). In homes where spouse abuse occurs, children are abused at a rate 1,500 percent higher than the national average. The presence of spouse abuse is, in fact, the most significant risk factor for child abuse (Martinez 1993).

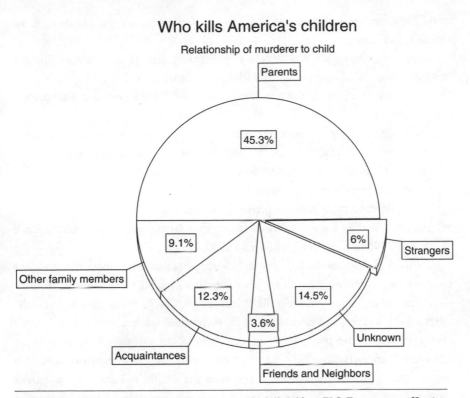

Who kills America's children

Relationship of murderer to child

Parents

45.3%

9.1%

6%

Strangers

Other family members

12.3%   14.5%

3.6%

Unknown

Acquaintances

Friends and Neighbors

Figure 23.1.   Relationship to the child of persons who kill children (U.S. Department of Justice 1995:280)

Violent families are not only dangerous for their members; they also teach children that violence is the way to solve life problems. When children watch parents and other family members deal with each other violently, they learn to be violent.

Research studies indicate that religious families do not differ from nonreligious families in the amount of violence and abuse they wreak on one another. Grant Martin states that the average pastor sees thirteen or fourteen situations of family violence each year (Martin 1987).

What Causes Family Violence

Family violence most often results from a confluence of social stresses and psychological factors that predispose a family member to use violence to impose his will. For example, in the case of child abuse, often there is a combination of the following factors:

□ a potential abuser who tends to act aggressively, having learned that this is a way to influence others to do one's wishes, or because of biological factors such as brain disease or injury, or the use of mind-altering substances, or a combination of these factors

□ the child is acting in some way that provokes a sense of powerlessness and anger in the potential abuser, thus fueling the adult's aggressive feelings

□ the adult and child are isolated, so that the adult has no one to provide assistance or exert control over the situation

□ the adult was already tense or physically exhausted

□ the adult lives in a community or family that sanctions interpersonal violence (Johnson 1996:6; Kadushin and Martin 1981:18-19)

In addition to these factors, research findings consistently show that a higher percentage of abusing parents are very young compared to nonabusive parents. Very few abusers are mentally ill. Mothers are likely to be developmentally delayed themselves, and fathers are likely to be addicted to alcohol. These families are likely to be poor. Stress in the parental relationship is very common (Kadushin and Martin 1981). Most parents who abuse see their behavior as a legitimate and necessary exercise of power to get a child to behave as the parent wants. From the parent's point of view, the physical violence is necessary punishment meted out for the child's own good (ibid.). Most instances of child abuse are, in effect, extensions of disciplinary actions, which at some point, and often inadvertently, crossed the ambiguous line between corporal punishment and child abuse.

This kind of child abuse falls into the category of what has been called "common family violence." Similarly, "common family violence" is experienced by adult partners when conflict has escalated, tempers are lost and someone slaps or throws something. This kind of violence is only occasional, motivated by a need to control a specific situation, rather than a need to be in power over others (Johnson 1995). There is another and more deadly form of family violence, however, that follows a pattern and is fed by the power needs of one family member.

Patterns of Family Battering
Researchers have found that parents who habitually abuse children are significantly more likely than nonabusing parents to have had a childhood character-

ized by insecure or anxious attachments (Bowlby 1988:84-85). These parents thus may look to their children to fulfill the unmet attachment needs, or they may repeat the parenting behaviors they themselves experienced. Insecurity does not in itself cause violence, but it significantly increases the sense of threat experienced, so that a much smaller provocation or stress becomes overwhelming and may lead to an attempt to overpower the other so as to maintain the relationship.

Patterned violence grows out of a threat to the batterer's sense of power, rather than out of the emotion of anger over a specific incident. The batterer's sense of self depends on the ability to overpower others and keep them dependent. This form of violence often underlies patterns of spouse abuse. It is qualitatively different from the action of the infuriated spouse who in a fit of rage slaps the other across the face or throws an object at the other. In patterned violence, the abuser is often *not* out of control with fury, but rather very much in control, and *using violence to attempt to control the other even further*. The batterer is almost always a male, because in our culture it is much more often the male whose sense of identity is dependent on his ability to control others.

These patterns of abuse often have three phases, which are repeated over and over. They apply to both adults and children. Phase one is tension-building. The woman (or child) tries to control things by attempting to please her partner and keep his world calm. At this point she does have some control over how rapidly the abuse progresses into the abusive phase that follows; this gives her and others the false impression that she can stop the battering if only she behaves better. In fact, all she can do is set the timing for when the battering incident will occur. Sometimes she can also influence where it occurs by speeding it up and "misbehaving." At times women do this to protect themselves by minimizing the abuse, not because they like to provoke or experience being beaten. For example, she may provoke him in the afternoon, before he has had any alcohol to further lower his inhibitions against harming her seriously.

In the second phase, something provokes him and he beats, rapes or otherwise abuses her. The third phase involves expressed contrition and overt affection; the tension is absent. He sometimes expresses his sorrow at what he has done, pleads for forgiveness and perhaps plies her with gifts or tender affection (Walker 1988). This phase is rewarding for both the abused and the abuser, and both may hope the abuse will not occur again. Nevertheless, tension is inevitable in any relationship, and as he begins to feel his sense of self threatened either within the marriage or from outside stressors, the cycle repeats.

Battering and rape in a marriage are more deeply traumatizing than violence at the hands of a stranger, because they undermine a woman's ability to trust and her basic confidence in herself and in forming relationships with others. Moreover, a woman raped or beaten by her husband has to live with her attacker, not just a frightening memory of a stranger's attack (Yllo and LeClerc 1988). Rape is a violent act, using sex as a weapon to humiliate, degrade and control the victim. Research shows that the closer the prior association of rapist and victim, the more violent the assault tends to be; that is, marital rape is generally much more violent than rape by a stranger. Marital rape is often accompanied by extreme violence, sometimes in the presence of children (Pagelow 1988).

One result of the psychological manipulation common among all types of family battering is victims' tendency to blame themselves. It is difficult for victims—abused children and battered wives—to avoid believing the rationalizations the abuser gives for what is happening. Indeed there is often some provocation—the child spilled milk at the table, the wife forgot to pick up the dry cleaning—but the violent response is all out of proportion to the victim's behavior. Nevertheless, victims commonly see themselves as having provoked the abuse or having deserved it, no matter how severe or arbitrary the violence is. Attachment to the abuser is often combined with a belief that the abuse will stop if only the victim can reform herself. The abused child or wife often feels shameful, believing that others could not possibly understand their situation. They often go to great lengths to keep the abuse secret (Finkelhor 1983).

Marriages characterized by this habitual pattern of battering carry great risks for homicide or suicide. She may become suicidal at the seeming hopelessness of her situation, or may use a suicide attempt as a desperate plea for help. Or she may feel the only way she can escape is to kill him before he kills her or harms a child. Research shows that almost all American wives convicted of killing their mates had previously been beaten by them. Women charged in the death of a mate have the least extensive criminal records of any female offenders. Yet women convicted of these murders are frequently sentenced to longer prison terms than are male murderers.

Women report that they felt hopeless, trapped in a desperate situation, in which staying meant the possibility of being killed, but attempting to leave also carried with it the threat of reprisal or death. For many homicidal women, the trigger event was the husband's abuse of a child (Browne 1988). On the other side, these men do sometimes follow through on their threats to kill the wife if she leaves.

Sexual Abuse of Children

Like patterned spouse battering, sexual abuse of children is a distortion of the power relationships in a family, in which an adult derives pleasure from coercing or convincing a child to engage in sexual behavior. The average age of onset of all forms of incest has been eight to nine years, and its duration about five years, or until the child either runs away or is old enough to stop the abuse (Kempe and Kempe 1984:15).

When children are sexually abused by a family member, the abuse occurs in a relationship that is likely one of trust and authority. The child looks to the adult to define good and bad, what is acceptable and unacceptable. As a consequence, the child may simply be unable to understand what has happened and that it is abuse. She has no other way of understanding than what the trusted adult has given her as the framework of reality (McFadyen 1996). Rarely does one form of maltreatment occur alone. Children who are sexually abused usually also experience physical and emotional abuse, particularly threats of harm if they expose the family secret.

What Congregations Can Do

One of the most significant ways to prevent family violence is to provide a community in which people look out for and know one another. Violent families are often isolated. Abusive family members may intentionally cut off relationships with others in order to consolidate their power over the family or to hide evidence of the abuse. Those who are abused often feel ashamed by the abuse and hold themselves in little esteem, which is fed by messages from the abuser about deserving the abuse. A community of persons who knows the family can be the first to pick up warning signals of violence. Unfortunately, the isolation of these families often means they are not involved in a community of faith.

Nevertheless, victims may seek help from the church. Each year more abuse victims, perpetrators and family members seek help from church leaders than all other helping professionals combined (Horton and Williamson 1988).

Provide support for those seeking to protect themselves or others in the family from violence. Battered family members very much need the church community's understanding and support when they take steps to protect themselves and other family members. Yet it appears that many church leaders encourage spouses to stay with their batterers, in a misguided understanding of the sanctity of marriage. In the 1980s a survey in thirty-four denominations disclosed that most pastors were more willing to accept marriage in which some violence was present, even though it is "not God's perfect will," than to advise a separation that might end in divorce. Of the respondents, 71 percent would not advise a battered woman to either leave or separate immediately because of abuse. One-third thought women should stay in the home until the abuse became "severe," and nearly half expressed concern that the husband's violence not be overemphasized and used as a "justification" for breaking the marriage commitment.

The study also suggested that these pastors do not perceive themselves as experiencing difficulty in counseling battered women and regard themselves as competent to perform the task. "Pastors who, in order to maintain a marriage, minimize the violence a victim reports to them and disregard her immediate need for safety have mistaken the purpose and substance of marriage in much the same way that the Pharisees mistook the intent of the Sabbath (Mk 2:27)" (Alsdurf and Alsdurf 1988:169).

Loving our neighbors means protecting them, even from those with whom they live (Blackburn 1995). The battered wife who flees with her children is not breaking the marital covenant; it was already broken by the violence. The most loving response she can make to her husband is to stop him from continuing to sin against her and the children. Women who feel the support of their congregation can take the actions they need to protect themselves and their children and to seek help in holding the violent partner accountable for his behavior.

Abusers almost always fail to realize the impact of their actions. A pastor or other church leader can help an abuser to take responsibility for what he has done. That is the only way he can stop. Some abusers tend to unload emotionally or even fall into depression. He needs help moving toward some course of action and away from self-pity. He needs to protect everyone by separating himself from the family, at least temporarily. A separation helps him begin to let go of the control issues underlying the abuse. Of course, and most important, it is the only way to ensure safety for everyone (Gondolf 1988).

For those confronted with family violence, here are some beginning guidelines. □ First deal with safety needs. The family cannot work on their problems until the breach in its responsibility to be a "safe place" is mended. Remember that both victims and abusers will tend to understate the extent of the abuse.

☐ Determine the level of danger: the presence of weapons, alcohol or drugs, sui-cide threats, intimidating behavior (following the spouse, threatening others, pre-vious violence, damage to property or harm to pets).

☐ Offer support, then move to protection—needed medical care, emergency shelter (either formal or with friends and relatives), law enforcement involve-ment, contacting government agencies responsible for child protection. Church leaders *should not attempt to deal alone with family violence.* Immediately seek assistance from family professionals in the community, and call the police if any-one has been hurt or seems to be in danger of being hurt. In cases of child abuse, church leaders are required by law to report the violence to the responsible gov-ernmental agency, and the same holds for other forms of violence in which family members could be considered to be in serious physical danger.

☐ A spouse abuse shelter, if available, may provide greater safety than friends or family. Shelter staff are equipped to deal with angry and upset husbands, and they offer the support of professionals and others who have had similar experi-ences.

☐ Encourage her to seek legal action. Legal intervention may help keep the abuser from imposing further injury or trauma and may be a way to get the family needed professional help.

Provide mentoring and support for healthy family relationships. Family life can be enormously stressful. Family members need help in learning to cope with that stress and to seek help when they have reached their limit. When parents experi-enced a childhood of abuse or insecurity themselves, they may need to nurtured, "reparented," such that they can experience the meeting of their emotional needs in an adult relationship—and stop expecting a child to provide nurture of which he or she is incapable. Some of the most successful child-abuse prevention pro-grams have provided young parents with a relationship with a loving, caring adult who can spend a significant period of time with them, sharing some household activities, showing the young parent how to care for and play with the child, giv-ing significant support and encouragement. In one program, volunteers spend an average of six hours per week with the family in its home during the child's infancy (Bowlby 1988). In the same way, spouses who witnessed abuse between their own parents can benefit from mentoring and modeling of healthier marital relating.

Provide a framework for all families to understand family violence. Church leaders can help by preaching and teaching about the sin of violence that breaks out in homes and the abuse of power from which it springs. Because abusers often convince abused family members that they have a *duty* to forgive, teaching about the process of forgiveness, repentance and restoration can be enormously helpful to hidden victims of family violence in a congregation. These victims need to know that the restoration of a covenant that has been destroyed by abuse depends on both forgiveness *and* repentance.

Many women stay and suffer abuse silently and unbeknownst to church leaders, precisely because they take their commitment seriously. Seldom does it occur to them that the covenant has already been broken by the violence itself. Any chance for restoration rests on the abuser's serious repentance, achieved by consistent participation in an abusers' treatment program (Eilts 1988).

Too often, the second half of the verse in which God says "I hate divorce" is ignored: "For I hate divorce, says the LORD, the God of Israel, *and covering one's garment with violence,* says the LORD of hosts. So take heed to yourselves and do not be faithless" (Mal 2:16). In Jesus' teaching, forgiveness is always the response of one with more power to one with less power, at least in a particular situation. It is the ability to pardon the other, to set them free of a debt they owe. Thus forgiveness by definition cannot be offered by one who has no power to pardon the other or to set them free. An abused mate who continues to be abused cannot forgive the abuser, because she is herself imprisoned by the abuse, as is he. She can forgive him only when she is free. She can forgive him only when she has the option of holding him accountable. That is why God is ultimately the source of forgiveness: only God has the power to hold us ultimately accountable.

Again and again throughout the Scriptures, it is God or one called by God (prophets such as Jeremiah, Isaiah and John the Baptist) who calls attention to the fact that the covenant has been broken. It is God who says, "If you want to be in a relationship with me you must change your ways—return to the promises you made with me." God, the One who has been faithful, is the One who says the covenant is broken; the covenant no longer stands. "It is the one who is faithful to the covenant who calls attention to the fact it has been broken" (Eilts 1988:210).

Keep a watchful eye for signs of violence in families. In addition to physical signs of violence—bruises, burns and broken bones—abused family members often show emotional signs of violence. Some children turn their troubles inward; adults may notice that they seem quiet and withdrawn or that they have reverted to behaviors left behind long ago, such as incontinence or thumb sucking. Other children act out their troubles through temper tantrums, aggression and other behavior problems. Teenagers may withdraw, spending long hours alone. They may become involved with drugs or a countercultural movement such as a gang or the occult. They may land in trouble with juvenile authorities. Or they may stop working in school or going to school at all. Adults may also withdraw, disappearing from community activities.

Being part of a faith community brings with it the responsibility to look out for one another. Community members should know the signs of abuse in children and in adults. Sometimes children and youths are the ones who become aware of abuse occurring in the families of others. Education about family violence and abuse provides everyone in the community with knowledge about the signs of abuse and about resources available to help families. When children or youths become concerned about what they have learned about a friend, they need to know that they can talk with a trusted adult.

IN CONCLUSION

Would that family ministry involved only helping prepare excited couples for marriage, providing toy and book libraries to support family life, setting up support groups where families can laugh and cry together, calling out the gifts in families as they seek to follow Christ by serving their community and world. It is all these things, of course, but it is also recognizing that we live in a broken world. Tragedies and catastrophes strike families in our community and congregation, and sometimes the family itself visits tragedy on its members through violence and betrayal.

No matter how effective the church is in preparing people for family life, in supporting and nurturing and challenging families, congregations will still face these crises and tragedies in the lives of families. In responding, however, the church has opportunity to communicate in its support—both tangible and verbal—that our God is the One who redeems, who makes all things new. No matter what we or others have done or have had done to us, we cannot be separated from God's love (Rom 8:35).

Appendix A

Social Justice &
Advocacy Organizations

Bread for the World
802 Rhode Island Avenue NE
Washington, DC 20018
Bread for the World is a Christian citizens' group working for programs to feed the
poor in America and elsewhere. It raises public support for government programs
that assist poor families.

Child and Family Justice Office
National Council of Churches of Christ
475 Riverside Drive, Room 572
New York, NY 10115-0050
The Child and Family Justice Office addresses justice issues that affect children and
families. It also coordinates and strengthens the ecumenical community's efforts to
respond to children's needs.

Child Welfare League of America
440 First Street NW, Suite 310
Washington, DC 20001
The Child Welfare League establishes standards and accredits child welfare agencies. It researches current policy and legislative agendas that affect children, reviews
innovative policies and programs, and publishes child welfare-related books and literature.

Children's Defense Fund
25 E Street NW
Washington, DC 20001

The Children's Defense Fund serves as an advocate for children's issues in public policy. CDF gathers and disseminates information on key issues affecting children at federal, state and local levels. It pursues an annual legislative agenda in the U.S. Congress and litigates selected cases of major importance to children. The Children's Defense Fund is supported by foundations, corporate grants and individual donations.

Family Resource Coalition
230 N. Michigan Avenue, Suite 1625
Chicago, IL 60601

The Family Resource Coalition is a cooperative network of professionals, including social workers, clergy, health professionals, academicians, early childhood educators, family therapists and others who are working in parent support programs. It reviews prevention program models, strategies and research and provides publications and information about parent support programs.

Appendix B

Resources for Family Ministry

Association for Couples in Marriage Enrichment (ACME)
P. O. Box 10596
Winston Salem, NC 27108
Phone: (800) 634-8325

Church Census and Audio Magazine for Family Ministry (AM/FM)
Center for Family and Community Ministries
Baylor University
P.O. Box 97120
Waco, TX 76798-7120
Phone: (254) 710-1199

Couples Communication Program
Interpersonal Communication Programs
7201 S. Broadway, Suite 6
Littleton, CO 80122
Phone: (800) 328-5099

Family Ministry: Empowering Through Faith
Louisville Presbyterian Theological Seminary
1044 Alta Vista Rd.
Louisville, KY 40205
Phone: (800) 264-1839

National Marriage Encounter
4704 Jamerson Place
Orlando, FL 32803
Phone: (800) 838-3351

PREPARE/ENRICH
Life Innovations
1300 Godward Street, Suite 6850
Minneapolis, MN 55413
Phone: (800) 441-1940

Prevention and Relationship Enhancement Program (PREP)
Center for Marriage and Family Studies
Psychology Department
University of Denver
Denver, CO 80208
Phone: (303) 750-8798

References

Achtemeier, E. 1976. *The committed marriage*. Philadelphia: Westminster Press.

———. 1987. *Preaching about family relationships*. Philadelphia: Westminster Press.

Acock, A. C., and D. H. Demo. 1994. *Family diversity and well-being*. Thousand Oaks, Calif.: Sage.

Adalist-Estrin, A. 1994. Family support and criminal justice. In *Putting families first: America's family support movement and the challenge of change*, ed. S. L. Kagan and B. Weissbourd, pp. 161-85. San Francisco: Jossey-Bass.

Ahlander, N. R., and K. S. Bahr. 1995. Beyond drudgery, power and equity: Toward an expanded discourse on the moral dimensions of housework in families. *Journal of Marriage and the Family* 57, no. 1:54-68.

Ahrons, C. R. 1980. Divorce: A crisis of family transition and change. *Family Relations* 29.

———. 1992. Twenty-first-century families: Meeting the challenges of change. *Family Therapy News*, no. 3 (October): 3, 16.

Ahrons, C. R., and R. H. Rodgers. 1987. *Divorced families: A multidisciplinary developmental view*. New York: W. W. Norton.

Aldous, J. 1978. *Family careers*. New York: Wiley.

———. 1996. *Family careers: Rethinking the developmental perspective*. Thousand Oaks, Calif.: Sage.

Allen, C. J. 1947. Our utmost for the highest. *Home Life: A Christian Family Magazine* 1, no. 1:1.

Alsdurf, J. M., and P. Alsdurf. 1988. A pastoral response. In *Abuse and religion: When praying isn't enough*, ed. A. L. Horton and J. A. Williamson, pp. 165-71. Lexington, Mass.: Lexington Books.

Amato, P. R., and A. Booth. 1996. A prospective study of divorce and parent-child relationships. *Journal of Marriage and the Family* 58, no. 2:356-65.

Anderson, R. S., and D. B. Guernsey. 1985. *On being family: A social theology of the family*. Grand Rapids, Mich.: Eerdmans.

Anthony, E. J., and B. J. Cohler. 1987. *The invulnerable child*. New York: Guilford.

Antonovsky, A., and T. Sourani. 1988. Family sense of coherence and family adaptation. *Journal of Marriage and the Family* 50:79-92.

Arditti, J. A. 1990. Noncustodial fathers: An overview of policy and resources. *Family Relations* 39, no. 4:460-65.

Arnett, J. J. 1995. Broad and narrow socialization: The family in the context of a cultural theory. *Journal of Marriage and the Family* 57, no. 3 (August): 617-28.

Astley, J. 1996. The role of the family in the formation and criticism of faith. In *The family in theological perspective*, ed. S. C. Barton, pp. 187-202. Edinburgh: T & T Clark.

Attneave, C. 1982. American Indians and Alaska Native families: Emigrants in their own homeland. In *Ethnicity and family therapy*, ed. M. McGoldrick, J. K. Pearce and J. Giordano, pp. 55-83. New York: Guilford.

Aymard, M. 1989. Friends and neighbors. In *A history of private life*, vol. 3, *Passions of the Renaissance*, ed. R. Chartier, pp. 447-91. Cambridge, Mass.: Harvard University Press.

Bahr, H. M., and K. S. Bahr. 1996. A paradigm of family transcendence. *Journal of Marriage and the Family* 58, no. 3:541-55.

Bailey, D. S. 1952. *The mystery of love and marriage*. London: SCM Press.

Balch, D. L. 1981. *Let wives be submissive: The domestic code in 1 Peter*. Chico, Calif.: Scholars Press.

Balswick, J. O., and J. K. Balswick. 1989. *The family: A Christian perspective on the contemporary home*. Grand Rapids, Mich.: Baker.

Barber, B. K., and C. Buehler. 1996. Family cohesion and enmeshment: Different constructs, different effects. *Journal of Marriage and the Family* 58, no. 2 (May): 433-41.

Barna, G. 1993. *The future of the American family*. Chicago: Moody Press.

Barth, M. 1974. *Ephesians.* Garden City, N.Y.: Doubleday.

Barton, S. C. 1996a. Biblical hermeneutics and the family. In *The family in theological perspective,* ed. S. C. Barton. Edinburgh: T & T Clark.

———. 1996b. Towards a theology of the family. In *Christian perspectives on sexuality and gender,* ed. A. Thatcher and E. Stuart, pp. 451-62. Grand Rapids, Mich.: Eerdmans.

Bayly, J. 1977. How basic the conflict? An open letter from Bill Gothard. *Eternity,* August, pp. 41-43.

Bayse, D. J., S. M. Allgood and P. H. Van Wyk. 1991. Family life education: An effective tool for prisoner rehabilitation. *Family Relations* 40, no. 3:254-57.

Beales, R. W. 1991. The preindustrial family (1600-1815). In *American families: A research guide and historical handbook,* ed. J. M. Hawes and E. I. Nybakken, pp. 35-82. New York: Greenwood.

Bean, F. D., R. L. J. Curtis and J. P. Marcum. 1977. Familism and marital satisfaction among Mexican Americans: The effects of family size, wife's labor force participation and conjugal power. *Journal of Marriage and the Family* 39:759-67.

Beavers, J. 1989. Physical and cognitive handicaps. In *Children in family contexts,* ed. L. Combrinck-Graham, pp. 193-212. New York: Guilford.

Beavers, J., R. B. Hampson, Y. F. Hulgus and W. R. Beavers. 1986. Coping in families with a retarded child. *Family Process* 25:365-78.

Beckerman, A. 1994. Mothers in prison: Meeting the prerequisite conditions for permanency planning. *Social Work* 39, no. 1:549-57.

Bedale, S. 1954. The meaning of *kephalē* in the Pauline epistles. *Journal of Theological Studies,* n.s. 5:211-15.

Bennett, C. E. 1992. *The black population in the United States: March 1992.* Current Population Reports, Population Characteristics, P20-471. Washington, D.C.: U.S. Department of Commerce, Bureau of the Census.

Benson, P. L., A. R. Sharma and E. C. Roehlkepartain. 1994. *Growing up adopted: A portrait of adolescents and their families.* Minneapolis: Search Institute.

Bernand, C., and S. Gruzinski. 1996. Children of the apocalypse: The family in Meso-America and the Andes. In *A history of the family,* vol. 2, *The impact of modernity,* ed. A. Burguiere, C. Klapisch-Zuber, M. Segalen and F. Zonabend, pp. 161-215. Oxford: Blackwell.

Bernard, J. 1982. *The future of marriage.* 2nd ed. New Haven, Conn.: Yale University Press.

Best, E. 1971. *1 Peter.* London: Oliphants.

Beutler, I. F., W. R. Burr, K. Bahr and D. A. Herrin. 1989. The family realm: Theoretical contributions for understanding its uniqueness. *Journal of Marriage and the Family* 51, no. 3 (August): 805-16.

Bigbee, J. L. 1992. Family stress, hardiness and illness: A pilot study. *Family Relations* 41, no. 2:212-17.

Billingsley, A. 1992. *Climbing Jacob's ladder: The enduring legacy of African-American families.* New York: Simon & Schuster.

Bird, C. E., and C. E. Ross. 1993. Houseworkers and paid workers: Qualities of the work and effects on personal control. *Journal of Marriage and the Family* 55, no. 4:913-25.

Blackburn, D. M. 1995. Spouse abuse: Shattered peace. In *Violence: A Christian response,* ed. P. Strickland and O. Bottorff, pp. 151-62. Atlanta: Cooperative Baptist Fellowship.

Blood, R. O. J., and D. M. Wolfe. 1960. *Husbands and wives: The dynamics of married living.* Glencoe, Ill.: Free Press.

Bobo, K., and P. Tom. 1996. Developing effective congregational-based advocacy ministries. In *Next steps in community ministry.* ed. C. S. Dudley, pp. 55-63. Washington, D.C.: Alban Institute.

Bockelman, W. 1976. *Gothard—the man and his ministry: An evaluation.* Santa Barbara, Calif.: Twill.

Bolger, N., A. DeLongis, R. C. Kessler and E. Wethington. 1989. The contagion of stress across multiple roles. *Journal of Marriage and the Family* 51:175-83.

Boss, P. 1988. *Family stress management.* Newbury Park, Calif.: Sage.

Boss, P. G., W. J. Doherty, R. LaRossa, W. R. Schumm and S. K. Steinmetz. 1993. *Sourcebook of family theories and methods: A contextual approach.* New York: Plenum.

Boukydis, Z. 1986. *Support for parents and infants: A manual for parenting organizations and professionals.* New York: Routledge and Kegan Paul.

Boulton, W. G. 1992. *Out of step: The family, American society and the Christian gospel.* Lanham, Md.: University Press of America.

Bowlby, J. 1969. *Attachment and loss.* Vol. 1, *Attachment.* New York: Basic Books.

―――. 1975. Attachment theory, separation anxiety and mourning. In *American handbook of psychiatry,* vol. 6, ed. D. A. Hamburg and H. K. M. Brodie. New York: Basic Books.

―――. 1988. *A secure base: Parent-child attachment and healthy human development.* New York: Basic Books.

Bowman, T. 1993. The father-son project. *Families in Society* 74, no. 1:22-27.

Boyer, E. 1984. *A way in the world.* San Francisco: Harper & Row.

Brady, M. D. 1991. The new model middle-class family (1881-1930). In *American families: A research guide and historical handbook,* ed. J. M. Hawes and E. I. Nybakken, pp. 83-123. New York: Greenwood.

Bresc, H. 1996. Europe: Town and country (thirteenth-fifteenth century). In *A history of the family,* vol. 1, *Distant worlds, ancient worlds,* ed. A. Burguiere, C. Klapisch-Zuber, M. Segalen and F. Zonabend, pp. 430-66. Cambridge: Polity.

Briggs, J., and P. Briggs. 1988. *Recreation Xtras: A prescription for family fun.* Nashville: Sunday School Board.

Broderick, C. B. 1993. *Understanding family process: Basics of family systems theory.* Newbury Park, Calif.: Sage.

Brody, G. H., D. F. Stoneman and C. McCrary. 1994. Religion's role in organizing family relationships: Family process in rural, two-parent African American families. *Journal of Marriage and the Family* 56, no. 4:878-88.

Bronfenbrenner, U. 1979. *The ecology of human development: Experiments by nature and design.* Cambridge, Mass.: Harvard University Press.

Browne, A. 1988. Family homicide. In *Handbook of family violence,* ed. V. B. Van Hasselt, R. L. Morrison, A. S. Bellack and M. Hersen, pp. 271-89. New York: Plenum.

Brubaker, T. H. 1990. Families in later life: A burgeoning research area. *Journal of Marriage and the Family* 52, no. 4:959-81.

Bruce, F. F. 1971. *1 and 2 Corinthians.* Grand Rapids, Mich.: Eerdmans.

Brueggemann, W. 1978. *The prophetic imagination.* Philadelphia: Fortress.

―――. 1982. *Genesis.* Atlanta: John Knox.

Brueggemann, W. G. 1996. *The practice of macro social work.* Chicago: Nelson-Hall.

Brundage, J. A. 1987. *Law, sex and Christian society in medieval Europe.* Chicago: University of Chicago Press.

―――. 1993. *Sex, law and marriage in the Middle Ages.* Brookfield, Vt.: Ashgate.

Burgess, E. 1926. The family as a unity of interacting personalities. *The Family* 7, no. 1 (March): 3-9.

Burgess, E. W., and H. J. Locke. 1945. *The family: From institution to companionship.* New York: American Book.

Burguiere, A., and F. Lebrun. 1996. Priest, prince and family. In *A history of the family,* vol. 2, *The impact of modernity,* ed. A. Burguiere, C. Klapisch-Zuber, M. Segalen and F. Zonabend, pp. 95-158. Oxford: Blackwell.

Burr, W. R. 1990. Beyond I-statements in family communication. *Family Relations* 39, no. 3:266-73.

Burr, W. R., and S. R. Klein. 1994. *Reexamining family stress: New theory and research.* Thousand Oaks, Calif.: Sage.

Burton, L. M., and C. B. Stack. 1993. Conscripting kin: Reflections on family, generation and culture. In *Family, self and society: Toward a new agenda for family research,* ed. P. A. Cowan et al., pp. 103-13. Hillsdale, N.J.: Lawrence Erlbaum Associates.

Buttry, D. L. 1997. Surfacing and analyzing conflict: A Bible study on the ministry of conflict medi-
ation. *Baptist Peacemaker* 17, no. 1:1011.
Byles, J., C. Byrne, M. H. Boyle and D. R. Offord. 1988. Ontario child health study: Reliability and
validity of the general functioning subscale of the McMaster family assessment device. *Family
Process* 27:97-104.
Caird, G. B. 1976. *Paul's letters from prison.* Oxford: Oxford University Press.
Caldwell, C. H., A. D. Greene and A. Billingsley. 1994. Family support programs in black churches:
A new look at old functions. In *Putting families first: America's family support movement and the
challenge of change,* ed. S. L. Kagan and B. Weissbourd. San Francisco: Jossey-Bass.
Campbell, W. 1995. Elvis Presley as redneck. *Baptist Peacemaker* 15, nos. 3-4:1-2.
Campolo, T. 1988. *Twenty hot potatoes Christians are afraid to touch.* Dallas: Word.
———. 1990. *The kingdom of God is a party.* Dallas: Word.
Campolo, T., and G. Aeschliman. 1993. *101 ways your church can change the world.* Ventura, Calif.: Regal.
Carey, P. W. 1993. *The Roman Catholics.* Westport, Conn.: Greenwood.
Carlson, B. E., and N. J. Cervera. 1991. Incarceration, coping and support. *Social Work* 36, no.
4:279-85.
Carroll, J. W., C. S. Dudley and W. McKinney, eds. 1986. *Handbook for congregational studies.* Nash-
ville: Abingdon.
Carter, B. 1995. Focusing your wide-angle lens. *Family Therapy Networker* 19, no. 6:31-35.
Carter, B., and M. McGoldrick. 1989. The changing family life cycle: A framework for family ther-
apy. In *The changing family life cycle,* ed. B. Carter and M. McGoldrick, pp. 3-28. Boston: Allyn
and Bacon.
Cartlidge, D. R. 1975. 1 Cor. 7 as a foundation for a Christian sex ethic. *Journal of Religion*
55:220-34.
CDF Reports. 1995. Friendly (but powerful) persuasion. *CDF Reports* 16, no. 6 (May): 10-11.
CDF Reports. 1998. New CDF studies look at status of former welfare recipients. *CDF Reports* 19,
nos. 4-5:4.
Centers, R., B. H. Raven and A. Rodrigues. 1971. Conjugal power structure: A reexamination.
American Sociological Review 36:264-78.
Chafin, K. 1991. The waiting father (Luke 15:11-24). *Preaching* 6, no. 6:21-24.
Chapman, S. F. 1991. Attachment and adolescent adjustment to parental remarriage. *Family Rela-
tions* 40, no. 2:232-37.
Cherlin, A. J. 1979. Work life and marital dissolution. In *Divorce and separation: Context, cause and
consequences,* ed. G. Levinger and O. C. Moles. New York: Basic Books.
———. 1992. *Marriage, divorce, remarriage.* Rev. ed. Cambridge, Mass.: Harvard University Press.
Cherlin, A. J., and C. Calhoun. 1996. *Public and private families: An introduction.* New York:
McGraw-Hill.
Children's Defense Fund. 1996. *The state of America's children.* Washington, D.C.: Children's Defense
Fund.
Clapp, R. 1993. *Families at the crossroads: Beyond traditional and modern options.* Downers Grove, Ill.:
InterVarsity Press.
Clinebell, H. J., and C. H. Clinebell. 1970. *The intimate marriage.* New York: Harper & Row.
Cluff, R. B., M. W. Hicks and C. H. Madsen. 1994. Beyond the Circumplex Model: Part I, A mor-
atorium on curvilinearity. *Family Process* 33, no. 4:455-70.
Cody, C. A. 1983. Naming, kinship and estate dispersal: Notes on slave family life on a South Caro-
lina plantation, 1786-1833. In *The domestic environment in early modern England and America,* ed.
M. Gordon, pp. 440-58. 3rd ed. New York: St. Martin's.
Cogle, F. L., G. E. and Tasker. 1982. Children and housework. *Family Relations* 31:395-99.
Cohen, N. J., J. C. Coyne and J. D. Duvall. 1996. Parents' sense of "entitlement" in adoptive and
nonadoptive families. *Family Process* 35, no. 4 (December): 441-56.

Coleman, M., and L. H. Ganong. 1990. Remarriage and stepfamily research in the 1990s: Increased interest in an old family form. *Journal of Marriage and the Family* 52, no. 4:925-40.

Collomp, A. 1989. Families: Habitations and cohabitations. In *A history of private life,* vol. 3, *Passions of the Renaissance,* ed. R. Chartier, pp. 493-529. Cambridge, Mass.: Harvard University Press.

Condran, J. G., and J. G. Bode. 1982. Rashomon, working wives and family division of labor: Middletown, 1980. *Journal of Marriage and the Family* 44:421-26.

Congregations. 1997. Trend scan: The view from here. *Congregations: The Alban Journal* 23, no. 2 (March-April): 5-11.

Connidis, I. A. 1992. Life transitions and the adult sibling tie: A qualitative study. *Journal of Marriage and the Family* 54, no. 4:972-82.

Cooksey, E. C., and M. M. Fondell. 1996. Spending time with his kids: Effects of family structure on fathers' and children's lives. *Journal of Marriage and the Family* 58, no. 3:693-707.

Coontz, S. 1988. *The social origins of private life: A history of American families, 1600-1900.* New York: Verso.

————. 1992. *The way we never were: American families and the nostalgia trap.* New York: BasicBooks.

Crosbie-Burnett, M. 1989. Application of family stress theory to remarriage: A model for assessing and helping stepfamilies. *Family Relations* 38, no. 3:323-31.

Crosbie-Burnett, M., and J. Giles-Sims. 1994. Adolescent adjustment and stepparenting styles. *Family Relations* 43, no. 4:394-99.

Curran, D. 1983. *Traits of a healthy family.* Minneapolis: Winston.

————. 1989. *Working with parents.* Circle Pines, Minn.: American Guidance Service.

Cutright, P. 1971. Income and family events: Marital instability. *Journal of Marriage and the Family* 33:291-306.

Daly, K. J. 1996. *Families and time: Keeping pace in a hurried culture.* Thousand Oaks, Calif.: Sage.

D'Antonio, W. V. 1995. Small faith communities in the Roman Catholic Church. In *Work, family and religion in contemporary society,* ed. N. T. Ammerman and W. C. Roof, pp. 237-59. New York: Routledge.

Dawson, D. A. 1991. Family structure and children's health and well-being: Data from the 1988 National Health Interview Survey on Child Health. *Journal of Marriage and the Family* 53, no. 3:573-84.

de la Ronciere, C. 1988. Ruscan notables on the eve of the Renaissance. In *A history of private life,* vol. 2, *Revelations of the medieval world,* ed. G. Duby, pp. 157-309. Cambridge, Mass.: Harvard University Press.

Delhaye, P. 1984. Propositions on the doctrine of Christian marriage. In *Contemporary perspectives on Christian marriage: Propositions and papers from the International Theological Commission,* ed. R. Malone and J. R. Connery. Chicago: Loyola University Press.

Demo, D. H., and A. C. Acock. 1993. Family diversity and the division of domestic labor: How much have things really changed? *Family Relations* 42, no. 3:323-31.

Devault, M. 1987. Doing housework: Feeding and family life. In *Families and work,* ed. N. Gerstle and H. Gross, pp. 178-91. Chicago: University of Chicago Press.

Deveaux, W. P. 1996. African Methodist Episcopal: Nurturing a sense of "somebodyness." In *Faith traditions and the family,* ed. P. D. Airhart and M. L. Bendroth, pp. 73-84. Louisville, Ky.: Westminster John Knox.

DeYoung, A. J. 1979. Marriage Encounter: A critical examination. *Journal of Marital and Family Therapy* 5:27-34.

Dicker, S. 1990. *Stepping stones: Successful advocacy for children.* New York: Foundation for Child Development.

Dinkmeyer, D., G. D. McKay and J. L. McKay. 1987. *New beginnings: Skills for single parents and stepfamily parents.* Champaign, Ill.: Research.

Doherty, W. J., and M. E. Lester. 1982. Casualties of marriage encounter weekends. *Family Therapy News* 13 no. 4:9.

Doherty, W. J., P. McCabe and R. G. Ryder. 1978. Marriage Encounter: A critical appraisal. *Journal of Marriage and Family Counseling* 4:99-106.

Doriani, D. 1996. The Puritans, sex and pleasure. In *Christian perspectives on sexuality and gender*, ed. A. Thatcher and E. Stuart, pp. 33-51. Grand Rapids, Mich.: Eerdmans.

Dornbusch, S. M., and M. H. Strober. 1988. *Feminism, children and the new families*. New York: Guilford.

Duby, G., D. Barthelemy and C. de La Ronciere. 1988. Portraits. In *A history of private life*, vol. 2, *Revelations of the medieval world*, ed. G. Duby, pp. 35-155. Cambridge, Mass.: Harvard University Press.

Dudley, C. S., and S. A. Johnson. 1993. *Energizing the congregation: Images that shape your church's ministry*. Louisville, Ky.: Westminster John Knox.

Duncan, S. F., and G. Brown. 1992. RENEW: A program for building remarried family strengths. *Families in Society* 73, no. 3:149-58.

Dundas, I. 1994. The family adaptability and cohesion scale III in a Norwegian sample. *Family Process* 33, no. 4:191-201.

Dunn, J. D. G. 1996. The household rules in the New Testament. In *The family in theological perspective*, ed. S. C. Barton, pp. 43-63. Edinburgh: T & T Clark.

Dunst, C. 1995. *Key characteristics and features of community-based family support programs*. Chicago: Family Resource Coalition.

Duvall, E., and R. Hill. 1948. *Report of the committee on the dynamics of family interaction*. Paper presented at the National Conference on Family Life, Washington, D.C.

Duvall, E., and B. Miller. 1985. *Marriage and family development*. 6th ed. New York: Harper & Row.

Eilts, M. N. 1988. Saving the family: When is covenant broken? In *Abuse and religion: When praying isn't enough*, ed. A. L. Horton and J. A. Williamson, pp. 207-14. Lexington, Mass.: Lexington Books.

Eisenman, T. L. 1996. *Temptations families face: Breaking patterns that keep us apart*. Downers Grove, Ill.: InterVarsity Press.

Elder, G. H. 1983. The life-course perspective. In *The American family in social-historical perspective*, ed. M. Gordon, pp. 54-60. 3rd ed. New York: St. Martin's.

Elkind, D. 1981. The family and religion. In *Family strengths*, vol. 3, *Roots of well-being*, ed. N. Stinnett. Lincoln: University of Nebraska Press.

Elliott, J. H. 1981. *A home for the homeless: A sociological exegesis of 1 Peter, its situation and strategy*. Philadelphia: Fortress.

Ellis, G. E. 1991. *New beginnings: Preparing families for remarriage in the church*. New York: The Pilgrim Press.

Erdman, C. W. 1995. *Beyond chaos: Living the Christian family in a world like ours*. Grand Rapids, Mich.: Eerdmans.

Erickson, R. 1993. Reconceptualizing family work: The effect of emotion work on perceptions of marital quality. *Journal of Marriage and the Family* 55, no. 4 (November): 888-900.

Erikson, E. H. 1968. *Identity: Youth and crisis*. New York: W. W. Norton.

Evans, A. F., R. A. Evans and W. B. Kennedy. 1987. *Pedagogies for the non-poor*. Maryknoll, N.Y.: Orbis.

Everett, W. J., and S. J. Everett. 1995. Couples at work: A study of patterns of work, family and faith. In *Work, family and religion in contemporary society*, ed. N. T. Ammerman and W. C. Roof, pp. 305-29. New York: Routledge.

Falicov, C. J. 1982. Mexican families. In *Ethnicity and family therapy*, ed. M. McGoldrick, J. K. Pearce and J. Giordano, pp. 134-63. New York: Guilford.

———. 1995. Training to think culturally: A multidimensional comparative framework. *Family Process* 34, no. 4:373-88.

Farrell, M. P., and G. M. Barnes. 1993. Family systems and social support: A test of the effects of cohesion and adaptability on the functioning or parents and adolescents. *Journal of Marriage and the Family* 55, no. 1:119-32.

Ferber, M. A. 1982. Labor market participation of young married women: Causes and effects. *Journal of Marriage and the Family* 44:457-68.

Ferguson, J. 1992. The congregation as context for social work practice. In *Church social work,* ed. D. R. Garland, pp. 36-57. St. Davids, Penn.: North American Association of Christians in Social Work.

Festinger, T. 1986. *Necessary risk: A study of adoptions and disrupted adoptive placements.* Washington, D.C.: Child Welfare League of America.

Fiese, B. H., K. A. Hooker, L. Kotary, J. Schwagler and M. Rimmer. 1995. Family stories in the early stages of parenthood. *Journal of Marriage and the Family* 57, no. 3 (August): 763-70.

Figley, C. R. 1989. *Treating stress in families.* New York: Brunner/Mazel.

Finkelhor, D. 1983. Common features of family abuse. In *The dark side of families: Current family violence research,* ed. D. Finkelhor, R. J. Gelles, G. T. Hotaling and M. A. Straus, pp. 17-30. Beverly Hills, Calif.: Sage.

Fisher, L., R. F. Kokes, R. E. Cole, P. M. Perkins and L. C. Wynne. 1987. Competent children at risk: A study of well-functioning offspring of disturbed parents. In *The invulnerable child,* ed. E. J. Anthony and B. J. Cohler, pp. 211-28. New York: Guilford.

Fitzpatrick, M. A. 1988. *Between husbands and wives: Communication in marriage.* Newbury Park, Calif.: Sage.

Fitzpatrick, M. A., and L. D. Ritchie. 1993. Communication theory and the family. In *Sourcebook of family theories and methods: A contextual approach,* ed. P. G. Boss et al., pp. 565-85. New York: Plenum.

Fletcher, A. 1996. The family, marriage and the upbringing of children in Protestant England. In *The family in theological perspective,* ed. S. C. Barton, pp. 107-28. Edinburgh: T & T Clark.

Foh, S. T. 1979. *Women and the word of God: A response to biblical feminism.* Phillipsburg, N.J.: Presbyterian & Reformed.

Forest, J. 1994. *Love is the measure: A biography of Dorothy Day.* New York: Orbis.

Forgatch, M. S. 1989. Patterns and outcome in family problem solving: The disrupting effect of negative emotion. *Journal of Marriage and the Family* 51:115-24.

Fossier, R. 1996. The feudal era (eleventh-thirteenth century). In *A history of the family,* vol. 1, *Distant worlds, ancient worlds,* ed. A. Burguiere, C. Klapisch-Zuber, M. Segalen and F. Zonabend, pp. 407-29. Cambridge: Polity.

Foster, R. 1978. *Celebration of discipline.* New York: Harper & Row.

Fowler, J. W. 1990. Faith development through the family life cycle. In *Catholic families: Growing and sharing faith.* New Rochelle, N.Y.: Don Bosco Multimedia.

———. 1991. *Weaving the new creation: Stages of faith and the public church.* San Francisco: Harper.

Freedman, E. B. 1997. The history of the family and the history of sexuality. In *The new American history,* ed. E. Foner. Philadelphia: Temple University Press.

Freedman, S. G. 1993. *Upon this rock: The miracles of a black church.* New York: HarperCollins.

Freeman, M. 1986. *Called to act: Stories of child care advocacy in our churches.* New York: Child Advocacy Office, Division of Church and Society, National Council of the Churches of Christ in the U.S.A.

Friedman, E. H. 1985. *Generation to generation: Family process in church and synagogue.* New York: Guilford.

Fristad, M. A. 1989. A comparison of the McMaster and circumplex family assessment instruments. *Journal of Marital and Family Therapy* 15:259-69.

Furr, J. 1997. How do parish consultants use research? Paper presented at the annual meeting of the Society for the Scientific Study of Religion, San Diego, November 8.

Furstenberg, F. F. 1991. As the pendulum swings: Teenage childbearing and social concern. *Family Relations* 40, no. 2:127-38.

Furstenberg, F. F., and A. J. Cherlin. 1991. *Divided families: What happens to children when parents part.* Cambridge, Mass.: Harvard University Press.

Gallagher, M. 1996. Re-creating marriage. In *Promises to keep: Decline and renewal of marriage in America,* ed. D. Popenoe, J. B. Elshtain and D. Blankenhorn, pp. 233-46. Lanham, Md.: Rowman and Littlefield.

Galvin, K. M. 1991. Supporting the stepfamily. *Journal of Family Ministry* 6 , no. 1:42.

Ganong, L. H., and M. Coleman. 1986. A comparison of clinical and empirical literature on children in stepfamilies. *Journal of Marriage and the Family* 48:309-18.

———. 1989. Preparing for remarriage: Anticipating the issues, seeking solutions. *Family Relations* 38:28-33.

Garbarino, J. 1979. Using natural-helping networks to meet the problem of child maltreatment. In *Schools and the problem of child abuse,* ed. R. Volpe, M. Breton and J. Mitton, pp. 129-36. Toronto: University of Toronto Press.

———. 1995. *Raising children in a socially toxic environment.* San Francisco: Jossey-Bass.

Garbarino, J., and K. Kostelny. 1994. Family support and community development. In *Putting families first: America's family support movement and the challenge of change,* ed. S. L. Kagan and B. Weissbourd, pp. 297-320. San Francisco: Jossey-Bass.

Garland, D. E. 1983. The Christian's posture toward marriage and celibacy: 1 Corinthians 7. *Review and Expositor* 80:351-62.

———. 1990. A biblical foundation for family ministry. In *The church's ministry with families: A practical guide,* ed. D. R. Garland and D. E. Pancoast, pp. 20-31. Dallas: Word.

———. 1993. *Reading Matthew.* New York: Crossroad.

Garland, D. R. 1983. The social worker and the pastoral counselor: Strangers or collaborators? *Social Work and Christianity* 10, no. 2:22-41.

———. 1989. An ecosystemic perspective for family ministry. *Review and Expositor* 86, no. 2:195-207.

———. 1990a. Creating and nurturing families. *Review and Expositor, 87,* 317-334.

———. 1990b. Developing and empowering parent networks. In *The church's ministry with families: A practical guide,* ed. D. R. Garland and D. L. Pancoast, pp. 91-109. Dallas: Word.

———. 1993. Family forum: Marriage and quilt-making. *The Western Recorder.*

———. 1994a. *Church agencies: Caring for children and families in crisis.* Washington, D.C.: Child Welfare League of America.

———. 1994b. Family stress: Reflections on personal experience and implications for congregational ministry. *Journal of Family Ministry* 8, no. 1:4-19.

———. 1995. Divorce and the church. *Review and Expositor* 92:419-34.

———. 1996. *Precious in his sight: A guide to child advocacy for the churches.* Birmingham, Ala.: New Hope.

Garland, D. R., K. C. Chapman and J. Pounds. 1991. *Christian self-esteem: Parenting by grace.* Nashville: Sunday School Board of the Southern Baptist Convention.

Garland, D. R., and D. E. Garland. 1986. *Beyond companionship: Christians in marriage.* Philadelphia: Westminster Press.

Garland, D. R., and D. L. Pancoast. 1990. *Churches ministering with families: A practical guide.* Dallas: Word.

Garland, D. R., R. Ross, W. Rowatt, and L. Chandler. 1995. *Life-changing events for youth and families.* Nashville: Convention Press.

Garland, D. R., and P. Yankeelov. 1998. The church census. *Family Ministry* 12, no. 3.

George H. Gallup International Institute. 1994. *Family volunteering: A report on a survey.* Washington, D.C.: Points of Light Foundation.

Gergen, K. J. 1991. The saturated family. *The Family Therapy Networker* 15, no. 5:27-35.

Gerson, M. J. 1998. A righteous indignation: James Dobson—psychologist, radio host, family-values crusader is set to topple the political establishment. *U.S. News & World Report*, May 4, pp. 20-25.

Gerstel, N., and H. E. Gross. 1987. *Families and work.* Philadelphia: Temple University Press.

Gies, F., and J. Gies. 1987. *Marriage and the family in the Middle Ages.* New York: Harper & Row.

Gilbreath, E. 1995. Manhood's great awakening: Promise Keepers' ambitious agenda for transforming Christian men. *Christianity Today* 39, no. 2:21-28.

Giles-Sims, J., and M. Crosbie-Burnett. 1989. Stepfamily research: Implications for policy, clinical interventions and further research. *Family Relations* 38:19-23.

Gilkes, C. T. 1990. "Until my change comes": Faith and social ministry in the African-American Baptist tradition. In *Faith and social ministry: Ten Christian perspectives,* ed. J. D. Davidson, C. L. Johnson and A. K. Mock, pp. 179-201. Chicago: Loyola Press.

———. 1995. The storm and the light: Church, family, work and social crisis in the African-American experience. In *Work, family and religion in contemporary society,* ed. N. T. Ammerman and W. C. Roof, pp. 177-98. New York: Routledge.

Glick, P. C. 1989. The family life cycle and social change. *Family Relations* 38:123-29.

Goddard, H. W., and B. C. Miller. 1993. Adding attributions to parenting programs. *Families in Society* 74, no. 2:84-92.

Goldscheiter, F. K., and L. J. Waite. 1991. *New families, no families: The transformation of the American home.* Berkeley: University of California Press.

Gondolf, E. 1988. Dealing with the abuser: Issues, options and procedures. In *Abuse and religion: When praying isn't enough,* ed. A. L. Horton and J. A. Williamson, pp. 101-11. Lexington, Mass.: Lexington Books.

Goody, J. 1996. Introduction to *A history of the family,* vol. 2, *The impact of modernity,* ed. A. Burguiere, C. Klapisch-Zuber, M. Segalen, and F. Zonabend, pp. 1-8. Oxford: Blackwell.

Gordon, T. 1975. *P.E.T.: Parent effectiveness training.* New York: New American Library.

Gottlieb, B. H., ed. 1988. *Marshaling social support: Formats, processes and effects.* Newbury Park, Calif.: Sage.

Gottman, J. M. 1991. Predicting the longitudinal course of marriages. *Journal of Marital and Family Therapy* 17, no. 1:3-7.

———. 1994a. *What predicts divorce? The relationship between marital processes and marital outcomes.* Hillsdale, N.J.: Lawrence Erlbaum Associates.

———. 1994b. *Why marriages succeed or fail.* New York: Simon & Schuster.

Governor's Advisory Task Force on Faith-Based Community Service Groups. 1996. *Faith in action: A new vision for church-state cooperation in Texas.* Austin, Tex.: Governor's Correspondence Office (P.O. Box 12428, Austin, TX 78711).

Gowan, D. E. 1987. Wealth and poverty in the Old Testament: The case of the widow, the orphan and the sojourner. *Interpretation* 41:341-53.

Grabill, W. H., C. V. Kiser and P. K. Whelpton. 1973. Demographic trends: Marriage, birth and death. In *The American family in social-historical perspective,* ed. M. Gordon, p. 375. New York: St. Martin's.

Greene, G. J. 1985. The effect of the Relationship Enhancement Program on marital communication and self-esteem. *The Journal of Applied Social Sciences* 10:78-94.

Grollman, E. 1984. The spiritual well-being of families in crisis. In *Family strengths,* vol. 5, ed. N. Stinnett, pp. 275-86. Newton, Mass.: Education Development Center.

Gudorf, C. E. 1985. Parenting, mutual love and sacrifice. In *Women's consciousness and women's conscience: A reader in feminist ethics,* ed. B. H. Andolsen, C. E. Gudorf and M. D. Pellauer, pp. 175-91. San Francisco: Harper & Row.

Guerney, B., and P. Maxson. 1990. Marital and family enrichment research: A decade review and look ahead. *Journal of Marriage and the Family* 52, no. 4:1127-35.

Guichard, P., and J.-P. Cuvillier. 1996. Barbarian Europe. In *A history of the family*, vol. 1, *Distant worlds, ancient worlds*, ed. A. Burguiere, C. Klapisch-Zuber, M. Segalen and F. Zonabend, pp. 318-78. Cambridge: Polity.

Guttman, H. A. 1989. Children in families with emotionally disturbed parents. In *Children in family contexts*, ed. L. Combrinck-Graham, pp. 252-76. New York: Guilford.

Hairston, C. F., and P. W. Lockett. 1987. Parents in prison: New directions for social services. *Social Work* 32:162-64.

Hall, C. 1990. The sweet delights of home. In *A history of private life*, vol. 4, *From the fires of revolution to the Great War*, ed. M. Perrot, pp. 47-93. Cambridge, Mass.: Belknap/Harvard University Press.

Hammar, R. R. 1995. Child abuse and churches: Legal implications. In *Violence: A Christian response*, ed. P. Strickland and O. Bottorff, pp. 125-34. Dallas: Texas Baptist Chrisian Life Commission.

Hancock, M. 1975. *Love, honor and be free*. Chicago: Moody Press.

Harder, C. S. 1997. Are we better off? An index to our not-so-civil society. *Foundation News and Commentary*, November-December, pp. 41-43.

Hartman, A., and J. Laird. 1983. *Family-centered social work practice*. New York: Free Press.

Hatch, R. C., D. E. James and W. R. Schumm. 1986. Spiritual intimacy and marital satisfaction. *Family Relations* 35:539-45.

Hauerwas, S. 1981. *A community of character: Toward a constructive Christian social ethic*. Notre Dame, Ind.: University of Notre Dame Press.

Hauk, G. H. 1988. *Family enrichment in your church*. Nashville: Convention Press.

Hawes, J. M., and E. I. Nybakken. 1991. The study of the American family. In *American families: A research guide and historical handbook*, ed. J. M. Hawes and E. I. Nybakken, pp. 3-13. New York: Greenwood.

Hawkins, A. J., and T.-A. Roberts. 1992. Designing a primary intervention to help dual-earner couples share housework and child care. *Family Relations* 41, no. 2:169-77.

Hawley, D. R., and L. DeHaan. 1996. Toward a definition of family resilience: Integrating life-span and family perspectives. *Family Process* 35, no. 3:283-98.

Hebbard, D. W. 1995. *The complete handbook for family life ministry in the church*. Nashville: Thomas Nelson.

Herlihy, D. 1985. *Medieval households*. Cambridge, Mass.: Harvard University Press.

Heyward, I. C. 1982. *The redemption of God: A theology of mutual relation*. New York: University Press of America.

Hill, M. D. 1988. Class, kinship density and conjugal role segregation. *Journal of Marriage and the Family* 50:731-41.

Hill, R., and R. H. Rodgers. 1964. The developmental approach. In *Handbook of marriage and the family*, ed. H. T. Christensen, pp. 171-211. Chicago: Rand McNally.

Hill, R. B. 1971. *The strengths of black families*. New York: Emerson Hall.

Hines, P. M., and N. Boyd-Franklin. 1982. Black families. In *Ethnicity and family therapy*, ed. M. McGoldrick, J. K. Pearce and J. Giordano, pp. 84-107. New York: Guilford.

Hochschild, A. 1989. *The second shift: Working parents and the revolution at home*. New York: Viking.

Holland, T. P., and A. C. Kilpatrick. 1993. Using narrative techniques to enhance multicultural practice. *Journal of Social Work Education* 29, no. 3:302-8.

Honeycutt, R. L. 1987. Risking the arm. Convocation address presented at Southern Baptist Theological Seminary, Louisville, Ky.

Hopper, J. 1993. The rhetoric of motives of divorce. *Journal of Marriage and the Family* 55, no. 4:801-13.

Horton, A. L., and J. A. Williamson, eds. 1988. *Abuse and religion: When praying isn't enough*. Lexington, Mass.: Lexington Books.

Hoskyns, E. C., and F. N. Davey. 1981. *Crucifixion, resurrection: The pattern of theology and ethics of the New Testament*. London: SPCK.

Howell, J. C. 1979. *Equality and submission in marriage.* Nashville: Broadman.

Hughes, L. 1988. *How to raise good children: Encouraging moral growth.* Nashville: Abingdon.

Hull, W. E. 1975. Woman in her place: Biblical perspectives. *Review and Expositor* 72:5-17.

Hunt, R. A. 1987. Marriage as dramatizing theology. *The Journal of Pastoral Care* 41, no. 2:119-31.

Hurley, J. B. 1981. *Man and woman in biblical perspective. A study in role relationships and authority.* Leicester, U.K.: Inter-Varsity Press.

Israeloff, R. 1989. The myth of quality time. *The Family Therapy Networker* 13:32-33.

James, P. S. 1991. Effects of a communication training component added to an emotionally focused couples therapy. *Journal of Marital and Family Therapy* 17, no. 3:263-75.

Jendrek, M. P. 1993. Grandparents who parent their grandchildren: Effects on lifestyle. *Journal of Marriage and the Family* 55, no. 3 (August): 609-22.

Johns, M. L. 1988. *Developing church programs to prevent child abuse.* Austin: Texas Conference of Churches.

Johnson, C. L. 1993. The prolongation of life and the extension of family relationships: The families of the oldest old. In *Family, self and society: Toward a new agenda for family research,* ed. P. A. Cowan et al., pp. 317-30. Hillsdale, N.J.: Lawrence Erlbaum Associates.

Johnson, H. C. 1996. Violence and biology: A review of the literature. *Families in Society* 77, no. 1:3-18.

Johnson, M. P. 1995. Patriarchal terrorism and common couple violence: Two forms of violence against women. *Journal of Marriage and the Family* 57, no. 2 (May): 283-94.

Jung, M. 1996. Family-centered practice with single-parent families. *Families in Society* 77, no. 9:583-90.

Kadushin, A., and J. A. Martin. 1981. *Child abuse: An interactional event.* New York: Columbia University Press.

Kagan, S. L., D. R. Powell, B. Weissbourd and E. R. Zigler. 1987. *America's family support programs: Perspectives and prospects.* New Haven, Conn.: Yale University Press.

Kain, E. L. 1990. *The myth of family decline.* Lexington, Mass.: D. C. Heath.

Kaplan, K. J., M. W. Schwartz and M. Markus-Kaplan. 1984. The family: Biblical and psychological foundations. *Journal of Psychology and Judaism* 8, no. 2.

Kaplan, M. 1996. *Clinical practice with caregivers of dementia patients.* Bristol, Penn.: Taylor and Francis.

Karpel, M. A. 1986. *Family resources: The hidden partner in family therapy.* New York: Guilford.

Kasl, S. V., and C. I. Cooper, eds. 1987. *Stress and health: Issues in research methodology.* Chichester, N.Y.: John Wiley & Sons.

Katz, M. 1997. *On playing a poor hand well: Insights from the lives of those who have overcome childhood risks and adversities.* New York: W. W. Norton.

Keith, V. M., and B. Finlay, Barbara. 1988. The impact of parental divorce on children's educational attainment, marital timing and likelihood of divorce. *Journal of Marriage and the Family* 50:797-809.

Kelly, P. 1992. Healthy stepfamily functioning. *Families in Society* 73, no. 10:579-87.

Kempe, R. S., and C. H. Kempe. 1984. *The common secret: Sexual abuse of children and adolescents.* New York: W. H. Freeman.

Kersten, K. K. 1990. The process of marital disaffection: Interventions at various stages. *Family Relations* 39, no. 3:257-65.

King, M. L., Jr. 1963. *Strength to love.* Philadelphia: Fortress.

Kingsolver, B. 1993. *Pigs in heaven.* New York: HarperPerennial.

Kolbenschlag, M. 1979. *Kiss sleeping beauty good-bye.* New York: Doubleday.

Kretzmann, J. P., and J. L. McKnight. 1993. *Building communities from the inside out.* Evanston, Ill.: Center for Urban Affairs and Policy Research.

Krueger, R. A. 1998a. *Developing questions for focus groups.* Thousand Oaks, Calif.: Sage.

————. 1998b. *Moderating focus groups.* Thousand Oaks, Calif.: Sage.

Krueger, R. A., and J. A. King. 1998a. *Analyzing and reporting focus group results.* Thousand Oaks, Calif.: Sage.

Krueger, R. A., and J. A. King. 1998b. *Involving community members in focus groups.* Thousand Oaks, Calif.: Sage.

Labyak, S. E. 1990. Ministry to the dying and their families. Paper presented at the NACSW 40th Annual Convention, St. Petersburg, Fla., September 29.

Laird, J. 1990. Developing and empowering parent networks. In *The church's ministry with families: A practical guide,* ed. D. R. Garland and D. L. Pancoast, pp. 110-30. Dallas: Word.

Lamb, M. E. 1982. Sibling relationships across the lifespan: An overview and introduction. In *Sibling relationships: Their nature and significance across the lifespan,* ed. M. E. Lamb and B. Sutton-Smith, pp. 1-11. Hillsdale, N.J.: Lawrence Erlbaum Associates.

Lamott, A. 1999. *Traveling mercies: Some thought on faith.* New York: Pantheon.

Lampe, P. 1992. "Family" in church and society of New Testament times. *Affirmation* (Union Theological Seminary in Virginia) 5, no. 1 (Spring):1-19.

Lasch, C. 1980. The family as a haven in a heartless world. In *Family in transition,* ed. A. Skolnick and J. H. Skolnick. 3rd ed. Boston: Little, Brown.

Lavee, Y., and D. H. Olson. 1991. Family types and response to stress. *Journal of Marriage and the Family* 53, no. 3:786-98.

Lazzari, M. M., H. R. Ford and K. J. Haughey. 1996. Making a difference: Women of action in the community. *Social Work* 21, no. 2:197-205.

Lebrun, F. 1989. The two reformations: Communal devotion and personal piety. In *A history of private life,* vol. 3, *Passions of the Renaissance,* ed. R. Chartier, pp. 69-109. Cambridge, Mass.: Harvard University Press.

Lee, C. 1988. Theories of family adaptabilty: Toward a synthesis of Olson's circumplex and the Beavers systems models. *Family Process* 27:73-96.

Lee, T. R., and H. W. Goddard. 1989. Developing family relationship skills to prevent substance abuse among high-risk youth. *Family Relations* 38, no. 3:301-5.

Leonard, B. J. 1996. Southern Baptist: Family as witness of grace in the community. In *Faith traditions and the family,* ed. P. D. Airhart and M. L. Bendroth, pp. 8-21. Louisville, Ky.: Westminster John Knox.

Leonard, J. H. 1984. Celebrate Christian marriage. *Educational Newsletter* (World Council of Churches) 2.

Leventhal, H., and A. Tomarken. 1987. Stress and illness: Perspectives from health psychology. In *Stress and health: Issues in research methodology,* ed. S. V. Kasl, pp. 27-55. Chichester, N.Y.: John Wiley & Sons.

Levine, C., ed. 1988. *Programs to strengthen families: A resource guide.* Chicago: Family Resource Coalition.

Lévi-Strauss, C. 1996. Introduction to *A history of the family,* vol. 1, *Distant worlds, ancient worlds,* ed. A. Burguiere, C. Klapisch-Zuber, M. Segalen and F. Zonabend, pp. 1-7. Cambridge: Polity.

Lewis, C. S. 1970. *God in the dock.* Grand Rapids, Mich.: Eerdmans.

Lewis, J. M., et al. 1976. *No single thread: Psychological health in family systems.* New York: Brunner/Mazel.

Lichtenstein, T., and R. Baruch. 1996. "I was born from the earth": Reconstructing the adoption self-narrative in the treatment of a preadolescent girl. *Families in Society* 77, no. 2:90-97.

Lillie, W. 1975. The Pauline house-tables. *Expository Times* 86:179-83.

Lindsay, J. W. 1993. *Teen dads: Rights, responsibilities and joys.* Buena Park, Calif.: Morning Glory.

Littell, J. H. 1986. *Building strong foundations: Evaluation strategies for family resource programs.* Chicago: Family Resource Coalition.

Locke, H., and G. Karlsson. 1952. Marital adjustment and prediction in Sweden and the United States. *American Sociological Reviews* 17:10-17.

Lohse, E. 1954. Paraenase und Kerygma im 1 Petrusbrief. *Zeitschrift für die Neutestamentliche Wissen-schaft* 45:68-89.

Loomis, L. S., and N. S. Landale. 1994. Nonmarital cohabiation and childbearing among black and white American women. *Journal of Marriage and the Family* 56, no. 4:949-62.

Louv, R. 1994. *101 things you can do for our children's future.* New York: Anchor.

Lowe, P. 1993. *Carepooling: How to get the help you need to care for the ones you love.* San Francisco: Berett-Koehler.

Lugtig, D., and D. Fuchs. 1992. *Building on the strengths of local neighborhood social network ties for the prevention of child maltreatment.* National Welfare Grant Project 4556-1-19. Winnipeg: Child and Family Service Research Group, Faculty of Social Work, University of Manitoba.

Lynch, T., S. Preister and Ad Hoc Committee on Marriage and Family Life. 1988. *A family perspective in church and society: A manual for all pastoral leaders.* Washington, D.C.: United States Catholic Conference.

Mace, D. R. 1982. *Close companions: The marriage enrichment handbook.* New York: Continuum.

Mace, D. R., and V. Mace. 1976. *Marriage enrichment in the church.* Nashville: Broadman.

Majonis, J. 1991. Discipline and socialization of children in abusive and nonabusive families. *Child and Adolescent Social Work Journal* 8, no. 3:203-24.

Malina, B. J. 1981. *The New Testament world: Insights from cultural anthropology.* Atlanta: John Knox.

Malone, A. P. 1992. *Sweet chariot: Slave family and household structure in nineteenth-century Louisiana.* Chapel Hill: University of North Carolina Press.

Marano, H. E. 1997. Rescuing marriages before they begin. *New York Times,* May 28.

Markman, H. J., F. Floyd and F. Dickson-Markman. 1982. Towards a model for the prediction and primary prevention of marital and family distress and dissolution. In *Personal relationships,* vol. 4, *Dissolving personal relationships,* ed. S. Dick. London: Academic Press.

Marler, P. L. 1995. Lost in the fifties: The changing family and the nostalgic church. In *Work, family and religion in contemporary society,* ed. N. T. Ammerman and W. C. Roof, pp. 23-60. New York: Routledge.

Martin, G. L. 1987. *Counseling for family violence and abuse.* Waco, Tex.: Word.

Martinez, J. 1993. The effects of spouse abuse on the children. Paper presented at the Children's Defense Fund annual conference, Charlotte, N.C.

Maxwell, J. W. 1979. A rational-emotive approach to strengthening marriage. In *Building family strengths: Blueprints for action,* ed. N. Stinnett, B. Chesser and J. DeFrain. Lincoln: University of Nebraska Press.

McCubbin, H. I., and C. Figley, eds. 1983. *Stress and the family,* vol. 1, *Coping with transitions.* New York: Brunner/Mazel.

McCubbin, H. I., and M. A. McCubbin. 1986. Resilient families, competencies, supports and coping over the life cycle. In *Faith and families,* ed. L. Sawyers, pp. 65-88. Philadelphi: Geneva.

McCubbin, H. I., and J. M. Patterson. 1981. *Systematic assessment of family stress resources and coping: Tools for research, education and clinical intervention.* St. Paul: University of Minnesota Press.

McCubbin, H. I., A. I. Thompson, P. A. Pirner and M. A. McCubbin. 1988. *Family types and strengths: A life cycle and ecological perspective.* Edina, Minn.: Bellwether.

McCubbin, M. A., and H. I. McCubbin. 1989. Theoretical orientations to family stress and coping. In *Treating stress in families,* ed. C. R. Figley, pp. 3-43. New York: Brunner/Mazel.

McDaniel, A., and S. P. Morgan. 1996. Racial differences in mother-child coresidence in the past. *Journal of Marriage and the Family* 58, no. 4:1011-17.

McFadyen, A. 1996. The abuse of family. In *The Christian family: A concept in crisis,* ed. H. Pyper, pp. 102-17. Norwich, Canterbury.

McGinnis, J. 1989. *Helping families care.* Bloomington, Ind.: Meyer-Stone Books; St. Louis: Institute for Peace and Justice.

McGoldrick, M., J. Giordano and J. K. Pearce, eds. 1996. *Ethnicity and family therapy*. 2nd ed. New York: Guilford.

McManus, M. J. 1993. *Marriage savers: Helping your friends and family stay married*. Grand Rapids, Mich.: Zondervan.

Meijer, A. M., and L. Oppenheimer. 1995. The excitation-adaptation model of pediatric chronic illness. *Family Process* 34, no. 4:441-54.

Meilaender, G. 1990. A Christian view of the family. In *Rebuilding the nest: A new commitment to the American family*, ed. D. Blankenhorn, S. Bayme and J. B. Elshtain, pp. 133-47. Milwaukee, Wisc.: Family Service America.

Melville, K. 1980. *Marriage and family today*. 2nd ed. New York: Random House.

Merk, K. 1997. Church wins grant to build apartments for low-income seniors. *The Courier-Journal* (Louisville, Ky.), January 1, 1997, p. B1.

Michel, A. 1967. Comparative data concerning the interaction in French and American families. *Journal of Marriage and the Family* 29:227-44.

Milardo, R. M. 1989. Theoretical and methodological issues in the identification of the social networks of spouses. *Journal of Marriage and the Family* 51:165-74.

Miles, J. 1975. *The feminine principle: A woman's discovery of the key to total fulfillment*. St. Louis: Bethany.

Miller, I. W., N. B. Epstein, D. S. Bishop and G. I. Keitner. 1985. The McMaster family assessment device: Reliability and validity. *Journal of Marital and Family Therapy* 11:345-56.

Miller, S., E. W. Nunnally and D. B. Wackman. 1975. *Alive and aware*. Minneapolis: Interpersonal Communication Programs.

Miller-McLemore, B. F. 1994. *Also a mother: Work and family as theological dilemma*. Nashville: Abingdon.

Moberg, D. O. 1984. *The church as a social institution*. Grand Rapids, Mich.: Baker.

Moorehouse, M. J. 1993. Work and family dynamics. In *Family, self, and society: Toward a new agenda for family research*, ed. P. A. Cowan et al., pp. 265-86. Hillsdale, N.J.: Lawrence Erlbaum Associates.

Morgan, D. L. 1998. *Planning focus groups*. Thousand Oaks, Calif.: Sage.

Morgan, M. 1975. *The total woman*. Old Tappan, N.J.: Fleming H. Revell.

Moss, B. F., and A. I. Schwebel. 1993. Defining intimacy in romantic relationships. *Family Relations* 42, no. 1:31-37.

Napier, A. 1980. Primary prevention: A family therapist's perspective. In *Family strengths: Positive models for family life*, ed. N. Stinnett. Lincoln: University of Nebraska Press.

National Marriage Encounter. 1978. *Marriage enrichment resource manual*. St. Paul, Minn.: National Marriage Encounter.

Neusner, J. 1979. *Method and meaning in ancient Judaism*. Missoula, Mont.: Scholars Press.

Northrup, W. B., and C. L. Bowan. n.d. *On the journey with Jesus: Family activities for Lent*. St. Louis: Institute for Peace and Justice.

O'Brien, M. U. 1989. The changing American family: Findings from a national survey. *Family Resource Coalition Report* 8, no. 3.

O'Hara, M. 1996. Divided we stand. *The Family Therapy Networker* 20, no. 5 (September-October): 46-53.

Olson, D. H. 1986. Circumplex model VII: Validation studies and FACES III. *Family Process* 25:337-51.

———. 1989. *Families: What makes them work*. Updated ed. Newbury Park, Calif.: Sage.

———. 1991. Commentary: Three-dimensional (3-D) circumplex model and revised scoring of FACES III. *Family Process* 30, no. 1:74-79.

Olson, D. H., C. S. Russell and D. H. Sprenkle, eds. 1988. *Circumplex model: Systemic assessment and treatment of families*. New York: Haworth.

Olson, L. 1997. Servant outings. *Journal of Family Ministry.*

Olson, M. R., and J. A. Haynes. 1993. Successful single parents. *Families in Society* 74, no. 5:259-67.

Oppenheimer, H. 1989. Two shall become one. In *Men and women: Sexual ethics in turbulent times*, ed. A. B. Ulanov et al., pp. 86-115. Cambridge, Mass.: Cowley.

Orbuch, T. L., and J. H. D. Veroff. 1993. Becoming a married couple: The emergence of meaning in the first years of marriage. *Journal of Marriage and the Family* 55, no. 4:815-26.

Osiek, C. 1996. The family in early Christianity: "Family values" revisited. *The Catholic Biblical Quarterly* 58:1-24.

Ozment, S. E. 1983. *When fathers ruled: Family life in Reformation Europe.* Cambridge, Mass.: Harvard University Press.

———. 1992. *The Protestants.* New York: Doubleday.

Pagelow, M. D. 1988. Marital rape. In *Handbook of family violence*, ed. V. B. Van Hasselt, R. L. Morrison, A. S. Bellack and M. Hersen, pp. 207-32. New York: Plenum.

Palmer, P. J. 1990. *The active life: A spirituality of work, creativity and caring.* San Francisco: Harper & Row.

Pannenberg, W. 1985. *Anthropology in theological perspective.* Trans. M. J. O'Connell. Philadelphia: Westminster Press.

Patlagean, E. 1996. Families and kinships in Byzantium. In *A history of the family*, vol. 1, *Distant worlds, ancient worlds*, ed. A. Burguiere, C. Klapisch-Zuber, M. Segalen and F. Zonabend, pp. 467-88. Cambridge: Polity.

Patton, J., and B. H. Childs. 1988. *Christian marriage and family: Caring for our generations.* Nashville: Abingdon.

Pearlin, L. I., and H. A. Turner. 1987. The family as a context of the stress process. In *Stress and health: Issues in research methodology*, ed. S. V. Kasl, pp. 143-65. Chichester, N.Y.: John Wiley & Sons.

Peck, J. S., and J. R. Manocherian. 1989. Divorce in the changing family life cycle. In *The changing family life cycle*, ed. B. Carter and M. McGoldrick, pp. 335-69. 2nd ed. Boston: Allyn and Bacon.

Peplau, L. A. 1983. Roles and gender. In *Close relationships*, ed. H. H. Kelley, pp. 220-64. New York: W. H. Freeman.

Perrot, M. 1990. The family triumphant. In *A history of private life*, vol. 4, *From the fires of revolution to the Great War*, ed. M. Perrot, pp. 99-165. Cambridge: Belknap/Harvard University Press.

Pieper, M. H., and W. J. Pieper. 1991. It's not tough, it's tender love. *Chicago Medicine* 94, no. 7:11-16.

Pill, C. 1990. Stepfamilies: Redefining the family. *Family Relations* 39, no. 2:186-93.

Pipher, M. 1996. *The shelter of each other: Rebuilding our families.* New York: Ballantine.

Pistole, M. C. 1994. Adult attachment styles: Some thoughts on closeness-distance struggles. *Family Process* 33, no. 2:147-59.

Plionis, E. M. 1990. Parenting, discipline and the concept of quality time. *Child and Adolescent Social Work Journal* 7, no. 6.

Pooley, L. E., and J. H. Littell. 1986. *Family resource program builder.* Chicago: Family Resource Coalition.

Power, D. 1987. Life in a parent support program: Research perspectives. *Family Resource Coalition Report* 6, no. 3:4-5.

Price, R. M. 1996. The distinctiveness of early Christian sexual ethics. In *Christian perspectives on sexuality and gender*, ed. A. Thatcher and E. Stuart, pp. 14-32. Grand Rapids, Mich.: Eerdmans.

Quale, G. R. 1988. *A history of marriage systems.* Westport, Conn.: Greenwood.

Qualls, S. H. 1997. Transitions in autonomy: The essential caregiving challenge. *Family Relations* 46, no. 1:41-45.

Rausch, H. L., W. A. Barry, R. K. Hertel and M. A. Swain. 1974. *Communication conflict and marriage.* San Francisco: Jossey-Bass.

Rawlings, S. W. 1994. *Household and family characteristics: March 1993.* Current Population Reports, Population Characteristics, P20-477. Washington, D.C.: U.S. Department of Commerce.

Reiss, D. 1981. *The family's construction of reality.* Cambridge, Mass.: Harvard University Press.

Reiss, D., and M. E. Oliveri. 1991. The family's conception of accountability and competence: A new approach to the conceptualization and assessment of family stress. *Family Process* 30, no. 2:193-214.

Religion News Service. 1996. Priest scandals hit St. Petersburg, Florida. *Christian Century* 113, no. 30:1005-6.

Renne, K. 1971. Health and marital experience in an urban population. *Journal of Marriage and the Family* 33:338-50.

Rexroat, C., and C. Shehan. 1987. The family life cycle and spouses' time in housework. *Journal of Marriage and the Family* 49:737-50.

Richards, S. P., and S. Hagemeyer. 1986. *Ministry to the divorced: Guidance, structure and organization that promote healing in the church.* Grand Rapids, Mich.: Zondervan.

Richardson, A. 1958. *An introduction to the theology of the New Testament.* London: SCM Press.

Rifner, L. J. 1997. We won't let it happen here. *Church and Society* 88, no. 1:17-23.

Robb, T. B. 1993. Aging and ageism: Implications for the church's ministry with families. *Church and Society* 84, no. 2:109-21.

Roberto, J. 1992. *Media, faith and families: A parish ministry guide.* New Rochelle, N.Y.: Don Bosco Multimedia.

Roberto, J., ed. 1995. *FamilyWorks.* Naugatuck, Conn.: Center for Youth Ministry Development (P.O. Box 699, Naugatuck, CT 06770).

Roberts, R. C. 1993. *Taking the word to heart: Self and other in an age of therapies.* Grand Rapids, Mich.: Eerdmans.

Rodgers, R. H. 1973. *Family interaction and transaction: The developmental approach.* Englewood Cliffs, N.J.: Prentice-Hall.

Roehlkepartain, E. 1993. *The teaching church: Moving Christian education to center stage.* Nashville: Abingdon.

Rohner, R. P., K. J. Kean and D. E. Cournoyer. 1991. Effects of corporal punishment, perceived care-taker warmth and cultural beliefs on the psychological adjustment of children in St. Kitts, West Indies. *Journal of Marriage and the Family* 53, no. 3:681.

Rohner, R. P., S. L. Bourque and C. A. Elordi. 1996. Children's perceptions of corporal punishment, caretaker acceptance and psychological adjustment in a poor, biracial southern community. *Journal of Marriage and the Family* 58, no. 4:842-52.

Rook, K., D. Dooley and R. Catalano. 1991. Stress transmission: The effects of husbands' job stressors on the emotional health of their wives. *Journal of Marriage and the Family* 53, no. 1 (February): 165-77.

Ross, C. E., and M. Van Willigen. 1996. Gender, parenthood and anger. *Journal of Marriage and the Family* 58, no. 3:572-84.

Ross, H. L., and I. V. Sawhill. 1975. *Time of transition: The growth of families headed by women.* Washington, D.C.: Urban Institute.

Roth, W., and R. R. Ruether. 1978. *The liberating bond: Biblical and contemporary.* New York: Friendship.

Russell, K. A. 1994. *In search of the church: New Testament images for tomorrow's congregations.* Bethesda, Md.: Alban Institute.

Sabourin, S., L. Laporte and J. Wright. 1990. Problem solving self-appraisal and coping efforts in distressed and nondistressed couples. *Journal of Marital and Family Therapy* 16, no. 1:89-97.

Sakenfeld, K. D. 1985. *Faithfulness in action: Loyalty in biblical perspective.* Philadelphia: Fortress.

Saluter, A. F. 1994. *Marital status and living arrangements: March 1993.* Current Population Reports, Bureau of the Census, P20-478. Washington, D.C.: U.S. Department of Commerce.

Sample, T. 1984. *Blue-collar ministry: Facing economic and social realities of working people.* Valley Forge, Penn.: Judson Press.

Sample, T. 1990. *U.S. lifestyles and mainline churches.* Louisville, Ky.: Westminster John Knox Press.

Sawin, M. M. 1979. *Family enrichment with family clusters.* Valley Forge, Penn.: Judson Press.

Scanzoni, J. 1978. *Sex roles, women's work and marital conflict: A study of family change.* Lexington, Mass.: Lexington Books.

Scanzoni, J., and G. L. Fox. 1980. Sex roles, family and society: The seventies and beyond. *Journal of Marriage and the Family* 42:743-56.

Scanzoni, L., and J. Scanzoni. 1976. *Men, women and change: A sociology of marriage and the family.* New York: McGraw-Hill.

Schaller, L. E. 1983. A practitioner's perspective: Policy planning. In *Building effective ministry: Theory and practice in the local church,* ed. C. S. Dudley, pp. 160-74. San Francisco: Harper & Row.

———. 1997. *The interventionist.* Nashville: Abingdon.

Schillebeeckx, E. 1965. *Marriage: Human reality and saving mystery.* London: Sheed & Ward.

Schnarch, D. M. 1991. *Constructing the sexual crucible: An integration of sexual and marital therapy.* New York: W. W. Norton.

Schnucker, R. V. 1990. Puritan attitudes towards childhood discipline, 1560-1634. In *Women as mothers in pre-industrial England: Essays in memory of Dorothy McLaren,* ed. V. Fildes, pp. 108-21. London: Routledge.

Schrage, W. 1974. Zur ethik der Neutestamentlichen Haustafeln. *New Testament Studies, 21,* 1-22.

Schweizer, E. 1975. *The good news according to Matthew.* Trans. D. E. Green. Atlanta: John Knox.

Scott, D. M., and B. Wishy. 1982. America's families: A documentary history. In *America's families: A documentary history,* ed. D. M. Scott and B. Wishy, pp. 2-8. New York: Harper & Row.

Sehested, N. H. 1994. Sparing the rod. *Baptist Peacemaker* 14, nos. 1-2:4.

Selwyn, E. G. 1947. *The first epistle of St. Peter.* London: Macmillan.

Senior, D. P. 1980. *1 and 2 Peter.* Wilmington, Md.: Michael Glazier.

Shamir, B. 1986. Unemployment and household division of labor. *Journal of Marriage and the Family* 48:195-206.

Shammas, C. 1983. The life-course perspective. In *The domestic environment in early modern England and America,* ed. M. Gordon, pp. 113-35. 3rd ed. New York: St. Martin's.

Shoemaker, N. 1991. Native American families. In *American families: A research guide and historical handbook,* ed. J. M. Hawes and E. I. Nybakken, pp. 291-317. New York: Greenwood.

Simons, R. L., C. Johnson, and R. D. Conges. 1994. Harsh corporal punishmnet versus quality of parental involvement as an explanation of adolescent maladjustment. *Journal of Marriage and the Family* 56, no. 3:591-607.

Sinclair, D., and Y. Stewart. 1992. *Christian parenting: Raising children in the real world.* Louisville, Ky.: Westminster John Knox.

Skolnick, A. S. 1993. Changes of heart: Family dynamics in historical perspective. In *Family, self and society: Toward a new agenda for family research,* ed. P. A. Cowan et al., pp. 43-68. Hillsdale, N.J.: Lawrence Erlbaum Associates.

Skolnick, A. S., and J. H. Skolnick. 1989. *Family in transition: Rethinking marriage, sexuality, child rearing and family organization.* 6th ed. Glenview, Ill.: Scott Foresman.

Smedes, L. B. 1988. *Caring and commitment: Learning to live the love we promise.* New York: Harper & Row.

———. 1990. The family commitment. In *Incarnational ministry: The presence of Christ in church, society and family—Essays in honor of Ray S. Anderson,* ed. C. D. Kettler and T. H. Speidel, pp. 241-53. Colorado Springs: Helmers and Howard.

Smith, W. C. 1985. *The church in the life of the Black family.* Valley Forge, Penn.: Judson Press.

Spanier, G. B. 1989. Bequeathing family continuity. *Journal of Marriage and the Family* 51:3-13.

Spitze, G. 1988. Women's employment and family relations: A review. *Journal of Marriage and the Family* 50:595-618.

Stack, C. 1974. *All our kin: Strategies for survival in the black community.* New York: Harper & Row.

Stanley, S., D. W. Trathen, S. C. McCain and B. M. Bryan. 1998. *A lasting promise: A Christian guide to fighting for your marriage.* San Francisco: Jossey-Bass.

Staples, R., and L. B. Johnson. 1993. *Black families at the crossroads: Challenges and prospects.* San Francisco: Jossey-Bass.

Stedham, M. 1989. Family ministry in the local church. *Review and Expositor* 86, no. 2:215-26.

Steinglass, P. 1995. The clinical power of research. *Family Process* 34, no. 2.

Sterner, M., and A. A. Zukowski. 1991. *Designing a parish media resource center.* Dayton, Ohio: Center for Religious Telecommunications, University of Dayton (300 College Park, Dayton, OH 45469-0314).

Stinnett, N., and J. DeFrain. 1985. *Secrets of strong families.* Boston: Little, Brown.

Stinnett, N., and N. Stinnett. 1995. Search for strong families. In *Handbook of family religious education,* ed. B. J. Neff and D. Ratcliff. Birmingham, Ala.: Religious Education Press.

Stitzinger, M. F. 1981. Genesis 1-3 and the male/female role relationship. *Grace Theological Journal* 2:23-44.

Stone, E. 1988. *Black sheep and kissing cousins: How our family stories shape us.* New York: Times Books.

Straus, M. A., J. R. Gelles and S. K. Steinmetz. 1980. *Behind closed doors: Violence in the American family.* New York: Anchor.

Straus, M. A., and C. L. Yodanis. 1996. Corporal punishment in adolescence and physical assaults on spouses in later life: What accounts for the link? *Journal of Marriage and the Family* 58, no. 4:825-41.

Strong, B., and C. DeVault. 1995. *The marriage and family experience.* 6th ed. Minneapolis: West.

Suitor, J. J., and K. Pillemer. 1994. Family caregiving and marital satisfaction: Findings from a one-year panel study of women caring for parents with dementia. *Journal of Marriage and the Family* 56 (August): 681-690.

Tapia, A. 1994. Can anything good come our of the 'hood? What a unique coalition of Atlanta churches and civic leaders is doing to resurrect a community. *Christianity Today* 38, no. 6:28-32.

Taubman, B. 1995. Single by choice and chance. *Kentucky Association for Marriage and Family Therapy News,* Winter, p. 5.

Terkelson, K. G. 1980. Toward a theory of the family life cycle. In *The changing family life cycle,* ed. E. A. Carter and M. McGoldrick, pp. 21-52. Boston: Allyn and Bacon.

Thornton, A. 1996. Comparative and historical perspectives on marriage, divorce and family life. In *Promises to keep: Decline and renewal of marriage in America,* ed. D. Popenoe, J. B. Elshtain and D. Blankenhorn, pp. 69-87. Lanham, Md.: Rowman and Littlefield.

Tidball, D. 1983. *An introduction to the sociology of the New Testament.* Exeter, U.K.: Paternoster.

Toubert, P. 1996. The Carolingina moment (eighth-tenth century). In *A history of the family,* vol. 1, *Distant worlds, ancient worlds,* ed. A. Burguiere, C. Klapisch-Zuber, M. Segalen and F. Zonabend, pp. 379-406. Cambridge: Polity.

Townsend, L. 1998. A walk in the wilderness without compass or map: Ministry with stepfamilies. *Journal of Family Ministry* 12, no. 2:52-68.

Trible, P. 1978. *God and the rhetoric of sexuality.* Philadelphia: Fortress.

Trout, C. R. 1993. Presbyterian mariners: An extended family ministry. *Church and Society* 84, no. 2:84-93.

Troyer, W. 1979. *Divorced kids.* New York: Harcourt Brace Jovanovich.

Turner, R. H. 1970. *Family interactions.* New York: Wiley.

Ulrich, D. N., and H. P. Dunne. 1986. *To love and work: A systemic interlocking of family, workplace and career.* New York: Brunner/Mazel.

U.S. Department of Justice. 1995. *Uniform Crime Reports: Crime in the United State, 1994.* Washington, D.C.: U.S. Department of Justice.

U.S. General Accounting Office, Health, Education and Human Services Division. 1995. *Child welfare: Complex needs strain capacity to provide services.* GAO/HEHS-95-208 Foster Care Overview. Washington, D.C.: U.S. General Accounting Office, Health, Education and Human Services Division.

Vaillant, G. E. 1977. *Adaptation to life.* Boston: Little, Brown.

Vance, B. 1989. *Planning and conducting family cluster.* Newbury Park, Calif.: Sage.

Vangelisti, A. L., and M. A. Banski. 1993. Couples' debriefing conversations: The impact of gender, occupation and demographic characteristics. *Family Relations* 42, no. 2:149-57.

Visher, E. B., and Visher, J. S. 1989a. *Old loyalties, new ties: Therapeutic strategies with stepfamilies.* New York: Brunner/Mazel.

———. 1989b. Parenting coalitions after remarriage: Dynamics and therapeutic guidelines. *Family Relations* 38:65-70.

Vogt, S. 1994. *Just family nights: Sixty activities to keep your family together in a world falling apart.* Elgin, Ill.: Brethren Press.

Vosler, N. R. 1996. *New approaches to family practice: Confronting economic stress.* Thousand Oaks, Calif.: Sage.

Voydanoff, P. 1990. Economic distress and family relations: A review of the eighties. *Journal of Marriage and the Family* 52, no. 4:1099-15.

Vuchinich, S. 1987. Starting and stopping spontaneous family conflicts. *Journal of Marriage and the Family* 49:591-601.

Walker, L. E. 1979. *The battered woman.* New York: Harper & Row.

———. 1988. Spouse abuse: A basic profile. In *Abuse and religion: When praying isn't enough,* ed. A. L. Horton and J. A. Williamson, pp. 13-20. Lexington, Mass.: Lexington Books.

Walker, L. S., F. J. McLaughlin and J. W. Greene. 1988. Functional illness and family functioning: A comparison of healthy and somaticizing adolescents. *Family Process* 27:317-25.

Wallerstein, J., and S. Blakeslee. 1989. *Second chances: Men, women and children a decade after divorce.* New York: Ticknor and Fields.

Walsh, A. 1998. The McCaughey babies. *Religion in the News* 1, no. 1:9-10.

Walsh, F. 1996. The concept of family resilience: Crisis and challenge. *Family Process* 35, no. 3:261-81.

Walsh, J. 1989. *Connections: Linking youth with caring adults* . Oakland, Calif.: Urban Strategies Council.

Wangerin, W., Jr. 1987. *As for me and my house.* Nashville: Thomas Nelson.

———. 1993. *Little lamb, who made thee?* Grand Rapids, Mich.: Zondervan.

Waters, D. B., and E. C. Lawrence. 1993. *Competence, courage and change: An approach to family therapy.* New York: W. W. Norton.

Watzlawick, P., J. H. Beavin and D. D. Jackson. 1967. *Pragmatics of human communication: A study of interactional patterns, pathologies and paradoxes.* New York: W. W. Norton.

Weaver, R. H. 1992. A subordinate loyalty: Christian teaching on the family. *Affirmation* (Union Theological Seminary in Virginia) 5, no. 1 (Spring): 21-49.

Weber, M. 1947. *The theory of social and economic organization.* Trans. A. M. Henderson and T. Parsons. New York: Oxford University Press.

Weems, R. 1996. Leah's epiphany. *The Other Side* 32, no. 3 (May-June): 8-11, 44-46.

Weiss, H. B., and F. H. Jacobs. 1988. *Evaluating family programs.* New York: Aldine de Gruyter.

Weiss, R. S. 1993. Attachment in adult life. In *Attachment across the life cycle,* ed. C. M. Parkes, J. Stevenson-Hinde, and P. Marris. London: Routledge.

———. 1996. Parenting from separate households. In *Promises to keep: Decline and renewal of marriage in America,* ed. D. Popenoe, J. B. Elshtain and D. Blankenhorn, pp. 215-30. Lanham, Md.: Rowman and Littlefield.

Weissbourd, B. 1994. The evolution of the family resource movement. In *Putting families first: America's family support movement and the challenge of change,* ed. S. L. Kagan and B. Weissbourd, pp. 28-47. San Francisco: Jossey-Bass.

Westerhoff, J. H. 1985. *Living the faith community.* Minneapolis: Winston.

Whipple, E. E., and S. R. Wilson. 1996. Evaluation of a parent education and support program for families at risk of physical child abuse. *Families in Society* 77, no. 4:227-39.

Whitaker, C. A., and D. V. Keith. 1977. Counseling the dissolving marriage. In *Klemer's counseling in marital and sexual problems: A clinician's handbook,* ed. R. F. Stahmann and W. J. Hiebert. 2nd ed. Baltimore: Williams and Wilkins.

White, J. M. 1991. *Dynamics of family development.* New York: Guilford.

White, L., and D. Brinkerhoof. 1987. Children's work in families: Its significance and meaning. In *Families and work,* ed. N. Gerstel and H. Gross, pp. 204-19. Philadelphia: Temple University Press.

White, L., and B. Keith. 1990. The effect of shift work on the quality and stability of marital relations. *Journal of Marriage and the Family* 52, no. 2:453-62.

White, L., and D. Peterson. 1995. The retreat from marriage: Its effect on unmarried chidren's exchange with parents. *Journal of Marriage and the Family 57,* no. 2 (May): 428-34.

Whitmore, E. 1991. *Evaluation and empowerment: It's the process that counts.* Networking Bulletin: Empowerment and Family Support 2, no. 2.

Wieman, R. W. 1937. *The modern family and the church.* New York: Harper & Brothers.

————. 1941. *The family lives its religion.* New York: Harper & Brothers.

Wilhelm, M. S., and C. A. Ridley. 1988. Stress and unemployment in rural nonfarm couples: A study of hardships and coping resources. *Family Relations* 37:50-54.

Wilkie, J. R. 1991. The decline in men's labor force participation and income and the changing structure of family economic support. *Journal of Marriage and the Family 53,* no. 1 (February): 111-22.

Williams, N. V. 1951. *How to have a family altar.* Chicago: Moody Press.

Willie, C. V., and S. L. Greenblatt. 1978. Four "classic" studies of power relationships in black families: A review and look to the future. *Journal of Marriage and the Family* 40:691-94.

Willimon, W. H. 1996. The people we're stuck with. In *Christian perspectives on sexuality and gender,* ed. A. Thatcher and E. Stuart. Grand Rapids, Mich.: Eerdmans.

Wilmes, D. J. 1988. *Parenting for prevention: How to raise a child to say no to alcohol/drugs.* Minneapolis: Johnson Institute Books.

Wimberly, A. 1994. *Soul stories: African American Christian education.* Nashville: Abingdon.

Winerip, M. 1998. He's getting by with a little help from his friends. *New York Times,* April 29, p. D11.

Witte, J., Jr. 1997. *From sacrament to contract: Marriage, religion and law in the Western tradition.* Louisville, Ky.: Westminster John Knox.

Witte, J. J. 1996. Consulting a living tradition: Christian heritage of marriage and family. *Christian Century 113,* no. 33 (November 13): 1108-11.

Wright, E. O., et al. 1992. The non-effects of class on the gender division of labor in the home: A comparative study of Sweden and the U.S. *Gender and Society 6,* no. 2: 252-82.

Wright, S. A. 1995. Religious innovation in the mainline church. In *Work, family and religion in contemporary society,* ed. N. T. Ammerman and W. C. Roof, pp. 261-81. New York: Routledge.

Wright, W. M. 1990. *Sacred dwelling: A spirituality of family life.* New York: Crossroad.

Wuerffel, J. 1990. How strong families use humor. *Family Perspective* 24:129-41.

Wuthnow, R. 1995. *Learning to care: Elementary kindness in an age of indifference.* New York: Oxford University Press.

Wynne, L. C. 1984. The epigenesis of relational systems: A model for understanding family development. *Family Process* 23:297-318.

Yankeelov, P., and D. R. Garland. 1998. The families in our congregations: Initial research findings. *Family Ministry* 12, no. 3.

Yankelovich, D. 1996. *Keynote address.* Paper presented at the Religion and the American Family Debate, Chicago, September 10-11.

Yllo, K., and D. LeClerc. 1988. Marital rape. In *Abuse and religion: When praying isn't enough,* ed. A. L. Horton and J. A. Williamson, pp. 48-57. Lexington, Mass.: Lexington Books.

Young, M., and P. Willmott. 1973. *The symmetrical family.* New York: Random House.

Ziegler, R. G., and P. Ziegler. 1992. *Homemade books to help kids cope: An easy-to-learn technique for parents and professionals.* New York: Magination.

Zigler, E. 1994. Foreword to *Putting families first: America's family support movement and the challenge of change,* ed. S. L. Kagan and B. Weissbourd, pp. xi-xix. San Francisco: Jossey-Bass.

For Instructors Using This Book as a Textbook

If you are using this book as a textbook or foundation for a workshop, the Baylor University Center for Family and Community Ministries has developed experiential exercises and case studies for classroom or workshop use. These resources are available at the Center's web site, <www.cfcm.baylor.edu>. Click on "Family Ministry Educational Resources." There is no charge for downloading and making copies of these resources. Additional resources are being added over time that will be useful to you in teaching family ministry. If you have difficulty with the web site, please contact the Center:

Center for Family and Community Ministries
Baylor University
P.O. Box 97120
Waco, TX 76798-7120
(254) 710-1199